HARCOURT HORIZONS

United States History:

Civil War to Present

TEACHER'S EDITION

VOLUME 2

Harcourt
SCHOOL PUBLISHERS

Orlando   Austin   New York   San Diego   Toronto   London

Visit *The Learning Site!*
www.harcourtschool.com

T71860

HARCOURT HORIZONS

Printed in the United States of America

ISBN 0-15-339637-7

3 4 5 6 7 8 9 10 030 10 09 08 07 06 05

Contents

Harcourt Horizons
Components

For content updates and additional information for teaching Harcourt Horizons, see The Learning Site: Social Studies Center at www.harcourtschool.com.

STUDENT SUPPORT MATERIALS	K	1	2	3	4	5	6
Pupil Editions		●	●	●	●	●	●
Big Book	●						
Unit Big Book		●	●				
Activity Books	●	●	●	●	●	●	●
Time for Kids Readers	●	●	●	●	●	●	●

TEACHER SUPPORT MATERIAL	K	1	2	3	4	5	6
Teacher's Editions	●	●	●	●	●	●	●
Activity Books, Teacher's Editions				●	●	●	●
Assessment Programs		●	●	●	●	●	●
Skills Transparencies		●	●	●	●	●	●
Reading and Vocabulary Transparencies		●	●	●	●	●	●
Audiotext Collections	●	●	●	●	●	●	●

TECHNOLOGY	K	1	2	3	4	5	6
The Learning Site: Social Studies Center	●	●	●	●	●	●	●
GeoSkills CD-ROM		●	●	●	●	●	●
Field Trip Videos		●	●	●	●	●	●

HARCOURT HORIZONS

United States History:

Civil War to Present

Harcourt
SCHOOL PUBLISHERS

Orlando   Austin   New York   San Diego   Toronto   London

Visit *The Learning Site!*
www.harcourtschool.com

HARCOURT HORIZONS

UNITED STATES HISTORY: CIVIL WAR TO PRESENT

General Editor

Dr. Michael J. Berson
Associate Professor
Social Science Education
University of South Florida
Tampa, Florida

Contributing Authors

Dr. Robert P. Green, Jr.
Professor
School of Education
Clemson University
Clemson, South Carolina

Dr. Thomas M. McGowan
Chairperson and Professor
Center for Curriculum and Instruction
University of Nebraska
Lincoln, Nebraska

Dr. Linda Kerrigan Salvucci
Associate Professor
Department of History
Trinity University
San Antonio, Texas

Series Consultants

Dr. Robert Bednarz
Professor
Department of Geography
Texas A&M University
College Station, Texas

Dr. Asa Grant Hilliard III
Fuller E. Callaway Professor
 of Urban Education
Georgia State University
Atlanta, Georgia

Dr. Thomas M. McGowan
Chairperson and Professor
Center for Curriculum and Instruction
University of Nebraska
Lincoln, Nebraska

Dr. John J. Patrick
Professor of Education
Indiana University
Bloomington, Indiana

Dr. Philip VanFossen
Associate Professor,
 Social Studies Education,
 and Associate Director,
 Purdue Center for Economic Education
Purdue University
West Lafayette, Indiana

Dr. Hallie Kay Yopp
Professor
Department of Elementary, Bilingual, and
 Reading Education
California State University, Fullerton
Fullerton, California

Content Reviewers

United States Geography

Dr. Phillip Bacon
Professor Emeritus
Geography and Anthropology
University of Houston
Houston, Texas

Native Americans and European Exploration

Dr. Susan Deans-Smith
Associate Professor
Department of History
University of Texas at Austin
Austin, Texas

Dr. John Jeffries Martin
Professor
Department of History
Trinity University
San Antonio, Texas

Richard Nichols
President
Richard Nichols and Associates
Fairview, New Mexico

Early Settlement and the American Revolution

Dr. John W. Johnson
Professor and Head
Department of History
University of Northern Iowa
Cedar Falls, Iowa

Dr. John P. Kaminski
Director, Center for the Study of
 the American Constitution
Department of History
University of Wisconsin
Madison, Wisconsin

Dr. Elizabeth Mancke
Associate Professor of History
Department of History
University of Akron
Akron, Ohio

The Constitution and United States Government

Dr. James M. Banner, Jr.
Historian
Washington, D.C.

Carol Egbo
Social Studies Consultant
Waterford Schools
Waterford, Michigan

Dr. John P. Kaminski
Director, Center for the Study of
 the American Constitution
Department of History
University of Wisconsin
Madison, Wisconsin

Dr. John J. Patrick
Professor of Education
Indiana University
Bloomington, Indiana

The National Period and Westward Expansion

Dr. Ross Frank
Professor
Department of Ethnic Studies
University of California at San Diego
La Jolla, California

Civil War and Reconstruction

Dr. Judith Giesburg
Assistant Professor
Department of History
Northern Arizona University
Flagstaff, Arizona

The United States in the Twentieth Century

Dr. Carol McKibben
Visiting Professor
Monterey Institute of International Studies
Monterey, California

Dr. Albert Raboteau
Henry W. Putnam Professor
Department of Religion
Princeton University
Princeton, New Jersey

Classroom Reviewers

Anne Hall
Teacher
Indian Prairie School District #204
Aurora, Illinois

Jennie Haynes
Teacher
A. Brian Elementary
Augusta, Georgia

Dr. Tom Jaeger
Assistant Superintendent:
 Curriculum/Instruction
Warren County R-III School District
Warrenton, Missouri

Ann Johnstone
Teacher
Stone-Robinson Elementary School
Charlottesville, Virginia

Merit Justice
Teacher
McDonald Elementary School
Georgetown, South Carolina

Karen Little
Teacher
Hubbertville School
Fayette, Alabama

Betty Morgan
Teacher
Hayes Elementary School
Kennesaw, Georgia

Deborah Neal
Teacher
Windsor Hill Elementary
North Charleston, South Carolina

Sondra Pair
Teacher
Johnson Elementary School
Pinson, Alabama

Debra Smallwood
Teacher
Dupont Elementary School
Hopewell, Virginia

Melody Wysong
Teacher
Big Valley Elementary School
Rupert, Idaho

Maps
researched and prepared by

MAPQUEST.COM

Readers
written and designed by

TIME FOR KIDS

Take a Field Trip
video tour segments provided by

CNN Turner Le@rning

Printed in the United States of America

ISBN 0-15-339621-0

1 2 3 4 5 6 7 8 9 10 048 13 12 11 10 09 08 07 06 05 04

Contents

Speaker of the House, 511
Spirit of St. Louis, 278–279
Sports, 287
Sports, women in, 441
Sprague, Frank, 211
Sputnik, 422–423, *423*
Squanto, 35
Square Deal, the, 215–217
Stalin, Josef, 334, 336, 390
Stamp Act, 47–48
Stamp Act Congress, 48
Standard Oil Company, 215
Stanton, Elizabeth Cady, 111, 247
Star of David, 367
State authority, 512
State congresses, 511–512
State governments, 60, 214–215, 510–513
State representatives, 512
States, Confederate, 119
States' rights, 100–101
States, secession of, 117–119
Statue of Liberty, 511, 516
Statute of Westminster, 543
Steamboats, 79–81, *80–81*
Steel industry, 159–161, 236–237, 277
Steel pennies, *352*
Steel production (1865–1900), *160*
Steinbeck, John (writer), 304
Stephens, Alexander, 117
Stock, 271, 297–299, 318–319
Stock certificate, *271*
Stock market, 271, 297–299
Stowe, Harriet Beecher, 112, *112*
Strategic Arms Reduction Treaty, 461
Strategy, 123
Streetcars, 211
Strike, 245
Student Nonviolent Coordination Committee (SNCC), 436
Submarines, 130, 235, 236, 373
Suburb, 281, 386–387, 418–419
Suffixes, 483
Suffrage, 247–249
Sugar Act, 47
Sulfa, 369
Sun Belt of the United States, 493, *m493*
Superpowers, 388–391, 422, 462
Supply, 160, 508–509
Supply and demand, *296–297,* 347–348
Supply of goods, 508–509
Supreme Court
    and the Cherokee Nation, 70
    Dred Scott decision, 104–105
    on segregation, 420–421, 422
    and the 2000 election, 471
Suspended bridge, 160
Symbols, patriotic

American flag, *472*
    identify, 516–517
    Liberty Bell, *18–19*
    purpose of, 511
    White House, *9*
Symbols on maps. *See* Map and globe skills
System of checks and balances, 61

T

Table activities, 64
Tables
    compare, 315
    Leading New Deal Programs, *315*
Taft, Howard, 216, 228
Tanaka, Shelley, 326
Taney, Roger B., 105
Tanks, 234, *339, 341*
Tarawa, 373
Tarbell, Ida, 214
Tariff, 100, 269
Tariff act, 302–303
Taxation, 47–49, 148
Taxes, 217, 312
Tea Act, 49
Technological innovations
    air brake, 159
    air conditioning, 493–494
    Arecibo Observatory, 532
    automobile, 202–203
    aviation, 204–205
    blood storage, 348
    brain scans, *506*
    cable cars, 209–211
    camera, *220*
    caravel, 29, *29*
    compass, *67, 74*
    elevators, 209
    high-tech industries, 505–506
    H. L. Hunley (submarine), 130
    lightbulb, 163
    machines, 200–201
    microchip, 496
    power station, 163
    radar, 369
    radio, 286–287
    satellite, *497*
    steel frames, 160, 208–209
    steel plow, 153
    streetcar/trolley car, 211
    telegraph system, 159
    television, 385
    water power, 77
    See also Inventions; Technology
Technology, 22, 496–497, 505–506
    See also Technological innovations
Teheran, Iran, 457
Teleconference, *497*
Telegraph, 159, 162
Telephone, 163, 201

Televisions, 385–386, 432
Temperance movement, 219
Temple, Shirley, 307, *307*
Tenements, 167, 206–207
Tennessee, 66, 118–119, 313–314
Tennessee (battleship), *343*
Tennessee River, 314
Tennessee Valley Authority (TVA), 313–314
Tenochtitlán, 32
Territory, 66
Terrorism, 472–473
Texas
    becomes a state, 525
    in the Dust Bowl, 305
    independence, 525
    population of, 493
    secession of, 117
    and slavery, 146
    war with Mexico, 71–72
Textile mill, 77
Textiles, 76
Theaters, *266–267,* 385
Theories, 20, 20–21, 31
Thirteen English Colonies, *m41*
Thirteenth Amendment, 141, *141*
Three Kings Day. *See* Epiphany
Thrust, 204
Time line activities, 205, 314, 381, 441, 461
Time lines, 380–381
Time zone, 546, 546–547, *m553*
Tisquantum, 35
Tobacco plantations, 43
Tojo, Hideki, 334
Tokyo, Japan, 376–377
Tom Thumb, locomotive, 80
Tomb of the Unknown Soldier, *224, 225*
Tompkins, Sally, 127
Tools of ancient Indians, 22
Towns, 151, 152, 161
Trade
    Canada and United States, 545
    with China, 452
    decline in world, *302*
    with Europe, 429
    European, 29
    international, *507–508*
    within North America, 528
    and the Panama Canal, 196
    slave, 44
    with Soviet Union, 452, 458
    United States and Western Hemisphere, *484–485*
Trade, international, 507–508
Trade-off, 355
Trail of Tears, 70–71
Transcontinental railroad. *See* Railroads
Transport planes, 368, *392*
Transportation
    air, 497
    automobiles. *See* Automobiles

aviation. *See* Aviation
    cable cars, 209–211, *209*
    canals, 78–79
    in the East, 1850, *m79*
    locomotive, 80
    paddle wheel steamboats, *80–81*
    public, 209–211, *209,* 278
    roads. *See* Road systems
    steamboats, 79–80
    streetcar/trolley car, 211
    See also Boats and ships; Railroads
Treaty, 53
    banning nuclear tests, 430
    of Paris, 53, 65
    Strategic Arms Reduction, 461
    of Versailles, 243, 244
Trench fighting, 234–235
Trial, 42, 368
Triangular trade routes, 44
Triborough Bridge, *312–313*
Trolley cars, 211
Trudeau, Pierre, 544
Truman, Harry S.
    becomes President, 367
    as President, 410–412
    with secretary of state, *391*
    Vice President, 375
    views on communism, 391
    and World War II, 377
Truman Doctrine, 391, 412
Trumbull, John (artist), 53
Tubman, Harriet, 111, *111*
Turks, Ottoman, 29
Turner, Nat, 109
Tuskegee Institute, 170
Tweed, William "Boss," *213,* 214
Twenty-first Amendment, 283

U

U-boats, *235,* 236
Uncle Sam, 512, 516
Uncle Tom's Cabin, 112
Underground, 110
Underground Railroad, 110–111, *m110, 111*
Unemployment, 301, *309,* 386, *469*
Uniforms, *123*
Union and Confederacy, The, *m124*
Union soldiers, *123, 175*
United Farm Workers (UFW), 439
United Nations (UN), 388–389, *388,* 412–413
Urban, 280
Urban and Rural Population, *83*
Urban Population, 82–83
USS *Arizona,* 343
USS *California,* 343
USS *Maryland,* 343
USS *Missouri,* 379, *381*

For permission to reprint copyrighted material, grateful acknowledgment is made to the following sources:

Atheneum Books for Young Readers, an imprint of Simon & Schuster Children's Publishing Division: Cover illustration from *Alexander Graham Bell* by Leonard Everett Fisher. Copyright © 1999 by Leonard Everett Fisher.

Candlewick Press, Inc., Cambridge, MA, on behalf of Walker Books Ltd., London: Cover illustration by P. J. Lynch from *When Jessie Came Across the Sea* by Amy Hest. Illustration copyright © 1997 by P. J. Lynch. Cover illustration by Gino D'Achille from *The Stone Age News* by Fiona Macdonald. Illustration copyright © 1998 by Walker Books Ltd.

Carolrhoda Books, Inc., a division of Lerner Publishing Group: Cover illustration by Rochelle Draper from *Georgia O'Keeffe* by Linda Lowery. Illustration copyright © 1996 by Linda Lowery.

Crown Publishers, a division of Random House, Inc.: Cover illustration from *My Dream of Martin Luther King* by Faith Ringgold. Copyright © 1995 by Faith Ringgold.

Dutton Children's Books, an imprint of Penguin Putnam Books for Young Readers, a division of Penguin Putnam Inc.: Cover photograph by Art Wolfe from *Journey Through the Northern Rainforest* by Karen Pandell. Photograph copyright © 1999 by Art Wolfe.

Farrar, Straus and Giroux, LLC: Cover illustration by David Wilgus from *My Wartime Summers* by Jane Cutler. Illustration copyright © 1994 by David Wilgus.

Harcourt, Inc.: From *Rose's Journal* by Marissa Moss. Copyright © 2001 by Marissa Moss. Cover photograph courtesy of the Library of Congress.

HarperCollins Publishers: From *Jason's Gold* by Will Hobbs. Text copyright © 1999 by Will Hobbs. Cover illustration by Mark Elliott from *Treasures in the Dust* by Tracey Porter. Illustration copyright © 1997 by Mark Elliott.

David Higham Associates Limited: Cover illustration by Martin Jordan from *Angel Falls: A South American Journey* by Martin and Tanis Jordan. Illustration copyright © 1995 by Martin Jordan. Published by Larousse Kingfisher Chambers Inc.

Henry Holt and Company, LLC: From *Betsy Ross: Patriot of Philadelphia* by Judith St. George, cover illustration by Sasha Meret. Text copyright © 1997 by Judith St. George; illustration copyright © 1997 by Sasha Meret.

Derek James: Cover illustration by Derek James from *Jason's Gold* by Will Hobbs. Illustration copyright © 1999 by Derek James.

Lee & Low Books, Inc., 95 Madison Avenue, New York, NY 10016: From *Dia's Story Cloth: The Hmong People's Journey to Freedom* by Dia Cha, illustrated by Chue and Nhia Thao Cha. Copyright © 1996 by Denver Museum of Natural History. Cover photograph by Mark T. Kerrin from *Dear Mrs. Parks: A Dialogue with Today's Youth* by Rosa Parks with Gregory J. Reed. Photograph copyright © 1996 by Mark T. Kerrin.

Madison Press Books: From *Attack on Pearl Harbor*, a Hyperion/Madison Press book by Shelley Tanaka, illustrated by David Craig. Copyright © 2001 by The Madison Press Limited.

Jack McMaster: Maps by Jack McMaster from *Attack on Pearl Harbor* by Shelley Tanaka, illustrated by David Craig.

Robin Moore and BookStop Literary Agency: Cover illustration by Robin Moore from *Across the Lines* by Carolyn Reeder. Illustration copyright © 1997 by Robin Moore.

Orion Books, a division of Random House, Inc.: From *All for the Union* by Robert Hunt Rhodes. Text and photograph copyright © 1985 by Robert Hunt Rhodes.

G. P. Putnam's Sons, an imprint of Penguin Putnam Books for Young Readers, a division of Penguin Putnam Inc.: Cover illustration by F. John Sierra from *My Mexico – México mío* by Tony Johnston. Illustration copyright © 1996 by F. John Sierra.

Scholastic Inc.: Cover illustration by Tim O'Brien from *Foster's War* by Carolyn Reeder. Illustration copyright © 1998 by Tim O'Brien.

Simon & Schuster Books for Young Readers, an imprint of Simon & Schuster Children's Publishing Division: Cover illustration by James Ransome from *Uncle Jed's Barbershop* by Margaree King Mitchell. Illustration copyright © 1993 by James Ransome.

Steck-Vaughn Company: Cover illustration by Debbe Heller from *Tales from the Underground Railroad* by Kate Connell. Illustration copyright © 1993 by Dialogue Systems, Inc.

Albert Whitman & Company: Cover illustration from *Theodore Roosevelt Takes Charge* by Nancy Whitelaw. Copyright © 1992 by Nancy Whitelaw.

Winslow Press: Cover illustration by Mark Summers from *Thomas Jefferson: Letters from a Philadelphia Bookworm* by Jennifer Armstrong. Illustration copyright © 2000 by Mark Summers.

Writers House LLC, on behalf of The Heirs to the Estate of Martin Luther King, Jr.: From "I Have a Dream" speech by Martin Luther King, Jr. Text copyright 1963 by Martin Luther King, Jr.; text copyright renewed 1991 by Coretta Scott King.

ILLUSTRATION CREDITS

Pages A18-A19, Studio Liddell; 12-13, Wayne Hovis; 20-21, Gregory Manchess; 24-25, Cliff Spohn; 44-45, Luigi Galante; 80-81, Don Foley; 88-89, Wayne Hovis; 92-93, Cliff Spohn; 94-97, George Gaadt; 118-119, Luigi Galante; 132, Bill Smith Studio; 158-159, Dennis Lyall; 176-177, Cliff Spohn; 180-181, Yuan Lee; 210-211, Nick Rotondo; 234-235, Jim Griffin; 251(t), Studio Liddell; 251(b), Patrick Gnan; 256-257, Yuan Lee; 260-261, Bill Maughan; 278-279, Don Foley; 279, Geoffrey McCormack; 320-321, Bill Maughan; 324-325, Andrew Wheatcroft; 364-365, Dennis Lyall; 374-375, Don Foley; 400-401, Andrew Wheatcroft; 404-405, Cliff Spohn; 432-433, Sebastian Quigley; 480-481, Cliff Spohn; 484-485, Rick Johnson; 510-511, Studio Liddell; 515, Bill Smith Studio; 516-517, Vincent Wakerley; 552-553, Rick Johnson.

All maps by MapQuest.com

PHOTO CREDITS

Cover: P. Frilet/Panoramic Images (astronaut); NASA (rocket); NASA (moon landing); H. Armstrong Roberts (pedestrians); Don Mason/Corbis Stock Market (computer chip).

PLACEMENT KEY: (t) top; (b) bottom; (l) left; (r) right; (c) center; (bg) background; (fg) foreground; (I) inset.

POSTER INSERT

Flag: Don Mason/Corbis Stock Market, Eagle: Minden Pictures

TITLE PAGE AND TABLE OF CONTENTS

Title page (fg) Ruth Dixon/Stock, Boston, (bg) Doug Armand/Stone; v Concord Museum; vi Smithsonian Institute; vii Stahlhelms Military Collectibles; viii Larry DeVito; ix Stahlhelms Military Collectibles; x The Image Bank.GRADE

INTRODUCTION

1(t) Ruth Dixon/Stock, Boston; (l) Doug Armand/Stone; 2 (t) Bettmann/Corbis; 2 (c) Brown Brothers; 2 (b) AP/Wide World Photos; 3 (t) Underwood & Underwood/Corbis; 3 (c) Bettmann/Corbis; 4 (b) W. L. Cenac; 5 (t) Bettmann/Corbis; 5 (tr) Owen Franken/Corbis; 7 (tl) Matthew Borkoski/Stock, Boston/PictureQuest; 7 (tr) Michael S. Yamashita/Corbis; 7 (bl) Kevin Alexander/Index Stock Imagery/PictureQuest; 7 (br) James Frank/Stock Connection/PictureQuest; 7 (cl) Peter Pearson/Stone; 7 (cr) Jeffrey Muir Hamilton/Stock, Boston/PictureQuest; 8 (c) Telegraph Colour Library/Getty Images; 8 (b) Gary Conner/PhotoEdit; 9 (b) Stone/Getty Images; 10 (t) Michael P. Gadomski/Photo Researchers; 10 (b) Bob Krist/Corbis.

UNIT 1

Unit Opener, (fg) Concord Museum; (bg) Eliot Cohen/Janelco Photographers; 14-15 The Granger Collection, New York; 15 (c) "Anonymous Loan", National Portrait Gallery, Smithsonian Institution/Art Resource, NY; 16 (b) The Granger Collection, New York; 16 (tr) Lee Snider/Corbis; 18-19 David Muench Photography; 20 (bl) Mark Newman/Alaska Stock Images; 22 (tl) Vera Lentz; 22 (tr) Place Stock Photo; 22 (b) Maxwell Museum of Anthropology Albuquerque, NM/Art Resource; 23 Dewitt Jones/Corbis; 24 (i) National Park Service, Sitka National Historical Park; 26 David Heald/National Museum of the American Indian; 28 (b) Werner Forman/Art Resource, NY; 28 (i) Made by Ivor Lawton, Courtesy of Regia/www.regia.org; 29 (t) Bibliotheque Nationale, Paris; 29 (b) Giraudon/Art Resource; 31 (b) Superstock; 31 (i) Courtesy of the Oakland Museum of California; 32 (b) George H. H. Huey Photography; 33 (tl) Library of Congress; 33 (tr) Canadian Museum of Civilization; 34 (t) Bettmann/Corbis; 34 (b) The Reformed Church of the Tarrytowns; 35 (t) Courtesy of the Pilgrim Society, Plymouth, Massachusetts; 38 Salem: Joseph Orme, c. 1765; Peabody Essex Museum; 39 (t) Blackwell History of Education Museum; 40 (t) Bettman/Corbis; 40 (b) Vince Streano/Corbis; 42 (b) Andre Jenny/Focus Group/PictureQuest; 43 (t) Hulton/Archive Photos; 43 (b) Hulton/Archive; 46 (b) Bettman Archive/Corbis; 47 (t) Courtesy of the National Portrait Gallery, London; 48 (tr) Contract Place Holder/Corbis; 48 (bl) Kevin Fleming/Corbis; 49 Hulton/Archive/Getty Images; 50 (b) Lee Snider Photo Images; 50 (tl) Bettman Archive/Corbis; 50 (tr) Hulton/Archive/Getty Images; 51 (tl) Barney Burstein/Corbis; 51 (bl) Corbis; 51 (br) Corbis; 53 (t) A detail, John Trumbull "The Surrender of Lord Cornwallis at Yorktown, 19 October 1781" Yale University Art Gallery, Trumbull Collection; 56-57 Tom Till Photography; 58 (bl) Hulton/Archive; 58 (br) Hulton/Archive Photos; 59 Bettmann/Corbis; 61 (b) North Wind Pictures Archives; 61 (bkgd) Harcourt; 62 Independence National Historical Park; 63 (t) Independence National Historical Park; 63 (b) Reprinted with permission of the Supreme Council, 33°, Scottish

Ray Juno/Corbis Stock Market; 319 (tc) Hulton/Archive; 319 (tr) Hulton/Archive; 319 (cr) Tony Perrottet/Omni-Photo Communications.

UNIT 5

Unit Opener; (fg) Stahlhelms Military Collectibles; (bg) Dennis Brock/Black Star; 330-331 James Blank/Stock, Boston; 332 (b) Hulton/Archive; 333 (t) Bettmann/Corbis; 334 (b) Bettmann/Corbis; 334 (i),(cr) Stahlhelms Military Collectibles; 336 (b) Hulton-Deutsch Collection/Corbis; 336 (t) Corbis; 336 (i),(cr) Culver Pictures; 337 (tl) William Vandivert/TimePix; 337 (tr) National Portrait Gallery, Smithsonian Institution/Art Resource, NY; 338 (b) William Vandivert/TimePix; 338 (tc) David E. Scherman/TimePix; 339 (t) Corbis; 340 (bl) Myron Davis/TimePix; 341 (t) Bettmann/Corbis; 341 (i),(cl) Bettmann/Corbis; 342 (b) TimePix; 343 (t) Bettmann/Corbis; 344 (tl) TimePix; 344 (tr) Corbis; 345 (br) Henry Groskinsky/TimePix; 346 (tl) Herbert Gehr/TimePix; 346 (i),(tr) Florida State Archives; 347 (b) George Strock/TimePix; 348 (tr) Scurlock Photo/Moorland-Spingarn Research Center/Howard University; 349 (bl) Library of Congress; 349 (br) Hulton/Archive; 350 (tc) Harcourt; 350 (bl) Peter Stackpole/TimePix; 350 (i),(br) Peter Stackpole/TimePix; 351 (tr) Hulton/Archive; 351 (br) Hulton/Archive; 352 (t) John Phillips/TimePix; 352 (br) Myron Davis/TimePix; 353 (b) Corbis; 353 (tr) Dean Wong/Corbis; 353 (i),(cr) Hulton-Deutsch Collection/Corbis; 354 (t) The Library of Virginia; 355 (br) Myron Davis/TimePix; 356 (b),(c) Corbis; 356 (tr) Hulton Archive/Getty Images; 357 (tl) Smithsonian Institution; 357 (cr) Smithsonian Institution; 358-359 Johnny Stockshooter/International Stock; 362 (bl) Corbis; 363 (b) Margaret Bourke-White/TimePix; 367 (b) Margaret Bourke-White/TimePix; 367 (cr) Yellow Star, Germany, 1930's. Printed cotton. Gift of Moriah Artcraft Judaica. Photograph by Greg Staley, Courtesy of B'nai B'rith Klutznick National Jewish Museum; 368 (tc) TimePix; 368 (bl) Hulton/Archive; 368-269 Stephen G. St. John/National Geographic Society; 369 (tl) Bettmann/Corbis; 372 (b) TimePix; 373 (tr) Bob Leavitt/TimePix; 374 (tc) Corbis; 376 (tc) Bettmann/Corbis; 376 (bl) Hulton/Archive; 378 (b) Bernard Hoffman/TimePix; 378 (cr) Office of War Information/National Archives/TimePix; 379 (tl) Hulton/Archive; 379 (tr) Hulton/Archive; 381 (t) Carl Mydans/TimePix; 382 (b) Yale Joel/TimePix; 383 (t) Hulton/Archive; 384 (b) Bettmann/Corbis; 384 (tl) Bettmann/Corbis; 385 (t) Bettmann/Corbis; 386 (bl) Catherine Redmond; 386 (br) Catherine Redmond; 387 (t) Margaret Bourke-White/TimePix; 388 (b) Gjon Mili/TimePix; 389 (br) Nat Farbman/TimePix; 390 (br) Alfred Eisenstaedt/TimePix; 391 (t) Bettmann/Corbis; 392 (b) Walter Sanders/TimePix; 392 (i),(cl) J. R. Eyerman/TimePix; 394 (b) Thomas D. McAvoy/TimePix; 394 (cl) Corbis; 395 (t) Bettman/Corbis; 398-399 Bill Bachmann/Mira; 399 (c) Carl Purcell/Mira; 399 (tc) Hulton-Deutsch Collection/Corbis; 399 (i),(tc) AP/Wide World Photos; 399 (i),(cr) AP/Wide World Photos; 399 (cr) AP/World Wide Photos.

UNIT 6

Unit Opener; (fg) The Image Bank; (bg) Lloyd Sutton/Masterfile; 408-409 Raymond Gehman/Corbis.; 411 (t) Corbis; 413 (b) Corbis; 413 (tc) William A. Bake/Corbis; 413 (i),(bl Carl Mydans/TimePix; 414 (b) John Dominis/TimePix; 414 (cl) Corbis; 415 (c) Bettmann/Corbis; 415 (tr) Bettmann/Corbis; 416 (b) Greg Mathieson/TimePix; 418 (b) Jack Moebes/Corbis; 418 (i),(cl Jack Moebes/Corbis; 419 (bc) Hulton/Archive; 419 (tl) Bettmann/Corbis; 420 (tl) Hank Walker/TimePix; 421 (bc) Carl Iwasaki/TimePix; 421 (tr) AP/Wide World Photos; 421 (br) Hank Walker/TimePix; 422 (b) Loomis Dean/TimePix; 422 (i) Bettmann/Corbis; 423 (i) Allan Grant/TimePix; 423 (tr) Howard Sochurek/TimePix; 425 (b) Bettmann/Corbis; 426 (tr) National Archives; 426 (bl) Bettmann/Corbis; 426 (br) Cold War Museum; 427 National Archives; 427 National Archives; 428 (b) John F. Kennedy Library; 429 (c) Peace Corps; 429 (tr) Al Fenn/TimePix; 430 (b) Carl Mydans/TimePix; 430 (i) UPI/Corbis; 431 (r) NASA; 432 (tl) Ralph Morse/TimePix; 434 (br) Corbis; 435 (b) Flip Schulke/Corbis; 436 (bl) UPI/Corbis; 437 (t) Flip Schulke/Corbis; 437 (br) Matt Herron/Black Star; 438 (tl) Ted Russell/TimePix; 438 (bl) Bettmann/Corbis; 439 (tr) Arthur Schatz/TimePix; 440 (t) Bettmann/Corbis; 441 (c) Theo Westenberger/Gamma Liasion International; 442 (b) Hulton Archive/TimePix; 448 (b) Corbis; 448 (i) Oscar White/Corbis; 449 (t) Bettmann/Corbis; 450 (b) Leif Skoogfors/Corbis; 450 (cl) Joe Munroe/TimePix; 451 (t) Larry Burrows/TimePix; 452 (tr) Bettmann/Corbis; 452 (bl) UPI/Bettmann/Corbis; 453 (b) Bettmann/Corbis; 455 (b) Bettmann/Corbis; 456 (bl) David Rubinger/TimePix; 457 (b) Bettmann/Corbis; 457 (tc) Owen Franklin/Corbis; 458 (b) Bettmann/Corbis; 460 (bc) Janet Wishnetsky/Corbis; 460 (tl) Dirck Halstead/Gamma Liaison International; 461 (tl) Chris Niedenthal/TimePix; 461 (i) David & Peter Turnley/Corbis; 462 (b) Dennis Brack/TimePix; 463 (t) David Valdez/TimePix; 464 (b) David Longstreath/AP/Wide World Photos; 464 (i) Terry Ashe/TimePix; 466 (b) Reuters NewMedia/Corbis; 467 (tl) Visar Kryeziu/AP/Wide World Photos; 468 (bl) AFP/Corbis; 469 (b) Mark Gibson/Index Stock Imagery/PictureQuest; 470 (b) Colin Braley/TimePix; 470 (i) Gary I. Rothstein/AP/Wide World Photos; 471 (tr) Reuters NewMedia/Corbis; 472 (b) AFP/Corbis; 472 (i) Thomas E. Franklin/The Record (Bergen County New Jersey)/Corbis SABA; 473 (t) Steve Liss/TimePix; 475 (tl) Alamy; 475 (tr) Alamy; 478 Mark Gibson; 479 (t) Raymond Gehman/Corbis; 479 (b) Birmingham Civil Rights Institute.

UNIT 7

Unit Opener, (bg) Werner J. Bertsch/Bruce Coleman, Inc.; 490-491 Miles Ertman/Masterfile; 492 Chuck Pefley/Stock, Boston; 494-495 (t) ML Sinibaldi/Corbis Stock Market; 494 (b) Steve Solum/Bruce Coleman Collection; 496 (b) Bettmann/Corbis; 497 (t) Denis Scott/Corbis Stock Market; 500 (b) Norman Owen Tomlin/Bruce Coleman Collection; 501 (t) Normwn Owen Tomlin/Bruce Coleman Collection; 501 (b) Debra P. Hershkowitz/Bruce Coleman Collection; 502 Tony Freeman/PhotoEdit/PictureQuest; 503 Robb Helfrick/Index Stock Imagery/PictureQuest; 504 (bl) Bob Daemmrich/Stock, Boston; 504 (br) Keith Bardin/Mira; 505 FPG International; 506 (t) Lester Lefkowitz/Corbis Stock Market; 506 (i) Pete Saloutos/Corbis Stock Market; 507 (b) Rei O'Hara/Black Star Publishing/PictureQuest; 507 (i) Erica Lanser/Black Star Publishing/PictureQuest; 508 Sonda Dawes/The Image Works; 509 Dave Bartruff/ Stock, Boston; 512 (c) Catherine Karnow/Corbis; 512 (tc) Corbis Stock Market; 513 (b) Jonathan Nourok/PhotoEdit; 513 (i) Dorothy Littel Greco/Stock, Boston; 514(b) Nubar Alexanian/Stock, Boston/PictureQuest; 515 (t) Raphael Macia/Photo Researchers, Inc.; 518(t) AP/Wide World Photos; 519(c) Bowling Green State University Library; 519(tr) Terry Heffernan/Kit Hinrichs and Delphine Hirasuna; 519(cr) Bowling Green State University Library; 519(cl) Terry Heffernan/Kit Hinrichs and Delphine Hirasuna; 522-523Larry Luxner; 524 Greg Von Doersten/Outside Images/PictureQuest; 526 (b) Bettmann/Corbis; 654 526 (cl) Carlos S. Pereyra/DDB Stock Photo; 527 (t) Carlos S. Pereyra/DDB Stock Photo; 528 (t) Reuters NewMedia Inc./Corbis; 529 Bob Daemmrich/Stock, Boston/PictureQuest; 531 (b) NOAA/APWideWorld; 531 (i) Yann Arthus-Bertrand/Corbis; 532 (t) Tom Haley/Sipa; 532 (b) David Parker/Science Photo Library/Photo Researchers; 533 AP Photo/Lynne Sladky); 534(b) Suzanne Murphy-Larronde/DDB Stock Photo; 536-537(b) H. Mark Weidman; 536(i) Jacques Jangoux/Photo Researchers; 538 (t) D. Donne Bryant/DDB Stock Photo; 538(b) Larry Luxner; 539(t) Peter Menzel/Stock, Boston; 539(b) Francis E. Caldwell/DDB Stock Photo; 540Walter Bibikow/Stock, Boston; 541(b) Pascal Quittemelle/Stock, Boston; 541(i) Martin Grosnick/Bruce Coleman, Inc.; 543(t) Owen Franken/Stock, Boston; 543(b) Walter Bibikow/Stock, Boston; 543 (i) The Parliament of Canada Photo Gallery; 544 (bl) J.A. Kraulis/Masterfile; 544 (bc) Mike Mazzaschi/Stock, Boston; 545 Public Archives, Canada/The St. Lawrence Seaway Management Corporation; 546 N. Devore/Bruce Coleman, Inc.; 550 (t) Miles Ertman/Masterfile; 550 (b) Russ Finley; 550-551 (bg) David R. Frazier; 551(tl) David R. Frazier; 551 (tr) Laurence Parent Photography; 551 (br) Lee Snider Photo Images; 551 (cl) National Geographic Society.

REFERENCE

R8-R10, All Presidential Portraits courtesy of National Portrait Gallery except page R10, (br) The Image Works

All other photos from Harcourt School Photo Library and/or Photographers: Weronica Ankarorn, Ken Kinzie, U. S. Color.

Reading in the Content Area

Reading in the Content Area

Reading is an important part of social studies. The Reading in the Content Area copying masters help you integrate the use of reading skills into your social studies instruction. At the top of each copying master, a reading skill is modeled, using text from the pupil edition. At the bottom, additional pupil edition text is provided for students to practice the reading skill.

Contents

Main Idea and Supporting Details

> The most important thought of a chapter, lesson, or paragraph is the main idea. The main idea may be stated in a sentence, or it may only be suggested. Facts or examples that provide information to support a main idea are known as **supporting details**.

Main Idea   Most of the first Americans, or ancient Indians, as archaeologists call them, were nomads who lived and hunted together in small groups.   **page 22**

Supporting Details   To survive, they gathered fruits and nuts and hunted mammoths and other large animals that wandered the land. They ate the meat and used the animals' fur, skins, and bones to make clothing, shelters, and tools.

Directions: Circle the main idea of the paragraph. Underline the supporting details.   **page 39**

Puritan life centered on religion. At the center of each town was a meetinghouse, where people worshiped and held town meetings. The government was controlled by a few powerful male church members.

Categorize

To **categorize** is to classify information by category. You can place people, places, and events into categories to make it easier to find facts.

page 110

By 1860 there were more than 500,000 free African Americans living in the United States. Some had been born to parents who were free. Some had bought their freedom or had been freed by their owners. Others had escaped slavery by running away.

The information can be sorted into this category:

African Americans Living in the United States by 1860			
Some had been born to parents who were free.	Some had bought their freedom.	Some had been freed by their owners.	Some had escaped slavery by running away.

Directions: Sort the information in the paragraphs into the category given.

page 127

In both the North and the South, only men were allowed to join the army. Women, however, found many ways to help. They took over factory, business, and farm jobs that men left behind. They sent food to the troops, made bandages, and collected supplies. Many women, such as Clara Barton and Sally Tompkins, worked as nurses. A few served as spies, and some even dressed as men, joined the army, and fought in battles.

Contributions of Women During the Civil War				

© Harcourt

Summarize

To **summarize**, restate the most important ideas or key points in your own words.

MODEL

New inventions also helped people shorten the amount of time it took to do housework. In the mid-1800s treadle, or foot-powered, sewing machines reduced the time needed to make clothes. Washing machines that people worked by turning a crank made doing laundry easier and saved time. By the early 1900s some homes had sewing machines and washing machines that were powered by electricity.

page 201

Summary Sewing machines and washing machines shortened the time it took to do housework.

TRY IT

Directions: Read the paragraph. Then write a summary of the paragraph.

page 215

President Theodore Roosevelt also believed in the progressive movement. In his first months as President, Roosevelt started a government program called the Square Deal to make sure that all Americans were given the same opportunities to succeed.

Summary _____

_____

© Harcourt

Sequence

The order in which events occur is their **sequence**. The sequence tells what happened first, next, then, and last.

Follow the sequence.

pages
228–230

First   In 1913 Woodrow Wilson becomes President.

Next   On May 7, 1915, a German submarine sinks the British passenger ship *Lusitania*. More than 1,000 people are killed including 128 United States citizens. The United States might have joined the Allies in the war right then, but Germany agrees not to attack any more passenger ships.

Then   Early in 1917, Germany begins firing upon any ships—even passenger ships—that try to sail to Britain.

Last   On April 6, 1917, the United States declares war on Germany.

Directions: Read the paragraphs. Determine the sequence. Then underline words that help show sequence.

pages
242–243

Long before the war was over, President Wilson began thinking about the peace to come. On January 8, 1918, he presented his peace ideas to Congress. He made a speech in which he described his Fourteen Points.

As the fighting continued in 1918, many people in the United States and people from other Allied nations cheered Wilson's plan. After the war ended and it was time to write a peace treaty, people began to question parts of the Fourteen Points.

In January 1919, representatives from more than 30 countries met near Paris to write a peace treaty. It took them five months. The treaty that came out of the negotiations was called the Treaty of Versailles for the palace in which the treaty was signed.

© Harcourt

Compare and Contrast

To **compare** people, places, events, or ideas, you find the ways in which they are alike. To **contrast** people, places, events, or ideas, you find the ways in which they are different.

Compare   Like radio, the movies began before the 1920s.   **page 287**

What is being compared—Radio and movies

Contrast   In the decade that followed World War I, the United States economy seemed to be getting stronger and stronger. The restrictions that had been placed on businesses during World War I were lifted when the war ended. Factories that had produced weapons and other war supplies went back to making consumer goods. . . . Factories made vacuum cleaners, washing machines, radios, and all kinds of new electric appliances for the home. Never before had consumers had so many ways to spend their money.   **pages 268–269**

What is being contrasted—The economy and spending habits of consumers during and after World War I

Directions: Read the paragraph. Identify what is being compared and contrasted.   **page 289**

In addition to listening to new music, people tried new dances. In earlier times, many people had enjoyed ballroom dances. Now the "flappers," as stylish women of the time were called, danced the Charleston with their dates. The Charleston had fast movements and high kicks.

© Harcourt

Generalize

When you **generalize**, you make a broad statement. Words such as *many*, *some*, and *most* usually signal a generalization.

By the end of the 1920s, many consumers already had washing machines, vacuum cleaners, and radios. Those who had bought these goods on installment plans continued to pay them off. However, they were not buying many new goods. As a result, consumer spending slowed. Suddenly, companies found that they had too many goods that they could not sell. Many companies soon cut workers' hours and wages. Some companies began to lay off workers. Other companies closed.

pages 296–297

Generalizations
- Most consumers only buy things they need.
- Less buying by consumers may lead to too much of certain products.
- When products do not sell, people may lose their jobs.

Directions: Read the paragraphs. Then make generalizations about what you have read.

page 308

In 1932 United States citizens elected Franklin D. Roosevelt as President. Roosevelt believed that in order to end the Great Depression, the federal government needed to take bold, new action. On his inauguration day, he said, "This great nation will endure as it has endured, will revive, and will prosper. So, first of all, let me assert my firm belief that the only thing we have to fear is fear itself. . . ." Roosevelt's words gave people hope that the economy would improve.

Generalizations _____

_____

Cause and Effect

An event or action that makes something else happen is a **cause**. What happens as a result of that event or action is the **effect**.

page 336

On September 1, 1939, nearly 2 million German soldiers invaded Poland from the west. At the same time, Soviet soldiers invaded from the east. The Germans attacked with tanks on land and planes in the air, and Poland was quickly defeated. The Germans called this style of fighting *blitzkrieg*, or "lightning war." When Poland fell, Stalin and Hitler divided the nation. Two days later Poland's allies, Britain and France, declared war on Germany. World War II had begun.

Cause	Effect
Germany and the Soviet Union attack Poland and after the attack divide it between both countries.	Britain and France declare war on Germany, and World War II begins.

Directions: Read the paragraph. Then identify any causes and their effects.

pages 344–345

The United States was shocked by the Japanese surprise attack on Pearl Harbor. President Roosevelt made a speech before Congress the next day to ask that war be declared on Japan. . . .

Three days later, Germany and Italy declared war on the United States, and Congress declared a state of war with them, too.

Cause	Effect

Make Inferences

When you read, sometimes you need to make inferences. An **inference** is an educated guess based on the facts you have read and your own knowledge and experience.

MODEL

By the time Johnson became President in November 1963, the Vietcong were winning the war. Then in August 1964 it was reported that a North Vietnamese gunboat had attacked a United States Navy ship in the Gulf of Tonkin near Vietnam. Johnson sent more soldiers to South Vietnam, hoping they could help defeat the Vietcong.

page 449

Inference

When United States citizens are attacked, the President of the United States takes action.

TRY IT

Directions: Read the paragraph. Then make an inference about what you have read.

page 465

The new countries in the former Soviet Union and Eastern Europe faced terrible problems. Communism had left their economies in ruins. Civil wars had also broken out in some places. Without communist control, old hatreds between people came to the surface.

Inference

_____

_____

Answer Key

Main Idea and Supporting Details

(Puritan life centered on religion.) At the center of each town was a meetinghouse, where people worshiped and held town meetings. The government was controlled by a few powerful male church members.

page C1

Categorize

page C2

Contributions of Women During the Civil War				
took over factory, business, and farm jobs	sent food to the troops, made bandages, and collected supplies	worked as nurses	served as spies	some dressed as men, joined the army, and fought in battles

Summarize

Possible response: The Square Deal was a program started by President Theodore Roosevelt that made sure all Americans had the same opportunities.

page C3

Sequence

Possible response:

First   Long <u>before the war was over</u>, President Wilson began thinking about the peace to come. On January 8, 1918, he presented his peace ideas to Congress.

Next   <u>After the war ended</u> and it was time to write a peace treaty, people began to question parts of the Fourteen Points.

Then   <u>In January 1919</u> representatives from more than 30 countries met near Paris to write a peace treaty.

Last   The treaty <u>that came about because of the meeting</u> was called the Treaty of Versailles for the palace in which the treaty was signed.

page C4

Compare and Contrast

What is being compared and contrasted—Types of dances before and during the "Roaring Twenties"

page C5

Generalize

Possible response:

page C6

- The words of a leader usually give people hope.
- Often, new leadership is needed to make things better for people.

Cause and Effect

page C7

Cause	Effect
The Japanese attack Pearl Harbor.	President Roosevelt asks Congress to declare war on Japan.
Germany and Italy declare war on the United States.	Congress declares war on Germany and Italy.

Make Inferences

Possible response: Countries undergoing a change in their form of government face economic problems and may have conflicts between groups of people with different cultural backgrounds.

page C8

© Harcourt

Thinking Organizers

Thinking Organizers

Ideas and concepts may be organized in many different ways. The contents of the following pages are intended to act as guides for that organization. These copying masters may be used to help students organize the concepts in the lessons they have read. They may also help students complete the wide variety of activities that are assigned throughout the school year.

Contents

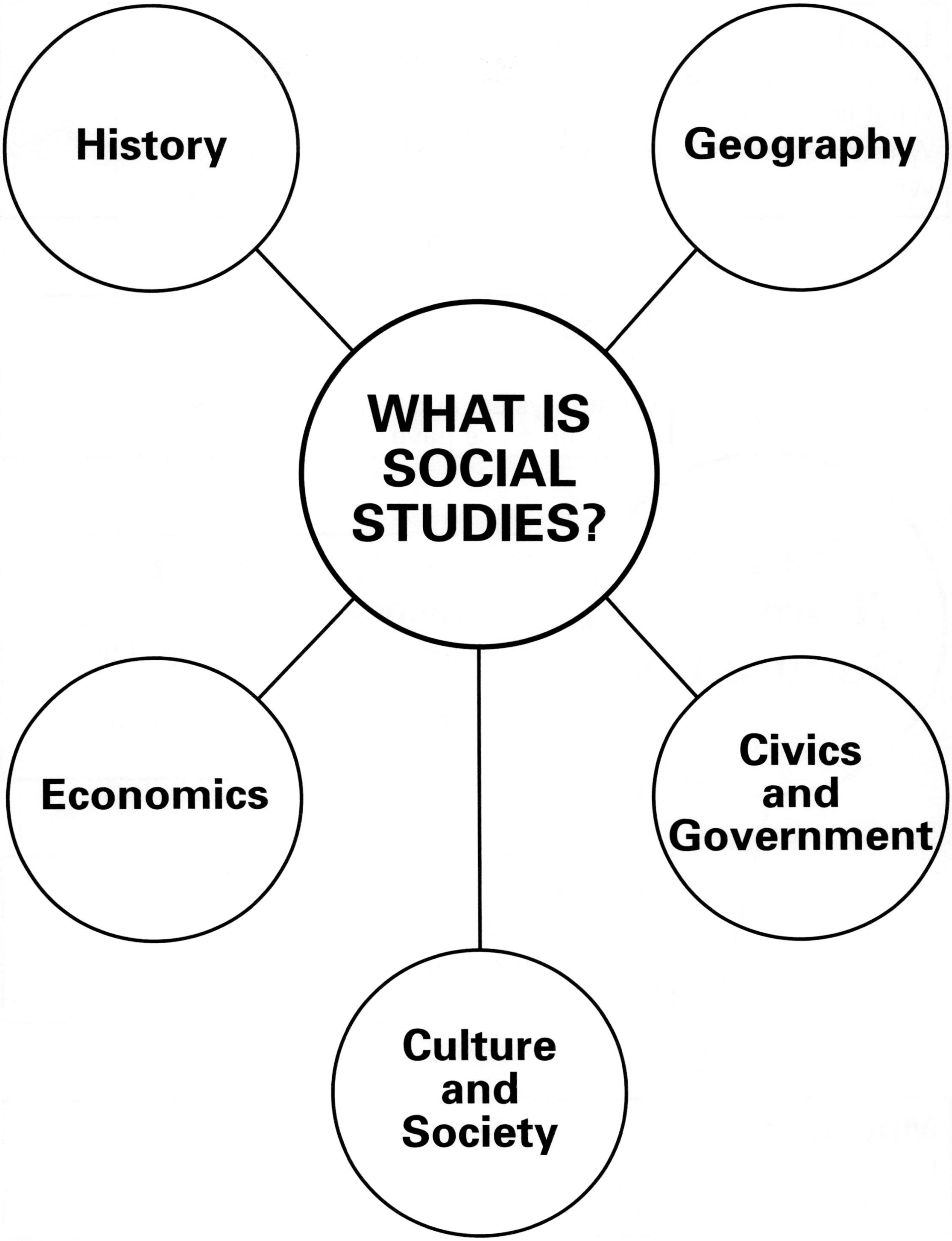
History
Geography
WHAT IS SOCIAL STUDIES?
Economics
Civics and Government
Culture and Society

Location

Where is the place located?

What is it near?

What direction is it from another place?

Why are certain features or places located where they are?

Place

What is it like there?

What physical and human features does the place have?

The Five Themes of Geography

Human-Environment Interactions

How are people's lives shaped by the place?

How has the place been shaped by people?

Regions

How is this place like other places?

What features set this place apart from other places?

Movement

How do people, products, and ideas get from one place to another?

Why do they make these movements?

© Harcourt

Essential Elements of Geography

The World in Spatial Terms

Why are things located where they are?

Human Systems

Where do people settle?

How do people earn their livings?

What laws do people make?

Places and Regions

What are the physical features of a region?

What are the human features?

Environment and Society

How do people affect the environment?

How does the environment affect people?

Physical Systems

How do wind, water, and precipitation affect Earth's surface?

How do living things create and change environments?

The Uses of Geography

What can I discover by looking at a map?

What kind of map should I use?

How can the map key help me?

© Harcourt

Reading About History

Ask yourself these questions as you read.

1. WHAT happened?

2. WHEN did it happen?

3. WHO took part in it?

4. HOW and WHY did it happen?

Current Events

Summary of an important event:

WHO:

WHAT:

WHEN:

WHERE:

HOW:

Where did it take place? Draw a map.

Why?

What was the cause? **What was the effect?**

Comparison

This event is similar to . . .

Prediction

What do I think will happen next?

Personal Reaction

My reaction to the event:

© Harcourt

Social Studies Journal

The single most important thing I learned was . . .

Something that confused me or that I did not understand was . . .

What surprised me the most was . . .

I would like to know more about . . .

Sources I can use to find answers to my questions . . .

The part that made the greatest impact on me was . . .

© Harcourt

Reading Guide

Questions I have before reading				New questions I have after reading
Question **1**	Question **2**	Question **3**	Question **4**	Question:
				Question:
Summary of what I learned after reading that answers my questions				**Other interesting information I learned while reading**
Question **1**	Question **2**	Question **3**	Question **4**	
General summary:				My reaction to what I read:

Visual Learning

Describe the artwork.

Explain what is happening in the artwork.

Explain what the artist is trying to show you.

Explain the mood set by the artwork.

Main Idea and Supporting Details

Supporting Detail	Supporting Detail

Main Idea

Supporting Detail	Supporting Detail

Fact and Opinion

✓	**Fact**
✓	**Fact**
✓	**Fact**
✓	**Fact**

✗	**Opinion**
✗	**Opinion**
✗	**Opinion**
✗	**Opinion**

Causes and Effects

What Caused the Event

Event

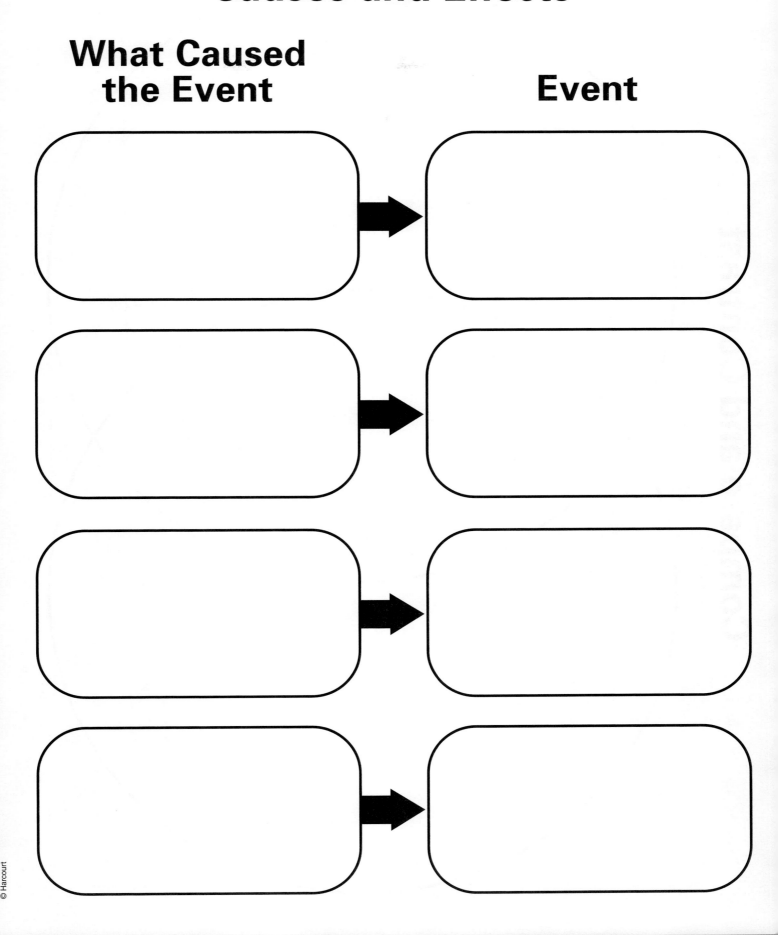

Compare and Contrast

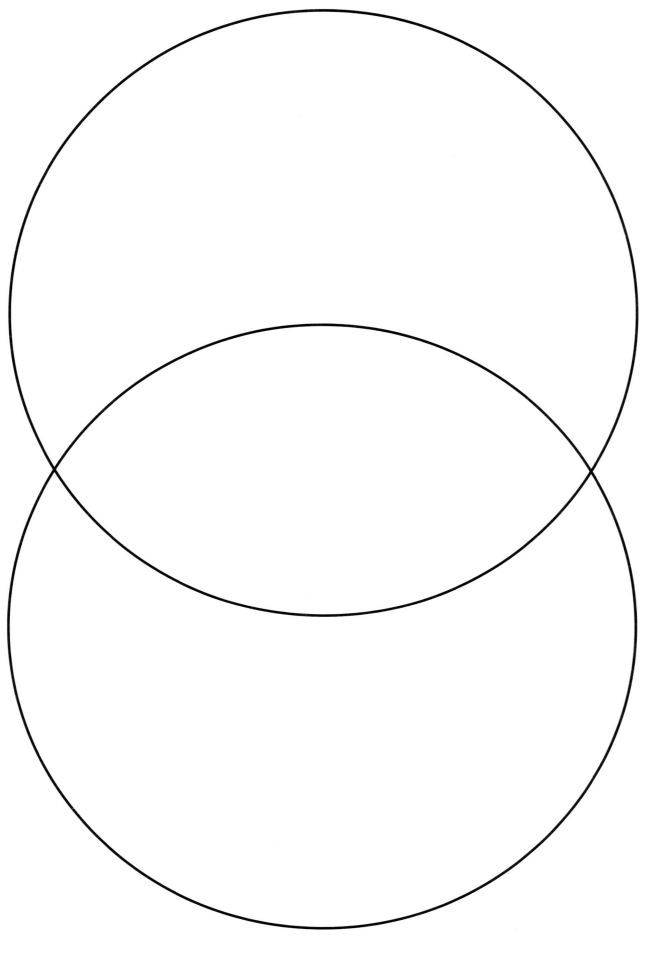

Categorize

Sequence

Event

Order

Event

Event

Event

Event

© Harcourt

Summarize

Important Facts

SUMMARY

Important Facts

Make a Generalization

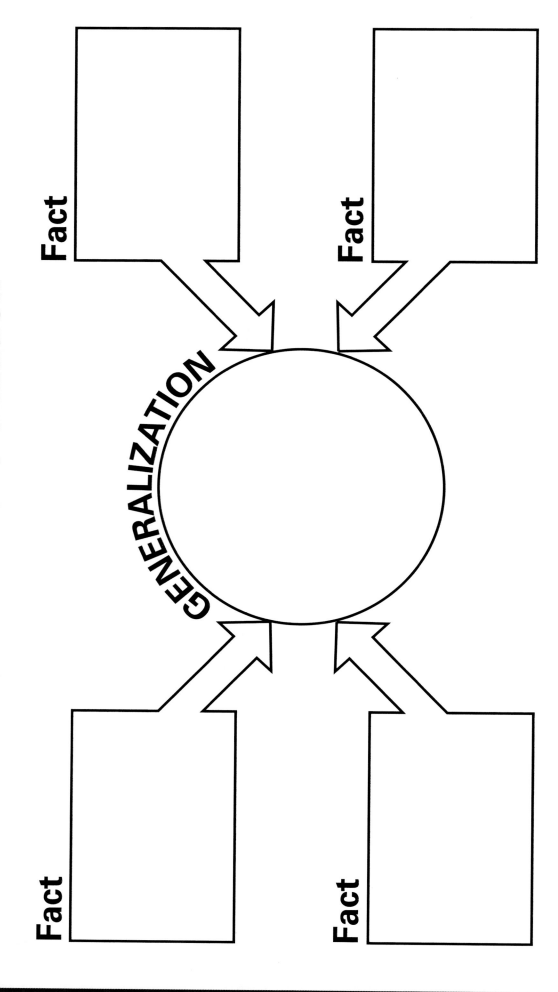

Fact

Fact

GENERALIZATION

Fact

Fact

Draw a Conclusion

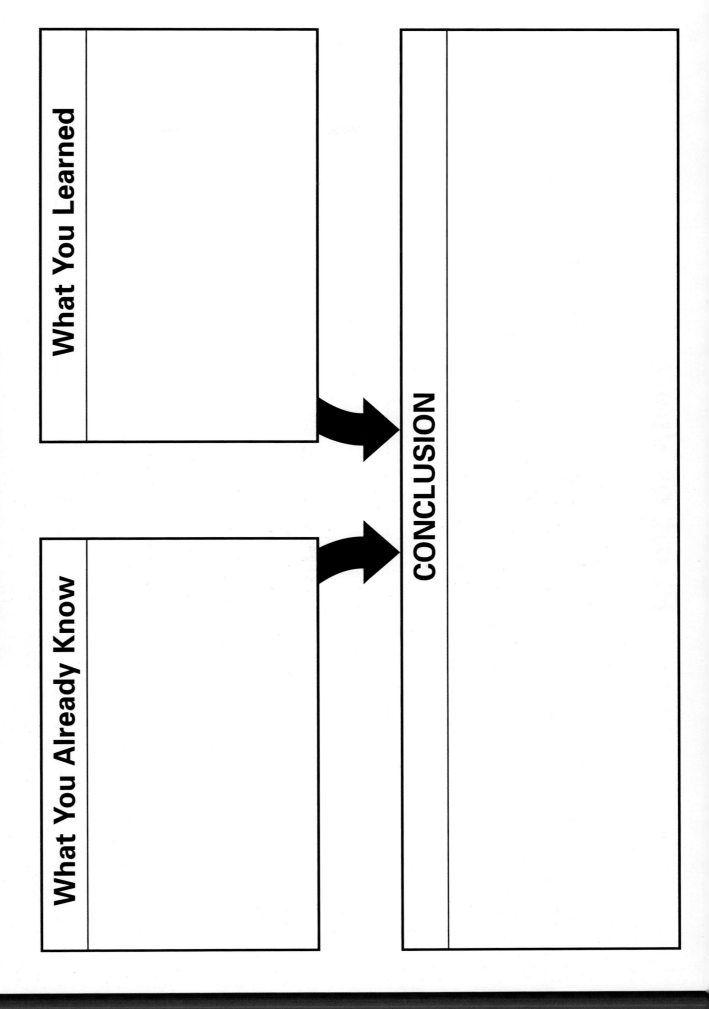

What You Learned

What You Already Know

CONCLUSION

Point of View

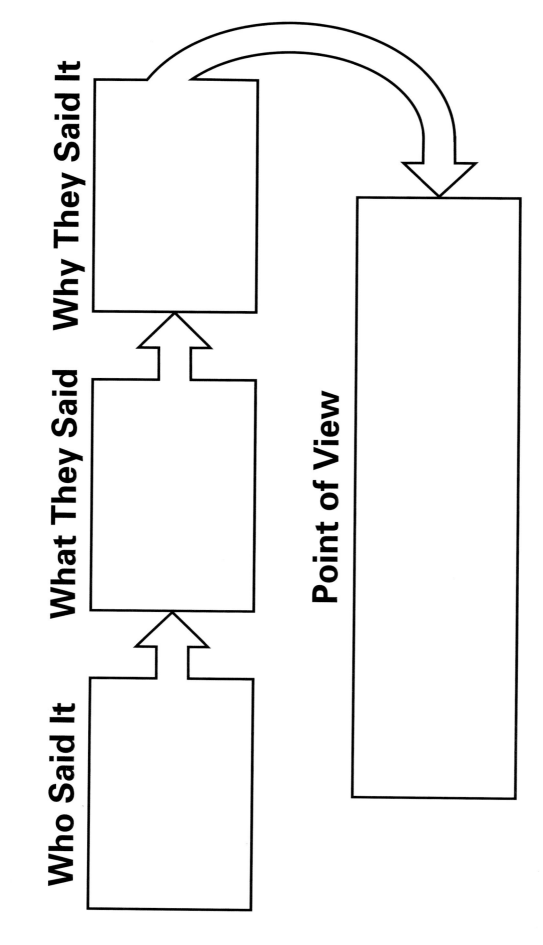

Who Said It

What They Said

Why They Said It

Point of View

Make Inferences

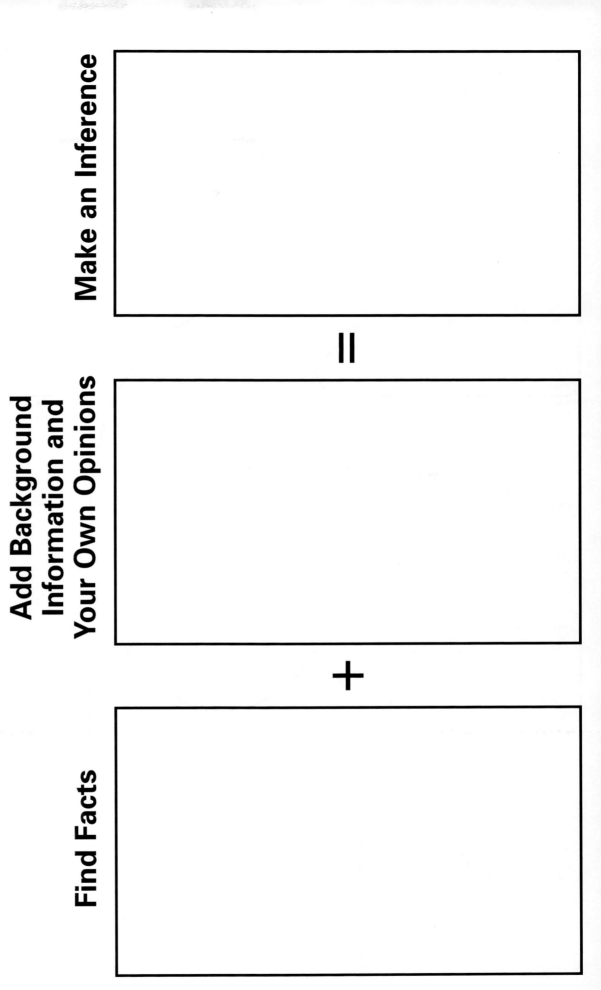

Make an Inference

Add Background Information and Your Own Opinions

Find Facts

=

+

© Harcourt

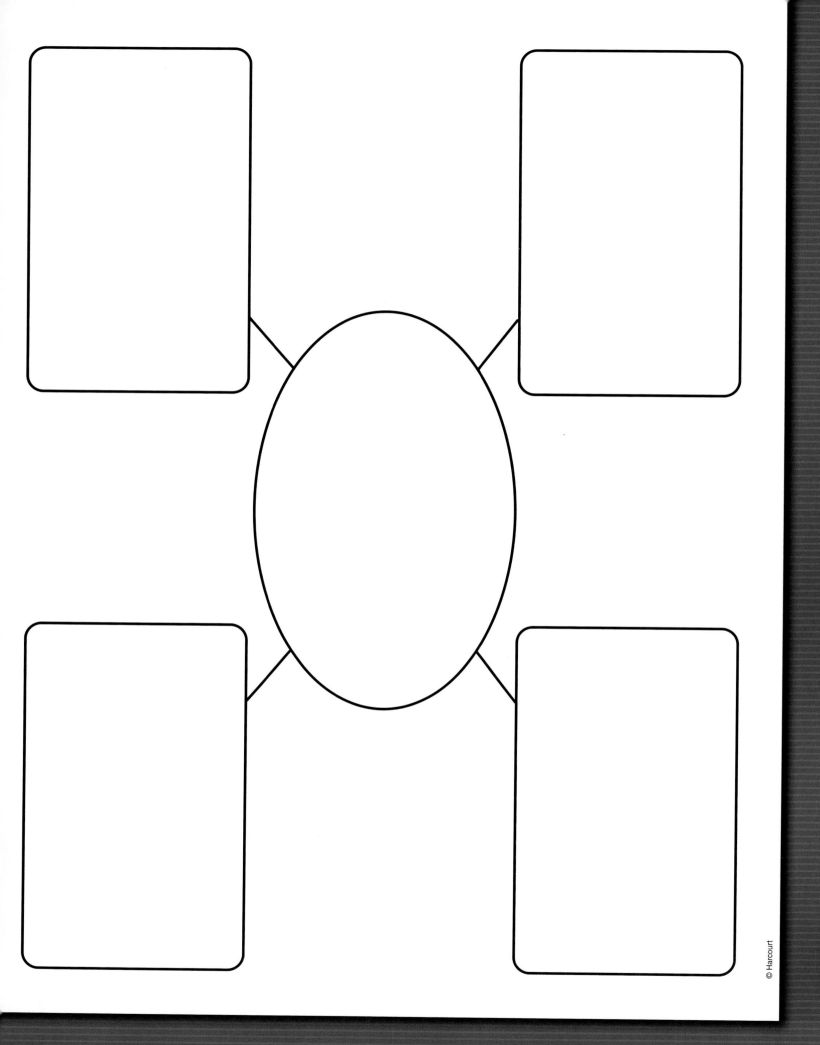

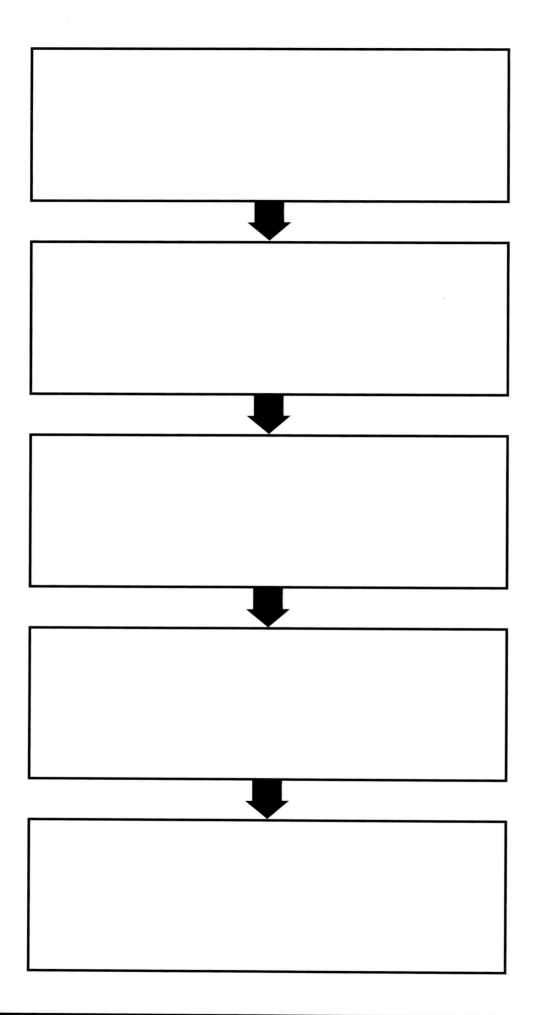

The United States

North America

The World

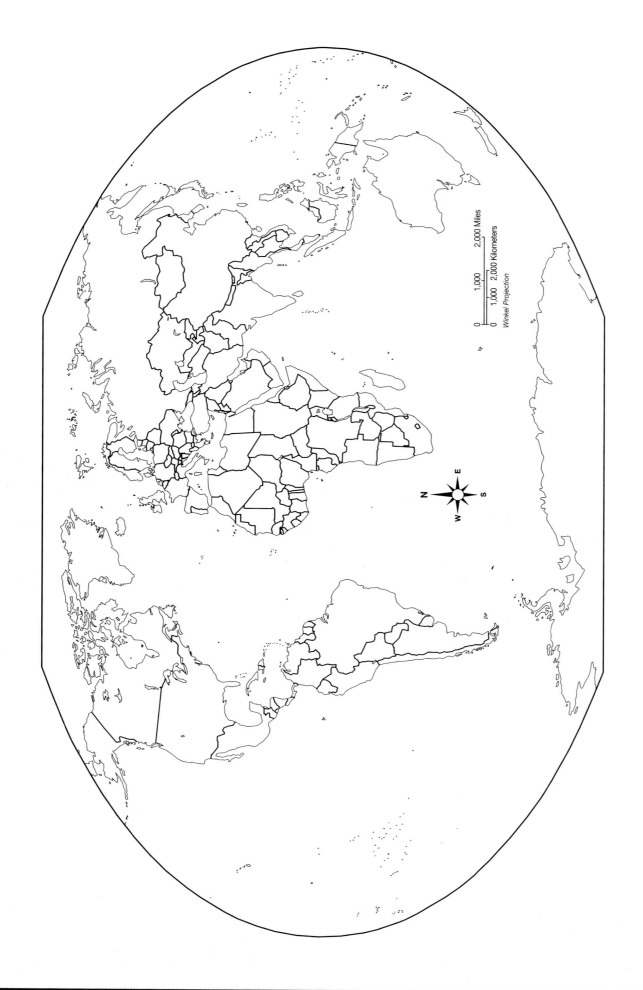

2,000 Miles

1,000

2,000 Kilometers

1,000

Winkel Projection

N
E
W
S

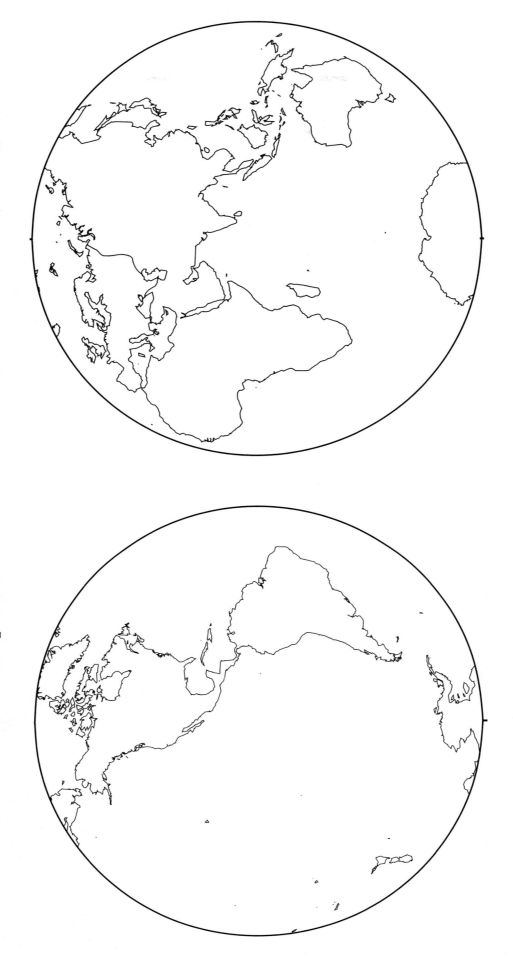

Eastern Hemisphere

Western Hemisphere

Northern Hemisphere

Southern Hemisphere

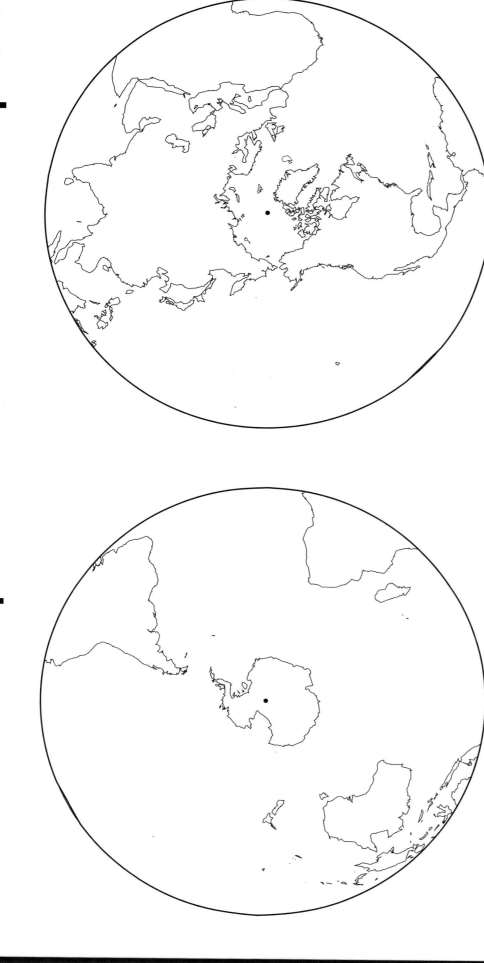

Labor Day

Labor Day

The first Monday in September marks the day dedicated to American workers— Labor Day. It signifies a national yearly tribute to the contributions workers have made to our country. The first Labor Day holiday was celebrated on September 5, 1882, in New York City. By 1885 many cities across the country had adopted this "workingman's holiday." In 1894, Congress passed an act making the first Monday in September a legal holiday.

- Today, Labor Day is celebrated with picnics and parades.
- To some, Labor Day marks the end of summer and the last three-day weekend of the year.

Risky Business

Have students poll their friends to find out which job or occupation they believe is the most dangerous. Then share with them information from the Census Bureau that lists some of the riskiest professions. Invite students to discuss those statistics.

Show Your Appreciation

Discuss how jobs can affect people's lives. Have students name jobs that impact their lives and think about the people who perform those jobs. Invite each student to select someone who does a job and to show that person his or her appreciation by creating a thank-you card.

Find a Job

1. Give each student a copy of the employment section of a newspaper.

2. Have students locate a job description.

3. Help students create a résumé that lists the skills needed to fill that job.

Career Fair

Have students invite people in different career fields to visit the class. Each career field can have a booth and handouts for more information. Or, have students research careers that they are interested in and set up career booths with handouts that tell others about their position and their job responsibilities. Invite other classes to visit these "experts" in their career fields.

Columbus Day

Columbus Day

Christopher Columbus was an explorer for Spain who sailed across the Atlantic Ocean. He was looking for a shorter route to use in trading valuable goods with people in the Indies. Columbus landed on San Salvador, an island in what is now the Bahamas. Instead of finding a new trade route, Columbus unknowingly visited an unknown continent between Europe and Asia. That continent was North America.

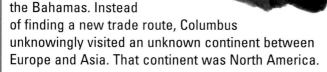

About four hundred years after Christopher Columbus first arrived in the Americas, people in the United States held the first celebration in his honor. Today, Columbus Day is a national holiday celebrated on the second Monday in October. It is celebrated with parades and speeches. Government offices and many businesses are closed.

- Calendars traditionally show the second Monday in October as Columbus Day.

- When Columbus landed in the Americas, he believed that he had reached the Indies, so he called the people that he met *Indians.*

- On Columbus's first voyage, he sailed with three ships, the *Niña,* the *Pinta,* and the *Santa María.*

Map It Out

Provide students with world maps, and help them locate Spain and San Salvador. Ask students to label the continents and oceans. With a colored pencil or marker, have students map the approximate route Columbus followed to get to San Salvador. Students should show and label his three ships en route.

Log Book

There have been several biographies written about the life of Christopher Columbus and his voyages. Columbus also kept a detailed log book of the daily events that took place on his voyage. The log book included the sailors' actions and behaviors as well as how they reacted toward one another and toward the native peoples they met along the way.

Explain that a log book is very similar to a diary or a journal. Choose and read aloud to students a few translated selections from Columbus's log book. Then have students begin their own log book and write about what happens each day, how others react, and what their feelings are about it.

Convince the Queen

Remind students that Columbus needed support from Spain in order to pay for his voyage. He made many appeals to Queen Isabella to provide money, ships, and supplies for his voyage. Have students take the role of Columbus and prepare and present to the class a short speech to convince the queen of the merits of a voyage.

Veterans Day

Veterans Day

Veterans Day is a day for remembering those who fought for our country. It was originally called Armistice Day, for the armistice ending the fighting in World War I but later became known as Veterans Day. In 1971, President Nixon declared Veterans Day, the second Monday in November, a federal holiday. Veterans Day is a day to honor all who have served in the armed forces of the United States. It is also a day to remember the sacrifices that men and women made during all wars fought by the United States. Veterans march in parades, give speeches, and are recognized in ceremonies throughout the United States. These ceremonies are often held at national monuments or memorials, such as the Vietnam Veterans Memorial in Washington, D.C. It was built to honor soldiers from the Vietnam War. The names of those lost in the war are etched into a black granite wall.

- In 1921 an unknown soldier was buried at Arlington National Cemetery to honor all who have died serving their country.
- The armistice that ended the fighting in World War I was signed in 1918 at 11:00 on the eleventh day of the eleventh month.

Letters to Home

Ask students to imagine they are soldiers far from home. Have them write letters describing their thoughts about serving their country.

Dear Mom and Dad,
    I am sitting on the deck of our battleship. We are headed into enemy territory.
    I am proud to serve my country. I am ready to fight for our freedom.
    Keep me in your thoughts and prayers.
                    I love you!
                    Robert

War Time Line

Let students research and make a time line showing the dates of major wars since World War I, listing relevant facts about each.

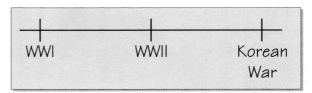

God Bless America

Irving Berlin's patriotic song "God Bless America" was first sung on Armistice Day, November 11, 1938, at the New York World's Fair. Today, the song remains a very popular patriotic tribute to America. Berlin donated all of the royalties from the song to charity. Invite students to find out more about Irving Berlin. Then, sing "God Bless America" together.

GOD BLESS AMERICA
by Irving Berlin

God bless America.
Land that I love.
Stand beside her and guide her,
Thru the night with a light from above.
From the mountains to the prairies
To the oceans white with foam,
God bless America
My home sweet home.
God bless America
My home sweet home.

Thanksgiving

Thanksgiving Day

Thanksgiving is a holiday that celebrates a special harvest in America a long time ago. Many people left Europe in the 1600s looking for a new life in the Americas. One group, the Pilgrims, left England to find a place where they could worship as they wished. They sailed across the ocean on the *Mayflower* and landed in North America at a place they called Plymouth. There they worked to clear the land, build houses, and make a new life.

During the first winter in Plymouth, half of the settlers died. In the spring an Indian named Squanto helped those who survived plant crops. Their fall harvest was a success, so the Pilgrims held a feast to give thanks to God. The Pilgrims shared the feast with the Wampanoag Indians.

Today, families gather at Thanksgiving to share good things to eat and to give thanks for the good things in their lives.

- Turkey is a traditional Thanksgiving food. People at the first Thanksgiving feast may have eaten wild turkey, but they probably also enjoyed other meats including venison, duck, goose, lobster, and clams.
- President Abraham Lincoln made Thanksgiving a national holiday in 1863.
- Schools, banks, government offices, and most businesses are closed on Thanksgiving.

What's for Dinner?

Most people associate pumpkin pie and cranberry sauce with Thanksgiving dinner, when in fact, neither of these were served at the Pilgrims' first Thanksgiving celebration. Have students research foods eaten in the 1600s and collect data regarding period games and activities. Then make a mural showing the similarities and differences between the Pilgrims' first Thanksgiving and a present-day celebration.

Compare Plant Growth

Squanto showed the Pilgrims how to grow corn. To fertilize the soil, the Indians mixed in fish and fish parts before planting the corn seeds. Do a science experiment with fish fertilizer. (This is a product for household plants that can be purchased at a nursery.) Put soil in two pots. Mix fish fertilizer with the soil in one of the pots. Plant the same kinds of seeds in each pot. Observe the plants over the next few weeks. Record the observations on a chart or in a journal. What conclusions can be drawn from the experiment?

Do Not Tip the Mayflower

When the Pilgrims left for North America, they could not take all their belongings with them. Choices were made as to what they really needed for that long voyage. Let students work in small groups to make a list of items the Pilgrims would need and the approximate weight of each. Tell students that only 100 lbs per group may be taken on the ship. Have students work together to decide which items should be taken on the trip. Ask each group to defend their choices.

Christmas Day

Christmas Day

On December 25 many people celebrate Christmas. For many people Christmas is a religious holiday honoring the birth of Jesus Christ. Christmas customs vary from family to family and are often based on traditions brought by ancestors from other countries.

In the United States many Christians go to church on Christmas Eve for a special ceremony in which they welcome the day when Christ was born. On Christmas morning some children hurry to see if Santa Claus has left them special gifts. In many homes families and friends come together to eat and exchange gifts.

- Homes are often decorated with holly, ivy, and evergreen trees as reminders of the beauty of nature. Houses and stores may be trimmed with outdoor lights, and festive music may be played.

- Christmas is celebrated in many countries. The holiday signifies the spirit of peace and goodwill.

Caroling, Caroling

Take part in one of the most popular traditions of the holiday season—caroling. Many carols have origins in other countries. For example, "Bring a Torch, Jeanette, Isabella" is a French carol. "Deck the Halls" is a Welsh carol, and "O Christmas Tree" is a favorite in Germany. Sing "O Christmas Tree" in English and German.

> O Christmas Tree, O Christmas Tree,
> Your branches green delight us.
> They're green when summer days are bright:
> They're green when winter snow is white.
> O Christmas Tree, O Christmas Tree,
> Your branches green delight us.

> O Tannenbaum, o Tannenbaum,
> Wie treu sind deine Blätter.
> Du grünst nicht nur zur Sommerzeit,
> Nein, auch im Winter, wenn es schneit.
> O Tannenbaum, o Tannenbaum,
> Wie treu sind deine Blätter.

Symbols of the Season

Many symbols and traditions are associated with the Christmas season. Let students pick a symbol (example: candy cane, Christmas tree, mistletoe) and research its history and any other information available. Have students report on their findings and then compile the information in a class book.

Thinking of Others

You will need:

12" x 18" pieces of heavy cardboard
Gold, green, and red yarn
Scissors
Strips of cloth

The Christmas season is a time to think of others. Have students weave Christmas placemats to be taken and given to a local nursing facility or hospital for use during the holiday season.

To make the placemats, have students cut small slits at 1 inch intervals down both long sides of the cardboard. Have them wrap a long piece of gold yarn across the cardboard, connecting the slits. Then, using lengths of yarn and cloth strips, students can weave in and out of the gold yarn until the cardboard is covered.

New Year's Day

New Year's Day

Nearly everywhere in the world, people celebrate the end of the old year and the beginning of the new one. New Year's Day in the United States is celebrated on January 1.

Many traditions are associated with New Year's Day. Perhaps the best-known tradition is to make New Year's resolutions. People make resolutions that will improve their lives, such as finding a new job. Another tradition is eating black-eyed peas, an idea thought to bring you good luck in the coming year. Celebrating the stroke of midnight is also very popular.

- January was named for the Roman god Janus, who had two faces. People believe one face looks forward and one looks back, just as we leave the old year behind and look forward to the new one.

New Year's Poem

> Fireworks
> Bright, colorful
> Boom, sparkle, explode
> Loud, exciting
> Celebration!

Have students brainstorm objects and images that are associated with New Year's Day celebrations. Then ask each student to choose one of the objects and create a New Year's Day poem about it. Have them use the poetic form known as cinquain. A cinquain poem has 5 lines and follows this format.

Line 1: 1 word title (noun)
Line 2: 2 adjectives that describe the title
Line 3: 3 verbs that relate to the title
Line 4: 2 adverbs that describe the verbs
Line 5: 1 noun that renames the title

Encourage volunteers to read their poems to the class.

Time Capsule

Have students make their own time capsule to be opened on a future date. Provide or have a student bring in a large coffee tin or cookie tin. Let students decorate the tin with paint or construction paper. Instruct students to put drawings of objects that are important to them now in the tin.

Seal the tin with tape, and tuck it away. Open it a few months from now, and have students determine if the same songs, games, clothes, and trends are still popular. Compare the current events now and then. Are they the same?

A Year in History

Invite students to reflect on events that have happened in the last year. They should think of events in history as well as events in their own lives. Begin a book "A Year in the Life of. . . ." Make a page for each event. This will serve as a reference of events in that particular year.

Old New Year

Sing a song of remembering old friendships and making new ones—"Auld Lang Syne." Explain that the title means "Old Long Since."

> AULD LANG SYNE
> by Robert Burns
>
> *Should auld acquaintance be forgot*
> *and never brought to mind?*
> *Should auld acquaintance be forgot*
> *and days of auld lang syne?*
> *For auld lang syne, my dear,*
> *for auld lang syne,*
> *we'll take a cup of kindness yet,*
> *for auld lang syne.*

Inauguration Day

Inauguration Day

The inauguration of a newly-elected President of the United States occurs every four years, following a presidential election. It is always on January 20 unless this is a Sunday, and then it would be on January 21. The swearing-in ceremony is the most important part of the day. This is when the President is given the oath of office. After the new President takes the oath of office, there is usually a parade down Pennsylvania Avenue from the United States Capitol to the White House.

■ Inauguration Day is considered a holiday only in Washington, D.C., two counties in Maryland, two counties in Virginia, and the cities of Alexandria and Falls Church, Virginia.

What It Takes

Have students research and list the qualifications for becoming President of the United States. Have students role-play using correct and incorrect information as the class decides if this person can be a candidate. (Example: I am 23 years old—No; I was born in the United States 50 years ago and have not been convicted of a felony—Yes.)

Design a New Seal

Show students a picture of the Seal of the President of the United States. Explain that it is the chief symbol of the presidency and is used to close envelopes containing messages or other documents from the President to the United States Congress. Have students study the objects shown on the seal. Explain that each symbol has its own meaning:

Eagle with shield—self-reliance
Olive branch—the desire for peace
Arrows—the ability to wage war
50 stars—the 50 states
Color *red*—hardiness and courage
Color *blue*—justice, vigilance, and perseverance
Color *white*—purity and innocence

Have students design a seal especially for a new President.

Dr. Martin Luther King, Jr., Day

Dr. Martin Luther King, Jr., Day

Dr. Martin Luther King, Jr., Day is one of our country's newest holidays. It honors a leader who was very important in helping Americans understand that everyone should be treated equally.

Dr. Martin Luther King, Jr., was born in Atlanta, Georgia, on January 15, 1929. While he was a minister in Montgomery, Alabama, an African American woman named Rosa Parks was arrested because she refused to give up her seat on a bus to a white man. Dr. King helped organize a bus boycott in Montgomery to protest the unfair treatment of African Americans. For 382 days, many people refused to ride the buses until the bus company finally agreed to change its rules. Dr. Martin Luther King, Jr., continued to speak out against the poor treatment of African Americans. He helped organize a historic march to Washington, D.C. There he gave a famous speech calling for freedom for all.

On April 4, 1968, Dr. King was assassinated. Today, Americans celebrate his birthday by remembering his fight for equal opportunity.

- On the third Monday in January each year, Americans honor Dr. King.
- Many cities celebrate Dr. Martin Luther King, Jr., Day with picnics, parades, and marches.

Time Line

Explain that we celebrate Dr. Martin Luther King, Jr., Day to honor a famous American who devoted his life to the struggle for equal rights for all people. Dr. King is particularly admired because he believed that people could and ought to peacefully protest against things that were unfair. Have students research Dr. King's life and illustrate the most important events in his life on a time line.

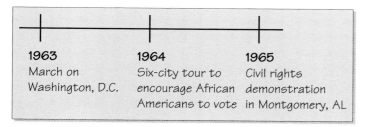

1963	1964	1965
March on Washington, D.C.	Six-city tour to encourage African Americans to vote	Civil rights demonstration in Montgomery, AL

"I have a dream…."

One of Dr. King's most famous speeches includes "I have a dream that my four little children will one day live in a nation where they will not be judged by the color of their skin but by the content of their character." Discuss the meaning of Dr. King's words. Then have students memorize and recite this thought-provoking sentence. Encourage them to add to King's speech, sharing their ideas for justice, fairness, or equality.

We Can Overcome

The song "We Shall Overcome" is associated with Dr. Martin Luther King, Jr., and the Civil Rights movement of the 1960s. Introduce the students to the version of the song that appears below. Read the first three verses aloud and talk about what the words mean. Then have the students sing the song with you. Challenge them to create their own verses for the song.

1. *We shall overcome*
   We shall overcome
   We shall overcome someday

   Chorus: *Oh, deep in my heart*
   I do believe
   We shall overcome someday

2. *We'll walk hand in hand*
   We'll walk hand in hand
   We'll walk hand in hand someday

   Chorus

3. *We shall all be free*
   We shall all be free
   We shall all be free someday

   Chorus

Presidents' Day

Presidents' Day

Presidents' Day celebrates the works of two great Presidents of the United States—George Washington and Abraham Lincoln. Both Presidents were born in February, so people honor them on the third Monday in that month. The lives of the other Presidents are celebrated on this holiday, too.

George Washington is called the Father of Our Country. He led the Continental Army when our nation was trying to gain its freedom from Britain. The people of the United States elected him the first President. As President, he worked to make the nation strong. He helped keep the new nation out of war and worked to keep the states from fighting with each other.

Abraham Lincoln was born in a log cabin. His family was so poor that he could not go to school. Instead, he studied at home and became a lawyer. In his lifetime, he saw many slaves being treated poorly. As President, Lincoln preserved the Union during the Civil War and freed the slaves in areas of the South that were fighting against the United States.

- During the first public celebration of George Washington's birthday, soldiers who fought in the Revolutionary War with Washington held a drum and fife concert for him. Cannons were fired in his honor, too.

- On Presidents' Day, people often think about the history of the United States. Some people visit the Washington Monument and the Lincoln Memorial in Washington, D.C.

Landmarks

Mount Rushmore, in South Dakota, is a monument to the first 150 years of our nation's history. The faces of Presidents Washington, Jefferson, Roosevelt, and Lincoln are carved out of the mountain. Each bust is 60 feet (about 18 m) high; the entire monument took 400 workers about 14 years to complete. Invite students to sculpt a model of Mount Rushmore out of clay, papier-mâché, or foam.

Yankee Doodle

Talk with the students about George Washington's role as leader of the Continental Army when our nation was trying to gain its freedom from Britain. Explain that the song "Yankee Doodle" was originally sung by the British to make fun of the Americans, but the Americans made the song their own and added their own words. Sing this version of "Yankee Doodle" together.

YANKEE DOODLE

Father and I went down to camp,
Along with Captain Gooding;
And there we saw the men and boys,
As thick as hasty pudding.

Yankee doodle, keep it up,
Yankee doodle dandy;
Mind the music and the step,
And with the girls be handy.

Conduct an Interview

Most adults have lived long enough to see several different Presidents in office. Have the students compile a list of questions and then interview an adult about his or her favorite President. Set up a mock TV station in the room, and let students share their reports with the classroom "audience."

Memorial Day

Memorial Day

Memorial Day is a day set aside to honor men and women who lost their lives while serving our country. What started in 1868 as citizens decorating the graves of Civil War veterans is now celebrated as the holiday that pays tribute to soldiers lost in later wars as well. Memorial Day is celebrated on the last Monday in May.

- Memorial Day was first called Decoration Day.

- Many people bring flowers or flags to the graves of those friends or family members who served in wars.

- People often observe Memorial Day with picnics, cookouts, and parades.

Memorial Day Essay

Share these lines, from Henry Wadsworth Longfellow, about soldiers who died in battle.

> *Your silent tents of green*
> *We deck with fragrant flowers;*
> *Yours has the suffering been,*
> *The memory shall be ours.*

Discuss the meaning of the poem with students and talk about why it is important to remember the men and women who died fighting for our country. Then ask students to write an essay about what Memorial Day means to them.

Family Memory Book

Memorial Day is the perfect time to start a family memory book. Have students think of family members who have died. Create one page for each person. Students should write facts and memories about the person and provide a picture, if possible.

Design a Badge

Memorial Day is sometimes called Decoration Day because people often decorate the graves of fallen soldiers. Decoration also refers to the decoration of a soldier with badges of honor or awards for bravery. Have students design a badge of honor for a soldier. Ask students to tell whom the badge was given to and what the badge was given for.

A Poppy to Remember

You will need:

Squares of red tissue paper
Craft wire

During World War I, soldiers fought many battles in Flanders in Belgium. Every spring the soldiers noticed red flowers blooming across the battlefields and on the graves of their friends who had been killed. Today, the poppy is worn to remind us of the many people killed in battle.

Have students make poppies by folding squares of red tissue paper back and forth like a fan. Twist a short section of craft wire to cinch the center of the folds. Then, unfold the "petals" of the flower. You can wrap the bottom of the flower with tape to hold it securely.

Flag Day

Flag Day

Our flag is more than just a cloth banner. It is a symbol of our country. In 1777 the Continental Congress adopted the Stars and Stripes pattern for our national flag. One hundred years later, in 1877, Flag Day was first celebrated. Many citizens and organizations wanted a national day to commemorate the United States flag. In 1949, President Harry Truman signed legislation making Flag Day a day of national observance.

- In 1983 the largest United States flag was displayed in Washington, D.C. The flag measured 411 feet (125 m) by 210 feet (64 m). Each star measured 13 feet (about 4 m) across.

- The United States flag has thirteen stripes, alternating red and white, with each stripe representing one of the thirteen original colonies.

- The United States flag has fifty stars, one for each state.

Create a Flag

Explain that George Washington's original pencil sketch for the flag indicated 6-pointed stars. Betsy Ross, however, recommended 5-pointed stars. At first, the Continental Congress protested that 5-pointed stars were too difficult to make, but the Congress eventually agreed to use them.

Ask students to work in groups and use the Internet or classroom reference books to research the history of the flag. Have each group create an original flag according to the specifications set out by the Continental Congress on June 14, 1777.

Our Flag

There are rules associated with our American flag. Discuss the guidelines for displaying a flag, the rules for folding the flag, and the proper disposal of an old flag.

1. The United States flag must never be lowered to any object or person while in a parade.

2. The flag should be raised quickly but lowered slowly.

3. The flag should never touch the ground.

4. The flag is customarily displayed from sunrise to sunset.

5. The flag should be folded lengthwise in half and then folded again. Then it is folded in a series of triangles starting with the stripes until only a blue field of stars is visible.

6. A worn-out flag should be burned.

Have students follow the guidelines for folding a flag. If possible, have a student be responsible for raising, lowering, and storing the flag that is displayed in front of your school.

The National Anthem

The national anthem of the United States is titled "The Star-Spangled Banner" and was written by Francis Scott Key. During the War of 1812, Key spent a night aboard a British warship in Chesapeake Bay while trying to arrange the release of an American prisoner. The next morning, Key saw that an American flag had survived the battle that had raged throughout the night. The flag inspired him to write the poem, which provides the words for our national anthem. Play a recording of the song, and have students sing the words of the song. The words appear on page R36 in the students' textbooks. Then divide the class into groups, with each group choosing a phrase from the song and explaining its meaning in their own words. Ask students to share their thoughts.

Independence Day

Independence Day

July 4, often called Independence Day, is a day Americans celebrate our country's freedom and independence. It is a legal holiday in all states. This date marks the anniversary of the day the Second Continental Congress adopted the Declaration of Independence in 1776. This document announced to the world that the 13 colonies were independent states and no longer belonged to Britain. Independence Day has become the most honored non-religious holiday in America.

- Firework displays have become a colorful tradition of this patriotic holiday.

- Independence Day is one of the few holidays that has not been moved to a Monday or a Friday to allow for a three-day weekend.

Famous Document

Ask students to fill in the missing words to the famous lines of this historic document:

The Declaration of Independence

We hold these truths to be self-evident, that all _____ are created _____ , that they are endowed by their Creator with certain unalienable _____ , that among these are Life, _____ , and the pursuit of Happiness.

Then, display and read a copy of the Declaration of Independence. Discuss what each line means. Have students copy the second paragraph onto a poster to display in the room.

Add Your "John Hancock"

Display a copy of the Declaration of Independence. Point out the signatures of each member of the Second Continental Congress. Challenge students to find the signature of the document's creator, Thomas Jefferson, and to look at John Hancock's signature. Invite students to speculate on the origin of the phrase "put your John Hancock here."

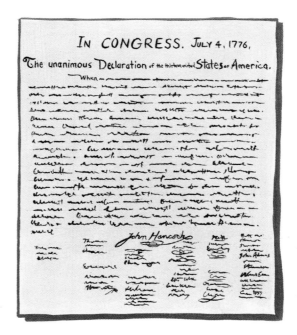

As American as Apple Pie

You will need:

> 1 9-inch piecrust in an aluminum pan
> 1 20-ounce can apple pie filling
> 1/2 cup sugar
> 1 teaspoon cinnamon
> Spoons

Explain that having picnics and making apple pie are two traditions often associated with Independence Day celebrations. Ask students to share how they celebrate the holiday. Then, make an apple pie to celebrate Independence Day in the classroom.

1. Mix apples, sugar, and cinnamon.

2. Pour into a pie pan.

3. Bake as directed on the can of pie filling.

Vocabulary Cards

This reproducible section will help you create word cards for the vocabulary found at the beginning of each lesson in your Teacher's Edition. The cards may be used to preview the unit, build vocabulary notebooks, assist ESL students, and review vocabulary at the end of the unit. Use blank cards to add vocabulary to meet the special needs of your class.

Contents

map title	compass rose
Atlas	*Atlas*
map key	cardinal directions
Atlas	*Atlas*
inset map	intermediate directions
Atlas	*Atlas*
grid system	history
Atlas	*Introduction*
locator	chronology
Atlas	*Introduction*
map scale	oral history
Atlas	*Introduction*

© Harcourt

A marker that shows directions on a map.	Words on a map that tells the subject of a map.
The main directions—north, south, east, and west.	A feature on a map that explains the symbols used on the map.
The directions between cardinal directions—northeast, northwest, southeast, and southwest.	A small map within a larger map.
What happened in the past.	A pattern of squares that appears on some maps.
The order in which events happen.	A small map or picture of a globe that shows where the place on the main map is located.
A story of an event or an experience told aloud by a person who did not have a written language or who did not write down what happened.	A feature on a map that compares a distance on the map to a distance in the real world and helps find the real distance between places on the map.

point of view Introduction	geography Introduction
historical empathy Introduction	modify Introduction
frame of reference Introduction	adapt Introduction
analyze Introduction	physical feature Introduction
primary source Introduction	human feature Introduction
secondary source Introduction	

© Harcourt

The study of Earth's surface and the way people use it.	How a person sees things.
To change.	An understanding of earlier people's actions and feelings.
To adjust.	A set of ideas that determine how a person understands something.
A land feature that has been made by nature.	To look closely at how the parts of an event connect with one another and how the event is connected to other events.
Something created by humans, such as a building or road, that alters the land.	A record of an event made by a person who saw or took part in it.
	A record of an event written by someone who was not there at the time.

location	civics
Introduction	Introduction
region	civic participation
Introduction	Introduction
economy	government
Introduction	Introduction
economics	culture
Introduction	Introduction
	heritage
	Introduction
	society
	Introduction

The study of citizenship.	The place where something can be found.
Being concerned with and involved in issues related to your community, state, or country or the entire world.	An area of Earth in which many features are similar.
A system of leaders and laws to help people live together in their community, state, or country.	The way people of a state, a region, or a country use resources to meet their needs.
A way of life.	The study of how people meet their needs.
Culture that has come from the past and continues today.	
A human group.	

theory Lesson 1	**confederation** Lesson 1
migration Lesson 1	**cause** Skill 1
technology Lesson 1	**effect** Skill 1
agriculture Lesson 1	**navigation** Lesson 2
civilization Lesson 1	**expedition** Lesson 2
diversity Lesson 1	**conquistador** Lesson 2

© Harcourt

A loose group of governments working together.	A possible explanation.
An event or an action that makes something else happen.	The movement of people.
Something that happens as a result of an event or action.	The use of scientific knowledge or tools to make or do something.
The study or act of planning and controlling the course of a ship.	Farming.
A journey.	A culture that usually has cities and well-developed forms of government, religion, and learning.
An explorer or soldier sent by Spain to conquer and claim large areas of North and South America.	Great differences among the people.

empire Lesson 2	**absolute location** Skill 2
colony Lesson 2	**lines of latitude** Skill 2
missionary Lesson 2	**parallels** Skill 2
mission Lesson 2	**lines of longitude** Skill 2
slavery Lesson 2	**meridians** Skill 2
legislature Lesson 2	**prime meridian** Skill 2

The exact location of any place on Earth.	A conquered land of many people and places governed by one ruler.
Lines that run east and west on a map or globe.	A settlement ruled by another country.
Lines of latitude.	A person sent out by a church to spread its religion.
Lines that run north and south on a map or globe.	A small religious settlement.
Lines of longitude.	The practice of holding people against their will and making them carry out orders.
The meridian marked 0 degrees and that runs north and south through Greenwich, England.	The lawmaking branch of a government

charter	cash crop
Lesson 3	Lesson 3
constitution	royal colony
Lesson 3	Lesson 3
proprietary colony	indentured servant
Lesson 3	Lesson 3
trial by jury	revolution
Lesson 3	Lesson 4
immigrant	representation
Lesson 3	Lesson 4
import	boycott
Lesson 3	Lesson 4

© Harcourt

A crop that is grown to be sold.	An official paper in which certain rights are given by a government to a person or business.
A colony ruled directly by a monarch.	A plan of government.
A person who agrees to work for another person for a certain length of time in exchange for passage to North America.	A colony owned and ruled by one person.
A sudden, complete change, such as the overthrow of a government.	The judging of a person accused of a crime by a jury of fellow citizens.
The action of having someone speak for another.	A person from one country who comes to live in another country.
The refusal to buy certain goods.	A product brought in from another country.

declaration	independence
Lesson 4	Lesson 4
competition	**treaty**
Lesson 4	Lesson 4

The freedom to govern on one's own.	An official statement.
An agreement between countries.	The contest among companies to get the most customers or sell the most goods.

republic 	**ratify** Lesson 1
compromise Lesson 1	**amendment** Lesson 1
federal system Lesson 1	**electoral college** Lesson 1
legislative branch Lesson 1	**pioneer** Lesson 2
executive branch Lesson 1	**territory** Lesson 2
judicial branch Lesson 1	**nationalism** Lesson 2

© Harcourt

To approve.	A form of government in which people elect representatives to govern the country.
A change.	To reach an agreement by having each party give up some of what it wants.
A group of electors who vote for the President and Vice President.	A system in which national and state governments share the responsibility of governing.
A person who first settles a place.	The part of government that makes the laws.
Land that belongs to a national government but is not a state and is not represented in Congress.	The part of government that carries out the laws.
Pride in one's country.	The part of government that settles differences about the meaning of laws.

© Harcourt

doctrine	bias
Lesson 2	Skill 1
democracy	**Industrial Revolution**
Lesson 2	Lesson 3
manifest destiny	**textile**
Lesson 2	Lesson 3
dictator	**interchangeable parts**
Lesson 2	Lesson 3
	mass production
	Lesson 3

A personal feeling for or against someone or something.	A government plan of action.
A time of complete change in how things were made, in which people began using machines instead of hand tools.	A government in which the people rule.
Cloth.	The belief that the United States should someday stretch from the Atlantic Ocean to the Pacific Ocean.
Identical machine-made parts, any of which may be used to make or repair an item.	A leader who has total authority to rule.
The system of producing large amounts of goods at one time.	

sectionalism	emancipation
Lesson 1	Lesson 2
tariff	resist
Lesson 1	Lesson 2
states' rights	code
Lesson 1	Lesson 2
free state	fugitive
Lesson 1	Lesson 2
slave state	underground
Lesson 1	Lesson 2
frame of reference	abolitionist
Skill 1	Lesson 2

© Harcourt

The freeing of enslaved peoples.	Regional loyalty.
To act against.	A tax on goods brought into a country.
A set of laws.	The idea that the states, rather than the federal government, should have final authority over their own affairs.
A person who is running away from something.	A state that did not allow slavery before the Civil War.
Done in secret.	A state that allowed slavery before the Civil War.
A person who wanted to end slavery.	A set of ideas that determine how a person understands something.

equality	border state
Lesson 2	Lesson 4
secede	strategy
Lesson 3	Lesson 4
Confederacy	casualty
Lesson 3	Lesson 4
retreat	address
Lesson 4	Lesson 5

© Harcourt

During the Civil War, a state—Delaware, Kentucky, Maryland, or Missouri—between the North and the South that was unsure which side to support.	Equal rights.
A long-range plan.	To leave.
A person who has been wounded or killed.	The group of eleven states that left the Union, also called the Confederate States of America.
A formal speech.	To fall back.

Reconstruction	carpetbagger
Lesson 1	Lesson 2
assassinate	scalawag
Lesson 1	Lesson 2
black codes	secret ballot
Lesson 1	Lesson 2
acquittal	segregation
Lesson 1	Lesson 2
freedmen	boom
Lesson 2	Lesson 3
sharecropping	refinery
Lesson 2	Lesson 3

A Northerner who moved to the South to take part in Reconstruction governments.	The time during which the South was rebuilt after the Civil War.
A rascal; someone who supports something for his or her own gain.	To murder a leader by sudden or secret attack.
A voting method in which no one knows how anyone else voted.	Laws limiting the rights of former slaves in the South.
The practice of keeping people in separate groups based on race or culture.	A verdict of not guilty.
A time of fast economic growth.	The men, women, and children who had once been slaves.
A factory in which materials, especially fuels, are cleaned and made into usable products.	A system of working the land in which the worker was paid with a "share" of the crop.

prospector Lesson 3	**climograph** Skill 1
bust Lesson 3	**free enterprise** Lesson 4
long drive Lesson 3	**transcontinental railroad** Lesson 4
homesteader Lesson 3	**entrepreneur** Lesson 4
open range Lesson 3	**petroleum** Lesson 4
reservation Lesson 3	**capital** Lesson 4

A chart that shows the average monthly temperature and the average monthly precipitation for a place.	A person who searches for gold, silver, or other mineral resources.
An economic system in which people are able to start and run their own businesses with little control by the government.	A time of quick economic decline.
The railway line that crossed North America.	A trip made by ranchers to lead cattle to the market or to the railroads.
A person who sets up and runs a business.	Person living on land granted by the government.
Oil.	Land on which animals can graze freely.
The money needed to set up or improve a business.	An area of land set aside by the government for use only by Native Americans.

human resource Lesson 4	**tenement** Lesson 5
old immigration Lesson 5	**prejudice** Lesson 5
new immigration Lesson 5	**regulation** Lesson 5
advertisement Lesson 5	

A poorly built apartment building.	A worker who brings his or her own ideas and skills to a job.
An unfair feeling of hate or dislike for members of a certain group because of their background, race, or religion.	People who came from northern and western Europe before 1890 to settle in North America.
A rule or an order.	People who came from southern and central Europe and other parts of the world after 1890 to settle in North America.
	A public announcement that tells people about a product or an opportunity.

panhandle	isthmus
Lesson 1	Lesson 2
imperialism	projections
Lesson 2	Skill 1
yellow journalism	distortions
Lesson 2	Skill 1
siege	assembly line
Lesson 2	Lesson 3
armistice	aviation
Lesson 2	Lesson 3
anarchist	
Lesson 2	

© Harcourt

A narrow strip of land that connects two larger landmasses.	A portion of land that sticks out like the handle of a pan.
The different kinds of maps cartographers use to show the Earth.	The building of an empire.
The purposeful errors that enable cartographers to make flat maps.	Style of newspaper writing in which reporters exaggerate the facts of a story in order to sell newspapers.
System of building things in which a moving belt carries parts from worker to worker.	A long-lasting attack.
Air travel.	An agreement to stop fighting a war.
	A person who is against any kind of government.

settlement house	merit system
Lesson 4	Lesson 5
skyscraper	monopoly
Lesson 4	Lesson 5
progressive	conservation
Lesson 5	Lesson 5
political boss	civil rights
Lesson 5	Lesson 5
commission	prohibition
Lesson 5	Lesson 5

© Harcourt

A system through which a person was tested to make sure he or she could do the job before the job was offered.	A community center where people can learn new skills.
A company that has little or no competition.	A tall steel-frame building.
The protection of the environment by keeping natural resources from being wasted or destroyed.	A person who worked to improve life for those who were not wealthy.
The rights guaranteed to all citizens by the Constitution.	An elected official—often a mayor—who has many dishonest employees and who is able to control the government with the help of those employees.
The plan to stop people in the United States from drinking alcoholic beverages.	A special committee.

militarism	military draft
Lesson 1	Lesson 1
alliance	prediction
Lesson 1	Skill 1
ally	propaganda
Lesson 1	Skill 1
dollar diplomacy	no-man's-land
Lesson 1	Lesson 2
neutral	communism
Lesson 1	Lesson 2

© Harcourt

A way of bringing the people of a nation into the armed forces.	The idea that using military force is a good way to solve problems.
A decision about what might happen next, based on the way things are.	A formal agreement.
Information designed to help or hurt a cause.	A partner in an alliance.
In a war, land not controlled by either side and filled with barbed wire, land mines, or bombs buried in the ground.	A policy in which the United States government gave money to other nations in return for some U.S. control over the actions of those nations.
A political and economic system in which all industries, land, and businesses are owned by the government.	Taking no side in a conflict.

isolation	strike
Lesson 3	Lesson 3
labor union	flow chart
Lesson 3	Skill 2

The stopping of work in protest of poor working conditions.	The policy of remaining separate from other countries.
A diagram that uses arrows to show the order in which events happen.	A group of workers who join together to improve their working conditions.

consumer good	land use
Lesson 1	Skill 1
installment buying	generalization
Lesson 1	Skill 1
interest	advertising
Lesson 1	Lesson 2
stock market	commercial industry
Lesson 1	Lesson 2
stock	urban
Lesson 1	Lesson 2
	rural
	Lesson 2

© Harcourt

The way in which most of the land in a place is used.	A product made for personal use.
A statement that summarizes the facts.	Taking home a product after paying only part of a price and then making monthly payments until the product is paid for.
Information that a business provides about a product or service to make people want to buy it.	The fee a borrower pays to a leader for the use of money.
An industry that is run to make a profit.	A place where people buy and sell shares of a company or business.
Of or like a city.	A share of a business or company.
Of or like the country; away from the city.	

suburb	renaissance
Lesson 2	Lesson 3
commute	fact
Lesson 2	Skill 2
architect	opinion
Lesson 2	Skill 2
jazz	
Lesson 3	

A time of great interest and activity in the arts.	A community or neighborhood that lies outside a city.
A statement that can be checked and proved true.	To travel back and forth to work.
A statement that tells what a person thinks or believes.	A person who designs buildings.
	A music style influenced by the music of West Africa as well as by spirituals and blues.

investor Lesson 1	**bureaucracy** Lesson 3
depression Lesson 2	**pension** Lesson 3
economist Lesson 2	**minimum wage** Lesson 3
unemployment Lesson 2	**hydroelectric dam** Lesson 3
balanced budget Lesson 2	**classify** Skill 1

© Harcourt

The many workers and groups that are needed to run government programs.	Someone who uses money to buy or make something that will yield a profit.
Retirement income paid to people who stop working at a certain age.	A time when industries do not grow and many people are out of work.
The lowest amount of money by law that a person can be paid per hour.	A person who studies the economy.
Dam that uses the water it stores to produce electricity.	The number of workers without jobs.
To sort.	A government plan for spending in which it does not spend more money than it makes.

© Harcourt

dictatorship	rationing
Lesson 1	Lesson 3
concentration camps	**recycling**
Lesson 1	Lesson 3
fascism	**relocation camp**
Lesson 1	Lesson 3
civilian	**trade-off**
Lesson 2	Skill 1
	opportunity cost
	Skill 1

© Harcourt

The limiting of the supply of what people can buy.	A government in which the dictator, or head of the government, has total authority.
Using items again.	A prison camp.
During World War II, an army-style settlement in which Japanese Americans were forced to live.	A political idea in which power is given to a dictator and the freedoms of individuals are taken away.
A giving up of one thing in return for another.	A person who is not in the military.
What a person gives up in order to get something he or she wants.	

front	V-J Day
Lesson 1	Lesson 2
segregated	parallel time lines
Lesson 1	Skill 2
D day	refugees
Lesson 1	Lesson 3
Holocaust	veteran
Lesson 1	Lesson 3
historical map	baby boom
Skill 1	Lesson 3
island hopping	
Lesson 2	

© Harcourt

Victory over Japan day; August 15, 1945, the day in World War II on which Japan agreed to surrender and fighting stopped.	A battle line.
Two or more time lines that show the same period of time.	Set apart or separated because of race or culture.
A person who seeks shelter and safety in a country other than his or her own.	June 6, 1944, the day the Allies worked together in Europe in the largest water-to-land invasion in history.
A person who has served in the armed forces.	The mass murder during World War II of European Jews and other people whom Adolf Hitler called "undesirable."
The 15 years following World War II during which 50 million babies were born in the United States.	A map which provides information about a place at a certain time in history.
	The fighting by the Allied forces to win only certain key islands as they worked their way toward an invasion of Japan.

superpower	free world
Lesson 4	Lesson 4
arms race	**cold war**
Lesson 4	Lesson 4

© Harcourt

The United States and its allies.	A nation that is one of the most powerful in the world.
A war fought mostly with propaganda and money rather than with soldiers and weapons.	A time during which one country builds up weapons to protect itself against another country.

desegregate Lesson 1	**developing country** Lesson 3
integration Lesson 2	**blockade** Lesson 3
nonviolence Lesson 2	**demonstration** Lesson 4
satellite Lesson 2	**migrant worker** Lesson 4

A country that does not have modern conveniences such as good housing, roads, schools, and hospitals.	To remove racial barriers.
The use of ships to isolate a port or island.	The bringing together of people of all races.
A public show of a group's feelings about a cause.	The use of peaceful ways to bring about change.
Someone who moves from place to place with the seasons, harvesting crops.	An object that orbits a planet.

inflation	scandal
Lesson 1	*Lesson 1*
hawk	**hostage**
Lesson 1	*Lesson 2*
dove	**deficit**
Lesson 1	*Lesson 2*
arms control	**recession**
Lesson 1	*Lesson 3*
détente	**candidate**
Lesson 1	*Lesson 3*
cease-fire	
Lesson 1	

© Harcourt

An action that brings disgrace.	An economic condition in which more money is needed to buy goods and services than was needed earlier.
A prisoner held until the captor's demands are met.	A person who supported the Vietnam War.
A shortage.	A person who was against the Vietnam War.
A period of slow economic activity.	Limiting the number of weapons that each nation may have.
A person chosen by a political party to run for office.	An easing of tensions, especially between the United States and the Soviet Union.
	A temporary end to a conflict.

veto	hijack
Lesson 4	Lesson 4
impeach	**population density**
Lesson 4	Skill 1
terrorism	
Lesson 4	

To illegally take control of an aircraft or other vehicle.	To reject.
The number of people living in 1 square mile or 1 square kilometer of land.	To accuse a government official, especially the President, of a crime.
	The use of violence to promote a cause.

Sun Belt Lesson 1	**diverse economy** Lesson 3
ethnic group Lesson 1	**high-tech** Lesson 3
Internet Lesson 1	**Information Age** Lesson 3
teleconference Lesson 1	**e-commerce** Lesson 3
cartogram Skill 1	**interdependent** Lesson 3
rapid-transit system Lesson 2	**international trade** Lesson 3

© Harcourt

An economy based on many kinds of industries.	A wide area of the southern United States that has a mild climate all year.
Based on computers and other kinds of electronic equipment.	A group of people from the same country, of the same race, or with a shared culture.
A period of history defined by the growing amount of information available to people.	A network that links computers around the world for the exchange of information.
The buying and selling of goods and services through computers.	A conference, or meeting, that uses electronic machines to connect people.
Depending on other states and regions for natural resources, finished products, and services.	A diagram that gives information about places by the size shown for each place.
Trade among nations.	A passenger transportation system that uses elevated or underground trains or both.

free-trade agreement Lesson 3	**informed citizen** Lesson 4
global economy Lesson 3	**jury** Lesson 4
responsibility Lesson 4	**volunteer** Lesson 4
register Lesson 4	**patriotism** Lesson 4

© Harcourt

Someone who knows what is happening in the community, the state, the nation, and the world.	A treaty in which countries agree not to charge tariffs, or taxes, on goods they buy from and sell to each other.
A group of citizens who decide a case in court.	The world market in which companies from different countries buy and sell goods and services.
A person who works without pay.	A duty; something a person is expected to do.
Love of one's country.	To sign up to vote by showing proof that the voter lives where the voting takes place.

© Harcourt

middle class	free election
Lesson 1	Lesson 2
interest rate	population pyramid
Lesson 1	Skill 1
commonwealth	life expectancy
Lesson 2	Skill 1
embargo	median age
Lesson 2	Skill 1

© Harcourt

Election that offers a choice of candidates instead of a single candidate.	An economic level between the poor and the wealthy.
A graph that shows the division of a country's population by age.	An amount that a bank charges to lend money.
The number of years a person can expect to live.	A kind of territory that governs itself.
An age in years that half of the people in a country are older than and half are younger than.	One nation's refusal to trade goods with another.

standard of living	province
Lesson 3	Lesson 4
liberate	**separatist**
Lesson 3	Lesson 4
deforestation	**time zone**
Lesson 3	Skill 2

A political region similar to a state in the United States.	A measure of how well people in a country live.
A person in a province who wants his or her province to become a separate nation to preserve a culture.	To set free.
A region in which a single clock time is used.	The widespread cutting down of forests.

School to Home Newsletter

School to Home Newsletters

These school to home newsletters offer a way of linking students' study of social studies to the students' family members. There is one newsletter, available in English and Spanish, for each unit. The newsletters include family activities as well as suggestions of books to read.

Contents

School to Home

Books To Read

The People Shall Continue by Simon Ortiz. Children's Book Press, 1988.

The Boston Tea Party by Laurie O'Neill. Millbrook, 1996.

A Pioneer Sampler: The Daily Life of a Pioneer Family in 1840 by Barbara Greenwood. Houghton Mifflin, 1995.

Content to Learn

Your child will be studying the earliest Americans and the eventual formation of the United States. Here are some of the topics that will be covered in the first unit, Making a New Nation:

- the environment's effect on early American peoples
- European exploration and settling of the Americas in the late 1400s and the 1500s
- movement of Europeans to the 13 English colonies during the 1600s and 1700s
- factors leading to the American Revolution
- cooperative efforts to change the government of the United States
- expansion of the United States from the Atlantic Ocean to the Pacific Ocean
- how technology changed life in the United States in the 1800s

Activities to Try

- Look at a world map or a globe with your child. Locate the routes that some of the early European explorers traveled in an effort to reach Asia. Discuss why some Europeans believed they could reach Asia by sailing west. Then talk about how people might have reacted when they learned a new continent had in fact been discovered.

- With your child, imagine that you are living in the colonies during the Revolutionary War period. Discuss how you, as a colonist, may feel about some of the laws that Parliament has passed. Talk about what it is like to live in the colonies during the American Revolution.

- With your child, use an encyclopedia or the Internet to find out more information about one of the inventions from the 1800s.

Ideas to Discuss

- How did gradual changes in the environment affect how and where the ancient Indians lived?

- What are some of the reasons that people founded new settlements in the thirteen English colonies during the 1600s and 1700s?

- Why were compromises so important to the formation of a new government?

 Visit **The Learning Site** at www.harcourtschool.com/socialstudies for additional activities, primary sources, and other resources to use in this unit.

© Harcourt

Carta para la casa

Libros

The People Shall Continue by Simon Ortiz. Children's Book Press, 1988.

The Boston Tea Party by Laurie O'Neill. Millbrook, 1996.

A Pioneer Sampler: The Daily Life of a Pioneer Family in 1840 by Barbara Greenwood. Houghton Mifflin, 1995.

Tema de estudio

Su niño comenzará a estudiar los primeros americanos y la formación final de Estados Unidos. Éstos son algunos de los temas que desarrollaremos en la primera unidad, Formar una nueva nación:

- el medio ambiente influye en los primeros americanos
- los europeos exploraron y se asentaron en las Américas a finales del siglo XV y en el siglo XVI
- muchos europeos emigraron a las 13 colonias inglesas durante los siglos XVII y XVIII
- factores que guiaron la Revolución Americana
- esfuerzos colectivos para cambiar el gobierno de Estados Unidos
- Estados Unidos se expandió desde el océano Atlántico hasta el océano Pacífico
- la tecnología cambió la vida en Estados Unidos en el siglo XIX

Actividades

- Con su niño, observe un mapa o un globo terráqueo. Ubique las rutas que algunos de los primeros exploradores europeos siguieron en su esfuerzo por llegar a Asia. Comente por qué algunos europeos pensaban que podrían llegar a Asia navegando hacia el oeste. Luego hable sobre cómo podrían haber reaccionado las personas cuando supieron que en lugar de llegar a Asia, habían descubierto un nuevo continente.

- Junto a su niño o niña, imagine que vive en las colonias durante la Guerra de la Independencia. Comente cómo usted, como colonizador se hubiera sentido ante algunas de las leyes aprobadas por el Parlamento. Hable sobre cómo hubiera sido vivir en las colonias durante la Revolución Americana.

- Con su niño o niña, use una enciclopedia o la Internet para buscar más información sobre uno de los inventos del siglo XIX.

Ideas para comentar

- ¿Cómo influyeron los cambios graduales en el medio ambiente en la forma de vida y el lugar dónde vivieron los antiguos indios?

- ¿Cuáles son algunas de las razones por las cuales se fundaron nuevos asentamientos en las trece colonias inglesas durante los siglos XVII y XVIII?

- ¿Por qué fueron tan importantes los compromisos en la formación del nuevo gobierno?

APRENDE en línea

Visiten The Learning Site en www.harcourtschool.com/socialstudies para obtener actividades adicionales, fuentes originales y otros recursos para usar en esta unidad.

© Harcourt

School to Home

Newsletter

Books To Read

Lincoln: A Photobiography by Russell Freedman. Clarion, 1987.

Lincoln in His Own Words by Milton Meltzer. Harcourt, 1993.

A House Divided: The Lives of Ulysses S. Grant and Robert E. Lee by Jules Archer. Scholastic, 1995.

Tales from the Underground Railroad by Kate Connell. Steck-Vaughn, 1993.

The Story of Thomas Alva Edison by Margaret Cousins. Random House Children's Publishing, 1997.

Immigrant Kids by Russell Freedman. Puffin Books, 1995.

Content to Learn

Your child is about to begin studying major events that occurred before, during, and after the Civil War. In the second unit, Civil War Times, these are some of the topics that will be covered:

- how regional differences caused conflict between the North and South
- the actions taken by some Americans to try to end slavery
- the effects of Lincoln's victory in the 1860 election
- the Civil War and Reconstruction
- the settlement of the West
- how industries and inventions changed life in the United States during the late 1800s
- opportunities and challenges faced by immigrants

✏ Activities to Try

- Discuss with your child the concept of frame of reference—where someone was when an event happened and what role he or she played in it. Then talk about how a child's frame of reference during the Civil War—whether that child was from the North or the South—might have influenced how he or she felt about the war.

- Imagine with your child that you are a witness to one of the debates that took place between Abraham Lincoln and Stephen Douglas in the summer of 1858. Describe what you see and hear at the debate, such as how the candidates look and what they say.

- Talk to your child about how settlers who moved from the East Coast to the Great Plains would have had to adjust to a new environment with a new climate and new kinds of resources. Work with your child to write a series of diary entries describing the life of a settler on the Great Plains and how that settler's life has changed since arriving there.

Dear Diary,

💡 Ideas to Discuss

- Why did Lincoln's victory in the 1860 election eventually lead to the outbreak of the Civil War?

- How did Lincoln's death affect Reconstruction in the South?

- What were the main incentives that led to settlement of the West?

Visit **The Learning Site** at www.harcourtschool.com/socialstudies for additional activities, primary sources, and other resources to use in this unit.

Carta para la casa

Libros

Lincoln: A Photobiography por Russell Freedman. Clarion, 1987.

Lincoln In His Own Words por Milton Meltzer. Harcourt, 1993.

A House Divided: The Lives of Ulysses S. Grant and Robert E. Lee por Jules Archer. Scholastic, 1995.

Tales from the Underground Railroad por Kate Connell. Steck-Vaughn, 1993.

The Story of Thomas Alva Edison por Margaret Cousins. Random House Children's Publishing, 1997.

Immigrant Kids por Russell Freedman. Puffin Books, 1995.

Tema de estudio

Su hijo comenzará a estudiar grandes hechos que tuvieron lugar antes, durante y después de la Guerra Civil. Éstos son algunos de los tópicos que cubrirá la segunda unidad, La Guerra Civil:

- cómo las diferencias regionales provocaron conflictos entre el Norte y el Sur
- las acciones emprendidas por algunos americanos para tratar de terminar con la esclavitud
- los efectos de la victoria de Lincoln en las elecciones de 1860
- la Guerra Civil y la Reconstrucción
- la colonización del Oeste
- cómo nuevas industrias e inventos cambiaron la vida en Estados Unidos a fines del siglo XIX
- oportunidades y desafíos enfrentados por los inmigrantes

Actividades

- Hablen con su hijo sobre el concepto de marco de referencia—dónde estaba alguien cuando ocurrió un hecho y qué papel jugó en el mismo. Entonces hablen sobre cómo el marco de referencia de un niño durante la Guerra Civil—sea el niño del Norte o del Sur—podría haber influido en cómo se sentían acerca de la guerra.

- Con su hijo, imagine que presencia uno de los debates entre Abraham Lincoln y Stephen Douglas en el verano de 1858. Describan lo que ven y lo que escuchan en el debate, cómo el aspecto que tienen los candidatos y qué dicen.

- Hable con su hijo de cómo debieron adaptarse al nuevo ambiente, clima y nuevos tipos de recursos los colonos que se trasladaron de la costa este a las Grandes Llanuras. Ayude a su hijo a escribir una serie de anotaciones en un diario describiendo la vida de un colono en las Grandes Llanuras y de cómo cambia su vida al llegar allí.

Ideas para comentar

- ¿Por qué la victoria de Lincoln en las elecciones de 1860 condujo al estallido de la Guerra Civil?

- ¿Cómo afectó la muerte de Lincoln a la Reconstrucción en el Sur?

- ¿Cuáles fueron los principales incentivos que impulsaron la colonización del Oeste?

Visiten The Learning Site en www.harcourtschool.com/socialstudies para obtener actividades adicionales, fuentes originales y otros recursos para usar en esta unidad.

© Harcourt

School to Home

Books To Read

Locks, Crocs, and Skeeters: The Story of the Panama Canal by Nancy Winslow Parker. Greenwillow, 1996.

The Story of Thomas Alva Edison by Margaret Cousins. Random House Children's Publishing, 1997.

You Want Women to Vote, Lizzie Stanton? by Jean Fritz. Putnam, 1995.

Content to Learn

Your child will be studying growth and changes in the United States during the late 1800s and early 1900s, and the role of the United States in World War I. Here are some of the topics that will be covered in the third unit, Becoming a World Power:

- addition of new lands in the late 1800s and early 1900s

- war with Spain and other events in the early 1900s, resulting in the United States becoming a world power

- how inventions in the late 1800s and early 1900s changed life in the United States

- problems of growing cities and how some people worked to solve them

- efforts of progressives to improve life in the United States

- the entrance of the United States into World War I

- how the United States helped Allied Powers win World War I

- how countries around the world were affected by the outcome of World War I

 ## Activities to Try

- Imagine with your child that you lived in the United States in the late 1800s. Gold has recently been discovered in Alaska. Discuss whether your family would be willing to go to

Alaska, a largely unsettled frontier, to look for gold and to settle there. Talk about the opportunities and challenges such an adventure would offer.

- With your child, talk about the many inventions that came about in the late 1800s and early 1900s. Discuss how these inventions changed the lives of people living at that time. Then discuss how these inventions still affect our lives today.

- Imagine with your child that your family is living during World War I. Talk about how the war would likely affect your daily lives.

Ideas to Discuss

- Why was the building of the Panama Canal important to the United States?

- In what ways did the efforts of progressives improve the lives of American citizens?

- How did women's contributions during World War I encourage the ratification of the Nineteenth Amendment, which gave women the right to vote?

 GO ONLINE Visit **The Learning Site** at www.harcourtschool.com/socialstudies for additional activities, primary sources, and other resources to use in this unit.

© Harcourt

Carta para la casa

Libros

Locks, Crocs, and Skeeters: The Story of the Panama Canal by Nancy Winslow Parker. Greenwillow, 1996.

The Story of Thomas Alva Edison by Margaret Cousins. Random House Children's Publishing, 1997.

You Want Women to Vote, Lizzie Stanton? by Jean Fritz. Putnam, 1995.

Tema de estudio

Su niño comenzará a estudiar el crecimiento y los cambios de Estados Unidos durante la segunda mitad del siglo XIX y su papel en la I Guerra Mundial a principios del siglo XX. Éstos son algunos de los temas que desarrollaremos en la tercera unidad, Convertirse en una potencia mundial:

- adquisición de nuevos territorios a finales del siglo XIX y principios del XX
- la guerra contra España y otros sucesos a principios del siglo XX trajeron como resultado que Estados Unidos se transformara en una potencia mundial
- cómo los inventos de finales del siglo XIX y comienzos del siglo XX cambiaron la vida en Estados Unidos
- problemas del crecimiento de las ciudades y cómo lo resolvieron
- esfuerzos crecientes por mejorar la vida en Estados Unidos
- Estados Unidos se oponía a entrar en la I Guerra Mundial
- Estados Unidos ayudó a las Fuerzas Aliadas a ganar la I Guerra Mundial
- los países de todo el mundo fueron afectados por los resultados de la I Guerra Mundial

Actividades

- Imagine que vivió con su niño o niña en Estados Unidos a finales del siglo XIX. El oro ha sido descubierto recientemente en Alaska. Comente con su familia si debieran ir a Alaska, una región extensamente despoblada, a buscar oro y asentarse allí. Hablen sobre las oportunidades y retos que ofrecería tal aventura.

- Con su niño o niña, hable sobre los inventos que aparecieron a finales del siglo XIX y principios del XX. Comente cómo estos inventos cambiaron las vidas de las personas de esa época. Luego comenten cómo esos inventos aún influyen en nuestra vida hoy.

- Con su niño o niña, imagine que su familia vive durante la I Guerra Mundial. Hablen sobre cómo la guerra afectaría sus vidas diarias.

Ideas para comentar

- ¿Por qué fue importante para Estados Unidos la construcción del canal de Panamá?

- ¿En qué forma los esfuerzos de los progresistas han mejorado las vidas de los ciudadanos americanos?

- ¿Cómo la I Guerra Mundial ayudó en los esfuerzos por ratificar la Novena Enmienda que le da el derecho al voto a la mujer?

APRENDE en línea

Visiten The Learning Site en www.harcourtschool.com/socialstudies para obtener actividades adicionales, fuentes originales y otros recursos para usar en esta unidad.

© Harcourt

School to Home

Newsletter

Books To Read

The Harlem Renaissance (African American Achiever series) by Veronica Chamber and B. Marvis. Chelsea House, 1997.

Eleanor Roosevelt: A Life of Discovery by Russell Freedman. Clarion, 1997.

Children of the Dust Bowl: The True Story of the School at Weedpatch Camp by Jerry Stanley. Crown, 1992.

Content to Learn

Your child will be studying events in the United States during the 1920s and 1930s. In the fourth unit, Good Times and Bad, these are some of the topics that will be covered:

- the booming United States economy in the early 1920s
- changes to daily life during the 1920s
- arts and entertainment during the 1920s
- the prosperity of the 1920s and the stock market crash of 1929
- the great hardships suffered by Americans during the Great Depression
- how Franklin Roosevelt's New Deal helped employ Americans and ease the effects of the Great Depression

✏️ Activities to Try

- With your child, discuss the significant changes that came about in people's lives as the automobile became available to more people. Talk about how it changed where people lived, where and how often they traveled, and the types of jobs and services that came about because of the automobile.

- The stock market crash of 1929 greatly affected the lives of many Americans. Together with your child, use the Internet or an encyclopedia to learn about efforts that have been taken to make sure such a crash does not happen again.

- Work with your child to find books or articles that describe what life was like for people living in the Dust Bowl region during the Great Depression. Examine pictures that show what the conditions were like. Talk about the hardships that people living in the region would have had to overcome.

💡 Ideas to Discuss

- How did installment buying allow more people to purchase consumer goods in the 1920s?

- In what ways did President Roosevelt's New Deal help many Americans?

- What major changes came about to radio and the movies during the 1920s?

GO ONLINE Visit **The Learning Site** at www.harcourtschool.com/socialstudies for additional activities, primary sources, and other resources to use in this unit.

© Harcourt

Carta para la casa

Libros

*The Harlem Renaissance
(African American Achiever
series)* by Veronica Chamber
and B. Marvis. Chelsea
House, 1997.

*Eleanor Roosevelt: A Life of
Discovery* by Russell
Freedman. Clarion, 1997.

*Children of the Dust Bowl: The
True Story of the School at
Weedpatch Camp* by Jerry
Stanley. Crown, 1992.

Tema de estudio

Su niño comenzará a estudiar los sucesos ocurridos en Estados Unidos durante las décadas de 1920 y 1930. En la cuarta unidad, Buenos y malos tiempos, desarrollaremos las siguientes ideas y temas:

■ la economía de Estados Unidos estaba en auge a principios de la década de 1920

■ cambios en la vida diaria durante la década de 1920

■ arte y entretenimiento durante la década de 1920

■ la prosperidad de la década de 1920 terminó con la caída del mercado de la bolsa en 1929

■ los americanos sufrieron grandes penurias durante la Gran Depresión

■ el New Deal (Nuevo Reparto) de Franklin Roosevelt ayudó a dar empleo a los americanos y a disminuir los efectos de la Gran Depresión

Actividades

■ Con su niño o niña, comente los cambios significativos que ocurrieron en la vidas de las personas a medida que el automóvil estuvo al alcance de muchas de ellas. Hablen sobre cómo éste cambió dónde vivían, a dónde y con qué frecuencia viajaban y los tipos de empleos y servicios que aparecieron por causa del automóvil.

■ La caída del mercado de la bolsa en 1929 afectó grandemente la vida de muchos americanos. Junto con su niño o niña, use la Internet o una enciclopedia para aprender sobre los esfuerzos que se han realizado para asegurar que no se produzca otra caída en la bolsa.

■ Trabaje con su niño o niña, para buscar libros o artículos que describan cómo era la vida de las personas que vivían en villas miseria o en la región del Dust Bowl durante la gran Depresión. Examine fotos que muestren en qué condiciones vivían. Hable sobre las penurias que tuvieron que vencer la personas que vivían en esos lugares.

Ideas para comentar

■ ¿Cómo el método de comprar a plazos permite que más personas puedan comprar artículos de consumo en la década de 1920?

■ ¿Qué cambios fundamentales se produjeron en la radio y el cine durante la década de 1920?

■ ¿En qué medida el New Deal (Nuevo Reparto) del presidente Roosevelt ayudó a muchos americanos?

Visiten The Learning Site en www.harcourtschool.com/socialstudies para obtener actividades adicionales, fuentes originales y otros recursos para usar en esta unidad.

© Harcourt

School to Home

Harcourt Horizons • United States History: From Civil War to Present, Unit 5

Newsletter

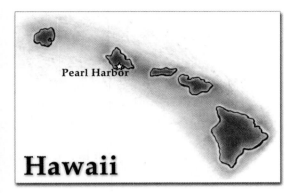

Hawaii

Pearl Harbor

Books To Read

A Boy at War: A Novel of Pearl Harbor by Harry Mazer. Simon & Schuster, 2001.

The 761st Tank Battalion by Katherine Browne Pfeiffer. Twenty-First Century Books, 1994.

I Am an American by Jerry Stanley. Crown, 1994.

Patriots Point in Remembrance by Steve Ewing. Pictorial Histories, 1999.

Content to Learn

Your child will be studying events that occurred before, during, and after World War II. Here are some of the topics that will be covered in the fifth unit, World War II:

- how World War II began
- world events that force the United States to enter World War II in 1941
- life in the United States during World War II
- how World War II affected countries in Africa and Europe
- why winning the war in the Pacific took longer
- how life in America changed after World War II
- the new threat of communism that many nations faced

Activities to Try

- With your child, look in an encyclopedia or on the Internet for maps that show countries that were invaded and conquered by Germany, Italy, and Japan before and during World War II. Talk about what life may have been like for citizens in these countries and in the United States during this time period.

- Imagine with your child that you are living during the time of World War II. Talk about the idea of rationing and its effects during World War II. Discuss why rationing is necessary. Make a list of items that you can only purchase by using government coupons. Then talk about how you can cut back on the use of rationed items to make them last longer.

- Work with your child to learn more about the formation of the United Nations (UN) or of the North Atlantic Treaty Organization (NATO). Both organizations were formed following World War II. Use an encyclopedia or the Internet to learn which countries joined the organization—and its purpose.

Ideas to Discuss

- Prior to the attack on Pearl Harbor, why were many Americans hesitant to become involved in World War II?

- How were the Allies able to win the war in Europe? in Japan?

- How did life change for many Americans after World War II?

© Harcourt

GO ONLINE Visit **The Learning Site** at www.harcourtschool.com/socialstudies for additional activities, primary sources, and other resources to use in this unit.

Pearl Harbor

Hawaii

Libros

A Boy at War: A Novel of Pearl Harbor by Harry Mazer. Simon & Schuster, 2001.

The 761st Tank Battalion by Katherine Browne Pfeiffer. Twenty-First Century Books, 1994.

I Am an American by Jerry Stanley. Crown, 1994.

Patriots Point in Remembrance by Steve Ewing. Pictorial Histories, 1999.

Tema de estudio

Su niño comenzará a estudiar los sucesos ocurridos antes, durante y después de la II Guerra Mundial. Éstos son algunas ideas y temas que desarrollaremos en la quinta unidad, La II Guerra Mundial:

- cómo comenzó la II Guerra Mundial
- sucesos mundiales que obligaron a Estados Unidos a entrar en la II guerra Mundial en 1941
- la vida en Estados Unidos durante la II Guerra Mundial
- cómo afectó la II Guerra Mundial a los países de África y de Europa
- ganar la guerra en el Pacífico tomó bastante tiempo
- la vida en América cambió después de la II Guerra Mundial
- muchas naciones enfrentaron la nueva amenaza del comunismo

Actividades

- Con su niño o niña, busque en una enciclopedia o en la Internet mapas que muestren los países que fueron invadidos y conquistados por Alemania, Italia y Japón, antes y durante la II Guerra Mundial. Hablen sobre cómo sería la vida de los ciudadanos en estos países y en América durante este período.

- Imagine que con su niño o niña, vive en los tiempos de la II Guerra Mundial. Hablen sobre el racionamiento y sobre cómo éste afecta sus vidas cotidianas. Comente por qué es necesario el racionamiento. Haga una lista de los artículos que sólo puede comprar con cupones del estado. Luego hable sobre cómo ahorrar estos productos para lograr que les dure más.

- Trabaje su niño o niña, para aprender más sobre la formación de la Naciones Unidas (NU) o sobre el Organización del Tratado del Atlántico Norte (OTAN). Ambas organizaciones se formaron durante la II Guerra Mundial. Use una enciclopedia o la Internet para buscar qué países se unieron a estas organizaciones y cuáles fueron sus propósitos.

Ideas para comentar

- ¿Por qué muchos americanos vacilaban ante la idea de entrar en la II Guerra Mundial, antes del ataque de Pearl Harbor?

- ¿Cómo los aliados fueron capaces de ganar la guerra en Europa? ¿y en Japón?

- ¿Cómo cambió la vida para muchos americanos después de la II Guerra Mundial?

Visiten The Learning Site en <u>www.harcourtschool.com/socialstudies</u> para obtener actividades adicionales, fuentes originales y otros recursos para usar en esta unidad.

© Harcourt

School to Home

Harcourt Horizons • United States History: From Civil War to Present, Unit 6

Newsletter

Books To Read

The Watsons Go to Birmingham: 1963 by Christopher Paul Curtis. Delacorte/BDD, 1995.

Flying to the Moon: An Astronaut's Story by Michael Collins. Farrar, Straus, and Giroux, 1994.

Maya Lin: Honoring Our Forgotten Heroes by Bob Italia. Lee and Low Books, 1997.

Content to Learn

Your child will be studying events that occurred during the second half of the twentieth century. In the sixth unit, The Cold War and Beyond, these are some of the topics that will be covered:

- the United States involvement in the Korean War to stop the spread of communism

- challenges inside and outside the United States during the 1950s

- how the United States and the Soviet Union shaped world events in the 1960s

- how individuals and groups worked to gain equal rights in the United States

- the causes and effects of the Vietnam War

- how individuals helped end the Cold War

- new challenges the United States faced after the Cold War

- changes in the United States and the world at the end of the twentieth century

Activities to Try

- Imagine with your child that you are living during the 1950s. Work together to write a diary entry that describes what life is like for you. Write about both the opportunities and the challenges that are faced by you and other Americans. Include your ideas about some of the issues.

- With your child, use an encyclopedia or the Internet to learn more about the Cuban Missile Crisis or the space race that took place between the United States and the Soviet Union during the 1960s. Create an information sheet describing the people, events, and issues important to your topic. Include a time line of significant events.

- The 2000 presidential election was very close. As a result, many Americans came to better understand the importance of the electoral college. With your child, use an encyclopedia or the Internet to learn more about the electoral college and how it works.

Ideas to Discuss

- In what ways do Americans continue to benefit from the efforts of those in the Civil Rights movement?

- What challenges did Americans face during the 1970s?

- Why did some people support the Vietnam War while others opposed it?

GO ONLINE Visit **The Learning Site** at www.harcourtschool.com/socialstudies for additional activities, primary sources, and other resources to use in this unit.

© Harcourt

Carta para la casa

Libros

The Watsons Go to Birmingham: 1963 by Christopher Paul Curtis. Delacorte/BDD, 1995.

Flying to the Moon: An Astronaut's Story by Michael Collins. Farrar, Straus, and Giroux, 1994.

Maya Lin: Honoring Our Forgotten Heroes by Bob Italia. Lee and Low Books, 1997.

Tema de estudio

Su niño comenzará a estudiar los sucesos ocurridos durante la segunda mitad del siglo XX. En la sexta unidad, La guerra fría y después, éstos son algunas ideas y temas que desarrollaremos:

- Estados Unidos entró en la Guerra de Corea para parar el avance del comunismo
- retos dentro y fuera de Estados Unidos durante la década del 1950
- Estados Unidos y la Unión Soviética dominaron todos los sucesos mundiales en la década de 1960
- personas y grupos de personas que trabajaron para lograr igualdad de derechos en Estados Unidos
- causas y efectos de la Guerra de Vietnam
- personas que ayudaron a terminar la Guerra Fría
- Estados Unidos enfrentó nuevos retos después de la Guerra Fría
- a finales del siglo XX, las personas trabajaron para lograr cambios en Estados Unidos y en el mundo

Actividades

- Con su niño o niña, imagine que viven en la década de 1950. Trabajen juntos para escribir una página de un diario que describa cómo era la vida de ustedes. Escriba tanto sobre las oportunidades como sobre los retos que enfrentaron usted y otros ameri-canos. Incluya sus apreciaciones sobre algunos de los aspectos tratados.

- Con su niño o niña, use una enciclopedia o la Internet para averiguar más sobre la Crisis de los Misiles Cubanos o sobre la Carrera Espacial que tuvo lugar entre Estados Unidos y la Unión Soviética durante la década de 1960. Cree una tarjeta de informa-ción donde describa las personas, los sucesos y los temas impor-tantes para su trabajo. Incluya una línea cronológica de los eventos más significativos.

- La elección presidencial del año 2000 fue muy cerrada. Como resultado, muchos americanos llegaron a comprender mejor la importancia del colegio electoral. Con su niño o niña, use una enci-clopedia o la Internet para buscar más información sobre el colegio electoral y su funcionamiento.

Ideas para comentar

- ¿En qué medida continúan be-neficiándose los americanos de los esfuerzos del movimiento de los Derechos Civiles?

- ¿Por qué algunas personas apoyaron la Guerra de Vietnam mientras otras se opusieron a ella?

- ¿Qué retos enfrentaron los ameri-canos en la década de 1970?

Visiten The Learning Site en www.harcourtschool.com/socialstudies para obtener actividades adicionales, fuentes originales y otros recursos para usar en esta unidad.

School to Home

Harcourt Horizons • United States History: From Civil War to Present, Unit 7

Newsletter

Books To Read

Celebrate! In Central America by Diane and Joe Viesti. Lothrop, Lee & Shepard, 1997.

Canada Facts and Figures by Susan Levert. Chelsea House, 1992.

Chico Mendes: Defender of the Rain Forest by Joann Burch. Millbrook, 1994.

Content to Learn

Your child is about to begin studying the United States today, its relationship with other nations, and its neighbors in the Western Hemisphere. In the seventh unit, The United States and the World, these are some of the topics that will be covered:

- how technology and cultural diversity have affected Americans' way of life

- how population growth has presented new challenges for the United States

- how changes in the American economy have changed the way many people earn a living

- the role of government and the rights and responsibilities of citizens

- the history of Mexico and its relationship with the United States

- nations in the Caribbean and Central America

- South America and its past and present challenges

- the history of Canada and its relationship with the United States

Activities to Try

- Share with your child information about your family's culture and heritage. Use an encyclopedia or the Internet to learn more about the country where your family or your ancestors came from.

- Discuss with your child similarities and differences in your school experiences and those of your child. For example, contrast the way in which you gathered and wrote information for research reports with the way your child is able to gather and write information.

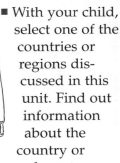

- With your child, select one of the countries or regions discussed in this unit. Find out information about the country or region, and create a travel brochure for it.

Ideas to Discuss

- How have new technologies and population growth affected people's daily lives?

- Why is the time in which we live called the Information Age?

- How is the United States interdependent with other countries?

© Harcourt

GO ONLINE Visit **The Learning Site** at www.harcourtschool.com/socialstudies for additional activities, primary sources, and other resources to use in this unit.

Carta para la casa

Libros

Celebrate! In Central America por Diane y Joe Viesti. Lothrop, Lee & Shepard, 1997.

Canada Facts and Figures por Susan Levert. Chelsea House, 1992.

Chico Mendes: Defender of the Rain Forest por Joann Burch. Millbrook, 1994.

Tema de estudio

Su hijo comenzará a estudiar Estados Unidos hoy, su relación con otras naciones, y sus vecinos en el hemisferio occidental. Éstos son algunos de los tópicos que cubrirá la séptima unidad, Estados Unidos y el mundo:

- los avances tecnológicos y la diversidad cultural han afectado el modo de vida de los estadounidenses
- el crecimiento de la población ha presentado nuevos desafíos para Estados Unidos
- los cambios en la economía americana han modificado el modo en que mucha se gana la vida
- el papel del gobierno y los derechos y responsabilidades del ciudadano
- la historia de México y su relación con Estados Unidos
- naciones del Caribe y América Central
- América del Sur y sus desafíos pasados y presentes
- la historia de Canadá y su relación con Estados Unidos

Actividades

- Comparta con su hijo información sobre la cultura y la herencia de su familia. Usen una enciclopedia o Internet para buscar más información sobre el país del que provienen sus antepasados o su familia.

- Hablen sobre las similitudes y diferencias entre su propia experiencia escolar y la de su hijo. Por ejemplo, comparen la forma en que usted reunía y escribía la información y el modo en que lo hace su hijo.

- Juntos, escojan uno de los países o regiones estudiados en esta unidad. Busquen información sobre el país o región y creen un folleto de viajes para ese sitio.

Ideas para comentar

- ¿Cómo han afectado la vida cotidiana los adelantos tecnológicos y el aumento de la población?

- ¿Por qué este período en el cual vivimos la Era de la Información?

- ¿Cómo es Estados Unidos interdependiente con otros países?

Visiten The Learning Site en www.harcourtschool.com/socialstudies para obtener actividades adicionales, fuentes originales y otros recursos para usar en esta unidad.

Index

· UNIT ·

1

Making a New Nation

· UNIT · 7

The United States and the World

Reference

Features You Can Use

Time Lines

Reading Your Textbook

Getting Started

Your textbook is divided into seven units.

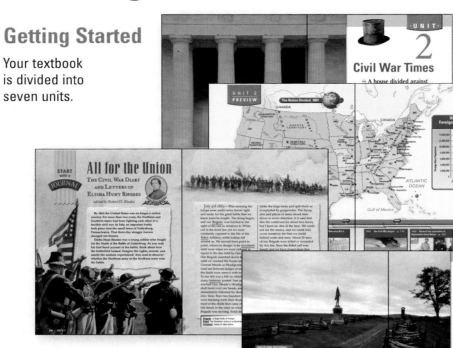

Each unit has a Unit Preview that gives facts about important events. The Preview also shows where and when those events took place.

Each unit is divided into chapters, and each chapter is divided into lessons.

Each unit begins with a song, poem, story, or other special reading selection.

The Parts of a Lesson

This statement gives you ideas to help you as you read a lesson.

This statement tells you why it is important to read the lesson.

These are the new vocabulary terms you will learn in the lesson.

Lesson title

This part of the time line shows the period when the events in the lesson took place.

Each new vocabulary term is highlighted in yellow and defined.

Each lesson is divided into several short sections.

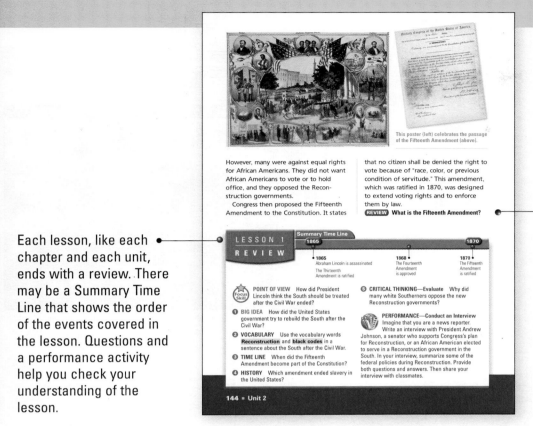

This poster (left) celebrates the passage of the Fifteenth Amendment (above).

However, many were against equal rights for African Americans. They did not want African Americans to vote or to hold office, and they opposed the Reconstruction governments.

Congress then proposed the Fifteenth Amendment to the Constitution. It states that no citizen shall be denied the right to vote because of "race, color, or previous condition of servitude." This amendment, which was ratified in 1870, was designed to extend voting rights and to enforce them by law.

REVIEW What is the Fifteenth Amendment?

LESSON 1 REVIEW

Summary Time Line

1865 — 1870

1865 Abraham Lincoln is assassinated
The Thirteenth Amendment is ratified

1868 The Fourteenth Amendment is approved

1870 The Fifteenth Amendment is ratified

POINT OF VIEW How did President Lincoln think the South should be treated after the Civil War ended?

1 BIG IDEA How did the United States government try to rebuild the South after the Civil War?

2 VOCABULARY Use the vocabulary words **Reconstruction** and **black codes** in a sentence about the South after the Civil War.

3 TIME LINE When did the Fifteenth Amendment become part of the Constitution?

4 HISTORY Which amendment ended slavery in the United States?

5 CRITICAL THINKING—Evaluate Why did many white Southerners oppose the new Reconstruction governments?

PERFORMANCE—Conduct an Interview Imagine that you are a news reporter. Write an interview with President Andrew Johnson, a senator who supports Congress's plan for Reconstruction, or an African American elected to serve in a Reconstruction government in the South. In your interview, summarize some of the federal policies during Reconstruction. Provide both questions and answers. Then share your interview with classmates.

144 ■ Unit 2

Each lesson, like each chapter and each unit, ends with a review. There may be a Summary Time Line that shows the order of the events covered in the lesson. Questions and a performance activity help you check your understanding of the lesson.

Each short section ends with a **REVIEW** question that will help you check whether you understand what you have read. Be sure to answer this question before you continue reading the lesson.

Skills

Your textbook has lessons that will help you build your reading, citizenship, chart and graph, and map and globe skills.

This statement tells you why it is important to learn the skill.

You will be able to practice and apply the skills you learn.

Special Features

The feature called Examine Primary Sources shows you ways to learn about different kinds of objects and documents.

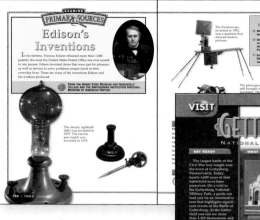

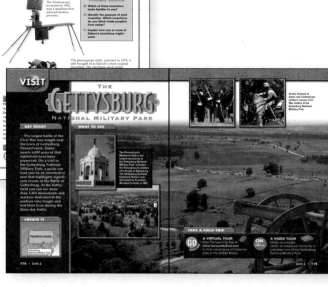

The Visit feature lets you "visit" many interesting places.

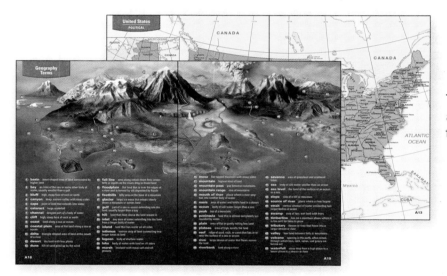

Atlas

The Atlas provides maps and a list of geography terms with illustrations.

For Your Reference

At the back of your textbook, you will find the reference tools listed below.

- Almanac
- American Documents
- Biographical Dictionary
- Gazetteer
- Glossary
- Index

You can use these tools to look up words and to find information about people, places, and other topics.

Atlas

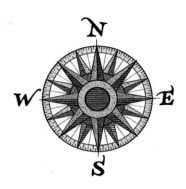

A1

Skill Lesson
PAGES A2–A3

OBJECTIVES

- Explain what a map is.
- Identify the parts of a map.
- Use a grid system to locate places.

Vocabulary

map title p. A2

map key p. A2

inset map p. A2

grid system
  p. A3

locator p. A3

map scale p. A3

compass rose
  p. A3

cardinal
  directions p. A3

intermediate
  directions p. A3

WORD CARDS

See pp. V1–V2.

1 Motivate

Why It Matters

Discuss why reading maps is an important skill. Have students brainstorm ways they can use maps in social studies. Emphasize that maps help us learn more about the world.

· SKILLS · MAP AND GLOBE
Read a Map

VOCABULARY		
map title	grid system	compass rose
map key	locator	cardinal directions
inset map	map scale	intermediate directions

► WHY IT MATTERS

Maps provide many kinds of information about the world around you. Knowing how to read maps is an important social studies skill.

► WHAT YOU NEED TO KNOW

A map is a drawing that shows all of or part of the Earth on a flat surface. Mapmakers add certain features to most of the maps they draw.

Mapmakers sometimes need to show places marked on the map in greater detail or places that are beyond the area shown on the map. Find Alaska and Hawaii on the map of the United States on pages A10–A11. This map shows the location of those two states in relation to the rest of the country.

- A **map title** tells the subject of the map. It may also identify the kind of map.
  - Political maps show cities, states, and countries.
  - Physical maps show kinds of land and bodies of water.
  - Historical maps show parts of the world as they were in the past.

- A **map key**, or legend, explains the symbols used on a map. Symbols may be colors, patterns, lines, or other special marks.

- An **inset map** is a small map within a larger map.

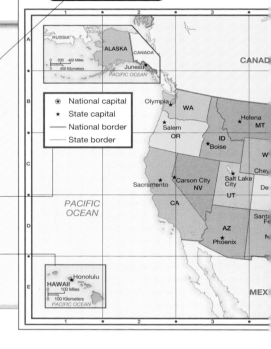

The United States

A2

BACKGROUND

Map Key Symbols Not all maps use the same symbols in the map key. However, a star is the most widely used symbol for national and state capital cities. The national capital is often represented with a bigger star than state capitals. In addition, the line for a national border is generally darker and thicker than the line for a state border.

Now find Alaska and Hawaii on the map below. To show this much detail for these states and the rest of the country on one map, the map would have to be much larger. Instead, Alaska and Hawaii are each shown in a separate inset map, or a small map within a larger map.

To help people find places on a map, mapmakers sometimes add lines that cross each other to form a pattern of squares called a grid system. Look at the map of the United States below. Around the grid are letters and numbers. The columns, which run up and down, have numbers. The rows, which run left and right, have letters. Each square on the map can be identified by its letter and number. For example, the top row of squares in the map includes square A1, square A2, and square A3.

➡ PRACTICE THE SKILL

Use the map of the United States to answer the following questions.
1. What cities can be found in square B7?
2. In which direction would you travel to go from Phoenix, Arizona, to Columbia, South Carolina?
3. About how many miles is it from Austin, Texas, to Montgomery, Alabama?
4. Which two oceans border Alaska?

➡ APPLY WHAT YOU LEARNED

Choose one of the maps in the Atlas. With a partner, identify the parts of the map and discuss what the map tells you. Ask each other questions that can be answered by reading the map.

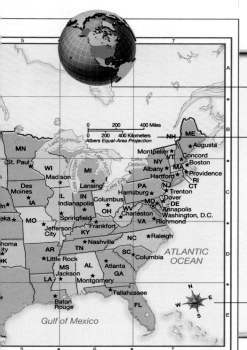

• A locator is a small map or picture of a globe that shows where the place on the main map is located.

• A map scale compares a distance on the map to a distance in the real world. It helps you find the real distance between places on a map.

• A compass rose , or direction marker, shows directions.
  • The cardinal directions, or main directions, are north, south, east, and west.
  • The intermediate directions, or directions between the cardinal directions, are northeast, northwest, southeast, and southwest.

MAP AND GLOBE SKILLS

A3

What You Need to Know

Ask students to read the labels describing the parts of a map. Point out to students that this is a political map. Discuss with students how the key, locator, scale, and compass rose make reading the map easier.

Q **What besides bodies of water and the shape of land does this map show?**

A capital cities, states, and countries

Practice the Skill—Answers

1. Phoenix
2. northeast
3. about 400 miles
4. Arctic Ocean and Pacific Ocean

3 Close

Apply What You Have Learned

Encourage students to reread the skill lesson if they are unable to identify parts of the map. You may wish to have students write down their questions and answers to share with the class.

ACTIVITY BOOK

Use ACTIVITY BOOK, p. 1, to give students additional practice using this skill.

TRANSPARENCY

Use SKILL TRANSPARENCY Atlas–1.

EXTEND AND ENRICH

Informative Writing Divide the class into small groups. Each group should write down as many uses for maps as they can think of. Then, ask groups to write an informative paragraph describing how maps influence and benefit people's lives.

RETEACH THE SKILL

Use the Map Scale Write four or five United States cities on the board. Have students use the map scale to estimate distances between the cities. Provide students with the correct distances. Direct students to compare their estimates with the true distances.

The World: Political

Set the Purpose

Main Idea Explain to students that a political map shows the names and borders of various political units, such as cities, states, provinces, and countries. This political map shows the names and borders of all the countries in the world.

Why It Matters Point out to students that this political map can be used to tell where a country is located and to see what size and shape that country is. The map can also be used to find out where a country is located in relation to other countries.

Visual Learning

Map Ask students how the map uses color to convey information. Guide them in recognizing that each country is a different color from the countries that surround it.

Also call students' attention to the map key. Tell students that a map key explains what the symbols used on a map stand for. This map key shows that gray lines indicate national borders.

Finally, point out the inset maps. Explain that inset maps are enlarged versions of a section of a map. Inset maps make it possible to show places in greater detail or to show places that are beyond the area shown on the main map.

Map Study

Geography Review latitude and longitude with students. Then ask them to identify the equator and the prime meridian.

Q If you were at a latitude of 20°N and a longitude of 100°W, in which country would you be?

A Mexico

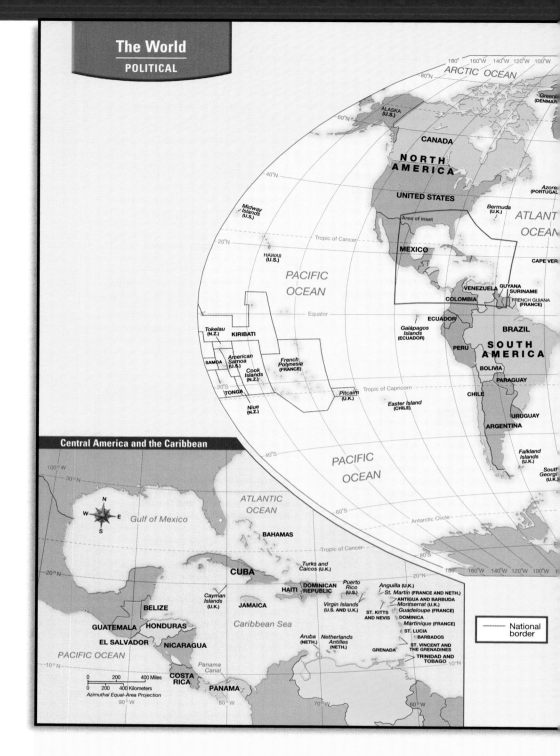

The World
POLITICAL

Central America and the Caribbean

National border

BACKGROUND

Changing Borders and Place Names National borders shift as wars and political change occur. In Europe many changes have occurred since 1989. The fall of communism gave birth to new independent nations. For instance, the 15 republics of the Soviet Union all became independent nations. Czechoslovakia split into two separate nations: the Czech Republic and Slovakia. East Germany and West Germany erased their border and became one nation: Germany.

QUESTIONS KIDS ASK

Q Why do some places have countries' names listed in parentheses?

A These islands and territories are not independent nations. These dependencies are governed or administered by the nation shown in parentheses.

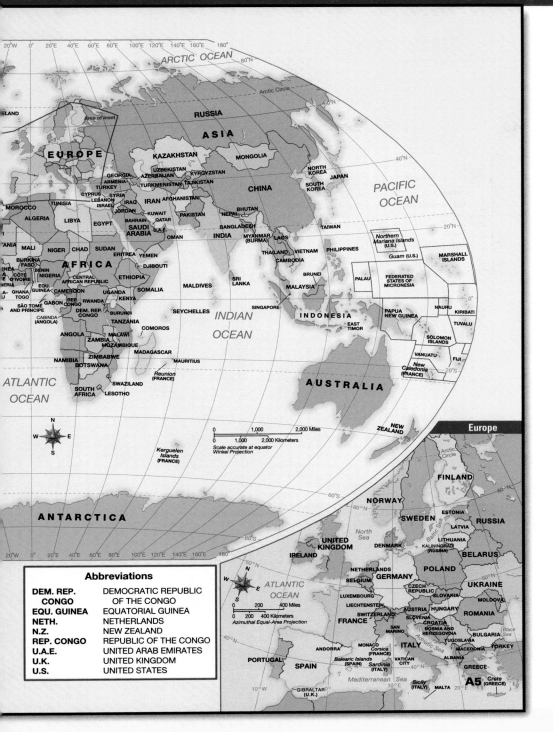

Abbreviations

DEM. REP. CONGO	DEMOCRATIC REPUBLIC OF THE CONGO
EQU. GUINEA	EQUATORIAL GUINEA
NETH.	NETHERLANDS
N.Z.	NEW ZEALAND
REP. CONGO	REPUBLIC OF THE CONGO
U.A.E.	UNITED ARAB EMIRATES
U.K.	UNITED KINGDOM
U.S.	UNITED STATES

Map Study

Geography Review the concept of regions with students. Explain that regions are areas that have specific characteristics that set them apart from other areas. A region may be defined, for example, by its landforms, by its cultural or political characteristics, or by other characteristics such as economic activities or the language people speak. For example, Latin America is a large region that refers to Central and South America, Mexico, and the Caribbean Islands. The term refers to the languages spoken in the countries that make up this region: Spanish, Portuguese, and French, all of which are languages that are derived from Latin.

Geography Call students' attention to the compass rose on the main map. Remind students that a compass rose is used to determine direction. Compass roses are useful for explaining where a country is located in relation to another country.

Q What direction would you travel to get from Sri Lanka to India?

A north

CD-ROM

Explore GEOSKILLS CD-ROM to give students additional practice using map and globe skills.

The Continent of North America You can use mental maps to judge students' level of knowledge and to correct any misconception students may have. Have students draw the continent of North America. They should label Canada, the United States, and Mexico. Have them include a compass rose on their drawings. After students have finished their drawings, have them compare their maps with an actual map of North America.

Make a Political Map Scrapbook Organize students in groups of four or five and ask them to search discarded newspapers and magazines as well as online sources for examples of political maps. Have them find three or four good examples to paste onto sheets of paper. For each map, have them identify the political units shown on the map and write a caption describing how the map was used in its original context.

The World: Physical

Set the Purpose

Main Idea Explain that the map on this page is a physical map of the world. A physical map shows what the surface of Earth looks like.

Why It Matters Physical maps are useful for getting an overview of the key physical features of the area shown on the map. This map can be used to find out where the world's mountains, lakes, rivers, oceans, and other physical features are located.

Visual Learning

Map Emphasize that this map's primary purpose is to show physical features. Landforms and bodies of water are the main focus and are labeled. National borders are shown but are not labeled. Have students study the map key and note how the map uses color to show terrain and vegetation patterns. If necessary review terms such as *arid* and *tundra* with students.

Map Study

Geography Point out the compass rose, and ask a volunteer to describe its purpose. Be sure students understand the concept of both cardinal and intermediate directions.

Q If you traveled from North America to Europe, which direction would you be going?

A east

Geography Have students locate the Tropic of Cancer and the Tropic of Capricorn on the map. Explain that the area between these lines is known as the tropics and the weather there is usually warm.

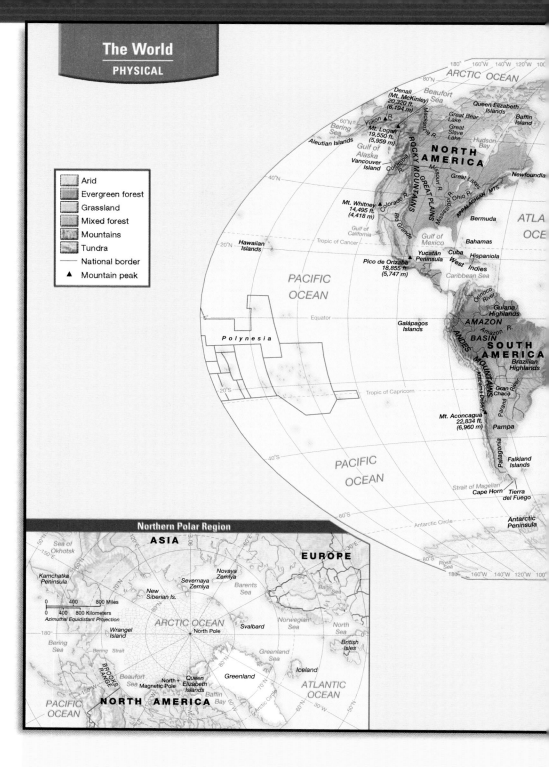

The World
PHYSICAL

Key:
- Arid
- Evergreen forest
- Grassland
- Mixed forest
- Mountains
- Tundra
- — National border
- ▲ Mountain peak

BACKGROUND

Map Projections Throughout history mapmakers have struggled with the difficulty of representing a spherical object—Earth—on a flat map. It is not possible to make a flat map completely accurate. The size and shape of some landmasses and areas become distorted, or changed.

Mapmakers must make compromises when they make flat maps. They use different projections, or ways of drawing Earth, depending on the main focus of the map. The main map on pages A6–A7, for example, is most accurate for the areas closest to the equator. Distortion increases as distance from the equator increases. The polar regions of the Arctic and Antarctic circles, for example, are quite distorted. Examine how different these two regions look on the inset maps, which use different projections to give a better representation.

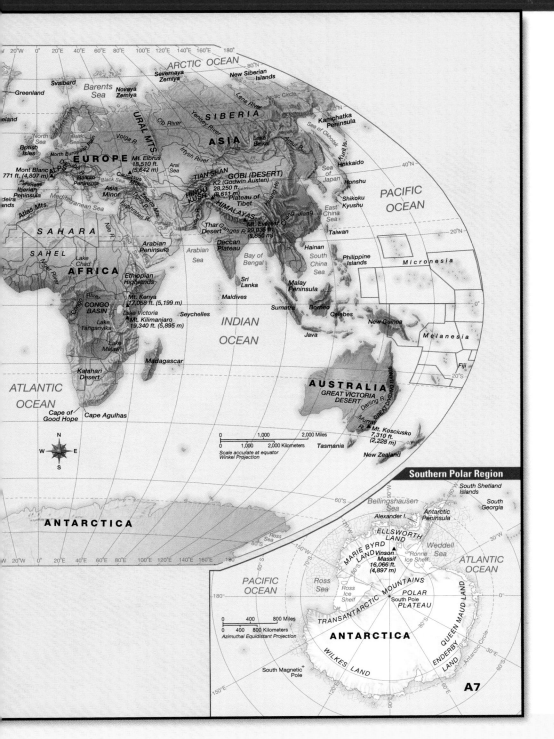

Map labels (from the world map):

20°W 0° 20°E 40°E 60°E 80°E 100°E 120°E 140°E 160°E 180°

ARCTIC OCEAN
80°N
Severnaya Zemlya
New Siberian Islands
Svalbard
Barents Sea
Novaya Zemlya
Greenland
Lena River
Arctic Circle
eland
Yenisey River
S I B E R I A
Kamchatka Peninsula
North Sea
Baltic Sea
Ob River
Sea of Okhotsk
British Isles
North European Plain
A S I A
Lake Baikal
Amur R.
Kuril Is.
EUROPE Mt. Elbrus 18,510 ft. (5,642 m)
Volga R.
Irtysh River
TIAN SHAN
40°N
Hokkaido
Mont Blanc ALPS 771 ft. (4,807 m)
Aral Sea
GOBI (DESERT)
Sea of Japan
Pyrenees
Caucasus
Black Sea
K2 (Godwin Austen) 28,250 ft. (8,611 m)
Honshu
PACIFIC OCEAN
Iberian Peninsula
Asia Minor
HINDU KUSH
Plateau of Tibet
Shikoku Kyushu
deira
Mediterranean Sea
Tigris R.
HIMALAYAS
Chang Jiang
East China Sea
nds
Atlas Mts.
Euphrates R.
Thar Desert
Mt. Everest 29,035 ft. (8,850 m)
Taiwan
20°N
S A H A R A
Nile R.
Arabian Peninsula
Ganges R.
Persian Gulf
Hainan
SAHEL
Lake Chad
Arabian Sea
Deccan Plateau
Bay of Bengal
South China Sea
Philippine Islands
Micronesia
Niger River
AFRICA
Ethiopian Highlands
Sri Lanka
Malay Peninsula
Congo River
Mt. Kenya 17,058 ft. (5,199 m)
Maldives
Sumatra
Borneo
Celebes
CONGO BASIN
Lake Victoria
Seychelles
New Guinea
Lake Tanganyika
Mt. Kilimanjaro 19,340 ft. (5,895 m)
INDIAN OCEAN
Java
Melanesia
Lake Malawi
20°S
Madagascar
Fiji
Kalahari Desert
ATLANTIC OCEAN
A U S T R A L I A
GREAT VICTORIA DESERT
GREAT DIVIDING RANGES
Cape of Good Hope
Cape Agulhas
Darling R.
0   1,000   2,000 Miles
0   1,000   2,000 Kilometers
Scale accurate at equator
Winkel Projection
Murray R.
Mt. Kosciusko 7,310 ft. (2,228 m)
Tasmania
New Zealand
N
W   E
S
ANTARCTICA
W 20°W 0° 20°E 40°E 60°E 80°E 100°E 120°E 140°E 160°E 180°

Southern Polar Region

South Shetland Islands
Bellingshausen Sea
60°S
Antarctic Peninsula
South Georgia
Alexander I.
ELLSWORTH LAND
Weddell Sea
Ross Sea
MARIE BYRD LAND
Vinson Massif 16,066 ft. (4,897 m)
Ronne Ice Shelf
ATLANTIC OCEAN
80°S
PACIFIC OCEAN
Ross Sea
Ross Ice Shelf
TRANSANTARCTIC MOUNTAINS
South Pole
POLAR PLATEAU
QUEEN MAUD LAND
ENDERBY LAND
0   400   800 Miles
0   400   800 Kilometers
Azimuthal Equidistant Projection
ANTARCTICA
WILKES LAND
South Magnetic Pole
Antarctic Circle

A7

Map Study

Geography Invite students to use the map key and the compass rose to formulate descriptive sentences about key physical features of each continent. For example, for Africa students might come up with the following sentence: "The northern part of Africa is mainly arid, but the central part of the continent has more forests and is more mountainous."

Geography Call students' attention to the symbol used for a mountain peak.

Q What is the highest mountain shown on the map and on which continent is it found?

A Mt. Everest is in Asia

Geography Have students notice the different kinds of bodies of water shown on the map. You might mention that there are four oceans: the Pacific, Atlantic, Indian, and Arctic Oceans. Seas, bays, and gulfs are all parts of these oceans.

Q What body of water lies between Africa and Europe?

A the Mediterranean Sea

CD-ROM

Explore GEOSKILLS CD-ROM to give students additional practice using map and globe skills.

Western Hemisphere: Political

Set the Purpose

Main Idea Remind students that the equator divides Earth into the Northern and Southern Hemispheres and that the prime meridian divides Earth into the Eastern and Western Hemispheres. Explain that the map on page A8 is a political map of the Western Hemisphere.

Why It Matters A map that focuses on a single hemisphere is useful because it can show more detail than a world map. The map on page A8, for example, can be used to find the location of national capitals and major cities as well as nations and national borders.

Visual Learning

Map Remind students that a political map shows political units. In this case, the political units are countries, each of which is a different color from those that surround it. Remind students that the map key identifies symbols used on the map, the scale is used to determine distances, and the compass rose is used to determine direction.

Map Study

Geography Be sure students understand that although the map shows all the national capitals, it does not show every city in the Western Hemisphere. It shows only the major cities.

Q What is the capital of Brazil?

A Brasília

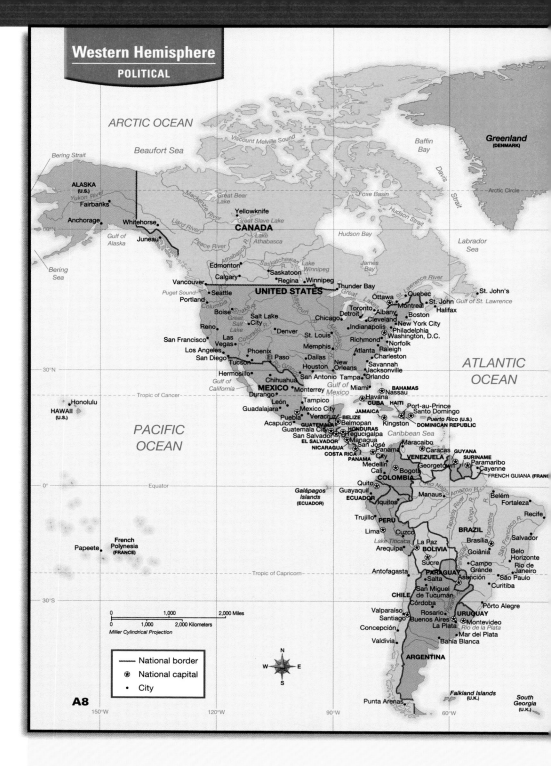

BACKGROUND

Compact Nations and Fragmented Nations Political geographers classify nations by their shapes and forms. Two classifications they use are compact nations and fragmented nations. A compact nation is one whose land areas are not separated by bodies of water or other countries. Uruguay, in South America, is an example of a compact nation. The United States, in contrast, is a fragmented nation because Alaska and Hawaii are separated from the rest of the country.

EXTEND AND ENRICH

Stage a Cultural Fair Organize students in small groups. Have each group choose a country in the Western Hemisphere (other than the United States) to research. Ask them to focus their research on cultural aspects of the country, such as music, art, or dance. Have students present a brief overview of the country to the rest of the class and then demonstrate or describe a traditional art form typical of the country.

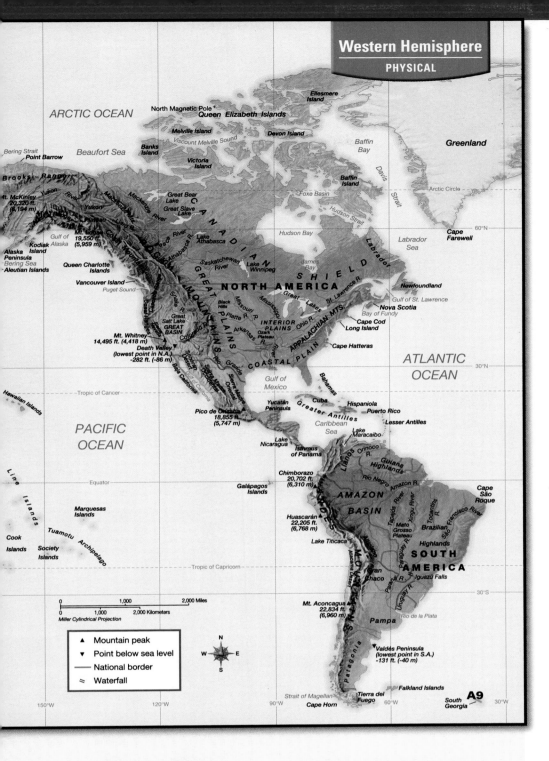

Map Labels

ARCTIC OCEAN

North Magnetic Pole
Queen Elizabeth Islands

Ellesmere Island

Greenland

Bering Strait
Point Barrow
Beaufort Sea

Banks Island

Melville Island

Devon Island

Baffin Bay

Viscount Melville Sound

Brooks Range

Victoria Island

Mt. McKinley
20,320 ft.
(6,194 m)

Yukon

Yukon River

Mackenzie Mts.

Great Bear Lake

Great Slave Lake

Baffin Island

Foxe Basin

Arctic Circle

60°N

Mackenzie River

Hudson Strait

Davis Strait

Gulf of Alaska

Mt. Logan
19,550 ft.
(5,959 m)

Kodiak Island

Alaska Peninsula

Bering Sea

Aleutian Islands

Queen Charlotte Islands

Vancouver Island

Puget Sound

Athabasca River

Lake Athabasca

Peace River

CANADIAN SHIELD

Hudson Bay

James Bay

Lake Winnipeg

Labrador

Cape Farewell

Labrador Sea

NORTH AMERICA

Snake R.

Columbia R.

GREAT PLAINS

Black Hills

Missouri R.

Mississippi R.

Great Lakes

St. Lawrence R.

Newfoundland

Gulf of St. Lawrence

Nova Scotia

Bay of Fundy

Great Salt Lake

GREAT BASIN

Platte R.

Arkansas R.

INTERIOR PLAINS

Ohio R.

Ozark Plateau

APPALACHIAN MTS.

Cape Cod
Long Island

Mt. Whitney
14,495 ft. (4,418 m)

Death Valley
(lowest point in N.A.)
-282 ft. (-86 m)

Colorado R.

Sierra Madre Oriental

Rio Grande

Sierra Madre Occidental

COASTAL PLAIN

Cape Hatteras

PACIFIC OCEAN

Tropic of Cancer

Hawaiian Islands

Baja California

Gulf of Mexico

Bahamas

ATLANTIC OCEAN

30°N

Pico de Orizaba
18,855 ft.
(5,747 m)

Yucatán Peninsula

Cuba

Greater Antilles

Hispaniola

Puerto Rico

Lesser Antilles

Lake Nicaragua

Caribbean Sea

Lake Maracaibo

Isthmus of Panama

Orinoco R.

Llanos

Guiana Highlands

Equator

Line Islands

Galápagos Islands

Chimborazo
20,702 ft.
(6,310 m)

Rio Negro

Amazon R.

AMAZON BASIN

Cape São Roque

Marquesas Islands

Huascarán
22,205 ft.
(6,768 m)

Tapajós River

Xingu River

Tocantins R.

São Francisco River

Tuamotu Archipelago

Cook Islands

Society Islands

Lake Titicaca

Mato Grosso Plateau

Brazilian Highlands

Tropic of Capricorn

SOUTH AMERICA

ANDES MOUNTAINS

Gran Chaco

Iguazú Falls

Atacama Desert

Paraguay R.

Paraná R.

30°S

Mt. Aconcagua
22,834 ft.
(6,960 m)

Uruguay R.

Río de la Plata

Pampa

Valdés Peninsula
(lowest point in S.A.)
-131 ft. (-40 m)

Patagonia

Falkland Islands

Strait of Magellan

Tierra del Fuego

Cape Horn

South Georgia

A9

0   1,000   2,000 Miles
0   1,000   2,000 Kilometers
Miller Cylindrical Projection

▲ Mountain peak
▼ Point below sea level
— National border
≈ Waterfall

150°W   120°W   90°W   60°W   30°W

Western Hemisphere: Physical

Set the Purpose

Main Idea Tell students that this map is a physical map of the Western Hemisphere. Remind students that a physical map's main purpose is to show what the surface of Earth looks like.

Why It Matters Because this is a map of the Western Hemisphere and not of the whole world, more detail about the Western Hemisphere's landforms and physical features can be shown.

Visual Learning

Map Allow students time to identify various kinds of physical features shown, such as mountains, lakes, rivers, highlands. Discuss how color and shading are used to distinguish these features. For example, rivers and bodies of water are shown in blue and mountains are shaded in a way that suggests the peaks and valleys of real mountains.

Map Study

Geography Point out the symbols in the map key. Ask students to identify the symbol that is used to show a mountain peak and the symbol used to show a point below sea level. Consider asking these questions:

- What is the lowest point in South America? the Valdés Peninsula
- What is the highest point in the Andes Mountains? Mt. Aconcagua

CD-ROM

Explore GEOSKILLS CD-ROM to give students additional practice using map and globe skills.

INTEGRATE SCIENCE

The North Poles Explain that the North Pole can be described in two ways. The geographic north pole is the place in the Northern Hemisphere where all the lines of longitude meet. There is also the north magnetic pole. Earth's rotation and its iron core create a magnetic field that, in fact, makes Earth act like a giant magnet. A compass needle aligns with the north magnetic pole, not the geographic north pole.

EXTEND AND ENRICH

Define Terms Ask students to use a geographical dictionary to find a description of each of the following physical features: altiplano, archipelago, highland, llano, pampas, point, range, strait, sierra, sound. Ask students to draw a picture of each feature and write a caption for it. Discuss the features with the class and then have students locate an example of each on the map.

United States Overview

Set the Purpose

Main Idea Explain to students that the map on these pages gives an overview, or general picture, of the United States. The map shows state borders, national borders, and major bodies of water that border the United States.

Why It Matters This map can be used to find the location of all the states in the United States and to see where they are located in relation to each other. The map is also helpful for identifying the countries that are the United States' closest neighbors.

Visual Learning

Map Point out to students that all parts of the United States are shown in pink and that each state is labeled with its name and the two-letter abbreviation used by the United States Postal Service.

Have students locate each of the 50 states as you call out state names.

Q Which state lies farthest north? farthest east?

A Alaska; Maine

Have students note that all other countries are simply labeled with their names. No internal borders, such as those of states or provinces, are shown for these other countries, as the focus of the map is the United States.

Map Study

Geography Have students identify the bodies of water that surround the United States.

Q Which ocean is located on the eastern border of Georgia?

A the Atlantic Ocean

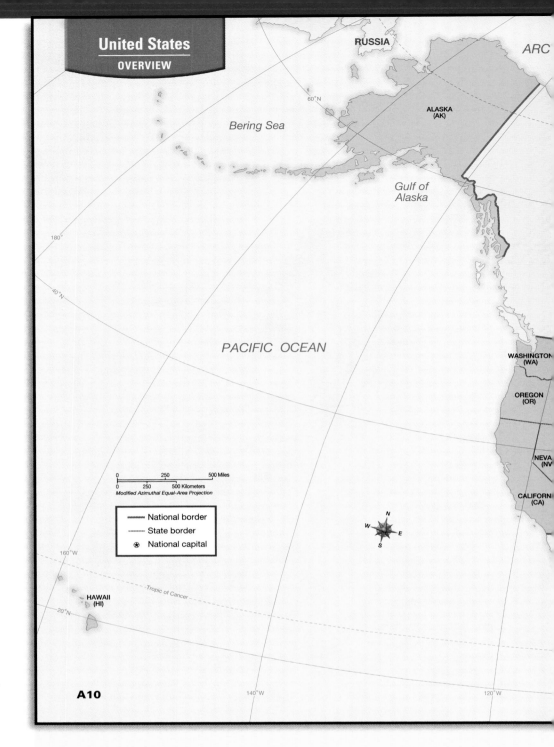

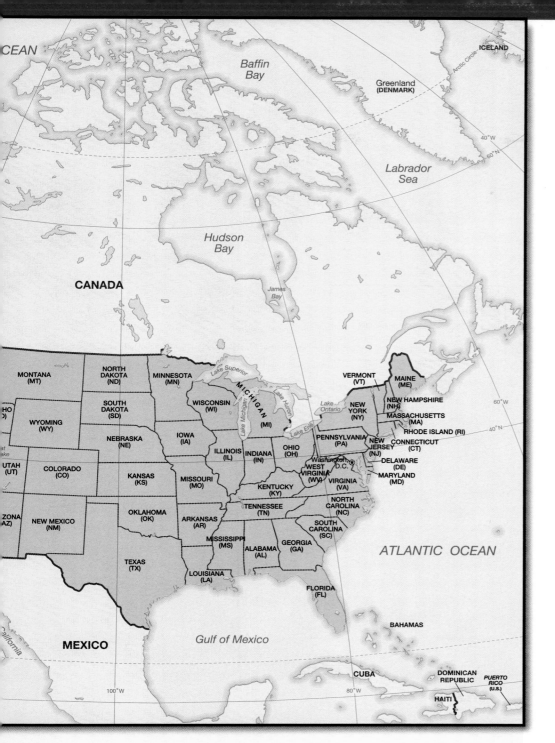

Map Study

Geography Ask students to explain the purpose of a map scale. If necessary, review how to use the map scale to measure distances. Point out that the scale can be used to measure distances in miles or kilometers.

Q **What is the distance in kilometers of the border between Arkansas and Louisiana?**

A about 250 kilometers

Geography Discuss with students how borders for countries and states are decided. Point out that some national and state borders follow the paths of physical features such as rivers. Invite students to look at the state borders on the map and hypothesize which ones might follow a physical feature. Have students consult the physical map of the United States on pages A14–A15 to check their hypotheses.

CD-ROM

Explore GEOSKILLS CD-ROM to give students additional practice using map and globe skills.

BACKGROUND

Alaska Alaska is the largest state in the United States. When Alaska became a state in 1959, it increased the size of the country by 20 percent! At the time of its purchase from Russia in 1867, many Americans thought of the area as a vast frozen wasteland. They sneeringly referred to it as Seward's Folly—a reference to the United States Secretary of State William S. Seward, who pushed the deal through. Alaska, however, proved to have a wealth of natural resources.

EXTEND AND ENRICH

Have a Class Discussion Invite students to name other states they have visited. List the states on the board, and have students locate them on the map. Then ask students to share their impressions of the other states' climate, cities, plant life, and so forth. Discuss how the other states compare with your state and what it might be like to live in one of the other states.

United States: Political

Set the Purpose

Main Idea Explain to students that the map on these pages is a political map of the United States. It shows the borders of states as well as the borders of the United States. The map also divides the United States into four regions.

Why It Matters A political map of the United States can be used to find out where a state is located and to see what size and shape that state is. This map can also be used to identify regions of the United States, each state capital, and a number of major cities.

Visual Learning

Map Students will probably notice that one of the key features of this map is that it divides the United States into four regions. Point out the map key and the color coding used to identify these regions. Explain that these regions are geographic regions. In other words, each region consists of several states located in the same part of the country. In general, the states in each region have similar physical features. For example, the West has many mountainous areas while the Middle West is known for its vast expanses of plains.

Map Study

Geography Ask a volunteer to name each geographic region. Consider asking these questions:

- Which region appears to be the largest? the West
- In which region do you live? Students should correctly identify the region in which they live.

Geography Have students practice identifying the 50 states on a map and telling which states are part of each of the four geographical regions.

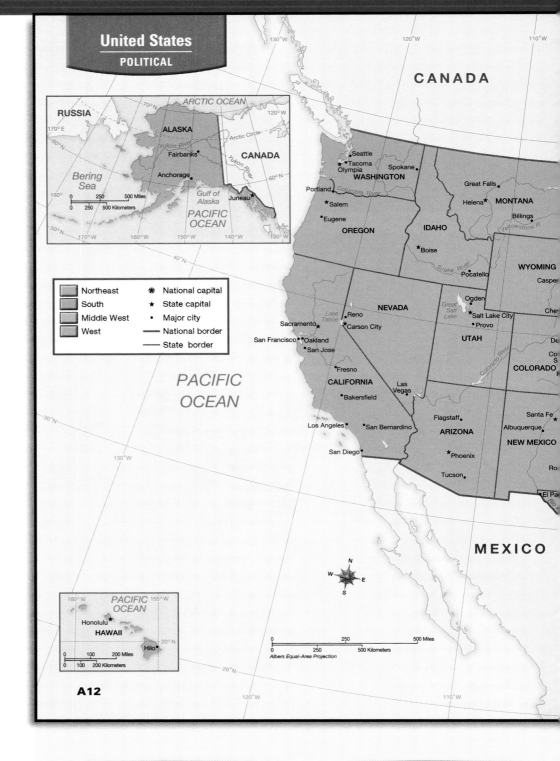

Map labels (main map):

CANADA

MAINE
Augusta ★
VERMONT
Burlington
Montpelier ★
NEW HAMPSHIRE
Portland •
Concord ★
NEW YORK
Manchester •
Boston
MASSACHUSETTS
Worcester
Albany ★
Syracuse
Rochester
Providence ★
RHODE ISLAND
Buffalo
Hartford ★
CONNECTICUT
Bridgeport •
Newark • • New York City
Trenton ★
NEW JERSEY
Philadelphia •
Wilmington •
Dover ★
DELAWARE
PENNSYLVANIA
Harrisburg ★
Pittsburgh •
Baltimore •
Annapolis ★
Washington, D.C.
MARYLAND
WEST VIRGINIA
Charleston ★
VIRGINIA
Richmond ★
Newport News •
Norfolk •
Roanoke •

NORTH DAKOTA
Grand Forks •
Fargo •
★ Bismarck
Duluth
Sault Sainte Marie
MICHIGAN
MINNESOTA
St. Paul ★
Minneapolis •
Green Bay •
WISCONSIN
Madison ★
Milwaukee •
Grand Rapids •
Flint •
Lansing ★
Detroit •
SOUTH DAKOTA
Pierre ★
Sioux Falls •
Sioux City •
IOWA
Cedar Rapids •
Davenport •
Des Moines ★
Rockford •
Chicago •
South Bend •
Gary
Toledo •
Cleveland •
Akron •
OHIO
Columbus ★
Wheeling •
NEBRASKA
Omaha •
Lincoln ★
ILLINOIS
Peoria •
Decatur •
Springfield ★
INDIANA
Indianapolis ★
Dayton •
Cincinnati •
Topeka ★
Kansas City •
KANSAS
Wichita •
MISSOURI
Jefferson City ★
St. Louis •
Springfield •
Louisville •
Frankfort ★
Lexington •
Evansville •
KENTUCKY
Charleston •
Greensboro •
Winston-Salem •
Raleigh ★
NORTH CAROLINA
Knoxville •
Nashville ★
Charlotte •
TENNESSEE
Chattanooga •
OKLAHOMA
Oklahoma City ★
Tulsa •
Amarillo •
ARKANSAS
Fort Smith •
Little Rock ★
Memphis •
Huntsville •
SOUTH CAROLINA
Columbia ★
Charleston •
Lubbock •
MISSISSIPPI
ALABAMA
Birmingham •
Atlanta ★
GEORGIA
Macon •
Columbus •
Savannah •
Meridian •
Montgomery ★
Jackson ★
Fort Worth •
Dallas •
Abilene •
Shreveport •
LOUISIANA
TEXAS
Austin ★
Beaumont •
Houston •
San Antonio •
Baton Rouge ★
Biloxi •
Mobile •
New Orleans •
Tallahassee ★
Jacksonville •
FLORIDA
Orlando •
Tampa •
St. Petersburg •
Lake Okeechobee
West Palm Beach •
Laredo •
Corpus Christi •
Miami •
ATLANTIC OCEAN
BAHAMAS
Gulf of Mexico
CUBA

Lake of the Woods
Lake Superior
Lake Michigan
Lake Huron
Lake Ontario
Lake Erie
Lake St. Clair
Lake Champlain
St. Lawrence River
Mississippi River
Missouri River
Platte River
Arkansas River
Red River
Lake Texoma
Ohio River
Rio Grande

A13

Map Study

Map Study

Geography Have students use the map key to find the symbol for the major cities. Then ask them what they think is meant by "major city." Guide them in understanding that major cities are those with large populations.

Geography Ask students to look at the map key and identify the symbol for the national capital.

Q In which region is the national capital?

A the South

Geography Call students' attention to the inset maps. Explain that in this case, the inset maps are used to show Alaska and Hawaii—places that are beyond the area shown on the main map.

CD-ROM

Explore GEOSKILLS CD-ROM to give students additional practice using map and globe skills.

BACKGROUND

Agriculture in the Middle West
Land use is another way of defining a region. The Middle West, for example, is one of the key agricultural regions of the United States. The region may be divided into subregions according to land use. Many of these subregions have nicknames. For example, a broad swath of land extending west from Ohio to South Dakota is often called the Corn Belt because so much of the land in the area is planted with corn.

EXTEND AND ENRICH

Explore Regional Cooking
Discuss the link between foods and regions and how traditional regional dishes tend to depend on foods locally available or on the ethnic or cultural backgrounds of the people that live in the region. In the Northeast, which is close to the Atlantic Ocean, seafood figures prominently in typical regional dishes such as clam chowder. Have students choose a region and then use cookbooks or online recipe archives to research recipes traditionally associated with that region.

United States: Physical

Set the Purpose

Main Idea Tell students that the map on these pages is a physical map of the United States. It shows important landforms and bodies of water found in the United States.

Why It Matters This map can be used to learn the names and locations of important physical features in the United States.

Visual Learning

Map Refer students to the map key. Point out that the colors represent different kinds of terrain, vegetation, or plant life. Review any unfamiliar terms. Ask a volunteer to explain how the map shows where the land is flat and where it is mountainous.

Map Study

Geography Remind students that the United States may be divided into geographic regions—the Northeast, the Middle West, the South, and the West.

Q Which region has the most arid areas?

A the West

Geography Have students describe the relative locations of major physical features of the United States.

Q How would you describe the location of the Mojave Desert?

A Possible response: The Mojave Desert lies on the border of California and Nevada not far from Death Valley and Lake Mead. It is in the western part of the country.

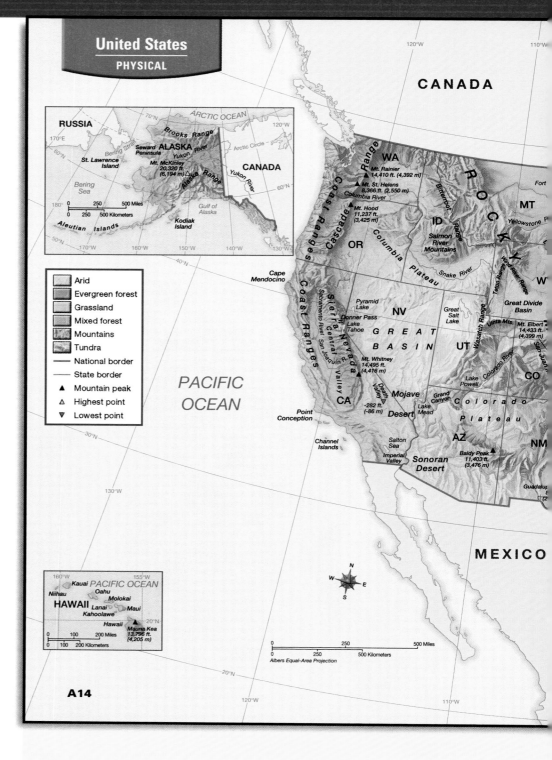

In Your State Have students spend a few minutes studying the physical features and bodies of water found in their state. Then discuss with students the challenges these features may pose for the residents of the state. For example, living in an arid area may mean that water conservation is an important issue. Living near a river may mean that residents have to be concerned about flooding.

The Great Lakes The Middle West is home to the world's largest group of freshwater lakes—the Great Lakes. Four of the five Great Lakes form part of the border between Canada and the United States. Both Native Americans and European settlers took advantage of the lakes as a transportation route and a source of fish. During the twentieth century manufacturing industries sprang up in cities near the lakes. The Great Lakes area became an industrial center of the United States.

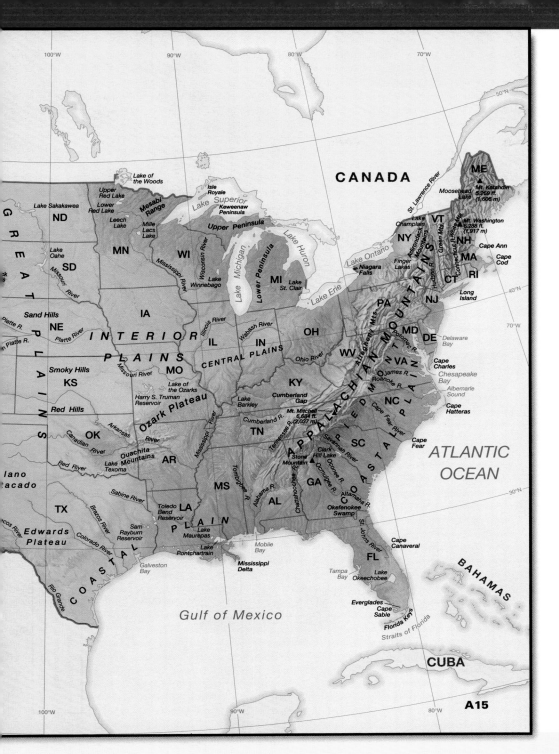

CANADA

ATLANTIC OCEAN

BAHAMAS

Gulf of Mexico

CUBA

A15

Map Study

Geography Allow students a few moments to identify the major mountain ranges in the United States. Call their attention to the map key and the symbol for mountain peaks.

Q **Are the tallest mountains found in the eastern or western mountain ranges?**

A the western mountain ranges

Geography Have students compare and contrast landforms and bodies of water in different parts of the country. You might ask questions like these:

- How is southern California different from northern California? Southern California is arid and northern California has evergreen forests.
- Which part of the United States is mostly flat grassland? the central part of the United States
- Which state has a large tundra area? Alaska

CD-ROM

Explore GEOSKILLS CD-ROM to give students additional practice using map and globe skills.

The Mountain Ranges of the United States Invite students to draw a map of the United States. Ask them to draw in and identify at least two major mountain ranges. Evaluate students' efforts by checking the accuracy of the location and the length of the mountain ranges.

Take a Virtual Hike Have groups of students do online research on one of the following long-distance hiking trails in the United States: the Appalachian Trail, the American Discovery Trail, the Continental Divide Trail, the North Country National Scenic Trail, or the Pacific Crest Trail. Have students mark the route on an outline map of the United States and then give a presentation to the rest of the class about the trail.

Canada

Set the Purpose

Main Idea Explain to students that this map of Canada shows political units as well as some physical features. The map shows Canada's ten provinces and three territories.

Why It Matters This map can be used to find out where Canada's provinces are located and to compare their sizes and shapes. This map can also be used to identify key cities and capitals and a number of important physical features.

Visual Learning

Map Have students notice Canada's huge size. Mention to students that Canada is larger than the United States and is, in fact, one of the largest nations in the world. Only Russia has more territory than Canada. Point out each province and territory for students. Have them note the difference in size between the province of Prince Edward Island and the provinces of Quebec or Ontario.

Map Study

Geography Like the United States, Canada may be divided into geographic regions. Newfoundland and Labrador, Nova Scotia, New Brunswick, and Prince Edward Island are known as the Atlantic Provinces; Quebec and Ontario are often called the Central Provinces; Manitoba, Saskatchewan, Alberta, and British Columbia are known as the West; and the territories are referred to as the North.

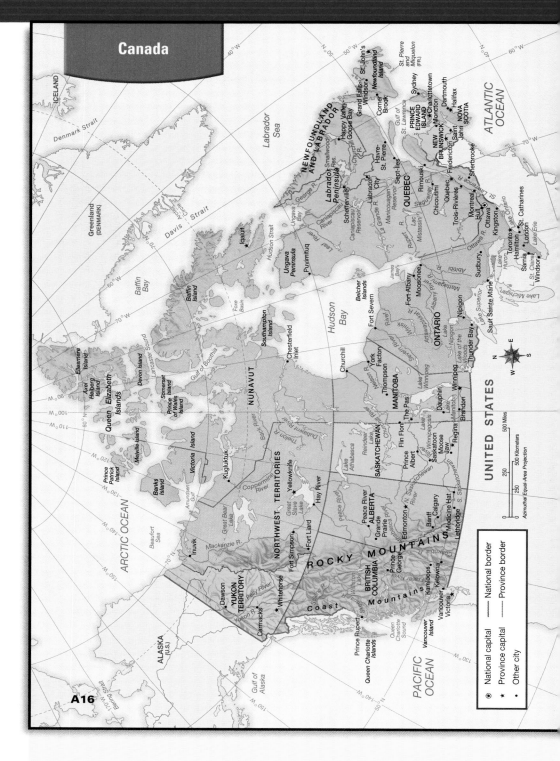

INTEGRATE LANGUAGE ARTS

Write a How-To Paragraph Have students imagine that they want to travel by boat from Banff to Winnipeg. Have them write a paragraph describing the route. Encourage them to give detailed instructions that include descriptions and names of physical features along the way, the names of provinces and cities they pass through or near, the direction they are traveling, and the names of rivers they cross.

EXTEND AND ENRICH

Find the Origins of Names Allow students a few minutes to study the names of Canada's provinces, territories, and major cities. Ask students to choose the name of a province, territory, or city and write down how they think it might have gotten its name. Then ask students to do some Internet research to find out the actual origin of the name. As a class, discuss the various origins of the names and how the names reflect the history, culture, or geography of the place.

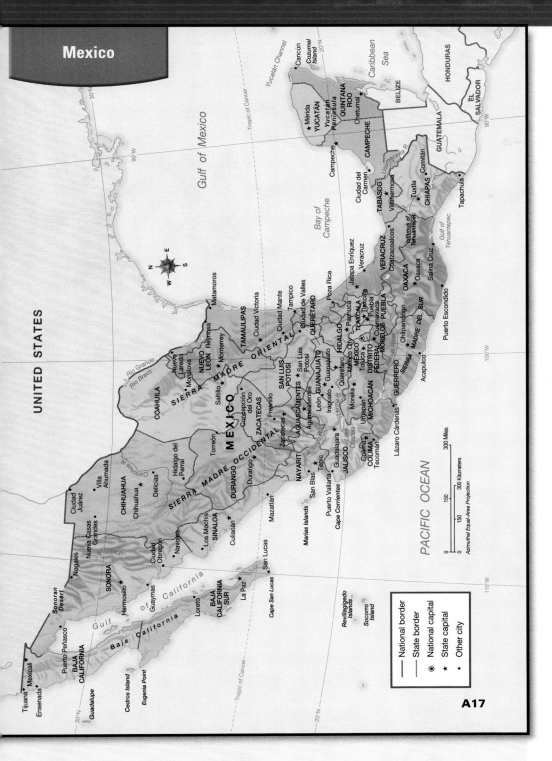

Mexico

Set the Purpose

Main Idea Explain to students that this map of Mexico shows key physical features and the names and borders of Mexico's 31 states. The map also shows the national borders between Mexico and other countries.

Why It Matters This map can be used to find out where states in Mexico are located and to see the size and shape of each state. This map can also be used to identify all the state capitals and the major cities in each state.

Visual Learning

Map Point out that each state is a different color from the states that surround it. Then call students' attention to the map key. Ask them to describe the difference between a state border and a national border. Mention that the map also shows the locations of the national capital, state capitals, and major cities.

Map Study

Geography Ask a volunteer to identify Mexico's capital city. Have students notice that Mexico City is located in what is known as the *Distrito Federal*, or Federal District. Explain that the *Distrito Federal* is a separate administrative area—not a state—somewhat like the District of Columbia in the United States.

Geography Have students notice the bodies of water that surround Mexico and the countries that border it.

Q Which Mexican states border the United States?

A Baja California, Sonora, Chihuahua, Coahuila, Nuevo León, and Tamaulipas

CD-ROM

Explore GEOSKILLS CD-ROM to give students additional practice using map and globe skills.

REACH ALL LEARNERS

English as a Second Language Invite Spanish-speaking students to pronounce some of the names and terms used on the map so that other students can hear the proper pronunciation. If students feel comfortable translating, they may want to explain what some of the terms and names mean. For example, they might explain that *ciudad* means "city," or that *sierra* means "mountain range," or that *puerto* means "port."

EXTEND AND ENRICH

Create a Travel Brochure Have students choose one of the cities shown on the map to research in order to make a travel brochure. Suggest they devote about half of the brochure to an overview of the city that includes information about the city's history, economy, and population and focus the rest of the brochure on sightseeing activities related to landmarks and culture.

Geography Terms

1 basin bowl-shaped area of land surrounded by higher land

2 bay an inlet of the sea or some other body of water, usually smaller than a gulf

3 bluff high, steep face of rock or earth

4 canyon deep, narrow valley with steep sides

5 cape point of land that extends into water

6 cataract large waterfall

7 channel deepest part of a body of water

8 cliff high, steep face of rock or earth

9 coast land along a sea or ocean

10 coastal plain area of flat land along a sea or ocean

11 delta triangle-shaped area of land at the mouth of a river

12 desert dry land with few plants

13 dune hill of sand piled up by the wind

14 fall line area along which rivers form waterfalls or rapids as the rivers drop to lower land

15 floodplain flat land that is near the edges of a river and is formed by silt deposited by floods

16 foothills hilly area at the base of a mountain

17 glacier large ice mass that moves slowly down a mountain or across land

18 gulf part of a sea or ocean extending into the land, usually larger than a bay

19 hill land that rises above the land around it

20 inlet any area of water extending into the land from a larger body of water

21 island land that has water on all sides

22 isthmus narrow strip of land connecting two larger areas of land

23 lagoon body of shallow water

24 lake body of water with land on all sides

25 marsh lowland with moist soil and tall grasses

#	Term	Definition
26	**mesa**	flat-topped mountain with steep sides
27	**mountain**	highest kind of land
28	**mountain pass**	gap between mountains
29	**mountain range**	row of mountains
30	**mouth of river**	place where a river empties into another body of water
31	**oasis**	area of water and fertile land in a desert
32	**ocean**	body of salt water larger than a sea
33	**peak**	top of a mountain
34	**peninsula**	land that is almost completely surrounded by water
35	**plain**	area of flat or gently rolling low land
36	**plateau**	area of high, mostly flat land
37	**reef**	ridge of sand, rock, or coral that lies at or near the surface of a sea or ocean
38	**river**	large stream of water that flows across the land
39	**riverbank**	land along a river
40	**savanna**	area of grassland and scattered trees
41	**sea**	body of salt water smaller than an ocean
42	**sea level**	the level of the surface of an ocean or a sea
43	**slope**	side of a hill or mountain
44	**source of river**	place where a river begins
45	**strait**	narrow channel of water connecting two larger bodies of water
46	**swamp**	area of low, wet land with trees
47	**timberline**	line on a mountain above which it is too cold for trees to grow
48	**tributary**	stream or river that flows into a larger stream or river
49	**valley**	low land between hills or mountains
50	**volcano**	opening in the earth, often raised, through which lava, rock, ashes, and gases are forced out
51	**waterfall**	steep drop from a high place to a lower place in a stream or river

A19

World War II

The Bronze Star

Unit 5 Planning Guide World War II

Introduce	CONTENT	RESOURCES
pp. 323–329 **Chapter 9**	**UNIT OPENER**, p. 323 **PREVIEW**, pp. 324–325 **START WITH A STORY** *Attack on Pearl Harbor: The True Story of the Day America Entered World War II*, pp. 326–329	Unit 5 Audiotext Unit 5 School-to-Home Newsletter, p. S9 Reading and Vocabulary Transparency 5-1 Internet Resources
The War Begins, pp. 330–359 **Chapter 10**	**INTRODUCE THE CHAPTER**, pp. 330–331 **LESSON 1** The Conflict Begins, pp. 332–339 **LESSON 2** The United States Enters the War, pp. 340–346 **LESSON 3** Life at Home, pp. 347–354 **CITIZENSHIP SKILLS** Make Economic Choices, p. 355 **EXAMINE PRIMARY SOURCES** War Posters, pp. 356–357 **CHAPTER REVIEW AND TEST PREPARATION,** pp. 358–359	Activity Book, pp. 84–91 Assessment Program, Chapter 9, pp. 73–76 Reading and Vocabulary Transparencies 5-2, 5-3, 5-4, 5-5 Skill Transparency 5-1 Internet Resources
The Allies Win the War, pp. 360–397 **Wrap Up**	**INTRODUCE THE CHAPTER**, pp. 360–361 **LESSON 1** War in Africa and in Europe, pp. 362–369 **MAP AND GLOBE SKILLS** Compare Historical Maps, pp. 370–371 **LESSON 2** War in the Pacific, pp. 372–379 **CHART AND GRAPH SKILLS** Read Parallel Time Lines, pp. 380–381 **LESSON 3** Life After World War II, pp. 382–387 **LESSON 4** A Changed World, pp. 388–395 **CHAPTER REVIEW AND TEST PREPARATION,** pp. 396–397	Activity Book, pp. 92–101 Assessment Program, Chapter 10, pp. 77–80 Reading and Vocabulary Transparencies 5-6, 5-7, 5-8, 5-9, 5-10 Skills Transparencies 5-2A, 5-2B, 5-3 Internet Resources GeoSkills CD-ROM
pp. 398–402	**VISIT** Berlin, Germany, pp. 398–399 **UNIT REVIEW AND TEST PREPARATION,** pp. 400–402	Internet Resources The Learning Site: Virtual Tours Take a Field Trip Video Time for Kids Readers Assessment Program, Unit 5, pp. 81–89

5 —— WEEKS	WEEK 1	WEEK 2	WEEK 3	WEEK 4	WEEK 5
Introduce the Unit	Chapter 9		Chapter 10		Wrap Up the Unit

Unit 5 Skills Path

Unit 5 features the reading skills of cause and effect and predicting a likely outcome. It also highlights the social studies skills of making economic choices, comparing historical maps, and reading parallel time lines.

FOCUS SKILLS

CHAPTER 9 READING SKILL

 CAUSE AND EFFECT

- INTRODUCE p. 331
- APPLY pp. 335, 336, 339, 345, 346, 353, 354, 358

CHAPTER 10 READING SKILL

 PREDICT AN OUTCOME

- INTRODUCE p. 361
- APPLY pp. 367, 369, 376, 379, 383, 387, 390, 395, 396

READING SOCIAL STUDIES

- Graphic Organizer, pp. 326, 328, 333, 383
- Personal Response, pp. 333, 339, 383, 387
- Study Questions, pp. 341, 346, 373, 379
- Create Mental Images, p. 342
- K-W-L Chart, pp. 348, 354, 389, 395
- Anticipation Guide, pp. 363, 369

CITIZENSHIP SKILLS

MAKE ECONOMIC CHOICES

- INTRODUCE p. 355
- APPLY p. 359

MAP AND GLOBE SKILLS

COMPARE HISTORICAL MAPS

- INTRODUCE pp. 370–371
- APPLY p. 397

CHART AND GRAPH SKILLS

READ PARALLEL TIME LINES

- INTRODUCE pp. 380–381
- APPLY p. 397

STUDY AND RESEARCH SKILLS

- Summarizing Information, p. 332
- Using Reference Sources, pp. 340, 351
- Using the Internet, p. 353
- Using Maps, p. 362
- Note Taking, p. 372
- Skimming and Scanning, p. 382
- Summarizing, p. 391

Multimedia Resources

The Multimedia Resources can be used in a variety of ways. They can supplement core instruction in the classroom or extend and enrich student learning at home.

Independent Reading

Easy

Coerr, Eleanor. **Sadako and the Thousand Paper Cranes.** Puffin, 1999. Based on the true story of the Japanese girl Sadako who is diagnosed with leukemia.

Granfield, Linda. **High Flight: A Story of World War II.** Tundra Books, 2001. Biography of Royal Canadian Air Force pilot John Magee, author of the famous poem "High Flight," who served and died in World War II.

Hest, Amy. **Love You, Soldier.** Candlewick Press, 2000. The story of how Katie and her mother rebuild their lives after Katie's father is killed in World War II.

Say, Allen. **Home of the Brave.** Walter Lorraine, 2002. Creative words and images portray a Japanese American family's hardships while living in the Japanese internment camps during World War II.

Average

Ambrose, Stephen E. **The Good Fight: How World War II Was Won.** Atheneum, 2001. Photographs, maps, personal stories, and descriptions present chronological details of the events of World War II.

Cretzmeyer, Stacy. **Your Name Is Renée: Ruth Kapp Hartz's Story as a Hidden Child in Nazi-Occupied France.** Oxford University Press, 1999. Set in Nazi-occupied France in 1941, Ruth lives as "Renée" while her family moves from home to home to hide from the Nazis.

Mazer, Harry. **A Boy at War: A Novel of Pearl Harbor.** Simon & Schuster Juvenile, 2001. Fourteen-year-old Adam is thrown into the chaos of the Pearl Harbor attack in 1941.

Osborne, Mary Pope. **My Secret War: The World War II Diary of Madeline Beck.** Scholastic, Inc., 2000. Thirteen-year-old Madeline organizes students to support the war effort, and bravely contacts the FBI when a German U-boat lands near her home.

Challenging

Lace, William W. **Leaders and Generals: World War II.** Lucent Books, 2000. Profiles of the lives and military careers of prominent World War II leaders, including MacArthur, Nimitz, Eisenhower, and Isoroku.

Kallen, Stuart A. **The War at Home.** Lucent Books, 2000. Discover how World War II affected daily life in the United States, including women's roles, air-raid drills, war bonds, and rationing.

Leapman, Michael. **Witnesses to War: Eight True-Life Stories of Nazi Persecution.**  Viking Children's Books, 1998. True World War II stories and photos of European children who were kidnapped and placed with German families.

Computer Software

Anne Frank House: A House With a Story. Cinegram Media, Inc., 2000. Mac/Windows 95. Explore the house in Amsterdam where Anne Frank and her family hid. Includes historical photos, film, and slide shows.

World War Two: Stories & Archives. Montparnasse Multimedia, 1996. Mac/Windows. Spans 1918 to 1945, concentrating on the events of World War II, including the rise of Hitler, the Holocaust, and the atomic bomb.

Videos and DVDs

The Battle for Midway: The Discovery of the U.S.S. Yorktown. National Geographic, 1999. Underwater expedition explores World War II Japanese and American aircraft carriers sunk during the Midway battle.

The World at War. HBO Video, 2001. Television documentary by Sir Jeremy Isaacs that presents a visual history of World War II.

Additional books also are recommended at point of use throughout the unit. Note that information, while correct at time of publication, is subject to change.

ISBNs and other publisher information can be found at **www.harcourtschool.com**

323D ■ UNIT 5 ORGANIZER

The Learning Site: Social Studies Center

The Learning Site at www.harcourtschool.com offers a special Social Studies Center. The center provides a wide variety of activities, Internet links, and online references.

Here are just some of the HARCOURT Internet resources you'll find!

Multimedia Biographies
www.harcourtschool.com

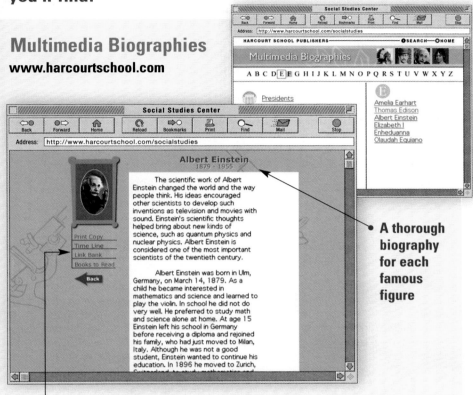

• A thorough biography for each famous figure

• Links to additional information and further reading

• Special features that include photographs, video clips, audio, and additional text

GO ONLINE — **INTERNET RESOURCES**

Find all this at
The Learning Site at
www.harcourtschool.com
- Activities and Games
- Content Updates
- Current Events
- Free and Inexpensive Materials
- Multimedia Biographies
- Online Atlas
- Primary Sources
- Video Updates
- Virtual Tours
- Your State

and more!

Free and Inexpensive Materials
- Addresses to write for free and inexpensive products
- Links to unit-related materials
- Internet maps
- Internet references

www.harcourtschool.com

Primary Sources
- Artwork
- Clothing
- Diaries
- Government Documents
- Historical Documents
- Maps
- Tools

and more!
www.harcourtschool.com

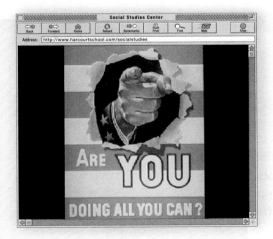

Virtual Tours
- Capitols and Government Buildings
- Cities
- Countries
- Historical Sites
- Museums
- Parks and Scenic Areas

and more!
www.harcourtschool.com

Integrate Learning Across the Curriculum

Use these topics to help you integrate social studies into your daily planning. See the page numbers indicated for more information about each topic.

Language Arts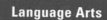

Produce a Historical Radio Broadcast, p. 328
Write to Compare and Contrast, p. 333
Write a Report, p. 341
Write a News Report, p. 364
Write a Persuasive Letter, p. 386

Health

Malaria, p. 375

Mathematics

Compare Distances, p. 336
Estimate, p. 363
Multiply, p. 385
Compute, pp. 392, 399

Physical Education

Research Physical Fitness Training, p. 365

Technology

GeoSkills CD-ROM, p. 371
Go Online, pp. 342, 343, 349, 351, 357, 365, 377, 390, 399
CNN Video, p. 399

Social Studies

Art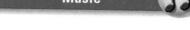

Make a Model, p. 327
Draw a Recruiting Poster, p. 348
Interpret Photographs, p. 366
Illustrate Time Lines, p. 380
Find Architectural Designs, p. 386

Science

Milkweed, p. 352
Atom Bombs, p. 376
Hydrogen Bomb, p. 391

Music

Listen to a Song, p. 349

Reading/Literature

Read Biographies, p. 345
Read a Biography, pp. 350, 376
Rosie the Riveter: Women Working on the Home Front in World War II, p. 402
Foster's War, p. 402
My Wartime Summers, p. 402

Reach All Learners

Use these activities to help individualize your instruction. Each activity has been developed to address a different level or type of learner.

English as a Second Language

Materials
- notebook paper
- textbook
- pen or pencils
- dictionary

PREVIEW THE UNIT Have students who are acquiring English scan Unit 5 to preview its content.

- Organize students who are learning English into groups.
- Invite students to scan the lesson titles, illustrations, and vocabulary terms to preview the war years of the United States.
- Encourage group members to list unfamiliar vocabulary terms in their journals.
- Have students illustrate or write definitions for unfamiliar words as they complete the unit.

Below-Level Learners

Materials
- textbook
- paper
- pen or pencil

COMPARE AND CONTRAST Have students work in pairs to compare and contrast the war in Africa and Europe with the war in the Pacific.

- Ask each student to use an index card to jot down notes about each war front.
- Have students work in pairs to fill in a Venn diagram to show the similarities and differences of the two fronts.
- Display students' work to encourage reinforcement of ideas.

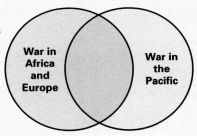

Advanced Learners

Materials
- library reference tools or Internet connection
- CD player

RESEARCH MUSIC Have advanced learners find out more about music from the World War II era.

- Provide students with a list of composers and musicians from the war years.
- Organize students into groups to research these individuals and their music.
- Encourage students to locate performances of the popular pieces of the time.
- Allow time in class for groups to present performances they found to the class.

Assessment Options

The Assessment Program gives all learners many opportunities to show what they know and can do. It also provides ongoing information about each student's understanding of social studies.

Formal Assessment

- **LESSON REVIEWS,** at ends of lessons
- **CHAPTER REVIEWS AND TEST PREPARATION,** pp. 358–359, pp. 396–397
- **CHAPTER TESTS**
  Assessment Program, pp. 73–76, pp. 77–80
- **UNIT REVIEW AND TEST PREPARATION,** pp. 400–401
- **UNIT ASSESSMENT
  STANDARD TEST,**
  Assessment Program, pp. 81–87
  INDIVIDUAL PERFORMANCE TASK,
    Assessment Program, p. 88
  GROUP PERFORMANCE TASK,
    Assessment Program, p. 89

Student Self-Evaluation

- **ANALYZE PRIMARY SOURCES AND VISUALS**
  within lessons of Pupil Book
- **GEOGRAPHY THEME QUESTIONS**
  within lessons of Pupil Book
- **INDIVIDUAL END-OF-PROJECT SUMMARY**
  Assessment Program, p. viii
- **GROUP END-OF-PROJECT CHECKLIST**
  Assessment Program, p. ix
- **INDIVIDUAL END-OF-UNIT CHECKLIST**
  Assessment Program, p. x

Informal Assessment

- **ANALYZE THE LITERATURE,** p. 329
- **REVIEW QUESTIONS,** throughout lessons
- **EXAMINE PRIMARY SOURCES,** pp. 356–357
- **SOCIAL STUDIES SKILLS CHECKLIST**
  Assessment Program, pp. vi–vii

- **SKILLS**
  Practice the Skill, pp. 355, 371, 381
  Apply What You Learned, pp. 355, 371, 381

Performance Assessment

- **PERFORMANCE ACTIVITY** in Lesson Reviews
- **UNIT ACTIVITIES,** p. 402
- **COMPLETE THE UNIT PROJECT,** p. 402
- **INDIVIDUAL PERFORMANCE TASK**
  Assessment Program, p. 88
- **GROUP PERFORMANCE TASK**
  Assessment Program, p. 89

Portfolio Assessment

STUDENT-SELECTED ITEMS MAY INCLUDE:
- **THINK AND WRITE,** pp. 358, 396
- **UNIT ACTIVITIES,** p. 402
- **COMPLETE THE UNIT PROJECT,** p. 402

TEACHER-SELECTED ITEMS MAY INCLUDE:
- **UNIT ASSESSMENT**
  Assessment Program, pp. 81–89
- **PORTFOLIO SUMMARY**
  Assessment Program, p. xv
- **GROUP END-OF-PROJECT CHECKLIST**
  Assessment Program, p. ix
- **INDIVIDUAL END-OF-UNIT CHECKLIST**
  Assessment Program, p. x

Unit 5 Test

·UNIT·

Name _____ Date _____

5 Test

Part One: Test Your Understanding

MULTIPLE CHOICE (2 points each)

Directions Circle the letter of the best answer.

1 Which political party did Hitler head?
A Democratic
B Fascist
C Nazi
D Communist

2 During World War II, the governments of Germany, Italy, Spain, Japan, and the Soviet Union were—
F democracies.
G dictatorships.
H communist.
J monarchies.

3 Who was the leader of the Soviet Union during World War II?
A Hideki Tojo
B Benito Mussolini
C Francisco Franco
D Joseph Stalin

4 In which two areas of the world were the battles of World War II mainly fought?
F Europe and the Pacific
G North Africa and Asia
H North America and Europe
J North Africa and Italy

5 Which of the following had the greatest influence on the United States' decision to enter World War II?
A the rise of dictatorships
B the invasion of Poland
C the attack on Pearl Harbor
D the rise of communism

6 How did most people in the United States respond once the United States entered World War II?
F by protesting against the military draft
G by working together to support war efforts
H by calling for a return to isolationism
J by doing all of the above

7 Which of the following statements describes United States industries during World War II?
A The number of industries grew, and new industries were created.
B Levels of production increased for many industries.
C Women worked in many fields in which only men had worked before the war.
D all of the above

(continued)

Unit 5 Test

Name _____ Date _____

8 To raise money for World War II, the United States—
F held a military draft.
G sold war bonds.
H rationed goods.
J recycled waste.

9 To defeat the Axis powers in Europe, the Allies first needed to—
A gain control of the Mediterranean Sea and invade Italy.
B land in Normandy, France, for the D day invasion.
C liberate the Netherlands.
D defeat Japan.

10 Concentration camps were—
F prisons in which Japanese Americans were forced to live during World War II.
G army training centers.
H prisons to which Nazi officials sent people with religious beliefs and ethnic backgrounds different from theirs.
J centers in which a country's best scientists gathered to build nuclear weapons.

11 Which Axis country was the last to surrender during World War II?
A Germany
B Italy
C Japan
D They all surrendered at the same time.

12 Which battle or battles marked a turning point in the war in the Pacific?
F Battle of Midway
G Battle of the Coral Sea
H Battle of the Bulge
J both F and G

13 The United States government helped soldiers readjust to civilian life after World War II by—
A passing the Servicemen's Readjustment Act, or G.I. Bill of Rights.
B encouraging them to move to the suburbs.
C making sure that all soldiers had jobs when they returned home.
D providing housing when they returned home.

14 Which statement best describes the role of the United States after World War II?
F The United States returned to a policy of isolation.
G Weakened by World War II, the United States took less of a leadership role in the world.
H Emerging as a superpower, the United States took on the responsibility of helping other nations.
J The United States began to take over other countries to ensure the spread of democracy.

(continued)

Unit 5 Test

Name _____ Date _____

COMPLETION (2 points each)

Directions Write the term from the box that correctly completes each statement. You will not use every term.

Holocaust	rationed
communism	relocation camps
neutral	cold war
free world	veterans
V-E Day	island hopping
V-J Day	fascism
arms race	dictatorships
civilian	

15 Hitler, Stalin, Franco, Mussolini, and Tojo ruled their countries under _____dictatorships_____

16 Although the United States had planned to remain _____neutral_____, it eventually entered World War II in 1941.

17 People used money and government coupons to buy _____rationed_____ goods during World War II.

18 The Allies' plan in the Pacific, in which they fought to take back only certain key islands on their way to Japan, was called _____island hopping_____.

19 On August 15, 1945, known as _____V-J Day_____, Japan surrendered to the Allies.

20 In the _____arms race_____ during the years following World War II, the United States and the Soviet Union each tried to build the most weapons to protect its people.

21 The United States and its allies who opposed communism became known as the _____free world_____.

(continued)

Unit 5 Test

Name _____ Date _____

SHORT ANSWER (3 points each)

Directions Answer each question in the space provided.

22 What happened on D day?

The Allies worked together in the largest water-to-land invasion in history, landing on the beach in Normandy, France, on June 6, 1944.

23 What was the turning point of World War II in Europe? Explain.

After D day the war turned in favor of the Allies. The Allies moved across Europe and freed countries that had been taken over by Germany.

24 What reasons did the Nazis give for the Holocaust?

The Nazis killed people because they did not like their religious and political beliefs or because they were ill or disabled and could not work. Hitler blamed the largest group of victims, the Jews, for Germany's problems.

25 What were three reasons many families in the United States moved to the suburbs in the years after World War II?

Possible answer: They wanted new houses, playgrounds, swimming pools, shopping centers, and better schools.

26 Describe the communist political and economic system.

Under communism all industries, land, and businesses are owned by the government, and people have few freedoms.

27 After World War II ended, how did life in the United States change?

Millions of soldiers returned home, and many went back to school. Colleges and universities had to build extra housing. Most rationing was over, and people began driving more. Drive-in movies and television were introduced. Soldiers started families, and millions of babies were born. Families moved out of the cities to suburbs.

(continued)

Unit 5 Test

Unit 5 Test

Name _____ Date _____

Part Two: Test Your Skills

READ PARALLEL TIME LINES (3 points each)

Directions Use these parallel time lines to answer the questions below.

Time Line A: World War II in Europe and the Pacific

1939	1940	1941	1942	1943	1944	1945	1946

1939 Germany invades Poland. Britain and France declare war on Germany

1940 Germany takes over most of Europe. Germany attacks Britain

1941 Japan attacks Pearl Harbor

1942 Battle of Midway

1943 Allies take back North Africa

1944 D day

1945 V-E Day V-J Day

Time Line B: World War II on the Home Front

1939	1940	1941	1942	1943	1944	1945	1946

1939 President Roosevelt asks for increase in defense spending. United States declares neutrality. United States economy booms

1940 First peacetime military draft

1941 Japan attacks Pearl Harbor. United States enters WWII

1942 Food rationing begins

1943 Victory gardens produce one-third of U.S. vegetables

1944 GI Bill of Rights

1945 First atomic bomb is tested

28 Did President Roosevelt ask for an increase in defense spending before or after Germany attacked Britain? _before_

29 Why do you think the attack on Pearl Harbor is shown on both time lines?
It was part of the war in the Pacific, and it was an attack on the United States and resulted in the entrance of the United States into the war.

30 Which happened first, V-E Day or the passing of the G.I. Bill of Rights?
the passing of the G.I. Bill of Rights

31 Did the United States enter the war before or after Hitler had taken over most of Europe? _after_

32 At what point in the war was the first atomic bomb tested?
near the end in 1945

(continued)

Unit 5 Test — Assessment Program ■ 85

Name _____ Date _____

Part Three: Apply What You Have Learned

DRAW CONCLUSIONS (3 points each)

Read the statements below. Then circle the letter of the conclusion that can be drawn from the information given.

33 The United States had many new soldiers who were inexperienced. The presence of Axis troops in North Africa was not as strong as it was in Europe. British troops had been fighting in North Africa for several years.
(A) North Africa was a good place for the United States to send its first troops.
B Europe was a good place for the United States to send its first troops.

34 During World War II, soldiers of the United States Armed Forces were segregated. Also, Japanese Americans were forced to leave their homes and live in prisons called relocation camps.
C As a result of World War II, the Army stopped segregating its soldiers.
(D) The United States still had problems with prejudice during World War II.

35 Manchuria is a region of China located close to Japan. Manchuria has many natural resources, including coal, iron, and fertile soil. In the 1920s and 1930s, China was experiencing internal fighting between its government and communists who wanted to take over the country. Japan took Manchuria in 1931.
A Japan was afraid that Chinese communists would take over their country, so they attacked first and claimed Manchuria.
(B) Japan took advantage of China's internal struggle and claimed some valuable land.

36 Britain and France promised to protect Czechoslovakia in case of a German invasion. When Germany decided to invade, British and French leaders met with Hitler and gave him control of western Czechoslovakia. In return, he promised to leave the rest of the country alone.
(C) Britain and France were trying to prevent a war.
D Czechoslovakia wanted to separate into two countries.

37 Germany took over Denmark in one day, Norway in weeks, Luxembourg in one day, the Netherlands in 5 days, and Belgium in 18 days. After taking over France, Germany attacked Britain. For months, German planes bombed Britain, but the British did not give up.
(A) Great Britain was better equipped to defend itself than were other European countries.
B Germany did not try hard enough in its attempt to take over Great Britain.

(continued)

86 ■ Assessment Program — Unit 5 Test

Name _____ Date _____

38 ESSAY (10 points)

Describe the leadership role that the United States took in the world after World War II ended. Give specific examples.

Possible response: The United States was a superpower after the war and felt a responsibility to help countries that were not as strong. Under the Marshall Plan, the United States helped European countries rebuild their businesses, factories, roads, and airports after the war. The United States also joined the United Nations to promote world peace. As one of five permanent members of the Security Council, the United States helps decide what to do when trouble breaks out somewhere in the world. Along with other democracies, the United States opposed the spread of communism and joined NATO. The United States gave money and supplies to countries that were fighting communist takeovers. When Russia blocked supplies from reaching Berlin by road or rail, in order to force the United States, Great Britain, and France to leave the city, the United States sent tons of supplies by plane in the Berlin Airlift, allowing the Allies to remain.

(continued)

Unit 5 Test — Assessment Program ■ 87

Name _____ Date _____

Individual Performance Task

Write an Advertisement

Imagine that you are working for the United States government in December 1941. The Japanese have just attacked Pearl Harbor and the United States has entered World War II. Your job is to persuade Americans to support the war effort. Create an advertisement designed to persuade people to do one of the following things:

- cooperate with rationing
- join the armed forces
- recycle
- buy war bonds
- volunteer for the Office of Civilian Defense
- work as a nurse

Start your project by rereading the information in your textbook that is related to your subject. You may also want to do further research in the library or on the Internet. Your ad should include the following:

- specific information about what you are asking people to do
- persuasive reasons for supporting the war in general
- an explanation of how the country will benefit from the person's help
- an attractive presentation of the information that is easy to read
- artwork or decoration to catch the reader's attention

You may prepare your advertisement as a poster or as a pamphlet. Completed advertisements can be displayed in the classroom.

Name _____ Date _____

Group Performance Task

Create a Game

As a group, choose one of the topics below. List events related to your topic and then reread the unit, gathering information. Write a list of questions and answers related to your topic to use in your game.

➡ TOPIC 1   Hitler and Germany in World War II

You will want to cover Hitler's rise to power, facts about the German government under Hitler, actions taken by Germany that led to World War II, events of the war involving Germany, and Germany's eventual defeat.

➡ TOPIC 2   Japan in World War II

Focus on actions taken by Japan that led to World War II, information about Japan's government and leaders, Japan's involvement in the war, and the part that atomic weapons played in Japan's defeat.

➡ TOPIC 3   The United States in World War II

Focus on why the United States entered a conflict it had tried to avoid. Be sure to include the point at which the United States entered the war, major battles, and the effect of the war on the home front.

Now, decide on a format for your game. Invent your own game, or model it on a popular board game or television game show. Prepare your game cards (and a game board, if necessary). Rank your questions, and assign points according to how hard they are. Write a list of rules and explain your game to the rest of the class. If time permits, exchange with another group and play the games.

RUBRICS FOR SCORING

SCORING RUBRICS The rubrics below list the criteria for evaluating the tasks above. They also describe different levels of success in meeting those criteria.

INDIVIDUAL PERFORMANCE TASK

SCORE 4	SCORE 3	SCORE 2	SCORE 1
• Rich description is provided. • Key concepts are well addressed. • Details fit historical period strongly. • Advertisements are well organized.	• Some description is provided. • Key concepts are addressed. • Details fit historical period. • Advertisements are somewhat organized.	• Little description is provided. • Key concepts are poorly addressed. • Details fit historical period weakly. • Advertisements are poorly organized.	• No description is provided. • Key concepts are not addressed. • Details do not fit historical period. • Advertisements are not organized.

GROUP PERFORMANCE TASK

SCORE 4	SCORE 3	SCORE 2	SCORE 1
• Game shows excellent planning. • Game shows excellent creativity. • Details fit historical period strongly.	• Game shows some planning. • Game shows some creativity. • Details fit historical period.	• Game shows little planning. • Game shows little creativity. • Details fit historical period weakly.	• Game shows no planning. • Game shows no creativity. • Details do not fit historical period.

Introduce the Unit

1

2

3

4

5

6

7

OBJECTIVES

- Identify the causes and events that led to United States involvement in World War II.
- Describe the major events and turning points of the war in Europe and in the Pacific.
- Analyze the impact of World War II on the homefront.

Access Prior Knowledge

Invite students to recall the major nations that battled each other during World War I. Copy on the board the graphic organizer below, and have students complete it.

Allied Powers		**Central Powers**
Britain		Germany
France		Austria-Hungary
United States		Ottoman Empire
Russia		Bulgaria
Italy		
Japan		

D-Day Memorial, Bedford, Virginia

BACKGROUND

D Day Operation Overlord was the formal name for the massive Allied invasion of northern France on June 6, 1944. Most people refer to the operation as D day. The previous night a fleet of 2,700 ships carrying 176,000 troops landed on the coast of Normandy and behind German lines. At dawn, troops from the United States, Canada, Great Britain, and France stormed ashore in the largest sea invasion in history. The Allies secured the coast and slowly advanced across France, pushing the German army back as they did. By August the Allies had reclaimed much of northwestern France, including Paris. The D day assault was a major victory in the war against Germany.

BACKGROUND

D Day Memorial The memorial, which opened on June 6, 2001, honors all soldiers who participated in the Allied invasion of Normandy, France, during World War II. The memorial was placed in Bedford, Virginia, a town that suffered a larger per capita loss of soldiers on D day than any other town in the United States. Although Bedford was a town of just 3,000 people in 1944, 35 of its residents took part in the invasion. Before the initial assault had ended, 23 soldiers from Bedford had died.

World War II

" The eyes of the world are upon you. The hopes and prayers of liberty-loving people everywhere march with you. "

—Dwight D. Eisenhower, order to troops preparing to invade Normandy, June 6, 1944

Preview the Content

Skim the unit. When you have finished, answer the following— *Who* and *What* is the unit about? *Where* are the places you will learn about? *When* did the events happen? *Why* are these events important? Make a graphic organizer, and fill in your responses.

WHO	→	_____
WHAT	→	_____
WHERE	→	_____
WHEN	→	_____
WHY	→	_____

Preview the Vocabulary

Related Words Use the Glossary to look up the vocabulary terms below. What do these terms have in common?

island hopping   **front**   **D day**   **arms race**

Unit 5 ■ 323

Visual Learning

Picture The background image shows the D day Memorial in Bedford, Virginia.

Analyze Primary Sources

WWII Officer's Medal Have students carefully examine the medal and describe it. Ask students what such a medal may represent. Possible answer: It represents the service and sacrifice of people in the military during World War II.

Quotation Have a volunteer read aloud the quotation from General Dwight D. Eisenhower.

Q Why did Eisenhower say that "the hopes and prayers of liberty-loving people everywhere" were with the troops?

A Many saw the D day invasion as an opportunity to stop the advance of the German army in Western Europe.

AUDIOTEXT

Use the Unit 5 AUDIOTEXT for a reading of the Unit narrative.

· Unit 5 ·

Preview the Content
Students' graphic organizers should resemble the one below.

Who	→	Germany, other European Nations, Japan, the United States
What	→	World War II
Where	→	Europe and in the Pacific
When	→	1940s
Why	→	to preserve democracy

Preview the Vocabulary
Explain that these terms are all related to World War II.

island hopping	Allied strategy of reclaiming Pacific islands from Japan during World War II
front	the place on a battlefield where opposing forces meet
D day	June 6, 1944—the date of the Allied invasion of Normandy
arms race	the competition for superior weapons among powerful nations

Preview the Unit

PAGES 324–325

OBJECTIVES

- Interpret information in databases and visuals.
- Use mathematical skills to interpret social studies data on maps and graphs.

Access Prior Knowledge

Ask students what they know about life in the United States in the early 1900s.

Visual Learning

Map Discuss as a class how the information in the map relates to that which is represented in the key. Explain to students that during World War II some American ships were sunk by German submarines off the Atlantic and Gulf coasts.

Time Line Have students work in pairs to ask and answer questions about the time line. For example, students might ask: *How long after the end of World War II was NATO founded?* four years

Time Line Illustrations Ask students to speculate about the significance of the events shown on the time line.

- Germany invaded Poland in 1939, which led Britain and France to declare war on Germany.
- Japan attacked Pearl Harbor, leading the United States to renounce its policy of neutrality and enter World War II.
- Millions of Americans served in the armed forces, and millions more aided the war effort at home.
- More than 170,000 Allied troops invaded Normandy, France, in what was called the D day invasion.
- The United States dropped a pair of atomic bombs on Japan, effectively ending World War II.
- NATO was formed in April 1945 to provide regional defense in Europe, Canada, and the United States.

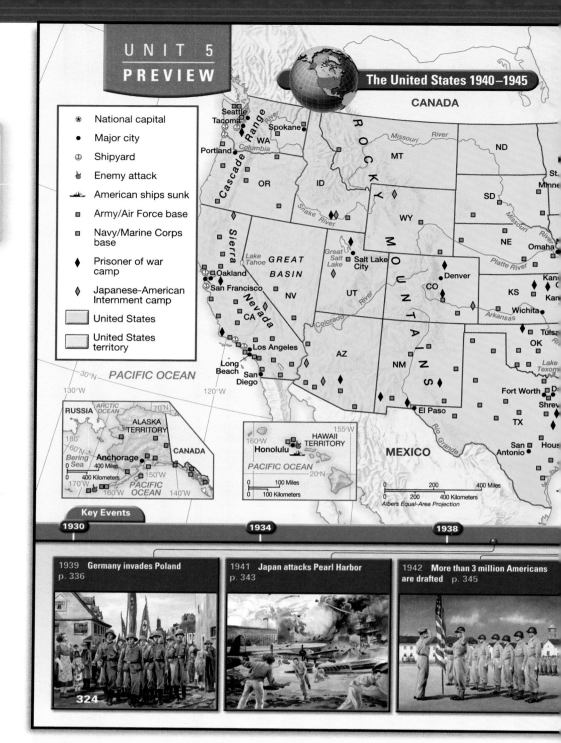

UNIT 5 PREVIEW — The United States 1940–1945

Key:
- National capital
- Major city
- Shipyard
- Enemy attack
- American ships sunk
- Army/Air Force base
- Navy/Marine Corps base
- Prisoner of war camp
- Japanese-American Internment camp
- United States
- United States territory

Key Events
1930 — 1934 — 1938

1939 Germany invades Poland p. 336

1941 Japan attacks Pearl Harbor p. 343

1942 More than 3 million Americans are drafted p. 345

REACH ALL LEARNERS

Advanced Learners Pair students, and have them research and write brief paragraphs about one of the events on the time line above. Encourage student pairs to use various references, such as encyclopedias, to research their chosen event. Have students use their findings as a basis for writing their paragraphs.

MAKE IT RELEVANT

In Your State Organize students into groups, and have them research the role their state played during World War II. Encourage students to use various primary and secondary sources in their research. Have groups write brief summaries of their findings. Compile the summaries into a binder titled *Our State in World War II*.

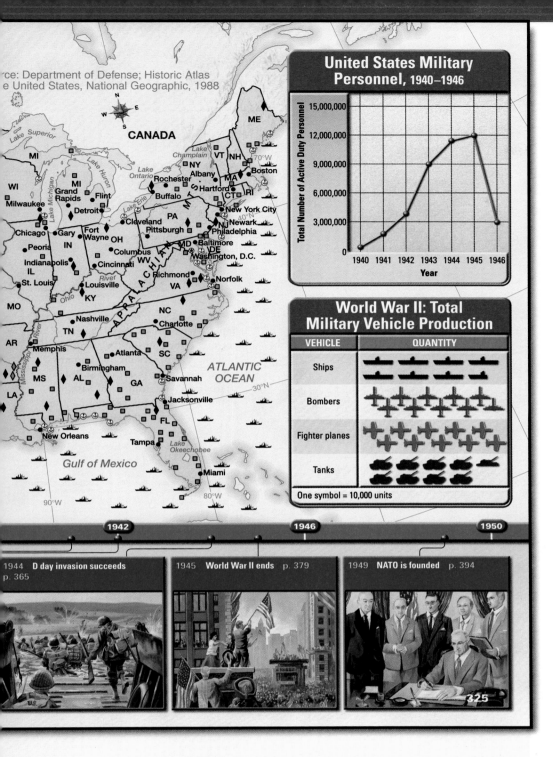

ce: Department of Defense; Historic Atlas
e United States, National Geographic, 1988

United States Military Personnel, 1940–1946

World War II: Total Military Vehicle Production

VEHICLE	QUANTITY
Ships	
Bombers	
Fighter planes	
Tanks	

One symbol = 10,000 units

1942   1946   1950

1944   D day invasion succeeds
p. 365

1945   World War II ends   p. 379

1949   NATO is founded   p. 394

325

Visual Learning

Line Graph Have students examine the line graph. Ask such questions as:

- *What does the line graph show?* the number of active duty personnel that served in the United States military from 1940 to 1946
- *What happened in the years from 1940 to 1945?* The number of United States military personnel increased each year.
- *In what year did the most United States personnel serve in the armed forces?* 1945

Picture Graph Work with students to interpret the data presented. You may want to ask such questions as:

- *What does the picture graph show?* the total number of ships, bombers, fighter planes, and tanks produced during World War II
- *Why do you think more bombers and fighter planes were produced than ships and tanks?* Students' answers may vary but should reflect that much of World War II was fought in the air.

Make Connections

Link Picture Graph and Line Graph
Ask students to use the picture graph and the line graph to make observations and draw conclusions about the relationship between the number of United States personnel in the armed forces and the production of ships, bombers, fighter planes, and tanks.

SCHOOL TO HOME

Use the Unit 5 SCHOOL-TO-HOME NEWSLETTER on pages S9–S10 to introduce the unit to family members and suggest activities they can do at home.

Start with a Story

PAGES 326–329

Summary

This selection describes the day that World War II came to the United States. It is told from the point of view of an 11-year-old named Peter Nottage.

1 Motivate

Set the Purpose

People throughout the nation were divided on whether to join the war. After the attack on Pearl Harbor, most citizens were eager to join the war.

Access Prior Knowledge

Ask students to tell what they know about the peace imposed upon Italy and Germany following World War I. Students should note that both countries lost land and had to pay huge sums in reparations.

READING SOCIAL STUDIES

Graphic Organizer Have students skim this story to fill in a time line tracing the major events associated with the attack on Pearl Harbor.

● USE READING AND VOCABULARY TRANSPARENCY 5-1.

5-1 TRANSPARENCY

START with a STORY

ATTACK ON PEARL HARBOR:
The True Story of the Day America Entered World War II
by Shelley Tanaka • paintings by David Craig

On Sunday, December 7, 1941, the roar of Japanese planes shattered the early-morning calm over the Hawaiian Islands. The planes dropped bombs on American ships docked at Pearl Harbor, an American naval base. Peter Nottage was 11 years old at the time. He witnessed the attack from nearby Kaneohe (kah·nay·OH·hay) Bay. Read now what Peter saw when World War II came to the United States.

Peter Nottage

326 ■ Unit 5

AUDIOTEXT

Text of this story can be found on the Unit 5 AUDIOTEXT.

REACH ALL LEARNERS

Auditory Learners
Some students may benefit from hearing the story read aloud prior to reading it themselves or while they read it. This can be accomplished in several ways. You may play the Unit 5 Audiotext. You also may have these learners work with partners who read the lesson aloud as they read it to themselves.

The Mitchell household was still asleep when Peter Nottage woke up. He slipped on a pair of shorts and an aloha shirt and went outside. Baby Girl shook herself awake and padded over to join him.

The house was built on a high bluff that overlooked Kaneohe (kah·nay·OH·hay) Bay. Across the water, the air station looked pretty quiet. Peter could see the two new hangars that housed the Navy's seaplanes. Most of the planes were neatly lined up on the ramp outside. Four planes were floating at anchor in the bay.

Peter heard a drone behind him. He looked up, and three silvery planes appeared above his head, coming in right over the house from the west. They were flying very close together and very low. He could see the goggled faces of the pilots.

Peter had never seen planes like these before. They weren't the usual P-26 fighters with the open cockpits, or even the sharp-nosed P-40s. Each plane had a big red circle painted on the underside of each wing. As he watched, the planes swerved over the bay and disappeared to the north.

Unit 5 ◾ 327

2 Teach

Read and Respond

Understand the Story Ask students to recount the details of the air station as Peter saw it when he woke up that historic morning. quiet; new hangars with Navy seaplanes in neat rows; four additional planes were floating at anchor in the bay

Understand the Story Have students list characteristics that Peter noticed about the incoming planes. Then ask students to share their lists with a partner. Lists may include planes flying low and close; goggled pilots; and unfamiliar models of planes with a big red circle under each wing.

Link History with Culture and Society Recall with students that the unfamiliar planes had a big red circle underneath each wing. Explain to the class that the Japanese flag is white with a big red circle in the center.

Q Who did Peter think was flying the planes, and what did he think the planes were doing?

A He thought that they were United States Navy pilots practicing maneuvers.

INTEGRATE ART

Make a Model Have groups of students create models of the naval base at Pearl Harbor. Students should refer to the description provided in the story. They also should use other sources to research details. Have students make labels for each feature their models show. Roles of group members may include researcher, designer, builder, writer, and presenter. When students have completed their models, call on each group's presenter to share the group's model with the class.

Read and Respond

Understand the Story Ask students to recount the damage being caused by the planes. Damage included bombing the hangar, blowing up an anchored seaplane, and burning many of the seaplanes.

Q Why do you think Peter's first thought would be that the Navy was holding maneuvers?

A It was probably common to see the Navy planes hold maneuvers, and people did not think that Pearl Harbor would be attacked.

3 Close

Summarize the Reading

- Early in the morning of December 7, 1941, the air station at Pearl Harbor is typically quiet.
- Unfamiliar planes arrive and begin to bomb the air station, causing serious damage before the people on the base can fight back.
- This is the surprise Japanese attack on Pearl Harbor.

READING SOCIAL STUDIES

Graphic Organizer Have students compare the events listed on their time lines with the events below.

- The airfield at Kaneohe Bay was quiet.
- Planes approached the air station.
- The planes began to fire on and bomb the air station.
- A bomb took out the ramp of the seaplane hangar.
- An anchored seaplane was hit.
- An attacking plane was hit.
- The pilot whose plane had been hit signaled the other planes to leave.
- As they left, the pilot whose plane had been hit crashed his plane into the armory.

● USE READING AND VOCABULARY TRANSPARENCY 5-1.

5-1 TRANSPARENCY

Within minutes they swooped in again. This time they sprayed machine-gun fire. Peter could see the water jump as the bullets splashed into the bay.

Wow, he thought. This was great. The Navy was holding maneuvers right before his eyes. Must be the red team's planes against the blue team.

The door opened behind him and Mr. Mitchell came out, still wearing his pajamas. He squinted as a group of nine planes came in over the air station.

"Never seen one of those," he said. "What kind of plane do you suppose that is, Peter?"

"I don't know. I guess—"

One of the planes dropped a bomb right on the ramp of the seaplane hangar, setting it on fire. Metal, concrete, and glass exploded from the ground.

Peter started. Had one of the Navy pilots gone crazy? Somebody was really going to get it for that.

And then one of the seaplanes anchored in the bay was hit, and it blew up in a burst of fire.

Kaneohe was suddenly a sea of smoke and flames. All the seaplanes seemed to be burning.

INTEGRATE LANGUAGE ARTS

Produce a Historical Radio Broadcast

Organize the class into groups that will create radio broadcasts covering the time before, during, and after the Japanese attack on Pearl Harbor. Broadcasts might begin with some 1940s Hawaiian music and an announcer commenting on the quiet morning at the air station before launching into a panicked account of the attack.

Thick black smoke began to pour from one of the buildings. Alarms brayed.

A group of fighter planes swooped in again, but this time they faced fire from below. One of the attacking planes seemed to be hit. The pilot turned and waggled his wings at the rest of his squadron, which broke formation and peeled off. He came in alone, heading right for the station armory, as straight and deliberate as an arrow. Then, as Peter watched, the plane slammed into the ground and burst into flames.

Peter's mother flung open the door behind them. "It's on the radio. It's war!" she shouted. "Those are the Japanese! We're under attack!" And she grabbed Peter's arm and yanked him into the house.

brayed called out loudly

Analyze the Literature

1. Why do you think Peter believed that the Navy was holding maneuvers?
2. Why did the pilot head toward the armory?
3. Write a paragraph explaining the clues that might have helped Peter realize that they were being attacked.

READ A BOOK

START THE UNIT PROJECT

Create an Illustrated Time Line
Work with your classmates to create an illustrated time line of World War II. As you read, make a list of the key events, people, and places you learn about. This list will help you decide which items to include on your time line.

USE TECHNOLOGY

GO ONLINE Visit The Learning Site at **www.harcourtschool.com** for additional activities, primary sources, and other resources to use in this unit.

Unit 5 ■ 329

Read a Book

Students may enjoy reading these leveled independent Readers or books of your choice. Additional books are listed on pages 323D of this Teacher's Edition.

Easy *Talking in Code* by Stephanie St. Pierre. Comanche and Najavo Indians devised codes that were essential to the war effort during World War II.

Average *Omaha Beach, Normandy* by Charles F. Hirsch. The landing of United States troops on D day at Omaha Beach, Normandy, was part of the greatest sea-to-land invasion in history.

Challenging *On the Home Front* by Madeline Boskey. While World War II was being fought overseas, those at home in the United States had battles of their own.

Start the Unit Project

Hint Suggest that students refer to the time lines that follow each lesson in the unit for examples of key events, people, and places. Have students begin compiling their own lists into a master time line that spans the time covered in this unit. Suggest that the entries depict people and places in the top portion of the time line and events in the bottom portion.

1930 ← → 1950

Use Technology

GO ONLINE **INTERNET RESOURCES**

THE LEARNING SITE Go to **www.harcourtschool.com** to view Internet resources for this unit.

TIME FOR KIDS Go to **www.harcourtschool.com** for the latest news in a student-friendly format.

Analyze the Literature
Answers

1. Students might suggest that Navy pilots had done practice maneuvers there before.
2. to destroy it by crashing into it
3. Students' paragraphs should note the unfamiliar plane models with a red circle under each wing as well as the machine-gun fire.

Chapter 9 Planning Guide The War Begins

Introducing the Chapter, pp. 330–331

LESSON	PACING	OBJECTIVES	VOCABULARY
Introduce the Chapter pp. 330–331	**1 Day**	■ Interpret information in visuals. ■ Apply critical-thinking skills to organize and use information. ■ Interpret excerpts from notable speeches.	**Word Work:** Preview Vocabulary, p. 331
1 The Conflict Begins pp. 332–339	**2 Days**	■ Describe how dictators came to power in Europe after World War I. ■ Analyze Japan and Italy's campaigns to form empires. ■ Compare republican forms of government to dictatorships and communism. ■ Identify major events and invasions of World War II.	dictatorship concentration camp fascism
2 The United States Enters the War pp. 340–346	**1 Day**	■ Examine the efforts of the United States to remain neutral in World War II. ■ Identify events that caused the United States to enter World War II. ■ Identify ways in which the United States prepared for World War II. ■ Describe how the United States' entrance into World War II affected Americans.	civilian

READING	INTEGRATE LEARNING	REACH ALL LEARNERS	RESOURCES
Cause and Effect, p. 331			
Reading Social Studies: **Personal Response,** p. 333 Reading Social Studies: **Graphic Organizer,** p. 333 **Cause and Effect,** p. 336 Reading Social Studies: **Personal Response,** p. 339	Language Arts **Write to Compare and Contrast,** p. 333 Mathematics **Compare Distances,** p. 336	**Advanced Learners,** p. 335 **Extend and Enrich,** p. 338 **Reteach the Lesson,** p. 339	**Activity Book,** pp. 84–85 **Reading and Vocabulary Transparency 5-2**
Reading Social Studies: **Study Questions,** p. 341 Reading Social Studies: **Create Mental Images,** p. 342 Reading Social Studies: **Study Questions Responses,** p. 346	Language Arts **Write a Report,** p. 341 Reading **Read Biographies,** p. 345	**English as a Second Language,** p. 340 **Auditory Learners,** p. 344 **Extend and Enrich,** p. 346 **Reteach the Lesson,** p. 346	**Activity Book,** pp. 86–87 **Reading and Vocabulary Transparency 5-3** Internet Resources

Chapter 9 Planning Guide The War Begins

LESSON	PACING	OBJECTIVES	VOCABULARY
3 **Life at Home** pp. 347–354	**2 Days**	■ Explain how United States factories mobilized for war. ■ Describe how World War II affected women in the United States. ■ Explain how people in the United States supported the effort to win World War II. ■ Describe and evaluate how World War II affected Japanese Americans.	**rationing** **recycling** **relocation camp** **Word Work:** Prefixes, p. 347
CITIZENSHIP SKILLS **Make Economic Choices** p. 355	**1 Day**	■ Explain the trade-offs and opportunity costs of economic decisions.	**trade-off** **opportunity cost**
EXAMINE PRIMARY SOURCES **War Posters** pp. 356–357	**1 Day**	■ Identify the purpose of World War II posters. ■ Describe the impact of World War II on the homefront and how people at home helped with the war effort.	
Chapter Review and Test Preparation pp. 358–359	**1 Day**		

READING	INTEGRATE LEARNING	REACH ALL LEARNERS	RESOURCES
Reading Social Studies: **K-W-L Chart,** p. 348 Reading Social Studies: **K-W-L Chart Responses,** p. 354	**Art** **Draw a Recruiting Poster,** p. 348 **Music** **Listen to a Song,** p. 349 **Reading** **Read a Biography,** p. 350 **Science** **Milkweed,** p. 352	**Below-Level Learners,** p. 347 **Advanced Learners,** p. 349 **Extend and Enrich,** p. 354 **Reteach the Lesson,** p. 354	**Activity Book,** p. 88 **Reading and Vocabulary Transparency 5-4** Internet Resources
		Extend and Enrich, p. 355 **Reteach the Skill,** p. 355	**Activity Book,** p. 89 **Skill Transparency 5-1**
		Extend and Enrich, p. 357 **Reteach,** p. 357	Internet Resources
		Test Preparation, p. 358	**Activity Book,** pp. 90–91 **Reading and Vocabulary Transparency 5-5** **Assessment Program, Chapter 9 Test,** pp. 73–76

Activity Book

Name _____ Date _____

The Conflict Begins

Directions Use the map and the following statements to help you answer the questions below.

1. Hitler's troops march into Austria and claim it for Germany.

2. Germany takes over Czechoslovakia.

3. With the help of the Soviet Union, Germany takes over Poland.

4. Denmark falls to Germany in hours.

5. Norway is taken over by Germany.

6. The Luxembourg invasion follows Norway's fall.

7. The Netherlands falls to Germany in five days.

8. Belgium is taken over by Germany.

9. France falls to Germany, leaving Britain alone against the Nazis.

Germany's Conquests in Europe

❶ Which countries bordering the seas west and north of Germany did Hitler quickly take over? Denmark, Norway, the Netherlands, and Belgium

❷ Which country helped Germany take over Poland? the Soviet Union

❸ Which was the last country to fall, leaving England alone to fight the Nazis? France

❹ Which is the only country bordering Germany that was not invaded by the German army? Switzerland

(continued)

Use after reading Chapter 9, Lesson 1, pages 332–339.

Name _____ Date _____

Directions Use the time line to help you answer the questions below.

Time Line

1930 1931 1932 1933 1934 1935 1936 1937 1938 1939 1940

1931 Japan seizes China's northeast corner, Manchuria.

1932 The Nazi Party, headed by Adolf Hitler, becomes the most powerful party in Germany

1933 Germany becomes a dictatorship when Hitler, the nation's prime minister, takes control and names himself as Germany's leader.

1935 Italy's dictator, Mussolini, conquers Ethiopia.

1936 The Japanese emperor loses control when Japan's military seizes its government.

1938 Hitler begins his aggressions against other countries; Austria is conquered first.

1939 Hitler takes Czechoslovakia and Poland; Mussolini conquers European Albania.

1940 Hitler takes over Denmark, Norway, Luxembourg, the Netherlands, Belgium, and France. In August, Germany uses air bombers to attack Britain.

❺ When did Germany become ruled by Hitler? 1933

❻ Which dictator conquered the most countries between 1930 and 1940?
Adolf Hitler

❼ How did Germany attack Britain in 1940? bombing by air

❽ In which part of China is Manchuria located? the northeast corner

❾ What African country did Italy conquer in 1935? Ethiopia

❿ How long after the Nazi Party became the most powerful party in Germany did the country become a dictatorship? one year

⓫ How many years did it take for Germany to take over Austria, Czechoslovakia, Poland, Denmark, Norway, Luxembourg, the Netherlands, Belgium, and France?
about two years

⓬ When did Japan's military take control of the country's government?
1936

Use after reading Chapter 9, Lesson 1, pages 332–339.

Name _____ Date _____

The United States Enters the War

Directions Imagine that you are a journalist covering the war. Answer the questions below to organize the following points of information.

- The United States declared war on Japan.
- about 1,100 sailors died on the ship.
- a day of tragedy for the United States
- 19 United States ships were damaged or destroyed.
- USS *Arizona*
- Because of the Pearl Harbor attack, the United States could no longer remain neutral.

- the morning of December 7, 1941
- December 8, 1941
- Pearl Harbor
- Japanese forces attacked the United States Pacific fleet.
- They came by air, in hundreds of airplanes with bombs.
- Relations between Japan and the United States were not good.
- Japan wanted to make sure the United States did not interfere with its plans to create a huge empire.

❶ Who? Japan; the United States; USS *Arizona*

❷ What? Japanese forces attacked the United States Pacific fleet; the United States declared war on Japan; about 1,100 sailors died on the ship; a day of tragedy for the United States; 19 United States ships were damaged or destroyed.

❸ When? the morning of December 7, 1941; December 8, 1941

❹ Where? Pearl Harbor

❺ Why? Relations between Japan and the United States were not good; Japan wanted to make sure that the United States did not interfere with its plans to create a huge empire; because of the Pearl Harbor attack, the United States could no longer remain neutral.

❻ How? They came by air, in hundreds of airplanes with bombs.

(continued)

Use after reading Chapter 9, Lesson 2, pages 340–346.

Name _____ Date _____

Directions Use the points of information you organized on page 86 to help you write a one-paragraph news story about the war.

United States Enters War!

Paragraphs will vary but should include some of the information below. Some students may include additional facts. On the morning of December 7, 1941, Japanese forces attacked the Pacific fleet of the United States at Pearl Harbor. Relations between Japan and the United States had not been good. Japan wanted to create a huge empire and did not want the United States to interfere with its plans. The Japanese came by air, in hundreds of airplanes, and dropped bombs on Pearl Harbor.

In the attack, 19 ships were damaged or destroyed. On the USS *Arizona*, about 1,100 sailors died on the ship. It was a day of tragedy for the United States. Because of the Pearl Harbor attack, the United States could no longer remain neutral. On December 8, 1941, the United States declared war on Japan.

Use after reading Chapter 9, Lesson 2, pages 340–346.

Name _____ Date _____

Life at Home

Directions Americans faced many challenges during World War II. Next to each statement below, write whether the situation relates to an economic challenge or a cultural challenge.

1 People were asked to save certain things for use in making war products. _____economic_____

2 Because many of the men drafted to serve in the war were fathers, many women were left alone to take care of children. _____cultural_____

3 Certain goods, such as food, shoes, and heating oil, cost not only money but also ration points. _____economic_____

4 Farmers worked extra hard to grow more crops. _____economic_____

5 Millions of volunteers were needed to help protect United States borders. _____cultural_____

6 Japanese American citizens were taken from their homes and moved to camps. _____cultural_____

7 American women learned to do jobs left empty by men who became soldiers. _____economic_____

8 Most drivers were allowed to buy only three gallons of gas per week. _____economic_____

Directions Write a paragraph about the challenges United States citizens faced during World War II.

Paragraphs will vary but should include some of the following information:
Americans faced many challenges during World War II. Some challenges were
economic. Items such as food and gasoline cost ration points. Farmers were asked
to grow more crops. Some items were recycled. Other challenges Americans faced
were cultural. Many people volunteered to help protect United States borders.
Some children had to be taken care of by their mothers alone when their fathers
went to war. Japanese American citizens were sent to camps to live during the war.

Name _____ Date _____

 CITIZENSHIP SKILLS
Make Economic Choices

Directions Read the paragraph and answer the questions below.

Rationing During World War II

During the war, goods such as meat, sugar, coffee, canned foods, shoes, tires, and gasoline cost ration points. Each person received a ration book with a certain number of ration points to spend. For example, red stamps were issued for meats, butter, fats, oils, and cheese. Each person was allowed 16 red stamp points per week. Additional red points could be earned by turning in fats to make other goods. Blue stamps, 48 per month per person, were for items such as canned fruits and vegetables, dried beans, baby food, and ketchup. Often the point value of certain goods changed. For example, grapefruit juice might cost 23 points one year but only 4 points another year. Ration coupons carried expiration dates, so people had to be wise in their spending choices.

1 If a pound of ham cost 8 ration points, how many pounds could a person buy in one week? Explain. Two pounds of ham could be purchased, but that purchase would use all the ration points for that week.

2 A family has used all of its blue stamp points for the week. Circle the items that cannot be purchased during this week.

steak   (canned peas)   cheese   oil   (dried beans)   (baby food)

3 How many blue ration points would a family of four be able to spend in one month? 192 points

4 Explain why it was important for citizens during World War II to make good economic choices. Answers will vary but should include the idea that citizens who made good economic choices were able to get what they needed.

Name _____ Date _____

World War II Begins

Directions Complete this graphic organizer to show that you understand the causes and effects of some of the key events that started World War II.

[Cause] → [Effect]

Cause	Effect
Adolf Hitler becomes chancellor of Germany.	The freedoms of German citizens are limited as German Jews are stripped of their rights.
Other dictators, such as Joseph Stalin, Benito Mussolini, and Hideki Tojo, rise to power in Europe and Asia.	**Democracy in Europe and Asia comes under attack.**
On September 1, 1939, German forces invade Poland.	World War II begins.
Japan continues its conquest of China and southeastern Asia.	**French Indochina falls to the Japanese.**
On December 7, 1941, Japanese forces attack Pearl Harbor.	The United States enters World War II.

▪ CHAPTER ▪

Name _____ Date _____

9   Test Preparation

Directions Read each question and choose the best answer. Then fill in the circle for the answer you have chosen. Be sure to fill in the circle completely.

1 Which country was not in the process of forming a dictatorship before World War II?
Ⓐ Germany
Ⓑ Italy
● France
Ⓓ Japan

2 For a while, the United States tried to remain _____ about the world's problems.
Ⓕ worried
● neutral
Ⓗ unconcerned
Ⓙ democratic

3 What event caused America to enter the war?
● Japan's attack on Pearl Harbor
Ⓑ Germany's attack on England
Ⓒ Italy's attack on Ethiopia
Ⓓ the Soviet Union's attack on Poland

4 The government _____ the goods that people could buy during the war.
Ⓕ ticketed
Ⓖ stamped
Ⓗ identified
● rationed

5 Which is a way Americans citizens helped in the war effort?
Ⓐ by issuing ration points for food
Ⓑ by using up gasoline
● by volunteering for the Office of Civilian Defense
Ⓓ by creating the War Production Board

NOTES

NOTES

COMMUNITY RESOURCES

Historical Societies

Museums

Experts on World War II

Veterans of World War II

Chapter 9 Assessment

STANDARD TEST

· CHAPTER ·

Name _____ Date _____

9 Test

Part One: Test Your Understanding

MULTIPLE CHOICE (4 points each)

Directions Circle the letter of the best answer.

1 Germany could not pay for Europe's World War I debts as the Treaty of Versailles required because—
A Hitler would not allow it.
B Germany needed the money to pay for a new war.
(C) the German economy was too weak after World War I and the Great Depression.
D none of the above

2 Which of the following did Hitler **not** believe?
F Germany had not been treated fairly after World War I.
G Jewish people were to blame for many of Germany's problems.
H Germans were better than all other peoples of the world.
(J) Germany should regain the power it had in ancient times.

3 In a dictatorship—
A all property is owned by the government.
(B) the head of the government has total authority.
C people elect representatives to run a country.
D a small group of leaders has total authority.

4 Benito Mussolini was dictator of—
(F) Italy.
G France.
H Spain.
J the Soviet Union.

5 On December 7, 1941, Japanese forces—
(A) attacked Pearl Harbor.
B invaded Indochina.
C took over Manchuria.
D took over Ethiopia and Albania.

6 Which country was **not** taken over by Germany during World War II?
F France
G Czechoslovakia
(H) Britain
J Poland

(continued)

Chapter 9 Test

Assessment Program ■ 73

STANDARD TEST

Name _____ Date _____

7 In World War II, Germany, Japan, and Italy were called the—
A Central Powers.
B Allies.
(C) Axis Powers.
D Nazis.

8 Why did the United States government ration certain goods during World War II?
F so old products could be turned into new goods
(G) so soldiers would have enough food and supplies
H so children could help in the war effort
J none of the above

9 Which of the following industries began in the United States during World War II?
A aircraft production
B recycling
C shipbuilding
(D) synthetic rubber production

10 During World War II Japanese Americans—
F volunteered to join the United States army.
G were suspected of being spies for Japan.
H were forced to leave their homes and live in relocation camps.
(J) all of the above

MATCHING (3 points each)

Directions Match the descriptions on the left with the terms on the right by writing the correct letter in the space provided. You will not use every term.

11 __G__ a political philosophy in which power is given to a dictator and the freedoms of individuals are denied

12 __B__ not taking sides in a conflict

13 __D__ a person who is not in the military

14 __A__ money a bank or borrower pays for using someone's money

15 __F__ a political and economic system in which all industries, land, and businesses are owned by the government

A. interest
B. neutral
C. war bond
D. civilian
E. riveter
F. communism
G. fascism

(continued)

74 ■ Assessment Program

Chapter 9 Test

STANDARD TEST

Name _____ Date _____

Part Two: Test Your Skills

MAKE ECONOMIC CHOICES (4 points each)

Directions Read about the two situations in the boxes below. Then use what you know about making economic choices to answer the following questions.

Emma's Situation	Mark's Situation
Emma has just received some money for her birthday. She wants to save enough money to buy a bicycle, but there are also some video games she wants to buy and some movies she wants to see with her friends.	Mark has started to cut lawns to make money. He is thinking about spending money on an advertisement for the local newspaper so that more people will know about his services.

16 If Emma decides to save her money for a bicycle, what will she be giving up?

She won't be able to buy the video games or go to the movies.

17 If Emma decides to go to the movies, what would the opportunity costs be?

She will not have the money to spend on video games or a bicycle.

18 If you were Emma, what decision would you make? Why?

Student answers will vary but should reflect the opportunity costs involved.

Possible answer: I would save up for a bicycle; you can ride a bicycle again

and again, but you can see a movie only once.

19 Describe the trade-offs involved in Mark's decision.

Spending money on an advertisement could bring Mark more business and

therefore more money in the future. Not spending the money on advertising

would allow him to use it for other things.

20 How might Mark get more customers without spending money on advertising?

Mark might put up flyers in local stores, ask his current customers for referrals, or

offer to work for friends and neighbors.

(continued)

Chapter 9 Test

Assessment Program ■ 75

STANDARD TEST

Name _____ Date _____

Part Three: Apply What You Have Learned

21 **MAIN IDEA AND SUPPORTING DETAILS** (5 points each)

You have learned about many ways in which life changed for Americans after the United States entered World War II. Use what you know to fill in supporting details for each main idea in the chart below.

Main Idea: After the attack on Pearl Harbor, Americans pulled together to help support the war effort.

Thousands of men enlisted in the armed forces; people paid higher taxes and bought war bonds; volunteers watched the skies for enemy planes; women filled the jobs left by soldiers and entered noncombat military service.

Main Idea: Many rights of Japanese Americans were taken from them during World War II.

Japanese Americans were forced to sell property, leave their homes, and stay in relocation camps.

Main Idea: American industries worked to supply the war materials needed during World War II.

The United States government controlled many industries during World War II in order to make sure that the needs of the Allied Forces were met. Companies that produced consumer goods began producing war materials, and many Americans went to work in the factories where these materials were made.

22 **ESSAY** (10 points)

Describe how the Japanese carried out their attack on Pearl Harbor. What were the results of this attack? Japanese ships traveled toward a

spot near Pearl Harbor. They awaited orders to attack while keeping radio

silence so the Americans would not know they were there. The Japanese

attacked Pearl Harbor on the morning of December 7, 1941. The United States

Pacific Fleet was badly damaged, and more than 2,000 Americans died. After the

attack, the United States declared war on Japan and entered World War II.

76 ■ Assessment Program

Chapter 9 Test

OBJECTIVES

- Interpret information in visuals.
- Apply critical-thinking skills to organize and use information.
- Interpret excerpts from notable speeches.

Access Prior Knowledge

Ask students what they know about World War II. Ask students whether they know why the United States became involved in World War II. What were some of the major events of World War II?

Visual Learning

Picture Have students examine the picture and the Locate It map. Using the images as a basis for discussion, ask students what they think the chapter will be about.

Locate It Map Pearl Harbor is a harbor on the Hawaiian Island of Oahu. The Pearl Harbor Naval Base covers more than 20,000 acres and is the center of the United States Navy's Pacific operations.

USS ARIZONA MEMORIAL

The USS *Arizona* Memorial is anchored at Pearl Harbor. It was built to honor the 1,177 sailors who lost their lives on December 7, 1941. The memorial is positioned above the sunken battleship that still lies on the ocean floor. President Dwight D. Eisenhower approved the creation of the memorial, which was dedicated in 1962.

LOCATE IT

HAWAII

Pearl Harbor

BACKGROUND

Picture The USS *Arizona* Memorial serves to commemorate those sailors who lost their lives on December 7, 1941. On that day, Japanese bombers destroyed or damaged twenty-one United States naval vessels. The single biggest loss was the USS *Arizona*, which sank in less than nine minutes. More than half of the total fatalities in the Pearl Harbor bombing were sailors on the USS *Arizona*. A marble wall on the memorial is engraved with the names of the sailers who died on the ship.

BACKGROUND

Quotation On the afternoon of December 7, 1941, President Franklin D. Roosevelt dictated a speech to his secretary. The speech called on Congress to declare war. Before he spoke to Congress the following day, he made several handwritten changes to his typed copy of the speech. One of those changes replaced the phrase "a date which will live in world history" with the words "a date which will live in infamy." The resulting speech was so powerful that it is sometimes referred to as the "Day of Infamy" speech.

9

The War Begins

" Yesterday, December 7, 1941—a date which will live in infamy. "

—Franklin D. Roosevelt, December 8, 1941, in a message to Congress

 Cause and Effect

An event or action that makes something else happen is a **cause**. What happens as a result of that event or action is the **effect**.

As you read this chapter, be sure to do the following.

• List the causes and effects of key events that led to World War II.

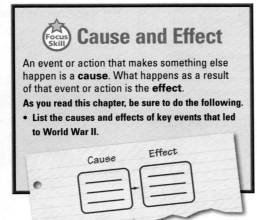

Cause   Effect

Read and Respond

Direct students' attention to the title of the chapter. Ask students to speculate about how World War II started.

Quotation Ask a volunteer to read the quotation aloud to the class.

Q What do you think it means for an event to "live in infamy"?

A To live in infamy means to always be remembered as something bad.

President Roosevelt delivered this speech to Congress the day after the Japanese attacked Pearl Harbor. The speech ended by asking Congress to declare war on Japan.

Cause and Effect

As students read the chapter, have them use a graphic organizer to help list the causes and effects of World War II.

• A blank graphic organizer can be found on page 90 of the Activity Book.

• Point out to students that the effect of one event can be the cause of another. Remind them that several events can be connected by cause and effect.

• A completed graphic organizer can be found on page 90 of the Activity Book, Teacher's Edition.

Cause   Effect

Preview Vocabulary Have students make a word web for each vocabulary term in the chapter. Tell them to put a term in the center of a web, to brainstorm other words they associate with the term, and to write those ideas in circles surrounding the term.

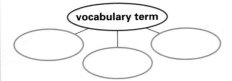

vocabulary term

Discussion Topics As you teach this chapter, you and your students might enjoy discussing some of the following topics. Each topic helps relate what students are learning about in this unit to their world today.

■ What can the United States do to help prevent wars?

■ For what reasons do you think nations make treaties today?

OBJECTIVES

- Describe how dictators came to power in Europe after World War I.
- Analyze Japan's and Italy's campaigns to form empires.
- Compare republican forms of government to dictatorships and communism.
- Identify major events and invasions of World War II.

 Cause and Effect pp. 331, 332, 335, 336, 339, 358

Vocabulary

SEE READING AND VOCABULARY TRANSPARENCY 5-2 OR THE WORD CARDS ON PP. V43–V44.

dictatorship p. 333   **fascism** p. 333

concentration camp p. 333

 When Minutes Count

Ask students to scan the lesson to find out who the dictators of Germany, Japan, Italy, and the Soviet Union were.

Quick Summary

This lesson describes the rise of dictators in Europe and their conquests that led to World War II.

 Motivate

Set the Purpose

Big Idea Inform students that World War II was fought in Asia, Europe, Africa, and the Pacific.

Access Prior Knowledge

Invite students to explain what they already know about the events leading up to World War II.

 · LESSON ·

1

Cause and Effect

As you read, look for causes and effects of World War II.

BIG IDEA
World War II began in Europe.

VOCABULARY
dictatorship
concentration camp
fascism

The Conflict Begins

1930   **1940**   **1950**

1930–1940

Franklin D. Roosevelt was reelected President in 1936. His New Deal programs had raised many people's spirits, but the worldwide depression continued. Europeans were still rebuilding their countries after World War I. Many of them had a hard time finding jobs to support their families. Also, food and other goods were scarce, making prices very high. In Asia some countries were running out of the resources needed to make their economies grow.

Powerful new leaders in some European and Asian countries promised to solve their countries' economic problems. They were willing to use force to do it.

The Rise of Dictators

The Treaty of Versailles marked the end of World War I. It made Germany pay other European countries for war damages. Germany could not afford to pay this debt. Like the economies of other countries, its economy had been badly damaged by the war. The Great Depression that soon followed left it unable to recover.

FAST FACT In 1923 German money became so low in value that German children were allowed to use bundles of German paper money as building blocks.

German leader Adolf Hitler addresses German soldiers at Nuremberg, Germany, in 1937.

332

STUDY/RESEARCH SKILLS

Summarize Information
Remind students that writing summaries can help them understand what they have read. Suggest that students write a short summary of each section as they read. Stress that a summary should include the main idea and only the most important details from each subsection.

BACKGROUND

Adolf Hitler Hitler's father wanted him to enter the civil service, but he wanted to be an artist. After his father died, Hitler did poorly in school and quit after the ninth grade. In 1907 Hitler was denied admission to the Vienna Academy of Fine Arts, and in 1908 his mother died. Hitler stayed in Vienna, living on an orphan's pension. When his pension ran out, he lived in a homeless shelter. He supported himself for a few years as an artist by painting and selling postcards.

Italian soldiers (at left) salute Benito Mussolini (center) with their knives.

Beginning in the 1920s an Austrian-born man who had fought in World War I started making angry speeches. His name was Adolf Hitler. He said that Germany had not been treated fairly after the war. He also said that Germans were better than all other peoples of the world. He was not speaking about all Germans, though. He blamed the Jewish people in Germany for many of the country's problems.

By 1932 the National Socialist party, or Nazis, who were led by Hitler, had become the most powerful political party in Germany. By 1933 Hitler was Germany's chancellor, or prime minister. Soon he had taken control of all of Germany and named himself its *führer* (FYOOR•er), which means "leader." Germany was now a dictatorship. A **dictatorship** is a government in which the dictator, or head of the government, has total authority.

Hitler soon took away the German people's right to vote and outlawed all political parties except the Nazi party. He also took control of the press and took away the rights of German Jews.

Hitler kept control by using a private army that he set up. Its soldiers, called storm troopers, arrested anyone who was even thought to disagree with Hitler. They put many of these people in terrible prisons called **concentration camps**.

Dictators rose to power in other European countries, too. This happened because of the rise of fascism. **Fascism** is a political idea in which power is given to a dictator and the freedoms of individuals are taken away. Since 1925 Italy had been under the rule of the fascist dictator Benito Mussolini (buh•NEE•toh moo•suh•LEE•nee). Mussolini wanted the nation to get back the power and glory it had had in ancient times, when it was the center of the Roman Empire.

Chapter 9 ■ 333

2 Teach

The Rise of Dictators

Read and Respond

Link Economics with Civics and Government Explain that political and economic conditions following World War I led to the rise of fascism. Tell students that many German people who had never voted before voted for the Nazi Party in the 1930 election because of the economic solutions it offered.

Q **Why do you think Germany's economic crisis made it easier for Hitler and the Nazi party to gain power?**

A Possible response: People had a difficult time finding jobs, so Hitler's promise to make Germany a world power again and to improve Germany's economy appealed to voters.

Explain that when the Nazi party won the election, Hitler demanded to be appointed chancellor. At first the German president refused, but his advisors believed that Hitler's popularity could be an advantage, so the president changed his mind.

Read and Respond

History Inform students that when Hitler and the Nazis took power in Germany, people of Jewish descent in Europe began to experience increased prejudice. The Nazis believed non-Jewish Germans were superior to Jews and non-Germans. Tell students that the night of November 7, 1938, marked a turning point in the lives of German Jews. Nearly 180 synagogues were destroyed that night, and thousands of Jewish-owned businesses were looted or destroyed. Because of the extensive damage, this date became known as *Kristallnacht,* German for "night of the broken glass." Other Nazi tactics to threaten Jews included boycotts of Jewish-owned businesses and the segregation of Jews into certain areas.

Civics and Government Japan's economic problems prompted a group of extremists to assassinate Prime Minister Inukai Tsuyoshi and take over the government. Ask students to use a Venn diagram to compare and contrast how dictatorships were formed in Germany and Japan.

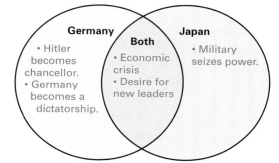

Germany
• Hitler becomes chancellor.
• Germany becomes a dictatorship.

Both
• Economic crisis
• Desire for new leaders

Japan
• Military seizes power.

Worldwide Troubles

Read and Respond

Culture and Society Discuss with students why Japan succeeded in taking over parts of China in the early 1930s.

Q How did fighting in China affect its ability to defend itself from Japan?

A Because the Chinese were fighting among themselves, they could not effectively defend themselves against the Japanese.

In Spain, Francisco Franco set up a dictatorship with help from Hitler and Mussolini.

In 1924 in the Soviet Union, Joseph Stalin took control as a dictator. The Soviet Union had formed after the Russian Revolution in 1917. Stalin did not believe in fascism, but he did believe in communism. Communism is a political and economic system in which all industries, land, and businesses are owned by the government and in which people have few freedoms.

Dictators also ruled Japan, in Asia. The Japanese emperor, Hirohito (hir•oh•HEE•toh), lost much of his power. Instead, military leaders had seized the government, and General Hideki Tojo was named prime minister. To get the resources Japan's industries needed, military leaders decided to conquer other nations in Asia and the Pacific.

REVIEW What countries were ruled by dictators before World War II? Germany, Italy, Spain, the Soviet Union, and Japan

Worldwide Troubles

In the 1920s and 1930s, China was torn by trouble. Communists were fighting to take over the nation. Japan made use of China's troubles to invade Chinese land. In 1931 Japan took Manchuria, a region in northeastern China. Manchuria was rich in resources such as coal and iron, which Japan needed. In 1937 Japan invaded the

Hirohito, the emperor of Japan, salutes as he inspects Japanese troops. The hat (right) was worn by a Japanese officer in World War II.

334 Unit 5

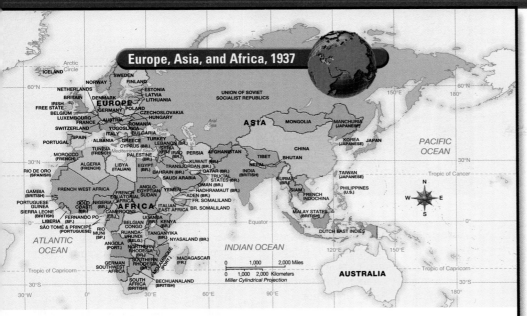

Europe, Asia, and Africa, 1937

Location **This map shows the names and the borders of countries in Europe, Asia, and Africa as they were in 1937.**

Which places in Asia were taken over by Japan?

---

rest of China. By the end of 1938, much of eastern China had been taken over by the Japanese.

Italy had also begun to take over other countries. In 1935 Italy took over the African nation of Ethiopia. Then, in 1939, Mussolini sent his soldiers to invade the European country of Albania.

Germany began to move against other countries in 1938. In March of that year, Hitler's troops marched into neighboring Austria and quickly took over.

Because of painful memories of World War I, other countries, including the United States, did little to stop these war-like acts. Most people hoped there would be no war.

REVIEW **Why did other countries do little to stop the warlike acts of some nations?**

🌐 CAUSE AND EFFECT

They had painful memories of World War I and hoped there would be no war.

War Breaks Out in Europe

After taking over Austria, Hitler next planned to invade the neighboring country of Czechoslovakia. Britain's prime minister, Neville Chamberlain, hoped to prevent the invasion. He met several times with both Hitler and Mussolini. At their last meeting in Munich, Germany, the three leaders and the leader of France signed the Munich Agreement. This treaty gave western Czechoslovakia to Germany. Britain and France hoped that in return, there would be no war. Hitler, however, did not stop at western Czechoslovakia. Within six months, he had broken the treaty. He sent German troops to take over the rest of Czechoslovakia.

Advanced Learners As they read the chapter, have students list the countries involved in World War II. Encourage them to note the changes in those countries during the war. Have them use research materials to find out what happened in those countries after the war.

Q **Why did Italy want to take over Ethiopia?**

A Italy had been interested in colonizing Ethiopia since the Suez Canal opened in 1869. Italy tried to take over Ethiopia in 1895 but failed. After Mussolini came to power, he conquered Ethiopia in 1935.

War Breaks Out in Europe

Read and Respond

Civics and Government Point out that a treaty or agreement is only worthwhile if all parties or nations comply with the terms of the agreement. Tell students that France had a mutual defense treaty with Poland before Germany invaded Poland. Explain that this meant Poland and France had agreed to come to each other's defense if necessary.

Visual Learning

Map Direct students' attention to the map on page 335. Encourage students to find Austria, Czechoslovakia, Poland, France, and Britain on the map.

CAPTION ANSWER: Manchuria, Korea, and Taiwan

Read and Respond

Geography Suggest that students complete a flow chart with the names of the European countries in the order that they were attacked by Germany.

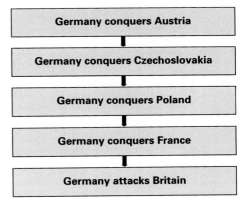

Germany conquers Austria
Germany conquers Czechoslovakia
Germany conquers Poland
Germany conquers France
Germany attacks Britain

Read and Respond

History Tell students that *blitzkrieg* also came to mean sudden, large-scale warfare. Its goal was to win a quick victory. Remind students that German bomber planes played a major role in a blitzkrieg.

Q How did Germany's blitzkrieg against Britain differ from its earlier attack against Poland?

A Germany used land and air forces to attack Poland. The attack on Britain came only from the air.

Read and Respond

History Tell students that the Soviet Union had been ignored by France, Britain, and Germany until it appeared that war was unavoidable. Explain that after Hitler threatened to invade Poland, France and Britain as well as Germany attempted to ally themselves with the Soviet Union. Point out that Germany gave the Soviet Union the best offer—the Soviet Union would not have to fight, only remain neutral. The German-Soviet Pact also gave Stalin unlimited powers over Finland, Estonia, Latvia, eastern Poland, and eastern Romania. Tell students that Hitler broke his agreement and attacked the Soviet Union in June 1941. The Soviet Union later joined the Allied Powers.

Visual Learning

Artifact Ask students what they can infer about the significance of Germany's invasion of Poland from the newspaper pictured on page 336. The article is the top story on the front page of a major American newspaper. Although the war was happening on another continent, it was important to people in the United States.

Signing the Munich Agreement are Chamberlain, Edouard Daladier of France, Hitler, and Mussolini.

Britain and France hoped that the Soviet Union would take action against Germany. To their surprise, the Soviet Union, which claimed to be against the Nazis, formed an alliance with Germany. By doing so, the Soviet Union hoped to keep Hitler from attacking it.

On September 1, 1939, nearly 2 million German soldiers invaded Poland from the west. At the same time, Soviet soldiers invaded from the east. The Germans attacked with tanks on land and planes in the air, and Poland was quickly defeated.

The Germans called this style of fighting *blitzkrieg*, or "lightning war." When Poland fell, Stalin and Hitler divided the nation. Two days later Poland's allies, Britain and France, declared war on Germany. World War II had begun.

German forces stormed across Europe with unbelievable speed, taking over Denmark in a matter of hours and Norway in a matter of weeks. German troops next conquered Luxembourg, the Netherlands, and Belgium.

German forces then attacked France. Germany's planes dropped bombs on France's cities and countryside for hours at a time, and France soon surrendered. One French soldier described the effects of these bombings: "This bombing has tired even the toughest. What can one do with light machine guns against 150 bombers? . . . Not to see the enemy face

German soldiers march to the Polish front during Germany's invasion of Poland in 1939. American newspapers (right) announce the news.

NAZI WAR PLANES BOMBING WARSAW

FRANCE MOBILIZES

POLAND INVADED!

WARSAW, OTHER CITIES BOMBED

336 Unit 5

Focus Skill

READING SKILL

Cause and Effect Ask students to reread the paragraphs on page 336 that deal specifically with Germany's invasion of Poland. After students have reread these paragraphs, encourage them to identify the cause-and-effect relationship described. Ask students what caused Britain and France to declare war on Germany.

INTEGRATE MATHEMATICS

Compare Distances Have students look at a map of Europe, and measure the distances between Berlin and the capitals of the countries that Germany invaded in World War II. Ask students to compare the distances between some of these European cities with distances between major cities in the United States.

Parts of London (left) burn during the Battle of Britain. Winston Churchill (above) spoke to the British people about never giving up.

to face, to have no means of defense, not to see the shadow of a French or Allied plane during the hours of bombing, this was one of the prime reasons for the loss of our faith in victory."

Although France had fallen, some French people kept up their fight. Many went to Africa or to Britain, where they set up a free French government. Within three months, much of western Europe had fallen to Hitler's forces. Events were happening so fast that one American warned that "before the snow flies again we may stand alone and isolated, the last great democracy on earth."

After the fall of France, Britain continued to fight, even though it was nearly alone. In August 1940 Germany took to the air to conquer Britain. For the next few months, wave after wave of German planes crossed the narrow

English Channel to bomb Britain. London alone saw German bombers in the air for 57 nights in a row! In fact, at times more than 1,000 German bombers filled the skies above Britain. This long air war became known as the Battle of Britain.

The British would not give up. Night after night, pilots from Britain's Royal Air Force (RAF) tried to stop the German bombers. By the end of the Battle of Britain, RAF pilots had shot down almost two German planes for every plane the RAF lost. Later, British Prime Minister Winston Churchill would honor those pilots when he said, "Never in the field of human conflict was so much owed by so many to so few."

Just as British pilots would not give up, neither would the British people. Edward R. Murrow was an American reporter in London during the Battle of Britain.

Chapter 9 ■ 337

Read and Respond

Link History with Civics and Government
Tell students that Winston Churchill became Britain's prime minister just as Germany invaded France. Emphasize that Churchill was an inspiring leader and an influential figure in the war. Explain that he decided not to send fighter planes to help France defeat Germany. Churchill believed that Britain's planes could not save France, and Britain needed the planes for its own defense.

History
The fall of France gave Germany control of northern France and the Atlantic coast.

Q Why was France an important conquest for Germany?

A When France was conquered by Germany, it could no longer help protect Britain. France also offered the shortest route for German bombers to reach Britain.

History
Point out that Germany conquered much of Europe through coordinated land and air attacks. Discuss why Hitler's first objective in the Battle of Britain was to neutralize the British air force. Hitler did not want British planes to bomb his forces on the European mainland.

MENTAL MAPPING

Germany's Neighbors Point out that Germany lies roughly in the center of Europe. Explain that Germany took advantage of its geographical position to conquer other countries. Have students arrange the following countries in relation to Germany without looking at a map of Europe.

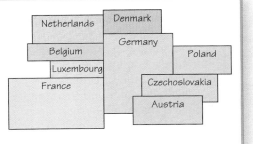

BACKGROUND

German Panzer Units German war strategy relied heavily on six panzer units made up of tanks and armored cars. The most powerful panzer tanks carried five soldiers, had three guns, weighed more than 17 tons, and reached speeds of 18 mph (29 kph). Panzer units were used throughout World War II. In the first week alone, panzers conquered 273 miles (about 439 km) of territory.

Analyze Primary Sources

Quotation Tell students that Edward R. Murrow did on-the-scene radio reporting from London during World War II. Ask for a volunteer to read aloud the quotation by Edward R. Murrow on page 338. Discuss with students what his opinion of the citizens of Britain was. He believed that British citizens were brave and committed to the fight.

War Breaks Out in Asia

Read and Respond

Geography Ask students to locate Vietnam, Laos, and Cambodia on a world map. Remind students that at the time of World War II, this region in southeastern Asia was called French Indochina.

Q Why did Japan want to invade French-controlled Indochina?

A Control over this region also gave Japan control over important resources found there.

3 Close

Summarize Key Content

- Germany, Italy, Spain, the Soviet Union, and Japan became dictatorships during the 1930s.
- Japan began invading China in 1931 in its quest to form a Japanese empire in eastern Asia.
- After Germany took over Austria, Britain, France, Italy, and Germany signed the Munich Agreement in exchange for peace. However, Germany broke the treaty and invaded the rest of Czechoslovakia and Poland, Denmark, Norway, Luxembourg, the Netherlands, Belgium, and France.
- Japan conquered Indochina, hoping to cut off supplies to China.

He explained how the British acted when faced with Germany's air war:

THIS SUBWAY IS NOT SAFE AS A SHELTER

Nearest air raid shelter

❝ The politicians who called this a 'people's war' were right. . . . I've seen some horrible sights in this city during these days and nights, but not once have I heard man, woman, or child suggest that Britain should throw in her hand [give up]. ❞

REVIEW **What action by Germany started World War II?** the invasion of Poland

War Breaks Out in Asia

Across the Pacific Ocean from the United States, another war was raging. Japan had continued its conquests in Asia. After Germany conquered France, Japan got Germany to agree to let the Japanese take over French Indochina. This East Asian region is in the southeastern corner of the Asian continent, on the edge of the South China Sea. It includes the present-day countries of Vietnam, Cambodia, and Laos. With control of this region, Japan

People of London spend the night in the basement of a large store during a German air raid. The sign (above) guided the city's people to safety.

338

BACKGROUND

The German and British Air War The fight between German bombers and the British Royal Air Force (RAF) during the 1940s is called the Battle of Britain. The RAF successfully defended the country against a massive German air assault. Winston Churchill, Britain's prime minister during the war, said, "Never in the field of human conflict was so much owed by so many to so few." Churchill meant that the relatively small group of pilots helped all British people by protecting the country.

EXTEND AND ENRICH

Simulation Organize students into four groups, representing France, Germany, Italy, and Britain. Tell them that Germany has just broken the Munich Agreement and invaded Czechoslovakia. Ask them to imagine that France and Germany have called a meeting to create a new treaty. Give each country time to decide what the terms of the new treaty should be. After the treaty has been negotiated, lead a discussion about the difficulties each group encountered.

Japanese tanks cross the Xinjiang (SHIN•JYAHNG) River in China in 1941. These special tanks traveled through water as well as on land.

could stop trains from taking needed supplies to China. The war between Japan and China went on as Japanese forces kept taking more of China's land.

For many years France had been in control of Indochina. However, at the time of the Japanese invasion, French forces there numbered only about 13,000 soldiers. This was too few to fight off the larger Japanese army.

REVIEW **How did the fall of France help Japan?** France could not hold on to French Indochina, so Japan took over the region.

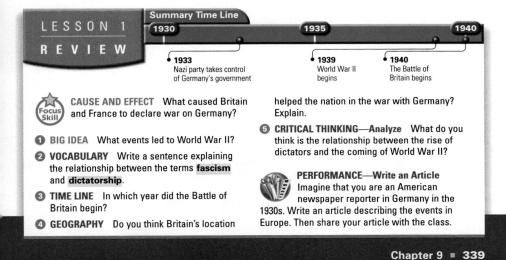

LESSON 1 REVIEW

Summary Time Line

1930 — 1935 — 1940

• 1933 Nazi party takes control of Germany's government

• 1939 World War II begins

• 1940 The Battle of Britain begins

CAUSE AND EFFECT What caused Britain and France to declare war on Germany?

❶ **BIG IDEA** What events led to World War II?

❷ **VOCABULARY** Write a sentence explaining the relationship between the terms **fascism** and **dictatorship**.

❸ **TIME LINE** In which year did the Battle of Britain begin?

❹ **GEOGRAPHY** Do you think Britain's location helped the nation in the war with Germany? Explain.

❺ **CRITICAL THINKING—Analyze** What do you think is the relationship between the rise of dictators and the coming of World War II?

PERFORMANCE—Write an Article Imagine that you are an American newspaper reporter in Germany in the 1930s. Write an article describing the events in Europe. Then share your article with the class.

Chapter 9 ■ 339

RETEACH THE LESSON

Graphic Organizer Have students complete a graphic organizer like the one below for each section of the lesson. They should write the main idea of each section in the center and supporting details on the sides.

The Rise of Dictators

Assess

Lesson 1 Review—Answers

 CAUSE AND EFFECT Both Britain and France were allies of Poland. When Hitler attacked Poland, Britain and France declared war on Germany.

❶ **BIG IDEA** Germany broke the Munich Agreement and later invaded Poland; Japan invaded Indochina.

❷ **VOCABULARY** **Fascism** is a political idea in which power is given to a dictator, and a dictator is the head of a **dictatorship**.

❸ **TIME LINE** 1940

❹ **GEOGRAPHY** Possible answer: Yes; because Britain was separated from the rest of Europe by the English Channel, Germany could only attack Britain by air.

❺ **CRITICAL THINKING—Analyze** Possible response: Dictators such as Hitler, Mussolini, and Tojo were determined to rebuild their countries' economies, even at the cost of going to war.

 Performance Assessment Guidelines Students' articles should describe the rise of dictators in Europe and the inability of France and Britain to negotiate a lasting peace.

ACTIVITY BOOK

Use ACTIVITY BOOK, pp. 84–85, to reinforce and extend student learning.

Lesson 2

OBJECTIVES

- Examine the efforts of the United States to remain neutral in World War II.
- Identify events that caused the United States to enter World War II.
- Identify ways in which the United States prepared for World War II.
- Describe how the United States' entrance into World War II affected Americans.

 Cause and Effect pp. 331, 340, 345, 346, 358

Vocabulary

SEE READING AND VOCABULARY TRANSPARENCY 5-3 OR THE WORD CARDS ON PP. V43–V44.

civilian p. 344

 When Minutes Count

Have students read about the attack on Pearl Harbor on pages 341 to 345. Then invite them to tell in their own words what happened.

Quick Summary

This lesson summarizes how the United States became involved in World War II.

 Motivate

Set the Purpose

Big Idea Ask students to think about events that might compel a country to go to war.

Access Prior Knowledge

Discuss with students what they know about why the United States entered World War II.

The United States Enters the War

 CAUSE AND EFFECT

As you read, look for causes and effects of Roosevelt's decision to enter World War II.

BIG IDEA
In 1941 world events forced the United States into World War II.

VOCABULARY
civilian

1930   1940   1950

1940–1942

The United States had planned to stay out of World War II. In fact, as late as October 1940, President Roosevelt told the American people, "I have said this before, but I shall say it again and again and again: Your boys are not going to be sent into any foreign wars." Soon, however, the actions of other countries would make it impossible for the United States to stay neutral, or take no sides, in the conflicts.

The United States Takes Action

Many Americans believed in a policy of isolation, or remaining separate from other countries. It soon became clear that even if the United States was neutral, its people were not. As the nation tried to stay out of the war, Americans began to take sides. Many of them sided with Britain.

President Roosevelt hoped for peace. Yet he knew the country should get ready for war, in case the United States was attacked. In his 1940 budget he asked for almost $2 billion for national defense. Five months later he asked for another $1 billion. Roosevelt also got the country ready for war by calling for the nation's first peacetime draft. He wanted to make sure there were enough American soldiers.

Through the Lend-Lease Act, Roosevelt helped Britain get war supplies without spending its limited amount of cash.

340

REACH ALL LEARNERS

English as a Second Language Instruct students who are acquiring English to add the lesson vocabulary to their vocabulary notebooks. Point out that they may encounter other unfamiliar terms in the lesson. Ask them to record these terms in their notebooks as well. Have students define the terms that they have recorded and write each one in a descriptive sentence that will help them remember the meaning.

STUDY/RESEARCH SKILLS

Using Reference Sources Emphasize to students that a good place to find additional information about Pearl Harbor and World War II is in reference sources, such as almanacs and encyclopedias. Remind students that information in encyclopedias is listed in alphabetical order. Encourage students to use reference sources throughout the lesson to find more information about events or people that interest them.

The Lend-Lease Act provided this tank (left) to Britain. It also helped other countries get supplies such as the American warships (above) given to the Cuban navy in 1943 to protect the Caribbean from German submarines.

President Roosevelt also looked for ways in which the United States could help Britain but stay out of the war. In September 1940 he announced the Destroyer-Bases Agreement. In this agreement the United States gave about 50 American warships to Britain in exchange for the right to use 8 British naval bases in Bermuda and the Caribbean. Then in March 1941 Roosevelt approved the Lend-Lease Act. This law allowed the United States to lend or rent supplies to warring countries whose defense was important to the United States. Soon the much-needed supplies of food and weapons were being sent to Britain.

REVIEW **What was the purpose of the Lend-Lease Act?** It provided a way for the United States to give aid to Britain during World War II.

Pearl Harbor

All during the 1930s, relations between Japan and the United States grew worse. The United States protested when Japan took over Manchuria. It protested again when Japan kept on fighting for more of China's land. Then, when Japan invaded Indochina, the United States decided to take action. Indochina is close to the Philippine Islands, which belonged to the United States at that time. Many American leaders feared that Japan would soon try to take over the Philippines and other places in the Pacific.

The United States government answered Japan's invasion of Indochina by placing a ban on resources, such as oil, that the United States exported to Japan.

Chapter 9 ■ 341

2 Teach

The United States Takes Action

Read and Respond

Culture and Society Remind students that Congress did not pass a Selective Service Act in World War I until after President Woodrow Wilson had asked for an official declaration of war. Ask students to speculate why President Roosevelt believed it was necessary to create a peacetime draft. Point out that American foreign policy evolved from neutrality to direct involvement as conflicts in Europe and Asia grew.

Pearl Harbor

Read and Respond

Link History and Geography Ask students to locate the Philippines, Manchuria, and French Indochina on the map on page 335.

Q How did Japan's policy of expansion threaten the United States' interests in the Pacific Ocean?

A The Philippine Islands, which are close to Japan, were a United States possession.

Read and Respond

Economics Explain to students that countries often employ economic sanctions to persuade other countries to change their policies. Point out that the oil ban imposed on Japan by the United States government was an economic sanction.

Q **What did the United States hope would happen when it banned trade with Japan?**

A It hoped Japan would stop trying to expand its empire.

Visual Learning

Map and Picture Direct students' attention to the map and photograph on page 342. Tell students that this photograph was taken by a Japanese pilot during the attack on Pearl Harbor. Have students use the map to locate the island of Oahu, and then Pearl Harbor, northwest of Honolulu. Then discuss with students why Pearl Harbor was an ideal port for many of the ships of the Pacific Fleet. Reinforce that both Japan and the Hawaiian Islands are in the Pacific Ocean.

Q **Why might Japan have wanted to destroy American warships and planes stationed in Hawaii?**

A Japanese leaders wanted to cripple United States military strength in the Pacific because they realized the United States Navy could block Japan's plans to control East Asia.
CAPTION ANSWER: Possible response: The distance was too great, and the planes would have run out of fuel.

 Students may enjoy learning more about other historic sites associated with World War II. Have them visit The Learning Site at **www.harcourtschool.com.**

Japan depended on the United States for more than half of its oil. The United States government hoped that cutting off part of Japan's oil supply would stop the Japanese from invading more countries. However, that did not stop them.

Pearl Harbor is a large natural harbor on the Hawaiian island of Oahu (oh•WAH•hoo). Its size and location made it a perfect home harbor for many of the ships in the United States Pacific Fleet. In December 1941 about 130 of those ships were at Pearl Harbor.

Many Americans believed the Pacific Fleet was so strong that no other country would attack it. However, the Japanese wanted to make sure the United States would not try to stop them from forming a huge empire.

In November 1941 a fleet of Japanese ships and aircraft carriers, or ships from which aircraft can take off and land,

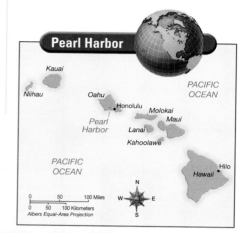

 Location Pearl Harbor is about 4,000 miles (6,400 km) from Japan. The planes that attacked the United States ships there (below) came most of the way on aircraft carriers.

◈ Why do you think the planes did not fly all the way from Japan to Pearl Harbor?

342

BACKGROUND

Pearl Harbor To make Pearl Harbor accessible to large naval vessels, the United States had to dig a channel at the mouth of the harbor. Workers started construction of a wide channel across the sandbar and coral reef at the mouth of the harbor in 1898 and finished it in 1911. The deepest point of the harbor is 60 feet (about 18 m).

READING SOCIAL STUDIES

Create Mental Images
Encourage students to close their eyes and imagine what is happening as you read aloud about the attack on Pearl Harbor. After students have heard the section, discuss with them the kinds of pictures they formed in their minds. Ask for volunteers to describe the images that they created. Discuss with students what they think the American soldiers were thinking as the attack was taking place.

The battleships USS *West Virginia* and USS *Tennessee* burn after the attack on Pearl Harbor. Both were later repaired.

arrived about 230 miles (370 km) north of Oahu. They had kept strict radio silence so no one would know they were there. On December 2 they received the order to attack the United States Pacific Fleet in five days.

On the morning of December 7, 1941, the calm at Pearl Harbor was shattered when Japanese forces attacked the Pacific Fleet. Hundreds of planes armed with thousands of pounds of bombs took off from the Japanese aircraft carriers. Some Japanese also attacked from the sea in small, two-person submarines. Together they attacked the ships and planes of the Pacific Fleet.

A few minutes after the first Japanese planes had dropped their first bombs, one hit the USS *Arizona*. The *Arizona* seemed to buck into the air as the bomb exploded hundreds of tons of gunpowder stored in the front of the battleship. It took less than nine minutes for the *Arizona* to sink into the harbor. Almost all its crew—more than 1,100 sailors—went down with the ship. Another 400 sailors were lost when the USS *Oklahoma* was hit by Japanese torpedoes, causing it to turn over in the water. During the raid, the USS *California* and the USS *West Virginia* also sank. Other ships, like the *Maryland*, the *Pennsylvania*, and the *Tennessee*, were badly damaged.

Chapter 9 ■ 343

Read and Respond

History Ask students why the main targets at Pearl Harbor were the Pacific Fleet's battleships. Point out that by destroying battleships, the Japanese thought they were destroying the part of the fleet that could do them the most harm.

Q How might the attack on Pearl Harbor have turned out if Japan had not surprised the United States forces at Pearl Harbor?

A The United States would have had time to prepare if it had known Japan was planning to attack. The loss of life and damage to ships might not have been as great.

Explain that today a memorial marks the spot where the USS *Arizona* sank.

Students may enjoy learning more about monuments and memorials. Have them visit The Learning Site at **www.harcourtschool.com.**

BACKGROUND

USS *Arizona* Memorial A memorial to the men who died on the USS *Arizona* was established in Honolulu in 1962. The floating white memorial sits over the sunken *Arizona*. The hull of the ship is visible from the memorial, lying 8 feet (2.4 m) below the surface. A marble wall within the memorial is engraved with the names of the men who died. More than 1,000 crewmembers remain buried at sea.

MAKE IT RELEVANT

In Your Community Ask students to find out how their community was affected by the attack on Pearl Harbor and World War II. Encourage them to start by talking to friends or family members old enough to remember the war. Suggest that they also look in the library for old newspaper articles from their community about the war. Ask students to share what they learned in informal presentations.

Analyze Primary Sources

Quotation Request that a volunteer read aloud the quotation by Jack Kelley on page 344. Discuss with students how the attack on Pearl Harbor probably changed many Americans' sense of security.

Read and Respond

Culture and Society Explain that the attack on the United States Pacific Fleet temporarily prevented the Navy from blocking Japanese aggression in the Pacific.

Q How do you think Americans reacted to the Japanese attack on Pearl Harbor?

A They were angry and their opposition to Roosevelt's policies about war preparations ended.

Civics and Government Inform students that only the United States Congress can formally declare war. Explain that most often the President asks Congress to declare war, as Roosevelt did in World War II. The Senate and the House of Representatives must both vote in favor of declaring war. After war has officially been declared, the President, as commander in chief, has broad powers to command the United States military forces.

History Tell students that almost a year before the attack on Pearl Harbor, President Roosevelt had met with Britain's prime minister Winston Churchill to discuss the war. They agreed that if the United States entered the war on the side of the Allies, they would try to defeat Germany before fighting Japan. This policy was known as Europe First.

Analyze Primary Sources

Quotation Direct students' attention to the quotation on page 345. Tell students that this is an excerpt from President Roosevelt's famous Day of Infamy speech, in which he asked Congress to declare war on the Empire of Japan. Ask students to think about the effect his words had on the American people.

Two Navy servicemen watch flames and smoke rise from Hickam Airfield during the attack on Pearl Harbor. Admiral Chester W. Nimitz pins the Navy Cross on Doris "Dorie" Miller (right) to honor him for his great courage during the attack.

Jack Kelley was a seaman aboard the USS *Tennessee*. He was below deck when the attack started. He said,

> 66 When I came topside . . . the *West Virginia* was settling on the bottom beside us, and I looked behind, and the *Arizona* was just one big ball of fire, and up ahead to the left the *Oklahoma* had turned upside down with the screws sticking up in the air. It made me wonder where we ever got the idea that we were so secure. 99

Some American sailors were able to fight back. Seaman Doris "Dorie" Miller was an African American cook on board the USS *West Virginia*. When the ship's commanding officer was wounded, Miller dragged him out of the line of fire.

Then Miller manned a machine gun and shot down four Japanese planes.

The Japanese attack lasted less than two hours. During the attack 19 warships were sunk or damaged in the harbor. About 150 planes were destroyed at nearby Hickam Airfield. More than 2,000 sailors and soldiers and 68 civilians were killed. A **civilian** is a person who is not in the military. As terrible as the losses were, they could have been even worse. The Japanese bomber planes did not hit the valuable oil supplies nearby. Also, the Pacific Fleet's three aircraft carriers were out of port on training exercises and escaped the attack.

The United States was shocked by the Japanese surprise attack on Pearl Harbor. President Roosevelt made a speech before Congress the next day to ask the members to declare war on Japan. He said,

344 ▪ Unit 5

"Yesterday, December 7, 1941—a date which will live in infamy—the United States of America was suddenly and deliberately attacked by naval and air forces of the Empire of Japan. . . . I ask that the Congress declare that since the . . . attack by Japan . . . a state of war has existed between the United States and the Japanese Empire."

Three days later, Germany and Italy declared war on the United States, and Congress declared a state of war with them, too. Germany, Italy, and Japan were known as the Axis Powers. The United States joined with the Allies, which included Britain, France, and the Soviet Union. The Soviet Union had once sided with Germany. However, Adolf Hitler had ordered Joseph Stalin to stay out of affairs in Europe. When Stalin did not agree, Germany invaded the Soviet Union in the summer of 1941.

REVIEW What event led the United States to enter the war? CAUSE AND EFFECT
the Japanese attack on Pearl Harbor

The United States Prepares for War

One of the biggest mistakes that the Japanese made while trying to take over lands and form an empire was to attack the United States. The surprise attack united most of the American people, even some who had been strongly against joining the war.

Thousands of men lined up to enlist, and thousands of others answered the draft's call. By 1942 more than 3 million American men had been drafted. Military camps and bases were soon built across the country to train pilots and soldiers.

DEMOCRATIC VALUES
The Common Good

The Japanese attack on Pearl Harbor brought together millions of Americans. They decided to put aside any differences they may have had and work together for the good of the country. This pulling together made it possible for the United States to supply the Allies with food, guns, bombs, tanks, medical equipment, and the other supplies that they needed in their fight against the Axis Powers.

Like Americans of the 1940s, Americans today often put aside their differences for the good of their community, their state, or their nation. Working together for the common good can help citizens overcome their differences.

Analyze the Value

❶ Why was it important for Americans to work together during World War II?

❷ **Make It Relevant** Ask your teacher or principal to name one change that would help your school be a better place. Then draw a poster that will encourage all the students to work for this common goal.

This United States flag was rescued from the sunken USS *California*.

Chapter 9 ■ 345

BACKGROUND

The Axis Treaties between Italy, Germany, and Japan prior to and during World War II created what was called the Rome-Berlin-Tokyo Axis. For this reason the collective term *Axis* came to refer to these three countries.

INTEGRATE LITERATURE

Read Biographies Direct students to work with their librarian to find biographies of World War II heroes. Ask students to read the biographies and then write short summaries about the war heroes and what they did in the war. Encourage them to share what they have learned with the class.

The United States Prepares for War

Read and Respond

Culture and Society Point out that although no battles took place in the continental United States, many people were directly affected by the United States' entrance into World War II.

Q **How did the United States' entrance into World War II directly affect the lives of Americans?**

A Families lost loved ones in the attack on Pearl Harbor, and many men were drafted into the military.

DEMOCRATIC VALUES
The Common Good

Have students consider why it would be important for people to work together during times of war.

Analyze the Value—Answers

❶ The cooperation of people in the United States allowed the country to provide the necessary soldiers and supplies for the war effort.

❷ Possible responses: more computers, more books and resources, more classrooms, more teachers

3 Close

Summarize Key Content

- President Roosevelt began preparing for war by requesting money for national defense and asking Congress to enact a peacetime draft.
- On December 7, 1941, the Japanese attacked the United States' Pacific Fleet in a surprise attack on Pearl Harbor, which led to the official entrance of the United States into World War II.
- More than 15 million Americans served in the armed forces during World War II.

READING SOCIAL STUDIES

Study Questions Have students answer the study questions.

1. He asked for billions of dollars for national defense and called for a peacetime draft.

2. the attack on Pearl Harbor

● USE READING AND VOCABULARY TRANSPARENCY 5-3.

5-3
TRANSPARENCY

Assess

Lesson 2 Review—Answers

Focus Skill

CAUSE AND EFFECT Japan's attack on Pearl Harbor

❶ **BIG IDEA** Poor relations between the countries led Japan to attack Pearl Harbor.

❷ **VOCABULARY** A **civilian** is a person who is not in the military.

❸ **TIME LINE** in 1941

❹ **GEOGRAPHY** Japanese forces in Indochina were very close to the Philippines, which was a United States possession.

❺ **CRITICAL THINKING—Evaluate**
Possible response: The men who were at Pearl Harbor grew up quickly because of the tragedies they witnessed and the new responsibilities they faced.

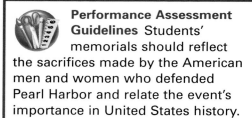
Performance Assessment Guidelines Students' memorials should reflect the sacrifices made by the American men and women who defended Pearl Harbor and relate the event's importance in United States history.

ACTIVITY BOOK

Use ACTIVITY BOOK, pp. 86–87, to reinforce and extend student learning.

After recruits were sworn in (left), their training began. In Miami, Florida, troops (above) exercise while wearing gas masks.

Some of the camps and bases did not have enough housing for all the troops, so hotels were used. In other camps, soldiers slept in tents.

During World War II, more than 15 million Americans—including about 338,000 women—served in the armed forces. Many women in the armed forces made maps, drove ambulances, and worked as mechanics, clerks, and nurses.

REVIEW Where were soldiers trained?
at training camps and military bases

LESSON 2 REVIEW

Summary Time Line

1940 — 1941 — 1942

1940 President Roosevelt announces the Destroyer-Bases Agreement

1941 Japan attacks Pearl Harbor and the United States enters World War II

1942 More than 3 million American men are drafted into military service

Focus Skill

CAUSE AND EFFECT What caused many Americans to change their minds about becoming involved in the war?

❶ **BIG IDEA** How did poor relations with the Japanese lead the United States into the war?

❷ **VOCABULARY** What is a **civilian**?

❸ **TIME LINE** When was Pearl Harbor attacked?

❹ **GEOGRAPHY** Why was Japan's attack on Indochina upsetting to the United States?

❺ **CRITICAL THINKING—Evaluate** One sailor who was there during the Pearl Harbor attack said, "I finished growing up on that day and learned that life was more than just a good-time roller coaster." What do you think he meant by that?

PERFORMANCE—Write a Memorial
Write a memorial paragraph honoring the American men and women who defended Pearl Harbor during the attack. In your memorial, also discuss the importance of the event in United States history.

EXTEND AND ENRICH

Write a News Story Have students write news stories about the attack on Pearl Harbor. Ask them to imagine that the stories will be published in a newspaper the day after the attack. Remind students to use information from the lesson and to create headlines for their articles.

RETEACH THE LESSON

Graphic Organizer Ask students to create flow charts similar to the one below, recounting how the United States became involved in World War II.

Peacetime draft is enacted.

↓

Lend-Lease aid to Britain begins.

↓

Japan attacks Pearl Harbor.

↓

United States enters World War II.

Life at Home

1930   1940   1950

1941–1945

Supplying war materials to the Allies had already helped the United States get ready for war. After the bombing at Pearl Harbor, however, the United States suddenly had to come up with even more airplanes, tanks, and other war supplies. This work provided jobs for many more Americans. The Great Depression was over.

Wartime Industries

Now that the United States had joined in the war, it found it had to help supply the Allied forces with food, weapons, and everything else they needed. This meant supplying goods to millions of people. To make sure the country could supply all these things, the government took control of many businesses and stopped the production of many consumer goods. Instead, manufacturers were asked to make weapons and other war materials.

Workers built ships in many coastal cities. This shipyard was in Tampa, Florida.

347

· LESSON ·

3

CAUSE AND EFFECT

As you read, look for causes and effects of the fighting in Europe.

BIG IDEA

American soldiers relied on the people at home to produce the supplies and weapons they needed.

VOCABULARY

rationing
recycling
relocation camp

Lesson 3
PAGES 347–354

OBJECTIVES

- **Explain how United States factories mobilized for war.**
- **Discuss how World War II affected women in the United States.**
- **Explain how people in the United States supported the effort to win World War II.**
- **Describe and evaluate how World War II affected Japanese Americans.**

 Cause and Effect pp. 331, 347, 353, 354, 358

Vocabulary

SEE READING AND VOCABULARY TRANSPARENCY 5-4 OR THE WORD CARDS ON PP. V43–V44.

rationing p. 351   **relocation camp**
recycling p. 351   p. 353

 ## When Minutes Count

Have students skim the lesson to find the meanings of the lesson vocabulary words. Encourage them to tell how each word relates to the Big Idea.

Quick Summary

This lesson examines how World War II affected the lives of people in the United States.

1 Motivate

Set the Purpose

Big Idea Ask students to suggest ways in which people in the United States could have helped provide for the soldiers fighting overseas.

Access Prior Knowledge

Have students discuss how people in the United States reacted to World War I.

WORD WORK

Prefixes Remind students that the prefix *re-* means "to do something again." Ask students to determine the root word of the terms in the chart, and to write the definitions.

Vocabulary Term	Root Word	Definition
recycle	cycle	to use again
relocation	locate	to put in a new or different place

REACH ALL LEARNERS

Below-Level Learners Encourage below-level learners to make an outline for each subsection of the lesson. Point out that outlining can help them make sure they understand what they have read. Remind them that they need to include only the main points of each subsection in their outlines.

2 Teach

Wartime Industries

Read and Respond

Link Economics with Civics and Government Inform students that the United States government created agencies such as the Office of Production Management and the War Production Board to help mobilize its industrial resources.

Q What kinds of problems might the government have had if it had not created these new agencies?

A The government might not have been able to produce all the war supplies it needed, which would have meant that it might have been more difficult for the Allies to fight the war.

Read and Respond

Link Economics and History Discuss how World War II changed industry and the goods produced. Have students consider the differences between goods produced in the early 1920s and in the early 1940s.

• SCIENCE AND TECHNOLOGY •

Blood Storage

Charles Drew

Before World War II, scientists were unable to store supplies of blood for long periods of time. As a result, many injured people who had lost too much blood died. Charles Drew, an African American doctor, helped change this. Drew discovered that the plasma, or liquid portion of blood, could be separated from the red blood cells. The two could then be frozen and stored for a long time. When a person needed a transfusion, or transfer of blood, the two parts could be put together again to form human blood. During the war Drew helped begin the American Red Cross Blood Program. It saved the lives of thousands of wounded soldiers.

Government actions also helped the growth of new industries. Before the war the United States had depended on Asian countries for the rubber used in making tires. After Japan took control of many of those countries, the supply of rubber nearly stopped. This might have caused a major problem for the United States military, which needed huge amounts of rubber for tires on trucks and airplanes. However, new industries were soon developed that made synthetic, or human-made, rubber.

To make the goods needed during wartime, hundreds of thousands of new workers were needed. Across the country people went to work in factories, steel mills, shipyards, and aircraft plants.

Working around the clock, American workers were able to produce huge amounts of war materials at record speed. At the beginning of the war, President Roosevelt asked American industries to produce as many as 60,000 aircraft a year. Many people believed this was impossible, but in 1943 alone, American workers built almost 86,000 aircraft.

Analyze Graphs The production of aircraft went up sharply during the first years of the war.

❖ About how many aircraft were produced in 1944?

United States Aircraft Production, 1941–1945

Aircraft Produced / Year

Source: *World War II: America at War, 1941-1945*

REVIEW How did the government get businesses to produce enough war supplies? It took control of many businesses and stopped the production of many consumer goods.

348 ■ Unit 5

Women During the War

As they had in World War I, American women rushed to take the jobs left empty as men became soldiers. In fact, between 1941, when the United States joined the war, and 1945, when the war ended, the number of working women in the nation increased by nearly 3 million!

Many of the jobs taken by women had been held mostly by men before the war. For example, in 1941 women made up only about 1 percent of all workers in the aviation industry. Just two years later, in 1943, 65 percent of the workers in that industry were women. Women worked building planes, ships, and tanks for use by American and other Allied soldiers. At this time, more women also entered professional careers as lawyers, doctors, and chemists.

Rosina Bonavita was one of the millions of women assembling airplanes. She and a partner welded 3,345 rivets in place to put together one wing of a bomber— and they did it in just one workday!

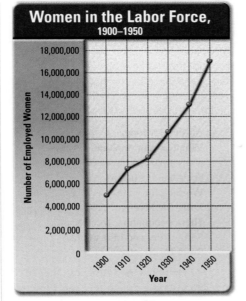

Source: Historical Statistics of the United States

Women in the Labor Force, 1900–1950

Analyze Graphs The graph shows how the number of women working outside the home grew between 1900 and 1950. The photograph below shows women building aircraft. At left men and women work on B-17F bombers.

◆ By 1950, about how many women had become part of the labor force?

Visual Learning

Line Graph Direct students' attention to the line graph on page 348.

Q How did President Roosevelt's asking American industries to produce 60,000 aircraft a year help the military?

A It provided the military with the aircraft it needed to win the war.

CAPTION ANSWER: about 98,000

Women During the War

Read and Respond

Culture and Society Point out that prior to World War II, most women performed jobs such as secretarial work and teaching. Lead students to realize that World War II enabled women to prove that they could do jobs traditionally reserved for men. In time, these women collectively came to be called "Rosie the Riveter."

Students might enjoy learning more about patriotic symbols, posters, and poetry and songs from the World War II era. Have them visit The Learning Site at **www.harcourtschool.com.**

Visual Learning

Line Graph Reinforce to students that factories depended on women workers during the war.

CAPTION ANSWER: about 17 million

Read and Respond

Link History with Culture and Society Inform students that many female factory workers during the war were young mothers. Tell students that in 1943 only 4,400 communities operated childcare centers for working mothers.

Q What might have been some of the problems young mothers faced in trying to care for their children and work at the same time?

A They probably faced the challenges of finding someone who was trustworthy and qualified to help care for their children, making time to spend with their children, and having enough money to pay the bills. The lack of childcare facilities was probably the most difficult challenge.

History Remind students that many women made important contributions to the armed forces. About 140,000 women enlisted in the Women's Army Corps. Another 100,000 women served in the United States Navy's women's auxiliary unit known as Women Accepted for Volunteer Emergency Service, or WAVES. About 1,000 female pilots served in the Air Force as well.

This feat helped earn Bonavita the nickname "Rosie the Riveter." In time, "Rosie the Riveter" came to stand for the millions of women who helped the United States produce 3 million machine guns, 89,000 tanks, and 300,000 planes during the war years. A song was even written about the nation's "Rosies." In part it said,

> 66 All the day long,
> Whether rain or shine,
> She's a part of the assembly line.
> She's making history,
> Working for victory,
> Rosie the Riveter. . . .
> There's something true about,
> Red, white, and blue about,
> Rosie the Riveter. 99

Other women joined American men in military service during the war. These women were not allowed to fight in battle. Instead, they carried out many important support tasks, which freed men for fighting. For example, pilot Jacqueline Cochran persuaded the government to start the WASPs, or Women's Air Force Service Pilots. These pilots flew military missions around the United States, which left male pilots free for war duties.

Some women worked in the Women's Army Corps, or WAC. They served their country at home and overseas in Europe. Beginning in 1942, the United States Navy recruited WAVES, or Women Accepted for Voluntary Emergency Service. Women also served as nurses. The American Red Cross sent nurses to help care for injured soldiers. Women who worked near the battlefields helped in camp hospitals where the men who had been wounded in battle were brought. In all, more than 60,000 American women served as nurses during the war.

REVIEW Whom did "Rosie the Riveter" come to stand for? the millions of women who helped produce machine guns, tanks, and planes during the war years

American women held many different jobs during the war. Some (below) worked as nurses overseas. Others (right) trained as pilots to fly military missions in the United States.

350 ▪ Unit 5

INTEGRATE READING

Read a Biography
Encourage students to read biographies of women leaders in the armed forces. Suggest women such as Oveta Culp Hobby, the highest-ranking officer of the Women's Army Corps, or Jacqueline Cochran, the head of the Women's Air Force Service Pilots. Ask volunteers to share what they learned about these women.

BACKGROUND

All-American Girls Professional Baseball League Philip K. Wrigley, the Chicago Cubs owner and chewing-gum tycoon, started the league in 1943, believing that baseball would lose men to the draft. Women were recruited from the United States, Canada, and Cuba to play for the four original teams, and were required to attend charm school, follow curfew, and be chaperoned while playing.

BACKGROUND

United Service Organizations (USO) The USO began in 1941 as a private nonprofit organization to provide entertainment for members of the United States military. By 1944 the USO had more than 3,000 clubs where soldiers and civilians could attend dances or watch movies. The USO also sent entertainers overseas to sing or dance at live shows for the troops.

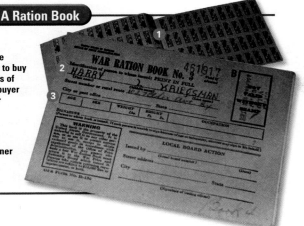

A Ration Book

Analyze Primary Sources

Ration books like the one shown here were used during World War II to enable people to buy rationed goods. Each family received books of coupons or stamps for certain goods. The buyer turned in the coupons as he or she paid for the goods.

❶ ration book stamps
❷ name of the ration book's owner
❸ traits that identify the ration book's owner
◆ How do you think rationing helped the United States during World War II?

The Home Front

World War II, like World War I, caused shortages of goods. To make sure there were enough goods for soldiers, new government rules in 1942 called for **rationing**, or limiting, what people could buy. For certain goods, people needed not only the money to buy them, but also government coupons. People could buy only the amount of butter, sugar, coffee, and meat that the coupons allowed. That way the government could control the amounts of these goods that were sold on the home front.

Among the most difficult things for Americans to get used to was the rationing of sugar and gasoline. The government limited the amount of gasoline people could buy by giving stamps to drivers. Most drivers were allowed to buy 3 gallons of gas a week. People who traveled in their line of work could get more. Other rationed items included fruits, vegetables, shoes, and tires.

People at home also helped by **recycling** items, or using them again.

In fact, recycling became a way of life during World War II. Recycled bacon grease and other fats, for example, were used in making bullets and tanning leather. Scrap iron from old lawn mowers, radiators, and shovels was used to make guns and grenades. Recycled paper was used to make cartons that were used to ship goods to soldiers overseas.

To help feed the thousands of people serving in the military, farmers planted more crops and raised more livestock.

Both coupons and money were needed to buy rationed goods.

351

The Home Front

Read and Respond

Economics Explain that rationing goods such as foodstuffs and gasoline allowed the federal government to be sure enough supplies were available to meet the military's needs. Automobile production was stopped in December 1941 to save steel, glass, and rubber. Soon production was halted on almost 300 items, including vacuums, radios, refrigerators, sewing machines, phonographs, coat hangers, and toothpaste tubes, that were not valuable to the war effort.

Analyze Primary Sources

A Ration Book Tell students that each family received a ration book with the stamps needed to purchase certain products. Each family had to combine their stamps to plan their meals. Sugar, butter, coffee, and beef were very limited.

CAPTION ANSWER: It helped the government make sure that supplies needed by the military would be available.

Read and Respond

Link History with Culture and Society Ask students to list ways that people in the United States were asked to make sacrifices during the war. rationing, recycling items, growing their own food Inform students that the Office of War Information coordinated artists and advertisers to make thousands of posters to inspire people to make these wartime sacrifices.

 Students may enjoy learning about posters that were used to inspire people in the United States during World War II. Have them visit The Learning Site at **www.harcourtschool.com.**

Read and Respond

Economics Point out that when wartime industrial production increased, income increased. When income rose, revenue from taxation also climbed because there was more income to tax. Those tax increases helped pay for about 30 percent of the war. Explain that people also bought war bonds to help finance the war effort.

Q **What did people in the United States buy to help pay for the war?**

A war bonds

Culture and Society Remind students that farmers had been struggling since before the Great Depression. Inform students that although World War II increased crop prices and demand, many farmers still could not eliminate their debt. Note that the war actually increased urban migration. More than 5 million rural residents moved to urban areas during World War II.

Analyze Primary Sources

Quotation Ask a volunteer to read aloud the quotation on page 352. Explain that Messerschmitts, Stukas, Mitsubishis, and Zeros were airplanes from different Axis countries. Tell students that many cities in the United States—even many inland cities such as Detroit—had air raid sirens to warn residents of possible attacks during World War II.

FAST FACT United States pennies are usually made from a combination of copper and zinc. In 1943 the government needed to save copper, which was used in military supplies, for the war effort. That year, pennies were made out of steel instead of copper.

Children helped in the war effort by gathering paper to recycle.

This demand for food brought about good times for many farmers.

There were many other ways that Americans helped the war effort. For example, millions of volunteers helped protect the nation's borders by working for the Office of Civilian Defense. Most of the volunteers were adults, but some were children. For example, Neil Shine was 11 years old and living in Detroit, Michigan, when the United States entered the war. He remembers how he and other children he knew pitched in to help protect the United States: "We had to protect our shores from this 'enemy.' We learned the silhouettes [outlines] of all the airplanes, and we spent countless hours lying on our backs at the playground, looking skyward, watching for Messerschmitts and Stukas [German planes] and Mitsubishis and Zeros [Japanese planes]. But all we ever saw were the planes from the local air base.

If they [the Germans or Japanese] had ever tried to slip one airplane over Detroit airspace, . . . some kid in my neighborhood would have sounded the alarm."

Americans helped pay for the war by paying higher taxes and by buying war bonds. A war bond is a piece of paper showing that the buyer had loaned the government money to help pay the cost of the war. When people bought war bonds, they were letting the government use their money for a certain amount of time. After the time was up, people turned in their bonds and got their money back with interest. Interest is the money a bank or borrower pays to a lender for the use of money.

These $50 war bonds were bought in 1942.

352 ■ Unit 5

INTEGRATE SCIENCE

Milkweed During World War II, scientists discovered that milkweed floss was 5 to 6 times more buoyant than cork. It was warmer than wool and 6 times lighter. When a few pounds were used in life jackets, milkweed floss held up a 150-pound (68-kg) man in the water. Flying suits lined with milkweed floss were light and warm to wear and also acted as a life preserver. Volunteers collected, dried, and shipped milkweed pods to collection points around North America.

BACKGROUND

V-Mail Because World War II was fought overseas, cargo space was desperately needed to ship supplies to the war front. To conserve space, the military and the U.S. Post Office encouraged people to send V-mail, preprinted pages that, once written on and addressed, were reduced, transferred to microfilm, and shipped overseas. Upon delivery, the microfilm was developed and delivered. More than one billion pieces of V-mail were sent between June 1942 and April 1945.

BACKGROUND

Children on the Home Front Children helped support the war effort in many ways during World War II. They planted victory gardens, bought war bonds, and recycled metal, rubber, and paper. Youth organizations sponsored fundraisers and collections for books, musical instruments, and razors to send to the troops overseas as well as clothing for people in Europe.

Companies and state and local governments also bought war bonds. Even children bought them. For 25 cents, children could buy a war-bond stamp. Then they pasted it into a stamp book. When the stamp book was filled, the child could turn it in for a $25 bond. To help sell bonds, movie stars and other famous people appeared at rallies. The effort was a huge success, raising more than $180 billion.

All over the nation, World War II caused families to pull together. However, many families also suffered because of the war. After all, millions of American men were fighting in Europe and the Pacific. When the men went overseas, many women were left alone to take care of their families. Worse yet, some of those men never came home.

REVIEW How did Americans help pay for the war? 🖊 CAUSE AND EFFECT
by paying higher taxes and buying war bonds

Japanese Americans

The war caused changes in people's lives. It also led to terrible problems for Japanese Americans. At the time of the attack on Pearl Harbor, about 125,000 Japanese Americans lived in the United States. Most had been born here and were citizens. The attack on Pearl Harbor had shocked them too.

After Pearl Harbor, however, anger against Japanese Americans grew. Some United States military officials believed that Japanese Americans might even help Japan invade the United States.

In February 1942 President Roosevelt ordered the army to put about 110,000 Japanese Americans in relocation camps. **Relocation camps** were army-style settlements in which the Japanese Americans were forced to live. All Japanese Americans had to wear identification tags. They also had to sell their homes, businesses, and belongings.

A Japanese American business (right) closes before its owner goes to a relocation camp. Below, Japanese Americans wait to enter a camp near Los Angeles.

Japanese Americans

Read and Respond

Culture and Society Discuss with students the anger that people in the United States felt about the attack on Pearl Harbor. Emphasize that Japan was the only country to seriously attack the United States on its own soil.

History Explain that the United States government attempted to justify placing Japanese Americans in relocation camps by saying that Japanese Americans might help Japan invade the United States, even though most Japanese Americans had been born in the United States and were citizens. Tell students that any person of Japanese heritage could be sent to a relocation camp.

3 Close

Summarize Key Content

- The United States government took control of many factories to ensure that it could meet the needs of the Allied forces.
- Because so many men joined the military to fight in the war, many women worked in factories that produced supplies for the war.
- People on the home front participated in rationing programs, recycled items such as scrap metal, and purchased war bonds.
- The government required about 110,000 Japanese Americans to move to relocation camps during World War II.

STUDY/RESEARCH SKILLS

Using the Internet Emphasize to students that the Internet can be a useful tool for finding more information about World War II. As they read about the anger that Japanese Americans encountered during the war, have students choose topics that they would like to study further, such as what the relocation camps were like or how long people were held there. Then have them use search engines to find reliable Web pages about that topic.

BACKGROUND

Japanese Relocation Camps There were 16 temporary detention compounds and 10 permanent relocation camps. The temporary detention compounds were set up at racetracks and fairgrounds. Most permanent camps were located on federal lands, mostly in the West. Each camp held between 8,000 and 20,000 Japanese Americans.

K-W-L Chart Direct students to complete the L column of their K-W-L chart.

What I Know	What I Want to Know	What I Learned
Factories made supplies for soldiers fighting overseas.	How did the lives of Americans change during the war?	People served in the military. More women worked in factories.

● USE READING AND VOCABULARY TRANSPARENCY 5-4.

5-4 TRANSPARENCY

Assess

Lesson 3 Review—Answers

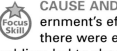

CAUSE AND EFFECT The government's efforts to make sure there were enough goods for soldiers led to shortages at home.

❶ **BIG IDEA** It took control of many businesses and rationed items.

❷ **VOCABULARY** **Rationing** limited what people at home could buy.

❸ **TIME LINE** in 1942

❹ **ECONOMICS** It stopped the production of many consumer goods and asked manufacturers to make weapons and other war materials instead.

❺ **CRITICAL THINKING—Analyze** Possible response: Although women did not serve in combat, the jobs they did at home were also very important.

Performance Assessment Guidelines Encourage students to explain on their posters why rationing is important to the war effort and why people should follow the rules.

ACTIVITY BOOK

Use ACTIVITY BOOK, p. 88, to reinforce and extend student learning.

Many of the soldiers in the 442nd Regimental Combat Team were Japanese Americans. They fought in Italy and Germany and received many service awards like the medal shown here.

Some of the camps were in California, Arizona, Wyoming, and Arkansas. "Our home was one room in a large . . . barracks, measuring 20 by 25 feet," remembers one woman. "The only furnishings were an iron pot-belly stove and cots."

While their families and friends were in the relocation camps, more than 17,000 Japanese Americans served in the armed forces. Most became members of the 442nd Regimental Combat Team, which fought in Italy and Germany. This unit received more service awards than any other unit its size in World War II.

REVIEW Why were many Japanese Americans sent to relocation camps? because some United States military officials believed that Japanese Americans might help Japan invade the United States

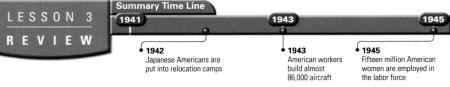

LESSON 3 REVIEW

Summary Time Line

1941	1943	1945

● **1942** Japanese Americans are put into relocation camps

● **1943** American workers build almost 86,000 aircraft

● **1945** Fifteen million American women are employed in the labor force

 CAUSE AND EFFECT What caused a shortage of goods for Americans?

❶ **BIG IDEA** What did the government do to make sure it had the food and supplies American soldiers needed?

❷ **VOCABULARY** Use the term **rationing** in a sentence about life at home during World War II.

❸ **TIME LINE** When were Japanese Americans placed in relocation camps?

❹ **ECONOMICS** In what ways did the United States government control businesses?

❺ **CRITICAL THINKING—Analyze** During World War II, the United States government called working women "soldiers without guns." What do you think the government meant by that?

 PERFORMANCE—Draw a Poster Imagine that it is 1942. Make a poster urging Americans to follow the rules for rationing any of the goods mentioned in this lesson. Display your poster in the classroom.

354 ■ Unit 5

EXTEND AND ENRICH

Research Have students use reliable Internet and reference sources to learn more about women who worked outside the home during World War II. Suggest that they find out how women's wages compared with men's and what happened to these women when the war was over.

RETEACH THE LESSON

Graphic Organizer Ask students to complete a cause-and-effect chart like the one below.

Causes	Effects
The Allies depended on the United States for food and supplies.	Goods were rationed and government took over factories.
Many jobs were left vacant.	Women began working in factories.
Many Americans were angry at the Japanese for attacking Pearl Harbor.	Japanese Americans were interned in relocation camps.

Make Economic Choices

VOCABULARY
trade-off
opportunity cost

▶ WHY IT MATTERS

When you buy something at a store, you are making an economic choice. Choosing between items to buy can be difficult. In order to buy something you want now, you must spend money that you cannot use to buy something in the future. This giving up of one thing in return for another is called a **trade-off**. What you give up is the **opportunity cost** of what you get. Understanding trade-offs and opportunity costs can help you make thoughtful economic choices.

▶ WHAT YOU NEED TO KNOW

You have read that in World War II, Americans supported the war effort by buying war bonds. The money helped the armed forces fight the war. Later, bond owners got their money back with interest.

▶ PRACTICE THE SKILL

Imagine that you are an American factory worker in 1944. At the end of every week you receive your paycheck. After paying your bills, you have some money left over. You might use it to buy something you want now, such as a

new sweater, or you might use it to buy a war bond.

❶ Think of the trade-offs. You could use the sweater, but you would not get any money back from this purchase. By buying war bonds, you are helping the war effort, but you would have to wait a while to earn interest on your bonds. What are the trade-offs of buying war bonds?

❷ Think of the opportunity costs. You don't have enough money to buy both, so you have to give up one. If you buy the sweater, you give up the chance to get back more than what you spent. What are the opportunity costs of buying war bonds?

▶ APPLY WHAT YOU LEARNED

Imagine that you want to buy a book and rent a movie, but you do not have enough money for both. Explain to a partner the trade-off and the opportunity costs of your choices.

Americans everywhere lined up to buy war bonds.

CITIZENSHIP SKILLS

Chapter 9 ■ 355

Skill Lesson
PAGE 355

OBJECTIVE

■ Explain the trade-offs and opportunity costs of economic decisions.

Vocabulary
trade-off p. 355
opportunity cost p. 355

WORD CARDS

See pp. V43–V44.

1 Motivate

Why It Matters

Understanding trade-offs and opportunity costs can help students make wise economic choices.

2 Teach

What You Need to Know

Explain that about $36 billion in war bonds were sold during World War II.

Practice the Skill—Answers

❶ You will not have money to buy a sweater.

❷ You will not get a new sweater.

3 Close

Apply What You Learned

Explanations should indicate an understanding of trade-offs and opportunity costs.

EXTEND AND ENRICH

Identify Economic Choices
Have small groups scan Chapter 9, looking for examples of economic choices. Have each group compile a list of both the trade-offs and the opportunity costs associated with each economic choice. Ask each group to have one person orally present the list to the class.

TRANSPARENCY

Use SKILL TRANSPARENCY 5-1.

RETEACH THE SKILL

Keep an Economic Journal
Ask students to keep journals of the economic choices they make for five days. For each decision, have students list possible trade-offs and opportunity costs.

ACTIVITY BOOK

Use ACTIVITY BOOK, p. 89, to give students additional practice using this skill.

Examine Primary Sources

PAGES 356–357

1 Motivate

Set the Purpose

Inform students that during World War II posters were used to rally public support for the war. Posters were placed in highly visible locations, such as schools, factories, offices, and store windows. Explain that posters appealed to citizens by telling them that they all could help the war effort in some way. Posters also featured various messages, such as explaining why the United States was involved in the war or exhorting civilians to give their time, money, and labor in support of the war effort.

Access Prior Knowledge

Ask students whether they have seen posters displayed in public areas. What might present-day posters encourage people to do?

2 Teach

Read and Respond

Have students study the posters on pages 356 and 357. Ask students to identify each poster's meaning and the response it wants to elicit from civilians. Posters encouraged women to join the workforce, civilians to buy war bonds, and everyone to participate in the war effort by growing, conserving, and saving.

EXAMINE PRIMARY SOURCES

War Posters

During World War II United States government agencies, businesses, and private organizations printed posters to support the war effort. Wartime posters were described as a visual call to arms—a way for making American war aims the personal goals of every citizen. Study the war posters on these pages, and identify the purpose of each one.

FROM THE SMITHSONIAN INSTITUTION, NATIONAL MUSEUM OF AMERICAN HISTORY, ONLINE EXHIBIT "PRODUCE FOR VICTORY"

Many posters encouraged all workers to participate in the war effort.

BACKGROUND

More About the Time Women were needed to fill many wartime labor shortages. Posters were used to encourage women to join defense industries, civilian service, and the Armed Forces. One popular poster image was of Rosie the Riveter. She was portrayed as a strong and competent woman, dressed in overalls with a bandanna around her head. Rosie became the symbol of patriotic women in the United States. Her slogan, "We Can Do It," inspired many women, especially those who had never before entered the workforce. Rosie and other images portrayed women as intelligent, confident, and resolved to do their part to help the war effort.

More About the Artifacts The posters addressed areas in which civilians could aid the war effort. The government along with corporations had some of the nation's top designers create posters. To oversee the content and imagery of war messages, the government created the U.S. Office of War Information.

Keep us flying!

BUY WAR BONDS

War bond posters asked citizens to share in the cost of the war. This poster shows one of the corps of fighter pilots trained at Tuskegee Institute in Alabama.

Some posters encouraged citizens to grow food or conserve resources.

GROW IT YOURSELF

PLANT A FARM GARDEN NOW

ACTIVITY

Make a Poster Imagine that you are working for the United States government during World War II. Design and make a poster of your choice. It should either encourage workers to help in the war effort or ask citizens to buy war bonds.

RESEARCH

Visit The Learning Site at **www.harcourtschool.com** to research other primary sources.

Analyze the Primary Source
Answers

1. Students should respond that the posters ask Americans to conserve rubber, participate in the war effort, buy war bonds, and plant gardens.

2. Students' responses will vary but may indicate that the "We Can Do It!" poster contains both a powerful message and imagery.

3. The posters presented simple but effective messages in a format that was easily accessible to many people in the United States.

3 Close

Activity

Make a Poster Encourage students to include artwork on their posters that relates to their topic and message. Check completed posters for historical accuracy.

Research

Students will find a variety of war posters at the Learning Site at **www.harcourtschool.com.**

Ask students to select one of the posters displayed at the site. Have them study the poster, and determine its message.

GO ONLINE   INTERNET RESOURCES

THE LEARNING SITE Go to **www.harcourtschool.com** for a DIRECTORY OF PRIMARY SOURCES.

EXTEND AND ENRICH

Civic Action Have students discuss messages today that the federal government might want to convey to citizens. Have them select one of the ideas and discuss ways to communicate that message to the public. Ask volunteers to share their ideas with the class.

RETEACH

Character Study Have students study the posters and describe any character qualities implied in them. Then ask students to express how these character qualities might have been beneficial to civilians in wartime efforts.

Chapter 9 Review
PAGES 358–359

 CAUSE AND EFFECT

Students may use the graphic organizer that appears on page 90 of the Activity Book. Answers appear in the Activity Book, Teacher's Edition.

Think & Write

Write a Diary Entry Student entries should reflect the shortages and rationing discussed in the chapter. Additional effects of the war will vary.

Write about a Career Students should use the Internet and other references to research women's roles during the war. Have volunteers share their completed reports with the class.

ACTIVITY BOOK

A copy of this graphic organizer appears in the ACTIVITY BOOK on page 90.

TRANSPARENCY

The graphic organizer appears on READING AND VOCABULARY TRANSPARENCY 5-5.

· CHAPTER ·

9 Review and Test Preparation

Summary Time Line
1930
• 1933
Nazi party takes control of Germany's government

Cause and Effect

Copy the following graphic organizer onto a separate sheet of paper. Use the information you have learned to show that you understand the causes and effects of some of the key events that started World War II.

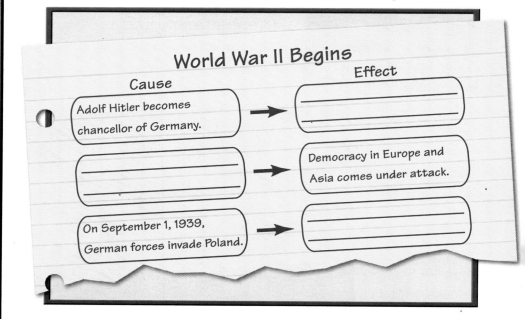

THINK & WRITE

Write a Diary Entry Imagine that you are living during World War II. Write a diary entry about going shopping with your family. Tell how the war has affected what you can buy. Also describe other ways the war has affected your family.

Write About a Career Reread the section in Lesson 3 called Women During the War. Choose a job that women began doing during World War II. Write a short report about that job. Tell what it is like to do that job today.

358 ■ Unit 5

TEST PREPARATION

Review these tips with students:

■ Read the directions before reading the questions.

■ Read each question twice, focusing the second time on all the possible answers.

■ Take the time to think about all the possible answers before deciding on an answer.

■ Move past questions that give you trouble, and answer the ones you know. Then return to the difficult items.

UNIT PROJECT

Progress Check Ask students to select six to eight significant events from the unit to include in their time lines. Suggest that students first sketch their key people or events before finalizing them on the time lines.

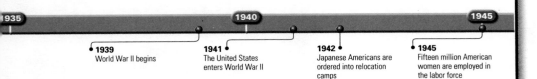

1939
World War II begins

1941
The United States enters World War II

1942
Japanese Americans are ordered into relocation camps

1945
Fifteen million American women are employed in the labor force

USE THE TIME LINE

Use the chapter summary time line to answer these questions.

1 Was the United States a nation at war in 1939?

2 In which year were there fifteen million working women in the United States?

USE VOCABULARY

Identify the term that correctly completes each sentence.

dictatorship (p. 333)

concentration camps (p. 333)

civilians (p. 344)

recycling (p. 351)

3 In a war, soldiers and _____ can be hurt or killed.

4 In a _____, the head of the government has total authority.

5 Hitler put people who did not agree with him into _____.

6 Many people helped by _____ items rather than throwing them away.

RECALL FACTS

Answer these questions.

7 Who was the dictator in Italy in the 1920s and 1930s?

8 What event brought the United States into World War II?

9 Why did American industries begin making synthetic rubber during World War II?

Write the letter of the best choice.

10 A political idea in which the power is given to a dictator is—
  A democracy.
  B capitalism.
  C fascism.
  D socialism.

11 The American government responded to Japan's invasion of Indochina by—
  F invading Japan.
  G placing a ban on resources that the United States exported to Japan.
  H sending the United States Pacific Fleet to the South China Sea.
  J issuing a written warning to Japan.

THINK CRITICALLY

12 Why do you think Japanese forces chose to attack the United States at Pearl Harbor rather than somewhere else?

13 Why did the Allies depend on the United States for supplies such as food and weapons?

APPLY SKILLS

Make Economic Choices
Read the following paragraph. Then use the information on page 355 to answer these questions.

Imagine you earn $6 for doing chores. You must choose between buying a new toy or putting the money into an interest-earning savings account.

14 What are the trade-offs of your choices?

15 What is the opportunity cost of each choice?

Chapter 9 ▪ 359

Think Critically

12 Most ships in the United States Pacific Fleet were stationed at Pearl Harbor.

13 Because the war was being fought in Europe and not in the United States, the United States was better equipped to produce and manufacture the needed goods and supplies.

Apply Skills

Make Economic Choices

14 You can use the $6 to buy the toy now, but you won't have the money in your savings account later.

15 If you buy the toy, your money will not earn interest. If you put the money into savings, you will not have the toy to play with.

ACTIVITY BOOK

Use the CHAPTER 9 TEST PREPARATION on page 91 of the Activity Book.

ASSESSMENT

Use the CHAPTER 9 TEST on pages 73–76 of the Assessment Program.

Use the Time Line

1 No; the United States entered World War II in 1941.

2 1945

Use Vocabulary

3 civilians

4 dictatorship

5 concentration camps

6 recycling

Recall Facts

7 Benito Mussolini (p. 333)

8 the Japanese attack on Pearl Harbor (pp. 344–345)

9 The supply of real rubber from other countries nearly stopped after Japan took control of those countries. (p. 348)

10 C (p. 333)

11 G (p. 341)

Chapter 10 Planning Guide The Allies Win the War

Introducing the Chapter, pp. 360–361

LESSON	PACING	OBJECTIVES	VOCABULARY
Introduce the Chapter pp. 360–361	1 Day	■ Apply critical-thinking skills to organize and use information. ■ Interpret excerpts from notable speeches. ■ Describe major events of World War II in the Pacific.	**Word Work:** Preview Vocabulary, p. 361
1 War in Africa and in Europe pp. 362–369	2 Days	■ Describe the importance of major military campaigns in North Africa and Italy. ■ Describe the D day invasion and other events that led to the Allies' victory in Europe. ■ Describe the Holocaust and the impact it had on Jews in Europe. ■ Explain how technological advances during World War II changed how wars were fought.	**front** **segregate** **D day** **Holocaust**
MAP AND GLOBE SKILLS **Compare Historical Maps** pp. 370–371	1 Day	■ Use geographic tools to collect, analyze, and interpret data. ■ Apply critical-thinking skills to organize and use information from maps.	**historical map**
2 War in the Pacific pp. 372–379	2 Days	■ Analyze difficulties the Allied forces encountered fighting against Japan in World War II. ■ Describe the events that led to the end of World War II.	**island hopping** **V-J Day**

READING	INTEGRATE LEARNING	REACH ALL LEARNERS	RESOURCES
Predict an Outcome, p. 361			
Reading Social Studies: **Anticipation Guide,** p. 363 Reading Social Studies: **Anticipation Guide Responses,** p. 369	Mathematics **Estimate,** p. 363 Language Arts **Write a News Report,** p. 364 Physical Education **Research Physical Fitness Training,** p. 365 Art **Interpret Photographs,** p. 366	**Advanced Learners,** p. 367 **Extend and Enrich,** p. 368 **Reteach the Lesson,** p. 369	**Activity Book,** pp. 92–93 **Reading and Vocabulary Transparency 5-6** Internet Resources
		Extend and Enrich, p. 371 **Reteach the Skill,** p. 371	**Activity Book,** pp. 94–95 **Skill Transparency 5-2A and 5-2B** **GeoSkills CD-ROM**
Reading Social Studies: **Study Questions,** p. 373 Reading Social Studies: **Study Questions Responses,** p. 379	Health **Malaria,** p. 375 Science **Atom Bombs,** p. 376 Reading **Read a Biography,** p. 376	**English as a Second Language,** p. 372 **Extend and Enrich,** p. 378 **Reteach the Lesson,** p. 379	**Activity Book,** p. 96 **Reading and Vocabulary Transparency 5-7** Internet Resources

Chapter 10 Planning Guide The Allies Win the War

LESSON	PACING	OBJECTIVES	VOCABULARY
CHART AND GRAPH SKILLS **Read Parallel Time Lines** pp. 380–381	**1 Day**	■ Use parallel time lines to compare events occurring at the same time in different places.	**parallel time lines**
3 Life After World War II pp. 382–387	**1 Day**	■ Describe some of the human costs of World War II. ■ Explain how the Servicemen's Readjustment Act helped World War II veterans adjust to civilian life in the United States. ■ Describe how society in the United States changed after World War II.	**refugees** **veteran** **baby boom**
4 A Changed World pp. 388–395	**2 Days**	■ Describe the purpose of the United Nations and the role of the United States in establishing it. ■ Explain how the United States accepted its role as a world superpower and helped to rebuild Europe and Japan after World War II. ■ Identify the role of the United States in world events during the Cold War. ■ Analyze the Truman Doctrine and Marshall Plan and their effects.	**superpower** **arms race** **free world** **cold war** **Word Work:** Historical Context, p. 388
Chapter Review and Test Preparation pp. 396–397	**1 Day**		

READING	INTEGRATE LEARNING	REACH ALL LEARNERS	RESOURCES
	Art **Illustrate Time Lines,** p. 380	**Extend and Enrich,** p. 381 **Reteach the Skill,** p. 381	**Activity Book,** p. 97 **Skill Transparency 5-3**
Reading Social Studies: **Personal Response,** p. 383 Reading Social Studies: **Graphic Organizer,** p. 383 Reading Social Studies: **Personal Response,** p. 387	**Mathematics** **Multiply,** p. 385 **Language Arts** **Write a Persuasive Letter,** p. 386 **Art** **Find Architectural Designs,** p. 386	**Below-Level Learners,** p. 384 **Extend and Enrich,** p. 387 **Reteach the Lesson,** p. 387	**Activity Book,** p. 98 **Reading and Vocabulary Transparency 5-8** **Internet Resources**
Reading Social Studies: **K-W-L Chart,** p. 389 Reading Social Studies: **K-W-L Chart Responses,** p. 395	**Science** **Hydrogen Bomb,** p. 391 **Mathematics** **Compute,** p. 392	**Auditory Learners,** p. 392 **Extend and Enrich,** p. 395 **Reteach the Lesson,** p. 395	**Activity Book,** p. 99 **Reading and Vocabulary Transparency 5-9** **Internet Resources**
		Test Preparation, p. 396	**Activity Book,** pp. 100–101 **Reading and Vocabulary Transparency 5-10** **Assessment Program, Chapter 10 Test,** pp. 77–80

Activity Book

LESSON 1

LESSON 1

Name _____ Date _____

War in Africa and in Europe

Directions Use the information below to complete the cause-and-effect chart.

Germany surrendered after Hitler's death.

German troops were sent to defend Italy after Mussolini's arrest.

American and British troops defeated the Axis forces in North Africa.

The Allies won a victory in Europe, and the war turned in their favor.

CAUSE	→	EFFECT

CAUSE	EFFECT
German troops were sent to defend Italy after Mussolini's arrest.	The Allied forces continued to fight in Italy.
Allied ships and planes along the Normandy coastline fought against German troops for an entire day.	The Allies won a victory in Europe, and the war turned in their favor.
American and British troops defeated the Axis forces in North Africa.	The Allies gained control of the Mediterranean Sea.
The Allies closed in on Berlin, and the Axis empire was defeated.	Germany surrendered after Hitler's death.

(continued)

© Harcourt

92 ■ Activity Book   Use after reading Chapter 10, Lesson 1, pages 362–369.

Name _____ Date _____

Directions Use the time line to help you answer the questions below.

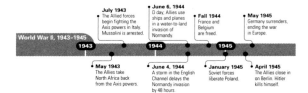

World War II, 1943–1945

July 1943 The Allied forces begin fighting the Axis powers in Italy. Mussolini is arrested.

June 6, 1944 D day; Allies use ships and planes in a water-to-land invasion of Normandy.

Fall 1944 France and Belgium are freed.

May 1945 Germany surrenders, ending the war in Europe.

1943 1944 1945

May 1943 The Allies take North Africa back from the Axis powers.

June 4, 1944 A storm in the English Channel delays the Normandy invasion by 48 hours.

January 1945 Soviet forces liberate Poland.

April 1945 The Allies close in on Berlin. Hitler kills himself.

❶ How long did it take for Germany to surrender after the Allies took back North Africa? two years

❷ What happened on June 4, 1944? A storm in the English Channel delayed the Normandy invasion.

❸ What kind of strategic attack was used for the D day invasion? a water-to-land invasion using planes and ships

❹ What important events happened one month before Germany's surrender? The Allies closed in on Berlin, and Hitler killed himself.

❺ Which countries were freed in 1944? France and Belgium

© Harcourt

Use after reading Chapter 10, Lesson 1, pages 362–369.   **Activity Book** ■ **93**

SKILL PRACTICE

SKILL PRACTICE

Name _____ Date _____

 MAP AND GLOBE SKILLS

Compare Historical Maps

Directions Use the maps to answer the questions on both pages.

Germany Before WWII

❶ Before the end of World War II, who had control of Berlin?
Germany

❷ In which zone was Berlin located after World War II ended?
the Soviet zone

❸ How much of Germany was controlled by the Axis powers before the war ended?
all of it

❹ Which countries had control of Germany after the war?
France, Britain, the United States, and the Soviet Union

❺ In what part of Germany was the British zone?
West Germany

(continued)

© Harcourt

94 ■ Activity Book   Use after reading Chapter 10, Skill Lesson, pages 370–371.

Name _____ Date _____

Germany After WWII

French Zone · American Zone · British Zone · Soviet Zone

❻ What two large German cities were controlled by the United States after the war?
Frankfurt and Munich

❼ Which country controlled the southeastern portion of Germany after the war?
the United States

❽ Which country controlled the southwestern portion of Germany after the war?
France

© Harcourt

Use after reading Chapter 10, Skill Lesson, pages 370–371.   **Activity Book** ■ **95**

War in the Pacific

Directions On the line provided, write the letter of the person or place that completes each statement.

A. Albert Einstein

B. General Douglas MacArthur

C. President Truman

D. Okinawa

E. The Coral Sea

F. Admiral Chester Nimitz

G. Dr. J. Robert Oppenheimer

❶ __B__ was ordered off the Philippine Islands but made a promise to return.

❷ __E__ was the site of the first naval battle in history in which enemy ships did not see each other.

❸ __D__ was where more than 7,600 Allied soldiers and Marines were killed or missing; 107,000 Japanese soldiers and civilians were dead.

❹ __A__ wrote a letter to President Roosevelt, warning him of Germany's plans to build a new kind of bomb.

❺ __G__ headed the Manhattan Project.

❻ __F__ led the Allied troops that met the Japanese fleet at Midway.

❼ __C__ made the decision to drop an atomic bomb on Hiroshima.

CHART AND GRAPH SKILLS

Read Parallel Time Lines

Directions Use the time lines to help you answer the questions.

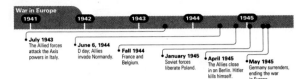

❶ Which happened first, the Battle of Midway or the Allied forces' entering Italy?

Battle of Midway

❷ How much time passed between the surrender of Germany and that of Japan?

three months

❸ What was happening in the United States a few months after Germany's surrender?

An atom bomb was being built and tested.

❹ What military events occurred in the Pacific in 1942?

the Battle of the Coral Sea and the Battle of Midway

Life After World War II

Directions Read each statement. On the lines provided, write *T* if the statement is true or *F* if it is false. Rewrite each false statement to make it true.

❶ The cost of World War II was measured not only in dollars but also in lost lives. T _____

❷ The GI Bill was created to give everyone an opportunity to receive a college education. F; The GI Bill was created to give veterans an opportunity to receive a college education or for job training.

❸ Because gasoline was still being rationed, people didn't drive their cars much after the war. F; Because gasoline was no longer being rationed, people drove their cars more after the war.

❹ Although unemployment increased after the war, the economy didn't suffer much. T _____

❺ Some industries that grew after World War II were electronics, plastics, and frozen foods. T _____

❻ The Employment Act of 1946 encouraged the government to keep a balanced budget, even if that meant keeping Americans from working. F; The Employment Act of 1946 created on economic council to advise the President and encouraged the government to keep Americans working.

❼ Because so many babies were born in this period, it became known as "the family boom." F; Because so many babies were born in this period, it became known as "the baby boom."

A Changed World

Directions Complete the graphic organizer by writing key events or ideas from the time following World War II. Then write a paragraph summarizing the challenges the world faced during this period.

Both the information in the graphic organizer and students' paragraphs may vary. Themes may include those shown in the graphic organizer. Paragraphs should summarize the challenges of this time and provide details to support the entries in the graphic organizer. The paragraph might include the following concepts:

After the war, the world faced many new challenges. The United Nations was organized for the purpose of promoting peace. Many democracies were threatened by the spread of communism. The Soviet Union wanted other countries to become communist. The Truman Doctrine was created to hold back the threat of Soviet invasion. NATO was created to help stop the spread of communism and to help nations work toward peaceful solutions to problems. The Marshall Plan helped European countries rebuild their economies. The Cold War between the Soviet Union and the United States began, and the two nations competed in building bigger bombs.

CHAPTER 10 REVIEW

Name ____________________ Date __________

Allied Victories in World War II

Directions Complete this graphic organizer by predicting outcomes about Allied victories in World War II.

EVENT	FACTS	OUTCOME
The D Day Invasion	On June 6, 1944, Allied forces stormed the beach at Normandy, France, in the largest water-to-land invasion in history.	After D day, the tide of war turned in favor of the Allied Forces.

EVENT	FACTS	OUTCOME
The Battle of Midway	From June 4 to June 8, 1942, the Battle of Midway raged. When it was over, four of Japan's nine aircraft carriers had been destroyed.	At Midway, the Allies began to force Japan out of the lands it had invaded.

 Use after reading Chapter 10, pages 360–395.

TEST PREPARATION

· CHAPTER · 10

Name ____________________ Date __________

Test Preparation

Directions Read each question and choose the best answer. Then fill in the circle for the answer you have chosen. Be sure to fill in the circle completely.

1. What major event turned the war in Europe in favor of the Allies?
   - Ⓐ the attack on Pearl Harbor
   - ● D day
   - Ⓒ Mussolini's arrest
   - Ⓓ the liberation of France
2. Anne Frank was a young girl who kept a diary about her days in hiding during—
   - Ⓕ World War I.
   - Ⓖ the "Red Scare."
   - ● the Holocaust.
   - Ⓙ the Normandy attack.
3. What major event helped turn the war in the Pacific in favor of the Allies?
   - Ⓐ Pearl Harbor
   - Ⓑ the Battle of the Coral Sea
   - Ⓒ the Battle of Midway
   - ● both B and C
4. What new electronic product were Americans buying after the war?
   - Ⓕ radios
   - Ⓖ cars
   - Ⓗ watches
   - ● television sets
5. Which country did **not** have a communist government after the war?
   - Ⓐ Czechoslovakia
   - Ⓑ Hungary
   - ● France
   - Ⓓ Poland

Use after reading Chapter 10, pages 360–395.

COMMUNITY RESOURCES

Historical Societies

____

Museums

____

Experts on World War II

____

National Parks

____

Chapter 10 Assessment

·CHAPTER·

Name _____ Date _____

10 Test

Part One: Test Your Understanding

MULTIPLE CHOICE (4 points each)

Directions Circle the letter of the best answer.

❶ Where did the United States Armed Forces fight first in World War II?
A Europe
B the Pacific
(C) North Africa
D none of the above

❷ Which statement best describes what happened on D day?
F France was freed from German rule.
G Germany surrendered and the Allies declared victory in Europe.
H Japan surrendered and World War II was finally over.
(J) The Allies attacked German forces in the largest water-to-land invasion in history.

❸ What happened during the Holocaust?
A More than six million men, women, and children were killed.
B People were killed for their religious or political beliefs.
C Hitler tried to rid Germany of people he considered undesirable.
(D) all of the above

❹ Which of the following was **not** the location of a battle in the Pacific during World War II?
F Okinawa
(G) Nuremberg
H Midway Island
J Iwo Jima

❺ The Manhattan Project was headed by—
(A) J. Robert Oppenheimer.
B Franklin D. Roosevelt.
C Albert Einstein.
D Harry S. Truman.

❻ Which of the following was **not** provided by the GI Bill for World War II veterans?
F money for college or job training
(G) free medical care
H loans with low interest rates
J income for one year when they could not find jobs

(continued)

Chapter 10 Test

Name _____ Date _____

❼ Which is the most accurate description of life in the United States after soldiers returned from World War II?
A Unemployment was higher than during the Great Depression.
B Gasoline continued to be rationed.
(C) There was a return to family life, many babies were born, and many people moved to the suburbs.
D Farm production slowed because people were used to eating less.

❽ The organization created to work for world peace is called the—
F free world.
G Peace Corps.
H North Atlantic Treaty Organization.
(J) United Nations.

❾ The goal of the Marshall Plan was to—
A stop the spread of communism.
(B) help the nations of Europe rebuild.
C develop nuclear weapons.
D stop the arms race.

❿ Countries that joined NATO promised to—
F help supply Berlin with goods during the Soviet blockade.
G trade freely with other member nations.
(H) keep peace among member nations and defend one another in case of a Soviet attack.
J limit the number of nuclear weapons they produced.

TRUE OR FALSE (5 points each)

Directions In the space provided, write whether each statement is true or false. Correct any false statements.

⓫ During World War II, United States soldiers were segregated.
True

⓬ Japan surrendered immediately after the United States dropped an atomic bomb on the city of Hiroshima.
False: Japan surrendered after another bomb was dropped on Nagasaki.

⓭ The demand for consumer goods in the United States was low in the years after World War II.
False: The demand for consumer goods in the United States was very high.

⓮ The Cold War lasted more than 40 years, but it never became an actual war.
True

(continued)

Chapter 10 Test

Name _____ Date _____

Part Two: Test Your Skills

COMPARE HISTORICAL MAPS (4 points)

Directions Compare the two maps of Asia and the Pacific during World War II. Then answer the following questions.

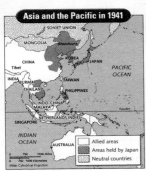
Asia and the Pacific in 1941

Asia and the Pacific in 1942

⓯ How did Asia and the Pacific change between 1941 and 1942?
Japan took over many other nations in the region.

⓰ When was Thailand taken over by Japan? in 1942

⓱ What was the largest country still considered an ally in the region in 1942?
China

⓲ Did Mongolia's borders change or stay the same between 1941 and 1942?
They stayed the same.

⓳ What area did Japan control south of the equator in 1942?
part of the Dutch East Indies

(continued)

Chapter 10 Test

Name _____ Date _____

Part Three: Apply What You Have Learned

⓴ **FACT AND OPINION** (10 points)
Read each statement and write *F* if it is a fact or *O* if it is an opinion.

F   After D day, the Allies began to free countries in Europe that had been taken over by Germany.

O   The Allies should not have used the strategy of island hopping because it cost too many lives.

F   The United States bomber *Enola Gay* dropped an atomic bomb on Hiroshima in 1945.

F   The United States lost over 400,000 troops in World War II.

O   In the years following World War II, it was better to live in the suburbs than in the city.

㉑ **ESSAY** (10 points)
The Soviet Union had been an ally of the United States during World War II, but it was a communist country. Joseph Stalin wanted all the countries the Soviet Union had taken over during World War II to become communist. President Truman believed that the spread of communism was a threat to the United States and the rest of the free world. Explain how communism is different from democracy and what the United States did to help countries deal with these problems.

In a communist country, the government owns all of the property and makes all of the economic decisions. In a democracy, people are free to own property and make economic decisions. These freedoms are important to Americans, and communism was a threat to these freedoms. After World War II, the United States was a superpower, and President Truman believed it had the responsibility to protect freedom for the rest of the world. To do this, the United States offered economic and military help to countries fighting communism. This policy became known as the Truman Doctrine.

Chapter 10 Test

Introduce the Chapter

OBJECTIVES

- Apply critical-thinking skills to organize and use information.
- Interpret excerpts from notable speeches.
- Describe major events of World War II in the Pacific.

Access Prior Knowledge

Ask students to think about times they have had to cooperate with their classmates or friends to accomplish something. How important was it to your goal that everyone work together?

Visual Learning

Picture Ask students to study the picture and the Locate It map. As a class, discuss what the images indicate the chapter will be about.

Locate It Map The United States Marine Corps War Memorial, located next to Arlington National Cemetery, is a tribute to marines who have died defending the United States.

U.S. MARINE CORPS WAR MEMORIAL

The Marine Corps War Memorial at Arlington National Cemetery shows the American flag being raised during the terrible battle for the Japanese island of Iwo Jima. It was designed by Felix W. de Weldon and is based on a photograph by Joe Rosenthal that became one of the most famous images of World War II.

LOCATE IT

Washington, D.C.

360 ▪ Unit 5

BACKGROUND

Picture Michael Strank, Harlon H. Block, Franklin R. Sousley, Rene A. Gagnon, Ira Hayes, and John H. Bradley were responsible for raising the flag on Mount Suribachi on Iwo Jima. Those men who survived the fighting that continued at Iwo Jima posed for sculptor Felix W. de Weldon as he made a life-size sculpture of the scene. To depict the marines who did not survive, de Weldon relied on photographs and physical descriptions. The sculpture was later used as a model for the much larger memorial. The inscription on the base of the memorial reads, "In honor and in memory of the men of the United States Marine Corps who have given their lives to their country since November 10, 1775."

BACKGROUND

Quotation Admiral Chester Nimitz was the commander in chief of the Pacific Fleet during World War II. Nimitz helped create the concept of island hopping, in which each island that was captured from the Japanese was used as a base to attack the next target. At the end of the war, Admiral Nimitz was the official United States representative to sign the document accepting the Japanese surrender.

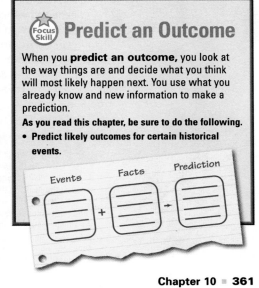

· CHAPTER ·

10

The Allies Win the War

" **Uncommon valor was a common virtue.** "

—Admiral Chester Nimitz, referring to United States soldiers in World War II, 1945

 Predict an Outcome

When you **predict an outcome,** you look at the way things are and decide what you think will most likely happen next. You use what you already know and new information to make a prediction.

As you read this chapter, be sure to do the following.

* **Predict likely outcomes for certain historical events.**

Read and Respond

Ask students to read the title of the chapter. Encourage them to speculate about its meaning. Ask students to think about how the Allies worked together to win the war.

Quotation Have a volunteer read the quotation aloud.

Q What do the words *valor* and *virtue* mean?

A *Valor* means "remarkable courage or bravery," and *virtue* is good moral quality.

Point out to students that this quotation is engraved on the United States Marine Corps War Memorial.

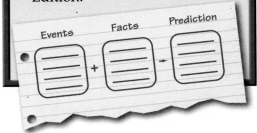 **Predict an Outcome**

As students read the chapter, have them use a graphic organizer to help them predict likely outcomes for events.

* A blank graphic organizer can be found on page 100 of the Activity Book.

* Point out to students that they should gather all of the information they know about an event and use this information to list possible outcomes. Then they should choose the most likely outcome from their list.

* A completed graphic organizer can be found on page 100 of the Activity Book, Teacher's Edition.

WORD WORK

Preview Vocabulary Have students make three-column charts for the terms in the lesson vocabulary lists. Students should write the terms in the first column, their definitions in the second column, and clues to remember what the terms mean in the third column.

Term	Definition	Clue

MAKE IT RELEVANT

Discussion Topics As you teach this chapter, you and your students might enjoy discussing some of the following topics. Each topic helps relate what students are learning about in this unit to their world today.

■ How do you feel when you see memorials and monuments dedicated to soldiers who died in battle?

■ Do you think it is important to have memorials?

■ How do you think life in the United States today is affected by what happened in World War II?

Lesson 1
PAGES 362–369

OBJECTIVES

- Describe the importance of major military campaigns in North Africa and Italy.
- Describe the D day invasion and other events that led to the Allies' victory in Europe.
- Describe the Holocaust and the impact it had on Jews in Europe.
- Explain how technological advances during World War II changed how wars were fought.

 Predict an Outcome
pp. 361, 362, 367, 369, 396

Vocabulary

SEE READING AND VOCABULARY TRANSPARENCY 5-6 OR THE WORD CARDS ON PP. V45–V46.

front p. 362   D day p. 364
segregate p. 363   Holocaust p. 368

 When Minutes Count

Direct students to the illustration on pages 364 and 365. Use the illustration as a springboard to discuss the D day invasion at Normandy.

Quick Summary

This lesson focuses on the Allied military campaigns in North Africa and Europe that led to Germany's defeat in World War II. It also examines the atrocities of the Holocaust.

 Motivate

Set the Purpose

Big Idea Remind students that Allied troops fought Axis troops in Africa and in Europe.

Access Prior Knowledge

Discuss with students what they know about major battles of World War II. Ask if they know who won the war.

362 ▪ UNIT 5

 PREDICT AN OUTCOME
As you read, predict likely outcomes of how World War II changed the world.

BIG IDEA
World War II affected countries in Africa and Europe.

VOCABULARY
front
segregated
D day
Holocaust

War in Africa and in Europe

1930	1940	1950

1942–1945

World War II was a new kind of war. Instead of fighting from trenches, as in World War I, soldiers used tanks, ships, and airplanes to move quickly from battle to battle. Bombs that were dropped from larger, faster airplanes destroyed whole cities.

World War II was also fought over a much larger area than any other war was—almost half the world. It was fought on two major **fronts**, or battle lines, at the same time. The first was in Africa and in Europe. The second was in the Pacific. The war would need to be won on both fronts.

North Africa and Italy

To defeat the Axis Powers in Europe, the Allied Powers needed to win control of the Mediterranean Sea. To do that, they would have to defeat the German and Italian forces in North Africa and then invade Italy. In 1942 British forces won a major battle at El Alamein in Egypt.

In June 1942 President Roosevelt put General Dwight D. Eisenhower (EYE•zin•how•er) in command of all the American troops in Europe. A respected leader and a skilled military planner, General Eisenhower led the Allied forces in their attack against the Axis forces in North Africa.

In November 1942 American forces landed in Morocco and Algeria in northwestern Africa. The American troops slowly fought their way east. At the same time, the British

FAST FACT During World War II, Dwight D. Eisenhower quickly advanced through the ranks of the United States Army. In 1942 he was a lieutenant colonel stationed in the Philippines. Less than two years later, he was a general commanding the most powerful military force in history.

362 ▪ Unit 5

STUDY/RESEARCH SKILLS

Using Maps Point out to students that maps can provide them with important information such as how a nation might have won a war. When studying maps, students should read the title of the map and decide whether it is historical or current. Students also should study the map key to help them interpret information on the map. Have students look at the maps in this chapter and ask them what they can learn about World War II by studying them.

QUESTIONS KIDS ASK

Q Why didn't the British and the Americans fight together?

A British and United States forces were able to trap the Axis troops in the middle of North Africa by coming from opposite sides. If British and United States troops had moved in from one direction, the Axis troops might have escaped.

pushed the Axis forces west, out of Egypt. On April 8, 1943, after five months of fighting, the American and the British troops met. Five weeks later, the Axis troops in North Africa surrendered. With that surrender, 240,000 German and Italian soldiers became prisoners of war.

The Allies then pushed north into Italy. They thought Italy might be close to surrendering, which would weaken the Axis Powers. They also thought that the Mediterranean Sea would be safer for Allied ships if the Allies pushed the Axis Powers out of Italy.

The Italian campaign began on July 10, 1943, on the island of Sicily. Fighting was fierce, but the Italian people were tired of the war. Cries of "Long live America!" and "Down with Mussolini!" greeted Allied soldiers as they took the Sicilian

city of Palermo. On July 24 Mussolini was told, "The soldiers don't want to fight anymore. At this moment, you are the most hated man in Italy." That same day, Mussolini was arrested and put into prison. However, the fighting in Italy did not end with Mussolini's arrest. Hitler sent more German troops to defend Italy and free Mussolini. As a result, it took Allied forces almost another year to reach Rome, Italy's capital.

One of the military units from the United States that helped the Allies in their battle for Italy was the 92nd Division. This division was made up of African American soldiers. During the war African American soldiers had to serve in **segregated**, or separate, units.

REVIEW Why did the Allies need to invade North Africa? so they could gain access to the Mediterranean Sea

African American soldiers of the 92nd Division load a gun behind sandbags during a battle in Italy.

Chapter 10 ▪ 363

INTEGRATE MATHEMATICS

Estimate Ask students to estimate the number of months between the Allied troops' meeting in North Africa and the invasion of Italy. April 8, 1943 – July 10, 1943 = about 3 months

---

BACKGROUND

Battle of Stalingrad The German siege of Stalingrad, now Volgograd, lasted about five months, from August 1942 until early 1943. In the struggle, the Soviets and Germans fought hand-to-hand for single streets, houses, and factories. The Soviets were finally able to win when the Volga River froze over and they were able to push supplies over the ice at night. By the end of the battle, the German army had lost about 300,000 soldiers.

READING SOCIAL STUDIES

Anticipation Guide Have students predict whether the following statements are true or false. Students may correct their predictions as they read.

1. Adolf Hitler was arrested toward the end of World War II. FALSE

2. About 6 million Jews were killed in the Holocaust. TRUE

● USE READING AND VOCABULARY TRANSPARENCY 5-6.

5-6 TRANSPARENCY

2 Teach

North Africa and Italy

Read and Respond

Link Geography and History Have students look at a map of Europe and North Africa. Ask them to locate Egypt, Morocco, and Algeria. Explain that it took the United States and Britain more than four months to defeat the Axis forces in North Africa. Based on what they learn from the map, have students speculate on why it took that much time to gain control of that area.

Explain to students that while Allied forces were fighting for control of North Africa, fierce fighting continued in eastern Europe. In a battle that lasted from August 1942 to early 1943, Soviet troops kept German troops from capturing Stalingrad, a city on the Volga River. The Soviet victory at the Battle of Stalingrad, which ended the Germans' eastward advance into the Soviet Union, was a turning point in the war in Europe.

History Explain that many Italians did not want Italy to be involved in the war, and most did not want to be aligned with Hitler and the Nazi party. Inform students that the Sicilians did not want their homeland destroyed in battle and therefore quickly surrendered when the Allies invaded. German and Italian troops retreated onto mainland Italy, where the fighting continued.

The D Day Invasion

Read and Respond

Link History and Geography Explain that the Germans believed that any invasion from Britain would land at Calais, France, because Calais is only 26 miles (42 km) from Britain across the English Channel. Instead, the Allies launched the invasion toward the Normandy beaches, west of Calais. Look at a map of France with students, and have them locate Normandy and Calais.

Q Why do you think the Allies chose France to begin their push into Europe, even though there were large numbers of German forces stationed there?

A Possible response: France is directly across the English Channel from England so ships could get there from England quickly.

History Describe to students the preparations of the Allied forces for the D day invasion. Inform students that it took about three years to plan and prepare for the invasion. During that time more than 170,000 soldiers, 20,000 vehicles, 1,500 tanks, and 12,000 planes were gathered at bases and ports in southern England. D day was the largest invasion over water in history.

The D Day Invasion

While the Allies were fighting in Italy, they were planning other invasions of Europe. General Eisenhower, now the commander of the Allied forces, would lead the largest of these invasions.

For months the Allies prepared for the attack. In fact, more than 170,000 soldiers and thousands of tanks, trucks, jeeps, and planes turned the southern part of Britain into one big army camp. The plan was for the Allied troops to cross the English Channel on June 4. They would come ashore on the beaches at Normandy, in France, and attack German forces there.

On Sunday, June 4, a terrible storm blew into the channel. However, weather forecasters told Eisenhower that there would be a break in the hurricane-like weather on Tuesday morning. General Eisenhower held off the attack. Now June 6, 1944, would be **D day**—the day the Allies would work together in the largest water-to-land invasion in history.

On June 6, in the early-morning darkness, the first of more than 4,000 ships began to leave Britain's coast to cross the English Channel. The slower ships went first, followed by the faster ships and airplanes, so that all the ships and planes would arrive at the same time in one giant striking force.

By 6:30 A.M., the first Allied soldiers had made it onto the beaches at Normandy. One soldier remembered:

INTEGRATE LANGUAGE ARTS

Write a News Report
Have students research the giant artificial harbors called mulberries, which were built specifically for support of the D day invasion. Have students imagine they are reporters writing stories about these new devices. Tell them to use the Internet and their library to research mulberries. Remind students to answer the journalistic questions of *who, what, when, where, how,* and *why* in their reports.

BACKGROUND

D day *D day* is the military term for the basic date from which an attack can be scheduled before the actual date of attack is known. This allows the military to plan and schedule various events relating to the attack. For example, if supplies are to be delivered two days after an attack, the delivery date is referred to as *D plus 2. H hour* is used to refer to the time. For instance, planes may bomb an area three hours before a ground attack, or *H minus 3.*

"Everything was confusion. Shells were coming in all the time; boats burning, vehicles with nowhere to go bogging down, getting hit; supplies getting wet; boats trying to come in all the time, some hitting mines, exploding."

Many soldiers died on D day, but the invasion was successful. The Allies broke through the German lines and began moving inland from the west, pushing the Germans back. One sailor said, "I felt thankful, of course, that I seemed to have survived the worst part. I took a few deep breaths and felt suddenly elated [joyful], proud to be having even a tiny part in what was maybe the biggest battle of all history. At that moment, soaked to the skin, seasick, dead tired, cold, still scared, I would not have wanted to be anywhere else."

In December 1944 the Germans fought back at the Battle of the Bulge, in Belgium, but American General George Patton and his troops turned the Germans back. In March 1945 Patton's troops were the first to enter Germany.

REVIEW On what date did the Allies attack the Germans at Normandy? *June 6, 1944*

A CLOSER LOOK
D Day Invasion at Normandy

Ships carried American, British, and Canadian soldiers across the English Channel to attack the German forces along the coast of France. This picture shows the American forces that took part.

1 German pillbox bunker
2 German soldiers
3 the English Channel
4 American soldier transports
5 American soldiers
6 American tanks
7 American tank transports
8 American destroyers and battleships
9 American fighter planes

◈ Why do you think ships and planes were used in the Allied invasion of Normandy?

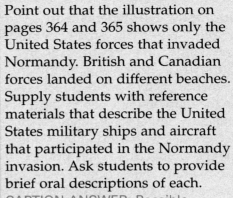

365

Point out that the illustration on pages 364 and 365 shows only the United States forces that invaded Normandy. British and Canadian forces landed on different beaches. Supply students with reference materials that describe the United States military ships and aircraft that participated in the Normandy invasion. Ask students to provide brief oral descriptions of each. CAPTION ANSWER: Possible response: Some ships carried landing craft and soldiers. Battleships fired toward the beaches. Planes dropped paratroopers behind German lines to capture bridges and railroad lines.

Visual Learning

Map Direct students to the map on page 365. Explain that Normandy is a northern region of France, not the name of the beach. Point out that Allied forces attacked five separate beaches that were controlled by Axis forces.

Analyze Primary Sources

Quotations Read the quotations on page 365 dramatically, as if you were the soldiers being quoted. Emphasize that soldiers had time to think about the invasion while crossing the English Channel. Point out that when they arrived, the troops had to travel from the ships to the beaches in small boats, and many of the soldiers got seasick and wet.

 Students might enjoy reading additional personal accounts. Have them visit The Learning Site at **www.harcourtschool.com.**

BACKGROUND

Invasion of Normandy The Allied forces attacked five separate beaches on D day. They had code names for each beach. The United States forces attacked Utah Beach and Omaha Beach. The Canadian forces attacked Juno Beach. British forces attacked Gold Beach and Sword Beach. By the end of the day on June 6, 1944, the Allies controlled all five beaches. By the end of June, there were 850,000 Allied soldiers and 150,000 Allied vehicles in Normandy, France.

INTEGRATE PHYSICAL EDUCATION

Research Physical Fitness Training Organize students into small groups, and encourage them to research the physical fitness training that soldiers underwent as they prepared for the D day invasion. Have each group compile a list of exercises soldiers performed. Lead a discussion about how this physical conditioning prepared soldiers for battle.

Victory in Europe

Read and Respond

Geography Tell students that the Allies defeated Germany in Europe in much the same way they did in North Africa—by advancing toward the enemy from opposite directions. Use the map on page 366 to show students how Soviet forces were pushing the Germans westward at the same time the United States and Britain were pushing the Germans eastward. Discuss with students how fighting on two fronts was a disadvantage for Germany.

Visual Learning

Map Tell students to study the map on page 366 of Europe and North Africa.

CAPTION ANSWER: Germany and Italy

Read and Respond

History Inform students that Soviet leader Joseph Stalin had lobbied hard for President Roosevelt and British Prime Minister Winston Churchill to open a second front in western Europe against the Germans. Explain that Soviet troops had shouldered the brunt of fighting against Germany since June 1941, when Germany invaded the Soviet Union.

Analyze Primary Sources

Quotation Ask a volunteer to read the quotation on page 366. Ask students to summarize in one word the emotion expressed by the Dutch woman in this quotation.

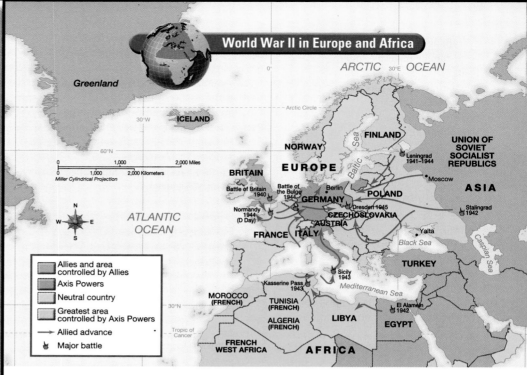

World War II in Europe and Africa

Allies and area controlled by Allies

Axis Powers

Neutral country

Greatest area controlled by Axis Powers

→ Allied advance

✊ Major battle

Location During the war, the areas controlled by the Axis Powers included much of Europe and Africa.

◈ Which European countries shown on the map were Axis Powers?

Victory in Europe

After D day, the tide of war began to turn in favor of the Allies. One by one, the countries Germany had conquered were freed as soldiers from the United States, Britain, Canada, and the Soviet Union forced the Germans out. In the fall of 1944, France and then Belgium were freed. Five months later, German troops in the Netherlands and Denmark surrendered to the Allies.

One Dutch woman, who was a little girl when the Netherlands was freed, remembered what it was like when the Allies came. She said, "Big tanks rolled through the streets, and for the very first time I saw people who smiled and waved to us. They were soldiers! It was like a miracle."

The Allies were closing in on Berlin, the capital of Germany. Hitler knew the war was lost. Mussolini had been captured and killed. The Axis Powers' control over Europe was gone. In May 1945 the Allied troops from the east and the west met near Berlin. There they learned that Hitler had killed himself.

MAKE IT RELEVANT

In Your Community Encourage students to research an important turning point in the war, such as the D day invasion, Truman's decision to use the atom bomb, or V-E Day, using newspapers from their community. Tell students to find stories about their community's reaction to that event. Ask volunteers to give brief oral presentations to the class.

INTEGRATE ART

Interpret Photographs Tell students that photographs of World War II soldiers and battles often show what is hard to describe in words. Have students find online or in their library famous photographs of World War II. Then have students work in groups to write captions for the photographs.

Berlin fell to the Soviets on May 2, 1945, and the German military leaders asked to surrender. On May 8, the Allies accepted their surrender. This day was called Victory in Europe Day, or V-E Day. It marked the end of the war in Europe.

President Roosevelt's health had grown worse. He did not live to see the end of the war. On April 12, 1945, Roosevelt died. Vice President Harry S. Truman became President.

REVIEW What happened to Axis leaders Hitler and Mussolini as World War II came to an end? **PREDICT AN OUTCOME** Mussolini was captured and killed, and Hitler killed himself.

The Holocaust

Not until the war in Europe was over did people discover all that Hitler and the Nazis had done. As Allied troops marched across Central Europe toward Berlin, they freed people in the Nazis' concentration camps. The largest group of victims was the Jews, the people Hitler had blamed for Germany's problems.

The Nazis had made life difficult for Jews in every country they controlled. The Nazis began arresting Jews in 1938, sending between 20,000 and 30,000 of them to concentration camps. In 1939 after Germany invaded Poland, the Nazis gained control of that country's more than 3 million Jews. Millions more came under Nazi control in 1940 and 1941, as German armies invaded Belgium, Denmark, France, Norway, the Netherlands, and the Soviet Union.

Anne Frank was a young Jewish girl living in the Netherlands when World War II began. After the Nazis invaded the Netherlands in 1940, Anne and her family went into hiding. They lived in secret rooms in a building in the Dutch city of Amsterdam. Then, on August 4, 1944, their hiding place was discovered. Anne and her family were sent to concentration camps.

Prisoners in concentration camps suffered horribly. The Nazis forced Jewish people to wear a yellow Star of David to make them stand out.

Read and Respond

History Inform students that Roosevelt and Churchill met in January 1943 and agreed that the Allies would fight until the Axis Powers agreed to an unconditional surrender. This meant that the Axis Powers would have to do whatever the Allies wanted after the war ended.

The Holocaust

Read and Respond

Link History with Culture and Society Lead a discussion on the Holocaust as an example of prejudice and discrimination taken to the extreme. Remind students that prejudice toward people of Jewish descent, or anti-Semitism, intensified when Hitler and the Nazis took power in Germany.

Holocaust The word *holocaust* comes from the Greek *holo,* meaning "whole," and *caustos,* meaning "burned." It was originally the term for a religious rite in which an offering was burned completely. Today it is used to refer to any widespread human destruction. However, if the word is capitalized, it refers to the Nazis' systematic attempt during World War II to rid Europe of all Jews.

Advanced Learners
Challenge advanced learners by having them read *The Diary of Anne Frank.* Ask each student to write three questions that could be used to stimulate conversation about the book. Give students time to discuss the book as a group, using their questions as a guide.

Visual Learning

Picture Ask students to study the photograph on page 368 of the war crimes trial at Nuremberg, Germany.

Q **Why do you think it was necessary for the people in this photograph to wear headsets?**

A The trial was being translated into German or English for the participants.

Changes in Technology

Read and Respond

History Inform students that some of the most severe fighting in Europe occurred late in the war. Allied bombing campaigns targeted German cities such as Dresden in an attempt to break the morale of the German people.

3 Close

Summarize Key Content

- In 1943 the Allies reclaimed North Africa from the Axis Powers.
- The D day invasion at Normandy on June 6, 1944, was a major turning point in the war. One by one, the Allies freed countries that had been conquered by Germany.
- More than 6 million Jews died in German concentration camps during World War II.
- New inventions, such as radar, during World War II changed the way soldiers fought.

---

the mass murder of all European Jews and others he considered "undesirable" in concentration camps

Seven months later, Anne died at a camp named Bergen-Belsen.

In those small secret rooms, Anne kept a diary of her days in hiding. One diary entry described what was happening to Jews on the streets of Amsterdam after the Nazi invasion:

Anne Frank (second from right) with family and friends in the Netherlands

❝ It is terrible outside. Day and night more of those poor miserable people are being dragged off, with nothing but a rucksack [backpack] and a little money. . . . Families are torn apart, the men, women, and children all being separated. ❞

In 1941 Hitler had begun what he called the "final solution to the Jewish question." It was the mass murder of all European Jews and other people he called "undesirable." The mass murder became known as the **Holocaust** (HOH•luh•kawst).

More than 6 million men, women, and children had been murdered in the camps. One of the largest camps was at Auschwitz (OWSH•vits), in Poland. About $1\frac{1}{2}$ million people were killed at this camp. The Nazis killed people for many reasons. Many were killed for their religious or political beliefs. Others were killed because they were ill or disabled and could not work.

Beginning in late 1945, Nazi leaders accused of these crimes were brought to trial by the Allies. The most important trials were held in the German city of Nuremberg. Many Nazi leaders were found guilty and sentenced to death for their crimes.

REVIEW What was Hitler's "final solution"?

Changes in Technology

During World War II, new technology changed the way war was fought. Improvements to airplanes made them an even more important part of warfare than they had been in World War I. In World War II planes were used in battle and put to many other uses.

Bombers dropped bombs from the sky. Special planes called drones flew without pilots and dropped bombs on cities. Transport planes parachuted soldiers into battle. Aircraft carriers launched planes from the sea to attack places that soldiers could not reach easily by land.

Other military inventions were also used in World War II. To fight the attacks by airplanes, special cannons called anti-aircraft guns were developed. They could

Many Nazi leaders were tried for their crimes in Nuremberg, Germany.

· SCIENCE AND TECHNOLOGY ·

Radar

Radar was developed in the 1930s by several countries. It was a way to use radio waves to locate faraway or hidden objects. Germany was one of the countries working to develop radar. However, Hitler ordered that the research be stopped. As a result, Allied radar systems were more advanced. By 1940, during the Battle of Britain, radar showed the Allies the number of German planes or ships that were approaching, as well as their speed and direction.

shoot large, exploding bullets to hit planes.

Another new invention helped find planes and ships in bad weather, at night, or over long distances. It was called radio detection and ranging, or radar. In addition, two-way radios let soldiers call for help or receive orders during battle.

Battlefield medicine also improved greatly during World War II. New drugs such as penicillin and sulfa helped keep soldiers' wounds from getting infected. In the Pacific a new chemical, DDT, was used to kill disease-carrying insects.

REVIEW **What new technologies were used for the first time in World War II?** antiaircraft guns, radar, two-way radios, penicillin, sulfa, and DDT

LESSON 1 REVIEW

Summary Time Line

| 1942 | 1943 | 1944 | 1945 |

- **1943** Allied forces take back North Africa
- **1944** General Eisenhower leads the D day invasion
- **1945** Germany surrenders

PREDICT AN OUTCOME How do you think the Allies would treat Germany after the war?

❶ **BIG IDEA** In what ways did World War II affect countries around the world?

❷ **VOCABULARY** Use the terms **D day** and **Holocaust** in a sentence about the war in Europe.

❸ **TIME LINE** Did the Allies win in North Africa before or after the D day invasion?

❹ **SCIENCE AND TECHNOLOGY** How did weather forecasters affect D day?

❺ **HISTORY** Who led the D day invasion?

❻ **CRITICAL THINKING—Evaluate** What do you think would have been most difficult for Anne Frank and her family during their time of hiding from the Germans?

PERFORMANCE—Write a Diary Entry Imagine that you are among the Allied troops freeing one of Germany's concentration camps. Write a diary entry in which you talk about what you saw when you entered the camp. Share your diary entry with a family member.

Chapter 10 ■ 369

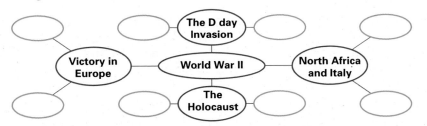
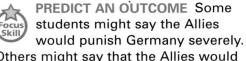
Assess

Lesson 1 Review—Answers

PREDICT AN OUTCOME Some students might say the Allies would punish Germany severely. Others might say that the Allies would help Germany rebuild.

❶ **BIG IDEA** World War II was fought over almost half the world—a much larger area than any other war was fought over.

❷ **VOCABULARY** In Europe thousands of soldiers died on **D day** and 6 million Jews were killed in the **Holocaust**.

❸ **TIME LINE** before

❹ **SCIENCE AND TECHNOLOGY** Forecasters predicted a storm on June 5 would lift the following morning, so General Eisenhower changed D day to June 6.

❺ **HISTORY** United States General Dwight D. Eisenhower

❻ **CRITICAL THINKING—Evaluate** Students' answers will vary but should indicate that they worried about whether they would be discovered by the Germans.

Performance Assessment Guidelines Students' diary entries should include specific descriptions of what they saw.

Skill Lesson

PAGES 370–371

OBJECTIVES

- Use geographic tools to collect, analyze, and interpret data.
- Apply critical thinking skills to organize and use information from maps.

Vocabulary

historical map p. 370

WORD CARDS

See pp. V45–V46.

1 Motivate

Why It Matters

Explain that historical maps show political borders at certain times in history. Inform students that having two maps of the same place at different times can help them see changes over time.

·SKILLS· MAP AND GLOBE

Compare Historical Maps

VOCABULARY
historical map

▶ WHY IT MATTERS

The end of World War II changed the map of Europe. The historical maps on pages 370 and 371 show those changes. A **historical map** provides information about a place at a certain time in history. Knowing how to use historical maps can help you learn how a region's borders have changed or how names given to an area changed at different times in history.

▶ WHAT YOU NEED TO KNOW

History books and many atlases contain historical maps. Often the title or key of a historical map tells what year or time period is shown on the map.

Map A: Europe in 1937

MENTAL MAPPING

Identify European Countries
Provide students with an outline map of Europe before World War II, similar to Map A. Ask them to write in the names of the countries without looking at a map for reference.

BACKGROUND

The Berlin Wall After World War II, East Germany was controlled by the Soviet Union, while the United States, France, and Great Britain supported West Germany. The city of Berlin also was divided into eastern and western parts. Between the end of World War II and 1961, more than 2.7 million people fled East Germany. More than half of them did so through Berlin. This prompted the Soviet Union to build a wall between the eastern and western parts of the city. In 1989 Germans began demolishing the wall. East Germany eventually removed the wall and Germany was reunified in 1990.

Map B: Europe in 1945

National capital

0   250   500 Miles
0   250   500 Kilometers
Azimuthal Equal-Area Projection

ATLANTIC OCEAN

ICELAND — Reykjavik
NORWAY — Oslo
SWEDEN — Stockholm
FINLAND — Helsinki
North Sea
Baltic Sea
IRELAND — Dublin
BRITAIN — London
DENMARK — Copenhagen
NETHERLANDS — Amsterdam
Brussels — BELGIUM
Paris — FRANCE
LUXEMBOURG
EAST GERMANY — Berlin
WEST GERMANY — Bonn
Warsaw — POLAND
Prague — CZECHOSLOVAKIA
Bern — SWITZERLAND
Vienna — AUSTRIA
Budapest — HUNGARY
ITALY — Rome
Belgrade — YUGOSLAVIA
ROMANIA — Bucharest
BULGARIA — Sofia
Black Sea
ALBANIA — Tiranë
GREECE — Athens
TURKEY — Ankara
Nicosia — Cyprus
Crete
Mediterranean Sea
Sicily
Sardinia
Corsica
SPAIN — Madrid
PORTUGAL — Lisbon
UNION OF SOVIET SOCIALIST REPUBLICS
Moscow
Caspian Sea
AFRICA
ASIA

As you can tell from the titles, both these maps are of Europe. Each shows the continent in a different year. Map A shows Europe in 1937 before World War II began. Map B shows Europe after World War II ended.

Colors are important map symbols. Sometimes colors help you tell water from land on a map. Colors on a map can also show you the areas claimed by different countries.

➡ PRACTICE THE SKILL

Compare Map A with Map B. Use what you learn to answer these questions about how World War II changed Europe.

❶ Was Germany broken into East Germany and West Germany before or after World War II was fought?

❷ Did Finland gain or lose land because of World War II?

❸ Did Portugal's borders change or stay the same after World War II ended?

❹ What happened to the country of Estonia between 1937 and 1945?

➡ APPLY WHAT YOU LEARNED

Write a paragraph that describes what these historical maps show. In your paragraph, also explain why historical maps are useful. Then share your paragraph with a classmate.

Practice your map and globe skills with the **GeoSkills CD-ROM**.

MAP AND GLOBE SKILLS

Chapter 10 ■ 371

2 Teach

What You Need to Know

Point out that historical maps can enable students to see how the world changed following a particular event, such as World War II. Ask students to study Maps A and B. Discuss the changes that occurred because of World War II.

Practice the Skill—Answers

❶ after

❷ Finland lost land to the Soviet Union.

❸ Portugal's borders stayed the same.

❹ It became part of the Soviet Union.

3 Close

Apply What You Learned

Students' paragraphs should describe why historical maps are useful. Encourage volunteers to present their completed paragraphs to the class.

ACTIVITY BOOK

Use ACTIVITY BOOK, pp. 94–95, to give students additional practice using this skill.

TRANSPARENCY

Use SKILL TRANSPARENCIES 5-2A and 5-2B.

CD-ROM

Explore GEOSKILLS CD-ROM to learn more about map and globe skills.

EXTEND AND ENRICH

Compare and Contrast Ask students to write brief but detailed comparison-contrast papers regarding the similarities and differences between Map A and Map B.

RETEACH THE SKILL

Write a Summary Instruct students to write paragraphs about how historical maps are useful. Ask them to describe in their summaries what is depicted in Maps A and B.

Lesson 2

PAGES 372–379

OBJECTIVES

- Analyze difficulties the Allied forces encountered fighting against Japan in World War II.
- Describe the events that led to the end of World War II.

 Predict an Outcome
pp. 361, 372, 376, 379, 396

Vocabulary

SEE READING AND VOCABULARY TRANSPARENCY 5-7 OR THE WORD CARDS ON PP. V45–V46.

island hopping   V-J Day p. 378
p. 373

 When Minutes Count

Model for students how to turn headings into questions.

Heading–Battles in the Pacific

Question–What battles were fought in the Pacific?

Then have pairs of students work together to write questions and answer them.

Quick Summary

This lesson summarizes military campaigns in the Pacific during World War II and the Allied victory over Japan.

 Motivate

Set the Purpose

Big Idea Remind students that World War II was fought on two fronts, in the Pacific and in Europe and North Africa.

Access Prior Knowledge

Encourage students to tell what they know about the war in Europe. What were some of the turning points in the war in Europe? How did the Allies win the war in Europe?

2

 PREDICT AN OUTCOME

As you read, predict likely outcomes of the fighting in the Pacific.

BIG IDEA
It took the Allies longer to win the war in the Pacific.

VOCABULARY
island hopping
V-J Day

War in the Pacific

1930   1940   1950
1942–1945

In the United States and in Europe, people cheered when they heard of Germany's surrender. However, they knew that although the Axis Powers had been defeated in Europe, the war was not yet over. Japan still had to be defeated.

Battles in the Pacific

Within days after the attack on Pearl Harbor, Japanese forces attacked and took over Hong Kong, Guam, Wake Island, and the Philippines. Other islands, too, fell to the Japanese. By the spring of 1942, it seemed that Japan might win the war in the Pacific.

After attacks from Japanese planes, the United States aircraft carrier *Lexington* burns during the Battle of the Coral Sea.

372

REACH ALL LEARNERS

English as a Second Language Pair students who are acquiring English with other students in the class. After students have read each section of the lesson, have each summarize the section verbally to his or her partner. Have English speakers in each pair do their summaries first so that those acquiring English can listen before giving their summaries.

STUDY/RESEARCH SKILLS

Note Taking Emphasize to students that taking notes can help them remember the main points of the lesson. It can be especially helpful if a lesson or section is long. Ask students to take simple and short notes while reading this lesson. Tell students that they can use their notes to recall information from the lesson.

Then two battles turned the war in favor of the Allies. One was the Battle of the Coral Sea. This battle took place when Allied ships sailed to the Coral Sea to try to stop Japan from advancing toward Australia. It was the first naval battle in history in which enemy ships did not see each other. Instead, the whole battle was fought by planes that had been launched from aircraft carriers. The Battle of the Coral Sea ended with no real victory. However, the Allies had stopped Japan from invading Australia.

Soon Japanese leaders sent a coded message to their navy. The message ordered Japan's forces to attack Midway Island, about 1,000 miles (1,609 km) west of Hawaii. If Japan won Midway, it would have a base from which its ships, submarines, and planes could threaten not only Hawaii but also the western coast of the United States.

However, the Allies had broken the Japanese codes and were now able to read Japan's plans. Admiral Chester Nimitz was in charge of the Allied fleet that rushed to meet the Japanese fleet. From June 4 to June 8, 1942, the Battle of Midway raged. When it was over, four of Japan's aircraft carriers had been destroyed with more than 200 planes aboard. For the first time since Pearl Harbor, the Japanese were on the run. Admiral Nimitz later said that ". . . the Battle of Midway would have ended

Naval Admiral Chester Nimitz served as the commander in chief of the United States fleet in the Pacific.

differently" if the United States had not broken Japan's codes.

After Midway the Allies began to force the Japanese out of the islands they had conquered. However, the Allies did not take back every island. Instead, they followed a plan of island hopping. **Island hopping** meant that the Allies would fight only for certain key islands as they worked their way toward an invasion of Japan. In November 1942, American soldiers won a fierce battle at the island of Tarawa. In July 1944, they won another important victory at the island of Saipan.

FAST FACT During World War II, battleships were named after states, submarines after fish and marine animals, cruisers after cities or territories, and destroyers after military heroes.

373

Study Questions Have students use these questions as guides to their reading.

1. What difficulties did United States forces encounter in fighting in the Pacific?

2. How was the United States finally able to get Japan to surrender in World War II?

● USE READING AND VOCABULARY TRANSPARENCY 5-7.
5-7 TRANSPARENCY

2 Teach

Battles in the Pacific

Read and Respond

Geography To help students understand the importance of the Pacific islands to both the Allies and the Axis Powers, have them look at a map of the world. Help them locate Hong Kong, Guam, Wake Island, Midway Island, and the Philippine Islands.

Q Why do you think it was important for Japan to control the Pacific Ocean if it wanted to win the war against the United States?

A Possible response: If Japan controlled the Pacific, it would be more difficult for the United States to attack the Japanese homeland.

Q Why was island hopping a sensible strategy?

A The military could concentrate its time, energy, resources, and personnel on fewer islands.

Visual Learning

Picture Ask students to study the photograph on pages 372 and 373 that depicts a scene of naval combat during the Battle of the Coral Sea. Ask them why they think naval battles were so crucial in the war against Japan.

Map Battle Sites in the Pacific Ask students to think about Japan's location in the Pacific Ocean. Then challenge students to draw the locations of major battles in the Pacific Ocean without looking at a map.

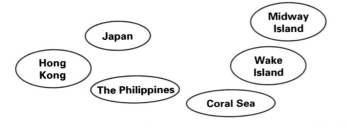

Japan
Midway Island
Hong Kong
Wake Island
The Philippines
Coral Sea

Read and Respond

History Ask students to speculate about how the Battle of Midway might have ended if the United States had not known Japanese forces would attack. Students should respond that the United States would not have been prepared and might have lost the island to the Japanese.

Geography Ask students to explain why some Pacific islands were considered strategically important. Make a list with students of characteristics of a strategically important island in World War II. The island lies along a direct route to Japan; it is a military base; it has an abundance of natural resources or war supplies. After the class has finished its list, have students check off the characteristics that apply to the Philippines.

Iwo Jima and Okinawa

Read and Respond

Link Geography and History Ask students to locate the islands of Iwo Jima and Okinawa on a map of the Pacific. Inform students that after World War II, both islands remained under United States control. Iwo Jima was returned to Japan in 1968 and Okinawa in 1972. Tell students that there is still a large United States military presence on Okinawa.

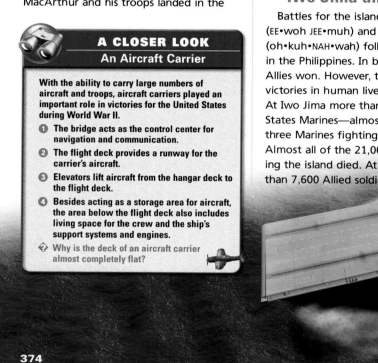

One group of islands they wanted to take back was the Philippine Islands because they had been a United States territory for many years. In early 1942, American and Philippine troops, led by General Douglas MacArthur, had fought the Japanese for four months but finally were forced to surrender. General MacArthur was ordered to leave the islands before the surrender. As he left, he made this promise to the people of the Philippines: "I shall return."

Two years later General MacArthur kept his promise. In October 1944 General MacArthur and his troops landed in the

United States soldiers raise the United States flag after the battle of Iwo Jima.

Philippines. By July 1945 the Allies had taken the Philippine Islands back from the Japanese. Victory in the Philippines did more than push the Japanese out of the islands. It left the southernmost island of Japan unprotected. It also gave the Allies a land base from which they could attack Japan.

REVIEW What was island hopping? the Allied plan to take certain key islands in the Pacific

Iwo Jima and Okinawa

Battles for the islands of Iwo Jima (EE•woh JEE•muh) and Okinawa (oh•kuh•NAH•wah) followed the victory in the Philippines. In both battles, the Allies won. However, the cost of these victories in human lives was very high. At Iwo Jima more than 25,000 United States Marines—almost one out of every three Marines fighting there—were killed. Almost all of the 21,000 Japanese defending the island died. At Okinawa more than 7,600 Allied soldiers

---

A CLOSER LOOK
An Aircraft Carrier

With the ability to carry large numbers of aircraft and troops, aircraft carriers played an important role in victories for the United States during World War II.

1. The bridge acts as the control center for navigation and communication.
2. The flight deck provides a runway for the carrier's aircraft.
3. Elevators lift aircraft from the hangar deck to the flight deck.
4. Besides acting as a storage area for aircraft, the area below the flight deck also includes living space for the crew and the ship's support systems and engines.

Why is the deck of an aircraft carrier almost completely flat?

374

BACKGROUND

Joe Rosenthal Photographer Joe Rosenthal was awarded a Pulitzer Prize for his photograph of soldiers raising the flag on Mount Suribachi after the fifth day of fighting at Iwo Jima. The photograph was reproduced and used as a war bond poster in 1945.

BACKGROUND

Navajo Code Talkers Tell students that Navajos served as code talkers in the Marines during World War II, transmitting information about war tactics and troop movements, orders, and other battlefield information. Philip Johnston, the son of a missionary to the Navajo, spoke Navajo fluently. Johnston knew that the language could be used as an unbreakable code because it is unwritten and complex. Navajos were respected for their speed and accuracy in transmitting messages during the war.

and Marines were killed or reported missing in action. Many thousands more were injured. More than 107,000 Japanese soldiers and civilians were killed.

The war in the Pacific was very different from the war in the Atlantic. The islands of the Pacific Ocean had a different geography from either Europe or North Africa. In the Pacific, soldiers faced tropical rain forests. One American soldier wrote of the difficulties of fighting in the heat, humidity, and heavy rains of the rain forests of the Pacific Islands: "[There was] always the rain and the mud, torrid heat and teeming [swarming] insect life. . . ." Because of the harsh conditions and the fierce battles, the numbers of those killed or wounded grew as the Allies moved closer to Japan.

REVIEW Who won the Battle of Iwo Jima?
The Allies

The Atom Bomb

On August 2, 1939, a scientist named Albert Einstein wrote a letter to President Franklin D. Roosevelt. In the letter, he warned of Germany's plans to build a new kind of bomb. This bomb, Einstein wrote, was an "extremely powerful bomb of a new type . . . [that when] carried by boat and exploded in a port might well destroy the whole port together with some of the surrounding territory."

Because of this letter, President Roosevelt created a secret group of scientists. The group was so secret that Vice President Harry S. Truman did not know of it until he himself became President! The goal of this group was to get ahead of Germany in creating this new kind of bomb.

Picture Ask students to study the photograph on page 374 of the Marines raising the flag at Iwo Jima. Ask volunteers to suggest what emotion this photograph conveys. You may wish to have students act out this famous photograph by Joe Rosenthal.

A CLOSER LOOK

An Aircraft Carrier

Have students examine the illustration on pages 374 and 375 of the aircraft carrier. Ask them to speculate why this type of ship was so important to the Allies' victory over Japan.
CAPTION ANSWER: so that aircraft can take off and land on it

The Atom Bomb

Read and Respond

Civics and Government Discuss with students the importance to the United States of building the atom bomb before Germany did. Point out that the Germans surrendered before they could complete their bomb.

Q Why did the Manhattan Project have to be so secret that even the Vice President did not know about it?

A Possible response: If Germany had known the United States was working on the bomb, it would have tried to build one faster.

INTEGRATE HEALTH

Malaria One challenge United States troops faced in the Pacific was the risk of catching tropical diseases such as malaria. Explain to students that malaria is a disease caused by a parasite. Ask for a volunteer to define *parasite*. Make sure students understand that it is an organism that lives off other organisms. Explain that the parasite that causes malaria lives in female mosquitoes and humans. Humans become infected if they are bitten by a mosquito that is carrying the parasite.

BACKGROUND

Henry "Red" Erwin During World War II Henry Erwin served as a radio operator on a B-29 bomber. During one flight over the Pacific, Erwin saved the lives of the plane's crew while disposing of a phosphorus bomb. In 1945 Henry "Red" Erwin was awarded the Congressional Medal of Honor for heroism above and beyond the call of duty.

Victory over Japan

Read and Respond

Culture and Society One of the issues that President Truman faced was the Japanese attitude toward surrender. During the war, not one Japanese military unit had surrendered, whereas mass suicides upon defeat were common. United States intelligence indicated that the Japanese had been defeated militarily even before Truman became President, but they continued to fight. Casualties grew higher and higher as United States troops got closer to Japan. Japan increased its troops by drafting every male from 15 to 60 and every woman from 17 to 45 into the army.

He wanted to warn the President about Germany's efforts to build a new kind of bomb.

Dr. J. Robert Oppenheimer was named to lead the scientists. He went from university to university, asking the nation's top scientists to come to Los Alamos, New Mexico, to help him with the Manhattan Project. This was the name by which this secret work would be known.

By July 1945 the Manhattan Project's scientists had built a new bomb. They called it an atom bomb, because its explosive power came from splitting atoms. On July 16 they tested it in the New Mexico desert.

J. Robert Oppenheimer

The explosion from this first atom bomb was very large. It had the force of more than 18,000 tons of dynamite, enough to shake the earth! Along with the explosion came a blinding flash and a cloud of smoke the shape of a giant mushroom. One scientist who watched the test bomb explode in New Mexico said, "I am sure that at the end of the world—in the last millisecond of the earth's existence—the last man will see something very similar to what we have seen."

REVIEW Why did Albert Einstein write President Roosevelt a letter?

PREDICT AN OUTCOME

Victory over Japan

By July 1945 Japan was in a difficult position. Its navy had been destroyed. Its air force was weakened. It had lost most of the territories it had invaded. With those losses came the loss of the raw materials Japan got from those territories. For example, in 1942 Japan got 40 percent of all the oil drilled in lands it had invaded. In 1943, as the Allies took back islands, they cut Japan off from those oil supplies.

In addition, Allied planes were fire-bombing Japanese cities, including Tokyo, in early March of 1945. High winds fanned the flames of the fires caused by the bombs until they had burned up 16 square miles (41 sq km) of Tokyo. The fires killed more than 80,000 people. They also left more than 1 million people homeless. One newspaper reporter wrote, "The city was as bright as at sunrise. . . . Clouds of smoke, soot, even sparks driven by the storm flew over it. That night we thought the whole of Tokyo was reduced

This photo shows United States and Filipino troops held in a Japanese prison camp.

---

to ashes." Similar damage was done during firebombing raids on other Japanese cities.

On July 26, 1945, the Allies sent Japan a message. It said that Japan had to surrender immediately. If it did not, the Allies would continue the bombing. Still, Japan would not surrender. President Harry S. Truman then made the difficult decision to drop an atom bomb on Japan. He said he wanted to end the war quickly and save American lives.

On August 6, 1945, the American bomber *Enola Gay* flew over the industrial city of Hiroshima (hir•uh•SHEE•muh),

Japan. It dropped a single bomb. The bomb destroyed almost all of Hiroshima and killed more than 70,000 people, mostly civilians who lived there.

The Allies were sure that the terrible destruction caused by the atom bomb would force Japan to surrender right away. Yet Japan still did not surrender. On August 9 the United States dropped a second atom bomb, this time on the city of Nagasaki (nah•guh•SAH•kee).

At that time Clarence Graham of the United States was a prisoner of war being held in Japan, just east of Nagasaki. He described the atomic explosion on the city.

Regions Several major battles of World War II were fought in the Pacific, where the war ended.

◈ In what general direction shown on the map did the Allied forces advance?

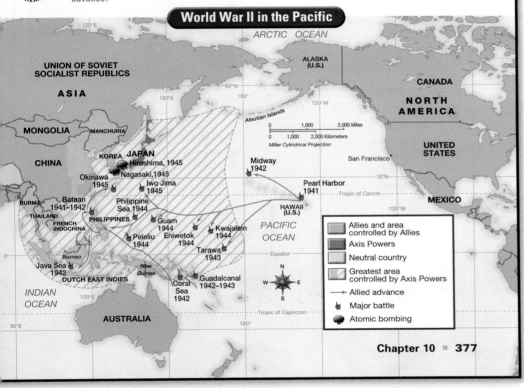

World War II in the Pacific

ARCTIC OCEAN

UNION OF SOVIET SOCIALIST REPUBLICS

ASIA

ALASKA (U.S.)

CANADA

NORTH AMERICA

MONGOLIA   MANCHURIA

CHINA   KOREA JAPAN

Hiroshima, 1945

Okinawa 1945   Nagasaki,1945

Iwo Jima 1945

BURMA   Bataan 1941–1942   Philippine Sea 1944

THAILAND   PHILIPPINES

FRENCH INDOCHINA   Guam 1944

Peleliu 1944   Eniwetok 1944   Kwajalein 1944

Tarawa 1943

Borneo

Java Sea 1942   New Guinea

DUTCH EAST INDIES   Coral Sea 1942   Guadalcanal 1942–1943

INDIAN OCEAN

AUSTRALIA

Aleutian Islands

Midway 1942

Pearl Harbor 1941

HAWAII (U.S.)

PACIFIC OCEAN

Equator

San Francisco

UNITED STATES

MEXICO

Tropic of Cancer

Tropic of Capricorn

0   1,000   2,000 Miles
0   1,000   2,000 Kilometers
Miller Cylindrical Projection

	Allies and area controlled by Allies
	Axis Powers
	Neutral country
	Greatest area controlled by Axis Powers
→	Allied advance
	Major battle
	Atomic bombing

N W E S

Chapter 10 ■ 377

Visual Learning

Map Ask students to study the map on page 377. Have students identify the areas that were controlled by the Allies.
CAPTION ANSWER: west

Read and Respond

Civics and Government Remind students that it was President Truman's decision to drop the atom bomb because the President is commander in chief of the United States military.

Link History and Geography Hiroshima and Nagasaki were chosen as sites on to which to drop the atom bombs because they had not been bombed previously in the war. Ask students to speculate what would have happened if Japan had refused to surrender after the second atom bomb was dropped.

GO ONLINE Students might enjoy reading more personal accounts and oral histories. Have them visit The Learning Site at **www.harcourtschool.com.**

BACKGROUND

After the Atom Bombs The atom bombs entirely destroyed about 5 square miles (8 sq km) in the centers of Hiroshima and Nagasaki. According to the United States, 70,000 people were killed in Hiroshima and 40,000 in Nagasaki. Japanese estimates put the total at 240,000 people. Since the end of the war, both cities have been rebuilt. The Peace Memorial Park was built in Hiroshima to honor the victims.

Explain to students that President Truman defended his decision to drop the atom bomb on the grounds that doing so would save the lives of many thousands of American soldiers who otherwise would be killed in a land attack on Japan. Since then some Americans have criticized the use of the bombs on two grounds: it should never have been used against civilians, and it launched the postwar nuclear arms race.

Analyze the Viewpoints—Answers

❶ Admiral Leahy opposed the use of the atom bomb against Japan. General Groves was in favor of using the bomb to end the war.

❷ Make sure that students' paragraphs summarize the arguments of two viewpoints.

Read and Respond

History Tell students that the USS *Missouri,* on which Japanese officials surrendered to the United States, was Admiral Nimitz's flagship during the war. It was involved in the attacks on Iwo Jima and Okinawa.

3 Close

Summarize Key Content

- The Allies faced challenges fighting the war in the Pacific unlike those they faced in Europe.
- Thousands of Allied soldiers were killed achieving victory at Iwo Jima and Okinawa.
- With the help of many scientists, the United States developed an atom bomb.
- The Japanese surrendered after atom bombs were dropped on Hiroshima and Nagasaki.

He said, "We saw a brilliant flash—there's no way to describe the brightness. You couldn't tell where the flash came from—just brilliant brightness. Then seconds later . . . you could feel the ground shaking."

The question of whether or not to use atom bombs was a difficult one to answer. President Truman asked a committee of scientists and officials whether the United States should use them. After reviewing the options, the committee said it should. Others opposed this advice.

ADMIRAL WILLIAM LEAHY, a top adviser to President Truman

❝ The use of this barbarous [cruel] weapon . . . was of no material assistance [real help] in our war against Japan. The Japanese were already defeated and ready to surrender. ❞

GENERAL LESLIE GROVES, the chief of the project developing the bomb

❝ The atomic bombings of Hiroshima and Nagasaki ended World War II. While they brought death and destruction on a horrifying scale, they averted [prevented] even greater losses—American, English, and Japanese. ❞

The explosion from the atom bomb (above) caused mass destruction in Nagasaki (below).

Analyze the Viewpoints
❶ What views did each person hold?
❷ **Make It Relevant** Look at the Letters to the Editor section of your newspaper. Find two letters that express different viewpoints about the same issue. Then write a paragraph that summarizes the viewpoint of each letter.

Japan then agreed to surrender, and fighting stopped. That day, August 15, 1945, became known as **V-J Day**—Victory over Japan Day.

The Allies cheered and laughed and wept. One American soldier fighting in

EXTEND AND ENRICH

Write a Journal Entry Challenge students to imagine that they are living at the end of World War II and that Japan has finally surrendered. Direct students to write journal entries describing the relief they feel now that the war is over.

All across the United States, Americans celebrated V-J Day at the end of World War II.

the Pacific remembered what happened after the atom bombs were dropped: "We . . . cried with relief and joy."

On September 2, 1945, representatives from Japan's government came aboard the USS *Missouri*, which was anchored in Tokyo Bay. There they and representatives of the United States government signed the surrender papers. The end of World War II had finally come.

REVIEW **Why did Japan finally surrender to the United States?** Two of their cities had been destroyed by atom bombs.

LESSON 2 REVIEW

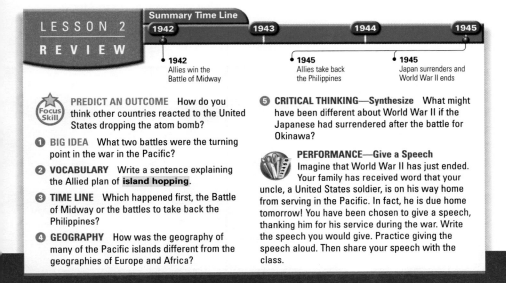

Summary Time Line

| 1942 | 1943 | 1944 | 1945 |

- **1942** Allies win the Battle of Midway
- **1945** Allies take back the Philippines
- **1945** Japan surrenders and World War II ends

 PREDICT AN OUTCOME How do you think other countries reacted to the United States dropping the atom bomb?

1 BIG IDEA What two battles were the turning point in the war in the Pacific?

2 VOCABULARY Write a sentence explaining the Allied plan of **island hopping**.

3 TIME LINE Which happened first, the Battle of Midway or the battles to take back the Philippines?

4 GEOGRAPHY How was the geography of many of the Pacific islands different from the geographies of Europe and Africa?

5 CRITICAL THINKING—Synthesize What might have been different about World War II if the Japanese had surrendered after the battle for Okinawa?

 PERFORMANCE—Give a Speech Imagine that World War II has just ended. Your family has received word that your uncle, a United States soldier, is on his way home from serving in the Pacific. In fact, he is due home tomorrow! You have been chosen to give a speech, thanking him for his service during the war. Write the speech you would give. Practice giving the speech aloud. Then share your speech with the class.

Chapter 10 ■ 379

Skill Lesson

PAGES 380–381

OBJECTIVE

■ Use parallel time lines to compare events occurring at the same time in different places.

Vocabulary

parallel time lines p. 380

WORD CARDS

See pp. V45–V46.

1 Motivate

Why It Matters

Inform students that parallel time lines can help make it easier to understand complex events such as those that took place on two fronts during World War II.

2 Teach

What You Need to Know

Direct students to study Time Lines A and B. Ask a volunteer to describe the characteristics of the time lines, such as the amount of time they show and the different places they cover. Next, ask students to find the event that is documented on both time lines. Point out that this event affected the war both in Europe and in the Pacific.

·SKILLS· Read Parallel Time Lines

VOCABULARY
parallel time lines

➤ WHY IT MATTERS

When there are many events happening at the same time in different places, it can be difficult to put the events in order on one time line. Parallel time lines can help. **Parallel time lines** are two or more time lines that show the same period of time. Parallel time lines can also show events that happened in different places.

➤ WHAT YOU NEED TO KNOW

The parallel time lines on these pages show events that took place during World War II, from 1941 to 1945. Time Line A shows the important events that affected the European front. Time Line B shows the important events that affected the Pacific front. You can use these parallel time lines to compare when different events in different places happened.

➤ PRACTICE THE SKILL

Use these parallel time lines to answer the following questions:

1 Which occurred first, D day or V-J Day?

2 Why do you think the label *Harry S. Truman becomes President of the United States* is shown on both time lines?

3 Did the Allies capture Guam before or after they won in North Africa?

4 In what year did V-E Day and V-J Day occur?

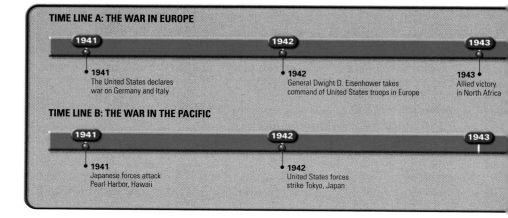

TIME LINE A: THE WAR IN EUROPE

1941	1942	1943
1941 The United States declares war on Germany and Italy	**1942** General Dwight D. Eisenhower takes command of United States troops in Europe	**1943** Allied victory in North Africa

TIME LINE B: THE WAR IN THE PACIFIC

1941	1942	1943
1941 Japanese forces attack Pearl Harbor, Hawaii	**1942** United States forces strike Tokyo, Japan	

INTEGRATE ART

Illustrate Time Lines
Explain to students that pictures often are included in time lines to illustrate an event. Ask students to draw pictures to accompany the time lines they create in this lesson.

On board the USS *Missouri*, a Japanese delegate signs the surrender papers that ended World War II.

➡ APPLY WHAT YOU LEARNED

Create parallel time lines of events that have happened in your lifetime. On one time line show the important events in your life, beginning with the year you were born and ending with the present year. On the other time line, show important events that have taken place in the United States during these same years. Share your time lines with a classmate.

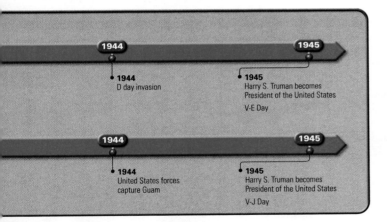

1944		1945
1944 D day invasion		**1945** Harry S. Truman becomes President of the United States V-E Day

1944		1945
1944 United States forces capture Guam		**1945** Harry S. Truman becomes President of the United States V-J Day

CHART AND GRAPH SKILLS

❶ D day

❷ because the event affected the war both in Europe and in the Pacific

❸ after

❹ 1945

 **Close**

Apply What You Learned

Make sure that students' time lines include information about their lives on the first time line and information about events of national importance on the second time line. Have students determine how national events have affected their own lives.

ACTIVITY BOOK

Use ACTIVITY BOOK, p. 97, to give students additional practice using this skill.

TRANSPARENCY

Use SKILL TRANSPARENCY 5-3.

EXTEND AND ENRICH

Research Events Ask students to choose an event that appears on both Time Line A and Time Line B. Suggest that they use the Internet and other reference sources to learn more about the event. Encourage them to find out how the event affected the war both in Europe and in the Pacific.

RETEACH THE SKILL

Make Time Lines Ask students to work in pairs to make parallel time lines of their previous days at school. Emphasize that partners must decide on a time period for their time lines before they begin. They also may wish to discuss the kinds of events they plan to include on the time lines.

OBJECTIVES

- Describe some of the human costs of World War II.
- Explain how the Servicemen's Readjustment Act helped World War II veterans adjust to civilian life in the United States.
- Describe how society in the United States changed after World War II.

Predict an Outcome
pp. 361, 382, 383, 387, 396

Vocabulary

SEE READING AND VOCABULARY TRANSPARENCY 5-8 OR THE WORD CARDS ON PP. V45–V46.

refugees p. 383   **baby boom**
veteran p. 383   p. 386

When Minutes Count

Invite pairs of students to examine the photographs in the lesson. Then have them come up with one question they think will be answered by reading the lesson. Encourage students to read the lesson to find the answers to their questions.

Quick Summary

This lesson describes life in the United States after World War II.

1 Motivate

Set the Purpose

Big Idea Ask students to think about why experts feared the United States economy would suffer after World War II.

Access Prior Knowledge

Discuss with students what they have learned about life in the United States during World War II.

PREDICT AN OUTCOME
As you read, predict likely outcomes of the end of World War II.

BIG IDEA
Life in the United States changed after World War II.

VOCABULARY
refugees
veteran
baby boom

American soldiers from many wars, including World War II, are buried in Arlington National Cemetery in Arlington, Virginia.

Life After World War II

1930   1940   1950
1944–1950

Many Americans were afraid that the end of the war might also mean the end of the jobs and money the war had brought to the United States. They wondered if there would be enough work for everyone. Yet Americans were to find that the end of the war did not bring economic hardships with it.

The Cost of the War

The cost of World War II in terms of human lives was great for all the countries involved. About 400,000 American soldiers and close to 17 million soldiers from other countries had died in the fighting. Germany alone lost more than 3 million soldiers. Millions of civilians also died in the fighting. Some died in fires caused by the bombing raids. Others died from diseases.

When the war ended, cities and towns in Europe and Japan and in other places where fighting had taken place were in ruins. In some cities nine out of every ten buildings were too badly damaged to be used. Many of the people who survived had no homes, no jobs, and often nothing to eat. Some of

382 ▪ Unit 5

BACKGROUND

Economic Costs of World War II World War II is estimated to have cost more than $1 trillion. The United States spent about $341 billion. Germany spent $272 billion, and the Soviet Union spent $192 billion. However, when the damages caused by the war are considered, the cost of the war becomes much higher. For example, Japan spent $56 billion on the war but actually lost a total of $562 billion because of damage to the country.

STUDY/RESEARCH SKILLS

Skimming and Scanning Remind students that they can find information in the lesson quickly by skimming and scanning the text. Have students practice this skill on the first page by skimming and scanning to find the following information:

- the number of United States soldiers who died in World War II
- the number of troops that Germany lost in World War II

Millions of American soldiers returning home after the war had a large effect on the country's economy.

these people were prisoners of war, some had been freed from concentration camps, and some had fled cities that were being invaded. All these people became **refugees**—people who seek shelter and safety elsewhere. Some traveled from place to place in search of food and a safe place to live.

To help the refugees, the Allies set up camps and provided them with food, shelter, and medical care until they could find homes. The United States also worked with other nations to create agencies to help these millions of people. People in the United States gave much of the money spent by these agencies.

REVIEW How did the United States help those who were left homeless by the war?

🔵 **PREDICT AN OUTCOME**

Soldiers Return

The war was over. Millions of soldiers were returning home. To help them re-adjust to civilian life, or settle into it, the government passed the Servicemen's Readjustment Act. Americans were soon calling it the GI Bill—the Government Issue Bill of Rights. The GI Bill was passed in 1944. Just as the United States had planned for the war, the nation also had planned for peace.

The GI Bill helped many **veterans**, or those who had served in the armed forces. It stated that veterans could get government money to pay for a college education or for job training. In addition, veterans would receive a monthly allowance while they were in school.

by providing money and setting up camps where the refugees could take shelter

Chapter 10 ■ 383

READING SOCIAL STUDIES

Personal Response As they read the lesson encourage students to think about how life changed in the United States after World War II.

● USE READING AND VOCABULARY TRANSPARENCY 5-8.

5-8 TRANSPARENCY

2 Teach

The Cost of the War

Read and Respond

Link Culture and Society with History Inform students that at the end of World War II, there were an estimated 21 million refugees in Europe. Many of these refugees had been forced out of their home countries by the Nazis to work in labor camps. Ask students if they think the United States has an obligation as a world power to help refugees.

Soldiers Return

Read and Respond

Culture and Society Lead students to understand the far-reaching impact of the GI Bill on education in the United States. By 1947 almost half of the college students in the United States were veterans. Also point out that under the GI Bill, married veterans attending school usually received larger monthly allowances because they often had families to support.

BACKGROUND

American Cemeteries Overseas The American Battle Monuments Commission manages 15 cemeteries in foreign countries. The bodies of 93,242 American soldiers from World War II are buried in these cemeteries.

READING SOCIAL STUDIES

Graphic Organizer Draw a problem-solution chart on the board. Point out to students that after World War II, the United States took many steps to prevent problems. In this chart, have students write the potential problem and then write in the steps the United States took either to prevent the problem from happening or to lessen its effects.

Problem	→	Solution
	→	

Read and Respond

Economics Explain to students that encouraging veterans to go back to school was very helpful for the transition from a wartime economy to a peacetime economy. Remind students that experts were worried that there would not be enough jobs for returning veterans.

Q **How did the educational benefits provided by the GI Bill help keep unemployment in the United States from skyrocketing?**

A Possible response: Because some veterans were in school and receiving monthly allowances, they did not need jobs. This left more jobs open for other veterans returning from the war.

Many veterans returned to school under the GI Bill. This photo shows veterans applying for educational courses.

Almost half of all the veterans took advantage of the GI Bill to get more education. In fact, General Dwight D. Eisenhower himself went back to school on the GI Bill.

With so many veterans going to school, many colleges and universities often ran out of room for housing and classes. The government helped by taking apart unused military buildings and sending them in pieces to be rebuilt and used by the nation's colleges.

The GI Bill also provided loans that had low interest rates. Because of the low interest rates, veterans would not have to pay back as much money as they would to repay a loan from a bank. Many veterans used these loans to buy houses and to start businesses. The government also provided one year of income to veterans who could not find work.

REVIEW What was the GI Bill? a bill that provided veterans with money for school, loans, and income

The use of automobiles increased after gas rationing ended.

384   Unit 5

 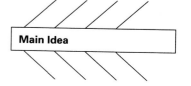

After the war, drive-in movie theaters became a popular place for entertainment. Some drive-in theaters, like this one in New York, held up to 1,200 cars!

Changes at Home

Most rationing ended with the end of the war. Many people were very happy that gasoline was no longer rationed. They could now get back in their automobiles and not worry about being able to get enough gas to go places.

A new place that people drove to was the drive-in movie theater. Between 1947 and 1950, about 2,000 drive-in theaters were built across the country. In these theaters people drove up to a parking spot in front of a huge movie screen, attached a speaker to their car, and then watched the movie.

Technology brought another new form of entertainment after the war. It was called the television. The first television sets were used in 1941, but it was not until after the war that television became popular. By 1949 Americans were buying almost 100,000 sets a week! In that same year, many TV stations started up. These stations broadcast everything from variety shows to sports games. Television also began to be used for education. For the first time, New York City high school students were able to watch a live meeting of national leaders on television.

People who had saved money during the war were ready to buy products. They wanted everything from houses to appliances to automobiles. Factories that had been making war supplies went back to producing consumer goods.

INTEGRATE MATHEMATICS

Multiply Direct students to determine about how many television sets were sold in the United States in 1949. 100,000 sets/week × 52 weeks/year = 5,200,000 television sets sold in 1949

MAKE IT RELEVANT

At Home Encourage students to start conversations with their family members about the role television plays in their lives. Ask them to keep logs of how much television they watch and which programs they watch over the course of one week. Have students share their logs in class. Discuss as a class what their findings suggest about how television influences their lives.

Changes at Home

Read and Respond

Link Culture and Society with Economics Discuss with students how new inventions, such as television, helped stimulate the United States economy. Ask students to make a list of all the jobs and industries that are affected by television. Stress that television affects electronics manufacturers, news broadcasters and stations, the entertainment industry, and the thousands of companies that run advertisements on television.

Economics Tell students that the unemployment rate is the percent of people in the labor force who do not have jobs but are actively looking for jobs. Emphasize that not everyone in the United States is in the labor force. For example, college students and retired people may not be seeking jobs.

Q **What does an unemployment rate of 3.8 percent mean?**

A It means that 3.8 percent of the people looking for jobs cannot find one.

Economics Tell students that after World War II, the economies of many other countries struggled to improve. Have students complete an idea map about the reasons the United States economy was able to stay strong after the war.

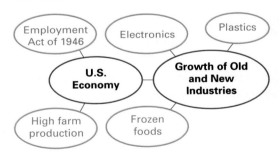

The Baby Boom

Read and Respond

Culture and Society Tell students that housing developments such as Levittown had an effect on life in large cities. As time went on, the centers of many cities became increasingly run down. Explain that by the 1970s many inner cities had become poor slum neighborhoods.

Economics After World War II more people than ever before were able to own their own homes. Discuss with students the advantages of owning a home over renting one. Point out that when a person buys a home, he or she is making an investment. Have students speculate on how home ownership is good for the economy.

3 Close

Summarize Key Content

- The cost of World War II was great. More than 400,000 United States soldiers died during the war, and many cities in Europe and Japan were in ruins.
- To help veterans readjust to civilian life, the United States government passed the Servicemen's Readjustment Act, known as the GI Bill of Rights. It provided money for tuition, low-interest loans, and a year of unemployment payments if needed.
- After World War II the United States economy was driven by new industries such as electronics, plastics, and frozen foods.
- About 50 million babies were born in the United States, and many families moved to the suburbs during the 15 years after World War II—a period known as the baby boom.

These factories could hardly keep up with consumers' demands. In fact, sometimes there were shortages of the goods that people wanted.

New industries did well after the war. The electronics industry grew rapidly, mainly because of the number of television sets people were buying. Other industries, such as the plastics and the frozen foods industries, also grew. Farm production stayed high after the war. For a while, the American farmer was also needed to provide the animals and the feed that would help start farms in war-torn countries.

The nation's economy remained strong. Some workers lost their jobs to returning soldiers, and many women left jobs at factories to care for their families. Still, the number of unemployed people stayed low. To make sure that unemployment stayed low, the government passed the Employment Act of 1946. This law created a council to advise the President on economic matters. This council also encouraged the government to take steps to keep Americans working.

REVIEW What product caused the electronics industry to grow after the war? television

The Baby Boom

After the war, soldiers returned home to their families. Others started families with wives they had met and married while they were away from home. In the years right after the war many babies were born. In fact, about 50 million babies were born in the United States during the 15 years after the war ended! So many babies were born that this period became known as the **baby boom**.

Many of these new and growing families went to live in housing developments in the suburbs. Suburbs were growing as fast as they could be built. Many suburbs

This photo (left) shows the wedding of a United States Army sergeant and a Red Cross worker from Northern Ireland. After World War II, the couple started a new life and a new family in Arlington, Virginia (below).

386 ■ Unit 5

INTEGRATE LANGUAGE ARTS

Write a Persuasive Letter Ask students to imagine that they have just moved to the suburbs with their families in the late 1950s. Direct them to write a persuasive letter encouraging a relative to move to the suburbs as well. Emphasize that their opinions should be supported with information from the lesson.

INTEGRATE ART

Find Architectural Designs Suggest that students use the Internet and architectural books to find designs of houses that were popular in suburbs in the United States after World War II. Have students create collages of housing styles from that time period. Display students' collages in the classroom.

The demand for housing became so strong in the postwar United States that new neighborhoods sprang up all over the country.

offered people new houses, playgrounds, swimming pools, and schools. Shopping centers were also built nearby. In the suburb of Levittown, on Long Island, New York, more than 17,000 new homes were built after the war. Sometimes as many as 36 houses were built in one day.

Life in the suburbs made Americans need their cars more than ever. Many people lived in the suburbs but worked in the cities. They needed their cars to get to and from work.

REVIEW **What encouraged American families to move to the suburbs?** Suburbs often offered new houses, playgrounds, new schools, and shopping centers nearby.

LESSON 3 REVIEW

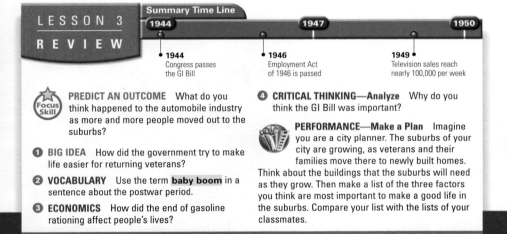

Summary Time Line

1944	1947	1950

1944 Congress passes the GI Bill

1946 Employment Act of 1946 is passed

1949 Television sales reach nearly 100,000 per week

PREDICT AN OUTCOME What do you think happened to the automobile industry as more and more people moved out to the suburbs?

1 **BIG IDEA** How did the government try to make life easier for returning veterans?

2 **VOCABULARY** Use the term **baby boom** in a sentence about the postwar period.

3 **ECONOMICS** How did the end of gasoline rationing affect people's lives?

4 **CRITICAL THINKING—Analyze** Why do you think the GI Bill was important?

 PERFORMANCE—Make a Plan Imagine you are a city planner. The suburbs of your city are growing, as veterans and their families move there to newly built homes. Think about the buildings that the suburbs will need as they grow. Then make a list of the three factors you think are most important to make a good life in the suburbs. Compare your list with the lists of your classmates.

Chapter 10 ■ 387

Lesson 4

OBJECTIVES

- Describe the purpose of the United Nations and the role of the United States in establishing it.
- Explain how the United States accepted its role as a world superpower and helped to rebuild Europe and Japan after World War II.
- Identify the role of the United States in world events during the Cold War.
- Analyze the Truman Doctrine and Marshall Plan and their effects.

 Predict an Outcome
pp. 361, 388, 390, 395, 396

Vocabulary

SEE READING AND VOCABULARY TRANSPARENCY 5-9 OR THE WORD CARDS ON PP. V47–V48.

superpower p. 388

arms race p. 390

free world p. 391

cold war p. 393

 When Minutes Count

Have students read the lesson and find at least one sentence that supports the Big Idea.

Quick Summary

This lesson describes the United Nations and the attempt by the United States to contain communism.

1 Motivate

Set the Purpose

Big Idea Discuss with students why some people in democratic nations felt communism was a threat.

Access Prior Knowledge

Ask students to tell how the economy in a communist country is different from the economy in a democracy.

4

 PREDICT AN OUTCOME
As you read, predict likely outcomes of the new threat of communism.

BIG IDEA
Some nations of the world faced a new threat—the threat of communism.

VOCABULARY

superpower
arms race
free world
cold war

A Changed World

1930   1940   1950

1945–1950

At the end of World War II, General Douglas MacArthur was present when Japan surrendered. Afterward, MacArthur spoke of his hopes for the future. He said, "It is my earnest hope . . . that from this solemn occasion a better world shall emerge."

In the years after the war, the United States and the Soviet Union became the world's most powerful nations. They were called the **superpowers** because of the important role they played in world events. The two superpowers were very different from each other, so there were many conflicts between them. Although the two nations never went to war with each other, the threat of war was always present. For this reason, the years following World War II were a frightening time for many people.

The United Nations

Just as world leaders did after World War I, they turned to the idea of an organization of nations after World War II. This time the United States supported the idea. In April 1945,

Representatives of countries discuss the formation of the United Nations.

388 ■ Unit 5

WORD WORK

Historical Context Remind students that new vocabulary terms come into use over time. Ask them to look at the vocabulary terms for this lesson. Point out that all the terms relate to events of the twentieth century. As students read the lesson, discuss the historical context of each vocabulary term they encounter.

BACKGROUND

The United Nations Delegates to the San Francisco conference worked for two months writing the charter for the United Nations. The charter includes the purpose, principles, and organizational structure of the United Nations. The charter was unanimously adopted on June 26, 1945, and the United Nations officially began when the charter took effect on October 24, 1945.

Divisions of the United Nations

GENERAL ASSEMBLY
- Each member nation has one vote.
- Makes decisions by two-thirds majority on important matters such as international peace and security, admitting new members, and the UN budget

SECURITY COUNCIL
- Fifteen council members, five of which are the permanent members from the United States, Britain, France, Russia, and China
- Is responsible for maintaining international peace and security
- Can order negotiations, economic bans, or military actions

ECONOMIC AND SOCIAL COUNCIL
- Fifty-four members elected by the General Assembly
- Works to improve economic and social conditions worldwide
- Individual groups work on issues such as human rights, crime prevention, and environmental protection.

INTERNATIONAL COURT OF JUSTICE
- Fifteen judges elected by the General Assembly and the Security Council
- Decides disputes among nations

SECRETARIAT
- Headed by the Secretary General, who is appointed by the General Assembly
- Is responsible for managing United Nations offices throughout the world

Analyze Charts The United Nations is organized into different areas of responsibility. Today almost 200 nations are members of the organization.

◈ Which division of the United Nations is responsible for deciding disputes between nations?

---

delegates from 50 countries met in San Francisco, California. They formed the United Nations, or UN. The purpose of the UN is to keep world peace and to promote cooperation among nations.

The United Nations soon found that keeping the peace was going to be a difficult task. The Nazis no longer threatened Europe or the rest of the world. Yet a new danger to the world's democracies had appeared—communism.

The United States and the Soviet Union had been allies during World War II.

British Prime Minister Winston Churchill works at his desk.

389

QUESTIONS KIDS ASK

Q Why did the United States and the Soviet Union become enemies if they fought on the same side during World War II?

A The United States and the Soviet Union had differences that they put aside to fight a more threatening enemy, the Nazis, during World War II. After the war they no longer had a common cause, so their differences became more evident.

QUESTIONS KIDS ASK

Q Where does the United Nations military force come from?

A The United Nations does not have its own army. Instead, it borrows troops from its member countries.

READING SOCIAL STUDIES

K-W-L Chart Direct students to complete the first two columns of a K-W-L chart before they begin reading the lesson.

K	W	L
The Soviet Union was communist.	What happened to many Eastern European countries under Soviet control after World War II?	
To many, communism is a threat to freedom.	How did the United States help Eastern European countries fight communism?	

● USE READING AND VOCABULARY TRANSPARENCY 5-9.

5-9 TRANSPARENCY

2 Teach

The United Nations

Read and Respond

Civics and Government Work with students to list at least three characteristics that define a superpower. Then have a volunteer read the definition of *superpower* from a dictionary. Discuss how students' definitions compare with the dictionary definition.

Link History with Civics and Government Have students recall the League of Nations and identify the similarities between the League of Nations and the United Nations.

Visual Learning

Charts Have students examine the chart and identify the roles for each division of the United Nations.
CAPTION ANSWER: the International Court of Justice

Read and Respond

Link Geography and History Locate a historical map that shows Europe just after World War II. Ask students to locate the Eastern European countries that became communist in the 1940s: Bulgaria, Czechoslovakia, Hungary, Poland, Romania, Albania, and Yugoslavia. Discuss why they were important to the Soviet Union. Because they bordered either the Soviet Union or a waterway that Soviets may have used. Then have students look at a current map of Europe. Direct them to locate the same countries. Emphasize to students that the borders and names of some countries have changed since World War II.

 Students might enjoy learning more about governments. Have them visit The Learning Site at www.harcourtschool.com.

Link History with Civics and Government Explain to students that the term *Iron Curtain* came to describe the Soviet Union's policy of isolation. Tell students that the Soviet Union did not allow travel into or out of the country and its satellite countries. Censorship of free expression also was a part of this policy. Explain that the effect of the Iron Curtain was the cutting off of communication and exchange of ideas between Soviet countries and the rest of the world.

Q Why do you think the Soviet Union wanted to cut off communication with the rest of the world?

A Allow students to express their opinions. Stress, however, that the Soviet government did not want its people to be exposed to Western ideas of democracy. Exposure to democratic ideas would have made it more difficult for the government to maintain control.

After the war this quickly changed. The Soviet Union was a communist country. It set up communist governments in the Eastern European countries it had invaded during the war. Joseph Stalin, the Soviet leader, felt that the Soviet Union had to control Eastern Europe to protect itself. He said that in this region, any "freely elected government would be anti-Soviet, and that we cannot allow." By 1948 Bulgaria, Czechoslovakia, Hungary, Poland, Romania, Albania, and Yugoslavia were communist countries. This happened so fast that Winston Churchill, the prime minister of Britain, said with alarm that the Soviets "are spreading across Europe like a tide."

Churchill was one of the first leaders to express concern about the spread of communism. In 1946 he spoke of his concerns at a university in the United States. He said that "an iron curtain has descended across the continent" between Eastern Europe and the West. He warned that the United States should remain ready for military conflict with the Soviet Union.

People across the world were also thinking about what the atom bombs had done to the Japanese cities of Hiroshima and Nagasaki. The Soviet Union feared the power of the United States, which had shown its ability to destroy a whole city with one bomb. Soon the Soviet Union was building its own atom bomb.

After the Soviet Union had the atom bomb, however, the United States made an even more powerful bomb—the hydrogen bomb. Scientists said that this bomb was 1,000 times more powerful than the atom bomb.

An arms race had begun. In an **arms race** one country builds up weapons to protect itself against another country. The other country then builds even more weapons to protect itself. Both the United States and the Soviet Union believed that having the most and the strongest weapons would keep their people safe.

REVIEW Why did Stalin want to control Eastern Europe? ⊜ PREDICT AN OUTCOME
He felt he needed to control Eastern Europe to protect the Soviet Union.

Scientists Albert Einstein (left) and J. Robert Oppenheimer (right) had played roles in the development of the atom bomb.

390 ▪ Unit 5

President Harry S. Truman (left) meets with Secretary of State George C. Marshall (right).

A New Role for the United States

President Truman watched the spread of communism. He wrote, "Unless Russia [the Soviet Union] is faced with an iron fist and strong language, another war is in the making." He felt that the spread of communism was a threat to freedom. In 1947 the United States began to help countries fight communism by giving them military and economic aid. In the fight against communism, the United States and its allies were known as the **free world**.

The policy of helping countries fight communism became known as the Truman Doctrine. The economic aid offered by the Truman Doctrine helped the United States contain, or hold back, the Soviet threat.

This policy was necessary, Truman said, because "the free peoples of the world look to us for support in maintaining their freedoms."

In 1948 Secretary of State George C. Marshall developed the Marshall Plan. This plan was to provide more aid to nations in war-torn Europe. According to the plan, the United States would help the nations of Europe rebuild their businesses, factories, roads, and airports over the next four years.

The Marshall Plan was a success. By the end of the four years, $12 billion had been sent to European countries in the form of money, machinery, livestock, and other materials that would help them rebuild. Many Europeans were pleased with the results of the plan.

REVIEW **Why was the Marshall Plan considered a success?** It succeeded in helping Europe rebuild.

A New Role for the United States

Read and Respond

Economics Lead a discussion on why the United States felt it was in its best interest to rebuild Europe and Japan after World War II and to prevent political and economic instability around the world. Ask students to describe what the Truman Doctrine meant to countries that were struggling to rebuild after World War II. Students should respond that it was very important in helping them improve their economies. Discuss with students how money and supplies could help prevent communist takeovers of countries. Remind students that after World War I, it was easy for dictators to take over countries with poor economies.

Civics and Government Discuss with students the benefits countries in Europe received from the Marshall Plan. Point out that the United States trades with many countries in Europe, so the rebuilding of those economies greatly benefited the United States as well.

Analyze Primary Sources

Quotation Ask students why they think President Truman said that people looked to the United States for support in maintaining their freedoms.

Hydrogen Bomb Inform students that a hydrogen bomb explodes with about 500 times more force than the atom bombs dropped on Hiroshima and Nagasaki. Explain that a hydrogen bomb explodes when atoms of hydrogen collide. Tell students that hydrogen bombs create great heat, high winds, and deadly radiation that can contaminate plants, soil, and water.

Summarizing Stress to students that writing summaries can help them understand what they have read. Emphasize that summaries are also good study tools. Ask students to write summaries of the main points of the section titled A New Role for the United States. Then have them exchange their summaries with a partner. Have partners read each other's summaries and add any important details that are missing.

New Threats to Peace

Read and Respond

Link History and Geography Inform students that after World War II, Germany was divided into two countries—East Germany and West Germany. Explain that the Soviet Union controlled East Germany and set up a communist government there, but West Germany was a democracy. Find a historical map of Germany that shows how the country was split from the end of World War II until 1990, when the country was reunified.

Link History with Civics and Government Remind students that Berlin was located in East Germany. Tell them that the city had been made up of 20 districts before the war and that these districts were distributed among the four Allies after the war. The Soviet Union controlled eight districts; the United States, six; Britain, four; and France, two. Explain that the districts controlled by the United States, Britain, and France were united to form West Berlin.

History After students read how the Soviet Union cut off the routes by which food and other supplies were delivered to Berlin, ask the following questions:

Q Why do you think the Soviet Union would not allow Eastern European countries to participate in the Marshall Plan?

A Possible response: The Soviet Union did not want Eastern Europe to be influenced by the United States in any way.

Q Why do you think West Berlin would have been seen as an island of freedom?

A Students may respond that West Berlin was an area of political freedom surrounded by areas of communist rule.

New Threats to Peace

At the end of World War II, the Allies divided Germany into four parts. Each of the major Allies controlled one part. The United States, Britain, and France worked together to build a strong West Germany out of their parts. The Soviet Union took charge of East Germany and formed a communist government there.

Berlin, the capital of Germany, was in East Germany. It was divided into four parts, too. In June 1948 the Soviet Union

challenged the other Allies by blocking all the highway, rail, and water routes into West Berlin. The Soviets hoped to drive the Western Allies out of Berlin by cutting off the routes by which food and other supplies were delivered.

Some Americans wanted to ignore what was happening in Berlin and pull out of the city. Others agreed with General Lucius Clay, who commanded American forces stationed in Germany after the war. He said, "If we mean . . . to hold [protect] Europe against communism, we must not budge. . . . I believe the future of democracy requires us to stay."

No one wanted to send supplies over land, because armed vehicles would be needed to break through the Soviet

United States Air Force pilots were trained to fly cargo transport planes (left) to deliver food and supplies to the people of West Berlin (below).

REACH ALL LEARNERS

Auditory Learners Some students may benefit from dramatic readings of the quotations throughout the lesson. Pair these students, and have them read each quotation dramatically to each other. Then ask them to tell each other what they think the quotation means.

INTEGRATE MATHEMATICS

Compute Help students compute the number of airplanes that landed in Berlin at the height of the Berlin Airlift. Ask students to find the approximate number of planes that landed in an eight-hour period if the planes landed every three minutes.

8 hours × 60 minutes/hour = 480 minutes

480 minutes ÷ 3 minutes = about 160 planes

Europe and the Cold War

- Communist country
- Noncommunist country
- Iron Curtain

0 250 500 Miles
0 250 500 Kilometers
Azimuthal Equal-Area Projection

FINLAND
NORWAY
SWEDEN
North Sea
Baltic Sea
IRELAND
BRITAIN
DENMARK
UNION OF SOVIET SOCIALIST REPUBLICS
NETHERLANDS
BRITISH ZONE
SOVIET ZONE
BELGIUM
EAST GERMANY
POLAND
LUXEMBOURG
FRENCH ZONE
WEST GERMANY
AMERICAN ZONE
CZECHOSLOVAKIA
ATLANTIC OCEAN
FRANCE
SWITZERLAND
AUSTRIA
HUNGARY
ROMANIA
PORTUGAL
SPAIN
ITALY
YUGOSLAVIA
BULGARIA
Black Sea
ALBANIA
TURKEY
GREECE
Mediterranean Sea
AFRICA
ASIA

GEOGRAPHY THEME

Place World War II changed Europe in ways that would affect the world for years to come.

❖ What does this map show about changes that took place in Germany after World War II?

blockade. That could mean war. General Clay thought about this problem. Then he called General Curtis LeMay of the Air Force. "Curt, can you transport coal by air?" he asked. The answer was "yes." Soon the United States was delivering coal and other supplies by plane.

Using three airports, American and British pilots made more than 272,000 flights over East Germany to West Berlin. They carried more than 2 million tons of food and supplies to the people there. On some days, planes landed on an average of once every 3 minutes all day long. This way of bringing supplies by plane became known as the Berlin Airlift. Six months later, the Soviet Union backed down and

ended the blockade. Supplies could again be delivered over land to West Berlin.

After the blockade ended, many people tried to leave East Berlin to escape from communist rule. In time, the East German government, with Soviet help, built a fence to keep people from leaving. Then East Germany took down the fence and put up a concrete wall with barbed wire on the top. The Berlin Wall, as it came to be known, was guarded by soldiers who were ready to shoot anyone who tried to cross it. The Berlin Wall became one of the best-known symbols of the Cold War. A **cold war** is a war that is fought mostly with ideas and money instead of with soldiers and weapons.

Chapter 10 ■ 393

BACKGROUND

The Collapse of the Soviet Union In 1989 many Eastern European countries began removing their communist governments. The Soviet Union was distracted by its own problems and agreed to withdraw troops from Eastern Europe. Shortly thereafter, republics of the Soviet Union began to secede. The Soviet parliament officially dissolved the Soviet Union on December 26, 1991.

QUESTIONS KIDS ASK

Q How big was the Berlin Wall?

A The Berlin Wall was 12 feet (4 m) tall and 103 miles (166 km) long. In places where a wall was not possible, buildings were bricked over.

Read and Respond

Economics Inform students that the Berlin Airlift also served to sustain West Germany's economy. Explain that just as airplanes carried food and supplies into West Berlin, so, too, did they carry exports out of West Berlin to other countries.

History Explain that although East Germans had limited access to Western ideas, they were aware of better opportunities elsewhere. Inform students that as a result, nearly 3 million people fled East Germany between 1949 and 1961. Explain that over time these defections did much to deplete East Germany's workforce.

Q Why did East Germany build the Berlin Wall?

A It wanted to prevent its people from leaving East Germany.

History Explain to students that the Cold War between the United States and the Soviet Union ended in 1991, when the Soviet Union dissolved.

Visual Learning

Map Direct students' attention to the map on page 393.

Q Which countries were considered to be behind the Iron Curtain?

A East Germany, Poland, Czechoslovakia, Hungary, Yugoslavia, Romania, Bulgaria, Albania, and the Union of Soviet Socialist Republics

CAPTION ANSWER: The map shows how after World War II Germany was divided and came under the control of other countries. West Germany was controlled by the United States, Britain, and France. East Germany was controlled by the Soviet Union.

Changes in Japan

Read and Respond

Civics and Government Inform students that the Japanese constitution written by MacArthur's advisers created a legislative body called the Diet. This group chose the nation's prime minister from its members. The constitution also created a judicial branch. Ask students why United States officials may have set up the Japanese government this way. Students may respond that the United States officials wanted to ensure a representative government in Japan.

Economics Remind students that Japan's industries were destroyed completely during World War II but grew rapidly in the years thereafter. Point out that these industries were rebuilt using the latest advances in technology and grew when they proved to be more efficient than other nations' industries.

Close

Summarize Key Content

- After World War II, the United Nations was formed to keep world peace and promote cooperation among nations.
- In the 1940s the Soviet Union established communist governments in many Eastern European countries, which led to increased tensions with Western nations.
- Policies such as the Truman Doctrine and the Marshall Plan called for the United States government to provide military and economic aid to countries battling communism. During the Berlin Airlift the United States and Britain got around a Soviet land blockade by delivering supplies by air into West Berlin.
- After World War II, Japan was rebuilt as an industrialized and democratic nation.

to keep the Soviet Union from spreading communism and attacking European nations The Berlin Wall stood for the division between the free world and the communist countries.

To make sure that the Soviet Union did not try to set up more communist governments in Europe, in 1949 most of the remaining European countries started a new alliance, the North Atlantic Treaty Organization, or NATO. The United States and Canada joined, too. NATO members promised that a Soviet attack on one member nation would be thought of as an attack on all. NATO also worked to find solutions to problems between member nations.

REVIEW What was the purpose of NATO?

This treaty (left) created the North Atlantic Treaty Organization. Representatives of NATO (below) give a press conference on the treaty.

Changes in Japan

After the war many Allied forces remained in Japan. They were under the command of General Douglas MacArthur. Most of these troops were American, since the United States had been the most involved in bringing about the Japanese surrender. The troops disarmed the Japanese military and stayed to help transform Japan into a democracy. In 1947 a constitution for Japan, written by MacArthur's advisers, went into effect. By its terms, the power to rule would be in the hands of the Japanese people, not their emperor or their military leaders.

In September 1951 most of the Allied nations, including the United States, signed a peace treaty with Japan. According to the treaty, Japan had to give up its overseas empire, but it was allowed to rebuild its military forces.

BACKGROUND

The Warsaw Pact In response to the forming of the NATO alliance, the Soviet Union established the Warsaw Pact. The pact served to strengthen the Soviet Union's military control over the Eastern European countries it had invaded during World War II. Albania, Bulgaria, Czechoslovakia, East Germany, Hungary, Poland, Romania, and the Soviet Union signed the pact in Warsaw in 1955. The pact ended in 1991 with the breakup of the Soviet Union.

MAKE IT RELEVANT

At School Point out that many areas of the world suffer from economic problems, just as many nations did after World War II. Explain that various organizations raise money and provide aid and supplies to these places every year. Have students research ways in which their school has helped people in other communities or countries.

General MacArthur (center) inspects the Honor Guard (left) outside the American Embassy during Japan's transformation to democracy.

Most of the Allied forces were then sent home. However, another treaty permitted the United States to keep some troops in Japan to help the Japanese change to a democratic government.

The war left many of Japan's factories and cities destroyed. Many of Japan's trading ships were also destroyed, leaving Japan cut off from the rest of the world. People were left homeless and jobless. In time, people began to move from farming villages to cities to find work. In the cities, they worked in the new industries that were being developed. It took almost ten years for Japan to fully recover from the war.

Over time, relations between Japan and the United States improved. Japan became an important trading partner and ally of the United States.

REVIEW Why did Allied forces remain in Japan after the Japanese surrendered? *to help transform Japan into a democracy*

LESSON 4 REVIEW

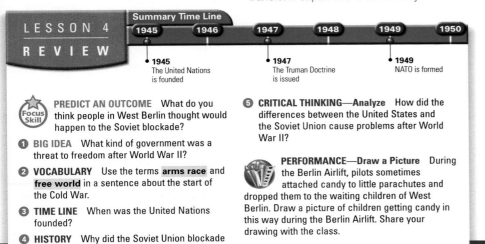

Summary Time Line

| 1945 | 1946 | 1947 | 1948 | 1949 | 1950 |

1945
The United Nations is founded

1947
The Truman Doctrine is issued

1949
NATO is formed

PREDICT AN OUTCOME What do you think people in West Berlin thought would happen to the Soviet blockade?

1 BIG IDEA What kind of government was a threat to freedom after World War II?

2 VOCABULARY Use the terms **arms race** and **free world** in a sentence about the start of the Cold War.

3 TIME LINE When was the United Nations founded?

4 HISTORY Why did the Soviet Union blockade West Berlin?

5 CRITICAL THINKING—Analyze How did the differences between the United States and the Soviet Union cause problems after World War II?

PERFORMANCE—Draw a Picture During the Berlin Airlift, pilots sometimes attached candy to little parachutes and dropped them to the waiting children of West Berlin. Draw a picture of children getting candy in this way during the Berlin Airlift. Share your drawing with the class.

Chapter 10 ■ 395

EXTEND AND ENRICH

Research the Cold War
Encourage students to use the Internet and other references to research more about the Cold War. Ask them to identify some of its major events and explain the effect it had on both the United States and the Soviet Union. Have students write summaries of their findings.

ACTIVITY BOOK

Use ACTIVITY BOOK, p. 99, to reinforce and extend student learning.

RETEACH THE LESSON

Sequence Events Ask students to place the following events related to the Cold War in correct order.

■ The Berlin Airlift ended. [3]

■ The United Nations was formed. [1]

■ Most Allied nations signed a peace treaty with Japan. [4]

■ Bulgaria, Czechoslovakia, Hungary, Poland, Romania, Albania, and Yugoslavia became communist countries. [2]

READING SOCIAL STUDIES

K-W-L Chart Instruct students to use what they have learned in the lesson to complete their K-W-L chart.

K	W	L
The Soviet Union was communist.	What happened to many Eastern European countries under Soviet control after World War II?	Many Eastern European countries became communist.
To many, communism is a threat to freedom.	How did the United States help Eastern European countries fight communism?	The United States helped Eastern European countries fight communism by giving them military and economic aid through policies such as the Truman Doctrine and the Marshall Plan.

● USE READING AND VOCABULARY TRANSPARENCY 5-9.

5-9
TRANSPARENCY

Assess

Lesson 4 Review—Answers

PREDICT AN OUTCOME Some people in West Berlin thought the Berlin Airlift would end the Soviet blockade.

1 BIG IDEA communist

2 VOCABULARY At the start of the Cold War, countries of the **free world** were in an **arms race** with Communist countries.

3 TIME LINE 1945

4 HISTORY The Soviet Union hoped to drive out the Allies by cutting off supply routes to West Berlin.

5 CRITICAL THINKING—Analyze Students' answers should indicate that differences in governments created tension between the countries as the Soviet Union tried to spread communism and the United States tried to contain it.

 Performance Assessment Guidelines Suggest students look in reference books or online for pictures of Berlin if they would like to include some of the city in their drawings.

PREDICT AN OUTCOME

Students may use the graphic organizer that appears on page 100 of the Activity Book. Answers appear in the Activity Book, Teacher's Edition.

Think & Write

Write a Compare-and-Contrast Essay Ask students to list the characteristics of World War I and World War II. Then have them use their lists as a basis to write their essays. Students' essays should accurately explain the similarities and differences between the wars.

Write a Letter Encourage students to use references to research their letters. Students' letters should accurately reflect life in the Pacific during World War II.

ACTIVITY BOOK

A copy of this graphic organizer appears in the ACTIVITY BOOK on page 100.

TRANSPARENCY

The graphic organizer appears on READING AND VOCABULARY TRANSPARENCY 5-10.

· CHAPTER ·

10 Review and Test Preparation

Summary Time Line
1942

● **1942**
Allies win the Battle of Midway

● **1943**
Allies take back North Africa

 Predict an Outcome

Copy the following graphic organizer onto a separate sheet of paper. Use the information you have learned to predict outcomes about Allied victories in World War II.

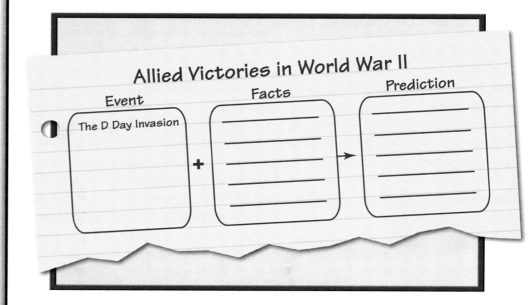

Allied Victories in World War II

Event | Facts | Prediction

The D Day Invasion

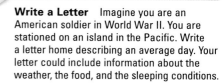

THINK & WRITE

Write a Compare-and-Contrast Essay Write an essay comparing and contrasting World War I with World War II. Include in your essay why the wars began, who fought in the wars, what weapons were used in the wars, and where the wars took place.

Write a Letter Imagine you are an American soldier in World War II. You are stationed on an island in the Pacific. Write a letter home describing an average day. Your letter could include information about the weather, the food, and the sleeping conditions.

396 ▪ Unit 5

TEST PREPARATION

Review these tips with students:

■ Read the directions before reading the questions

■ Read each question twice, focusing the second time on all the possible answers.

■ Take the time to think about all the possible answers before deciding on an answer.

■ Move past questions that give you trouble, and answer the ones you know. Then return to the difficult items.

UNIT PROJECT

Progress Check Ask students to work in pairs to place their time line events in the correct order. Encourage students to check their time line dates against those listed in the text.

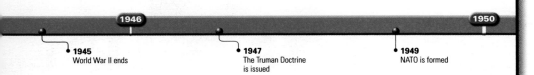

1946

1945
World War II ends

1947
The Truman Doctrine
is issued

1949
NATO is formed

1950

USE THE TIME LINE

Use the chapter summary time line to answer these questions.

1 When did World War II end?

2 When was NATO formed?

USE VOCABULARY

Use each of the following terms in a sentence that will help explain its meaning.

front (p. 362)

V-J Day (p. 378)

refugee (p. 383)

veteran (p. 383)

cold war (p. 393)

RECALL FACTS

Answer these questions.

3 Where did the D day invasion take place?

4 Who was Anne Frank?

5 Why did Albert Einstein write a letter to President Franklin D. Roosevelt in 1939?

6 What was the GI Bill?

Write the letter of the best choice.

7 World War II was fought on two main fronts in—
  A the United States and Asia.
  B Europe and Africa, and in the Pacific.
  C Australia and South America.
  D Canada and Mexico.

8 The United States' policy of helping countries fight communism was called—
  F Americans Against Communism.
  G the Free World Plan.
  H the Truman Doctrine.
  J the Marshall Plan.

THINK CRITICALLY

9 How do you think the scientists on the Manhattan Project felt about building such a destructive weapon?

10 Why did President Truman feel that the spread of communism was a threat to freedom?

APPLY SKILLS

Compare Historical Maps
Use the information and maps on pages 370 and 371 to help answer these questions.

11 When would you use historical maps?

12 Where can you find historical maps?

13 How can you tell if a map is a historical map?

Read Parallel Time Lines
Use the information and time lines on pages 380 and 381 to answer these questions.

14 What is shown on Time Line A? Time Line B?

15 How does using two time lines help you in viewing the events?

Chapter 10 ■ 397

5 He wanted to warn President Roosevelt of Germany's plan to build a new kind of bomb. (p. 375)

6 The GI Bill helped veterans pay for education, new homes, and living expenses. (p. 383)

7 B (p. 372)

8 H (p. 391)

Think Critically

9 Students' answers may vary but should reflect the idea that the scientists were concerned about building a weapon that was so destructive.

10 He was concerned that communist countries such as the Soviet Union might become powerful enough to start another world war.

Apply Skills

Compare Historical Maps

11 You would use historical maps to learn how a region's borders have changed over time.

12 You can find historical maps in references such as textbooks and atlases.

13 You can tell by looking at the map's title or key.

Read Parallel Time Lines

14 key events that affected the front in Europe; key events that affected the front in the Pacific

15 Events appear better organized on parallel time lines.

ACTIVITY BOOK

Use the CHAPTER 10 TEST PREPARATION on page 101 of the Activity Book.

ASSESSMENT

Use the CHAPTER 10 TEST on pages 77–80 of the Assessment Program.

Use the Time Line

1 1945

2 1949

Use Vocabulary

Possible sentences:

- Africa and Europe were the sites of major **fronts** during World War II. (p. 362)
- **V-J Day** marks Japan's surrender on August 15, 1945. (p. 378)
- During wartime many people were forced to leave their homes and become **refugees**. (p. 383)
- After the war many **veterans** returned home to their families and friends. (p. 383)
- During the **Cold War** some people in the United States worried about an attack by the Soviet Union. (p. 393)

Recall Facts

3 It took place on the beaches in Normandy, France. (p. 364)

4 A young Jewish girl living in the Netherlands at the beginning of World War II; she and her family hid from the Germans. (p. 367)

Visit
Berlin, Germany
PAGES 398–399

OBJECTIVES

■ **Identify Berlin, Germany, as an important historic site of World War II.**

■ **Use visual materials to learn about the history of the United States.**

Summary

Berlin is Germany's capital city. Though the city was at one time divided by a huge wall, the removal of the wall reunited East Berlin and West Berlin into Germany's largest city.

1 Motivate

Get Ready

Point out that the Berlin Wall was built in 1961 to separate East Berlin from West Berlin. After the wall came down in 1989, the city reunited and faced a bright future. But the past has not been forgotten. Parts of the wall and other structures remain standing as memorials. Ask whether any students have visited a memorial or monument. Encourage them to share their experiences with the class.

2 Teach

What to See

Have students look carefully at the photographs of Berlin. Ask the following questions:

• *What do people see when they visit Tempelhof Airport?*

• *What was the purpose of the Berlin Wall?*

• *Why do you think parts of the Berlin Wall were preserved?*

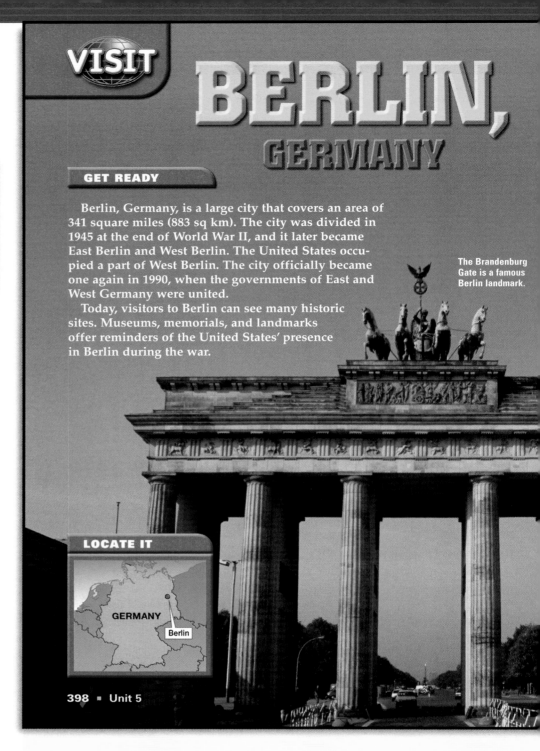

VISIT BERLIN, GERMANY

GET READY

Berlin, Germany, is a large city that covers an area of 341 square miles (883 sq km). The city was divided in 1945 at the end of World War II, and it later became East Berlin and West Berlin. The United States occupied a part of West Berlin. The city officially became one again in 1990, when the governments of East and West Germany were united.

Today, visitors to Berlin can see many historic sites. Museums, memorials, and landmarks offer reminders of the United States' presence in Berlin during the war.

The Brandenburg Gate is a famous Berlin landmark.

LOCATE IT

GERMANY

Berlin

398 ■ Unit 5

BACKGROUND

Berlin's Museums Art lovers in Germany hope to make Museum Island a national showplace. Museum Island, which is surrounded by the Spree River, is home to four museums. City officials hope that these museums will become the "Louvre of the Spree." The museums on the island were built between 1830 and 1930. All are undergoing major remodeling and will be connected by underground passageways. When the $10 million project is complete, Berlin hopes to attract about 6 million visitors per year.

MAKE IT RELEVANT

In Your Community Ask students to identify a memorial or monument in their community. Have them write short reports on the memorial or monument, including when it was built and whom or what it honors. Invite volunteers to read their reports to the class.

A memorial honors members of the United States Air Force who participated in the Berlin Airlift.

During the Berlin Airlift transport planes unloaded food and supplies at Tempelhof Airport.

The Berlin Wall was built in 1961.

Work to tear down the Berlin Wall began in 1989. Today visitors can see pieces of the wall that have been preserved as part of history.

Visitors can see Checkpoint Charlie, a famous guard station of the Berlin Wall.

TAKE A FIELD TRIP

GO ONLINE **A VIRTUAL TOUR** Visit The Learning Site at www.harcourtschool.com to find virtual tours of parks and scenic areas.

CNN Turner Learning **A VIDEO TOUR** Check your media center or classroom library for a videotape tour of Berlin, Germany.

Unit 5 ■ 399

---

3 Close

Take a Field Trip

Direct students to research one memorial or museum that can be found in Berlin. Students may be interested in learning how the airlift provided tons of food, fuel, machinery, and other supplies to the citizens of Berlin.

A Virtual Tour Depending on the availability of computers, have students work individually, with partners, or in small groups to view the virtual tour. Encourage them as they explore the Web sites to research the events that led to the building of the Berlin Wall and then to its destruction. Remind students to use what they learn on their virtual tours as background information for the Unit Project.

GO ONLINE **INTERNET RESOURCES**

THE LEARNING SITE Go to www.harcourtschool.com for a listing of Web sites focusing on places of interest in Europe.

A Video Tour Have students fill in the first two columns of a K-W-L chart about Berlin, Germany, before they watch the videotape. After they view the videotape, have students fill in the last column, listing what they learned. Ask volunteers to share their charts with the class.

VIDEO

Use the CNN/Turner Learning TAKE A FIELD TRIP videotape of Berlin, Germany.

INTEGRATE MATHEMATICS

Computation Remind students that the Berlin Wall was built in 1961. Ask students to compute the following:

How old was the wall when it was torn down in 1989? 1989 − 1961 = 28 years

How old are the portions of the wall that are still standing today? Students' should find the answer by subtracting 1961 from the current year.

EXTEND AND ENRICH

Write a Letter Have students imagine that they are about to visit Berlin, Germany. Ask them to write letters to friends or relatives and describe what they plan to see. Ask students to include specific details about the sites on their travel itineraries.

Unit 5 Review and Test Preparation

PAGES 400–402

Visual Summary

Students' descriptions should clearly describe one of the events pictured from the perspective of a radio announcer.

- **Germany invades Poland** Germany's invasion of Poland prompted Britain and France to declare war on Germany.

- **Japan attacks Pearl Harbor** The attack on Pearl Harbor brought the United States into the war, joining the Allied nations of Britain, France, and the Soviet Union.

- **More than 3 million Americans are drafted** The government spent more than $23 billion to train about 10 million Americans who were drafted into military service.

- **D day invasion succeeds** Allied Forces landed on the beach in Normandy in the largest water-to-land invasion in history.

- **World War II ends** Berlin fell to the Soviets on May 2, 1945. Then, on August 15, 1945, Japan surrendered to the United States.

- **NATO is founded** Several European countries, the United States, and Canada developed an alliance called the North Atlantic Treaty Organization to protect themselves against aggressive countries.

Use Vocabulary

Possible answers:

- Many people were put in concentration camps in Europe during the Holocaust.

- After the war, many veterans had to become used to being civilians again.

- During the world wars, people learned the importance of rationing food and recycling items.

- The superpowers competed in an arms race because they each wanted to have the most weapons.

·UNIT·

5 Review and Test Preparation

VISUAL SUMMARY

Write Descriptions Imagine that you are a radio announcer. Your job is to describe the events in the Visual Summary to your audience. Write a description for each event. Make sure you include enough detail that someone could match the description with its event.

USE VOCABULARY

Use each pair of terms in a sentence that explains the meanings of the terms.

concentration camp, Holocaust (pp. 333, 368)

civilian, veteran (pp. 344, 383)

rationing, recycling (p. 351)

superpowers, arms race (pp. 388, 390)

RECALL FACTS

Answer these questions.

1. What were the main messages in Hitler's speeches?

2. What was one of the biggest mistakes the Japanese made while trying to build an empire?

3. What happened to Japanese Americans during World War II?

4. Who was the commander of the Allied forces in Europe after the Americans entered World War II?

5. In the years after World War II, which nations became superpowers?

Write the letter of the best choice.

6. Which of the following events brought the United States into World War II?
   A Japan's attack on Pearl Harbor
   B D day
   C Germany's invasion of Austria
   D Japan's attack on Midway Island

7. The period after World War II in which the United States' population grew by about 50 million became known as—
   F the population explosion.
   G the bountiful era.
   H the post-war expansion.
   J the baby boom.

Visual Summary

1930   1934   1938

1939 **Germany invades Poland** p. 336

1941 **Japan attacks Pearl Harbor** p. 343

1942 **More than 3 million American are drafted** p. 345

400

Recall Facts

1. Germany had not been treated fairly after World War I; German people were superior. (p. 333)

2. the attack on the United States (p. 345)

3. The United States government sent them to relocation camps. (p. 353)

4. General Dwight D. Eisenhower (p. 362)

5. the United States and the Soviet Union (p. 388)

6. A (pp. 344–345)

7. J (p. 386)

THINK CRITICALLY

❽ What impact did the Treaty of Versailles have on the beginning of World War II?

❾ What do you think would have happened if Germany had taken control of Britain before the United States entered World War II?

❿ Why do you think World War II was fought over a larger area than World War I?

⓫ Do you think it was difficult for American soldiers returning from the war to readjust to everyday life? Explain.

APPLY SKILLS

Compare Historical Maps
Use the maps of Germany on this page to answer the following questions.

⓬ What city became the capital of West Germany?

⓭ Why do you think the land area of Germany in 1937 is larger than the combined land areas of West and East Germany?

Germany, 1937

Germany, 1949

1942 1946 1950

44 **D day invasion succeeds**
365

1945 **World War II ends** p. 379

1949 **NATO is founded** p. 394

Think Critically

❽ The Treaty of Versailles brought financial ruin and depression to Germany. This in turn gave German people, such as Hitler, a reason to blame other nations for Germany's problems. This way of thinking helped lead to the beginning of the war.

❾ Possible response: Germany would have controlled most of Europe. The Axis Powers may have won World War II.

❿ The driving forces in World War II—the Germans and the Japanese—both had visions of establishing great empires around the world; their desire to conquer brought the war to many areas of the world.

⓫ Students' answers will vary but may include the idea that the United States government helped the readjustment period for the veterans.

Apply Skills

Compare Historical Maps

⓬ Bonn

⓭ Some parts of Germany became parts of other countries following World War II.

TEST PREPARATION

Review these tips with students:

- Read the directions before reading the questions.

- Read each question twice, focusing the second time on all the possible answers.

- Take the time to think about all the possible answers before deciding on an answer.

- Move past questions that give you trouble, and answer the ones you know. Then return to the difficult items.

ASSESSMENT

Use the UNIT 5 TEST on pages 81–89 of the Assessment Program.

Unit Activities

Make a Newspaper

Give students real newspapers to use as examples for their activity. As a class, label the articles in the real newspapers as news stories, editorials, letters to the editor, or feature articles. This will help students include each kind of article in their newspapers.

 Performance Assessment Guidelines Check that students' newspapers accurately report events that took place during World War II.

Develop a Secret Code

Tell students that writing a secret code is similar to developing their own secret language. Students can use numbers or other symbols to stand for the real words or letters in their codes. Have groups trade messages. They may wish to try to crack the codes before looking at the translations.

Performance Assessment Guidelines Make sure that students use their codes to write about an event in World War II, such as the attack on Pearl Harbor or D day.

Complete the Unit Project

Provide students with art supplies such as posterboard, markers, and crayons to use in creating their time line. Tell students to review their lists and choose the events to include in their time lines.

Performance Assessment Guidelines Make sure that students have used accurate dates on their time lines.

Unit Activities

 Make a Newspaper

Work in a group to make a newspaper that could have been printed during World War II. Your newspaper should include news stories, editorials, letters to the editor, feature articles, cartoons, advertisements, and illustrations. Share your newspaper with the class.

 Develop a Secret Code

Work in groups to develop a secret code. The secret code can either use whole words or letters. Be sure to include a translation for your secret code. Use your secret code to write about one of the major events of World War II. Give your finished secret code and writing to another group to translate.

GO ONLINE Visit The Learning Site at www.harcourtschool.com for additional activities.

VISIT YOUR LIBRARY

- *Rosie the Riveter: Women Working on the Home Front in World War II* by Penny Colman. Crown Publishers.

- *Foster's War* by Carolyn Reeder. Scholastic Press.

- *My Wartime Summers* by Jane Cutler. Farrar, Straus, & Giroux.

COMPLETE THE UNIT PROJECT

Create an Illustrated Time Line
Work as a class to complete the unit project—create an illustrated time line. Review the events, people, and places that you listed during your reading. Make sure that each item on your list has a date. Next, create a variety of scenes and captions to go with your items. Complete the project by placing dates, scenes, and captions on a time line.

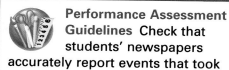

1939   1941   1943   1945

Visit Your Library

Encourage independent reading after students' study of World War II with these books or books of your choice. Additional books are listed on the Multimedia Resources, on page 323D of this Teacher's Edition.

Easy *Rosie the Riveter: Women Working on the Home Front in World War II* by Penny Colman. Crown Publishers, 1998. A look at the jobs women took, the impact women had on the workplace, and what happened to working women at war's end.

Average *Foster's War* by Carolyn Reeder. Scholastic Press, 1998. While his older brother fights in the war, young Foster fights his own battles at home with his stern and demanding father.

Challenging *My Wartime Summers* by Jane Cutler. Farrar, Straus & Giroux, 1994. Ellen's favorite uncle is drafted in the war, and she sees how it changes them both forever.

The Cold War and Beyond

A 1950s television

Unit 6 Planning Guide The Cold War and Beyond

Introduce	CONTENT	RESOURCES
pp. 403–407	**UNIT OPENER**, p. 403 **PREVIEW**, pp. 404–405 **START WITH A SPEECH** "I Have a Dream," pp. 406–407	Unit 6 Audiotext Unit 6 School-to-Home Newsletter, p. S11 Reading and Vocabulary Transparency 6-1 Internet Resources
Chapter 11 **At Home and Abroad**, pp. 408–445	**INTRODUCE THE CHAPTER**, pp. 408–409 **LESSON 1** The Korean War Years, pp. 410–415 **MAP AND GLOBE SKILLS** Identify Changing Borders, pp. 416–417 **LESSON 2** The 1950s, pp. 418–423 **CHART AND GRAPH SKILLS** Compare Graphs, pp. 424–425 **EXAMINE PRIMARY SOURCES** Civil Defense, pp. 426–427 **LESSON 3** New Opportunities and New Challenges, pp. 428–433 **CITIZENSHIP SKILLS** Resolve Conflicts, p. 434 **LESSON 4** Working for Equal Rights, pp. 435–441 **CITIZENSHIP SKILLS** Act as a Responsible Citizen, pp. 442–443 **CHAPTER REVIEW AND TEST PREPARATION**, pp. 444–445	Activity Book, pp. 102–113 Assessment Program, Chapter 11, pp. 91–94 Reading and Vocabulary Transparencies 6-2, 6-3, 6-4, 6-5, 6-6 Skills Transparencies 6-1A and 6-1B, 6-2A and 6-2B, 6-3, 6-4 Internet Resources GeoSkills CD-ROM
Chapter 12 **Into Modern Times**, pp. 446–477	**INTRODUCE THE CHAPTER**, pp. 446–447 **LESSON 1** The Vietnam War Years, pp. 448–454 **LESSON 2** The Cold War Ends, pp. 455–461 **LESSON 3** New Challenges, pp. 462–467 **LESSON 4** The End of the Twentieth Century, pp. 468–473 **MAP AND GLOBE SKILLS** Read a Population Map, pp. 474–475 **CHAPTER REVIEW AND TEST PREPARATION**, pp. 476–477	Activity Book, pp. 114–123 Assessment Program, Chapter 12, pp. 95–98 Reading and Vocabulary Transparencies 6-7, 6-8, 6-9, 6-10, 6-11 Skills Transparency 6-5 Internet Resources GeoSkills CD-ROM
Wrap Up pp. 478–482	**VISIT** The Birmingham Civil Rights Institute, pp. 478–479 **UNIT REVIEW AND TEST PREPARATION**, pp. 480–481	Internet Resources The Learning Site: Virtual Tours Take a Field Trip Video Time for Kids Readers Assessment Program, Unit 6, pp. 99–107

5 WEEKS	WEEK 1	WEEK 2	WEEK 3	WEEK 4	WEEK 5
	Introduce the Unit	Chapter 11		Chapter 12	Wrap Up the Unit

Unit 6 Skills Path

Unit 6 features the reading skills of drawing conclusions and making inferences. It also highlights the social studies skills of identifying changing borders, reading a population map, comparing graphs, resolving conflicts, and acting as a responsible citizen.

FOCUS SKILLS

CHAPTER 11 READING SKILL

 DRAW CONCLUSIONS

- INTRODUCE p. 409
- APPLY pp. 413, 415, 422, 423, 430, 433, 438, 441, 444

CHAPTER 12 READING SKILL

 MAKE INFERENCES

- INTRODUCE p. 447
- APPLY pp. 450, 451, 454, 456, 461, 465, 467, 470, 473, 476

READING SOCIAL STUDIES

- Study Questions, pp. 411, 415
- Reread Aloud, p. 413
- Personal Response, pp. 419, 423, 436, 441, 469, 473
- Summarize, pp. 407, 421, 442
- K-W-L Chart, pp. 429, 432, 449, 454
- Cause and Effect, p. 437
- Reread to Clarify, p. 452
- Graphic Organizer, pp. 456, 461
- Anticipation Guide, pp. 463, 467

MAP AND GLOBE SKILLS

IDENTIFY CHANGING BORDERS

- INTRODUCE pp. 416–417
- APPLY p. 445

READ A POPULATION MAP

- INTRODUCE pp. 474–475
- APPLY p. 477

CHART AND GRAPH SKILLS

COMPARE GRAPHS

- INTRODUCE pp. 424–425
- APPLY p. 445

CITIZENSHIP SKILLS

RESOLVE CONFLICTS

- INTRODUCE p. 434
- APPLY p. 445

ACT AS A RESPONSIBLE CITIZEN

- INTRODUCE pp. 442–443
- APPLY p. 445

STUDY AND RESEARCH SKILLS

- Using the Internet, pp. 419, 459
- Using Maps, pp. 430, 449
- Using Reference Sources, pp. 418, 471
- Summarizing Information, pp. 435, 468
- Use Maps, p. 458
- Outlining, p. 466

Multimedia Resources

The Multimedia Resources can be used in a variety of ways. They can supplement core instruction in the classroom or extend and enrich student learning at home.

Independent Reading

Easy

Dunham, Montrew. ***Ronald Reagan: Young Leader.*** Aladdin Publishing Co., 1999. Fictionalized biography of former President Reagan's childhood.

Kramer, Barbara. ***John Glenn: A Space Biography.*** Enslow Publishers, Inc., 1998. Read about the life of John Glenn and his space travel.

Stein, R. Conrad. ***The Assassination of Martin Luther King, Jr.*** Children's Press, 1998. An account of the events surrounding King's assassination in Memphis.

Turck, Mary. ***The Civil Rights Movement for Kids.*** Chicago Review Press, 2000. Activities and stories about the impact children had on the Civil Rights movement.

Average

Karr, Kathleen. ***Dwight D. Eisenhower: Letters from a New Jersey Schoolgirl.*** Winslow Press, 2002. Fictional letters between Eisenhower and 13-year-old Annie, a New Jersey farm girl.

Mead, Alice. ***Soldier Mom.*** Farrar, Straus & Giroux, 1999. A family faces emotional and financial struggles when a single mother is called to serve overseas in the Gulf War.

Pinkney, Andrea Davis. ***Let It Shine: Stories of Black Women Freedom Fighters.*** Gulliver Books, 2000. Biographies of ten black women whose actions made a difference in history.

Zeinert, Karen. ***The Valiant Women of the Vietnam War.*** Millbrook Press, 2000. Highlights women's involvement in the Vietnam War, both at home and overseas, through first-person accounts and photos.

Challenging

Burgan, Michael. ***The Threats.*** Raintree-Steck Vaughn, 2001. Learn about threats to the United States during the Cold War of the 1950s and 1960s.

Marsh, Carole. ***The Day That Was Different: September 11, 2001—When Terrorists Attacked America.*** Gallopade Publishing Group, 2001. Background on the people and cultures involved in the events related to the September 11 attack on the United States.

Uschan, Michael V. ***The Korean War.*** Lucent Books, 2001. Maps, photos, quotes, and sidebars provide insight into the causes, events, and politics of the Korean War.

Computer Software

American Social Issues. ABC-Clio, Inc., 1999. Windows. Interactive encyclopedia presents over 800 topics relevant to the United States today such as immigration, welfare reform, the environment, civil rights, and education.

Civil Rights Movement in the United States. ABC-Clio, Inc., 2000. Windows. Interactive encyclopedia chronicles the Civil Rights movement from the Civil War to the present day.

JFK Assassination: A Visual Investigation. Wilbur Films Multimedia, Inc., 1993. Mac. Investigate the assassination through a collection of four films that include eyewitness interviews, book excerpts, and photos.

Videos and DVDs

Post-War U.S.A. Schlessinger Media, 1996. Examine life in the United States after World War II.

Apollo 13. NASA Space Series, 1997. Discover how NASA and the *Apollo 13* crew helped bring the disabled spacecraft safely back to Earth.

The Learning Site: Social Studies Center

The Learning Site at www.harcourtschool.com offers a special Social Studies Center. The center provides a wide variety of activities, Internet links, and online references.

Here are just some of the HARCOURT Internet resources you'll find!

Multimedia Biographies
www.harcourtschool.com

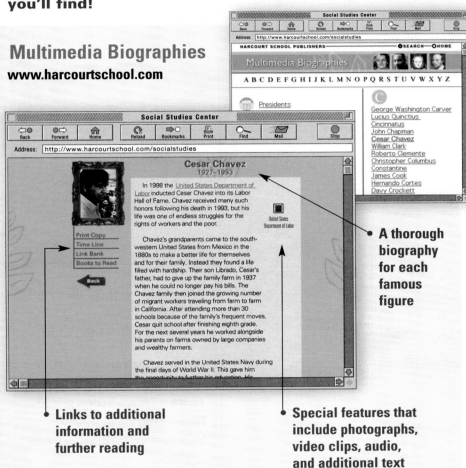

- **A thorough biography for each famous figure**

- **Links to additional information and further reading**

- **Special features that include photographs, video clips, audio, and additional text**

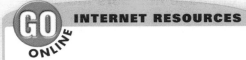

INTERNET RESOURCES

Find all this at
The Learning Site at
www.harcourtschool.com

- Activities and Games
- Content Updates
- Current Events
- Free and Inexpensive Materials
- Multimedia Biographies
- Online Atlas
- Primary Sources
- Video Updates
- Virtual Tours
- Your State

and more!

Free and Inexpensive Materials
- Addresses to write for free and inexpensive products
- Links to unit-related materials
- Internet maps
- Internet references

www.harcourtschool.com

Primary Sources
- Artwork
- Clothing
- Diaries
- Government Documents
- Historical Documents
- Maps
- Tools

and more!
www.harcourtschool.com

Virtual Tours
- Capitols and Government Buildings
- Cities
- Countries
- Historical Sites
- Museums
- Parks and Scenic Areas

and more!
www.harcourtschool.com

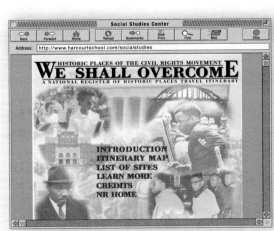

Integrate Learning Across the Curriculum

Use these topics to help you integrate social studies into your daily planning.
See the page numbers indicated for more information about each topic.

Technology

Go Online, pp. 407, 427, 430, 438, 460, 479

GeoSkills CD-ROM, pp. 417, 475

CNN Video, p. 479

Science

Research the Space Race, p. 404

Make a Double-Bar Climograph, p. 414

Recognizing the Effect of Television on Civil Rights, p. 438

Research Energy Sources, p. 456

Art

Draw a Picture, p. 431

Draw a Poster, p. 437

Design a Poster, p. 457

Design a Memorial, p. 472

Social Studies

Language Arts

Write and Perform an Oral History, p. 406

Persuasive Writing, pp. 414, 430, 463

Write an Advertisement, p. 432

Stage a Debate, p. 450

Write a News Story, p. 453

News Interview, p. 464

Informative Writing, pp. 466, 468

Write a Poem, pp. 479

Languages
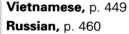

Vietnamese, p. 449

Russian, p. 460

Reading/Literature

"I Have a Dream," pp. 406–407

Read a Biography, pp. 439, 458

President George W. Bush: Our Forty-third President, p. 482

My Dream of Martin Luther King, p. 482

Dear Mrs. Parks: A Dialogue with Today's Youth, p. 482

Mathematics

High Tide, p. 413

Determine Population Growth, p. 424

Multiplication, p. 429

Make a Circle Graph, p. 466

Reach All Learners

Use these activities to help individualize your instruction. Each activity has been developed to address a different level or type of learner.

English as a Second Language

Materials
- textbook
- paper
- pen or pencil
- thesaurus

BUILD VOCABULARY Have students who are acquiring English work in pairs to find synonyms and antonyms for vocabulary terms.

- Present the thesaurus as a tool for building vocabulary. Explain ways in which it is and is not like a dictionary.
- Have students work in pairs to complete graphic organizers showing synonyms and antonyms for as many vocabulary terms as possible.
- Ask students to write sentences using the new terms to show that they understand the meanings of these words.

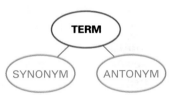

Below-Level Learners

Materials
- paper
- pen or pencil
- word list
- dictionary

REVIEW USAGE Have below-level learners review the definitions of nouns and verbs. Discuss with students differences between nouns and verbs.

- Give students a list of words that appear in this unit that can be used as either nouns or verbs. Allow students to use the dictionary as needed to define these words.
- Ask each student to write two sentences for each word. One sentence should illustrate the word's meaning as a noun. The other sentence should use the word as a verb.
- If students find this task difficult, ask them to make simple drawings that illustrate the meanings of the words.

Advanced Learners

Materials
- library resources
- paper
- pen or pencil

LEARN ABOUT NONVIOLENT PROTESTS Have advanced learners work in groups to research Mohandas Gandhi and his influence on the Civil Rights movement in the United States.

- Encourage students to read about Gandhi's work in India, using either library materials or online resources. You may wish to assign groups different aspects of nonviolent protests, such as hunger strikes, fasts, or peace marches.
- Ask students in each group to find ways in which Dr. Martin Luther King, Jr., adapted Gandhi's ideas. Challenge them to find current applications for nonviolent practices.
- Allow each group time to present its research to the class.

Assessment Options

The Assessment Program gives all learners many opportunities to show what they know and can do. It also provides ongoing information about each student's understanding of social studies.

Formal Assessment

- **LESSON REVIEWS,** at ends of lessons
- **CHAPTER REVIEWS AND TEST PREPARATION,** pp. 444–445, pp. 476–477
- **CHAPTER TESTS**
  Assessment Program, pp. 91–94, pp. 95–98
- **UNIT REVIEW AND TEST PREPARATION,** pp. 480–481
- **UNIT ASSESSMENT**
  STANDARD TEST,
    Assessment Program, pp. 99–105
  INDIVIDUAL PERFORMANCE TASK,
    Assessment Program, p. 106
  GROUP PERFORMANCE TASK,
    Assessment Program, p. 107

Student Self-Evaluation

- **ANALYZE PRIMARY SOURCES AND VISUALS**
  within lessons of Pupil Book
- **GEOGRAPHY THEME QUESTIONS**
  within lessons of Pupil Book
- **INDIVIDUAL END-OF-PROJECT SUMMARY**
  Assessment Program, p. viii
- **GROUP END-OF-PROJECT CHECKLIST**
  Assessment Program, p. ix
- **INDIVIDUAL END-OF-UNIT CHECKLIST**
  Assessment Program, p. x

Informal Assessment

- **ANALYZE THE LITERATURE,** p. 407
- **REVIEW QUESTIONS,** throughout lessons
- **EXAMINE PRIMARY SOURCES,** pp. 426–427
- **SOCIAL STUDIES SKILLS CHECKLIST**
  Assessment Program, p. vi

- **SKILLS**
  Practice the Skill, pp. 417, 425, 434, 443, 475
  Apply What You Learned, pp. 417, 425, 434, 443, 475

Performance Assessment

- **PERFORMANCE ACTIVITY** in Lesson Reviews
- **UNIT ACTIVITIES,** p. 482
- **COMPLETE THE UNIT PROJECT,** p. 482
- **INDIVIDUAL PERFORMANCE TASK**
  Assessment Program, p. 106
- **GROUP PERFORMANCE TASK**
  Assessment Program, p. 107

Portfolio Assessment

STUDENT-SELECTED ITEMS MAY INCLUDE:

- **THINK AND WRITE,** pp. 444, 476
- **UNIT ACTIVITIES,** p. 482
- **COMPLETE THE UNIT PROJECT,** p. 482

TEACHER-SELECTED ITEMS MAY INCLUDE:

- **UNIT ASSESSMENT**
  Assessment Program, pp. 99–107
- **PORTFOLIO SUMMARY**
  Assessment Program, p. xv
- **GROUP END-OF-PROJECT CHECKLIST**
  Assessment Program, p. ix
- **INDIVIDUAL END-OF-UNIT CHECKLIST**
  Assessment Program, p. x

Unit 6 Test

·UNIT·

Name _____ Date _____

6 Test

Part One: Test Your Understanding

MULTIPLE CHOICE (2 points each)

Directions Circle the letter of the best answer.

1 Which of the following was designed to stop the spread of communism?
- A the Fair Deal
- (B) the Truman Doctrine
- C the United Nations
- D the Armed Forces Act

2 What role did the United States play in the Korean War?
- F It remained neutral.
- G It supported North Korea.
- (H) It supported South Korea.
- J It had no role in the Korean War.

3 Which of the following was true about the Korean War?
- A It became a major issue in the 1952 presidential election.
- B Most of the troops sent to South Korea were from the United States.
- C When the war ended, South Korea remained an independent nation.
- (D) All of the above

4 Which statement does **not** relate to life in the 1950s?
- F New businesses, schools, and churches opened.
- G The nation's economy grew as people purchased more goods.
- H New household appliances helped make people's lives easier.
- (J) Listening to the radio became a regular family activity.

5 What effect did *Brown v. Board of Education of Topeka* have on education?
- A Schools in Kansas remained segregated.
- (B) The Supreme Court overturned a previous ruling and ordered an end to segregation.
- C Schools across the nation immediately became desegregated.
- D It had no effect on education.

6 How did the United States react to the Cuban Missile Crisis?
- (F) It set up a blockade to keep Soviet ships away from Cuba.
- G It launched more satellites into space.
- H It sent Peace Corps workers to Cuba.
- J It did nothing about the Cuban Missile Crisis.

(continued)

Unit 6 Test   Assessment Program ■ 99

Name _____ Date _____

7 The Equal Rights Amendment would have—
- A stopped discrimination against African Americans.
- B provided health insurance and better wages to Mexican American farmworkers.
- C restored many rights of Native Americans.
- (D) guaranteed equal rights to women under federal law.

8 Which act, passed during Lyndon Johnson's presidency, banned segregation in public places?
- F the Voting Rights Act of 1965
- G the Equal Rights Amendment
- (H) the Civil Rights Act of 1964
- J none of the above

9 In what way was the Vietnam War similar to the Korean War?
- A In both, the United States supported communist countries.
- B In both, the United States remained neutral.
- (C) In both, the United States supported independent nations against the threat of communism.
- D The wars were not similar.

10 Which of the following events occurred during Jimmy Carter's presidency?
- (F) the Soviet invasion of Afghanistan and the Iran hostage crisis
- G the end of communism and a civil war in Bosnia
- H the Cuban Missile Crisis and the space race
- J the end of the Vietnam War and the Gulf War

11 The collapse of the Soviet Union resulted in—
- (A) the formation of a loose confederation of states.
- B an Olympic boycott.
- C an increase in arms production in the United States.
- D prosperity for the economies of the former Soviet republics.

12 President Clinton's time in office was noted for—
- F bringing about the end of communism.
- (G) a long period of economic growth.
- H the start of a global war on terror.
- J the beginning of national health care.

13 The 2000 presidential election—
- A was won by former Vice President Al Gore.
- B was decided on election night.
- (C) was the closest in 40 years.
- D did not include any recounts.

14 What challenges face the United States in the twenty-first century?
- F developing good foreign relations
- G working against terrorist threats
- H defending democratic values around the world
- (J) all of the above

(continued)

100 ■ Assessment Program   Unit 6 Test

Name _____ Date _____

MATCHING (3 points each)

Directions Match each definition on the left with the correct term on the right. Then write the letter of the term in the space provided.

15 __E__ to remove racial barriers, as President Truman did for those in the military in 1948

16 __C__ a Supreme Court case that ended segregation in public schools in the United States

17 __D__ peaceful actions designed to solve a problem without threatening or harming people

18 __B__ a temporary end to a conflict

19 __F__ a person chosen by a political party to run for public office

20 __A__ a limit on the number of weapons that nations may have

- A. arms control
- B. cease-fire
- C. *Brown v. Board of Education of Topeka*
- D. nonviolence
- E. desegregate
- F. candidate

(continued)

Unit 6 Test   Assessment Program ■ 101

Name _____ Date _____

SHORT ANSWER (3 points each)

Directions Answer each question in the space provided.

21 What do you think might have happened if the United States had not become involved in the Korean War?

Students may suggest that communism might have spread to more countries.

_____

22 What did Rosa Parks do that led to a victory for equal rights?

She refused to give up her seat on a bus in Montgomery, Alabama. In support

of her action, African Americans in Montgomery organized a bus boycott that

resulted in the rules being changed.

23 What effect did President Nixon's visit to China have on relations between China and the United States?

As a result of his visit, the two nations agreed to trade with each other and to

allow visits from each other's scientific and cultural groups.

_____

24 How did *perestroika* and *glasnost* help to end communism in Europe?

Perestroika, in which people could own their businesses, and *glasnost*, in which

they could speak out without fear of being punished, showed the Soviets how

much better life would be without communism.

25 What events led to the decision of the United States in late 2001 to lead a global war on terrorism?

Various acts of terrorism, such as the bombing of the World Trade Center in

1993 and its destruction in 2001, caused terrible loss of life.

_____

(continued)

102 ■ Assessment Program   Unit 6 Test

Unit 6 Test

Name _____ Date _____

Part Two: Test Your Skills
RESOLVE CONFLICTS (3 points each)

During the Korean War, the United Nations wanted to keep the fighting inside of Korea to prevent the conflict from becoming another world war. However, when UN troops neared the Chinese border, China felt threatened and sent troops to help North Korea. The Chinese troops pushed the UN troops out of North Korea. General MacArthur was frustrated. He wanted to attack mainland China, believing that would end the war. President Truman disagreed. He did not want to start a world war. He also knew that he would not bring together North Korea and South Korea, so he decided to try to stop the communist invasion of South Korea. President Truman wanted to work toward a peace agreement between North Korea and South Korea. When General MacArthur publicly disagreed with President Truman's plans, President Truman asked for his resignation.

(Directions) **Use the historical conflict referred to above and the conflict resolution steps taught in this unit to answer the questions.**

26 What did President Truman want?

He wanted to stop the communist invasion of South Korea and prevent a

world war.

27 What did General MacArthur want?

He wanted to attack China, believing that would end the war.

28 What are the differences in the two plans?

Truman wanted peace with China and MacArthur wanted to fight the Chinese.

29 How might the two leaders have reached a compromise?

Students' answers will vary but should reflect a compromise between the two

leaders.

30 Considering President Truman's role as commander in chief of the armed forces, do you think a compromise was necessary?

Students might suggest that his role gave him the right to decide how the

situation would be handled.

(continued)

Name _____ Date _____

Part Three: Apply What You Have Learned
31 MAKING INFERENCES (2 points each)

Match the correct inference to each related fact by writing the letter of the correct inference in the space provided.

	Fact	Inference
C	The Supreme Court decided to integrate all public schools in the United States.	A. Many Americans blamed President Carter for the nation's troubles.
G	Dr. Martin Luther King, Jr., and Malcolm X worked to achieve equal rights.	B. Communism was beginning to collapse.
F	After 13 days, the United States and the Soviet Union reached a compromise to end the Cuban Missile Crisis.	C. Until the ruling, schools had not offered African American students equal opportunities.
E	Cesar Chavez and others helped organize a group called the United Farm Workers.	D. The 2000 election was so close that at first no one knew who had won.
A	During his presidency, inflation rose and Americans were held hostage in Iran.	E. Migrant workers needed better wages and improved working conditions.
B	In the late 1980s, the Berlin Wall was torn down, and the ideas of *perestroika* and *glasnost* were welcomed in the Soviet Union.	F. With the agreement, the superpowers had avoided going to war.
D	George W. Bush was elected President after the Supreme Court stopped a recount of Florida votes in 2000.	G. African Americans were being treated unfairly.

(continued)

Name _____ Date _____

32 ESSAY (10 points)

Describe the technological changes that occurred in the second half of the twentieth century, and explain how they affected the American way of life.

Possible response: New appliances, such as washing machines and

dishwashers, made life easier for people in the United States and provided them

with more leisure time. Watching television soon became a regular family

activity. The development of the first satellites led to the start of the space race.

The development of smaller, more fuel-efficient cars allowed people to drive

farther on less gas. The many technological changes also resulted in the

creation of millions of new jobs during the 1990s, a time of record economic

growth in the United States.

(continued)

Name _____ Date _____

Individual Performance Task

Decade Summary

Select and summarize one of the decades listed below, describing the highs and lows of that period. Begin your project by rereading the information in the unit that is related to your decade. You may want to further research the period. In your summary, make sure to include the items listed below as well as others that you find during your research. Write your summary using a formal language.

1950s
- Truman Doctrine
- the Korean War
- the hydrogen bomb
- suburbs
- desegregation

1960s
- New Frontier
- Cuban Missile Crisis
- the Vietnam War
- the space race
- the Civil Rights movement

1970s
- Equal Rights Amendment
- Watergate
- détente
- the Soviet invasion of Afghanistan
- the Iran hostage crisis

1980s
- improved relations with Soviet Union
- *perestroika* and *glasnost*
- the fall of the Berlin Wall

1990s and beyond
- the Gulf War
- a new Eastern Europe
- the elections of 1992 and 2000
- the threat of terrorism

(continued)

© Harcourt

Name _____ Date _____

Group Performance Task

Presidential Panel Interview

Choose one of the following panels of Presidents to interview about their experience leading the United States. The panel interview should be written as if the selected Presidents are reflecting upon their presidencies soon after they have ended. Have each President discuss the condition of the United States when his presidency began and end with recommendations to the next President. Find information in your text, in the school library, or on the Internet about the political, technological, and lifestyle conditions during each selected President's time period. Perform your presidential panel interview before the class.

➡ **PRESIDENTIAL PANEL 1**   Harry S. Truman and Dwight D. Eisenhower

The interview should discuss the Truman Doctrine and the effect it had on United States involvement in Cold War events. Important events to cover include the desegregation of armed forces, the end of the Korean War, and the prosperity and challenges of the 1950s.

➡ **PRESIDENTIAL PANEL 2**   John F. Kennedy and Lyndon B. Johnson

The interview should discuss Kennedy's New Frontier. Important events include increasing minimum wage, forming the Peace Corps, begining the space race, and successfully ending the Cuban Missile Crisis. The struggle for equal rights continued under both Presidents.

➡ **PRESIDENTIAL PANEL 3**   Richard M. Nixon, Gerald Ford, and Jimmy Carter

Important events to cover include Nixon's ending of United States involvement in Vietnam. The economy began to weaken, and the Watergate scandal ended his time as President. Ford's pardon of Nixon disappointed many people. Jimmy Carter began some domestic programs but faced a challenge in foreign affairs.

➡ **PRESIDENTIAL PANEL 4**   Ronald Reagan, George Bush, and Bill Clinton

The interview should cover the fact that during Reagan's presidency, the economy slowly improved as high inflation ended. Reagan's work to improve relations with the Soviet Union was continued by Bush. Bush witnessed the fall of the Berlin Wall and the collapse of communism. The United States experienced a period of record economic growth during Clinton's time in office, but scandal challenged his presidency.

© Harcourt

RUBRICS FOR SCORING

SCORING RUBRICS The rubrics below list the criteria for evaluating the tasks above. They also describe different levels of success in meeting those criteria.

INDIVIDUAL PERFORMANCE TASK

SCORE 4	SCORE 3	SCORE 2	SCORE 1
• Rich description is provided. • Key concepts are well addressed. • Details fit historical period strongly. • Summaries are well organized.	• Some description is provided. • Key concepts are addressed. • Details fit historical period. • Summaries are somewhat organized.	• Little description is provided. • Key concepts are poorly addressed. • Details fit historical period weakly. • Summaries are poorly organized.	• No description is provided. • Key concepts are not addressed. • Details do not fit historical period. • Summaries are not organized.

GROUP PERFORMANCE TASK

SCORE 4	SCORE 3	SCORE 2	SCORE 1
• Interview shows excellent research. • Interview shows creativity. • Details fit historical period strongly.	• Interview shows some research. • Interview shows some creativity. • Details fit historical period.	• Interview shows little research. • Interview shows little creativity. • Details fit historical period weakly.	• Interview shows no research. • Interview shows no creativity. • Details do not fit historical period.

Introduce the Unit

OBJECTIVES

- **Use artifacts and primary sources to acquire information about the United States during and after the Cold War.**
- **Interpret information in visuals.**

Access Prior Knowledge

Challenge students to fill in the graphic organizer below with events or people they associate with the term *Cold War*.

military
communism
arms race
freedom
Soviet Union — **Cold War** — nuclear war
democracy
Korean War
Cuban Missile Crisis

A suburban neighborhood in Riverside, California

BACKGROUND

Construction Boom Much of the construction of suburban communities after World War II occurred in California. After the war, there was so much demand for housing in the state that on a single day in 1946, salespeople at a planned community near Los Angeles sold 107 houses in one hour. Suburban communities in California continue to grow rapidly. Between 1980 and 1990, the population of Riverside County, in southern California, grew by more than 76 percent.

BACKGROUND

Television Television was first developed in the 1920s. In 1936 the National Broadcasting Company (NBC) broadcast the cartoon *Felix the Cat* to 150 homes in the New York City area. In 1939 NBC set up the first regular broadcasts in the United States. The earliest broadcasts reached only areas of the East Coast. In fact, not until 1951 could the same television broadcast be seen coast to coast.

·UNIT·

6

The Cold War and Beyond

" We stand today at the edge of a new frontier. **"**

—John F. Kennedy, presidential nomination acceptance speech, Democratic National Convention, Los Angeles, July 15, 1960

Preview the Content

Skim the chapter and lesson titles. Use them to make an outline of the unit. Write down any questions that occur to you about the time in United States history known as the Cold War years.

Preview the Vocabulary

Multiple Meanings A word can often have several meanings. You may know one meaning but not another. Use the Glossary or a dictionary to look up each of the terms listed below. Then use each term in two sentences that show its different meanings.

| HAWK ⇒ _____ | DOVE ⇒ _____ |
| SATELLITE ⇒ _____ | RECESSION ⇒ _____ |

Unit 6 ■ 403

Visual Learning

Picture The background image shows Riverside, California. Inform students that many suburban communities today, such as Riverside, are modeled after the kind of planned suburban community that became popular in the years following World War II.

Analyze Primary Sources

1950s TV Set Have students examine the television set. Ask them to compare and contrast this set with a television set of today. Students should notice the set's bulkiness, much smaller picture area, and knobs and dials to change channels. Also, tell students that early television sets showed programs only in black and white.

Quotation Have a volunteer read aloud the quotation from John F. Kennedy.

Q Why does Kennedy refer to the future as a "frontier"? Does he seem optimistic or pessimistic about it?

A Kennedy sees the future as unknown territory that Americans must explore. The quote seems to suggest optimism and interest in the possibilities of the future.

AUDIOTEXT

Use the Unit 6 AUDIOTEXT for a reading of the Unit narrative.

· Unit 6 ·

Preview the Content
Students' outlines for Unit 6 should resemble the one below:

Preview the Vocabulary
Make sure students' sentences use each word correctly and that the social studies meaning of each word has been written.

hawk - a person who supports military action

dove - a person who does not support military action

satellite - an object in orbit around Earth

recession - a period of slow economic activity

Preview the Unit

PAGES 404–405

OBJECTIVES

- Interpret information in databases and visuals.
- Use mathematical skills to interpret social studies data on maps and graphs.

Access Prior Knowledge

Ask students what they know about life in the United States following World War II.

Visual Learning

Map Ask students to examine the map and share their observations. Students may notice that interstate highways tend to connect large cities.

Time Line Have students work in pairs to ask and answer questions about the time line. For example, students might ask: *What wars were waged in the second half of the twentieth century?* The United States fought in both the Korean and Vietnam Wars. Although it was not officially a war, the Cold War was a period of tense relations between the United States and the Soviet Union.

Time Line Illustrations Have students speculate about the significance of events on the time line.

- The United States aided South Korea in its war against North Korea.
- The Supreme Court decision in 1954 to end segregation in public schools refuted the idea of "separate but equal."
- In 1957 the Soviet Union launched *Sputnik,* the world's first satellite.
- United States involvement in the Vietnam War escalated throughout the 1960s.
- Astronauts from the *Apollo 11* mission landed on the moon in 1969.
- Starting in the 1980s United States and Soviet leaders worked to end the Cold War. The Cold War came to an end with the breakup of the Soviet Union in 1991.

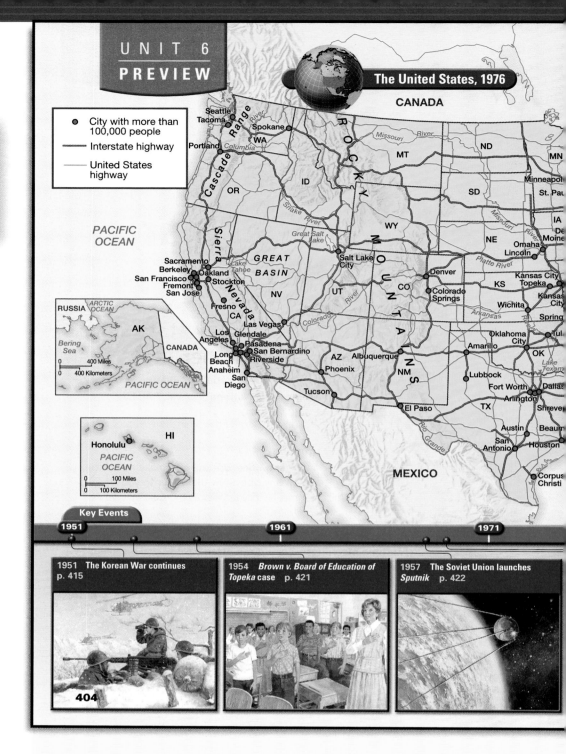

UNIT 6 PREVIEW

The United States, 1976

- City with more than 100,000 people
- Interstate highway
- United States highway

Key Events

1951 | 1961 | 1971

1951 The Korean War continues p. 415

1954 *Brown v. Board of Education of Topeka* case p. 421

1957 The Soviet Union launches *Sputnik* p. 422

INTEGRATE SCIENCE

Research the Space Race Invite students to research the space race between the United States and the Soviet Union in the 1960s. Encourage students to use various sources in their research. Ask volunteers to report their findings to the class.

MAKE IT RELEVANT

At Home Ask students to log for one week their television viewing habits. Have them write down the television programs and times as they watch throughout the week. Have students use their findings to write brief summaries of their viewing habits.

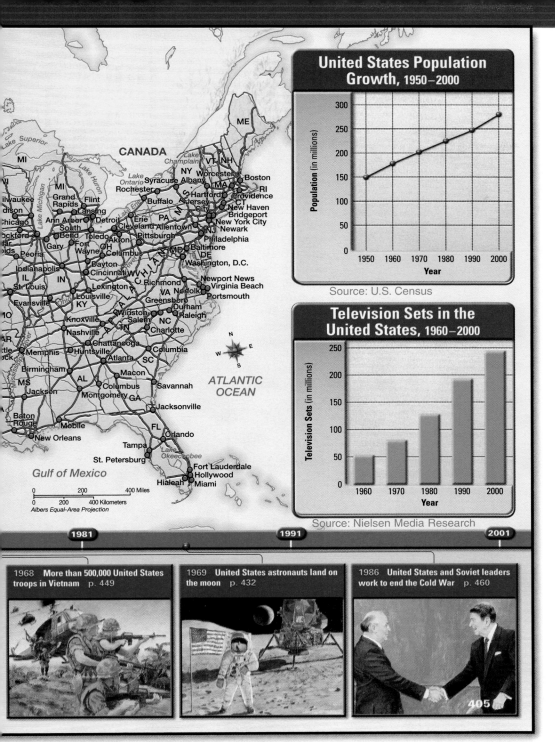

United States Population Growth, 1950–2000

Population (in millions)

300
250
200
150
100
50
0

1950   1960   1970   1980   1990   2000
Year

Source: U.S. Census

Television Sets in the United States, 1960–2000

Television Sets (in millions)

250
200
150
100
50
0

1960   1970   1980   1990   2000
Year

Source: Nielsen Media Research

1981   1991   2001

1968   More than 500,000 United States troops in Vietnam   p. 449

1969   United States astronauts land on the moon   p. 432

1986   United States and Soviet leaders work to end the Cold War   p. 460

405

Visual Learning

Line Graph Have students examine the line graph. Ask such questions as:
- *What does the line graph show?* It shows population growth in the United States between 1950 and 2000.
- *What trend can you see in United States population growth between 1950 and 2000?* It increased in each decade from 1950 to 2000.
- *How many more people were living in the United States in 2000 than in 1950?* about 130 million more

Bar Graph Work with students to interpret the data presented. You may want to ask such questions as:
- *What does the bar graph show?* It shows the number of television sets in the United States from 1960 to 2000.
- *Which decade saw the largest increase in television sets in the United States?* The largest increase occurred between 1980 and 1990.
- *What happened to the number of television sets in the United States between 1970 and 2000?* It tripled.

Make Connections

Link Bar Graph and Line Graph Ask students to use the bar graph and the line graph to make observations and draw conclusions about the relationship between population growth in the United States and the number of television sets in the country.

SCHOOL TO HOME

Use the Unit 6 SCHOOL-TO-HOME NEWSLETTER on pages S11–S12 to introduce the unit to family members and suggest activities they can do at home.

Start with a Speech

OBJECTIVES

- Identify the goals that Martin Luther King, Jr., had for the United States.
- Analyze historical speeches.

Summary

This selection is part of a famous speech Martin Luther King, Jr., delivered at a march for civil rights.

1 Motivate

Set the Purpose

Following World War II many citizens worked for equal rights.

Access Prior Knowledge

Invite students to tell what they know about past struggles for equal rights in the United States. Students might mention the Civil War as well as the abolition and suffrage movements.

READING SOCIAL STUDIES

Summarize Tell students to create summaries of the speech after they have read it.

- USE READING AND VOCABULARY TRANSPARENCY 6-1.

6-1 TRANSPARENCY

2 Teach

Read and Respond

Understand the Speech Ask students to identify what works King quotes in his speech. the Declaration of Independence and the patriotic song "My Country 'Tis of Thee (America)" by Samuel F. Smith

START with a SPEECH

I HAVE A DREAM
by Dr. Martin Luther King, Jr.
illustrated by Leonard Jenkins

In the years after World War II, many people across the country worked for civil rights. Martin Luther King, Jr., became a leader of the Civil Rights movement in the United States. He worked hard for racial justice, and his peaceful protests caught the attention of people around the world. In 1963 about 250,000 people gathered for a march in Washington, D.C. The marchers were supporting a proposed civil rights bill that was in Congress. As the crowd stood in front of the Lincoln Memorial, King spoke to them about his dream for African Americans. Read now part of King's speech.

406 ■ Unit 6

Focus Skill — READING SKILL

Draw Conclusions Explain to students that conclusions are judgments reached after examining facts. Help students draw conclusions about King's dream. Have them recall King's goals for the United States. freedom and equality Then have students draw conclusions about why these two qualities mattered so much to King. Freedom and equality are qualities upon which the country is built, but not all citizens benefited equally from them.

INTEGRATE LANGUAGE ARTS

Write and Perform an Oral History Organize students into small groups. Have each group research the March on Washington, which culminated with King's speech. Ask each group to create an oral history of a family or group who participated in the march. Each group of students should write and memorize its story, and then perform it for the class.

I say to you today, my friends, that in spite of the difficulties and frustrations of the moment I still have a dream. It is a dream deeply rooted in the American dream.

I have a dream that one day this nation will rise up and live out the true meaning of its creed: "We hold these truths to be self-evident; that all men are created equal. . . ."

This will be the day when all of God's children will be able to sing with new meaning, "My country 'tis of thee, sweet land of liberty, of thee I sing. Land where my father died, land of the Pilgrims' pride, from every mountainside, let freedom ring."

And if America is to be a great nation, this must become true. So let freedom ring from the prodigious [gigantic] hilltops of New Hampshire. Let freedom ring from the mighty mountains of New York. Let freedom ring from the heightening Alleghenies of Pennsylvania!

Let freedom ring from the snowcapped Rockies of Colorado! Let freedom ring from the curvaceous peaks of California! But not only that; let freedom ring from Stone Mountain of Georgia! Let freedom ring from Lookout Mountain of Tennessee!

Let freedom ring from every hill and molehill of Mississippi. From every mountainside, let freedom ring.

Analyze the Literature

❶ What was King's dream?

❷ Imagine that you are one of the marchers in Washington, D.C., and write an article describing people's reactions to King's words.

READ A BOOK

START THE UNIT PROJECT

Make a Class Magazine With your classmates, create a class magazine about the United States during the Cold War. As you read the unit, make a list of the key people, places, and events discussed. This list will help you decide what to include in your magazine.

USE TECHNOLOGY

GO ONLINE Visit The Learning Site at **www.harcourtschool.com** for additional activities, primary sources, and other resources to use in this unit.

Unit 6 ▪ 407

Analyze the Literature
Answers

❶ freedom and equality for all

❷ Students might suggest that the marchers were moved by his eloquence and inspired by his perseverance and continued hopefulness.

Use Technology

INTERNET RESOURCES

THE LEARNING SITE
Go to **www.harcourtschool.com** to view Internet resources for this unit.

TIME FOR KIDS
Go to **www.harcourtschool.com** to link to the latest news in a student-friendly format.

3 Close

Summarize the Reading

- Martin Luther King, Jr., worked for equal rights.
- King gave this speech to about 250,000 people in Washington, D.C., in 1963.
- The speech states his dream for the country.

READING SOCIAL STUDIES

Summarize Have partners compare their summaries. You may wish to read them the summary in the Close section to use as a guide.

⬤ USE READING AND VOCABULARY TRANSPARENCY 6-1. **6-1 TRANSPARENCY**

Read a Book

Students may enjoy reading these leveled independent Readers or books of your choice. Additional books are listed on page 403D of this Teacher's Edition.

Easy *Malcolm X* by Richie Chevat. The views of Malcolm X, a supporter of black nationalism, evolved as he developed into an important figure.

Average *Welcome to the Space Age* by Dina Anastasio. The story of Cape Canaveral, NASA, and the United States space program.

Challenging *U.S. Highways* by Dina Anastasio. The development of the interstate highway system began with the enactment of the Interstate Highway Act.

Start the Unit Project

Hint Suggest that students use a graphic organizer to list people, places, and events during and after the Cold War. Students also may wish to designate group members' roles at this time.

Chapter 11 Planning Guide At Home and Abroad

LESSON	PACING	OBJECTIVES	VOCABULARY
Introduce the Chapter pp. 408–409	1 Day	■ Interpret information in visuals. ■ Apply critical-thinking skills to organize and use information. ■ Interpret excerpts from notable speeches.	**Word Work:** Preview Vocabulary, p. 409
1 The Korean War Years pp. 410–415	1 Day	■ Describe the Korean War, the factors leading up to it, and its conclusion. ■ Analyze reasons for the United States' involvement in the Korean War. ■ Identify the role of the United States military in defending freedom during the Korean War.	desegregate
MAP AND GLOBE SKILLS **Identify Changing Borders** pp. 416–417	1 Day	■ Identify borders on a map. ■ Identify reasons that countries' borders change. ■ Evaluate how war changed the border between North Korea and South Korea.	
2 The 1950s pp. 418–423	1 Day	■ Identify cultural changes that occurred in the United States during the 1950s. ■ Explain how the fear of communism led to an air of distrust. ■ Describe the beginnings of the Civil Rights movement in the United States.	integration nonviolence satellite **Word Work:** Historical Context, p. 418
CHART AND GRAPH SKILLS **Compare Graphs** pp. 424–425	1 Day	■ Identify and interpret different kinds of graphs. ■ Evaluate the purpose and effectiveness of different kinds of graphs.	
EXAMINE PRIMARY SOURCES **Civil Defense** pp. 426–427	1 Day	■ Identify the purpose of the United States Federal Civil Defense Administration (FCDA). ■ Describe the services and information provided by the FCDA. ■ Interpret visual information.	

READING	INTEGRATE LEARNING	REACH ALL LEARNERS	RESOURCES
(Focus Skill) **Draw Conclusions,** p. 409			
Reading Social Studies: **Study Questions,** p. 411 Reading Social Studies: **Reread Aloud,** p. 413 Reading Social Studies: **Study Questions Responses,** p. 415	Mathematics **High Tide,** p. 413 Science **Make a Double-Bar Climograph,** p. 414 Language Arts **Persuasive Writing,** p. 414	**Advanced Learners,** p. 410 **English as a Second Language,** p. 411 **Tactile Learners,** p. 412 **Extend and Enrich,** p. 415 **Reteach the Lesson,** p. 415	**Activity Book,** pp. 102–103 **Reading and Vocabulary Transparency 6-2**
		Tactile Learners, p. 416 **Extend and Enrich,** p. 416 **Reteach the Skill,** p. 417	**Activity Book,** pp. 104–105 **Skill Transparencies 6-1A and 6-1B** **GeoSkills CD-ROM**
Reading Social Studies: **Personal Response,** p. 419 Reading Social Studies: **Summarize,** p. 421 Reading Social Studies: **Personal Response,** p. 423		**Kinesthetic Learners,** p. 422 **Extend and Enrich,** p. 423 **Reteach the Lesson,** p. 423	**Activity Book,** p. 106 **Reading and Vocabulary Transparency 6-3** Internet Resources
	Mathematics **Determine Population Growth,** p. 424	**Extend and Enrich,** p. 425 **Reteach the Skill,** p. 425	**Activity Book,** p. 107 **Skill Transparencies 6-2A and 6-2B**
		Extend and Enrich, p. 427 **Reteach,** p. 427	Internet Resources

Chapter 11 Planning Guide At Home and Abroad

LESSON	PACING	OBJECTIVES	VOCABULARY
3 New Opportunities and New Challenges pp. 428–433	1 Day	■ Analyze the effect of President Kennedy's New Frontier on the nation. ■ Evaluate relationships between the United States and the communist countries of Cuba and the Soviet Union. ■ Describe how the United States entered the space race.	**developing country** **blockade**
CITIZENSHIP SKILLS **Resolve Conflicts** p. 434	1 Day	■ Identify compromise as the key to resolving conflicts. ■ Recognize steps to take to resolve conflicts.	
4 Working for Equal Rights 435–441	2 Days	■ Identify the achievements of individuals and leaders in the fight for equal rights. ■ Describe and evaluate the actions of various groups who worked to gain equal rights.	**demonstration** **migrant worker**
CITIZENSHIP SKILLS **Act as a Responsible Citizen** pp. 442–443	1 Day	■ Discuss specific examples of responsible citizenship. ■ Understand the importance of voluntary individual participation in the democratic process. ■ Evaluate the difference one responsible citizen can make.	
Chapter Review and Test Preparation pp. 444–445	1 Day		

READING	INTEGRATE LEARNING	REACH ALL LEARNERS	RESOURCES
Reading Social Studies: K-W-L Chart, p. 429 **Reading Social Studies:** K-W-L Chart Responses, p. 432	Mathematics **Multiplication**, p. 429 Language Arts **Persuasive Writing**, p. 430 **Write an Advertisement**, p. 432 Art **Draw a Picture**, p. 431	**English as a Second Language**, p. 428 **Tactile Learners**, p. 429 **Extend and Enrich**, p. 433 **Reteach the Lesson**, p. 433	**Activity Book**, p. 108 **Reading and Vocabulary Transparency 6-4** Internet Resources
		Extend and Enrich, p. 434 **Reteach the Skill**, p. 434	**Activity Book**, p. 109 **Skill Transparency 6-3**
Reading Social Studies: Personal Response, p. 436 **Reading Social Studies:** Graphic Organizer, p. 437 **Reading Social Studies:** Personal Response, p. 441	Art **Draw a Poster**, p. 437 Science **Recognizing the Effect of Television on Civil Rights**, p. 438 Reading **Read a Biography**, p. 439	**Auditory Learners**, p. 436 **Advanced Learners**, p. 438 **Extend and Enrich**, p. 441 **Reteach the Lesson**, p. 441	**Activity Book**, p. 110 **Reading and Vocabulary Transparency 6-5** Internet Resources
Reading Social Studies: Summarize, p. 442		**Extend and Enrich**, p. 443 **Reteach the Skill**, p. 443	**Activity Book**, p. 111 **Skill Transparency 6-4**
		Test Preparation, p. 444	**Activity Book**, pp. 112–113 **Reading and Vocabulary Transparency 6-6** **Assessment Program, Chapter 11 Test**, pp. 91–94

Activity Book

Name _____ Date _____

The Korean War Years

Directions Read the information below, and study the map. Then answer the questions on page 103.

The Truman Doctrine stated that the United States would support any country that was resisting armed minorities or resisting outside pressures threatening to destroy that country's democracy. The United States followed this policy in its attempt to stop the spread of communism. Several European nations, some of which had been allies of the United States in World War II, also supported this policy. The leaders of these countries believed that if one country in a region fell to communism, others in that region would likely follow. This idea is known as the domino theory.

The European Powers

(continued)

Name _____ Date _____

Directions Use the map and information on page 102 to answer the questions below.

1 Where were most of the Soviet-controlled countries located?
near the Soviet border

2 Where were most of the nations allied with the United States located?
in the western part of Europe

3 Which countries do you think the United States was most concerned about protecting against communism? Why? Answers may vary but could include the nations closest to the Soviet Union. These countries would be more likely to be influenced by the Soviet Union.

4 In 1953 elections were held in Yugoslavia, a communist country. Would the Truman Doctrine have applied to this election? No; the country was already a communist country and not in danger of losing democracy.

5 Which countries separated the United States allies from the Soviet-controlled countries? Austria, Switzerland, and Italy

---

Name _____ Date _____

MAP AND GLOBE SKILLS

Identify Changing Borders

Directions Use the maps below to answer the questions on page 105.

Vietnam Area Before 1954

Vietnam Area After 1954

(continued)

Name _____ Date _____

Directions Use the maps on page 104 to answer the questions below.

1 Before 1954, what were the names of the countries and regions that made up the Vietnam area? Tonkin, Laos, Annam, Cambodia, Cochinchina

2 After 1954, what were the names of the countries that made up the former Vietnam area? Laos, Cambodia, North Vietnam, South Vietnam

3 Which nation received more land, North Vietnam or South Vietnam?
South Vietnam

4 After 1954, South Vietnam was formed from what two regions?
Annam and Cochinchina

5 What river follows the western borders of Laos and Cambodia?
Mekong River

6 From what you know about Germany and Korea after World War II, what might be a reason for dividing a nation? A country might be divided so that half could be a democracy and half could be communist.

Name _____ Date _____

The 1950s

Directions Imagine that you are living during the late 1950s. Write a letter to a pen pal about how your life has changed over the past decade. Here are some words to help you compose your letter.

suburbs	television	rock and roll	appliances
communism	civil rights	cold war	satellite

Letters will vary but should include several ideas related to the words provided above. Students may choose to focus on the changes brought about by suburban living, including the movement of people and economy from the inner cities to the suburbs. The 1950s also saw an increased interest in television, and people were introduced to rock and roll music. Students also may write about appliances. Students may concentrate on the fears of communism that started the activities of Senator Joseph McCarthy. Students may write of the fight for civil rights, both to integrate schools—following the 1954 Supreme Court ruling in *Brown v. Board of Education of Topeka*—and to integrate buses and other services after Rosa Parks's nonviolent protest on a Montgomery, Alabama, bus. Students may focus on the space race between the Soviet Union and the United States, after the launch of *Sputnik.*

Use after reading Chapter 11, Lesson 2, pages 418–423.

© Harcourt

Name _____ Date _____

CHART AND GRAPH SKILLS

Compare Graphs

Directions Use the graphs below to answer the questions that follow.

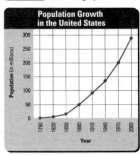

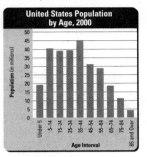

1 How many people lived in the United States in 1970? 200 million

2 How many people lived in the United States in 2000? about 275 million

3 What is the largest age group in the United States? How many people are in this group? 35-44; 45 million

4 What is the smallest age group in the United States? How many people are in this group? 85 and over; about 5 million

5 What statement can be made about the United States population from 1790 to 2000? The population always increased.

6 Why is it important to read the title of a graph? The title tells important information, such as which areas are being included and what the graph is about.

© Harcourt

Use after reading Chapter 11, Skill Lesson, pages 424–425.

Name _____ Date _____

New Opportunities and New Challenges

Directions The following graphic organizer reviews new opportunities and new challenges that people faced in the United States during the early 1960s. Fill in the blanks with information from the lesson.

John F. Kennedy is inaugurated.

The Soviet Union places missiles in Cuba.

The Soviets put the first human into space.

The Cuban Missile Crisis causes tensions with the Soviet Union.

President Kennedy challenges the country to put an American on the moon before 1970.

President Kennedy orders a blockade of Cuba.

Alan Shepard is the first American in space.

The Soviets agree to remove their missiles.

John Glenn, Jr., orbits Earth three times.

Use after reading Chapter 11, Lesson 3, pages 428–433.

© Harcourt

Name _____ Date _____

CITIZENSHIP SKILLS

Resolve Conflicts

Directions Read the statements below about the Korean War. Number the events from 1 to 8, starting with the event that happened first (1) and ending with the one that happened last (8). Then answer the question that follows.

1 _5_ UN forces pushed the North Koreans back above the thirty-eighth parallel.

2 _1_ The Soviet Union did not allow free elections for all of Korea.

3 _7_ Eisenhower promised to end the Korean War.

4 _2_ North Korean soldiers crossed into South Korea.

5 _6_ By this time, more than 300,000 Chinese troops had entered North Korea.

6 _8_ North and South Korea signed an armistice.

7 _3_ The United Nations called for a cease-fire.

8 _4_ General Douglas MacArthur was named commander of the United Nations force in Korea.

9 Why did the Korean War become a major issue in the 1952 presidential election. because so many American soldiers lost their lives in Korea

© Harcourt

Use after reading Chapter 11, Skill Lesson, page 434.

Name _____ Date _____

Working for Equal Rights

Directions Look at the pictures of these leaders who worked for equal rights. Then write the initials of the person next to the phrases that apply to him or her.

Martin Luther King, Jr.

Cesar Chavez

Malcolm X

Betty Friedan

❶ _CC_ asked people to boycott California grapes

❷ _MLK_ gave one of the most unforgettable speeches in United States history

❸ _BF_ worked for equal rights for women

❹ _MX_ changed name to show loss of African ancestral name

❺ _MLK_ led a march on Selma, Alabama

❻ _MX_ at one time believed violence was acceptable in fighting for rights

❼ _BF_ helped start the National Organization for Women

❽ _CC_ worked with organizations for farm workers' rights

Name _____ Date _____

 CITIZENSHIP SKILLS

Act as a Responsible Citizen

Directions Read each passage below. Write a brief description of what your role, responsibilities, actions, and goals would be in each situation.

❶ As part of a community service project, you have decided to organize a group of your classmates to help keep the school grounds clean. Saturday crews will patrol the school grounds for litter and dispose of it properly.

Answers will vary but should include some of the following: The role of organizer would include the responsibility for setting up teams, assigning each team specific hours, and checking to see that the work was done. The actions would be to encourage participation and follow-through and to monitor the teams, as well as to lead by example. The goals would be cleaner school grounds.

❷ A local dry cleaner is collecting used winter coats for area children in need. You decide to advertise information about the drive at school so students will know about the chance to recycle their outgrown coats.

Answers will vary but should include some of the following: The role of advertiser would include the responsibility for determining how to advertise the event and creating the advertisements. The actions might include making posters, distributing flyers and buttons, and writing announcements for the school P. A. system or community radio station. The goal would be to increase donations of coats.

Name _____ Date _____

The 1950s

Directions Use this graphic organizer to help you draw conclusions about the 1950s.

EVIDENCE		CONCLUSION
The growth of suburbs that began after World War II increased greatly in the 1950s.	→	As America's urban and suburban areas grew, the need for more
KNOWLEDGE		
When the population of an area grows, more services are needed.	→	services continued to grow as well.
EVIDENCE		**CONCLUSION**
During the prosperous 1950s, homes, cars, and appliances sold faster than ever before.	→	During the economic boom of the 1950s, the lifestyle of
KNOWLEDGE		
In a good economy, people have more money to spend.	→	many Americans improved greatly.
EVIDENCE		**CONCLUSION**
In 1954, the Supreme Court put an end to segregation in America's schools.	→	Many people disagreed with the Supreme Court's decision to end
KNOWLEDGE		
Many people did not agree with the Supreme Court decision.	→	segregation in schools, and other public places remained segregated.
EVIDENCE		**CONCLUSION**
African Americans of Montgomery decided not to ride the city buses until the buses were integrated.	→	African Americans brought about the
KNOWLEDGE		
One way to bring about change is through peaceful actions.	→	end of segregated buses in Montgomery.

CHAPTER   Name _____ Date _____

11   Test Preparation

Directions Read each question and choose the best answer. Then fill in the circle for the answer you have chosen. Be sure to fill in the circle completely.

❶ President Truman showed his commitment to equality by—
Ⓐ desegregating the country's armed forces.
Ⓑ encouraging people to vote for the Equal Rights Amendment.
Ⓒ appointing Thurgood Marshall to the Supreme Court.
Ⓓ returning Native Americans' lands.

❷ Which of the following conflicts was a result of following the Truman Doctrine?
Ⓐ World War II
Ⓑ the Korean War
Ⓒ World War I
Ⓓ the D day invasion

❸ The Supreme Court ruled in the case of *Brown v. the Board of Education of Topeka* that—
Ⓐ African Americans should be allowed to sit anywhere on a city bus.
Ⓑ restaurants had to serve African Americans.
Ⓒ separate-but-equal schools were unfair.
Ⓓ all teachers should receive the same salaries, regardless of race.

❹ As part of his New Frontier, President Kennedy created—
Ⓕ the Peace Corps.
Ⓖ the American Indian Movement.
Ⓗ the Civil Rights Act.
Ⓙ a national park system.

❺ Lyndon Baines Johnson became President after—
Ⓐ President John F. Kennedy was impeached.
Ⓑ the Senate held a runoff vote after a close election.
Ⓒ he was elected in 1960.
Ⓓ President John F. Kennedy was assassinated.

Chapter 11 Assessment

·CHAPTER·

Name _____ Date _____

11 Test

Part One: Test Your Understanding

MULTIPLE CHOICE (4 points each)

Directions Circle the letter of the best answer.

1 The Truman Doctrine—
A committed the United States to fighting communism worldwide.
B was designed to stop communism from spreading.
C led the nation into the Korean War.
D all of the above

2 After World War II, Korea was divided in half and was—
F run by the United Nations under a democratic government.
G occupied by the Soviet Union.
H run by the United States.
J occupied partly by the Soviet Union and partly by the United States.

3 Which event occurred first?
A UN soldiers recaptured Seoul.
B North Korean soldiers retreated behind the 38th parallel.
C North Korea's surprise attack drove South Korean troops in the Pusan area.
D MacArthur led a surprise attack on Inchon.

4 Suburban life in the 1950s was characterized by—
F newspaper closings, urban decay, and declining businesses.
G television, shopping malls, and time-saving appliances.
H jazz clubs, automobile trips, and tax increases.
J rock and roll, declining population, and less free time.

5 What caused Cold War tensions to grow during the 1950s?
A Soviet bombing raids
B television
C a build-up of weapons
D underground bunkers

6 President Kennedy's New Frontier program—
F increased the minimum wage and created the Peace Corps.
G defended the United States against communism.
H led to the spread of democracy.
J all of the above

(continued)

Chapter 11 Test

Name _____ Date _____

7 Why were Soviet missiles in Cuba a threat to the United States?
A because it could have led to a blockade
B because Cuba is close to Florida
C because exiles fled to Florida
D because the Soviets kept blocking American cargo ships to Cuba

8 Which occurred first?
F Soviet astronaut Yury Gagarin orbited Earth.
G United States astronaut Alan Shepard went into space.
H United States astronauts walked on the moon.
J United States astronaut John Glenn, Jr., orbited Earth.

9 President Kennedy's civil rights bill—
A was proposed because southern politicians demanded it.
B passed in the House but not in the Senate.
C made segregation in public places against the law.
D was vetoed by Lyndon Johnson.

10 Cesar Chavez—
F believed in using nonviolent means to protest.
G led Mexican American farm workers in a fight for better wages.
H asked people in the United States to boycott California grapes.
J all of the above

TRUE OR FALSE (4 points each)

Directions Indicate whether the following statements are true or false by writing T or F. Correct false statements in the space provided.

11 General Douglas MacArthur was the commander of the UN forces in Korea.

T _____

12 As suburbs grew in the 1950s, cities began to decay. F; Cities near suburbs grew

and prospered as new businesses, schools, and churches opened.

13 Watching television was not popular in the 1950s.

F; Watching television became a regular family activity in the 1950s.

14 In the 1950s teenagers listened to rock and roll music.

T _____

15 Malcolm X was awarded the Nobel Peace Prize for his use of nonviolent protests.

F; Dr. Martin Luther King, Jr., won the Nobel Peace Prize.

(continued)

Chapter 11 Test

Name _____ Date _____

Part Two: Test Your Skills

COMPARING GRAPHS (4 points)

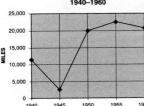

Federal Highway Miles Completed 1940–1960

Percentage of Federal Highway Miles Completed 1940–1959

- 1940–1944 12%
- 1945–1949 19.5%
- 1950–1954 30%
- 1955–1959 38.5%

Directions Use the graphs to answer these questions about miles of federal highway systems completed between 1940 and 1960.

16 Which graph is better for showing the trend in the construction of federal highways during the 1940s and 1950s? the line graph

17 What was the trend in the construction of highways during the late 1940s?

Highway construction increased rapidly during that time.

18 During which period were the least miles of highways built?

the early 1940s

19 Which graph is better for showing the percentages of highway miles that were

built at different times? the circle graph

20 What percentage of highway miles were completed during the late 1950s?

38.5 percent

(continued)

Chapter 11 Test

Name _____ Date _____

Part Three: Apply What You Have Learned

21 **CATEGORIZE** (10 points)

Complete the chart below by listing each feature of the 1950s in the correct column. Then add two entries of your own in each column.

Lifestyle/Entertainment	Politics
shopping malls	the Korean War
suburbs	the Truman Doctrine
appliances	Malcolm X
television	nonviolent protests
rock and roll	the Cold War

- suburbs
- television
- the Truman Doctrine
- nonviolent protests
- the Cold War

- the Korean War
- rock and roll
- Malcolm X
- shopping malls
- appliances

21 **ESSAY** (10 points)

Choose two events, movements, or trends from the 1950s, and explain their importance. One of your choices should be related to politics. The other should be related to lifestyle.

Students' choices will vary. Choices related to politics may include the Korean War,

the space race, the Civil Rights movement, the Cuban missile crisis, or the

death of John F. Kennedy. Choices related to lifestyle may include the rise of

suburban living, the way of life created around suburbs, rock and roll music, the

increased popularity of television, or any of the movements for equality or civil

rights.

Chapter 11 Test

Introduce the Chapter

OBJECTIVES

- Interpret information in visuals.
- Apply critical-thinking skills to organize and use information.
- Interpret excerpts from notable speeches.

Access Prior Knowledge

Lead students in a discussion of what they know about the Civil Rights movement. What was the Civil Rights movement? Who were some of the people involved?

Visual Learning

Picture Direct students' attention to the picture and the Locate It map. Ask students to think about what the chapter might be about, on the basis of the picture.

Locate It Map The Civil Rights Memorial is located in Montgomery, Alabama. It was built at the entrance to the Southern Poverty Law Center, just a few blocks from where the first White House of the Confederacy stood.

408 ▪ Unit 6

· CHAPTER ·

11

At Home and Abroad

" . . . until justice rolls down like water and righteousness like a mighty stream. "

—Martin Luther King, Jr., speech at the Lincoln Memorial in Washington, D.C., August 28, 1963

 Draw Conclusions

A **conclusion** is a decision or an idea reached by using evidence from what you read and what you already know about a subject. To draw a conclusion, you combine new facts with the facts you already know.

As you read this chapter, be sure to do the following.

• Use evidence and what you already know to draw conclusions about the United States.

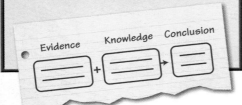

Evidence   Knowledge   Conclusion

Chapter 11 ▪ 409

WORD WORK

Preview Vocabulary Have students make a list of the vocabulary terms in this chapter. Then have students read through the lessons and write brief definitions of the terms. Ask students to concentrate on the words that have multiple meanings. Students should list the alternate meanings of these words next to the definitions from the chapter.

MAKE IT RELEVANT

Discussion Topics As you teach this chapter, you and your students might enjoy discussing some of the following topics. Each topic helps relate what students are learning about in this chapter to their world today.

■ In what ways do Americans continue to work for equal rights today?

■ How does the government make sure all citizens are treated equally?

Read and Respond

Instruct students to read the title of the chapter and think about what it means. Encourage them to speculate about the kinds of events that were going on in the United States during the time covered by the chapter.

Quotation Have a volunteer read the quotation aloud.

Q What do you think the quotation means?

A Allow students to express their viewpoints.

Dr. Martin Luther King, Jr., gave his "I Have a Dream" speech to more than 200,000 civil rights supporters who had gathered in Washington, D.C.

 Draw Conclusions

As students read the chapter, have them complete a graphic organizer to help them draw conclusions about the United States.

• A blank graphic organizer can be found on page 112 of the Activity Book.

• Remind students that they should use information they know combined with new information they have learned to help them draw conclusions.

• A completed graphic organizer can be found on page 112 of the Activity Book, Teacher's Edition.

Evidence   Knowledge   Conclusion

Lesson 1

PAGES 410–415

OBJECTIVES

- Describe the Korean War, the factors leading up to it, and its conclusion.
- Analyze reasons for the United States' involvement in the Korean War.
- Identify the role of the United States military in defending freedom during the Korean War.

 Draw Conclusions
pp. 409, 410, 413, 415, 444

Vocabulary

SEE READING AND VOCABULARY TRANSPARENCY 6-2 OR THE WORD CARDS ON PP. V49–V50.

desegregate
  p. 411

 When Minutes Count

Have pairs of students work together to find the answers to the subsection review questions.

Quick Summary

This lesson examines the Korean War, the factors leading up to it, and the eventual involvement of the United States in it.

 Motivate

Set the Purpose

Big Idea Explain to students the strategic importance of the United States' attempt to end the spread of communism in Korea.

Access Prior Knowledge

Have students discuss what they have learned about the spread of communism following World War II.

1

 DRAW CONCLUSIONS
As you read, draw conclusions about the United States' entry into the Korean War.

BIG IDEA
The United States entered the Korean War to stop the spread of communism in the world.

VOCABULARY
desegregate

The Korean War Years

1951   1976   2001

1950–1953

The Berlin crisis was just the beginning of the conflict between the free world and communism. In 1950, the United States, along with other members of the United Nations, entered a war to stop communist forces from taking control of Korea. This conflict became known as the Korean War. The Korean War showed the world that the United States still wanted to defend freedom.

The 1948 Election

When Harry S. Truman became President after the death of Franklin D. Roosevelt, he understood the great challenge of his new office. During his first years as President, he worked hard to meet that challenge. Still, many people did not think he could win the 1948 presidential election.

FAST FACT Late on election night in 1948, the editors of the *Chicago Daily Tribune* realized that they had incorrectly predicted the election's winner. However, thousands of morning newspapers had already been delivered.

Many people, including the editors of the *Chicago Daily Tribune*, did not think Truman (below) had enough support to win the presidential election.

410 ▪ Unit 6

Election Predictions Few experts believed that Truman would win the 1948 presidential election. In fact, the October 11, 1948, issue of *Newsweek* published the results of a poll that asked 50 political experts to predict the election result. All of the 50 experts predicted that Dewey would win.

Advanced Learners
Remind students that President Truman believed communism to be the opposite of democracy. Organize students into groups, and have them research communism and democracy. Have them create charts from their findings that illustrate the differences between the two political philosophies.

Prior to 1948, African American soldiers had to serve in separate units.

As Election Day drew near, most reporters predicted Truman's opponent, Republican Thomas E. Dewey, would win. After voting ended on Election Day, the *Chicago Daily Tribune* printed a headline for the next day's paper. It read, "Dewey Defeats Truman." The next morning, however, after all the votes had been counted, Truman had won the election by just over 2 million votes. Harry Truman had won one of the biggest surprise victories in the history of United States presidential elections.

REVIEW Why were many people surprised by Harry Truman's victory in the 1948 presidential election? because most newspapers had predicted Thomas Dewey would win

Changes Continue at Home

President Truman was a strong believer in the New Deal. He wanted to expand the programs that Franklin D. Roosevelt had begun. Soon after his election he said, "Every individual has a right to expect from his government a fair deal."

In 1949 Truman presented to Congress a plan that became known as the Fair Deal. It extended many of the economic programs the New Deal had created. Under the Fair Deal, for example, the minimum wage was increased. Social Security payments for the elderly continued. In addition, federal funds were used to help rebuild run-down areas in many of the nation's cities.

President Truman also believed in civil rights. In 1946 he formed the Presidential Committee on Civil Rights to advise him about civil rights in the country. Then, in 1948, he desegregated the nation's armed forces. To **desegregate** is to remove racial barriers. This meant that African Americans, for example, would no longer be put in separate units.

Truman's relations with other countries were influenced by the fact that he did not trust communism. He believed that communism was the opposite of democracy. He believed, too, that the United States should stop the spread of communism. He said, "I believe that it must be the policy of the United States to support free peoples who are resisting attempted subjugation [control] by armed minorities or by outside pressures."

Chapter 11 ■ 411

Causes of the War

Read and Respond

History Explain that entering the twentieth century, Korea had enjoyed a long and rich history as an independent country. Inform students that in 1910, Japan forcibly annexed Korea and controlled it until the end of World War II, when the United States and Soviet Union began occupying it.

Q Why do you think the United States decided to occupy South Korea?

A Students' answers may vary but could indicate that the United States was concerned about the possible spread of communism in Korea.

Visual Learning

Map Direct students' attention to the map on page 412. Ask students to locate the capitals of North Korea and South Korea. Pyongyang and Seoul

Q About how far away was the capital city of South Korea from the prewar boundary line?

A about 30 miles (50 km)
CAPTION ANSWER: at the thirty-eighth parallel

The War Begins

Read and Respond

History Explain that China and the Soviet Union, both communist countries, aided North Korea in the Korean War. Inform students that the United States provided most of the troops, equipment, and supplies sent to South Korea. Explain that the United States offered such assistance as part of a United Nations "police action" and did not issue a formal declaration of war.

 Regions After World War II, Korea was divided into two parts—North Korea and South Korea.

◈ Where was the prewar boundary?

The policy of stopping communism from spreading became known as the Truman Doctrine. In 1950 the United States went to war to uphold the Truman Doctrine and to defend the people of South Korea.

REVIEW How did President Truman change the armed forces? He desegregated the nation's armed forces.

Causes of the War

Like Germany, the Asian country of Korea was divided after World War II. The border that divided the country was known as the thirty-eighth parallel. Soviet troops occupied the northern part, and United States troops occupied the southern part.

412 ■ Unit 6

The division of Korea was supposed to last only a short time. So, in 1947, the United Nations called for elections that would choose a government for all of Korea. However, the Soviet Union was against the plan. Instead, each part of Korea chose a government. Each government said it was the lawful government for both North Korea and South Korea.

North Korea, which set up a communist government, was known as the People's Democratic Republic of Korea. South Korea, which set up a free government, became known as the Republic of Korea. Between 1948 and 1950, troops from both sides often battled near the border. These battles would soon lead to a much larger conflict.

REVIEW What two countries sent troops to occupy Korea after World War II? the United States and the Soviet Union

The War Begins

On June 25, 1950, North Korean soldiers crossed the thirty-eighth parallel and invaded South Korea. Immediately, the United Nations called for a cease-fire. When North Korean troops would not stop fighting, the United Nations voted to send in troops to restore peace. For the first time in history, a world organization went to war to stop one country's attack on another country. Many of the member nations sent troops to South Korea. Most of the troops, however, were from the United States or were South Korean.

REACH ALL LEARNERS

Tactile Learners
Organize students into small groups. Supply each group with a globe. Review with students the meaning of the words *longitude* and *latitude*. Have students take turns placing their index fingers on the globe's 38°N line of latitude. Have each student trace the 38°N line of latitude around the globe until he or she locates Korea.

BACKGROUND

Douglas MacArthur (1880–1964)
Douglas MacArthur was born in Arkansas, the son of a decorated Civil War hero. Like his father before him, Douglas MacArthur entered military service. He served in World War I and was supreme commander of the United States' successful Pacific operations during World War II. In 1950 MacArthur was named to command United Nations forces in Korea.

This Congressional Medal of Honor was awarded to a soldier who fought in the Korean War.

The United Nations named United States General Douglas MacArthur as commander of all UN forces in Korea. MacArthur had commanded troops in the Pacific during World War II and knew the region well.

North Korea's surprise attack had driven South Korean troops farther and farther south. By September 1950 the South Koreans held only the area around the city of Pusan, in the southeast corner of the nation. However, UN troops held the line around Pusan. This proved to be a turning point in the war.

REVIEW Why did the United Nations vote to send troops to South Korea? to restore peace

DRAW CONCLUSIONS

UN Forces Move North

General MacArthur had a plan to cut off North Korean forces. According to this plan, some UN troops would attack North Korean forces at the line around Pusan. Others would approach secretly from the sea. They would surprise communist troops at a city called Inchon, 150 miles (241 km) deep into communist-held South Korea.

The attack at Inchon would be very dangerous, for each day the city had tides 30 feet (9 m) high. If the troops missed high tide, their ships would be stuck in mud. Then escape would be impossible. However, Inchon remained the target. A victory there would cut some of the North Korean forces' supply lines.

General MacArthur (left) commanded the UN troops in South Korea. The soldiers (right) are watching for North Korean troops.

Read and Respond

History Explain that in the summer of 1950 North Korea appeared to be on the verge of winning the war. At one point North Korean forces occupied about 90 percent of South Korea. In August UN forces kept control of the city of Pusan, a key step in halting the southward advance of North Korean forces.

Q **Why was the defense of Pusan considered a key victory by UN forces?**

A It stopped North Korean forces from claiming the city and moving closer to victory in the war.

UN Forces Move North

Read and Respond

History Inform students that MacArthur's decision to attack at Inchon provided momentum to UN forces. Within six weeks UN forces had pushed North Korean forces out of South Korea and had advanced into North Korea.

Geography Explain that Inchon did not have a wide, sandy beach where troops could be dropped off for an invasion. Inchon is located off a shallow body of water called the Yellow Sea. At low tide the "beach" at Inchon was said to resemble mud flats. This meant that troops could land only at high tide, which restricted troop landings to just a few hours in a day.

READING SOCIAL STUDIES

Reread Aloud Display on the wall a map of North Korea and South Korea. Ask a volunteer to read aloud the events of the war as described on pages 412–414, including the fighting at Pusan, the invasion at Inchon, and the unexpected arrival of Chinese troops at the Yalu River. Each time the volunteer reads a place-name, have a second volunteer locate the place on the wall map.

INTEGRATE MATHEMATICS

High Tide Inform students that Inchon had modern industries and port facilities. The tidal basin was constructed to overcome the 30-foot (9-m) difference between high and low tides. Have students measure and mark a distance of 30 feet (9 m) on the floor. Ask them to visualize that measurement vertically. Lead students to understand the danger to the UN forces had they missed landing at high tide.

Advance and Retreat

Read and Respond

History Explain to students that when fighting ended in Korea, a buffer zone was formed that separated the northern half and the southern half. This *demilitarized zone* runs 2.5 miles (4 km) wide along the final battle line on the peninsula.

The Korean War Ends

Read and Respond

History Explain that by 1952 the casualty rate among United States soldiers was so high that presidential candidate Dwight D. Eisenhower made ending the war a key part of his campaign.

Q Why did Dwight D. Eisenhower promise during his presidential campaign to end the Korean War if he was elected?

A Students may infer that Eisenhower understood that people in the United States were upset by the war's high casualty rate and that an end to the conflict would appeal to voters.

3 Close

Summarize Key Content

- Harry S. Truman surprised many people by winning the 1948 presidential election.
- Truman presented to Congress his Fair Deal plan, which expanded the programs of the New Deal.
- Truman believed strongly that the United States should act to contain communism.
- The Korean War began with North Korea's invasion of South Korea.
- Early in the war, North Korean troops took over most of South Korea, but UN troops pushed them back to the north.
- China's involvement in the Korean War brought the war to a deadlock.
- After three years of battles, the Korean War ended on July 27, 1953.

The attack on the troops at Inchon started early in the morning on September 15. It so surprised the North Koreans that the battle was over in one day. At the same time, UN troops broke through enemy lines around Pusan and started heading north. By the end of September, UN soldiers had recaptured the city of Seoul, South Korea's capital. And by early October, UN forces had pushed the North Koreans back above the thirty-eighth parallel.

REVIEW Why was the attack on Inchon dangerous? The tides at Inchon were 30 feet (9m) high each day. The attack had to be timed perfectly.

LOCATE IT

Heartbreak Ridge

NORTH KOREA

SOUTH KOREA

Advance and Retreat

For several weeks UN troops kept moving northward, pushing communist forces up toward the Yalu River. The Yalu River forms the border between North Korea and China. Most people did not believe China would become involved in the war. However, China's communist government supported North Korea. Soon Chinese troops and equipment were moving across the border. By the end of November more than 300,000 Chinese troops had entered North Korea.

On November 26, 1950, Chinese and North Korean forces attacked. UN troops were forced to fall back below the thirty-eighth parallel. Soon UN troops made another try and pushed the communist forces back into North Korea.

REVIEW How did China become involved in the Korean War?

This ridge (below) near the thirty-eighth parallel was called Heartbreak Ridge because of the great number of soldiers who were killed defending the position. These soldiers (left) were at the ridge and were only 45 yards (41 m) from North Korean troops.

China's communist government supported North Korea and sent troops and equipment to help the North Koreans.

INTEGRATE SCIENCE

Make a Double-Bar Climograph Remind students that UN forces struggled with the harsh weather along the Korean peninsula. Have small groups research the climates of the Korean peninsula and of their home state. Have them use that information to make a double-bar graph. One set of bars should show the average temperature for each month in the Korean peninsula. The other set of bars should show their state's average temperature for each month. Have students make climate comparisons from their graphs.

INTEGRATE LANGUAGE ARTS

Persuasive Writing Tell students to imagine that they are living at the time of the Korean War. Have them write letters to a newspaper suggesting an end to the war. Students' letters should persuade the American public to agree with their position. Have volunteers read their letters to the class.

The Korean War Ends

The Korean War became a war fought in feet, not in miles. The front lines moved very little in either direction for the next two years as UN troops battled the North Koreans and the Chinese. The weather, too, became a problem. Freezing cold winters made it hard to get supplies to the troops. Under these difficult conditions, soldiers had a hard time staying prepared for battle.

So many American soldiers lost their lives in Korea that the war became a major issue in the 1952 presidential election. General Dwight D. Eisenhower, who had commanded troops in World War II, promised that he would work to end the war if elected. Soon after his election he kept his promise. By 1953 communist troops had been pushed back into North Korea. That same year, an

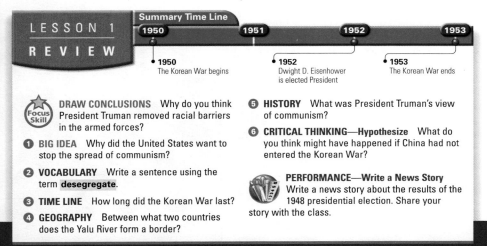

General Dwight D. Eisenhower (above, with his wife, Mamie) was elected President in 1952. Supporters carried signs with his nickname, Ike.

armistice was signed, ending the fighting. The Korean War was over, and South Korea remained an independent country.

REVIEW Why did the Korean War become an issue in the 1952 presidential election? Many soldiers were killed in the war, and Eisenhower promised to end the war if elected.

LESSON 1 REVIEW

Summary Time Line

1950 — 1951 — 1952 — 1953

- 1950 The Korean War begins
- 1952 Dwight D. Eisenhower is elected President
- 1953 The Korean War ends

 DRAW CONCLUSIONS Why do you think President Truman removed racial barriers in the armed forces?

❶ **BIG IDEA** Why did the United States want to stop the spread of communism?

❷ **VOCABULARY** Write a sentence using the term **desegregate**.

❸ **TIME LINE** How long did the Korean War last?

❹ **GEOGRAPHY** Between what two countries does the Yalu River form a border?

❺ **HISTORY** What was President Truman's view of communism?

❻ **CRITICAL THINKING—Hypothesize** What do you think might have happened if China had not entered the Korean War?

 PERFORMANCE—Write a News Story Write a news story about the results of the 1948 presidential election. Share your story with the class.

OBJECTIVES

- **Identify borders on a map.**
- **Identify reasons that countries' borders change.**
- **Evaluate how war changed the border between North Korea and South Korea.**

1 Motivate

Why It Matters

Review with students some of the countries, such as the United States, whose borders have changed during the last 200 years. Discuss how the Civil War threatened to change the border of the United States. Point out that the borders of countries around the world have changed throughout history and that maps can be used to illustrate those changes.

➡ WHY IT MATTERS

Historical maps give important information about places as they were in the past. By studying a historical map, you can see how a place and its borders have changed over time. Seeing those changes on a historical map can help you better understand the changes and how they came about.

➡ WHAT YOU NEED TO KNOW

In Lesson 1 you read that when World War II ended, Korea was broken into two parts—North Korea and South Korea. You also read that the border was set on a line of latitude—the thirty-eighth parallel, or 38°N.

The two maps on page 417 show how the border between North Korea and South Korea changed over time. One map shows the national border before the Korean War. The second map shows the border after the war.

This soldier is standing guard at the border of South Korea.

➡ PRACTICE THE SKILL

Use the two maps to answer these questions:

1. What color is used to show North Korea?
2. What color is used to show South Korea?
3. Which map shows North and South Korea's prewar border?
4. Is North and South Korea's present-day border mostly north or mostly south of the prewar border?

Tactile Learners Point out that the change in Korea's borders came as a result of war. Organize students into small groups, and assign each group one of the two world wars. Have groups compare maps of Europe from before and after the war to determine how country borders changed. Then display a wall map of Europe with its present-day borders. Have a volunteer from each group come to the wall map and trace with his or her finger the borders that were drawn after the war. Volunteers can ask for help from group members to accurately trace the borders.

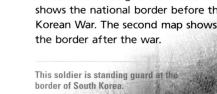

Listen to Directions Supply students with a political map of Korea that does NOT show the border between North and South. Organize students into small groups. Have one person in each group try to describe orally where the border runs as the other students try to draw the corresponding line. When students have finished, discuss how information like this can be presented more effectively visually than verbally.

Korea, 1945

⊛ National capital

0   50   100 Miles
0   50   100 Kilometers
Conic Projection

CHINA

NORTH KOREA
Pyongyang ⊛
Hüngnam
Sea of Japan

Yellow Sea

Panmunjom
Inchon ⊛ Seoul

SOUTH KOREA

Pusan

Cheju Island

JAPAN

Korea, 1953

⊛ National capital

0   50   100 Miles
0   50   100 Kilometers
Conic Projection

CHINA

NORTH KOREA
Pyongyang ⊛
Hüngnam
Sea of Japan

Yellow Sea

Panmunjom
Inchon ⊛ Seoul

SOUTH KOREA

Pusan

Cheju Island

JAPAN

⑤ According to the maps, did South Korea win or lose land at the end of the Korean War?

▶ **APPLY WHAT YOU LEARNED**

Many states today do not have the same borders they had when they joined the United States. Find a historical map of the United States, and choose one of the states it illustrates. Then use an encyclopedia or an atlas to

find a map showing the state's present-day borders. On a sheet of paper, draw a map showing the original borders of the state. Then draw another map showing the present-day borders of the state. Share your maps with the class.

Practice your map and globe skills with the **GeoSkills CD-ROM**.

MAP AND GLOBE SKILLS

2 Teach

What You Need to Know

Have students look at the map key to identify how the map uses colors. Explain that the colors show how the border between North and South Korea changed over time. Help students locate the border on both maps.

Practice the Skill—Answers

❶ orange
❷ green
❸ the 1945 map
❹ mostly north
❺ gained land

3 Close

Apply What You Learned

As students display their maps, have them describe how the borders have changed.

- Identify cultural changes that occurred in the United States during the 1950s.
- Explain how the fear of communism led to an air of distrust.
- Describe the beginnings of the Civil Rights movement in the United States.

Draw Conclusions
pp. 409, 418, 422, 423, 444

Vocabulary
SEE READING AND VOCABULARY TRANSPARENCY 6-3 OR THE WORD CARDS ON PP. V49–V50.

integration p. 421   **satellite** p. 423
nonviolence p. 421

When Minutes Count

Have students read about Rosa Parks and the Montgomery bus boycott on pages 421–422. Then invite them to tell in their own words what they just read.

Quick Summary

This lesson examines the people and events that helped shape the 1950s. It also describes the challenges people in the United States faced as they dealt with the fear of communism and worked toward civil rights.

1 Motivate

Set the Purpose

Big Idea Explain that the United States faced various political and social challenges throughout the 1950s.

Access Prior Knowledge

Have students discuss what they have learned about the spread of communism. Ask students to predict how the United States will respond as communism overtakes other countries.

2

 DRAW CONCLUSIONS
As you read, draw conclusions about the challenges faced by the United States.

BIG IDEA
The United States faced challenges both outside and inside the nation during the 1950s.

VOCABULARY
integration
nonviolence
satellite

The 1950s

1951	1976	2001

1950–1960

The 1950s were years when many Americans were doing well. Thanks to the GI Bill, the men and women who had served in World War II were given the chance to go to college. Many found good jobs and were able to buy homes in suburbs. Suburbs grew rapidly during the 1950s, and so did many Americans' sense of community. However, throughout the 1950s, Americans also were worried about communism, the arms race, and equal rights for all.

Life in the 1950s

Suburbs that began after World War II grew even more in the 1950s. In fact, of the 13 million houses built between 1948 and 1958, 11 million were in suburbs. Suburbs changed the look of the United States. As more people moved out to suburbs,

The popularity of television grew in the 1950s (left). Children (below) of families who moved to suburbs walked to neighborhood schools.

418

Historical Context Have groups of students look up the definitions of the lesson vocabulary terms. Tell students that these terms provide clues about the lesson's content. Have groups use the vocabulary terms to predict the lesson content. Then have them locate each term and read the paragraph in which it appears to see whether their predictions were correct.

Use Reference Sources Encourage students to use primary and secondary sources to learn about Andrew Wyeth. Explain that Wyeth is a famous artist who has painted scenes in American life from the 1940s up to the present, and that his works were particularly popular in the 1950s. Ask students to write a short paragraph about Wyeth's paintings.

By 1960, millions of people in the United States had television sets.

singers such as Elvis Presley, Buddy Holly, and Chuck Berry. A new youth culture had begun to develop.

During the 1950s the economy of the United States boomed. Homes, cars, and appliances were sold faster than ever before. Many of these items were bought on credit, which meant they were paid for over time. The number of Americans buying goods on credit grew. The first credit cards were introduced in the 1950s. Soon many people used them for instant credit.

One reason for the growth of the economy during this time was the growing number of building projects. In 1956 President Eisenhower signed the Federal Aid Highway Act. This led to the building of highways across the country. These new highways helped the number of automobile sales grow. They also led to the building of thousands of new hotels, restaurants, and gas stations across the country.

The growing number of automobiles and highways also led to the growth of shopping centers. In 1945 there were only 8 shopping centers in the United States. By 1960 there were almost 4,000. New shopping centers and malls became places where families from the suburbs gathered.

the population of many older cities dropped. Cities near suburbs, however, grew and did well as new businesses, schools, and churches opened there.

Family life also changed in the 1950s. New appliances such as washers and dryers and dishwashers made life easier and gave people more free time. Watching television became a thing to do as a family. By the end of the decade, nine out of ten homes in the United States had televisions.

Television also brought a new kind of music into the nation's homes. It was called rock and roll. It combined country music and rhythm and blues. Teenagers of the 1950s danced to the rock and roll songs of musicians and sales led to the building of highways, restaurants, hotels, and shopping centers.

REVIEW How did the United States economy grow during the 1950s? Many people bought homes, appliances, and automobiles. Automobile

Chuck Berry was a popular rock and roll singer.

Chapter 11 ■ 419

QUESTIONS KIDS ASK

Q Why do people use credit to buy goods?

A Credit allows people to buy goods or services and pay for them later. One form of consumer credit is a credit card, which can be used to charge purchases at restaurants, businesses, or online. Another type of consumer credit is an installment plan, which allows the buyer to make small payments over a period of time. Many people use installment plans to buy furniture or large household appliances.

STUDY/RESEARCH SKILLS

Use the Internet Encourage students to use the Internet to learn more about popular television shows during the 1950s. Explain that "I Love Lucy," "The Mickey Mouse Club," and "American Bandstand" are three examples of successful 1950s programs. Ask students to discuss how these shows seem similar or dissimilar to modern television programs.

2 Teach

Life in the 1950s

Read and Respond

Link Geography and Economics Tell students that the migration of people from cities to the suburbs during the 1950s was very costly to the cities. Explain that the drop in city populations resulted in a decrease in their tax bases. This meant some cities could not offer the same services as before.

Visual Learning

Picture Direct students' attention to the photograph of the family watching television on page 419. Discuss with students whether they consider television watching today to be a family activity as it was in the 1950s.

Read and Respond

Link Culture and Society with Economics Explain to students that when President Eisenhower ran for re-election in 1956 his campaign slogan was "peace and prosperity." Have students discuss why his slogan linked peace with economic prosperity. Students may respond that peaceful times after World War II coincided with an economic boom.

Fears of Communism

Read and Respond

History Explain that in the early 1950s Joseph McCarthy accused various high-profile people, including actors and politicians, of being communists. Inform students that although McCarthy seldom provided proof of his accusations, few people dared to criticize him. McCarthy's tactics gave rise to the term "Red Scare," which referred to the panic over communism in the 1950s.

Q Why did few people question McCarthy's claims?

A Students should indicate that if people spoke out against McCarthy, they too might be labeled as communists.

A Supreme Court Ruling

Read and Respond

Civics and Government Explain that the Supreme Court heard arguments in the *Brown* case in 1952, but did not render a decision that year. Inform students that the Supreme Court was very divided at the time and it was only after Earl Warren became Chief Justice that it became more unified. Chief Justice Warren persuaded the other justices in 1954 to support a decision ending segregation.

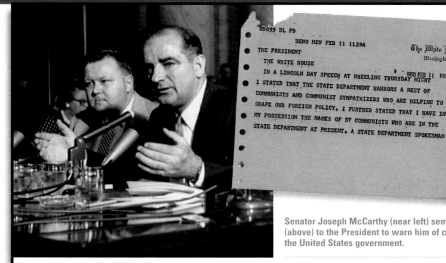

Senator Joseph McCarthy (near left) sent a telegram (above) to the President to warn him of communists in the United States government.

Fears of Communism

During the 1950s Americans had more money than ever before. At the same time, people were worried about the future. Much of this concern had to do with the spread of communism around the world. However, the events in China and North Korea were not the only ones that troubled people in the United States. At home several citizens were tried for and found guilty of being communist spies.

In 1950 Senator Joseph McCarthy began holding hearings to look into possible communist threats in the United States. McCarthy made people's fears grow by saying that communist spies were working in every branch of the national government. He also ruined the lives of many innocent people by falsely accusing them of being communists.

However, for several years few people dared to say anything against McCarthy and his hearings. Those who did were often accused of being communists themselves. In time, people fought back against McCarthy. In 1954 he said that communist spies were working in the United States Army. Joseph Welch, the lawyer for the Army, challenged McCarthy during a hearing shown on television. Soon most Americans refused to believe McCarthy any longer.

REVIEW Who was Joseph McCarthy? *a senator who falsely accused some Americans of being communist spies*

A Supreme Court Ruling

In the early 1950s Linda Brown of Topeka, Kansas, wanted to go to school with other children in her neighborhood. She did not understand why state laws in Kansas said that African American children had to attend separate schools.

In 1896 the United States Supreme Court had made a ruling in a case called *Plessy v. Ferguson*. The court said that separate public places for whites and African Americans were lawful as long as the places were equal. In most cases, however, they were not equal. This ruling applied to all public places, including schools. As a result, African American

420 Unit 6

QUESTIONS KIDS ASK

Q Why were people in the United States so concerned about communism?

A It had spread to other parts of the world, such as North Korea, leading people in the United States to fear it might spread here, too.

BACKGROUND

The Hollywood "Blacklist" As tensions about communism grew, many people in Hollywood's movie industry spoke out against communist ideas in films. Actors, screenwriters, and any other employees suspected of communist beliefs were "blacklisted," or banned from any employment. Today many people believe the "blacklist" was harsh and unfair.

BACKGROUND

Joseph McCarthy (1908–1957) Joseph McCarthy was a senator from Wisconsin who first began attracting national attention in 1950 with his claims of communist activity in the United States. McCarthy's charges ruined the lives of many innocent people he accused. Eventually McCarthy was censured by fellow senators for making charges without proof. His influence in the Senate and elsewhere on the national political scene was never the same again.

children often had to attend run-down schools with few study materials.

Linda Brown's family and 12 other African American families decided to fight laws that upheld segregated schools. The NAACP agreed to help in 1951. One of its lawyers, Thurgood Marshall, presented the case before the Supreme Court. The case, which became known as *Brown v. Board of Education of Topeka*, would help change history. Marshall argued that separate schools did not provide an equal education. He called for **integration**, or the bringing together of people of all races, in public schools.

In 1954 Supreme Court Chief Justice Earl Warren said, "In the field of education the doctrine of 'separate but equal' has no place." The court ordered an end to segregation in public schools. Some states protested the court's ruling. In 1957 there were riots in Little Rock, Arkansas, because of integration. President Eisenhower had to send 1,000 soldiers to restore order. Still, many other schools remained segregated.

REVIEW What did the Supreme Court say about segregation in public schools?
The Supreme Court ruled that segregation in public schools must end.

Rosa Parks is fingerprinted after her arrest for refusing to move to the back of the bus.

The Montgomery Bus Boycott

On December 1, 1955, a young African American woman named Rosa Parks got on a bus in Montgomery, Alabama. She took a seat in the middle of the bus. Under Alabama law, African Americans had to sit in the back. They could sit in the middle section only if the seats were not needed for white passengers.

When the bus filled up, the bus driver told Rosa Parks to give up her seat to a white man. She refused. The bus driver called the police, and Parks was arrested.

After Parks's arrest, the African Americans of Montgomery decided to boycott, or refuse to ride, the city buses until they were integrated. A minister named Dr. Martin Luther King, Jr., led the boycott. He believed in **nonviolence**, or peaceful actions to bring about change.

Thurgood Marshall (far left) argued against school segregation so that students like Linda Brown (left) could get an equal education.

Chapter 11 ▪ 421

READING SOCIAL STUDIES

Summarize Remind students that in the *Plessy v. Ferguson* decision, the Supreme Court ruled that "separate but equal" was acceptable. Have students write brief summaries contrasting that notion with the decision rendered in *Brown v. the Board of Education of Topeka*. Ask volunteers to share their summaries with the class.

Read and Respond

History Explain that in issuing its ruling in the *Brown* case, the Supreme Court essentially overruled its *Plessy v. Ferguson* ruling of 1896. Inform students that although the Court's *Brown* ruling was issued in 1954, it would be many years before certain states complied with it.

The Montgomery Bus Boycott

Economics Remind students that a boycott is a refusal to do business with an individual, company, group, or country. Protesters hope that by boycotting a business, they will cause financial harm to it, which might lead it to change its practices.

Q **Is a boycott an effective means of protest? Why or why not?**

A Students' answers will vary but should reflect that a boycott can be an effective form of protest.

Q **What role did Rosa Parks play in the struggle for civil rights?**

A Her refusal to give up her bus seat led to a bus boycott and the eventual end of segregation on public transportation.

Culture Ask students to explain what Martin Luther King, Jr., meant when he said that nonviolence would help bring about change. How might a non-violent struggle such as that advocated by King affect not only the cause but also society? A nonviolent protest might bring attention to a problem and show the need for change.

Cold War Tensions Grow

Read and Respond

History Review with students some of the ways in which tensions increased between the United States and the Soviet Union during the Cold War. Emphasize to students that the United States and the Soviet Union had been rivals in the areas of science and engineering.

Q **Why did the Cold War extend into space?**

A Students may respond that the race into space was an extension of other rivalries between the United States and the Soviet Union.

3 Close

Summarize Key Content

- The advent of suburbs, television, and rock and roll helped shape life in the 1950s.
- Fear of communism made some Americans act in ways that were not constitutional.
- The Supreme Court's ruling in the case of *Brown v. the Board of Education of Topeka* made school segregation illegal in the United States.
- The actions of African Americans such as Rosa Parks and Martin Luther King, Jr., helped further the cause of civil rights.
- Cold War tensions between the United States and the Soviet Union extended into a race into space.

For more than a year, African Americans stayed off the buses. Finally, in November 1956 the Supreme Court ruled that all public transportation companies had to end segregation. The bus company had to change its rules. Rosa Parks had helped change the law.

REVIEW What was the purpose of the Montgomery bus boycott?

DRAW CONCLUSIONS
to force the bus company to end segregation in public transportation

Cold War Tensions Grow

As people like Rosa Parks and Dr. Martin Luther King, Jr., worked to change laws in the nation, the Cold War tensions between the United States and the Soviet Union grew. Both nations continued to build up the number of weapons they had. People in the United States and around the world closely followed the actions of both nations.

Some people in the United States feared that a Soviet bombing raid could come at any moment. They built underground bunkers, or bomb shelters, and filled them with food and supplies. There they hoped they could survive any bombs that were dropped. Government officials also wanted people to be prepared. They made comic books to illustrate to schoolchildren what they should do in case of an attack.

The two superpowers also took the Cold War into space. In 1957 the Soviet Union surprised the United States by launching *Sputnik* (SPUT•nik). *Sputnik* was

People prepared for bombing raids by building bomb shelters (below). During drills (right), students were trained to take cover.

After the launching of *Sputnik* (model shown at right), the United States formed NASA (above).

the world's first human-made **satellite**. A satellite is an object that orbits a planet.

Because of *Sputnik*, the United States sped up its own efforts to explore space. In 1958 the National Aeronautics and Space Administration, or NASA, was formed to develop the nation's space program.

REVIEW **Why was NASA formed?** NASA was formed to develop the nation's space program.

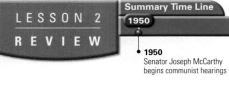

LESSON 2 REVIEW

Summary Time Line

1950 — 1955 — 1960

1950 Senator Joseph McCarthy begins communist hearings

1954 The Supreme Court declares segregation of public schools illegal

1957 The Soviet Union launches *Sputnik*

 DRAW CONCLUSIONS Why do you think the bus boycott in Montgomery, Alabama, helped change the bus company's rules?

1 **BIG IDEA** What challenges did the United States face during the 1950s?

2 **VOCABULARY** Write a sentence explaining how Dr. Martin Luther King, Jr., and others used **nonviolence** to achieve **integration**.

3 **TIME LINE** In what year was *Sputnik* launched?

4 **HISTORY** Why did some people build underground bunkers?

5 **CRITICAL THINKING—Analyze** How do you think Rosa Parks's actions helped the Civil Rights movement?

 PERFORMANCE—Simulation Activity Imagine that it is December 1, 1955, and you are on the bus with Rosa Parks. With a partner, role-play a conversation between you and a fellow passenger.

Chapter 11 ■ 423

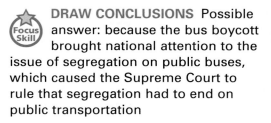

OBJECTIVES

- Identify and interpret different kinds of graphs.
- Evaluate the purpose and effectiveness of different kinds of graphs.

1 Motivate

Why It Matters

Point out that pages 424 and 425 show a variety of graphs. Ask students to examine the graphs and tell which they think are easiest to read. Ask volunteers to provide brief explanations that support their choices.

·SKILLS· **Compare Graphs**

CHART AND GRAPH

➡ **WHY IT MATTERS**

Suppose you want to prepare a report on the population of the United States after World War II. You want to show a lot of information in a brief, clear way. One way you might do this is by making graphs. Knowing how to read and make graphs can help you compare large amounts of information.

➡ **WHAT YOU NEED TO KNOW**

Different kinds of graphs show information in different ways. A line graph shows change over time. The line graph to the right shows how the number of people living in the United States changed between 1930 and 1960.

Bar graphs make it easy to compare a lot of information quickly. The bar graph to the right shows the number of immigrants in the United States between 1930 and 1960.

A circle graph, or pie chart, can also help you make comparisons. The circle graphs on page 425 show the percentage of Americans living in urban and rural areas in two different years.

➡ **PRACTICE THE SKILL**

Use the information in these four graphs to answer the following questions.

424 ▪ Unit 6

As you work, think about the advantages and disadvantages of each kind of graph.

❶ In 1960, about how many people lived in this country?

❷ Did the United States population get bigger or smaller between 1930 and 1960?

Source: United States Census Bureau

Source: United States Census Bureau

INTEGRATE MATHEMATICS

Determine Population Growth Remind students that the population figures shown in the graphs on page 424 are in millions. Ask students to find how much the United States population grew between 1930 and 1960. 175 million − 125 million = 50 million Ask students which graph provides this information. the line graph

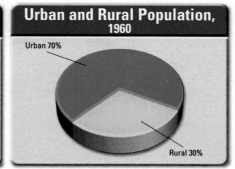

Urban and Rural Population, 1930

Urban 56%

Rural 44%

Source: United States Census Bureau

Urban and Rural Population, 1960

Urban 70%

Rural 30%

Source: United States Census Bureau

❸ In which year was this statement true? *About two-thirds of all Americans live in cities.*

❹ About how many people who were foreign born lived in the United States in 1960?

❺ When the percentage of the urban population increases, why does the percentage of the rural population decrease?

➡️ **APPLY WHAT YOU LEARNED**

Use the graphs on these pages to write a paragraph summarizing information about changes in the United States population between 1930 and 1960. Share your paragraph with a partner, and compare your summaries.

In 1960 most of the people in the United States lived in or near cities.

CHART AND GRAPH SKILLS

425

2 Teach

What You Need to Know

Explain that the names of the graphs on pages 424 and 425 also describe them. For example, circle graphs are made of circles divided into pieces, line graphs use lines to show change over time, and bar graphs compare information shown with bars. Inform students that the sum of percentages in each circle graph should equal one hundred percent.

Practice the Skill—Answers

❶ about 175 million

❷ It got bigger.

❸ 1960

❹ about 9 million

❺ because people are moving from rural areas to urban areas

3 Close

Apply What You Learned

Students' paragraphs should accurately reflect population changes in the United States from 1930 to 1960.

EXTEND AND ENRICH

Identify Different Kinds of Graphs Have small groups of students look for graphs in recent newspapers and magazines. Ask students to cut out and mount on colored paper any graphs they find. For each graph, ask the groups to write on the colored background paper the kind of graph and the information it provides. Have groups share their findings with the class. Discuss whether one kind of graph seems to be used more than others in certain newspapers and magazines.

RETEACH THE SKILL

Experiment with Graphs Have students use data from the graphs on pages 424 and 425 to make different graphs that illustrate the same data. For example, have them use the data to make a circle graph from the graphs on page 424. Have them make bar graphs from the circle graphs on page 425. Encourage students to think of other ways in which data may be depicted differently.

Examine Primary Sources

OBJECTIVES

- Identify the purpose of the United States Federal Civil Defense Administration (FCDA).
- Describe the services and information provided by the FCDA.
- Interpret visual information.

1 Motivate

Set the Purpose

During the Cold War many people in the United States feared a nuclear attack by the Soviet Union. Prompted by the Soviets' first atom bomb test, the FCDA was formed to protect civilians. The administration was mostly involved in the publishing of public awareness materials. It had limited involvement in the construction of shelters.

Access Prior Knowledge

Remind students that people often are given instructions for what to do in an emergency. Ask students to suggest times and places today when directions for emergencies are given.

2 Teach

Read and Respond

Have volunteers read aloud the information on the brochures. Ask students to explain the procedures for seeking shelter when a person is in a house at the time of a nuclear attack. Students should state that people should seek shelter either in an underground shelter, a basement shelter, or at the center of the house.

EXAMINE PRIMARY SOURCES

Civil Defense

The United States Federal Civil Defense Administration (FCDA) began operating in 1951. The purpose of this government agency was to prepare the American people for a possible nuclear war with the Soviet Union. It did so through programs during the 1950s and 1960s. The FCDA encouraged citizens to build fallout shelters as protection from the tiny radioactive particles that fall to Earth after a nuclear explosion. The agency also provided printed information.

FROM THE NATIONAL ARCHIVES AND RECORDS ADMINISTRATION IN WASHINGTON, D.C.

A fallout shelter

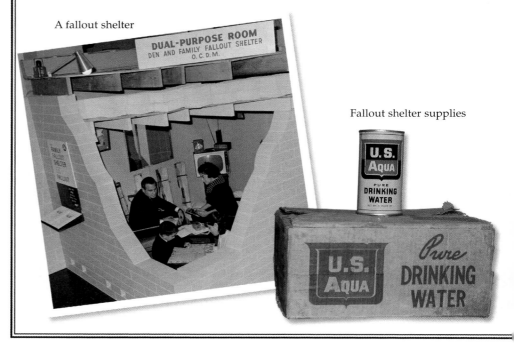
Fallout shelter supplies

BACKGROUND

More About the Time When the Federal Civil Defense Administration was created in 1951, the agency was not very effective because of its limited budget. By the late 1950s, however, civil defense had become a priority. More funding was made available to the administration and the FCDA became the Office of Civil Defense Mobilization. By 1962 the Department of Defense reported that more than 112,000 fallout shelters had been built that could protect about 60 million civilians.

More About the Artifacts The Federal Civil Defense Administration encouraged families to build fallout shelters in their backyards or basements. Brochures explaining survival kit preparation were published, and children practiced duck and cover drills in case of nuclear attack. Fallout shelter signs were posted on public buildings to indicate shelter.

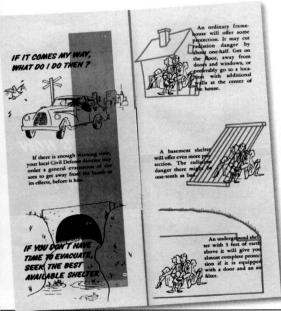

Analyze the Primary Source

Answers

❶ Citizens could learn of a nuclear attack by listening to the radio.

❷ People were to report to shelters to protect themselves from radiation fallout during an attack.

3 Close

Activity

Compare and Contrast Have students compare the FCDA with today's Office of Homeland Security. Students should compare the purposes of these government agencies and their methods of communicating information. Students should understand that both agencies work to ensure the safety of the nation's people.

Research

Students will find more posters at The Learning Site at **www.harcourtschool.com.**

Ask each student to select one poster and write a brief description of the poster and its purpose.

INTERNET RESOURCES

THE LEARNING SITE
Go to **www.harcourtschool.com** for a DIRECTORY OF PRIMARY SOURCES.

EXTEND AND ENRICH

Role-Play Have students imagine that they are living in the United States during the Cold War era. Organize students into small groups to research safety drills. Then have students in each group role-play a scenario in which they pretend to be taking part in a safety drill.

RETEACH

Write Questions Have students work in groups to develop questions that could be answered from the brochures on this page. Suggest that students trade questions with another group and find the answers to the questions. Compile a list of the groups' questions into a classroom guide for analyzing the artifacts.

Lesson 3

PAGES 428–433

New Opportunities and New Challenges

1951	1976	2001

1960–1969

OBJECTIVES

- Analyze the effect of President Kennedy's New Frontier on the nation.
- Evaluate relationships between the United States and the communist countries of Cuba and the Soviet Union.
- Describe how the United States entered the space race.

 Draw Conclusions
pp. 409, 428, 430, 433, 444

Vocabulary

SEE READING AND VOCABULARY TRANSPARENCY 6-4 OR THE WORD CARDS ON PP. V49–V50.

developing   **blockade** p. 429
country p. 429

 ## When Minutes Count

Invite students to examine the photographs and captions. Then have them tell which photographs belong in the category *New Opportunities* and which belong in the category *New Challenges*.

Quick Summary

This lesson identifies the opportunities and challenges the United States faced during the 1960s. It also identifies international issues, specifically the events of the Cold War.

1 Motivate

Set the Purpose

Big Idea Encourage students to explain the difference between the Cold War and an actual war, such as World War II.

Access Prior Knowledge

Have students discuss what they have learned about the Cold War.

DRAW CONCLUSIONS
As you read, draw conclusions about the competition between the United States and the Soviet Union.

BIG IDEA
The actions of the United States and the Soviet Union shaped world events in the 1960s.

VOCABULARY
developing country
blockade

President Kennedy takes the oath of office at his inauguration.

All during the 1960s, the United States and the Soviet Union challenged each other both on Earth and in space. The election of a new President in 1960 raised the hopes of many Americans. Then a tragic event just three years later would forever change the nation. Even before then, however, people worried about what was going on in Cuba and the possibility of war. Yet, the accomplishments of the space program inspired people everywhere.

A "New Frontier"

In 1961 John F. Kennedy took the oath of office as President of the United States. Only 43 years old, Kennedy was the youngest person ever elected President. Young people liked his energy and enthusiasm. At his inauguration, the new President

428

BACKGROUND

Kennedy's Inauguration At President John F. Kennedy's inauguration in 1961, Robert Frost read his poem "The Gift Outright," about the United States gaining independence through its devotion to the land. In 1962 President Kennedy presented Frost with a Congressional Medal.

REACH ALL LEARNERS

English as a Second Language Pair students learning English with English-proficient students, and have them look up the vocabulary terms in the narrative. Have them read each term in context. Ask students to determine whether each term has something to do with the Cold War. If the answer is yes, have students write the term and its connection to the Cold War.

urged Americans to work for the good of their country: "And so, my fellow Americans: Ask not what your country can do for you—ask what you can do for your country."

President Kennedy wanted to bring people with new ideas into the government. To fill his Cabinet he chose people who shared his views. Among them was his 35-year-old brother, Robert Kennedy. He became attorney general and the President's closest adviser.

President Kennedy's program to improve life in the United States and elsewhere became known as the New Frontier. Among the successes of the New Frontier was an increase in the minimum wage. Also, Congress voted to spend more money on rebuilding poor areas in the nation's older cities. Kennedy also signed a European trade deal that made trade between the United States and Europe easier.

One of the best-known and longest-lasting parts of the New Frontier remains the Peace Corps. Started in 1961, the Peace Corps is a program that sends volunteers from the United States to live and work with people in developing countries. A **developing country** is a country that does not have modern conveniences such as good housing, roads, schools, and hospitals. Many people in developing countries are very poor. Peace Corps volunteers teach classes in everything from farming to reading and writing English. Since 1961 more than 150,000 Peace Corps volunteers have worked in countries around the world.

REVIEW What was the New Frontier?
President Kennedy's program to improve life in the United States

These volunteers are applying to become members of the Peace Corps.

The Cuban Missile Crisis

Soon after President Kennedy took office, the problems of the Cold War began to take up much of his time. In October 1962 he learned that the Soviet Union had built several launch sites for missiles on the island of Cuba, just 90 miles (145 km) off the tip of Florida. Fidel Castro had taken control of Cuba in 1959. With the help of the Soviet Union, he had formed a communist government. The missiles that Castro let the Soviets set up in Cuba had a range of more than 1,000 miles (1,609 km). This meant that these missiles could reach many of the United States' largest cities.

Kennedy demanded that the Soviets remove the missiles. When they did not, he ordered United States Navy ships to **blockade**, or prevent other ships from entering or leaving, the island nation. Their orders were to stop Soviet ships carrying missiles from reaching Cuba.

Chapter 11 ■ 429

Visual Learning

Map Ask students to locate the U.S. aircraft carriers on the map on page 430. Explain that the Cuban Missile Crisis of 1962 brought the United States and the Soviet Union to the brink of nuclear conflict.

CAPTION ANSWER: The aircraft carriers were placed so that they could block ships taking missiles to Cuba.

Students might enjoy researching artifacts from the Cold War. Have them visit The Learning Site at **www.harcourtschool.com.**

Read and Respond

Geography Discuss with students why the Soviet Union wanted the United States to remove its missiles that were near the Soviet Union. Those missiles were as much a threat to the Soviet Union as the missiles in Cuba were to the United States.

Q What prevented the start of a nuclear war during the Cuban Missile Crisis?

A The two superpowers were able to come to a peaceful agreement in which both sides compromised.

History Explain to students that the Cuban Missile Crisis was one of the most significant events of the Cold War. Having come close to nuclear war, the superpowers decided to establish a better relationship. In 1963 a telephone "hot line" linked Washington and Moscow to provide instant communication.

Q How would an instant communication link be helpful to the two nations?

A Misunderstandings could be taken care of immediately. If, for example, a United States plane strayed across a Soviet border, the two countries could immediately contact each other to explain that the mistake was not an act of war.

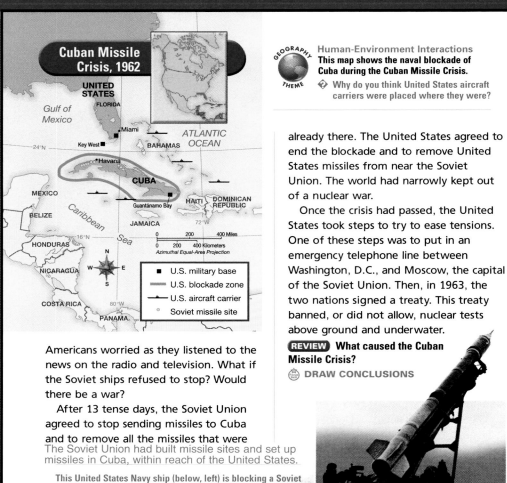

Cuban Missile Crisis, 1962

UNITED STATES

Gulf of Mexico

FLORIDA

Miami

Key West

BAHAMAS

ATLANTIC OCEAN

24°N

Havana

CUBA

MEXICO

Guantánamo Bay

HAITI

DOMINICAN REPUBLIC

BELIZE

Caribbean Sea

JAMAICA

72°W

16°N

0   200   400 Miles

0   200   400 Kilometers
Azimuthal Equal-Area Projection

HONDURAS

NICARAGUA

N W E S

COSTA RICA

80°W

PANAMA

■ U.S. military base
━ U.S. blockade zone
━ U.S. aircraft carrier
○ Soviet missile site

Human-Environment Interactions
This map shows the naval blockade of Cuba during the Cuban Missile Crisis.

◆ Why do you think United States aircraft carriers were placed where they were?

Americans worried as they listened to the news on the radio and television. What if the Soviet ships refused to stop? Would there be a war?

After 13 tense days, the Soviet Union agreed to stop sending missiles to Cuba and to remove all the missiles that were already there. The United States agreed to end the blockade and to remove United States missiles from near the Soviet Union. The world had narrowly kept out of a nuclear war.

Once the crisis had passed, the United States took steps to try to ease tensions. One of these steps was to put in an emergency telephone line between Washington, D.C., and Moscow, the capital of the Soviet Union. Then, in 1963, the two nations signed a treaty. This treaty banned, or did not allow, nuclear tests above ground and underwater.

REVIEW What caused the Cuban Missile Crisis? DRAW CONCLUSIONS

The Soviet Union had built missile sites and set up missiles in Cuba, within reach of the United States.

This United States Navy ship (below, left) is blocking a Soviet ship (below, right) from reaching Cuba. Soviet missiles (right) were being set up in Cuba.

878

430

INTEGRATE LANGUAGE ARTS

Persuasive Writing
Have small groups of students pretend that they are presidential advisers. Word has just come that Soviet missiles have been spotted in Cuba. Have each group debate the possible courses of action the United States could take. Have groups list pros and cons for each course of action to help them choose the most appropriate action to take. Have groups write reports supporting their final choices. Have each group present its final choice to the class.

STUDY/RESEARCH SKILLS

Using Maps Remind students that Soviet missiles could carry bombs a distance of 1,100 miles (1,770 km). Supply small groups with political maps of North America that include Cuba. Have groups use the map scale and their rulers to determine which cities were potential targets for the missiles in Cuba.

A National Tragedy

President Kennedy became more and more well liked. He knew, however, that he would have to work hard to be reelected. On November 22, 1963, the President and Jacqueline, his wife, visited Dallas, Texas, to meet with supporters there. They were waving to the crowds as their car drove through the streets. Suddenly shots rang out. President Kennedy had been assassinated.

A couple of hours later, Vice President Lyndon Johnson took the oath of office and became the thirty-sixth President of the United States. Kennedy's sudden death shocked the world. Thousands of people lined the streets of Washington, D.C., as his coffin was taken for burial to Arlington National Cemetery.

REVIEW Who became President after John F. Kennedy's death? Lyndon B. Johnson

The Space Race

Starting in 1958, the United States began to launch satellites into orbit. Many of these satellites contained devices that did scientific experiments in space. The United States was behind the Soviet Union in the space race, but NASA scientists were catching up fast.

In 1961 President Kennedy had set a goal for the United States. Kennedy wanted scientists to put a person on the moon by the end of the 1960s. Many people thought this would not be possible. However, the scientists in the space program immediately began working toward President Kennedy's goal.

In April 1961 the Soviet Union became the first nation to launch a spacecraft with a person on board. The spacecraft's

• GEOGRAPHY •

John F. Kennedy Space Center

Understanding Places and Regions

Most of our nation's spacecraft are sent into space from the launch pads located at the Kennedy Space Center. People come to watch as space shuttles and rockets are launched into orbit around Earth. A special part of the center, named Spaceport U.S.A., has exhibits and activities that teach people about the space program.

The *Freedom 7* was launched into space with Alan Shepard, Jr., on board. The flight lasted 15 minutes.

name was the *Vostok*, and its pilot's name was Yury Gagarin. Gagarin orbited Earth one time before returning to Earth's surface. His flight became international news. Many Americans began to worry that the Soviet Union would control space. However, the United States was preparing a manned mission of its own.

Chapter 11 ■ **431**

A National Tragedy

Read and Respond

History Tell students that, as Kennedy's body lay in state in the Capitol rotunda, an estimated 250,000 mourners filed by. An eternal flame marks Kennedy's grave site.

The Space Race

Read and Respond

History Discuss with students the start of the space race. Remind them that the space race was really a technology race. Better technology in the Cold War also meant better weapons. That is, a nation that could put a probe on the moon also could fire a missile accurately to the other side of the world.

Q What did the first United States satellites do?

A They carried instruments that performed scientific experiments in space.

History The satellites the United States put into orbit were much smaller than Soviet satellites. For example, the early Vanguard satellite weighed just 3 pounds 4 ounces (1.5 kg) and was only 6.4 inches (16 cm) in diameter.

• GEOGRAPHY •

John F. Kennedy Space Center

Understanding Places and Regions Inform students that on November 28, 1963, President Lyndon B. Johnson announced in a televised address that Cape Canaveral would be renamed Cape Kennedy in memory of President John F. Kennedy, who had been assassinated six days earlier. The name was later changed back to Cape Canaveral.

Direct students' attention to the illustrations on pages 432–433. Point out the different steps involved in landing people on the moon. Then have students answer the question in the caption.

CAPTION ANSWER: He piloted the orbiter around the moon while Armstrong and Aldrin walked on the moon's surface.

3 Close

Summarize Key Content

- President Kennedy put in place a program that became known as the New Frontier.
- The Cuban Missile Crisis led the United States and the Soviet Union to the brink of war.
- President Kennedy was assassinated on November 22, 1963.
- The Soviet Union and the United States began a race to put a person on the moon.

READING SOCIAL STUDIES

K-W-L Chart Encourage students to review the lesson as they complete the last column of the K-W-L chart.

What I Know	What I Want to Know	What I Learned
In the 1950s many people in the United States were afraid of communism.	What happened in the 1960s?	In the 1960s the Cold War led to a missile crisis and a space race.

● USE READING AND VOCABULARY TRANSPARENCY 6-4.

6-4 TRANSPARENCY

These astronauts were trained to fly spacecraft that would orbit Earth.

In May 1961 United States astronaut Alan Shepard, Jr., climbed aboard the *Freedom 7* spacecraft. The *Freedom 7* was not designed to orbit Earth. Instead, it rocketed more than 115 miles (185 km) into the sky and then curved back down. A parachute helped the *Freedom 7* land safely in the ocean. This flight marked the first time the United States had managed to put a person into space.

One year later John Glenn, Jr., became the first United States astronaut to orbit Earth. Glenn orbited the Earth three times in the *Friendship 7* spacecraft.

In 1965 NASA launched the *Gemini 4* spacecraft. While the *Gemini 4* was orbiting Earth, Edward H. White became the first United States astronaut to venture outside of a spacecraft. A 26-foot (8-m) cord connected White to the spacecraft during his spacewalk. White moved in space by using a handheld device filled with gas. The United States had caught up to the Soviet Union in the space race.

President Kennedy had been one of the strongest supporters of the space program. After his death, NASA continued working to land a person on the moon.

432 ■ Unit 6

A series of explorations called the Apollo program prepared for a moon landing. In 1968 astronauts in *Apollo 8* first circled the moon. By the next year, NASA was ready to attempt a landing.

On July 16, 1969, *Apollo 11* blasted off from Cape Canaveral, Florida. On board were astronauts Neil Armstrong, Edwin "Buzz" Aldrin, Jr., and Michael Collins. Four days later, on July 20, Armstrong and Aldrin became the first two people to walk on the moon.

The astronauts used television cameras to record their moonwalk. People all around the world watched with amazement as the historic event was broadcast on television. Eight years after Kennedy had challenged scientists to put a person on the moon, his goal had been met.

REVIEW What was the Apollo program? the space program that prepared to land a person on the moon

INTEGRATE LANGUAGE ARTS

Write an Advertisement Tell students to imagine that it is the early 1960s. Now that the United States has entered the space race, it is necessary to find people to train as astronauts. Have small groups of students discuss what traits would be important for that career. Then ask each group to write an advertisement to recruit people to train as astronauts. Ask groups to read their ads to the class.

BACKGROUND

Huntsville, Alabama The space race had a direct effect on the growth of many American cities. In 1950 Huntsville, Alabama, was a small cotton market town. That year a team of rocket scientists arrived to work on the rocket that launched America's first satellite. Soon Huntsville became a central spot for the development of rocket technologies. Today the city has more than 180,000 residents and is home to the United States Space Camp.

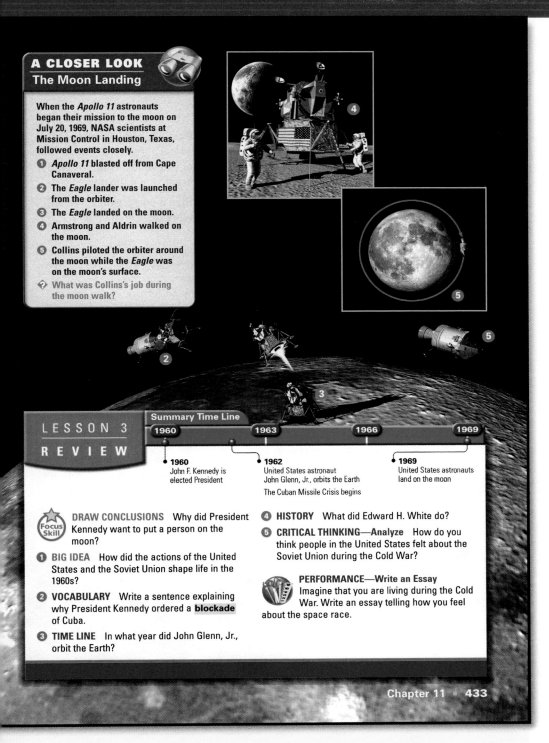

LESSON 3 REVIEW

Summary Time Line

1960	1963	1966	1969

• **1960** John F. Kennedy is elected President

• **1962** United States astronaut John Glenn, Jr., orbits the Earth
The Cuban Missile Crisis begins

• **1969** United States astronauts land on the moon

DRAW CONCLUSIONS Why did President Kennedy want to put a person on the moon?

① **BIG IDEA** How did the actions of the United States and the Soviet Union shape life in the 1960s?

② **VOCABULARY** Write a sentence explaining why President Kennedy ordered a **blockade** of Cuba.

③ **TIME LINE** In what year did John Glenn, Jr., orbit the Earth?

④ **HISTORY** What did Edward H. White do?

⑤ **CRITICAL THINKING—Analyze** How do you think people in the United States felt about the Soviet Union during the Cold War?

PERFORMANCE—Write an Essay Imagine that you are living during the Cold War. Write an essay telling how you feel about the space race.

Chapter 11 ▪ 433

Assess

Lesson 3 Review—Answers

DRAW CONCLUSIONS Possible answer: because he wanted the United States to compete with and work to stay ahead of the Soviet Union

① **BIG IDEA** The constant threat of nuclear war made people afraid, but the space race gave people hope.

② **VOCABULARY** President Kennedy dealt with the Cuban Missile Crisis by having the Navy form a **blockade** around Cuba.

③ **TIME LINE** 1962

④ **HISTORY** Edward H. White was the first United States astronaut to venture outside of a spacecraft.

⑤ **CRITICAL THINKING—Analyze** Students may indicate that people feared or felt hatred toward the Soviet Union.

Performance Assessment Guidelines Students' essays should clearly reflect their opinions regarding the space race.

ACTIVITY BOOK

Use ACTIVITY BOOK, p. 108, to reinforce and extend student learning.

EXTEND AND ENRICH

Diplomacy Organize students into two groups. Have one group represent the Soviet Union and the other the United States. Have the groups role-play representatives at a meeting between the two countries during the Cuban Missile Crisis. Have groups first meet separately to plan what they will ask for and what they are willing to give up. Then bring the groups together for a diplomatic discussion.

RETEACH THE LESSON

Write a Biography Remind students that this lesson identifies several people who affected the course of history in the 1960s. Have each student choose for individual study one of the people mentioned in this lesson. Have each student research the person chosen and write a one-page biography about him or her. When students have finished, staple all the reports together to make a booklet titled "Important People of the 1960s."

OBJECTIVES

- Identify compromise as the key to resolving conflicts.
- Recognize steps to take to resolve conflicts.

1 Motivate

Why It Matters

Tell students that just as many days have pleasant moments, many days also have conflicts to resolve. Because of this, students will be able to practice this skill daily.

2 Teach

What You Need to Know

Have a volunteer read aloud the steps listed in "What You Need to Know." Have students identify the step that introduces the idea of compromise. Step 3

Practice the Skill—Answers

The Soviet Union agreed to withdraw its missiles from Cuba, and the United States agreed to remove its missiles that were near the Soviet Union.

3 Close

Apply What You Learned

Students should explain how each step brings them closer to a resolution.

ACTIVITY BOOK

Use ACTIVITY BOOK, p. 109, to give students additional practice using this skill.

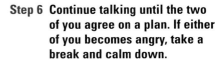

· SKILLS · Resolve Conflicts

CITIZENSHIP SKILLS

➡ **WHY IT MATTERS**

There are many ways to handle a disagreement. You can walk away and let the strong feelings fade over time. You can talk about the disagreement and explain your thoughts about it. You also can compromise. Knowing how to compromise gives you another way to resolve, or settle, conflicts.

➡ **WHAT YOU NEED TO KNOW**

To resolve a conflict through compromise, you can follow these steps:

Step 1 Tell the other person clearly what you want.

Step 2 Decide which of the things you want are most important to you.

Step 3 Present a plan for a possible compromise and listen to the other person's plan.

Step 4 Talk about differences in the two plans.

Step 5 Present another plan, this time giving up one of the things that is important to you.

Step 6 Continue talking until the two of you agree on a plan. If either of you becomes angry, take a break and calm down.

Step 7 Plan a compromise that will work for a long time.

➡ **PRACTICE THE SKILL**

Lesson 3 explained the events that took place during the Cuban Missile Crisis. The Soviet Union was threatening the United States by putting missiles in Cuba. The United States answered by blockading the island. How did the United States and the Soviet Union resolve this conflict?

➡ **APPLY WHAT YOU LEARNED**

With your classmates, think of an issue on which not all the students agree. Form groups to talk about the issue, using the steps outlined on this page. Have each group share with the class how any conflicts were resolved.

Government officials met during the Cuban Missile Crisis to try to find a way to get the Soviets to take their missiles out of Cuba.

434 ■ Unit 6

EXTEND AND ENRICH

Keep a Conflict Journal Tell students that for one day they are to write down any conflicts that they face and record how they resolved those conflicts. When the day is finished, have students determine whether they followed the seven steps on this page to resolve the conflicts they faced.

TRANSPARENCY

Use SKILL TRANSPARENCY 6-3.

RETEACH THE SKILL

Identify Conflicts and Their Resolutions Organize students into small groups. Have group members skim through their textbooks, looking for a time in history when conflict arose. When students have identified a conflict, have them research to determine how it was resolved.

Working for Equal Rights

1951 — **1976** — **2001**

1960–1980

The Civil Rights movement that began in the 1950s continued in the decades that followed. As the movement grew and got national attention, other groups joined African Americans in the fight for equal rights. Among these groups were Hispanic Americans, Native Americans, and women. During the 1960s and 1970s, Americans saw the nation change greatly.

Civil Rights Demonstrations

After the Montgomery bus boycott, the actions of Martin Luther King, Jr., and his followers got thousands of people in the United States to protest segregation laws. These civil rights demonstrations were reported in newspapers and on radio and television. A **demonstration** is a public show of group feelings about a cause. As more Americans learned about the demonstrations, they began to center their attention on the problems that caused them.

These people attended a march in Washington, D.C., to show their support for a bill that was in Congress.

435

· LESSON ·

4

DRAW CONCLUSIONS

As you read, draw conclusions about the movement for equal rights.

BIG IDEA
Individuals and groups in the United States worked to gain equal rights.

VOCABULARY
demonstration
migrant worker

Lesson 4
PAGES 435–441

OBJECTIVES

- Identify the achievements of individuals and leaders in the fight for equal rights.
- Describe and evaluate the actions of various groups who worked to gain equal rights.

Draw Conclusions
pp. 409, 435, 438, 441, 444

Vocabulary
SEE READING AND VOCABULARY TRANSPARENCY 6-5 OR THE WORD CARDS ON PP. V49–V50.

demonstration
p. 435

migrant worker
p. 439

When Minutes Count

Read aloud the Big Idea statement at the beginning of the lesson. Then ask students to examine the photographs and captions in the lesson and identify how each one relates to the Big Idea.

Quick Summary

This lesson looks at the struggle for equal rights that took place in the 1960s.

1 Motivate

Set the Purpose

Big Idea Make sure that students understand the meaning of the term *equal rights*.

Access Prior Knowledge

Have students discuss what they have learned about the struggle for equal rights in this country.

BACKGROUND

Martin Luther King, Jr. Martin Luther King, Jr., first came to national attention when he was asked to serve as leader of the bus boycott that followed Rosa Parks's arrest. At that time, he was serving as pastor of the Dexter Avenue Baptist Church in Montgomery, Alabama. King was an ordained minister with a Ph.D. in theology. King's philosophy of nonviolence was part of his religious beliefs.

STUDY/RESEARCH SKILLS

Summarizing Information Tell students that summaries help people make sure that they have understood the main idea of what they were reading. As students read the lesson, give them time at the end of each section to write summaries of that section. Tell students to keep their summaries to use when they are studying for the chapter test.

2 Teach

Civil Rights Demonstrations

Read and Respond

Civics and Government Have students identify rights people in the United States enjoy today. Ask them what the loss of those rights would mean to their lives. Ask why civil rights marches took place in the early 1960s. African Americans were trying to get equal rights in the United States.

• HERITAGE •

Dr. Martin Luther King, Jr., Day

Inform students that before Dr. King's birthday was made a national holiday, several states had declared it a state holiday. The first state to do so was Illinois, in 1973. The bill declaring the day a national holiday was passed and signed into law by President Reagan on November 2, 1983.

Analyze Primary Sources

Quotation Ask a volunteer to read the excerpt of King's speech. Inform students that this speech has become one of the most famous public addresses of the twentieth century. Have students hypothesize why King used the metaphor of people sitting at a table together. Sitting at a table together symbolizes friendship and equality.

In 1960 black and white college students formed the Student Nonviolent Coordinating Committee. These students challenged segregation laws at places such as restaurants, churches, and movie theaters. They also set an example by riding together on buses all over the South. The students and those who joined them were known as freedom riders. However, not everyone agreed with the students' actions. Sometimes the students were threatened by angry mobs.

• HERITAGE •

Dr. Martin Luther King, Jr., Day

Dr. Martin Luther King, Jr., was born on January 15, 1929, in Atlanta, Georgia. With the Montgomery bus boycott, he became a leader in the Civil Rights movement. He worked tirelessly for racial justice, in spite of many arrests and many threats against his life. On April 4, 1968, King was assassinated. Just four days later, members of Congress began working to make his birthday a federal holiday. However, it was not until 1983 that such a law was signed. The third Monday in January became Dr. Martin Luther King, Jr., Day. The holiday was first celebrated on January 20, 1986. Today people celebrate the day with parades and other events. The special activities remind Americans of the continuing fight for equality, justice, and peace.

He organized the Montgomery bus boycott, led marches in Birmingham, Alabama, and Washington, D.C., and spoke for racial equality.

In April 1963 Martin Luther King, Jr., led a series of marches in Birmingham, Alabama. Much of the city was segregated, and the marchers wanted to put a stop to it. For eight days there were marches. Many of the marchers were arrested. King was one of those taken to jail. While he was in jail, he wrote, "We know through painful experience that freedom is never voluntarily given. . . . It must be demanded."

Later that year, close to 250,000 people gathered for a march in Washington, D.C. The marchers were there to show they were for a civil rights bill that Congress was debating. Standing in front of the Lincoln Memorial, Martin Luther King, Jr., gave one of the most unforgettable speeches in United States history. He spoke about his dream for the nation's future. He said,

> ❝ I have a dream that one day on the red hills of Georgia the sons of former slaves and former slaveowners will be able to sit down together at the table of brotherhood. . . . ❞

King's words brought hope to millions of people. The year after the march in Washington, he was awarded the Nobel Peace Prize for his work.

REVIEW How did Martin Luther King, Jr., work for civil rights?

Working for Change

Shortly after he became President, Lyndon Johnson asked Congress to pass the civil rights bill that President Kennedy had introduced. Congress agreed. In 1964 both Democrats and Republicans voted to pass what became

---

People in Selma, Alabama, marched in support of voting rights for African Americans.

Working for Change

Read and Respond

Linking History with Civics and Government Tell students that the Civil Rights Act of 1964 had several major provisions. As the textbook points out, it made discrimination in employment or in public accommodations illegal. In addition, it gave the government the power to help integrate public schools, and it helped protect minority voting rights.

Q Under which President was the Civil Rights Act of 1964 passed?

A President Lyndon B. Johnson

Analyze Primary Sources

Quotation Have a volunteer read aloud President Johnson's quotation regarding the march in Selma. Inform students that, in the speech, the President compared Selma to Lexington, Concord, and Appomattox. Have students look up those three cities to find out their significance. Point out that President Johnson considered the fight against discrimination to be a kind of war.

known as the Civil Rights Act of 1964. This law made segregation in public places against the law. It also said that people of all races should have equal job opportunities.

Even after the Civil Rights Act was passed, not all Americans were treated the same. In many places African Americans were kept from voting or were threatened if they tried to vote. Once again, Martin Luther King, Jr., led a march to try to bring about change. The march took place in Selma, Alabama. Those who were against it used violence to break up the march. The events in Selma were broadcast on television and troubled many Americans.

In response to the events in Selma, President Johnson appeared before Congress to ask for a

voting rights law. He wanted to make sure that every United States citizen had the chance to vote. Afterward, in a speech broadcast on television, President Johnson said, "There is no issue of states' rights or national rights. There is only the struggle for human rights." Working together, Congress and President Johnson passed the Voting Rights Act of 1965. By 1968 more than half of all African Americans who were old enough to vote were registered voters.

REVIEW **What did the Civil Rights Act of 1964 do?** This law made segregation in public places illegal.

Many civil rights workers helped African Americans register to vote.

437

Other Ideas, Other Leaders

Read and Respond

History Remind students that not all African Americans agreed with King's nonviolent approach to the Civil Rights movement. Help them identify Malcolm X as an African American who advocated immediate change, using force if necessary.

Q How did Malcolm X's views change as he grew older?

A His views softened and he talked more about cooperation among groups.

Civics and Government Explain to students that the voter base changed with the registration of African American voters. It was only a matter of time until more African Americans were elected to office. Shirley Chisholm was elected to the Ninety-first Congress and to six succeeding Congresses.

Q Why would newly registered African Americans make a difference to elections?

A People generally elect candidates they relate to or who seem to have an understanding of the voters' issues.

 Students might enjoy learning more about the Civil Rights movement in the United States. Have them visit The Learning Site at **www.harcourtschool.com**.

After traveling to Mecca, Malcolm X encouraged groups to cooperate with one another.

Other Ideas, Other Leaders

Some African American leaders disagreed with Martin Luther King, Jr.'s, belief in nonviolent protest. Malcolm X was one of them. He was a member of the Nation of Islam, or Black Muslims. He wanted change to happen faster.

Malcolm X was born Malcolm Little, but he changed his last name to X to stand for the unknown African name his family had lost through slavery. In his early speeches, Malcolm X called for strict separation between white people and African Americans. Only in this way, he said, could African Americans truly be free. Later, after a trip to the Islamic holy city of Mecca in 1964, he talked less about separation and more about cooperation among groups. Malcolm X had little time to act on his new ideas. He was assassinated in 1965. Three years later, in April 1968, Martin Luther King, Jr., was also assassinated. Even though African Americans had lost two important leaders, other leaders continued to work for equal rights.

In 1966 Robert Weaver became the first African American to serve in the President's Cabinet when he became secretary of housing and urban development. In 1967 Thurgood Marshall became the first African American justice to sit on the Supreme Court of the United States. Two years later Shirley Chisholm became the first African American woman elected to Congress. These leaders worked for change from inside the government rather than from outside.

REVIEW How did Malcolm X's ideas change over time? **DRAW CONCLUSIONS**
At first he called for separation of the races but later urged cooperation instead of separation.

Robert Weaver was the first African American Cabinet member.

438 ■ Unit 6

 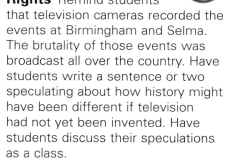

Civil Rights for Other Groups

Following the lead of the African American Civil Rights movement, other groups in the United States began to organize for change. They, too, wanted equal rights under the law.

To help improve the lives of farm workers, Cesar Chavez, Dolores Huerta (HWAIR•tah), and others organized a group that would become the United Farm Workers. Most of its members were Mexican American migrant workers. A migrant worker is someone who moves from place to place with the seasons, harvesting crops.

Like Martin Luther King, Jr., Cesar Chavez called for nonviolent action to solve problems. In 1965 he organized a strike by California grape pickers and started a nationwide boycott of grapes. Chavez's goal was to get better wages and improve working conditions for migrant workers. Many of the nation's people showed their support for the movement by not buying grapes. In 1970 Chavez reached an agreement with California's grape growers and helped the migrant workers get greater rights.

American Indians also formed groups to work for the rights that they had been promised in earlier treaties with the United States government. In many cases those treaties had not been honored. Then, in 1975, Congress passed the Self-Determination and Educational Assistance Act. For the first time, Indian tribes could run their own businesses and health and education programs.

REVIEW What did Cesar Chavez accomplish?
He got better wages and better working conditions for migrant workers.

Cesar Chavez worked to improve conditions for migrant workers.

The Women's Rights Movement

Although the Civil Rights Act of 1964 said that all people should have equal job opportunities, many jobs were still not open to women. When men and women did have the same kinds of jobs, women were often paid less than men. To help women achieve equal rights, Betty Friedan and others started the National Organization for Women, or NOW, in 1966.

NOW and other women's rights groups helped elect many women to public office. These groups felt that having women in the government would make it easier to change unfair laws.

By the 1970s new laws had been passed saying that employers must treat men and women equally. No job could be open to men only or to women only.

Chapter 11 ■ 439

Civil Rights for Other Groups

Read and Respond

Culture and Society Explain that Cesar Chavez did much to improve migrants' working conditions.

Q How was Cesar Chavez's situation similar to that of Rosa Parks?

A Both were important figures in boycotts that led to civil rights improvements.

History Have students orally describe the methods used by Mexican Americans in their efforts to gain equal rights.

Q How did the methods used by Mexican American migrant workers compare with those used by Martin Luther King, Jr.?

A They were also nonviolent methods.

The Women's Rights Movement

Read and Respond

Civics and Government Explain to students that people with common interests sometimes form groups so that they might become more politically effective. These groups then lobby, or work to influence, politicians so that they will vote for laws that favor the group. NOW is one such group. Challenge students to think of other such groups.

INTEGRATE READING

Read a Biography Point out to students that this lesson includes the names of people who affected the direction the United States took in the 1960s. Have each student choose for study one of the people mentioned in this lesson or a person they find in their research. Have students read biographies about that person. Ask each student to draw pictures of three important events in that person's life. Then have students present and describe their drawings to the class.

Read and Respond

Culture and Society Discuss with students the purpose of the Equal Rights Amendment. Ask students whether they think it would still be worthwhile to have an Equal Rights Amendment added to the Constitution.

Q **Why did the Equal Rights Amendment not become part of the Constitution?**

A The required number of states had not ratified the amendment by the deadline.

Visual Learning

Graph Direct students' attention to the graph on page 440. Ask students to draw conclusions about the number of women in the workforce over the past fifty years. It has increased dramatically.
CAPTION ANSWER: about 67 million women

3 Close

Summarize Key Content

- Under the leadership of Martin Luther King, Jr., African Americans used nonviolent methods to achieve equal rights.
- President Johnson asked for the passage of a voting rights law that would ensure every American the opportunity to vote.
- Malcolm X initially opposed using nonviolent forms of protest to end racial discrimination.
- Groups such as Mexican Americans, Native Americans, and migrant workers also worked for equal rights during the 1960s.
- Women worked with groups such as NOW to increase their civil rights.

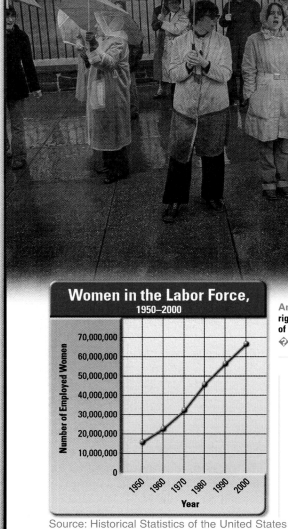

Women in the Labor Force, 1950–2000

Source: Historical Statistics of the United States

Analyze Graphs In the 1970s women worked for equal rights (above) and equal pay. During this time the number of women in the labor force continued to increase.

◈ About how many women were employed in 2000?

As a result, many women began careers in fields such as law, medicine, and business. Some became astronauts, construction workers, and firefighters.
    Many women also called for a new amendment to the Constitution. The amendment that was introduced in Congress became known as the Equal Rights Amendment. The purpose of this amendment was to make sure that

440 ■ Unit 6

MAKE IT RELEVANT

In Your Community Since the Civil Rights movements of the 1960s and 1970s, women have found more employment for higher pay in a wider variety of jobs. Ask students to find out how women are employed in their community. Have students find out how many women are in local government. Ask students to present their findings to the class.

women would always have equal rights under the law.

The Equal Rights Amendment was passed by Congress. However, it did not become part of the Constitution. For an amendment to be added to the Constitution, it must be ratified by three-fourths of the states. Since the Equal Rights Amendment was not ratified by the required number of states, it was never adopted.

Although the Equal Rights Amendment failed to pass, a number of education laws were passed in 1972. These laws helped guarantee women equal treatment in colleges. As a result, the number of women in law schools and medical schools went up.

In addition, women's sports programs also were helped by these new laws. For the first time, colleges and universities had to fund and support women's sports just as they did men's sports.

Today American women have the same rights and responsibilities as American men. In 1981 Sandra Day O'Connor became the first woman appointed to the United States Supreme Court. In the 1990s Madeleine Albright became the first woman secretary of state, and Janet Reno became the first woman attorney general. Women also serve their country in the armed forces.

REVIEW What did NOW do to help women gain equal rights? NOW helped elect many women to public offices.

Justice Sandra Day O'Connor

LESSON 4 REVIEW

Summary Time Line

1960	1970	1980
• 1964 The Civil Rights Act is signed into law	• 1965 Cesar Chavez organizes migrant workers • 1972 Congress passes education reforms	

DRAW CONCLUSIONS Why do you think marches were a good way for groups to show support for civil rights?

❶ **BIG IDEA** How did individuals and groups try to get equal rights?

❷ **VOCABULARY** Write a sentence explaining how Cesar Chavez helped improve the lives of **migrant workers**.

❸ **TIME LINE** When was the Civil Rights Act signed into law?

❹ **CULTURE** What group was helped by the Self-Determination and Educational Assistance Act?

❺ **CRITICAL THINKING—Analyze** Why is it important for everyone to be treated equally?

PERFORMANCE—Create a Time Line Create a year-by-year time line of the 1960s. On the time line, include all the dates in this lesson that marked important events in Americans' struggle for equal rights. Compare your completed time line with the time line of a classmate.

Chapter 11 ▪ 441

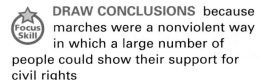
READING SOCIAL STUDIES

Personal Response Have students review their paragraphs on how the struggle for equal rights might affect them. Encourage them to revise their responses on the basis of what they learned in the lesson.

● USE READING AND VOCABULARY TRANSPARENCY 6-5. **6-5 TRANSPARENCY**

Assess

Lesson 4 Review—Answers

DRAW CONCLUSIONS because marches were a nonviolent way in which a large number of people could show their support for civil rights

❶ **BIG IDEA** Individuals and groups used nonviolent protests, such as boycotts and marches, as well as the legal system to get equal rights.

❷ **VOCABULARY** Possible response: Cesar Chavez's use of the boycott eventually won better contracts for Mexican American **migrant workers**.

❸ **TIME LINE** in 1964

❹ **CULTURE** Native Americans

❺ **CRITICAL THINKING—Analyze** Possible answer: because all persons should be given equal opportunities to develop their talents and contribute to society

Performance Assessment Guidelines Students' time lines should mention all the dates identified in this lesson as important to Americans' struggle for equal rights.

ACTIVITY BOOK

Use ACTIVITY BOOK, p. 110, to reinforce and extend student learning.

EXTEND AND ENRICH

Write a Biographical Sketch Assign each student a leader or achiever who worked for equal rights. Examples include Martin Luther King, Jr., President Lyndon Johnson, Malcolm X, Cesar Chavez, Betty Friedan, Thurgood Marshall, and Shirley Chisholm. Ask students to use library resources to write and illustrate a biographical sketch about the person, focusing on his or her contribution to the struggle for equal rights.

RETEACH THE LESSON

Graphic Organizer Ask students to create a web diagram that identifies a group of people who worked for equal rights, details the methods they used, and describes the gains they made.

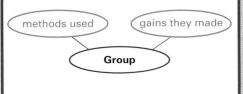

CHAPTER 11 ▪ 441

OBJECTIVES

- **Discuss specific examples of responsible citizenship.**
- **Understand the importance of voluntary individual participation in the democratic process.**
- **Evaluate the difference one responsible citizen can make.**

1 Motivate

Why It Matters

Point out that students act as responsible citizens in many ways every day. For example, if they have voted for class officers or if they have recycled their soft-drink cans, they have acted as responsible citizens. Discuss with students other ways in which they may act responsibly every day.

·SKILLS·
CITIZENSHIP

Act as a Responsible Citizen

▶ WHY IT MATTERS

Democratic nations depend on their citizens to act responsibly. For a democracy to work, its citizens must learn about important issues, choose wise leaders, and take part in government. In addition, when a nation faces a problem, its citizens must take responsible action to solve it.

▶ WHAT YOU NEED TO KNOW

You have read about the fight for civil rights in the United States during the 1950s and 1960s. Many citizens took part in the Civil Rights movement. The peaceful protests of Dr. Martin Luther King, Jr., and others caught the attention of people around the world.

Acting as a responsible citizen is not always as difficult as it was during the fight for civil rights. It can be as simple as voting or sitting on a jury. It does, however, require both thought and action.

Some of the steps that citizens working for civil rights followed to

Dr. Martin Luther King, Jr., led people in the civil rights march in Washington, D.C.

442

MAKE IT RELEVANT

In Your Community Have students work together to plan an event that demonstrates responsible citizenship. Examples might include cleaning up the sidewalks of a city street, picking up litter alongside a rural road, repainting the school stadium's bleachers, and so on. Students can make posters that advertise the event and encourage other students to participate.

READING SOCIAL STUDIES

Summarize Have students select a compromise they learned about in this chapter. Ask them to write a summary, identifying the steps listed on page 443 that may have been followed to reach a peaceful solution. Ask volunteers to share their summaries with the class.

Cesar Chavez (center) was still working for the rights of farm workers when he died in 1993.

act as responsible citizens are listed below. They followed these steps to bring about change.

Step 1 **They learned about problems of injustice that affected people in the nation.**

Step 2 **They thought about what could be done to bring about change.**

Step 3 **They decided how to bring about change in a way that would be good for the whole country.**

Step 4 **Each person decided what contribution he or she could best make.**

Step 5 **People worked as individuals or with others to bring about change.**

➡ **PRACTICE THE SKILL**

Those citizens and the others who took part in the Civil Rights movement risked their lives to fight injustice. Some even died in the fight for civil rights.

In Lesson 4, you read about people who acted responsibly as they worked for civil rights. Choose two of them, and explain how they showed they were responsible citizens.

➡ **APPLY WHAT YOU LEARNED**

Some acts of citizenship, such as voting, can be done only by adults. Others can be done by citizens of almost any age. Use the five steps on this page as you decide on ways you and your classmates might act as responsible citizens of your community.

Chapter 11 ■ **443**

CITIZENSHIP SKILLS

 Teach

What You Need to Know

Ask students to imagine that they are Martin Luther King, Jr. Have them follow the steps listed in "What You Need to Know" as they consider actions they need to take to achieve equal rights.

Practice the Skill—Answers

Make sure the students' choices are people who were mentioned in Lesson 4. Students should demonstrate knowledge of the problem, think about the solutions, and explain how the people they chose were responsible citizens.

 Close

Apply What You Learned

Students should use the five steps to think about how they might act as responsible citizens in their community. For example, as a first step they should identify a problem in their community. Discuss the remaining steps with students, writing their suggestions on the board.

ACTIVITY BOOK

Use ACTIVITY BOOK, p. 111, to give students additional practice using this skill.

TRANSPARENCY

Use SKILL TRANSPARENCY 6-4.

EXTEND AND ENRICH

Perform a Public Service
List on the board students' suggestions from the Apply What You Learned activity. Organize students into groups and have them select activities to pursue. Lead them as they make and enact plans for performing their selected public services.

RETEACH THE SKILL

Identify Present-Day Responsible Citizens Organize students into small groups, and supply them with recent news magazines and newspapers. Tell the groups to use these resources to identify two citizens who are acting responsibly. Ask the groups to write down the names and the deeds that make the people fit in the category of Responsible Citizen. Lead a class discussion about the groups' findings.

DRAW CONCLUSIONS

Students may use the graphic organizer that appears on page 112 of the Activity Book. Answers appear in the Activity Book, Teacher's Edition.

Think & Write

Write a Story Students' stories should reflect the changes in their family life brought about by television.

Write a Descriptive Paragraph Provide students with pictures of the moon's surface to aid them in writing their paragraphs. Students' paragraphs should be imaginative and well-written.

ACTIVITY BOOK

A copy of this graphic organizer appears in the ACTIVITY BOOK on page 112.

TRANSPARENCY

The graphic organizer appears on READING AND VOCABULARY TRANSPARENCY 6-6.

11 Review and Test Preparation

Summary Time Line
1950

• **1950** The Korean War begins
• **1953** The Korean War ends
• **1954** *Brown v. Board of Education*

 Draw Conclusions

Copy the following graphic organizer onto a separate sheet of paper. Use the information you have learned to help you draw conclusions about the 1950s.

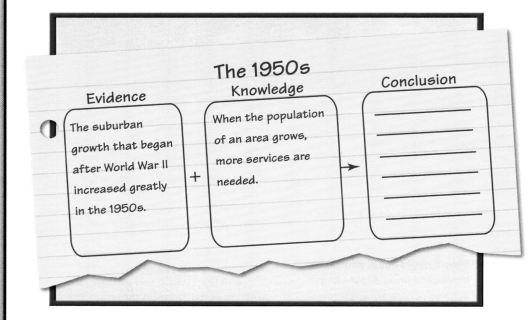

The 1950s

Evidence
The suburban growth that began after World War II increased greatly in the 1950s.

+

Knowledge
When the population of an area grows, more services are needed.

Conclusion
_____

THINK & WRITE

Write a Story Imagine you are living in the early 1950s. Your family has just bought its first black-and-white television set. Write a story about how the television set has affected your family life. Share your story with a classmate.

Write a Descriptive Paragraph Imagine you are either Neil Armstrong or Buzz Aldrin. Write a descriptive paragraph about your first step onto the moon's surface. Describe what you see, what you hear, and how you feel.

444 ■ Unit 6

TEST PREPARATION

Review these tips with students:

■ Read the directions before reading the questions

■ Read each question twice, focusing the second time on all the possible answers.

■ Take the time to think about all the possible answers before deciding on an answer.

■ Move past questions that give you trouble, and answer the ones you know. Then return to the difficult items.

UNIT PROJECT

Progress Check Ask students to select about 10 significant people, places, or events from the unit to include in their magazine. Encourage students to use the Internet or other references to research pictures that could be used in the magazine.

1960   1970   1980

1962 The Cuban missile crisis   **1964** The Civil Rights Act is passed   **1965** Cesar Chavez begins a nationwide grape boycott   **1966** The National Organization for Women is formed   **1969** *Apollo 11* astronauts land on the moon   **1972** Congress passes education reforms

USE THE TIME LINE

Use the chapter summary time line to answer these questions.

1 When was the Civil Rights Act passed?

2 When did the moon landing happen?

USE VOCABULARY

Use each term in a complete sentence that will help explain its meaning.

3 **desegregate** (p. 411)

4 **satellite** (p. 423)

5 **migrant worker** (p. 439)

RECALL FACTS

Answer these questions.

6 What kind of government ruled North Korea in 1950?

7 Who was the commander of all UN forces in Korea?

8 What was the Civil Rights Act of 1964?

Write the letter of the best choice.

9 Shortly after his election, President Harry S. Truman presented a plan to Congress that became known as—
 A the New Deal.
 B the Big Deal.
 C the Fair Deal.
 D the Truman Deal.

10 Which of the following was the name of the United States space program to land astronauts on the moon?
 F Apollo
 G Discovery
 H Explorer
 J Atlantis

THINK CRITICALLY

11 Why do you think most people felt that Harry S. Truman could not win the 1948 presidential election?

12 How did the Civil Rights movement inspire change in people around the United States?

APPLY SKILLS

Identify Changing Borders
Use the maps on page 417 to answer the question.

13 Where was the border between North Korea and South Korea set in 1945?

Compare Graphs
Use the information and graphs on pages 424 and 425 to answer these questions.

14 How are bar graphs different from circle graphs? How are they the same?

Resolve Conflicts
Use the information on page 434 to answer the question.

15 How can compromise solve conflicts?

Act as a Responsible Citizen

16 Identify a person who you think is a responsible citizen. Write a paragraph explaining why you think that person is acting responsibly.

Chapter 11 ■ **445**

Think Critically

11 Students' answers may reflect the idea that because Truman had finished out Roosevelt's term, many people believed that he could not win an election on his own.

12 Possible response: It enabled people to see the need for change; inspired other groups, such as migrant workers, to work toward equal rights; and made jobs available to groups such as women, who previously had not worked in certain fields.

Apply Skills

Identify Changing Borders

13 38°N, the thirty-eighth parallel

Compare Graphs

14 Bar graphs are shaped differently from circle graphs. Unlike bar graphs, circle graphs divide information into parts. Both graphs are used to compare information.

Resolve Conflicts

15 The people involved in the conflict agree to give up some things they want in exchange for other things they want more.

Act as a Responsible Citizen

16 Responses should identify an action the person has taken and should explain why that action showed responsibility.

ACTIVITY BOOK

Use the CHAPTER 11 TEST PREPARATION on page 113 of the Activity Book.

ASSESSMENT

Use the CHAPTER 11 TEST on pages 91–94 of the Assessment Program.

Use the Time Line

1 1964

2 1969

Use Vocabulary

3 Possible response: President Truman wanted to **desegregate** the armed forces so white and African American soldiers would serve in the same units.

4 Possible response: The **satellite** *Sputnik* orbited Earth.

5 Possible response: The apricots were picked by **migrant workers**.

Recall Facts

6 a communist government (p. 412)

7 General Douglas MacArthur (p. 413)

8 A law that outlawed segregation in public places and stated that people of all races should have equal job opportunities. (p. 437)

9 C (p. 411)

10 F (p. 432)

Chapter 12 Planning Guide Into Modern Times

Introducing the Chapter, pp. 446–447

LESSON	PACING	OBJECTIVES	VOCABULARY
Introduce the Chapter pp. 446–447	1 Day	■ Interpret information in visuals. ■ Apply critical-thinking skills to organize and use information. ■ Interpret excerpts from notable speeches.	**Word Work:** Preview Vocabulary, p. 447
1 The Vietnam War Years pp. 448–454	2 Days	■ Identify the role of the United States military during the Vietnam War. ■ Analyze the events surrounding the decrease in the number of United States troops in Vietnam. ■ Discuss the significance of President Nixon's visits to China and the Soviet Union. ■ Describe the events that led to President Nixon's resignation.	**inflation** **hawk** **dove** **arms control** **détente** **cease-fire** **scandal** **Word Work:** Preview Vocabulary, p. 448
2 The Cold War Ends pp. 455–461	1 Day	■ Identify the foreign, political, and economic crises that the United States faced in the latter part of the twentieth century. ■ Discuss President Reagan's economic policies and their effect on people in the United States. ■ Recognize the role of individuals in bringing an end to the Cold War.	**hostage** **deficit**

READING	INTEGRATE LEARNING	REACH ALL LEARNERS	RESOURCES

Make Inferences, p. 447

Reading Social Studies:
K-W-L Chart, p. 449

Make Inferences, p. 451

Reading Social Studies:
Reread to Clarify, p. 452

Reading Social Studies:
K-W-L Chart Responses, p. 454

Languages
Vietnamese, p. 449

Language Arts
Stage a Debate, p. 450

Write a News Story, p. 453

Advanced Learners, p. 450
Advanced Learners, p. 452
Extend and Enrich, p. 454
Reteach the Lesson, p. 454

Activity Book, pp. 114–115
Reading and Vocabulary Transparency 6-7

Reading Social Studies:
Graphic Organizer, p. 456

Reading Social Studies:
Graphic Organizer Responses, p. 461

Science
Research Energy Sources, p. 456

Art
Design a Poster, p. 457

Reading
Read a Biography, p. 458

Languages
Russian, p. 460

Tactile Learners, p. 456
Below-Level Learners, p. 459
Extend and Enrich, p. 461
Reteach the Lesson, p. 461

Activity Book, p. 116
Reading and Vocabulary Transparency 6-8
Internet Resources

Chapter 12 Planning Guide Into Modern Times

LESSON	PACING	OBJECTIVES	VOCABULARY
3 New Challenges pp. 462–467	**1 Day**	■ Identify challenges that the United States faces today as the world's only superpower. ■ Describe the circumstances of the Gulf War and the role that the United States played in defending democracy. ■ Describe the breakup of Yugoslavia and the factors behind its civil war. ■ Identify the role the United States played in ending conflicts in Yugoslavia.	**recession** **candidate**
4 The End of the Twentieth Century pp. 468–473	**1 Day**	■ Identify the role of the President in changing economic conditions. ■ Describe how life in the United States had changed at the end of the twentieth century. ■ Discuss the circumstances of the 2000 presidential election. ■ Identify and discuss challenges faced today by the United States and its citizens.	**veto** **impeach** **terrorism** **hijack**
MAP AND GLOBE SKILLS **Read a Population Map** pp. 474–475	**1 Day**	■ Identify and determine population density. ■ Organize and interpret information from a map.	**population density**
Chapter Review and Test Preparation pp. 476–477	**1 Day**		

READING	INTEGRATE LEARNING	REACH ALL LEARNERS	RESOURCES
Reading Social Studies: **Anticipation Guide,** p. 463 *(Focus Skill)* **Make Inferences,** p. 465 **Reading Social Studies:** **Anticipation Guide** **Responses,** p. 467	**Language Arts** **Persuasive Writing,** p. 463 **News Interview,** p. 464 **Informative Writing,** pp. 466, 468 **Mathematics** **Make a Circle Graph,** p. 466	**Advanced Learners,** p. 464 **Kinesthetic Learners,** p. 465 **Extend and Enrich,** p. 467 **Reteach the Lesson,** p. 467	**Activity Book,** p. 117 🌐 **Reading and Vocabulary** **Transparency 6-9**
Reading Social Studies: **Personal Response,** p. 469 **Reading Social Studies:** **Personal Response,** p. 473	**Art** **Design a Memorial,** p. 472	**Advanced Learners,** p. 469 **Extend and Enrich,** p. 473 **Reteach the Lesson,** p. 473	**Activity Book,** pp. 118–119 🌐 **Reading and Vocabulary** **Transparency 6-10** 💻 Internet Resources
		Extend and Enrich, p. 475 **Reteach the Skill,** p. 475	**Activity Book,** pp. 120–121 🌐 **Skill Transparency 6-5** 💿 **GeoSkills CD-ROM**
		Test Preparation, p. 476	**Activity Book,** pp. 122–123 🌐 **Reading and Vocabulary** **Transparency 6-11** ✔ **Assessment Program,** **Chapter 12 Test,** pp. 95–98

Activity Book

Name _____ Date _____

The Vietnam War Years

Directions Use the words in the box to complete the time lines below. Then use the time lines to answer the questions on page 115.

Watergate	Nixon	Great Society	Neil Armstrong	Air Quality
Gulf of Tonkin	China	Cambodia	the Soviet Union	South Vietnam

Domestic events:

- 1975
- 1974 — Gerald R. Ford becomes President
  - Nixon resigns
- 1973 — Richard M. Nixon reelected
- 1972 — Watergate break-in
- 1971
- 1970
- 1969 — Neil Armstrong walks on the moon
- 1968 — Richard M. Nixon elected President
- 1967 — Air Quality Act
- 1966
- 1965 — Lyndon Johnson's Great Society government programs expands
- 1964 — Civil Rights Act

Foreign events:

- 1975 — South Vietnam surrenders
- 1974
- 1973 — Cease-fire takes place in Vietnam
- 1972 — Nixon first visits China and then the Soviet Union
- 1971
- 1970 — Nixon orders invasion of Cambodia
- 1969
- 1968 — More than 500,000 United States soldiers in Vietnam
- 1967
- 1966
- 1965
- 1964 — United States Navy ship attacked in the Gulf of Tonkin

(continued)

114 ■ Activity Book   Use after reading Chapter 12, Lesson 1, pages 448–454.

Name _____ Date _____

Directions Use the time lines on page 114 to answer the questions below.

1. Which event came first, the attack on the United States Navy in the Gulf of Tonkin or the Air Quality Act? the attack on the United States Navy in the Gulf of Tonkin

2. What was the name of Lyndon Johnson's expansion of government programs? Great Society

3. How many United States soldiers were in Vietnam in 1968? more than 500,000

4. What domestic event could also be considered an international scientific breakthrough? Neil Armstrong's walk on the moon

5. How did President Nixon expand the Vietnam War in 1970? He ordered the invasion of Cambodia.

6. What 1972 event led to President Nixon's resignation? the Watergate break-in

7. When did Richard Nixon resign? 1974

8. What communist countries did President Nixon visit in 1972? China and the Soviet Union

Use after reading Chapter 12, Lesson 1, pages 448–454.   Activity Book ■ 115

Name _____ Date _____

The Cold War Ends

Directions Read each sentence below. If the statement is a Fact, write *F* on the line before it. If the statement is an Opinion, write *O* on the line.

_O_ 1. The Watergate scandal proves that politicians can't be trusted.

_F_ 2. By 1975 unemployment rates were the highest they had been since World War II ended.

_O_ 3. President Ford was wrong to grant former President Nixon a pardon.

_O_ 4. The United States should use less oil in order to depend less on the Middle East.

_F_ 5. President Carter refused to allow athletes from the United States to participate in the 1980 Olympic Games in Moscow.

_F_ 6. The Iran hostage crisis was part of the reason President Carter lost the 1980 election.

_O_ 7. The Cold War was a struggle between right and wrong.

_F_ 8. President Reagan and Soviet leader Mikhail Gorbachev agreed to limit arms production.

116 ■ Activity Book   Use after reading Chapter 12, Lesson 2, pages 455–461.

Name _____ Date _____

New Challenges

Directions Fill in the outline below to give the main ideas and supporting details of the lesson. Some of the points have been done for you. Answers may vary but should contain key elements from the lesson. Examples are provided.

I. Domestic Challenges
   - A. Businesses fail
   - B. A recession causes unemployement
   - C. Taxes go up

II. A New World Order
   - A. The United States tries to protect freedom all over the world
   - B. Civil war is fought in Bosnia
   - C. Civil war is fought in Kosovo
   - D. The United States and NATO stopped the wars

III. The Gulf War
   - A. Iraqi forces invade Kuwait
   - B. allied forces fight Iraq
   - C. United States conducts air strikes and ground war
   - D. The Gulf War ends

Use after reading Chapter 12, Lesson 3, pages 462–467.   Activity Book ■ 117

Name _____ Date _____

The End of the Twentieth Century

Directions Write at least three sentences to describe events at the end of the twentieth century. Use the vocabulary words in the box below to explain what you learned in the chapter.

veto
impeach
terrorism
hijack

Sentences will vary but should correctly use the vocabulary words. Possible responses are provided.

1 Congress passed bills that President Clinton wanted to veto. _____
_____

2 In 1999 President Clinton became only the second United States President to be impeached. _____
_____

3 The United States experienced acts of terrorism at home and abroad. _____
_____

4 The worst act of terrorism in the history of the United States occurred when terrorists hijacked four American commercial airplanes. _____
_____

(continued)

Name _____ Date _____

Directions Using the terms in the box, write a paragraph describing the events that occurred in the 2000 election.

vote
Supreme Court
Florida
candidate
recount
county

Paragraphs will vary but should accurately describe the events using the terms. The following is an example paragraph: Since the 2000 election was the closest presidential election in 40 years, it showed how important each person's vote is. Texas Governor George W. Bush was the Republican party's candidate. Vice President Al Gore was the Democrat party's candidate. When the votes were counted, the results were very close. The winner would be decided by votes in Florida. For five weeks, many counties in Florida began recounting votes to make sure the totals were correct. On December 12, 2000 the United States Supreme Court ruled that the counting must stop. The officials that recounted the votes found that George W. Bush had won by about 600 votes.
_____
_____
_____

Name _____ Date _____

MAP AND GLOBE SKILLS

Read a Population Map

Directions Use the map below to answer the questions on page 121.

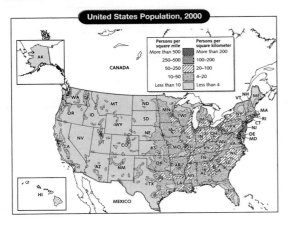

United States Population, 2000

(continued)

Name _____ Date _____

Directions Use the map on page 120 to answer the questions below.

1 What is the lowest population density shown on the map?
The lowest density is less than 10 persons per square mile.

2 What is the highest population density shown on the map?
more than 500 persons per square mile

3 Which state in the West has areas of more than 500 persons per square mile?
California

4 What is the highest population density found in North Carolina?
50–250 persons per square mile

5 Which region of the United States has the greatest population density?
the Northeast

6 Which state has the greater population density—Nevada or Georgia?
Georgia

7 Which state in the Northeast has the fewest people per square mile?
Maine

8 What do you notice about most of the states in the West?
Almost all are in the lowest category of population density.

Name _____ Date _____

Into Modern Times

Directions Complete this graphic organizer by using information you have learned from the chapter to make inferences about the end of the Soviet Union and communist rule in Europe.

The End of the Soviet Union and Communist Rule in Europe

WHAT YOU HAVE READ

As leader of the Soviet Union, Mikhail Gorbachev introduces reforms that give the Soviet people more freedom.

WHAT YOU KNOW

The Soviet Union had been _____ under communist rule. _____

INFERENCE

For the first time in their lives, many Soviet citizens were experiencing freedoms unheard of under Soviet rule. _____

WHAT YOU HAVE READ

In 1991, Soviet President Gorbachev outlaws the communist party.

WHAT YOU KNOW

Since the end of World War II, the communist government had control over much of Europe.

INFERENCE

With communism gone, each of the 15 Soviet republics will declare its independence. _____

Use after reading Chapter 12, pages 446–475.

© Harcourt

Name _____ Date _____

12 Test Preparation

Directions Read each question and choose the best answer. Then fill in the circle for the answer you have chosen. Be sure to fill in the circle completely.

❶ Which of the following was **not** a part of President Johnson's Great Society?
Ⓐ the largest expansion of government since the New Deal
Ⓑ attempting to make life better for all Americans
Ⓒ fighting communism
Ⓓ the passage of 435 bills through Congress

❷ Which United States President signed an agreement with the Soviet Union to limit nuclear arms?
Ⓕ Ronald Reagan
Ⓖ Jimmy Carter
Ⓗ Lyndon B. Johnson
Ⓙ Gerald Ford

❸ Why did United States troops and NATO troops go to Bosnia?
Ⓐ to force that nation to lower its prices
Ⓑ to encourage free trade
Ⓒ to keep grain prices down
Ⓓ to try to end a civil war

❹ Which two recent Presidents faced possible impeachment charges?
Ⓕ Bill Clinton and Jimmy Carter
Ⓖ Richard Nixon and George W. Bush
Ⓗ Richard Nixon and Bill Clinton
Ⓙ Gerald Ford and George Bush

❺ The destruction of the World Trade Center towers is an example of—
Ⓐ embargo.
Ⓑ terrorism.
Ⓒ veto.
Ⓓ coalition.

© Harcourt

Use after reading Chapter 12, pages 446–475..

COMMUNITY RESOURCES

Experts on the Cold War

_____
_____
_____
_____
_____

Museums

_____
_____
_____
_____
_____

Experts on the Vietnam War

_____
_____
_____
_____
_____

National Parks

_____
_____
_____
_____
_____

Chapter 12 Assessment

STANDARD TEST

Name _____ Date _____

12 Test

Part One: Test Your Understanding

MULTIPLE CHOICE (4 points each)

Directions Circle the letter of the best answer.

1 President Johnson's Great Society included government programs to—
A give tax relief.
B help people retire early.
C prepare Americans for war.
(D) make life better for all Americans.

2 According to the domino theory,—
F if one country became democratic, surrounding countries would as well.
G Asian countries were more likely to become communist than other countries were.
H when the domestic programs of a nation work well, its international programs will also.
(J) if one Asian country fell to communism, others would follow.

3 People in the United States who were against the Vietnam War became known as—
A domestics.
(B) doves.
C hawks.
D all of the above

4 Which of the following was **not** a domestic problem following Nixon's presidency?
F a high unemployment rate
(G) fuel shortages
H President Ford's pardon of Richard Nixon
J high inflation

5 When the Soviets invaded Afghanistan, President Carter—
A launched a secret mission to rescue hostages.
B increased the national defense budget.
(C) reduced trade and boycotted the 1980 Olympic Games in Moscow.
D began arms control talks with Gorbachev.

6 The first meeting between Reagan and Gorbachev resulted in—
(F) improved relations and treaties limiting nuclear missiles.
G a program to limit the number of weapons in other countries.
H the United States' taking responsibility for increased freedoms for Soviet people.
J actions by both governments to increase the number of weapons.

(continued)

STANDARD TEST

Name _____ Date _____

7 The collapse of the Soviet Union eventually resulted in—
A the destruction of the Berlin Wall.
B the end of the Cold War.
C new freedoms and independence for other communist nations.
(D) both B and C

8 The Gulf War—
F helped bring Middle Eastern oil resources under United States control.
G ended Saddam Hussein's leadership.
(H) resulted from Iraq's invasion of Kuwait.
J lasted seven years.

9 Under President Clinton—
(A) the United States economy became stronger and stronger.
B Congress was unable to pass any budget reforms.
C government spending increased and higher taxes followed.
D universal health care was provided for all Americans.

10 Which of the following was **not** an issue in the 1990s?
F defending Kuwait from Iraq
G helping the people of Bosnia
H improving the United States economy
(J) freeing the American hostages in Iran

COMPLETION (4 points each)

Directions Fill in each blank with a word or phrase that correctly completes the sentence.

11 During Nixon's presidency there was an easing of tensions, known as _____détente_____, between the United States and the Soviet Union.

12 The Watergate _____scandal_____ eventually resulted in the end of Nixon's presidency.

13 _____George Bush_____ was President when the Berlin Wall came down and the Soviet Union collapsed, ending the Cold War.

14 _____Kosovo_____ fought a civil war after it declared independence from Yugoslavia.

15 _____The Supreme Court_____ ruled that the recounting of Florida's votes in the 2000 election must stop.

(continued)

STANDARD TEST

Name _____ Date _____

Part Two: Test Your Skills

READ A POPULATION MAP (5 points each)

Directions Use the map below to answer the questions.

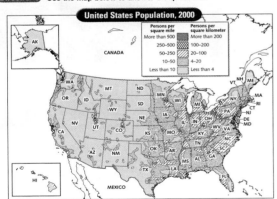

United States Population, 2000

Persons per square mile	Persons per square kilometer
More than 500	More than 200
250–500	100–200
50–250	20–100
10–50	4–20
Less than 10	Less than 4

16 What does this map show?
United States population in persons per square mile or square kilometer in 2000

17 Using persons per square mile, which population ranges are found in Florida?
less than 10 persons per square mile, 10–50 persons per square mile, 50–250 persons per square mile

18 Which population range, in kilometers, is equal to 250–500 persons per square mile?
100–200 persons per square kilometer

19 Is the population greater in the eastern or western United States?
East

(continued)

STANDARD TEST

Name _____ Date _____

Part Three: Apply What You Have Learned

20 **DRAW CONCLUSIONS** (10 points)

For each set of statements, draw a conclusion as to what historical event or situation is being discussed. Name the event or situation on the line provided.

a. President Johnson sent planes and soldiers to halt communist forces in Asia. Some people in the United States disapproved of the conflict from the beginning. As the conflict continued through the Nixon presidency, more and more people disapproved. In the year Nixon resigned, the fighting was resolved.
the Vietnam War

b. President George Bush continued talks with Soviet leader Gorbachev, who worked toward *glasnost* and *perestroika* in his country. The Berlin Wall was destroyed, reuniting East and West Germany. In 1991 the Soviet Union collapsed.
the end of the Cold War

21 **ESSAY** (10 points)

The United States economy has been through several ups and downs since Nixon's presidency. Discuss these periods, their causes and effects, and how the Presidents involved contributed to creating or resolving them.

Students should note that Nixon left a struggling economy for Ford, as the nation tried to pay for the Vietnam War. Unemployment increased and inflation was high. Fuel shortages during the Carter administration made things worse. Reagan's economic policies and increased defense spending resulted in tripling the nation's deficit, leaving George Bush in an economic recession. Bush's administration passed laws to help failing industries but still had to raise taxes to try to reduce the deficit. During Bill Clinton's presidency, businesses created millions of new jobs and unemployment was reduced to its lowest level in decades. Clinton's presidency saw one of the greatest periods of economic growth in the nation's history.

Introduce the Chapter

OBJECTIVES

- Interpret information in visuals.
- Apply critical-thinking skills to organize and use information.
- Interpret excerpts from notable speeches.

Access Prior Knowledge

Encourage students to discuss what they know about the Berlin Wall. Where was it? Why was it built? Why was it taken down?

Visual Learning

Picture Ask students to examine the picture and the Locate It map. Discuss with students what they think the chapter will be about, on the basis of the picture.

Locate It Map The Ronald Reagan Presidential Library is located in Simi Valley, California, which is just northwest of Los Angeles. It was dedicated on November 4, 1991. The library also has a museum chronicling the life and presidency of Ronald Reagan.

LOCATE IT

CALIFORNIA

Simi Valley

RONALD REAGAN PRESIDENTIAL LIBRARY

The Ronald Reagan Presidential Library is one of ten presidential libraries. In this photograph taken from inside the library, a piece of the Berlin Wall is displayed. The original wall was 96 miles (154 km) long and divided Germany for almost 30 years. Helping bring down the wall was one of President Reagan's greatest accomplishments.

446 ▪ Unit 6

Picture In addition to housing nearly 50 million pages of documentation and more than 1 million photographs, the library includes exhibits about Ronald Reagan's early childhood years, his career in movies, and his campaign for the presidency. More than 2,000 gifts that the former President received from other heads of state are also on display, as is a deactivated land-based cruise missile. This missile was one of only a few of its kind remaining after President Reagan and Mikhail Gorbachev signed the 1987 INF Treaty, which eliminated an entire class of nuclear weapons.

Quotation President Reagan visited the city of Berlin twice during his presidency. In his speech there in 1987, he called on the Soviet Union to tear down the Berlin Wall and bring freedom to the people of Eastern Europe. President Reagan also pledged the support of the United States and its allies in helping Eastern European nations establish democratic governments.

12

Into Modern Times

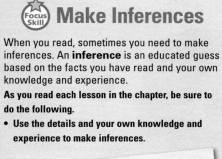

" Mr. Gorbachev, tear down this wall. "

—Ronald Reagan, in a speech at the Berlin Wall, June 12, 1987

⭐ Focus Skill Make Inferences

When you read, sometimes you need to make inferences. An **inference** is an educated guess based on the facts you have read and your own knowledge and experience.

As you read each lesson in the chapter, be sure to do the following.

• **Use the details and your own knowledge and experience to make inferences.**

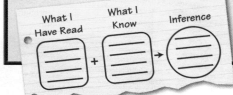

Chapter 12 ■ 447

Read and Respond

Direct students' attention to the title of the chapter. Ask them to speculate about the meaning of the title.

Quotation Have a volunteer read the quotation aloud.

 Why was Gorbachev the person Ronald Reagan asked to tear down the Berlin Wall?

A In 1987 Gorbachev was the leader of the Soviet Union. The Soviet Union controlled the government of East Germany, which had put up the wall and had the authority to tear it down.

Reagan delivered this speech at the Brandenburg Gate in West Berlin. Although the speech was given to the people of West Berlin, it could be heard clearly in part of East Berlin.

⭐ Focus Skill Make Inferences

As students read the chapter, have them complete a graphic organizer to help them make inferences throughout the lesson.

• A blank graphic organizer can be found on page 122 of the Activity Book.

• Remind students to make inferences based on facts and on their own knowledge and experiences.

• A completed graphic organizer can be found on page 122 of the Activity Book, Teacher's Edition.

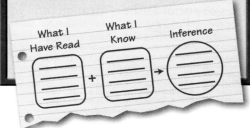

WORD WORK

Preview Vocabulary Have students list the chapter vocabulary terms in the first column of a three-column chart. Then ask students to write in the second column what they think each term means. Students should write in the third column the definitions they find in the chapter.

Vocabulary Chart		
Term	Student Definition	Chapter Definition

MAKE IT RELEVANT

Discussion Topics As you teach this chapter, you and your students might enjoy discussing some of the following topics. Each topic helps relate what students are learning about in this unit to their world today.

■ What are some countries today in which people do not have the same freedoms we have in the United States?

■ What effect do you think the President of the United States can have on leaders of other countries?

■ Do you think the United States should become involved in the problems of other countries?

Lesson 1
PAGES 448–454

 Make Inferences pp. 447, 448, 450, 451, 454, 476

Vocabulary

SEE READING AND VOCABULARY TRANSPARENCY 6-7 OR THE WORD CARDS ON PP. V51–V52.

inflation p. 450	**détente** p. 453
hawk p. 450	**cease-fire** p. 453
dove p. 450	**scandal** p. 453
arms control p. 453	

 When Minutes Count

Have students examine the map of Vietnam on page 449. Use the map as a springboard to discuss the main events in the lesson.

Quick Summary

Explain that the 1960s and 1970s were times of social and political change in the United States.

1 Motivate

Set the Purpose

Big Idea Explain that the Vietnam War and events of the 1970s resulted in great change in the United States.

Access Prior Knowledge

Have students discuss what they know about the Cold War.

---

1 The Vietnam War Years

 MAKE INFERENCES

As you read, make inferences about how the events of the 1970s divided Americans.

BIG IDEA

The Vietnam War and the events of the 1970s changed the United States.

VOCABULARY

inflation
hawk
dove
arms control
détente
cease-fire
scandal

1951 — 1976 — 2001

1963–1975

While many groups were trying to win better treatment and equal rights, President Lyndon Johnson was working on government programs to make life better for all Americans. These programs were part of Johnson's dream—what he called the Great Society. However, Johnson also faced challenges outside the nation as the United States became involved in the Vietnam War. This war and the events of the 1970s divided the American people.

The Vietnam War

Like Korea, Vietnam was divided into two countries after World War II. North Vietnam became a communist country, and South Vietnam became a republic. In the late 1950s South Vietnamese communists, called the Vietcong, tried to take over

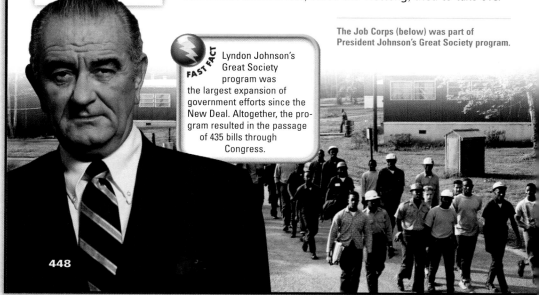

FAST FACT Lyndon Johnson's Great Society program was the largest expansion of government efforts since the New Deal. Altogether, the program resulted in the passage of 435 bills through Congress.

The Job Corps (below) was part of President Johnson's Great Society program.

448

WORD WORK

Preview Vocabulary Have students list and define vocabulary terms as they read the lesson.

Term	Definition
inflation	
hawk	
dove	
arms control	
détente	
cease-fire	
scandal	

BACKGROUND

Johnson's Great Society
President Johnson first mentioned the idea of a Great Society during a speech in 1964. Almost immediately thereafter more than a dozen secret task forces began studying various domestic issues. The result was a series of sweeping legislative actions that included improvements to elementary, secondary, and higher education; a program called Medicare that helped people pay for medical care; and the Voting Rights Act of 1965, which improved minority voter registration.

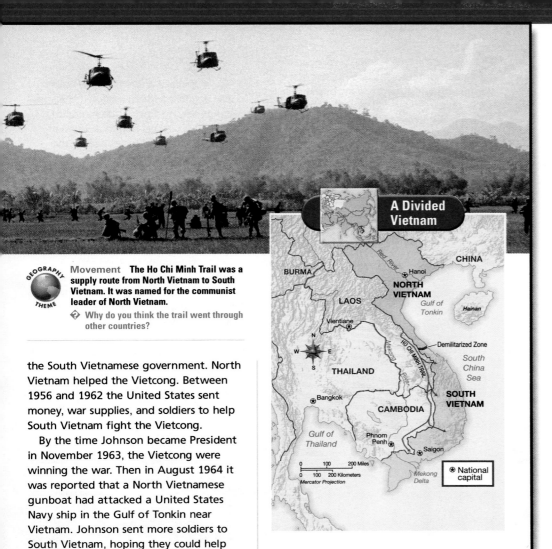

GEOGRAPHY THEME

Movement The Ho Chi Minh Trail was a supply route from North Vietnam to South Vietnam. It was named for the communist leader of North Vietnam.

◆ Why do you think the trail went through other countries?

A Divided Vietnam

⊛ National capital

the South Vietnamese government. North Vietnam helped the Vietcong. Between 1956 and 1962 the United States sent money, war supplies, and soldiers to help South Vietnam fight the Vietcong.

By the time Johnson became President in November 1963, the Vietcong were winning the war. Then in August 1964 it was reported that a North Vietnamese gunboat had attacked a United States Navy ship in the Gulf of Tonkin near Vietnam. Johnson sent more soldiers to South Vietnam, hoping they could help defeat the Vietcong.

When United States and South Vietnamese troops failed to defeat the Vietcong quickly, the United States sent planes to bomb North Vietnam. Johnson thought the bombing would stop the flow of supplies from North Vietnam to the Vietcong. He also sent more troops to South Vietnam. By 1968 more than

500,000 United States soldiers were serving there.

The Vietnam War now was costing the United States billions of dollars each year. At the same time, President Johnson was building many of his Great Society programs. Johnson said that the nation could afford both. It turned out that he was wrong.

Chapter 12 ▪ **449**

2 Teach

The Vietnam War

Read and Respond

Economics Inform students that by 1970 the Vietnam War had become very costly to the United States. Explain that more than 40,000 U.S. soldiers had died in a war that was costing the nation more than $20 billion per year. Point out that as a result of financing both the war effort and the Great Society programs, the U.S. economy suffered.

Visual Learning

Map Direct students' attention to the map on page 449. Explain that the Ho Chi Minh Trail was the primary route the North Vietnamese used to secretly transport supplies to communist troops fighting in South Vietnam. CAPTION ANSWER: Students' responses will vary and may indicate that the reason the Ho Chi Minh Trail ran through other countries was so the North Vietnamese could avoid detection by South Vietnamese and United States troops.

Citizens Are Divided

Read and Respond

History Explain that over time it became clear to the United States government that the Vietnam War had no end in sight. Inform students that increased United States troops deployments resulted in higher casualty numbers. Tell students that nationwide protests against the war affected the government's decision to start withdrawing troops. Tell students that those in the United States government eventually saw the communist takeover of South Vietnam as inevitable. Explain that by 1972 President Nixon had reduced the number of United States troops in Vietnam from 543,000 to 24,000.

Visual Learning

Photograph Explain that during the 1960s and 1970s, many college students protested against the Vietnam War. Inform students that the protests became increasingly violent. In 1970, at an antiwar protest at Kent State University in Ohio, four people were killed and dozens more were injured when members of the Ohio National Guard attempted to contain the protest by firing into the crowd.

Q What effect do you think protests had on the war?

A Students may respond that the protests pressured the U.S. government to end the nation's involvement in the war.

To pay for the Vietnam War and the programs of the Great Society.

To pay for both the Vietnam War and the programs of the Great Society, the government had to borrow a lot of money. This borrowing led to inflation. When there is **inflation**, people need more money to buy the same goods and services. This weakens a country's economy.

REVIEW Why did the government have to borrow money in the 1960s?

MAKE INFERENCES

Citizens Are Divided

The Vietnam War divided American public opinion. Some people felt that the war was needed to stop the spread of communism. Others said that it was a civil war that should be settled by the Vietnamese without outside help.

The nation's leaders were also divided. Most government leaders were either hawks or doves. **Hawks**—named for the fierce bird of prey—were people who supported the war. They thought that if South Vietnam became a communist country, its neighbors—Laos and Cambodia—would soon also become communist. The idea that once one country fell to communism, neighboring countries would follow was called the domino theory. **Doves**, named for the traditional symbol of peace, were those who wanted the war to end. They believed that people were dying needlessly in a war that South Vietnam could not win. Each side believed that it was right and that the other side was wrong.

Some Americans (above, left) wanted the United States to leave Vietnam. Others (below) supported American involvement.

450

During the Vietnam War, United States soldiers joined with South Vietnamese troops to fight communist forces.

The number of Americans killed in Vietnam rose into the thousands. Many others were listed as MIA, or Missing In Action. Some were captured and held as Prisoners Of War, or POWs. At home, groups of Americans marched to protest against these losses. Many young Americans did not want to be drafted for the war. They burned their draft cards in protest. Some even moved to Canada to avoid military service.

By the end of Johnson's term, just one in four Americans thought he was doing a good job in Vietnam. Johnson announced that he would not run for President again. In 1968 the American people elected a new President—Richard Nixon. Nixon promised, "I'm going to end that war. Fast." However, the war did not end. War protests grew, and some became violent. In 1970 four students died during a march at Kent State University in Ohio.

As the war continued, Nixon developed his plan to end the war as quickly as possible. He wanted to prevent more American soldiers from being injured or killed. He also wanted to keep South Vietnam from becoming a communist country.

Nixon's plan was to train the South Vietnamese troops better. Then they could fight the Vietcong and the North Vietnamese on their own. This would allow the United States to bring some American soldiers home. Other soldiers would stay and continue the bombing raids on North Vietnam. As the number of troops that were sent home grew, Nixon announced a new plan. After learning the Vietcong were launching some of their attacks from neighboring Cambodia, Nixon ordered an invasion of Cambodia. Soon troops were sent there to destroy the Vietcong bases.

REVIEW What was the domino theory?
It was the idea that once one country fell to communism its neighbors would follow.

Chapter 12 ■ 451

History Inform students that a turning point in the Vietnam War occurred during the Vietnamese New Year's holiday known as Tet. Explain that on January 31, 1968, North Vietnam launched a major offensive and attacked more than 40 cities and 20 airfields and military bases in South Vietnam. Casualties were high on both sides, but it was a political and psychological victory for the communists. Lead students to understand that the Tet Offensive signaled the beginning of the end of U.S. involvement in the conflict.

Culture and Society Tell students that returning Vietnam War veterans did not always feel they were treated as heroes. Ask students to discuss why some veterans felt this way. Students may respond that many Americans opposed the war and did not consider it a heroic cause.

Civics and Government Explain that most political experts expected President Johnson to seek a second full term in 1968 and that his decision to retire instead surprised many people. Johnson's decision came amid lagging support for his leadership and the entry of a number of Democratic challengers into the race. Richard Nixon, a Republican, won the election after promising to end United States involvement in Vietnam.

Q **What effect did Nixon's plan for ending United States involvement in the Vietnam War have on his election as President?**

A Students' responses may vary, but should reflect that many voters supported Nixon and his plan to end U.S. involvement in the Vietnam War.

READING SKILL

Make Inferences Ask students to reread pages 450 and 451 and infer the effect that protests, mounting casualties, and continued attacks by North Vietnam on South Vietnam had on the United States' decision to end its involvement in the Vietnam War. Students should infer that those issues helped lead the United States to end its involvement in the war.

BACKGROUND

Jeremiah Denton In 1965 Commander Jeremiah Denton was taken prisoner after his plane was shot down in Vietnam. North Vietnamese officials asked Denton to speak out against the United States but he refused, saying that he would support his government as long as he lived. For the next seven years he remained in North Vietnam as a prisoner of war. When Denton was released he was welcomed home as a national hero.

DEMOCRATIC VALUES
Popular Sovereignty

One argument used to justify the lowering of the voting age was the United States government's drafting of 18-year-olds to fight in Vietnam. The rallying cry for many who supported the amendment was "If we're old enough to fight, we're old enough to vote!"

Analyze the Value—Answers

❶ It lowered the voting age to 18.

❷ **Make It Relevant** Students should research and write detailed essays explaining how the passage of the Twenty-sixth Amendment has affected elections.

Improved Relations

Read and Respond

History Explain that President Nixon's talks with China and the Soviet Union represented a shift in Cold War policy. Ask students why Nixon wanted to open relations with these countries. Students may suggest that he did so to reduce the threat of war and to increase trade options.

Nixon Resigns and the War Ends

Read and Respond

Civics and Government Explain that an investigation led by a special prosecutor found that the Watergate incident was one of many scandals involving Nixon's White House. Inform students that for more than a year President Nixon denied knowledge of any wrongdoing. Then in August 1974 he was forced to release a series of audiotapes that proved he had participated in the Watergate cover-up.

DEMOCRATIC VALUES
Popular Sovereignty

During the 1960s many of the nation's high school and college students began a movement to give 18- to 20-year-olds the right to vote. Before this time the minimum voting age was 21. In 1971, West Virginia Senator Jennings Randolph proposed a constitutional amendment to lower the voting age to 18. The amendment was quickly approved by Congress and was ratified by the states in less than four months— faster than any earlier constitutional amendment. The Twenty-sixth Amendment states that the voting rights of citizens 18 years or older "shall not be denied or abridged by the United States or by any state on account of age."

Analyze the Value

❶ What did the Twenty-sixth Amendment do?

❷ **Make It Relevant** Write an essay explaining how you think elections have or have not changed since the passage of the Twenty-sixth Amendment.

After the Twenty-sixth Amendment was ratified, President Nixon signed the new law.

Improved Relations

In 1972, as the war raged on, President Nixon accepted an invitation from China's leader, Mao Zedong (MOW zeh•DUNG), to visit China. The United

452

States had not traded or carried on foreign relations with China since 1949 when China became a communist country. As a result of Nixon's visit, the two nations agreed to trade with each other and to allow visits from each other's scientific and cultural groups.

Three months after visiting China, President Nixon flew to Moscow to meet with Soviet leader Leonid Brezhnev (BREZH•nef). This was the first time a United States President had visited both China and the Soviet Union. As a result of the meeting in Moscow, the United States and the Soviet Union agreed to increase trade and to work together on scientific and cultural projects.

During their 1972 visit to China, President Nixon and his wife, Patricia, visited the Great Wall of China.

REACH ALL LEARNERS

Advanced Learners
Point out to students that the Watergate scandal and the related hearings lasted several months. Have students research these events and design flow charts tracing the Watergate scandal and President Nixon's resulting resignation.

READING SOCIAL STUDIES

Reread to Clarify Ask students to reread the lesson, pausing after each section to list concepts or ideas that they do not fully understand. When students have finished the lesson, have them work with you or a partner to answer any questions they have about the reading.

During the meeting Nixon and Brezhnev also agreed to **arms control**, or limiting the number of weapons that each nation could have. This marked the beginning of a period of **détente** (day•TAHNT), or an easing of tensions, between the United States and the Soviet Union. However, that did not last long.

REVIEW What was détente? an easing of U.S.–Soviet relations under Nixon's presidency

Nixon Resigns and the War Ends

In 1972 Nixon was reelected President. The next year he agreed to a cease-fire in Vietnam. A **cease-fire** is a temporary end to a conflict. He also agreed to bring the remaining American soldiers home. The last ground troops left Vietnam in March 1973.

During the election campaign, some people working to help Nixon, a Republican, had done some things that were against the law. One thing they did was to break into an office of the Democratic party in the Watergate building in Washington, D.C. It was later shown that when Nixon learned about this unlawful act, he tried to cover it up.

OKLAHOMA CITY **TIMES** 10¢
Thursday evening ——— August 9, 1974

NIXON RESIGNING OFFICE

President to go on TV tonight at 8 p.m.

White House aide, House leader reveal decision

Nixon announced his decision to resign in a national television speech.

The Watergate scandal ended Nixon's presidency. A **scandal** is an action that brings disgrace. On August 9, 1974, Nixon became the first United States President to resign, or give up, the presidency. On that same day, Vice President Gerald Ford became President.

Soon after the last American ground troops had left Vietnam, fighting broke out yet again. Without the support of American troops, South Vietnam could not win the war. On April 30, 1975, the government of South Vietnam surrendered.

When United States forces left the city of Saigon in South Vietnam, there was much confusion. Thousands of South Vietnamese people asked to leave on United States helicopters.

453

K–W–L Chart Encourage students to review the lesson as they complete the K–W–L chart.

What I Know	What I Want to Know	What I Learned
The United States military fought in the Vietnam War.	How did the war affect people in the United States?	Some people did not support the war because it cost many soldiers' lives.

● USE READING AND VOCABULARY TRANSPARENCY 6-7.

6-7
TRANSPARENCY

Assess

Lesson 1 Review—Answers

MAKE INFERENCES Some people were surprised, and others were relieved.

❶ **BIG IDEA** The Vietnam War and events of the 1970s resulted in protests against, and a lack of trust in, the federal government.

❷ **VOCABULARY** Possible sentence: A **hawk** was someone who supported the Vietnam War, and a **dove** was someone who opposed it.

❸ **TIME LINE** after

❹ **CRITICAL THINKING—Analyze** Students may indicate that President Nixon thought that by visiting China and the Soviet Union, he could improve U.S. relations with both countries.

Performance Assessment Guidelines Students' reports should reflect information from the lesson as well as various reference sources.

ACTIVITY BOOK

Use ACTIVITY BOOK, pp. 114–115, to reinforce and extend student learning.

Veterans Day

To celebrate the signing of the armistice that ended World War I, Armistice Day was first observed on November 11, 1919. In 1954 President Dwight D. Eisenhower changed the name of Armistice Day to Veterans Day. This day honors all veterans of the United States armed forces.

Today Veterans Day is still observed on November 11. People celebrate with parades and speeches that honor the service that members of the military have given their country. Veterans Day is a time for families and friends of Vietnam veterans to visit the Vietnam Veterans Memorial. Volunteers help visitors find the names of friends and relatives on the memorial's wall.

A Vietnam veteran and his son search for people's names on the Vietnam Veterans Memorial.

The government of North Vietnam gained control of the whole country. The Vietnam War was over.

On Veterans Day in 1982, the Vietnam Veterans Memorial in Washington, D.C., was opened to visitors. The memorial's wall lists the names of more than 58,000 American men and women who lost their lives or were reported missing during the Vietnam War.

REVIEW Who became President after Nixon resigned? Vice President Gerald Ford became President of the United States.

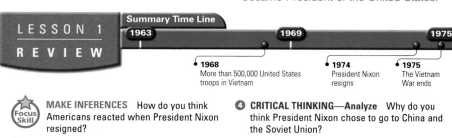

LESSON 1 REVIEW

Summary Time Line
1963   1969   1975

● 1968 More than 500,000 United States troops in Vietnam

● 1974 President Nixon resigns

● 1975 The Vietnam War ends

MAKE INFERENCES How do you think Americans reacted when President Nixon resigned?

❶ **BIG IDEA** How did the Vietnam War and the events of the 1970s change the nation?

❷ **VOCABULARY** Write a sentence explaining the political difference between a **hawk** and a **dove**.

❸ **TIME LINE** Did the Vietnam War end before or after President Nixon resigned?

❹ **CRITICAL THINKING—Analyze** Why do you think President Nixon chose to go to China and the Soviet Union?

PERFORMANCE—Write a Report Use the Internet or library sources to write a report about the Vietnam Veterans Memorial. Share your report with the class.

EXTEND AND ENRICH

Conduct an Interview Have students interview an older family member about how they felt when the United States pulled out of South Vietnam. Encourage volunteers to share what they learned with the rest of the class.

RETEACH THE LESSON

Make a Graphic Organizer Ask students to complete a graphic organizer like the one below, showing the challenges the United States faced in the late 1960s and early 1970s.

Vietnam War   higher inflation

Challenges to the U.S.

Watergate scandal   Nixon's resignation

The Cold War Ends

1951   1976   2001

1975–1991

Although the Watergate scandal ended his time in office, President Nixon accomplished many things. His most important achievement may have been reducing tensions between the free world and communist nations. However, the Cold War did not end until 1991.

A New President

Just a few weeks after taking office, President Ford granted Richard Nixon "a full, free and absolute [total] pardon." This pardon included forgiveness "for all offenses against the United States which he . . . has committed or may have committed or taken part in." Ford said that putting Nixon on trial would have divided the American people even more than they were already.

President Ford also faced a troubled economy during his presidency. The nation was still paying for the Vietnam War. Businesses were making less money, and prices continued to rise.

· LESSON ·

2

MAKE INFERENCES
As you read, make inferences about how the end of the Cold War affected the world.

BIG IDEA
Events brought about the end of the Cold War.

VOCABULARY
hostage
deficit

As Gerald Ford took office as President, the nation's economy faced many problems. Unemployed workers seeking benefits and new jobs formed long lines at employment offices throughout the country.

Chapter 12 ■ 455

QUESTIONS KIDS ASK

Q What is a pardon?

A A pardon is a release from punishment by the government for a person who has done something illegal.

BACKGROUND

Gerald Ford (1913–) Gerald Ford was the first and only President who was not elected as President or as Vice President. After a 25-year career as a U.S. representative from Michigan, Ford was chosen by President Nixon in 1973 to succeed Spiro Agnew as Vice President. Less than a year later, Ford became President after Nixon resigned from office. President Ford served out the remainder of Nixon's second term and lost a bid for election in 1976.

Lesson 2

OBJECTIVES

■ Identify the foreign, political, and economic crises that the United States faced in the latter part of the twentieth century.

■ Discuss President Reagan's economic policies and their effect on people in the United States.

■ Recognize the role of individuals in bringing an end to the Cold War.

 Make Inferences
pp. 447, 455, 456, 461, 476

Vocabulary
SEE READING AND VOCABULARY TRANSPARENCY 6-8 OR THE WORD CARDS ON PP. V51–V52.

hostage p. 457   **deficit** p. 459

 When Minutes Count

Ask students to examine the photographs and captions in this lesson. Then have them write a brief summary that describes the main ideas of the lesson.

Quick Summary

This lesson examines the many political and economic challenges faced by the United States in the years following the Vietnam War.

1 Motivate

Set the Purpose

Big Idea Inform students that a series of events in the 1980s and 1990s led to the end of the Cold War.

Access Prior Knowledge

Ask students to discuss what they have learned about the Cold War. Ask them to predict whether the Cold War would continue or come to an end soon.

Graphic Organizer Ask students to complete the chart by listing the challenges faced by Presidents Ford, Carter, Reagan, and Bush.

President	Challenges
Ford	
Carter	
Reagan	
Bush	

● USE READING AND VOCABULARY TRANSPARENCY 6-8.

6-8 TRANSPARENCY

2 Teach

A New President

Read and Respond

Civics and Government Explain that President Ford's pardoning of Richard Nixon negatively affected Ford's presidency. Tell students that the congressional elections of 1974, held two months after the pardon, gave Democrats control of Congress and made it difficult for President Ford to enact his legislative agenda.

Visual Learning

Graphs Ask students to examine the line graph showing the changes in the rate of inflation.

CAPTION ANSWER: about 10

Tensions Rise

Read and Respond

Economics Inform students that Presidents Ford and Carter faced economic and energy crises during their administrations. Explain that increased inflation and unemployment, combined with rising fuel costs, soon frustrated many Americans.

Source: Historical Statistics of the United States

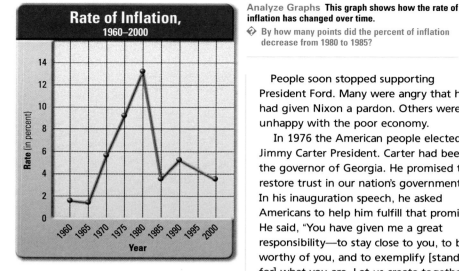

Rate of Inflation, 1960–2000

Analyze Graphs This graph shows how the rate of inflation has changed over time.

◆ By how many points did the percent of inflation decrease from 1980 to 1985?

The number of people who were unemployed grew and inflation was high. Ford tried to lower inflation by slowing down the economy. He also started a program called Whip Inflation Now, or WIN, to help lower inflation. However, the nation still faced economic problems.

President Carter (center) is shown shaking hands with President Sadat of Egypt (left) and Prime Minister Begin of Israel at the signing of their peace agreement.

People soon stopped supporting President Ford. Many were angry that he had given Nixon a pardon. Others were unhappy with the poor economy.

In 1976 the American people elected Jimmy Carter President. Carter had been the governor of Georgia. He promised to restore trust in our nation's government. In his inauguration speech, he asked Americans to help him fulfill that promise. He said, "You have given me a great responsibility—to stay close to you, to be worthy of you, and to exemplify [stand for] what you are. Let us create together a new national spirit of unity and trust."

REVIEW Why did President Ford decide to not put Richard Nixon on trial?

MAKE INFERENCES because he said it would divide the American people even more.

Tensions Rise

Two years after Carter was elected President, he helped bring peace to the countries of the Middle East. Together, Southwest Asia and Northeast Africa are often called the Middle East. For centuries people in this region have been divided by religious, cultural, and political differences. In 1978 Carter brought the prime minister of Israel, Menachem Begin (BAY•guhn), and Egypt's president, Anwar Sadat (suh•DAT), to Camp David in Maryland.

456 ▪ Unit 6

Together they set up a peace agreement for these longtime enemies. The agreement became known as the Camp David Accords.

The following year President Carter faced another challenge in the Middle East. In February 1979 a revolution took place in the nation of Iran. The leaders of the revolution caused the shah, the country's ruler, to flee from Iran. These leaders became angry when the United States supported the shah.

To show their anger, the revolutionaries attacked the United States embassy in Teheran, the capital of Iran. They captured 53 Americans and made them hostages. A **hostage** is a prisoner held until the captors' demands are met. The captors demanded that the United States make the shah return to Iran for punishment. The United States, however, refused.

During the hostage crisis, Americans across the country counted the number of days in captivity for the American hostages held in Iran.

For more than a year, President Carter tried, but failed, to get the hostages freed. At the same time, the nation's economy slowed and unemployment rose. Inflation remained very high, and there were fuel shortages.

The United States did not produce as much oil as Americans needed. In fact, by 1972 almost one-third of the nation's oil needs were met by countries in the Middle East. In 1973 many Middle Eastern leaders were angered when the United States supported Israel in a war against Arab countries. This anger was one reason that Arab leaders decided to join together to control the amount of oil shipped to the United States.

Looking exhausted, the American hostages sit inside the United States embassy during a press conference.

457

Read and Respond

Geography Use a wall map of the world to show students the location of the Middle East, including Egypt and Israel. Inform students that Israel and Egypt had been enemies for many years before agreeing to the Camp David Accords in 1978.

Civics and Government Explain that President Carter spent much of the last year of his term working to free the United States hostages in Iran. Inform students that various tactics failed, and many people blamed Carter for the continued crisis.

Visual Learning

Pictures Direct students' attention to the pictures at the bottom of pages 456 and 457. Ask students to compare and contrast the images. Students may say that in one picture, the president of Egypt and the prime minister of Israel are shaking hands on a peace agreement, and in the other picture, hostages are being held captive in Iran.

Read and Respond

Economics Explain that the Organization of Petroleum Exporting Countries (OPEC) coordinates the oil policies and prices of its member nations. In 1973 OPEC placed an embargo on the United States for its support of Israel in a war between Israel, Egypt, and Syria. By the late 1970s oil prices had reached record highs.

Q What effect did rising oil prices have on life in the United States?

A People were forced to pay more money for less fuel, which led to various sacrifices by consumers and an energy crisis in the United States.

History Explain that the Soviet Union occupied Afghanistan from 1979 to 1988. During that time the Soviet Union installed a communist government and made many changes in Afghanistan. Inform students that these changes, along with the ongoing war between the Soviet Union and the Afghan rebels, led many people to leave Afghanistan. In the 1980s the United States supplied the rebel forces with military and financial aid in their war against the Soviet Union.

Visual Learning

Picture Direct students' attention to the picture of the New York Stock Exchange on page 458. Explain that each day millions of shares of stock and other securities are traded on the floor of the New York Stock Exchange.

Into the 1980s

Read and Respond

Civics and Government Inform students that during the Reagan administration defense spending more than doubled.

Q Why did President Reagan more than double spending on the U.S. military during his administration?

A Students may respond that Reagan wanted the United States to remain a superpower and at the same time help end communism.

Since gasoline is made from oil, Americans now had to wait in long lines to get gasoline for their cars. The price of traveling by car and of heating a home rose as oil prices soared.

To conserve energy, people made many sacrifices during this time. Americans heated their homes less. In some areas, schools met only every other day, and factories closed early. Americans also began buying smaller cars that used less gasoline.

The United States also had to deal with troubles outside the nation. In 1979 Soviet troops invaded the country of Afghanistan (af•GA•nuh•stan) in Southwest Asia. The invasion moved Soviet troops much closer to the region's rich oil fields. President Carter called the invasion a threat to world peace.

Carter demanded that the Soviets leave Afghanistan. When they refused, he cut back American trade with the Soviet Union and stopped supporting arms control. He also kept American athletes from taking part in the 1980 Olympic Games, because they would be held in the Soviet Union's capital city, Moscow.

The fighting in Afghanistan continued for years. The Afghan rebels fought so hard that it was difficult for the Soviets to win control of the country. Finally, in 1988, the Soviet Union began to remove its troops.

REVIEW What were the Camp David Accords?
A peace agreement between Israel and Egypt

Into the 1980s

Many people blamed President Carter for the nation's troubles. He ran for President again in 1980 but lost the election to the former governor of California Ronald Reagan. The day that Reagan

This photo shows a busy day of trading in the New York Stock Exchange. The United States economy began to grow stronger after Ronald Reagan took office.

458

INTEGRATE READING

Read a Biography Ask each student to select a famous figure from this lesson and work with a librarian to locate a book about that person. Famous figures may include people such as Presidents Ford, Carter, Reagan, and Bush, as well as Soviet president Mikhail Gorbachev, Egyptian president Anwar Sadat, or Israeli prime minister Menachem Begin. Have each student write a brief report about his or her chosen figure, including any new information he or she learned.

STUDY/RESEARCH SKILLS

Use Maps Encourage students to consult world maps as they read the lesson. Explain that by using the maps, students may better understand the locations of countries mentioned in the text.

The New York Times

❸ **REAGAN TAKES OATH AS 40TH PRESIDENT; PROMISES AN 'ERA OF NATIONAL RENEWAL'**

MINUTES LATER, 52 U.S. HOSTAGES IN IRAN FLY TO FREEDOM AFTER 444-DAY ORDEAL

became President, the Iranians finally freed the hostages.

When Ronald Reagan ran for President, he had promised to help the economy. He quickly won approval from Congress for large tax cuts. The economy slowly grew stronger, and high inflation ended. At the same time, however, the government's budget **deficit**, or shortage, increased. When there is a deficit, the government spends more money than it takes in each year in taxes and other income. Reagan borrowed some of the money for deficit spending from other countries.

President Reagan soon increased defense spending. He believed that to win the Cold War the nation needed a stronger military. He said that the Cold War was a "struggle between right and wrong, good and evil." Reagan also said the Soviet Union was "the evil empire."

The Soviet Union continued to build more weapons, too, and it helped communist governments all over the world. Then, in 1985, a new leader named Mikhail Gorbachev (mee•KAH•eel gawr•buh•CHAWF) came to power in the Soviet Union. Nothing would be the same again.

REVIEW **What causes a deficit in the government's budget?** The government spends more money than it brings in.

Reduced Tensions

When Gorbachev took over, President Reagan said he would welcome the chance to meet the new Soviet leader in the "cause of world peace." In April 1985 Gorbachev agreed to a meeting. He said that better relations between the United States and the Soviet Union were "extremely necessary—and possible."

Chapter 12 ■ 459

Analyze Primary Sources

A Daily Newspaper Ask students to carefully examine the newspaper pictured on page 459. Have students consider the effect that the timing of the release of the United States hostages had on people's early perceptions of President Reagan. Students may suggest that after the release of the hostages, people in the United States had a very positive perception of President Reagan.

CAPTION ANSWER: Students may respond that the picture caption and news stories provide additional details about the photograph and headlines.

Read and Respond

History Ask students to study President Reagan's quotations about the Soviet Union on page 459. Explain that under President Reagan the United States increased aid and supplies to countries battling communism.

Q How did President Reagan's policy toward the Soviet Union differ from that of previous United States Presidents?

A Students' responses should indicate that unlike Presidents Nixon and Carter, who relaxed relations with communist countries, Reagan believed U.S. opposition to the Soviet Union was a matter of right against wrong.

Reduced Tensions

Read and Respond

History Emphasize that improved relations between the United States and the Soviet Union came as a result of continued meetings between Presidents Reagan and Gorbachev. Discuss with students the importance of open dialogue between nations.

Analyze Primary Sources

Quotation Direct students' attention to President Reagan's quotation on page 460.

Q What did President Reagan mean when he said he and Gorbachev were the only men "who could bring about World War III" and the only men "who might be able to bring peace to the world"?

A He meant that as leaders of the world's main superpowers, they could lead the way in global relations.

Students might be interested in learning more about the end of the Cold War. Have them visit The Learning Site at **www.harcourtschool.com.**

3 Close

Summarize Key Content

- Many people blamed President Ford for a failing economy and were angry that he gave a pardon to Richard Nixon.
- During President Carter's administration tensions increased between the United States and Soviet Union.
- President Reagan increased military spending in an attempt to end the spread of communism.
- In the late 1980s Presidents Reagan and Gorbachev helped usher in a new era of relations between the United States and Soviet Union.

Soviet leader Gorbachev (left) and President Reagan (right) shake hands at their first meeting. They met each year from 1985 through 1988.

Reagan later spoke of the meeting with Gorbachev:

> Here we were, I said, two men from humble beginnings. Now we were probably the only two men in the world who could bring about World War III. At the same time, I said, we were possibly the only two men who might be able to bring peace to the world.

The meeting between the two leaders marked a change in the Cold War. President Reagan called it a "fresh start" in United States–Soviet relations. Soon the United States and the Soviet Union agreed to more treaties limiting nuclear missiles.

In the Soviet Union, Gorbachev was already changing many of the old ways of doing things. He called for *perestroika* (pair•uh•STROY•kuh), or a restructuring of the Soviet government. Under perestroika,

Soviet people could start their own businesses. Gorbachev also called for *glasnost* (GLAZ•nohst), or openness. He wanted the Soviet people to have more freedoms. Soviet citizens could now speak out without fear of being punished.

Reforms in the Soviet Union led to changes in many other communist nations. In Poland, Czechoslovakia, and Hungary, people gained new freedoms. In time these nations became independent. In 1989 the government leaders of East Germany removed the armed guards from the Berlin Wall and opened its gates. As East Germans poured into West Berlin, people from both sides of the wall began to use hammers, bricks, and anything else they could find to start breaking down the wall. The following year Germany was reunited.

A political poster in Moscow, Russia, shows support for perestroika.

460 ▪ Unit 6

BACKGROUND

Mikhail S. Gorbachev (1931–)
During his tenure president Gorbachev presided over key reforms in the Soviet Union. He legalized political parties, allowed people to run private businesses, and implemented a policy of *glasnost* that increased individual freedoms. Some communists opposed Gorbachev's reforms and in 1991 staged a coup, or sudden overthrow, of Gorbachev's government. Although the coup failed, Gorbachev resigned four months later.

INTEGRATE LANGUAGES

Russian Two Russian words were widely used in the English-speaking world at the end of the Cold War: *perestroika* and *glasnost*. *Perestroika* comes from the Russian words *pere-*, meaning "re-," and *-stroika*, meaning "construction." *Glasnost* was first used earlier in the century and comes from the Russian word *glas*, meaning "voice." Ask students how these words' origins relate to the policies they describe.

Tearing down the Berlin Wall became an important part of the celebration of West Germans and East Germans after their border opened.

In 1989 George Bush became the new President of the United States. That year he met with Mikhail Gorbachev.

The leaders talked about the many changes taking place in Europe and the Soviet Union. At the end Gorbachev looked Bush in the eye. "I have heard you say that you want *perestroika* to succeed," he said, "but frankly I didn't know this. Now I know." The Cold War was finally ending. On July 31, 1991, Bush and

Gorbachev signed a new agreement called the Strategic Arms Reduction Treaty. This treaty was aimed at reducing each country's number of short-range nuclear weapons. As 1991 went on, Bush reduced the number of weapons in the United States even more, and he challenged Gorbachev to do the same in the Soviet Union.

REVIEW What new policies did Gorbachev bring to the Soviet Union? glasnost and perestroika

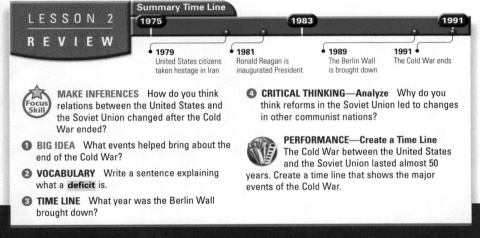

LESSON 2 REVIEW

Summary Time Line

1975	1983	1991

- 1979 United States citizens taken hostage in Iran
- 1981 Ronald Reagan is inaugurated President
- 1989 The Berlin Wall is brought down
- 1991 The Cold War ends

 MAKE INFERENCES How do you think relations between the United States and the Soviet Union changed after the Cold War ended?

1 **BIG IDEA** What events helped bring about the end of the Cold War?

2 **VOCABULARY** Write a sentence explaining what a **deficit** is.

3 **TIME LINE** What year was the Berlin Wall brought down?

4 **CRITICAL THINKING—Analyze** Why do you think reforms in the Soviet Union led to changes in other communist nations?

PERFORMANCE—Create a Time Line The Cold War between the United States and the Soviet Union lasted almost 50 years. Create a time line that shows the major events of the Cold War.

Graphic Organizer Check students' charts against the one below.

President	Challenges
Ford	troubled economy, rising unemployment, lack of support from U.S. citizens
Carter	Iran hostage crisis, fuel shortages, high unemployment
Reagan	improved economy, built up military
Bush	reduced number of nuclear weapons

● USE READING AND VOCABULARY TRANSPARENCY 6-8.

 6-8 TRANSPARENCY

Assess

Lesson 2 Review—Answers

MAKE INFERENCES Relations improved between the United States and Soviet Union.

1 **BIG IDEA** Arms treaties between the United States and Soviet Union and various reforms by the Soviet Union led to the end of the Cold War.

2 **VOCABULARY** A budget **deficit** is a shortage of funds that occurs when the government spends more money than it takes in.

3 **TIME LINE** 1989

4 **CRITICAL THINKING—Analyze** Students may suggest that other nations followed the lead of the Soviet Union's reforms.

 Performance Assessment Guidelines Time lines should accurately depict the main events of the Cold War.

ACTIVITY BOOK

Use ACTIVITY BOOK, p. 116, to reinforce and extend student learning.

EXTEND AND ENRICH

Narrative Writing Have students skim the lesson and take notes on the accomplishments of individual leaders mentioned in this lesson. Then have them write essays about how individuals can change the course of history. Have students use their notes to provide detailed examples.

RETEACH THE LESSON

Research Have students select one of the Presidents mentioned in this lesson and research his accomplishments. Encourage students to use reference sources such as encyclopedias and the Internet in their research. Ask volunteers to report their findings to the class.

Lesson 3

OBJECTIVES

- Identify challenges that the United States faces today as the world's only superpower.
- Describe the circumstances of the Gulf War and the role that the United States played in defending democracy.
- Describe the breakup of Yugoslavia and the factors behind its civil war.
- Identify the role the United States played in ending conflicts in Yugoslavia.

 Make Inferences
pp. 447, 462, 465, 467, 476

Vocabulary

SEE READING AND VOCABULARY TRANSPARENCY 6-9 OR THE WORD CARDS ON PP. V51–V52.

recession p. 463   **candidate** p. 465

 When Minutes Count

Have pairs of students read the lesson. Then ask them to write a summary paragraph for the lesson.

Quick Summary

This lesson describes the economic and social challenges that faced the United States during the late 1980s.

 Motivate

Set the Purpose

Big Idea Point out that today the United States is the world's only superpower. Discuss the responsibilities associated with this role.

Access Prior Knowledge

Ask students to predict ways in which the world might change as a result of improved relations between the United States and the Soviet Union.

· LESSON ·

3

 MAKE INFERENCES
As you read, make inferences about the way the United States worked to ensure stability at home and around the world.

BIG IDEA
The United States faced many new challenges after the Cold War ended.

VOCABULARY
recession
candidate

Vice President George Bush speaks at the Republican National Convention before being elected President.

New Challenges

1951	1976	2001

1989–1995

President George Bush faced many challenges during his presidency. One of the biggest was trying to improve the nation's economy. Also during this time, the United States emerged as the world's only superpower. As such, the United States played an important role in the conflicts that took place in other nations.

Challenges at Home

In his 1989 inauguration speech, President Bush urged Americans to volunteer their time to help one another. He described those that do so as "a thousand points of light . . . spread like stars throughout the nation." To encourage Americans to become more involved in their communities, President Bush helped begin the Points of Light Foundation to promote volunteer work.

462 ▪ Unit 6

BACKGROUND

George Herbert Walker Bush (1924–) George Bush grew up in Connecticut, the son of a United States senator. He was a bomber pilot during World War II and later graduated with honors from Yale University. He worked in the oil industry before beginning a career of public service. Bush served in the U.S. House of Representatives, as director of the Central Intelligence Agency, and as Vice President of the United States. In 1988 he was elected the forty-first President of the United States.

BACKGROUND

Balancing the Budget One way that President Bush tried to balance the budget was to cut military spending. He pushed Congress to authorize a 25 percent cut in the nation's military. Even with the cuts in military spending, however, more tax money was needed. Bush could not stand by a famous statement he made during his campaign: "Read my lips, no new taxes."

President George Bush (seated in the chair on the right) meets with his advisers, including General Colin Powell (far left).

Bush wanted to improve life for all Americans, but he had difficulty improving the nation's economy. In 1990 the United States entered a **recession**, or a period of slow economic activity. This recession lasted for more than two years. During that time millions of Americans lost their jobs.

President Bush tried to boost the nation's economy by passing laws to help failing industries. However, the changing world economy meant that many jobs were moving. Factory jobs once done by workers in the United States were now being done by workers elsewhere. Bush had promised not to raise taxes, but he hoped that by raising some taxes, he would be able to lower the deficit.

Although President Bush was busy with problems at home, he also dealt with world events. Talking about the idea of a world without the Cold War, he said, "Now we can see . . . the very real prospect of a new world order." By "a new world order," Bush meant a world without the conflicts of the past. Despite his hopes, new conflicts soon developed.

REVIEW What is a recession?
It is a time of slow economic activity.

The Gulf War

In August 1990 the nation of Iraq, led by its dictator, Saddam Hussein (hoo•SAYN), invaded and took control of the small country of Kuwait (koo•WAYT). Kuwait, a major producer of oil in the Middle East, borders Iraq and Saudi Arabia. Since Kuwait and Saudi Arabia were both allies of the United States, Bush quickly sent troops to Saudi Arabia to help defend it in case it, too, was attacked.

Chapter 12 ■ 463

2 Teach

Challenges at Home

Read and Respond

Economics Explain that by 1990 the federal debt had grown tremendously. Inform students that President Bush believed that the incomes of most people in the United States would not increase if the nation's economy was built on debt. Consequently, Bush attempted to bring the budget deficit under control. That ultimately resulted in tax revenue increases, which went against his campaign promise to not raise taxes.

The Gulf War

Read and Respond

Economics Explain that when Iraq seized Kuwait, it also assumed control of 10 percent of the world's oil reserves. Point out that Iraq's own 10 percent share of world oil reserves, coupled with a possible takeover of Saudi Arabia and its 25 percent share, meant that Iraq was close to controlling nearly half of the world's oil.

Read and Respond

History Point out that the Allied forces that attacked Iraq included a number of Arab nations, such as Egypt and Syria.

Q Why was it important that the alliance included a broad base of nations?

A The broad alliance showed that many nations were united in their efforts to stop Iraq and free Kuwait.

Civics and Government Explain that General Colin L. Powell was the first African American to become Chairman of the Joint Chiefs of Staff. Inform students that in 2001 Powell achieved another first when he became the first African American secretary of state.

Q What was Colin Powell's contribution to the Gulf War?

A He used his military leadership and experience to help the Allied forces win the Gulf War.

A New Eastern Europe

Read and Respond

History Inform students that the communist governments in Eastern Europe, backed by the Soviet Union, had forced different groups, such as Muslims and Christians, to live together. When the Soviet Union broke up, these groups, which had different ways of life, had little to keep them together. Soon these groups began fighting each other. Explain that the United States and NATO intervened to stop the fighting.

Q Why did the United States and NATO decide to help end the fighting among groups in Eastern Europe?

A Students' responses should indicate that the United States and NATO wanted to end the fighting before it worsened or spread elsewhere.

When Iraq refused to remove its troops from Kuwait, allied forces from 27 countries, including the United States, attacked Iraq. The United States led this attack, called Operation Desert Storm, or the Gulf War. Among President Bush's advisers during Operation Desert Storm was General Colin L. Powell. He was Chairman of the Joint Chiefs of Staff—the leaders of all the branches of the military. General Powell, who had commanded troops in the Vietnam War, had military experience and leadership qualities.

Allied planes bombed the country of Iraq, and Iraqi forces in Kuwait. Then ground troops swept into Kuwait and drove out the Iraqi forces. Within seven months the allied forces had defeated the Iraqis and returned Kuwait's leaders to power. Saddam Hussein, however, stayed in power in Iraq.

General Powell won fame during the Gulf War and became a national hero. In 2001 he became the United States secretary of state.

REVIEW What event caused the Gulf War to begin? Iraq's invasion of Kuwait

A New Eastern Europe

The early 1990s marked the end of communism in Eastern Europe. In 1991 Soviet president Gorbachev outlawed the Communist party. Once communism was gone, there was little to unite the many different peoples in the Soviet Union. Each of its 15 republics declared its

General Colin Powell (left) helped the United States win the Gulf War. During the war, burning oil fields (below) were a common sight.

464

INTEGRATE LANGUAGE ARTS

News Interview
Organize students into small groups, and have them imagine that they are reporters during Operation Desert Storm. Ask each student to plan and conduct an interview with people in the United States to find out how they are showing their support for the soldiers fighting in the Gulf War. Have students take turns playing the parts of reporter and citizen.

REACH ALL LEARNERS

Advanced Learners
Ask students to select a former Soviet republic and research its transition from communism to capitalism. Encourage students to use various references in their research. Have students write brief summaries of the republic on the basis of their findings and present them to the class.

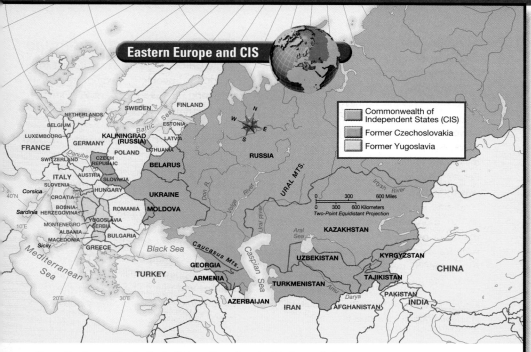

Eastern Europe and CIS

Commonwealth of
Independent States (CIS)
Former Czechoslovakia
Former Yugoslavia

Regions After the Soviet Union collapsed, each of the former Soviet republics declared independence. New countries were also formed in what were once Czechoslovakia and Yugoslavia.

❖ How does the size of Russia compare with the size of the CIS?

independence. Most of the newly independent countries—including the largest, Russia—joined to form a loose confederation called the Commonwealth of Independent States (CIS).

The new countries in the former Soviet Union and Eastern Europe faced terrible problems. Communism had left their economies in ruins. Civil wars had also broken out in some places. Without communist control, old hatreds between people came to the surface.

REVIEW Why did many Eastern European countries face problems after the end of communism? **MAKE INFERENCES**
Communism had left their economies in ruins and civil wars soon broke out.

The 1992 Election

The 1992 presidential election was different from most because it featured three major candidates. A **candidate** is a person chosen by a political party to run for office. In 1992 George Bush was the Republican candidate. Bill Clinton was the Democratic candidate. And H. Ross Perot was the Reform party candidate.

Perot, a Texas businessperson, was popular with voters who wanted a change from the two major parties. Perot's decision to enter the race greatly changed the election. Early on, he appeared to be leading both Bush and Clinton.

Chapter 12 ▪ 465

Visual Learning

Map Direct students' attention to the map on page 465. Ask students to determine which republics joined the Commonwealth of Independent States. Armenia, Azerbaijan, Belarus, Georgia, Kazakhstan, Kyrgyzstan, Moldova, Russia, Tajikistan, Turkmenistan, Ukraine, and Uzbekistan CAPTION ANSWER: The Commonwealth of Independent States is much larger than Russia.

The 1992 Election

Read and Respond

History Inform students that following the Gulf War, President Bush held a voter approval rating of 90 percent. Explain that his popularity fell as the recession in the United States continued. Many people blamed President Bush for the recession, contending that he paid more attention to foreign policy than to domestic issues.

Civics and Government Explain that Ross Perot's candidacy hurt President Bush's reelection bid in 1992. Inform students that the Republican party was divided. Some members voted for Bush and other members voted for Perot. These factors helped Bill Clinton, a Democrat, become elected President of the United States.

Q What effect did Ross Perot have on the outcome of the 1992 presidential election?

A Since the Republican Party was divided, Bill Clinton won the election.

Conflicts in Eastern Europe

Read and Respond

Economics Explain that the war in Bosnia took a heavy toll on that country and its economy. Inform students that during the war, inflation and unemployment increased dramatically. By 1995 three of every four workers in Bosnia were unemployed. In addition, nearly half of Bosnia's industrial plants had been destroyed, damaged, or looted.

3 Close

Summarize Key Content

- A recession prompted President Bush to raise taxes.
- The United States led Allied forces in Operation Desert Storm, a successful effort that forced Iraq to end its occupation of Kuwait.
- The end of communism brought the beginning of new hostilities between ethnic groups in Eastern Europe.
- Bill Clinton defeated George Bush and Ross Perot in 1992 to claim the presidency.
- In the 1990s, the United States and NATO stepped in to end violence in the former Yugoslavia.

As Election Day drew near, however, Clinton and Bush were the two leading candidates.

After all the votes had been counted, Bill Clinton was the winner. Clinton received only 43 percent of the popular vote, but he won 370 electoral votes. The rest of the popular vote was divided between Bush's 38 percent and Perot's 19 percent. Perot's percent was the highest ever for a third-party candidate.

Also, more voters voted in this election than ever before. More than 104 million Americans cast their votes in the election. Altogether 55 percent of all those who could vote did so.

REVIEW How was the 1992 presidential election different from most elections?
It had three major candidates.

Conflicts in Eastern Europe

The United States tried to protect the freedom of people in many parts of the world. In 1993 President Bill Clinton faced serious challenges in Bosnia, a small country located near Yugoslavia. One group there, called the Serbs, wanted to clear the country of the other two groups, the Croats (KRO•ats) and the Muslims. The Serbs forced members of those groups into concentration camps.

President Clinton said Americans had a responsibility to help the Bosnians. In 1995 he sent 20,000 United States soldiers to join troops led by NATO. The NATO forces stopped the killing of Bosnian civilians and maintained a cease-fire. Clinton told Americans, "We stood for peace in Bosnia."

President George Bush (on stage at left) and Bill Clinton (on stage at right) look on as H. Ross Perot (on stage at center) speaks during the 1992 presidential debates.

466

INTEGRATE MATHEMATICS

Make a Circle Graph
Organize students into groups, and ask them to research the results of the 1992 presidential election. Have groups illustrate both the popular and electoral votes in separate circle graphs. Have groups share their completed graphs with the class.

INTEGRATE LANGUAGE ARTS

Informative Writing
Remind students that the United Nations and NATO were designed to keep world peace after World War II. Have students write paragraphs explaining how successful these organizations were in accomplishing their goal. Paragraphs should contain specific examples from the textbook and other resources. Have volunteers share their paragraphs with the class.

STUDY/RESEARCH SKILLS

Outlining Ask students to outline the material in this lesson. Have students use section headings as main points and include supporting details beneath them.

Children of Kosovo watch United States peacekeepers set up a soccer goal at a school.

In 1998 another problem arose in Kosovo, a small region controlled by Yugoslavia. The people of Kosovo wanted independence, but the Yugoslav leader Slobodan Milosevic (mil•OH•seh•vitch) refused their request. Milosevic sent troops into Kosovo to destroy its people. In 1999 President Clinton again sent United States troops to join NATO forces. After NATO air strikes, Yugoslavia agreed to withdraw its forces from Kosovo. Once again, the United States had stepped in to protect the rights and freedoms of people in other nations.

REVIEW Why did the United States send troops to Bosnia and Kosovo? To protect the rights and freedoms of people in other nations.

LESSON 3 REVIEW

Summary Time Line

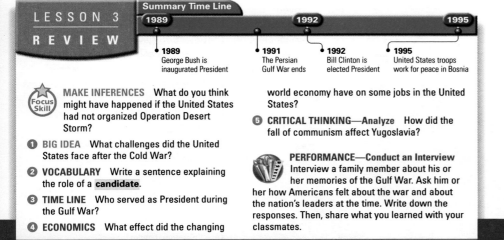

1989	1992	1995

1989 George Bush is inaugurated President
1991 The Persian Gulf War ends
1992 Bill Clinton is elected President
1995 United States troops work for peace in Bosnia

MAKE INFERENCES What do you think might have happened if the United States had not organized Operation Desert Storm?

① **BIG IDEA** What challenges did the United States face after the Cold War?

② **VOCABULARY** Write a sentence explaining the role of a **candidate**.

③ **TIME LINE** Who served as President during the Gulf War?

④ **ECONOMICS** What effect did the changing world economy have on some jobs in the United States?

⑤ **CRITICAL THINKING—Analyze** How did the fall of communism affect Yugoslavia?

PERFORMANCE—Conduct an Interview Interview a family member about his or her memories of the Gulf War. Ask him or her how Americans felt about the war and about the nation's leaders at the time. Write down the responses. Then, share what you learned with your classmates.

Chapter 12 ■ 467

CHAPTER 12 ■ 467

Make Inferences
pp. 447, 468, 470, 473, 476

Vocabulary
SEE READING AND VOCABULARY TRANSPARENCY 6-10 OR THE WORD CARDS ON PP. V53–V54.

veto p. 468   **terrorism** p. 472

impeach p. 470   **hijack** p. 472

When Minutes Count

Have students scan the lesson to find the meaning of each of the lesson vocabulary terms. Then ask them to use the terms in sentences about the lesson.

Quick Summary

This lesson examines and describes new challenges facing the United States in the twenty-first century.

Motivate

Set the Purpose

Big Idea Explain that the United States and its citizens experienced various changes at the end of the twentieth century.

Access Prior Knowledge

Have students discuss what they know about challenges that people in the United States faced during the twentieth century.

· LESSON ·

4

The End of the Twentieth Century

MAKE INFERENCES

As you read, make inferences about the challenges Americans have faced as they worked to build a better nation.

BIG IDEA

Americans worked to make changes in the United States and the world at the end of the twentieth century.

VOCABULARY
veto
impeach
terrorism
hijack

1951	1976	2001

1992–2001

The end of the twentieth century brought many changes to the United States. Americans watched as the nation's economy grew stronger and stronger. Americans also saw how important each person's civic responsibilities are. During this time the United States worked with other nations to help resolve conflicts. At home, Americans came together as they faced new dangers.

Changes at Home

President Clinton's programs helped change life in America. However, not all of his programs were successful. In his first year in office, Clinton promised to find a way to offer health care to the 30 million Americans who had no health insurance. Clinton's plan was presented before Congress, but it was not approved.

Other Clinton programs ran into problems after the 1994 congressional election. That election gave Republicans a majority of members in both the House and the Senate. Many times Congress passed bills that Clinton had **vetoed**, or rejected. Also, Clinton suggested bills that Congress did not pass.

One of the issues the President and Congress began to work on together was the national budget. A part of the budget dealt with money spent on the welfare program of

President Clinton worked with Congress to help balance the national budget.

468

Analyze Graphs During the 1990s, the number of unemployed people steadily decreased.

◈ What does this graph tell you about the nation's economy in the 1990s?

the nation. Welfare is aid that needy people can receive from the government. Some people apply for welfare to help feed their families. Others rely on welfare for housing. The law was not exactly what either Congress or the President wanted. Yet both the Congress and the President were able to reach a compromise and change welfare spending. The new law put a time limit on welfare benefits. People could receive welfare for a period of only two years.

As President, Clinton oversaw one of the greatest periods of economic growth in the nation's history. Businesses created millions of new jobs, and unemployment dropped to its lowest level in many years.

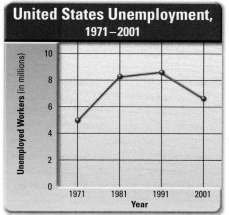

United States Unemployment, 1971–2001

Source: Bureau of Labor Statistics

When Clinton left office in 2001, the strong economy was one reason he had the support of many Americans.

Clinton also worked with Boris Yeltsin, the new president of Russia, to further reduce the number of nuclear weapons.

During the 1990s jobs were created in many new industries. These workers are helping put together computers.

Chapter 12 • 469

READING SOCIAL STUDIES

Personal Response Ask students to write personal responses about an event or a challenge faced by the United States in this lesson. Have students revise their thoughts as they read the lesson.

● USE READING AND VOCABULARY TRANSPARENCY 6-10.

6-10 TRANSPARENCY

2 Teach

Changes at Home

Visual Learning

Graph Direct students' attention to the line graph on page 469. Inform students that unemployment is a leading indicator of the state of a country's economy.

Q What happened to unemployment in the United States between 1991 and 2001?

A It dropped from a little more than 8 million to a little more than 6 million.
CAPTION ANSWER: The graph indicates that the nation's economy grew in the 1990s as more people joined the workforce.

REACH ALL LEARNERS

Advanced Learners Ask students to research unemployment figures in their state over the last decade and illustrate their findings in line graphs. Then have students use their graphs to draw conclusions about unemployment in their state during the past ten years. Ask volunteers to share their conclusions with the class.

BACKGROUND

William Jefferson Clinton (1946–) Bill Clinton was born in Hope, Arkansas, where he became known as a bright and diligent student. He went on to graduate from Georgetown University and then Yale University Law School before beginning a career of public service. In 1978 he was elected to the first of five terms as governor of Arkansas. In 1992 Clinton was elected President of the United States, a position to which he was reelected in 1996.

Read and Respond

Civics and Government Explain that Bill Clinton's tenure as President featured both achievements and controversies. In the 1990s he oversaw one of the greatest periods of economic growth in United States history. In 1999 he became the second United States President to be impeached.

Q **What was the most significant challenge faced by President Clinton?**

A Students' responses will vary but could include turning around the nation's economy, working with Congress to pass legislation, or overcoming impeachment proceedings.

The 2000 Election

Visual Learning

Pictures Direct students' attention to the pictures on page 470. Explain that the so-called "butterfly ballot" was a source of confusion for many voters in Florida and led to a number of recounts in that state.

Read and Respond

Civics and Government Explain that in the 2000 election Al Gore received about 500,000 more votes than George W. Bush, but Bush won more electoral votes. Inform students that the closeness of the election led to numerous recounts and legal decisions. As a result of the Supreme Court decision, Bush became the first candidate in more than 100 years to win the electoral vote and the election while losing the popular vote.

He wanted to reduce the number of nuclear weapons each nation had.

In his 1995 State of the Union Address, Clinton said, "Tonight . . . is the first State of the Union Address ever delivered since the beginning of the Cold War when not a single Russian missile is pointed at . . . America."

President Clinton also experienced controversy during his presidency. In 1999 he became only the second United States President to be **impeached**, or accused of a crime. Clinton's 37-day trial for obstructing justice and lying under oath could have resulted in his removal from office. As a result of the Senate vote, however, he was allowed to finish his term.

REVIEW Why did President Clinton work with Russian leader Boris Yeltsin?
MAKE INFERENCES

The 2000 Election

The presidential election of 2000 showed how important each person's vote is. Texas governor George W. Bush was the Republican party's candidate. Vice President Al Gore was the Democratic party's candidate. When the more than 100 million votes had been counted, both candidates were very close to winning the presidency. In fact, it was the closest presidential election in 40 years.

The winner would be decided by votes in the state of Florida. But the numbers of votes were so close that for five weeks nobody could tell who had won. During that time, many counties in Florida began to recount their citizens' votes to make

The voting system (left) used in Palm Beach County, Florida, confused some voters. Palm Beach election officials (below) had to recount thousands of votes by hand.

On January 20, 2001, George W. Bush was sworn in as President. He became the first President of the twenty-first century.

sure the totals were correct. On December 12, 2000, the United States Supreme Court ruled that the counting must stop. The officials in Florida who recounted the votes found that George W. Bush had won by about 600 votes. He became President of the United States.

President George W. Bush began working on issues he had discussed during his campaign for the presidency. He proposed laws for tax cuts and worked to make changes in education. However, Bush soon faced challenges in foreign relations. Communist China is a powerful nation. The United States and China are not enemies, but they also are not allies. On April 1, 2001, a spy plane from the United States was flying off the coast of China. A Chinese fighter jet collided with the spy plane. The jet crashed, and its pilot was killed. The spy plane was also badly damaged. The crew had to make an emergency landing at a Chinese military base on the island of Hainan [HY•NAHN].

China's leaders were angry about the accident, and they kept the 24 members of the American crew as prisoners.

United States leaders asked the Chinese government to send the plane and its crew back home, but the Chinese refused. They demanded that the United States government apologize for the incident. Many Americans did not believe that the United States was at fault, but President Bush knew that he needed to avoid war with China. The two nations reached a compromise, and the plane and its crew were soon returned to the United States.

President Bush also dealt with problems in the Middle East when war broke out between Israel and the Palestinian people. The two groups had fought each other many times before, and other nations had volunteered to help bring about a peace agreement. President Bush agreed to attend talks between Israeli and Palestinian representatives. He hoped to play a role in bringing peace to the Middle East. Part of the President's job is to help other nations. It is a way to make the world better for citizens of every nation.

REVIEW How did the presidential election of 2000 show that each person's vote counts?
The election was so close that a few hundred votes in Florida helped decide the winner.

Chapter 12 ■ 471

Read and Respond

Civics and Government Discuss the importance to the United States of strong foreign relations. Explain that as the world's only remaining superpower, the United States faces many challenges, such as mediating disputes between opposing nations.

Q **Why is it important for the United States to try to bring peace to the Middle East?**

A Students' responses should reflect that events in the Middle East affect life in the United States and various other places.

History Inform students that relations between the United States and China have improved since the days of the Cold War. Explain that economic reforms in China have resulted in an expansion of privately owned businesses. Tell students that although the United States and China maintain relations today, they are still divided over certain issues.

BACKGROUND

George W. Bush (1946–) George W. Bush was born into a family of politicians. His grandfather, Prescott, was a United States senator from Connecticut and his father, George Herbert Walker Bush, was the forty-first President of the United States. George W. Bush was elected governor of Texas in 1994 and again in 1998. In 2000 he defeated Al Gore for the presidency and in so doing became the first son to follow his father into the White House in nearly 200 years.

STUDY/RESEARCH SKILLS

Using Reference Sources
Inform students that the presidential winners in the elections of 1876 and 1888 also received fewer popular votes than did their opponents. Ask students to use the Internet and other reference sources to research these elections. Have students use their findings to write brief summaries comparing those elections with the election of 2000.

Facing New Dangers

Read and Respond

Civics and Government Explain that the global war on terrorism began in October 2001 with air strikes against the country of Afghanistan.

History Discuss with students the terrorist attacks of September 11, 2001. Point out that while other acts of terrorism have occurred in the United States, this was the worst attack in our nation's history. Emphasize that since that attack new laws have been enacted to strengthen the nation's security.

3 Close

Summarize Key Content

- Bill Clinton's two terms as President of the United States featured many challenges, achievements, and controversies.
- George W. Bush was elected President of the United States in 2000.
- The September 11, 2001, terrorist attacks shocked the world and changed the lives of many people forever.

Facing New Dangers

At the end of the twentieth century, the United States faced new dangers from both outside and inside its borders. The nation's military forces continued to defend democratic values in missions around the world—from Haiti in the Caribbean to Bosnia in Europe. The nation also experienced acts of terrorism as bombs exploded at two United States embassies in Africa and next to a United States Navy ship in the Middle East. **Terrorism** is the deliberate use of violence to promote a cause.

Acts of terrorism occurred inside the United States, too. In the early 1990s, a bomb rocked the World Trade Center in New York City. Then, in 1995, an American citizen who was angry with the government set off a bomb outside the federal office building in Oklahoma City, Oklahoma. That blast killed 168 men, women, and children.

However, the worst act of terrorism in the nation's history occurred on September 11, 2001. That morning, terrorists **hijacked**, or illegally took control of, four American commercial airplanes. Again, terrorists targeted the World Trade Center. Two of the hijacked planes were flown directly into the center's twin towers, causing huge explosions. The third plane was flown into the side of the Pentagon, the nation's military headquarters, near Washington, D.C. The fourth

After the terrorist attacks on September 11, 2001, the twin towers of the World Trade Center caught fire and later collapsed. Firefighters (right) stand among the ruins and raise the American flag as a symbol of patriotism.

472   Unit 6

In the days after the terrorist attacks, Americans around the nation came together in public ceremonies to remember the victims.

plane crashed in an empty field near Pittsburgh, Pennsylvania.

Less than two hours after the attacks on the World Trade Center, both towers collapsed, killing thousands of people. At the Pentagon, nearly 200 people died.

President Bush, with the support of Congress, pledged that the United States would lead the world in a war against terrorism. As the United States works to make our nation and the world more secure, the Constitution will continue to make sure that our basic freedoms as Americans are protected.

REVIEW In what ways has terrorism affected the United States? Terrorist attacks both inside and outside the country have destroyed property and caused a great loss of life.

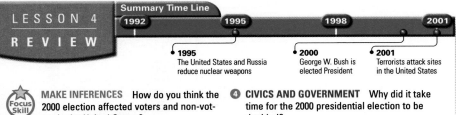

LESSON 4 REVIEW

Summary Time Line

1992 — 1995 — 1998 — 2001

- **1995** The United States and Russia reduce nuclear weapons
- **2000** George W. Bush is elected President
- **2001** Terrorists attack sites in the United States

 MAKE INFERENCES How do you think the 2000 election affected voters and non-voters in the United States?

1 BIG IDEA What challenges did Americans face at the end of the twentieth century?

2 VOCABULARY Use the word **veto** in a sentence about the President.

3 TIME LINE In what year was George W. Bush elected President?

4 CIVICS AND GOVERNMENT Why did it take time for the 2000 presidential election to be decided?

5 CRITICAL THINKING—Hypothesize What do you think will be the most difficult challenge the United States will face in the future?

 **PERFORMANCE—Make a Poster** Research more information about one of the events in this lesson. Then make a poster that illustrates what you learned.

Chapter 12 ■ 473

OBJECTIVES

- Identify and determine population density.
- Organize and interpret information from a map.

Vocabulary
population density p. 474

WORD CARDS

See pp. V53–V54.

1 Motivate

Why It Matters

Explain that population density maps have many uses, such as helping urban planners decide where certain services are needed and dividing areas into balanced segments or precincts for voting purposes.

SKILLS

MAP AND GLOBE

Read a Population Map

VOCABULARY
population density

▶ WHY IT MATTERS

Like most other geographic information, population can be shown on maps in many different ways. One way to show the population of a place is with color. Knowing how to read a population map can make it easier for you to find out the number of people who live in different areas of the United States and the world.

▶ WHAT YOU NEED TO KNOW

The map below is a population map of the United States. A population map shows where people live. It also shows the population density of each place. **Population density** is the number of people who live in 1 square mile or 1 square kilometer of land. A square mile is a square piece of land. Each of its four

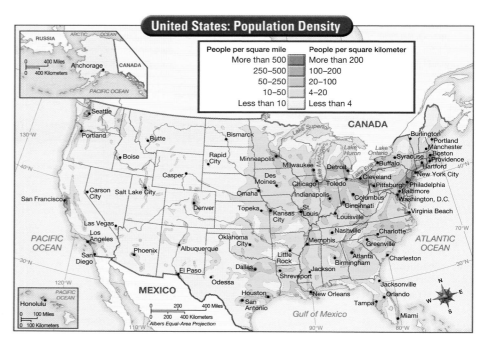

United States: Population Density

People per square mile	People per square kilometer
More than 500	More than 200
250–500	100–200
50–250	20–100
10–50	4–20
Less than 10	Less than 4

Albers Equal-Area Projection

474 ▪ Unit 6

MAKE IT RELEVANT

In Your State Ask students to use the Internet and other references to research their state's population density over the past decade. Have students note any patterns in their state and write brief summaries from their findings.

BACKGROUND

Growing Population According to the 2000 census, the population in the United States has grown to more than 281 million people. Much of that growth is spread across states in the South and West, such as Georgia, North Carolina, Arizona, and California. The population growth has affected congressional representation across the nation. Some states, such as Texas and Florida, have gained congressional seats; others, such as Pennsylvania and New York, have lost them.

Many people today live in large cities like Seattle, Washington (left). Others live in small, rural communities like this New England town (right).

sides is 1 mile long. A square kilometer is a square piece of land with sides that are each 1 kilometer long.

Look at the key on the map. It shows colors that stand for different population densities.

On the map, the light-tan color stands for the least crowded areas. Red stands for the most crowded areas. Use the map key to find areas that have more than 500 people per square mile or fewer than 10 people per square mile.

➡ PRACTICE THE SKILL

Use the map on page 474 to answer the following questions:

❶ What is the lowest population density shown on the map?

❷ What is the highest population density shown on the map?

❸ Do most people live in the eastern half of the country or the western half?

❹ Which city has greater population density—Miami, Florida, or Los Angeles, California?

➡ APPLY WHAT YOU LEARNED

Study the population information given on the map on page 474. Then show some of the same information by using a chart, graph, or table.

Practice your map and globe skills with the **GeoSkills CD-ROM**.

Chapter 12 ■ 475

2 Teach

What You Need to Know

Explain that the areas shown on population maps are divided into irregular segments according to their use. Inform students that an area zoned residential will have a higher population density than will an area zoned commercial.

Practice the Skill

❶ The lowest population density on the map indicates less than 10 people per square mile (4 per sq km).

❷ The highest population density on the map indicates more than 500 people per square mile (200 per sq km).

❸ More people live in the eastern half of the United States.

❹ Los Angeles, California

3 Close

Apply What You Learned

Have students select ten cities from the map and make a graph that shows their population densities.

ACTIVITY BOOK

Use ACTIVITY BOOK, pp. 120–121, to give students additional practice using this skill.

TRANSPARENCY

Use SKILL TRANSPARENCY 6-5.

EXTEND AND ENRICH

Write a Summary Instruct students to summarize in writing the information they learned from the map. Summaries should include descriptions of the most and least populated areas and references to the largest and smallest cities.

RETEACH THE SKILL

Find Population Trends Provide students with population density maps from several states in your region. Ask students to study the maps and draw conclusions about the population in the region. Have volunteers share their conclusions with the class.

CD-ROM

Explore GEOSKILLS CD-ROM to learn more about map and globe skills.

MAKE INFERENCES

Students may use the graphic organizer that appears on page 122 of the Activity Book. Answers appear in the Activity Book, Teacher's Edition.

Think & Write

Write an Interview Students may use information in this chapter as a basis for writing interview questions. Encourage volunteers to share their completed interviews with the class.

Write a Report Students' reports should contain accurate information about their chosen countries' geography, people, cultures, religions, and economy.

ACTIVITY BOOK

A copy of the graphic organizer appears in the ACTIVITY BOOK on page 122.

TRANSPARENCY

This graphic organizer appears on READING AND VOCABULARY TRANSPARENCY 6-11.

---

12 Review and Test Preparation

Summary Time Line
1961

● **1968**
More than 500,000
United States troops
in Vietnam

● **1974**
President Nixon
resigns

Make Inferences

Copy the following graphic organizer onto a separate sheet of paper. Use the information you have learned to make inferences about the end of the Soviet Union and communist rule in Europe.

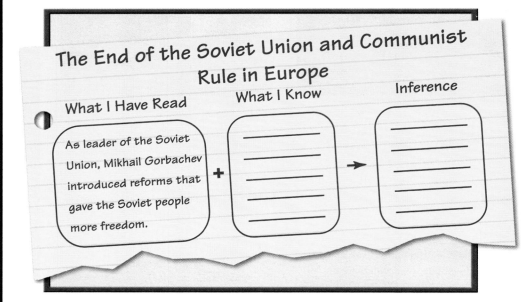

The End of the Soviet Union and Communist Rule in Europe

What I Have Read

As leader of the Soviet Union, Mikhail Gorbachev introduced reforms that gave the Soviet people more freedom.

What I Know

Inference

THINK & WRITE

Write an Interview Interview a grandparent, parent, or other family member who was alive during one of the following presidencies: Nixon, Ford, Carter, Reagan, or Bush. Ask questions about what life was like during that time period. Write out the interview questions and answers.

Write a Report Research one of the countries you read about in Chapter 12. Write a report about that country. Include in your report information about the country's geography, people, cultures, religions, and economy. Share your report with a classmate.

TEST PREPARATION

Review these tips with students:

■ Read the directions before reading the questions.

■ Read each question twice, focusing the second time on all the possible answers.

■ Take the time to think about all the possible answers before deciding on an answer.

■ Move past questions that give you trouble, and answer the ones you know. Then return to the difficult items.

UNIT PROJECT

Progress Check Have students determine the order in which the significant people, places, or events they listed will appear in their magazine. Suggest that students order them either by topic, importance, or chronology.

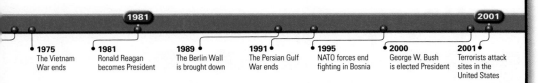

1975
The Vietnam
War ends

1981
Ronald Reagan
becomes President

1989
The Berlin Wall
is brought down

1991
The Persian Gulf
War ends

1995
NATO forces end
fighting in Bosnia

2000
George W. Bush
is elected President

2001
Terrorists attack
sites in the
United States

USE THE TIME LINE

Use the chapter summary time line to answer these questions.

1 In what year did the Vietnam War end?

2 When was George W. Bush elected president?

USE VOCABULARY

Identify the correct term that completes each sentence.

| arms control (p. 453) |
| cease-fire (p. 453) |
| deficit (p. 459) |
| candidate (p. 465) |
| impeached (p. 470) |

3 A _____ temporarily stops a conflict but does not end a war.

4 In 1992 Bill Clinton was chosen to be the presidential _____ for the Democrats.

5 Nations that agree to _____ must limit the number of weapons that they have.

6 The government caused a _____ when it spent more money than it had.

7 The representatives wanted the President to be _____ after he was caught lying.

RECALL FACTS

Answer these questions.

8 Why did the United States support South Vietnam during the Vietnam War?

9 How did the Vietnam War divide people in America?

10 What meeting marked the beginning of the end of the Cold War?

11 What was Operation Desert Storm?

12 Who was the second American President to be impeached?

Write the letter of the best choice.

13 The first American President to resign was—
A George Bush.
B Bill Clinton.
C Richard Nixon.
D Jimmy Carter.

14 In 2001 President George W. Bush, supported by Congress, declared a war on—
F drugs.
G crime.
H terrorism.
J fraud.

THINK CRITICALLY

15 How do you think citizens of the Soviet Union felt about *perestroika* and *glasnost*?

16 Why do you think the 2000 presidential election was so close?

APPLY SKILLS

Read a Population Map
Use the information on pages 474 and 475 and the map on page 474 to help answer these questions.

17 What do population maps show?

18 When would you use a population map?

19 According to the map, which region of the United States has the lowest population density, the Northeast or the West?

Chapter 12 ▪ 477

---

11 It was the name for the Allied forces' attack on Iraq; also called the Gulf War. (p. 464)

12 Bill Clinton (p. 470)

13 C (p. 453)

14 H (p. 473)

Think Critically

15 Students' answers will vary but may include the idea that Soviet citizens were likely excited about having new freedoms under *perestroika* and *glasnost*.

16 Possible response: The candidates had nearly equal support among voters.

Apply Skills

Read a Population Map

17 Population maps show where people live and the population densities of various areas.

18 You would use a population map in order to find out the number of people who live in a particular place.

19 the West

ACTIVITY BOOK

Use the CHAPTER 12 TEST PREPARATION on page 123 of the Activity Book.

ASSESSMENT

Use the CHAPTER 12 TEST on pages 95–98 of the Assessment Program.

Use the Time Line

1 1975

2 2000

Use Vocabulary

3 cease-fire

4 candidate

5 arms control

6 deficit

7 impeached

Recall Facts

8 The United States wanted to stop the spread of communism in Southeast Asia. (p. 450)

9 Some people in the United States felt that the war was needed to stop the spread of communism. Others said that it was a civil war that should be settled by the Vietnamese without outside help. (p. 450)

10 the meeting in 1985 between President Reagan and Soviet leader Gorbachev (pp. 459–460)

Visit the Birmingham Civil Rights Institute

PAGES 478–479

OBJECTIVES

- Identify important events of the Civil Rights movement.
- Describe segregation faced by African Americans in the 1950s and 1960s.

Summary

The Birmingham Civil Rights Institute honors the courage of the men and women who fought for equal rights for African Americans.

1 Motivate

Get Ready

Point out that many important events in the Civil Rights movement happened in Alabama. Tell students that many people visit the Institute to learn more about the Civil Rights movement. Ask whether any students have visited a civil rights museum. If any have, ask them to share their experiences with the class.

2 Teach

What to See

Have students look carefully at the photographs on page 479. Ask students the following questions:

- *What is happening in the lunch counter exhibit on page 479?*
- *Why do you think the museum chose to use life-size figures in the exhibits rather than showing only photographs and other images?*

VISIT

THE BIRMINGHAM Civil Rights Institute

GET READY

The Birmingham Civil Rights Institute celebrates the many people who worked to gain full rights for African Americans. On a visit there, you seem to travel back in time. You will see, feel, and hear what it was like in this important time in American history. After you explore the life-size scenes and watch the video presentations in the institute's different galleries, you will feel as if you had lived through the events of the Civil Rights movement.

LOCATE IT

Birmingham

ALABAMA

478 ▪ Unit 6

BACKGROUND

Birmingham, Alabama

Birmingham was the site of several major events in the Civil Rights movement. Martin Luther King, Jr., outlined his commitment to nonviolent protest in a letter he wrote while being held in Birmingham's jail in April 1963. In September 1963 the nation was shocked when members of the Ku Klux Klan bombed the Sixteenth Street Baptist Church, killing four children attending Sunday school.

REACH ALL LEARNERS

Tactile Learners Ask these learners to research a famous event of the Civil Rights movement, such as King's "I Have a Dream" speech. Have these students make a sketch that depicts the event. Encourage them to present their sketches and describe what the sketches show.

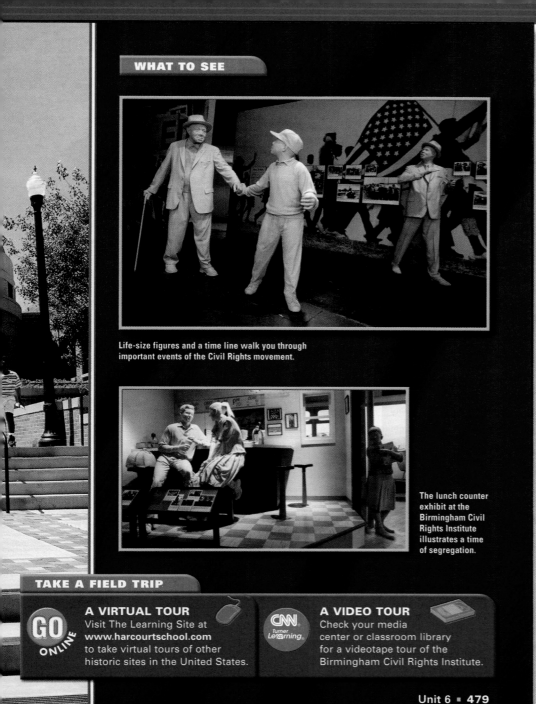

Life-size figures and a time line walk you through important events of the Civil Rights movement.

The lunch counter exhibit at the Birmingham Civil Rights Institute illustrates a time of segregation.

TAKE A FIELD TRIP

GO ONLINE

A VIRTUAL TOUR
Visit The Learning Site at **www.harcourtschool.com** to take virtual tours of other historic sites in the United States.

CNN Turner Le@rning

A VIDEO TOUR
Check your media center or classroom library for a videotape tour of the Birmingham Civil Rights Institute.

Unit 6 ■ 479

3 Close

Take a Field Trip

Direct students to research one important event or person from the Civil Rights movement. Students may wish to learn more about the exhibits that can be found at the Birmingham Civil Rights Institute.

A Virtual Tour Depending on the availability of computers, have students work individually, in pairs, or in small groups to view the virtual tour. Encourage them to research events of the Civil Rights movement as they explore the Web sites. Remind students to use what they learn on their virtual tours as background information for the Unit Project.

GO ONLINE **INTERNET RESOURCES**

THE LEARNING SITE
Go to **www.harcourtschool.com** for a listing of Web sites focusing on historical sites in the United States.

Video Tour Before students watch the CNN video tour of the Birmingham Civil Rights Institute, have them write down three questions about the institute. Invite them to answer the questions as they watch the videotape. Ask for volunteers to share their questions and answers with the class.

VIDEO

Use the CNN/Turner Learning TAKE A FIELD TRIP videotape of the Birmingham Civil Rights Institute.

INTEGRATE LANGUAGE ARTS

Write a Poem Ask students to imagine that they are fighting for civil rights in the 1960s. Challenge them to write short poems about their experiences or about a civil rights issue. Inform them that Maya Angelou, a famous African American poet and writer, has written many poems about strong and courageous African American women. Encourage them to locate one of her poems and use it as a model.

EXTEND AND ENRICH

Write a Contrast Essay Ask students to look at the picture of the lunch counter exhibit closely. Have them write paragraphs describing how the African American girl is being treated at the lunch counter. Ask for volunteers to read their paragraphs to the class.

Unit 6 Review and Test Preparation

PAGES 480–482

Visual Summary

Students' poems should imaginatively yet accurately interpret the events portrayed in the Visual Summary. You may wish to have volunteers share their poems in class.

- **The Korean War continues** United Nations troops, which consisted mostly of United States soldiers, tried to stop communist forces from taking control of Korea.

- *Brown v. the Board of Education* **case** Thurgood Marshall presented this case to the Supreme Court. He stated that separate schools did not provide equal education and called for integration in schools.

- **The Soviet Union launches** *Sputnik* *Sputnik* was the world's first satellite. It helped speed up United States efforts during the space race.

- **More than 500,000 United States troops in Vietnam** When United States and South Vietnamese troops failed to defeat the Vietcong quickly, President Johnson sent more United States troops to South Vietnam.

- **United States astronauts land on the moon** *Apollo 11* carried astronauts to the moon. Neil Armstrong and Edwin "Buzz" Aldrin became the first two people to walk on the moon.

- **The Cold War ends** A 1985 meeting between United States President Reagan and Soviet leader Gorbachev was the start of eased relations between the two countries. The Cold War ended with the breakup of the Soviet Union in 1991.

VISUAL SUMMARY

Write a Poem Look at the Visual Summary below and choose one of the events to write a poem about. Use the captions, your imagination, and what you have learned in your reading to interpret what is taking place in the picture. In your poem, describe what is happening in the picture and how the picture makes you feel.

USE VOCABULARY

Identify the term that correctly matches each definition.

| integration (p. 421) |
| blockade (p. 429) |
| détente (p. 453) |
| recession (p. 463) |

1. a period of slow economic activity
2. the bringing together of people of all races
3. an easing of tensions
4. to isolate a place

RECALL FACTS

Answer these questions.

5. Which United States President created the Presidential Committee on Civil Rights?
6. How did Martin Luther King, Jr., protest segregation?
7. Who was the first United States astronaut to orbit Earth?
8. Why did President Nixon resign from the presidency?
9. Why did the Soviet Union break up in 1991?
10. Which President helped bring peace to the Middle East in 1978?
    - A Jimmy Carter
    - B Gerald Ford
    - C Richard Nixon
    - D Bill Clinton
11. Which group of people demanded independence from the Yugoslavian government in 1998?
    - F the Serbs
    - G the Croats
    - H the people of Bosnia
    - J the people of Kosovo

Visual Summary

1951   1961   1971

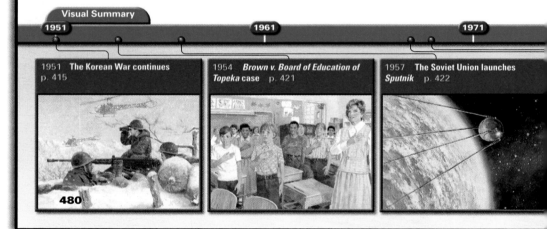

1951 The Korean War continues p. 415

1954 *Brown v. Board of Education of Topeka* case p. 421

1957 The Soviet Union launches *Sputnik* p. 422

480

Use Vocabulary

1. recession
2. integration
3. détente
4. blockade

Recalls Facts

5. Harry S. Truman (p. 411)
6. by working for change in nonviolent ways (p. 421)
7. John Glenn (p. 432)

8. because the public learned that he had tried to cover up an illegal act (p. 453)
9. There was no longer communism to unite all the different peoples. (pp. 464–465)
10. A (p. 456)
11. J (p. 467)

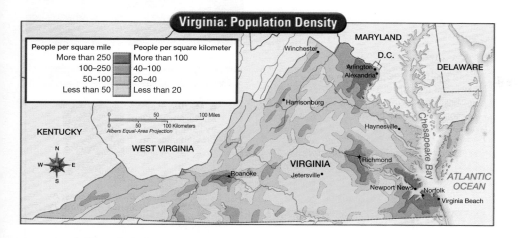

Virginia: Population Density

People per square mile
- More than 250
- 100–250
- 50–100
- Less than 50

People per square kilometer
- More than 100
- 40–100
- 20–40
- Less than 20

0   50   100 Miles
0   50   100 Kilometers
Albers Equal-Area Projection

MARYLAND

D.C.

DELAWARE

Winchester

Arlington
Alexandria

Harrisonburg

Haynesville

Chesapeake Bay

KENTUCKY

WEST VIRGINIA

VIRGINIA

Richmond

Jetersville

Roanoke

ATLANTIC
OCEAN

Newport News   Norfolk

Virginia Beach

N W E S

THINK CRITICALLY

12 How were the Korean War years similar to the Vietnam War years? How were they different?

13 Why do you think it was important to President Kennedy to put an astronaut on the moon by the end of the 1960s?

14 How do you think the American people felt when they learned President Nixon was resigning?

APPLY SKILLS

Read a Population Map
Use the map on this page to answer the following questions.

MAP AND GLOBE SKILLS

15 Which city has a higher population density—Winchester or Virginia Beach?

16 Which city has a lower population density—Norfolk or Harrisonburg?

| 1981 | 1991 | 2001 |

1968 More than 500,000 United States troops in Vietnam   p. 449

1969 United States astronauts land on the moon   p. 432

1986 United States and Soviet leaders work to end the Cold War   p. 460

481

Think Critically

12 Possible response: During both the Korean War and the Vietnam War many new laws were passed in the United States and the country was fighting the spread of communism. Unlike during the Vietnam War, during the Korean War there were not as many public protests about the fighting.

13 Students' answers will vary but may include the idea that the United States was trailing the Soviet Union in the space race.

14 Students' responses will vary but they may state that the American people felt worried, upset, relieved, betrayed, or satisfied. Students should base their answers on facts from the chapter.

Apply Skills

15 Virginia Beach

16 Harrisonburg

TEST PREPARATION

Review these tips with students:

- Read the directions before reading the questions.
- Read each question twice, focusing the second time on all the possible answers.
- Take the time to think about all the possible answers before deciding on an answer.
- Move past questions that give you trouble, and answer the ones you know. Then return to the difficult items.

ASSESSMENT

Use the UNIT 6 TEST on pages 99–107 of the Assessment Program.

Unit Activities

Make a Collage

Provide groups with appropriate art supplies such as paints, markers, and posterboard to complete their collages. Also give them old magazines and newspapers from which they can cut words, phrases, and photographs.

 Performance Assessment Guidelines Make sure that students' collages give an accurate portrayal of the decades from the 1950s through the 1990s.

Complete the Unit Project

Make sure that each student chooses a different person, place, or event to write about in the magazine. Students may need art supplies such as paints and markers to illustrate their articles. Combine finished articles into a class magazine.

 Performance Assessment Guidelines Make sure that students have used accurate information for their magazine articles and have presented the information imaginatively.

Unit Activities

GO ONLINE Visit The Learning Site at www.harcourtschool.com for additional activities.

 Make a Collage

In a group, work together to make a collage of the decades from the 1950s to the 1990s. Divide the collage into sections. In each section, use drawings, words, and photographs to represent a different decade. Make sure to include the following subjects in your collage: Korean and Vietnam Wars, Civil Rights movement, the Cold War, and the fall of Communism.

COMPLETE THE UNIT PROJECT

Make a Class Magazine Work as a class to complete the unit project—make a class magazine. Review the list you took during your reading. Then, choose one key person, place, or event to write a magazine article about. You can also draw pictures and design advertisements to go along with your article.

VISIT YOUR LIBRARY

■ *My Dream of Martin Luther King* by Faith Ringgold. Crown Publishers.

■ *Dear Mrs. Parks: A Dialogue with Today's Youth* by Rosa Parks and Gregory J. Reed. Lee and Low Books.

■ *President George W. Bush: Our Forty-third President* by Beatrice Gormley. Aladdin Paperbacks.

482 ■ Unit 6

Visit Your Library

Encourage independent reading of these books or books of your choice. Additional books are listed on the Multimedia Resources, on page 403D of this Teacher's Edition.

Easy *My Dream of Martin Luther King* by Faith Ringgold. Dragonfly, 1998. This book recounts the author's dream of a new world of peace and unity.

Average *Dear Mrs. Parks: A Dialogue with Today's Youth* by Rosa Parks, Gregory J. Reed. Lee and Low Books, 1997. For the last 40 years, Rosa Parks has received thousands of letters, most of them from children. This book features some of these letters. Parks's replies are simple and reassuring.

Challenging *President George W. Bush: Our Forty-third President* by Beatrice Gormley. Aladdin Paperbacks, 2001. This book tells the life story of George W. Bush, from childhood to his presidency.

The United States and the World

Patriotic folk art

Unit 7 Planning Guide The United States and the World

Introduce	CONTENT	RESOURCES
pp. 483–489	**UNIT OPENER**, p. 483 **PREVIEW**, pp. 484–485 **START WITH A STORY** *Dia's Story Cloth*, pp. 486–489	Unit 7 Audiotext Unit 7 School-to-Home Newsletter, p. S13 Reading and Vocabulary Transparency 7-1 Internet Resources

Chapter 13		
The United States Today, pp. 490–521	**INTRODUCE THE CHAPTER**, pp. 490–491 **LESSON 1** The American People Today, pp. 492–497 **CHART AND GRAPH SKILLS** Use a Cartogram, pp. 498–499 **LESSON 2** The Challenges of Growth, pp. 500–503 **LESSON 3** The American Economy, pp. 504–509 **LESSON 4** Government and the People, pp. 510–515 **CITIZENSHIP SKILLS** Identify Political Symbols, pp. 516–517 **EXAMINE PRIMARY SOURCES** Political Buttons, pp. 518–519 **CHAPTER REVIEW AND TEST PREPARATION**, pp. 520–521	Activity Book, pp. 124–133 Assessment Program, Chapter 13, pp. 109–112 Reading and Vocabulary Transparencies, 7-2, 7-3, 7-4, 7-5, 7-6 Skills Transparencies, 7-1A, 7-1B, 7-2 Internet Resources GeoSkills CD-ROM

Chapter 14		
Partners in the Hemisphere, pp. 522–549	**INTRODUCE THE CHAPTER**, pp. 522–523 **LESSON 1** Mexico, pp. 524–528 **LESSON 2** Central America and the Caribbean, pp. 529–533 **CHART AND GRAPH SKILLS** Read Population Pyramids, pp. 534–535 **LESSON 3** South America, pp. 536–540 **LESSON 4** Canada, pp. 541–545 **MAP AND GLOBE SKILLS** Use a Time Zone Map, pp. 546–547 **CHAPTER REVIEW AND TEST PREPARATION**, pp. 548–549	Activity Book, pp. 134–143 Assessment Program, Chapter 14, pp. 113–116 Reading and Vocabulary Transparencies, 7-7, 7-8, 7-9, 7-10, 7-11 Skills Transparencies, 7-3, 7-4 Internet Resources GeoSkills CD-ROM

Wrap Up		
pp. 550–554	**VISIT** Washington, D.C., pp. 550–551 **UNIT REVIEW AND TEST PREPARATION**, pp. 552–554	Internet Resources The Learning Site: Virtual Tours Take a Field Trip Video Time for Kids Readers Assessment Program, Unit 7, pp. 117–125

4 WEEKS	WEEK 1	WEEK 2	WEEK 3	WEEK 4
Introduce the Unit	Chapter 13		Chapter 14	Wrap Up the Unit

Unit 7 Skills Path

Unit 7 features the reading skills of telling fact from opinion and comparing and contrasting. It also highlights the social studies skills of using a cartogram, reading population pyramids, identifying political symbols, and using a time zone map.

 FOCUS SKILLS

CHAPTER 13 READING SKILL

 FACT AND OPINION

• INTRODUCE p. 491
• APPLY pp. 495, 497, 502, 503, 506, 509, 514, 515, 520

CHAPTER 14 READING SKILL

 COMPARE AND CONTRAST

• INTRODUCE p. 523
• APPLY pp. 525, 528, 531, 533, 539, 540, 542, 545, 548

READING SOCIAL STUDIES

• Personal Response, pp. 486, 488
• Predictions, pp. 493, 497
• Summarize, pp. 495, 542, 545
• Graphic Organizer, pp. 501, 502, 526, 530, 533
• Create Mental Images, p. 501
• Study Questions, pp. 505, 508, 537, 540
• Read Aloud, p. 505
• K-W-L Chart, pp. 511, 515
• Anticipation Guide, pp. 525, 528
• Graphic Organizer, p. 526
• Reread to Clarify, p. 532

 CHART AND GRAPH SKILLS

USE A CARTOGRAM

• INTRODUCE pp. 498–499
• APPLY p. 521

READ POPULATION PYRAMIDS

• INTRODUCE pp. 534–535
• APPLY p. 549

 CITIZENSHIP SKILLS

IDENTIFY POLITICAL SYMBOLS

• INTRODUCE pp. 516–517
• APPLY p. 521

 MAP AND GLOBE SKILLS

USE A TIME ZONE MAP

• INTRODUCE pp. 546–547
• APPLY p. 549

STUDY AND RESEARCH SKILLS

• Using the Internet, pp. 496, 505, 531
• Note Taking, p. 506
• Using Reference Sources, pp. 493, 502, 536
• Outlining, p. 538

7

Multimedia Resources

The Multimedia Resources can be used in a variety of ways. They can supplement core instruction in the classroom or extend and enrich student learning at home.

Independent Reading

Easy

Cherry, Lynne. **The Great Kapok Tree: A Tale of the Amazon Rainforest.**  Voyager Picture Book, 2000. Modern fable of a man who is sent to the rainforest to cut down a kapok tree and is visited in a dream by animals who plead with him not to destroy their home.

Halperin, Wendy Anderson. **Once Upon A Company…: A True Story.** Orchard Books, 1998. Three young children become entrepreneurs in this story that provides an introduction to business.

Johnston, Tony. **My Mexico-México Mío.** G. P. Putnam's Sons, 1996. Slice-of-life poems about Mexico in both English and Spanish.

Average

Jordan, Martin and Tanis. **Angel Falls: A South American Journey.** Kingfisher, 1995. Follow two travelers on an expedition that highlights the unique geographic wonders of South America.

Krull, Kathleen. **A Kids' Guide to America's Bill of Rights: Curfews, Censorship, and the 100-Pound Giant.** Avon Books, 1999. Overview of the Bill of Rights and how it affects the daily life of every American, including children.

Lesinski, Jeanne M. **Bill Gates.** Lerner Publishing Group, 2000. Biography of software pioneer who founded Microsoft, a multi-billion dollar company.

Challenging

Creeden, Sharon. **Fair is Fair.** August House Publishers, Inc., 1997. Thirty international folktales relating to law and justice that illuminate today's legal issues. Many stories followed by commentary on current legal debates and court cases.

Isler, Claudia: **Volunteering to Help in Your Neighborhood.** Children's Press, 2000. Provides students with advice on volunteerism and what to expect in a service-learning program.

Pandell, Karen. **Journey Through the Northern Rainforest.** Penguin Putnam Books for Young Readers, 1999. Chronicles the changes taking place in the rainforest region.

Computer Software

Inspirer: International Inspirer. Tom Snyder Productions, 1997. Mac/Windows. Students learn about international issues such as alliances, economics, and geographic and economic ties countries have to one another.

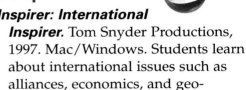

Videos and DVDs

My America: Becoming an Active Citizen. Sunburst, 1997. Provides students with an understanding of what the role of an active citizen should be.

Symbols and Ceremonies: Celebrating America. Sunburst, 1999. Provides students with information about the origin and meanings of symbols and ceremonies such as the flag, the Pledge of Allegiance, The Great Seal, and Statue of Liberty.

The Learning Site: Social Studies Center

The Learning Site at www.harcourtschool.com offers a special Social Studies Center. The center provides a wide variety of activities, Internet links, and online references.

Here are just some of the HARCOURT Internet resources you'll find!

Multimedia Biographies

www.harcourtschool.com

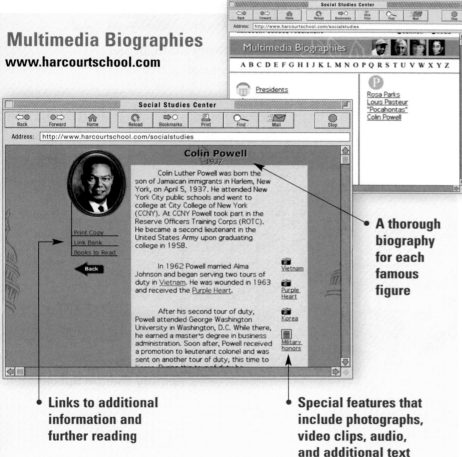

A thorough biography for each famous figure

Links to additional information and further reading

Special features that include photographs, video clips, audio, and additional text

INTERNET RESOURCES

Find all this at
The Learning Site at
www.harcourtschool.com

- Activities and Games
- Content Updates
- Current Events
- Free and Inexpensive Materials
- Multimedia Biographies
- Online Atlas
- Primary Sources
- Video Updates
- Virtual Tours
- Your State

and more!

Free and Inexpensive Materials

- Addresses to write for free and inexpensive products
- Links to unit-related materials
- Internet maps
- Internet references

www.harcourtschool.com

Primary Sources

- Artwork
- Clothing
- Diaries
- Government Documents
- Historical Documents
- Maps
- Tools

and more!

www.harcourtschool.com

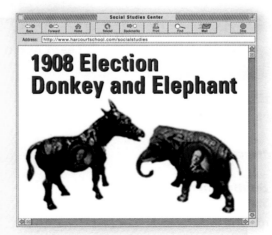

Virtual Tours

- Capitols and Government Buildings
- Cities
- Countries
- Historical Sites
- Museums
- Parks and Scenic Areas

and more!

www.harcourtschool.com

Integrate Learning Across the Curriculum

Use these topics to help you integrate social studies into your daily planning. See the page numbers indicated for more information about each topic.

Mathematics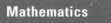

Figuring Percentages, p. 494

Art

Sketch a Story Cloth, p. 488
Make a Symbol, p. 516

Language Arts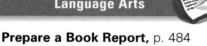

Prepare a Book Report, p. 484
Descriptive Writing, p. 495
Write a Report, p. 502
Write a Letter, p. 514
Expressive Writing, p. 518
Informative Writing, p. 527
Write a Scientific Summary, p. 534

Music

Canadian Music, p. 544

Science

Hurricanes, p. 531
Identify Unique Species, p. 537

Technology

GeoSkills CD-ROM, p. 547
Go Online, pp. 489, 494, 519, 537, 542, 551
CNN Video, p. 551

Languages

Learn About Hmong, p. 486

Reading/Literature

Dia's Story Cloth, pp. 486–489
Discussing the National News, p. 513
My Mexico—México mío, p. 554
Angel Falls: A South American Journey, p. 554
Journey Through the Northern Rainforest, p. 554

Social Studies

Reach All Learners

Use these activities to help individualize your instruction. Each activity has been developed to address a different level or type of learner.

English as a Second Language

15 minutes a day

Materials
- notebook paper
- textbook
- pens or pencils

WRITE PERSONAL RESPONSES Have students who are acquiring English write personal responses to the issues discussed in Unit 7.

- Prepare students by asking them to set aside a few pages in a notebook for personal responses to Unit 7.
- Have students read or review the lessons of the unit and take notes on issues that relate in some way to their own experiences.
- Invite students to write a paragraph explaining their responses to one of the issues they selected. Challenge them to use vocabulary from the unit.
- Allow students to meet with a partner to proofread each other's writing.
- Prompt volunteers to share their responses with the class.

Below-Level Learners

30 minutes for 3 days

Materials
- paper
- pencils
- scissors
- sample newspaper front page

PREPARE A FRONT PAGE Have students work in groups to prepare the front page of a newspaper, based on the issues in Unit 7.

- Organize students into groups, and ask them to identify key issues in the unit.
- Direct each student in the group to prepare a short news article, complete with a headline and an illustration with a caption, about one of the issues in the unit.
- When students have written their articles, provide students with a sample newspaper front page. Have the group lay out their own newspaper front page, using their articles and images. Encourage students to name their newspaper.
- Ask students to share their completed pages with the class.

Advanced Learners

45 minutes for 2 days

Materials
- notebook paper
- pens or markers
- textbook

ACT OUT A SUMMIT MEETING Have students work in groups to role play a meeting in which they discuss issues raised in Unit 7.

- Organize students into groups of three. Assign one person in each group to represent the United States, Mexico, or Canada.
- Have students who represent the same country leave their original groups and meet together. Instruct them to review Unit 7 for information about the country they represent.
- Direct students to return to their original groups and to participate in a round-table discussion of the problems their country faces.
- Ask each group to summarize its discussion for the class.

Assessment Options

The Assessment Program gives all learners many opportunities to show what they know and can do. It also provides ongoing information about each student's understanding of social studies.

Formal Assessment

- **LESSON REVIEWS,** at ends of lessons
- **CHAPTER REVIEWS AND TEST PREPARATION,** pp. 520–521, pp. 548–549
- **CHAPTER TESTS**
  Assessment Program, pp. 109–112, pp. 113–116
- **UNIT REVIEW AND TEST PREPARATION,** pp. 552–553
- **UNIT ASSESSMENT**
  STANDARD TEST,
  Assessment Program, pp. 117–123
  INDIVIDUAL PERFORMANCE TASK,
  Assessment Program, p. 124
  GROUP PERFORMANCE TASK,
  Assessment Program, p. 125

Student Self-Evaluation

- **ANALYZE PRIMARY SOURCES AND VISUALS** within lessons of Pupil Book
- **GEOGRAPHY THEME QUESTIONS** within lessons of Pupil Book
- **INDIVIDUAL END-OF-PROJECT SUMMARY** Assessment Program, p. viii
- **GROUP END-OF-PROJECT CHECKLIST** Assessment Program, p. ix
- **INDIVIDUAL END-OF-UNIT CHECKLIST** Assessment Program, p. x

Informal Assessment

- **ANALYZE THE LITERATURE,** p. 489
- **REVIEW QUESTIONS,** throughout lessons
- **EXAMINE PRIMARY SOURCES,** pp. 518–519
- **SOCIAL STUDIES SKILLS CHECKLIST** Assessment Program, p. iv

- **SKILLS**
  Practice the Skill, pp. 499, 517, 535, 546
  Apply What You Learned, pp. 499, 517, 535, 547

Performance Assessment

- **PERFORMANCE ACTIVITY** in Lesson Reviews
- **UNIT ACTIVITIES,** p. 554
- **COMPLETE THE UNIT PROJECT,** p. 554
- **INDIVIDUAL PERFORMANCE TASK** Assessment Program, p. 124
- **GROUP PERFORMANCE TASK** Assessment Program, p. 125

Portfolio Assessment

STUDENT-SELECTED ITEMS MAY INCLUDE:
- **THINK AND WRITE,** p. 520, 548
- **UNIT ACTIVITIES,** p. 554
- **COMPLETE THE UNIT PROJECT,** p. 554

TEACHER-SELECTED ITEMS MAY INCLUDE:
- **UNIT ASSESSMENT** Assessment Program, pp. 117–123
- **PORTFOLIO SUMMARY** Assessment Program, p. xv
- **INDIVIDUAL END-OF-UNIT CHECKLIST** Assessment Program, p. x
- **GROUP END-OF-PROJECT CHECKLIST** Assessment Program, p. ix

Unit 7 Test

STANDARD TEST

7 Test

Name _____ Date _____

Part One: Test Your Understanding

MULTIPLE CHOICE (2 points each)

Directions Circle the letter of the best answer.

1 Today most immigrants into the United States come from countries in—
A Europe and Asia.
B Latin America and Europe.
C Asia and Australia.
D Latin America and Asia. *(circled)*

2 Today most immigrants enter the United States through—
F a train station.
G an airport. *(circled)*
H a ship's dock.
J a bus depot.

3 In recent years the number of people in the United States over the age of 65 has—
A grown steadily. *(circled)*
B fallen sharply.
C stayed about the same.
D declined only slightly.

4 Computers were first developed—
F during World War II. *(circled)*
G after the creation of the World Wide Web.
H before the development of air conditioning.
J during World War I.

5 The Internet was first developed for—
A research needs.
B military communication. *(circled)*
C personal shopping.
D financial transactions.

6 Why would a community want to find methods to reduce urban growth?
F to limit shopping opportunities for consumers
G to protect farmland from being sold and developed *(circled)*
H to provide more housing for workers in new industries
J to encourage the development of modern highway systems

7 States that received more seats in Congress because their populations grew between 1990 and 2000 were located—
A in the Northeast.
B in the Sun Belt. *(circled)*
C in the Northwest.
D in the Great Plains.

(continued)

Unit 7 Test   Assessment Program ▪ 117

STANDARD TEST

Name _____ Date _____

8 One result of responsible conservation in the United States is—
F the extinction of some types of wildlife.
G the presence of chemicals in the water supply.
H the creation of large amounts of trash.
J the increase of the American bald eagle population. *(circled)*

9 A person who works in a service job might—
A repair appliances or automobiles. *(circled)*
B build electronic equipment.
C work on a farm.
D work in a factory.

10 The first Native American to be elected president of Mexico was—
F Porfirio Díaz.
G Vicente Fox.
H Benito Juárez. *(circled)*
J Father Miguel Hidalgo.

11 For more than 70 years, the Partido Revolucionario (PRI) controlled—
A which people were elected to the Mexican Congress.
B railroads and factories in Mexico.
C Mexican farming and agriculture.
D which people were elected president of Mexico. *(circled)*

12 Which Mexican city is surrounded by the Federal District?
F Mexico City *(circled)*
G Monterrey
H Puebla
J the Sierra Madre

13 Except for El Salvador, every country in Central America has—
A a border on the Pacific Ocean.
B a border on the Caribbean Sea. *(circled)*
C active volcanoes.
D set aside 25 percent of its land for nature preserves.

14 Canada is located—
F west of the United States.
G east of the United States.
H north of the United States. *(circled)*
J south of the United States.

(continued)

118 ▪ Assessment Program   Unit 7 Test

STANDARD TEST

Name _____ Date _____

FILL IN THE BLANK (3 points each)

Directions Complete each sentence in the space provided.

15 A meeting that links people through electronic equipment is called a _____teleconference_____.

16 An automobile with a ___Global Positioning System___ uses receiver satellites to determine the vehicle's location.

17 The development of the ___microchip___ allowed computers to become smaller and less expensive.

18 The United States produces more ___manufactured___ goods than any other nation in the world.

19 The states that we today call ___Texas, Arizona, California, Colorado, New Mexico, and Utah___ were once a part of Mexico.

(continued)

Unit 7 Test   Assessment Program ▪ 119

STANDARD TEST

Name _____ Date _____

SHORT ANSWER (3 points each)

Directions Complete each statement in the space provided.

20 An invention that made life more comfortable and spurred population growth in the Sun Belt was ___air conditioning___.

21 A(n) ___ethnic group___ is a collection of people who share the same country, race, or culture.

22 When urban areas spread into land that was once used for farming, the result is called ___urban growth___.

23 Countries that have a ___free-trade agreement___, such as Canada, the United States, and Mexico, charge no taxes on goods they sell to each other.

24 Mexico City, located in the Mexican Plateau, is the world's largest ___metropolitan area___.

25 Central America contains fertile land on which crops such as ___Possible responses: bananas, sugarcane, coffee, corn, cotton, beans___ are grown.

26 Nations such as Puerto Rico and Canada are called ___commonwealth nations___ because they are united with another country.

27 Some scientists worry that the greenhouse effect could lead to ___Possible responses: rising temperatures, melting polar ice caps, flooding___.

28 Cuba has had a ___communist___ government since 1959.

(continued)

120 ▪ Assessment Program   Unit 7 Test

Unit 7 Test

STANDARD TEST

Name _____ Date _____

Part Two: Test Your Skills
USE A TIME ZONE MAP (10 points)

Directions Use the time zone map to answer the following questions.

Time Zone Map of North and Central America

29 When it is 11 A.M. in Saskatchewan, what time is it in Costa Rica?

The time would be the same, 11 A.M.

30 Find Alaska and Mexico City on the map. At 8 A.M. in Alaska, what time is it in

Mexico City? 11 A.M.

31 Name two countries that lie in more than one time zone.

Possible responses: Mexico, Canada, and the United States

32 What is the time difference between Mexico City and Boston? In which city is it

later? 1 hour; Boston

33 What generalization can you make about how time changes when a person

travels from south to north? The time does not change when a person travels
from south to north. It changes only when a person travels east or west.

(continued)

STANDARD TEST

Name _____ Date _____

Part Three: Apply What You Have Learned
34 CATEGORIZE AND DESCRIBE (10 points)

Some countries in North America, Central America and the Caribbean, and South America have had many types of government. Look at the types of government, the examples, and the details that are already shown in the chart. Choose the correct terms from the list below and write them in the blanks to complete the chart.

Governments in North America		
Type	**Democracy**	Commonwealth	**Communist Government**
Example	Haiti	Canada	Cuba
Details	a. has a history of military takeovers b. in 1990 elected Jean-Bertrand Aristide in a free election	a. has local self-government b. government headed by a prime minister	a. has been governed by both Spain and the United States b. government headed by Fidel Castro since 1959
	Costa Rica	Puerto Rico	
	a. government structure similar to the United States b. has three branches of government and a president elected for a four-year term	a. is a territory of the United States b. citizens hold United States citizenship	

Terms:
- is a territory of the United States
- government structure similar to the United States
- government headed by a prime minister
- has a history of military takeovers
- government headed by Fidel Castro since 1959
- Commonwealth
- Cuba
- Haiti

(continued)

STANDARD TEST

Name _____ Date _____

35 ESSAY (10 points)

British, French, and Native American traditions have brought both diversity and conflict to Canada's government. Write a paragraph that describes the Canadian model of self-government and compare it to the other examples of government you have read about in Unit 7.

Possible response: Canada, like other countries in North America, was

once governed entirely by European nations. Unlike countries such as the

United States and Mexico, Canada did not have a revolution to change its

government. Canada is politically independent, but it still has political ties

to Great Britain. Quebec attempted to secede from Canada. The territory

of Nunavut was created in 1999 and will be governed by the Inuit

tradition of consensus.

NOTES

Name _____ Date _____

Individual Performance Task

Advertisement

Write an advertisement for one of the types of companies described below. Your advertisement should contain information about why people should be interested in the company or service.

- A business that makes silicon chips for computers
- A company that sells farm equipment over the Internet
- A company that teaches businesses how to set up teleconferences
- A bank that specializes in international trade

Before you begin to create your advertisement, you may need more information about the type of company you will be promoting. You can look in the library or on the Internet for this information. Make up a creative name for your company and include eye-catching illustrations or design. Be sure that you provide factual information about the kind of product or service such a business would offer.

© Harcourt

Name _____ Date _____

Group Performance Task

Round-Table Discussion

Hold a round-table discussion with any historical figures you have read about in Unit 7. Choose six to eight historical people who worked to shape their country and who played an important role in their government. Be sure to have a broad selection of governments represented, with characters such as Father Miguel Hidalgo and Simón Bolívar. Find information about your character in your textbook, in the school library, or on the Internet. Then help write questions that a moderator can use to direct your discussion. Your round-table discussion should take 10 to 15 minutes.

© Harcourt

RUBRICS FOR SCORING

SCORING RUBRICS The rubrics below list the criteria for evaluating the tasks above. They also describe different levels of success in meeting those criteria.

INDIVIDUAL PERFORMANCE TASK

SCORE 4	SCORE 3	SCORE 2	SCORE 1
• Rich description is provided.	• Some description is provided.	• Little description is provided.	• No description is provided.
• Advertisement is well organized.	• Advertisement is somewhat well organized.	• Advertisement is poorly organized.	• Advertisement is not organized.
• Advertisement includes excellent designs or illustrations.	• Advertisement includes average designs or illustrations.	• Advertisement includes poor designs or illustrations.	• Advertisement includes designs or illustrations.
• Topic is very well researched.	• Topic is fairly well researched.	• Topic is minimally researched.	• Topic is not researched.

GROUP PERFORMANCE TASK

SCORE 4	SCORE 3	SCORE 2	SCORE 1
• Performance shows excellent creativity.	• Performance shows some creativity.	• Performance shows little creativity.	• Performance shows no creativity.
• Characters chosen are very relevant to discussion.	• Characters chosen are somewhat relevant to discussion.	• Characters chosen are minimally relevant to discussion.	• Characters chosen are not relevant to discussion.
• Discussion is historically accurate.	• Discussion is mostly historically accurate.	• Discussion is partially historically accurate.	• Discussion is not historically accurate.

Introduce the Unit

OBJECTIVES

- Use artifacts and primary sources to acquire information about the United States.
- Interpret information in visuals.

Access Prior Knowledge

Lead the class in a discussion about the changing global relations during the Cold War. Have students think about how those relations have changed over time.

Statue of Liberty, Liberty Island, New York

BACKGROUND

The Statue of Liberty The Statue of Liberty is one of the largest statues in the world. Lady Liberty, as it is sometimes called, holds in her left hand a tablet inscribed with the date of the Declaration of Independence. At her feet a broken shackle symbolizes the overthrow of tyranny. The statue was erected on Liberty Island in 1886.

BACKGROUND

The United States With the collapse of the Soviet Union in 1989, the United States became the world's sole remaining superpower. As such, the United States maintains an active role in foreign relations throughout the world.

UNIT 7

The United States and the World

" History and destiny have made America the leader of the world that would be free. "

—Colin Powell, Chairman of the United States Joint Chiefs of Staff, in a speech, September 28, 1993

Preview the Content
Read the title and the Big Idea for each lesson. Then write a short paragraph for each lesson, telling what you think it is about.

Preview the Vocabulary
Suffixes A suffix is a word part that is added to the end of a root word. Use the root words and suffixes in the chart below to learn the meaning of each vocabulary word.

SUFFIX	ROOT WORD	VOCABULARY WORD	POSSIBLE MEANING
-ity	responsible	responsibility	
-ism	patriot	patriotism	

Unit 7 ■ 483

Preview the Unit

OBJECTIVES

- Interpret information in data-bases and visuals.
- Use appropriate mathematical skills to interpret social studies information such as maps and graphs.

Access Prior Knowledge

Have students describe what they have already learned about global relations in the twentieth century.

Visual Learning

Map Have students examine the map and locate the United States, Canada, and Mexico.

Q **What are the capitals of the United States, Canada, and Mexico?**

A Washington, D.C.; Ottawa; and Mexico City

Story Line To help students prepare for their reading, have them work in pairs to ask and answer questions about the story line. For example, a student might ask: *What industry employs more people than any other?* the service industry

Story Line Illustrations Ask students to speculate about the significance of the events shown on the story line.

- The United States is home to people from all over the world.
- Today more people in the United States work in the service industry than any other field.
- In the twenty-first century, Mexico City became one of the largest metropolitan areas in the world.
- Jean-Bertrand Aristide becomes Haiti's first elected president.
- South American General Simón Bolívar fought for independence for many Latin American countries.
- The St. Lawrence Seaway allows ships to travel from the Atlantic Ocean to the Great Lakes.

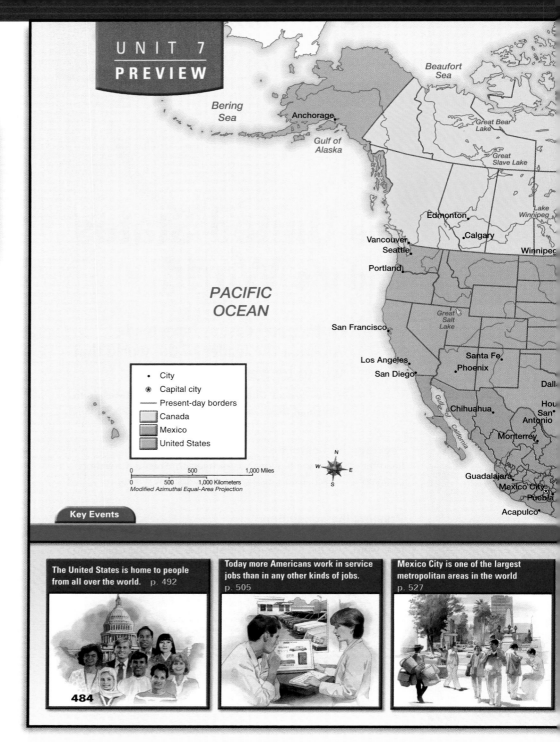

UNIT 7 PREVIEW

Key Events

- City
- ⊛ Capital city
- — Present-day borders
- Canada
- Mexico
- United States

0   500   1,000 Miles
0   500   1,000 Kilometers
Modified Azimuthal Equal-Area Projection

The United States is home to people from all over the world. p. 492

Today more Americans work in service jobs than in any other kinds of jobs. p. 505

Mexico City is one of the largest metropolitan areas in the world p. 527

484

INTEGRATE LANGUAGE ARTS

Prepare a Book Report
Suggest that each student select and read a nonfiction book about an event shown. Students can use the information gathered to write a short report that focuses on changes that occurred in the United States, Canada, or Mexico.

United States Trading Partners, Western Hemisphere

Bar graph showing Total Amount of Exports and Imports (in millions) by Country:

- Canada: ~400,000
- Mexico: ~245,000
- Brazil: (small)
- Venezuela: (small)
- Colombia: (small)
- Dominican Republic: (small)
- Argentina: (small)

Source: Bureau of the Census, U.S. Department of Commerce

North America

Baffin Bay
Labrador Sea
Hudson Bay
Quebec
Montreal
Ottawa
Toronto
Boston
Detroit
Chicago
New York
Philadelphia
Washington, D.C.
St. Louis
Atlanta
Charleston
New Orleans
Orlando
Gulf of Mexico
Miami
Merida
Caribbean Sea
ATLANTIC OCEAN

Jean-Bertrand Aristide becomes Haiti's president. p. 533

Simón Bolívar helps win independence for many present-day Latin American countries. p. 538

The St. Lawrence Seaway allows ships to travel from the Atlantic Ocean to the Great Lakes. p. 545

485

Visual Learning

Bar Graph Have students examine the bar graph. Pose such questions as the following:
- *What does this bar graph show?* It shows the United States' trading partners in the Western Hemisphere.
- *According to the graph, which country is America's most important trading partner?* Canada

Make Connections

Link Bar Graph and Map Ask students to use the information presented in the bar graph and map to draw conclusions about physical proximity and trade relationship.

Link Map and Key Events Have students identify the countries that were affected by each of the key events.
- People from all over the world have come to live in the United States. United States
- The service industry employs more people in the United States than does any other industry. United States
- Mexico City is now one of the largest metropolitan areas in the world. Mexico
- The St. Lawrence Seaway allows ships to travel between the Great Lakes and the Atlantic Ocean. Canada, United States
- Simón Bolívar won independence for the present-day countries in Latin America. Latin America
- Jean-Bertrand Aristide was elected as Haiti's president. Haiti

Start with a Story
PAGES 486–489

Summary

Many Hmong people have come to the United States from Asia. The embroidered story cloths tell the story of Dia Cha, who immigrated to the United States when she was fifteen years old.

1 Motivate

Set the Purpose

People have different ways of recording their history. For the Hmong, story cloths show important things in their history and culture.

Access Prior Knowledge

Ask students to share what they know about the countries in Asia.

READING SOCIAL STUDIES

Personal Response Encourage students to ask questions about the text. After they have read the text, have them write one question about something in the text they did not understand or were curious about. As a class, work together to answer the students' questions.

● USE READING AND VOCABULARY TRANSPARENCY 7-1.

7-1 TRANSPARENCY

START with a STORY

Dia's Story Cloth
The Hmong People's Journey of Freedom

by Dia Cha
stitched by Chue and Nhia Thao Cha

This hand-embroidered story cloth tells the story of the Hmong and their long journey from Laos to the United States. The name *Hmong* means "free people."

People from all over the world have come to live in the United States, and the freedoms and economic opportunities offered by our country continue to attract newcomers. Many immigrants today tell stories of how they came to the United States. Some tell their stories in letters. Others tell their stories in poems and songs. This immigrant story was inspired by a Hmong [MONG] hand-sewn story cloth. Hmong needleworkers sew pictures on cloth, using no patterns or measurements, to remember their past. The story cloth on these pages tells the story of how Dia Cha [DEE·ah CHAY] and her family left Asia, to come to the United States in 1979.

WORD WORK

Vocabulary Chart Ask students to make a list of unfamiliar words as they read. Encourage students to write down what they think the words mean based on the context. When they have finished reading, have them look up the definitions of the words in the dictionary, correcting their definitions if necessary.

Vocabulary Chart	
Word	Definition

INTEGRATE LANGUAGES

Learn About Hmong
Explain to students that the Hmong language has eight different tones. The tones indicate the meaning of a word. Tell students that the very last letter of a word tells what tone the word has.

Only 15 years old when she arrived in the United States, Dia Cha found life in America very different from life in Laos.

When my people first arrived in America, most didn't speak or write English. Many families had sponsors, who picked us up at the airport.

Everything about life in America was different for the Hmong.

I was 15 years old when I came to this country. I'd never been to school, so I had to start everything from scratch. They wanted to put me in high school, but I didn't know anything. Then they wanted to put me in adult school, but the teachers said I was too young.

Shoulder baskets (left) are made in adult and child sizes for carrying crops and other items. The stool, gourd water jar, and bamboo table (right) are like those found in many Hmong households.

2 Teach

Read and Respond

Understand the Story Challenge students to imagine that they have immigrated to a country where they do not speak the language. Ask students to describe their feelings. Some students in the class may be immigrants to the United States and may have gone through this experience. Encourage them to share their stories with the class.

Q What are some of the challenges new immigrants face in the United States?

A They may not speak English. They need to find jobs and a place to live. They may have very little money.

Visual Learning

Illustration Explain to students that the story cloth made by Chue and Nhia Thao Cha is shown in its entirety on page 486. Sections of the story cloth are on pages 487–488. Ask students to study the scene shown on page 487. Use the following question to begin a discussion about the story cloth.

- How did Dia Cha's family get to the United States? by airplane

AUDIOTEXT

Text of this story can be found on the Unit 7 AUDIOTEXT.

BACKGROUND

The Hmong The Hmong are an Asian ethnic group that live mostly in China and Southeast Asia. Only 300,000 to 600,000 live in the countries of Vietnam, Laos, and Thailand, whereas 8 million live in southern China. Hmong immigrants have settled in Australia, Canada, France, and the United States.

Read and Respond

Understand the Story Ask students to think about how Dia Cha's story may inspire other immigrants.

Civics and Government Explain to students that most of the Hmong that immigrated to the United States were refugees from the Vietnam War. They were displaced from their homes during the war and the United States became a new home to more than 110,000 of them. They settled primarily in California, Minnesota, and Wisconsin.

Visual Learning

Illustration Ask students to examine the scene shown on page 488. Discuss with students what it shows about life in Laos. Ask students to list some of the differences between life in Laos and life in the United States.

3 Close

Summarize the Reading

- The Hmong people use story cloths to tell about their history and culture.
- Dia Cha is an immigrant from Laos who came to the United States.

READING SOCIAL STUDIES

Personal Response Have students use reference materials to help answer the questions. Then ask them to write a summary about what they learned.

● USE READING AND VOCABULARY TRANSPARENCY 7-1.

7-1 TRANSPARENCY

The Hmong are known for their beautiful needlework, which is called *pa'ndau* (pan•DOW), or "flower cloth." Each design follows a theme. Those shown above, from left to right, are called "lightning", "snail house," and "frog legs."

Finally, I started high school. Thirteen years later, I received my master's degree from Northern Arizona University. I went back to Laos as an anthropologist in 1992 to work with Hmong and Lao women in the refugee camps in Thailand.

This story cloth reminds me of the history of my family and of my people. Some of the memories it brings are good, and some are bad. But it is important for me to remember everything the Hmong have been through.

Dia Cha believes that each memory sewn into the story cloth is important. This part of the story cloth shows Cha's home in Laos.

INTEGRATE ART

Sketch a Story Cloth
Ask students to draw a story cloth depicting some event or events in their life. Suggest they choose a special event. Tell them to study the story cloths in the lesson for ideas. Then have them draw their story on a piece of paper. Ask for volunteers to show their story cloths to the class.

The Hmong's heavily embroidered clothes set them apart from neighboring peoples in Asia. Hmong clothes sometimes combine green, pink, black, dark blue, and white, as seen in the child's jacket and sash above.

Hmong women in America continue to stitch new story cloths. We all have vivid memories about our lives and culture and history. The story cloth is a bridge to all the generations before us. When I show the story cloth to my niece and nephew, who were both born here in the United States, I point to different pictures and tell them that this is what it was like.

Analyze the Literature

❶ What is the purpose of a Hmong story cloth?

❷ Why do you think many people feel it is important to remember their past?

READ A BOOK

START THE UNIT PROJECT

A Cultural Fair With your classmates, hold a cultural fair. As you read the unit, take notes about the different cultures discussed. Your notes will help you decide what to include in your cultural fair.

USE TECHNOLOGY

 Visit The Learning Site at **www.harcourtschool.com** for additional activities, primary sources, and other resources to use in this unit.

Unit 7 ■ 489

Read a Book

Students may enjoy reading these leveled Independent Readers. Additional books are listed on pages 483D of this Teacher's Edition.

Easy *A Certain Courage* by Renee Skelton. Students learn how students, with the help of federal marshals, integrated Central High School in Little Rock, Arkansas.

Average *The Berlin Airlift* by Heather Miller. This book explains how the United States dropped supplies into the blockaded city of West Berlin following World War II.

Challenging *The Surprising Mr. Birdseye* by Roberta Ann Cruise. Students can read about Clarence Birdseye, the man best known for inventing the process for making frozen foods.

Start the Unit Project

Hint Suggest that students use an outline to help them organize their notes about the different cultures in the unit.

Use Technology

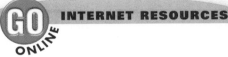

Go to **www.harcourtschool.com** to view Internet resources for this unit.

Go to **www.harcourtschool.com** for the latest news in a student-friendly format.

Analyze the Literature
Answers

❶ Hmong story cloths tell stories of the past.

❷ People feel it is important to remember their past because they want to stay connected to their family, culture, and history.

Chapter 13 Planning Guide The United States Today

Introducing the Chapter, pp. 490–491

LESSON	PACING	OBJECTIVES	VOCABULARY
Introduce the Chapter pp. 490–491	1 Day	■ Interpret information in visuals. ■ Use critical-thinking skills to organize and analyze information.	**Word Work:** Preview Vocabulary, p. 491
1 The American People Today pp. 492–497	2 Days	■ Explain the reasons for population growth in the United States. ■ Analyze cultural and ethnic diversity within the United States. ■ Explain how cultural differences affect life in the United States. ■ Describe the influence of technology on the way people in the United States live and work.	**Sun Belt** **ethnic group** **Internet** **teleconference** **Word Work:** Prefixes, p. 492
CHART AND GRAPH SKILLS **Use a Cartogram** pp. 498–499	1 Day	■ Use diagrams and maps to collect, analyze, and interpret data. ■ Apply critical-thinking skills to organize and use information from diagrams and maps.	**cartogram** **Word Work:** Word Origins, p. 498
2 The Challenges of Growth pp. 500–503	1 Day	■ Analyze the effects of the growth of the American population. ■ Analyze environmental challenges that result from population growth in the United States.	**rapid-transit system**
3 The American Economy pp. 504–509	2 Days	■ Identify how the American economy has changed in recent years. ■ Explain how international trade has affected the United States. ■ Describe how the free enterprise system works in the United States.	**diverse economy** **high-tech** **Information Age** **e-commerce** **interdependent** **international trade** **free-trade** **agreement** **global economy** **Word Work:** Historical Context, p. 504

READING	INTEGRATE LEARNING	REACH ALL LEARNERS	RESOURCES
Focus Skill **Fact and Opinion,** p. 491			
Focus Skill **Fact and Opinion,** p. 492 Reading Social Studies: **Predictions,** p. 493 Reading Social Studies: **Summarize,** p. 495 Reading Social Studies: **Predictions Responses,** p. 497	**Mathematics** **Figuring Percentages,** p. 494 **Language Arts** **Descriptive Writing,** p. 495 **Technology** **Discussion,** p. 496	**Advanced Learners,** p. 493 **Extend and Enrich,** p. 496 **Reteach the Lesson,** p. 497	**Activity Book,** pp. 124–125 **Reading and Vocabulary Transparency 7-2** Internet Resources
		Extend and Enrich, p. 499 **Reteach the Skill,** p. 499	**Activity Book,** pp. 126–127 **Skill Transparencies 7-1A and 7-1B**
Reading Social Studies: **Graphic Organizer,** p. 501 Reading Social Studies: **Create Mental Images,** p. 501 Reading Social Studies: **Graphic Organizer Responses,** p. 502	**Language Arts** **Write a Report,** p. 502	**English as a Second Language,** p. 500 **Extend and Enrich,** p. 503 **Reteach the Lesson,** p. 503	**Activity Book,** p. 128 **Reading and Vocabulary Transparency 7-3**
Reading Social Studies: **Study Questions,** p. 505 Reading Social Studies: **Read Aloud,** p. 505 Reading Social Studies: **Study Questions Responses,** p. 508		**Below-Level Learners,** p. 504 **Advanced Learners,** p. 507 **Extend and Enrich,** p. 508 **Reteach the Lesson,** p. 509	**Activity Book,** p. 129 **Reading and Vocabulary Transparency 7-4** Internet Resources

LESSON	PACING	OBJECTIVES	VOCABULARY
4 Government and the People pp. 510–515	2 Days	■ Identify the roles of the federal government. ■ Compare and contrast the responsibilities of state and federal governments. ■ Describe the duties and responsibilities of citizens. ■ Explain the importance of patriotism and good citizenship.	**responsibility** **register** **informed citizen** **jury** **volunteer** **patriotism** **Word Work:** Suffixes, p. 510
CITIZENSHIP SKILLS **Identify Political Symbols** pp. 516–517	1 Day	■ Identify important political symbols that represent American beliefs and principles. ■ Explain how political symbols contribute to our national identity.	
EXAMINE PRIMARY SOURCES **Political Buttons** pp. 518–519	1 Day	■ Identify political buttons as an effective campaigning technique. ■ Compare and contrast the effectiveness of examples of political memorabilia from our nation's past.	
Chapter Review and Test Preparation pp. 520–521	1 Day		

READING	INTEGRATE LEARNING	REACH ALL LEARNERS	RESOURCES
Reading Social Studies: K-W-L Chart, p. 511 **Reading Social Studies: K-W-L Chart Responses,** p. 515	**Reading** **Discussing the National News,** p. 513 **Language Arts** **Write a Letter,** p. 514	**English as a Second Language,** p. 510 **Advanced Learners,** p. 511 **Kinesthetic Learners,** p. 512 **Extend and Enrich,** p. 514 **Reteach the Lesson,** p. 515	**Activity Book,** p. 130 ⬤ **Reading and Vocabulary Transparency 7-5** 🖥 Internet Resources
	Art **Make a Symbol,** p. 516	**Extend and Enrich,** p. 517 **Reteach the Skill,** p. 517	**Activity Book,** p. 131 ⬤ **Skill Transparency 7-2**
	Language Arts **Expressive Writing,** p. 518	**Extend and Enrich,** p. 519 **Reteach,** p. 519	🖥 Internet Resources
		Test Preparation, p. 520	**Activity Book,** pp. 132–133 ⬤ **Reading and Vocabulary Transparency 7-6** ✓ **Assessment Program, Chapter 13 Test,** pp. 109–112

Activity Book

Name _____ Date _____

The American People Today

Directions Choose two of the items shown. Write a paragraph explaining the effect that each item has had on life in the United States. Describe what life might be like without the item. Students' answers may vary; possible answers are given.

Cellular telephone—Effect: helps people stay connected; makes communications/

businesses move faster. Without: would be harder to reach people when they were

away from home or office. Personal computer—Effect: allows people to complete

many tasks, even run businesses from home; allows people to connect via Internet

and World Wide Web to sources of information around the world; allows instant

sharing of documents, images, and sounds via e-mail. Without: would have to

physically travel to accomplish many tasks (shopping, banking, researching); sharing

information would take longer. Air conditioner—Effect: spurred population and

economic growth and environmental change in the Sun Belt by making life there

more comfortable. Without: population of South would probably be much smaller;

population of West would probably not be fastest-growing in the United States.

(continued)

Name _____ Date _____

Directions Use the clues to complete the word puzzle. The letters in the outlined box will spell a word that describes a characteristic of the United States population.

Clues

❶ Many people who come to live in the United States are looking for _____ and opportunity.

❷ More than 1 million _____ came to the United States during each year of the 1990s.

❸ The United States population grows when more people are born and when more people _____ to this country.

❹ The Sun _____ stretches across the southern United States.

❺ Texas and _____ have the largest Hispanic populations.

❻ Currently, most people who come to live in the United States are from Latin American or _____ countries.

❼ Of the 20 percent of United States school children who do not speak English at home, most speak _____.

❽ A group of people from the same country, of the same race, or with the same culture is called a(n) _____ group.

❾ A decade is a period of ten _____.

```
¹F  R  E  E  D  O  M
    ²I  M  M  I  G  R  A  N  T  S
          ³M  O  V  E
          ⁴B  E  L  T
⁵C  A  L  I  F  O  R  N  I  A
                ⁶A  S  I  A  N
    ⁷S  P  A  N  I  S  H
              ⁸E  T  H  N  I  C
              ⁹Y  E  A  R  S
```

SKILL PRACTICE

Name _____ Date _____

CHART AND GRAPH SKILLS
Use a Cartogram

The cartogram below shows the population of North America.

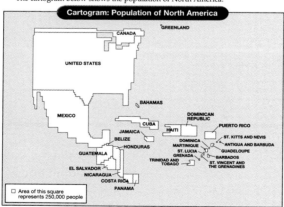

Cartogram: Population of North America

□ Area of this square represents 250,000 people

Directions Write a brief paragraph that defines the term *population cartogram*, and discusses appropriate and inappropriate uses of a population cartogram.

Definition: The size of each geographical area represents the size of the population

of the area rather than the physical size of the area.

Appropriate: to compare populations of various locations

Inappropriate: to determine distances between locations

(continued)

SKILL PRACTICE

Name _____ Date _____

Directions Use the population cartogram of North America on the previous page and a political map of North America from your textbook to answer the following questions. Remember that Puerto Rico is a territory of the United States.

❶ Which country has the largest population? United States

❷ What country has the second largest population? Mexico

❸ Which country has the greatest land area? Canada

❹ Which country has the smaller population, Cuba or Jamaica?
Jamaica

❺ Which is larger: the population of Canada or the population of Mexico?
Mexico

❻ Which country has the larger population, Costa Rica or Belize?
Costa Rica

❼ Which two countries have the largest populations? United States and Mexico

❽ What does the size of Mexico on the cartogram tell you about the population of
Mexico? that Mexico has a large population

❾ What does the size of Canada on the cartogram and on the map tell you about
the population of Canada? that Canada does not have a very large population

---

Name _____ Date _____

The Challenges of Growth

Directions The table shows six challenges that face a growing population. Write each solution from the list below in the appropriate box in the table. Some challenges will have more than one solution. Some solutions may help solve more than one challenge.

Solutions

add more bus routes

adjust number of seats in Congress to match current states' populations

build rapid-transit systems

pass laws to protect endangered species

improve public transportation

prevent building on some land

recycle glass, metal, plastic, and paper

use electronic highway signs

use computer-controlled traffic lights

pass laws to stop land and water pollution

improve technology

Challenges	Solutions
❶ Damage to wildlife	pass laws to protect endangered species; pass laws to stop land and water pollution; prevent building on some land
❷ Large amounts of trash	recycle glass, metal, plastic, and paper
❸ Demands on natural resources	pass laws to stop land and water pollution; recycle glass, metal, plastic, and paper; improve technology
❹ Keeping government fair	adjust number of seats in Congress to match current states' populations
❺ Roads jammed with cars and trucks	add more bus routes; build rapid-transit systems; use computer-controlled traffic lights; use electronic highway signs; improve public transportation

Use after reading Chapter 13, Lesson 2, pages 500–503.

© Harcourt

Name _____ Date _____

The American Economy

Directions Use the terms from the lesson to solve the crossword puzzle.

Across: 1 INFORMATIONAGE
FREEE TRADE AGREEMENT (down)
3 E-COMMERCE
4 DIVERSE
5 GLOBAL (down)
6 HIGH-TECH (down)
7 INTERNATIONALTRADE
8 INTERDEPENDENT

Across

❶ A period when people can find and share rapidly-growing knowledge

❸ Buying products on the Internet

❹ An economy that is not based on just one kind of industry

❼ Buying and selling between companies in more than one country

❽ Businesses that rely on each other for resources, products, or services

Down

❷ A promise between nations not to tax the products that they buy from or sell to each other

❺ An economy that includes businesses from around the world

❻ Businesses that design, produce, or use electronic equipment

© Harcourt

Use after reading Chapter 13, Lesson 3, pages 504–509.

Name _____ Date _____

Government and the People

Directions Complete the Web page below by filling in certain responsibilities of United States citizens. The home page on the left lists some constitutional rights. Use the items below to fill in the pop-up windows with citizens' matching responsibilities.

• Stay informed about local, state, and national events; respect the views of others

• Register and take part in local, state, and national elections

• Treat others fairly

• Be willing to serve on a jury

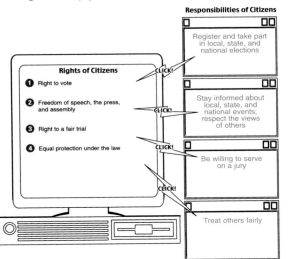

Rights of Citizens

❶ Right to vote

❷ Freedom of speech, the press, and assembly

❸ Right to a fair trial

❹ Equal protection under the law

CLICK!

Responsibilities of Citizens

Register and take part in local, state, and national elections

Stay informed about local, state, and national events; respect the views of others

Be willing to serve on a jury

Treat others fairly

© Harcourt

Use after reading Chapter 13, Lesson 4, pages 510–515.

Name _____ Date _____

CITIZENSHIP SKILLS
Identify Political Symbols

Directions Match each symbol below with the appropriate description. Write the letter of the description on the line next to the symbol. Some descriptions will be used more than once.

❶  _e_

❷  _a_

❸ _d_   ❻ _b_

❹  _f_   ❼ _c_

❺ _f_   ❽ _g_

a. United States government

b. Democratic party

c. United States Congress

d. Republican party

e. President of the United States

f. The United States of America

g. freedom

© Harcourt

Use after reading Chapter 13, Skill Lesson, pages 516–517.

Name _____ Date _____

Facts and Opinions About the United States

Directions Complete this graphic organizer by identifying facts and opinions about the United States.

THE POPULATION OF THE UNITED STATES

FACT	OPINION
More than 291 million people live in the United States.	→ Student answers will vary. Sample answer: The larger the population of the United States, the better.
Most immigrants come to the United States seeking freedom and a better way of life.	→ Student answers will vary. Sample answer: The United States is one of the best countries to live in.

THE UNITED STATES GOVERNMENT AND THE PEOPLE

FACT	OPINION
Citizens who feel strongly about an issue can contact their representative by making phone calls.	→ Student answers will vary. Sample answer: If you feel strongly about an issue, you should call your representative.
Today e-mail makes staying in touch with government leaders simpler than ever.	→ Student answers will vary. Sample answer: Because communicating with government leaders has become so easy, Americans should take a more active role in their government.

132 ▪ Activity Book   Use after reading Chapter 13, pages 490–519.

• CHAPTER •   Name _____ Date _____

13   Test Preparation

Directions Read each question and choose the best answer. Then fill in the circle for the answer you have chosen. Be sure to fill in the circle completely.

1 Today, from where do most immigrants to the United States come?
Ⓐ Asia and Europe
Ⓑ Africa and Europe
● Asia and Latin America
Ⓓ Africa and Latin America

2 How can a rapid-transit system prevent traffic jams?
● by providing people with alternate ways to travel
Ⓖ by adding traffic lights to highways
Ⓗ by adding more highways
Ⓙ by limiting the number of people who travel by train

3 Which is an example of a service job?
Ⓐ miner
● nurse
Ⓒ farmer
Ⓓ factory worker

4 In a free-enterprise economy, which is a result of an increased demand for a product?
● The price of the product will go up.
Ⓖ The product's price will be set by the government.
Ⓗ Fewer people will want to buy the product.
Ⓙ Fewer companies will want to sell the product.

5 What is the role of the federal government?
Ⓐ To organize the two main political parties
Ⓑ To oversee the work of the state governments
Ⓒ To stop local laws from conflicting with state laws
● To make and apply the laws that run the United States

Use after reading Chapter 13, pages 490–519.   Activity Book ▪ 133

Government Employees

_____
_____
_____
_____
_____

Elected Officials

_____
_____
_____
_____
_____

Experts in Economics

_____
_____
_____
_____
_____

Experts in Political Science

_____
_____
_____
_____
_____

Chapter 13 Assessment

CONTENT / VOCABULARY

13 Test

Part One: Test Your Understanding

MULTIPLE CHOICE (4 points each)

Directions Circle the letter of the best answer.

1 Four of every five people in the United States live in—
   A the Sun Belt.
   B metropolitan areas.
   C New York and Pennsylvania.
   D California and Texas.

2 The state that has the highest percentage of Hispanic residents is—
   F Texas.
   G Florida.
   H California.
   J New Mexico.

3 Why was the Internet created?
   A The University of Washington wanted to develop a database to keep better records of its students.
   B The Department of Defense established a computer network for military communications.
   C The Library of Congress needed a database to track its library collection.
   D The Department of Commerce wanted a computer program to help banks record credit card purchases.

4 A passenger transportation system that uses elevated or underground trains is called—
   F urban growth.
   G land use.
   H a rapid-transit system.
   J a rush-hour system.

5 Reusing old materials to create new products is called—
   A reducing materials.
   B recycling materials.
   C naturalizing materials.
   D rebranding materials.

6 Most residents of the United States today work in what kinds of jobs?
   F construction jobs
   G farming jobs
   H service jobs
   J factory jobs

(continued)

CONTENT / VOCABULARY

7 People in high-tech industries—
   A make up about four of every five workers.
   B work in banks or insurance companies.
   C are mainly government or transportation workers.
   D invent or build computers or electronic equipment.

8 Two countries that are interdependent—
   F trade very few products.
   G rely on each other for products or resources.
   H have unstable economic systems.
   J have similar natural resources.

9 Which of the following documents set up the federal system of government and protects the rights and freedoms of United States citizens?
   A the Declaration of Independence
   B the Articles of Confederation
   C the Constitution
   D the Emancipation Proclamation

10 In order to vote, United States citizens must—
   F pass a reading and citizenship test.
   G register to show they live where the voting is taking place.
   H serve on a jury at least two times.
   J volunteer to serve on an election campaign.

TRUE OR FALSE (4 points each)

Directions Indicate whether the following statements are true or false by writing *T* or *F* in the spaces provided.

11 __T__ People who belong to the same ethnic group share the same race, country, or culture.

12 __F__ Almost no schoolchildren in the United States today speak a language other than English.

13 __F__ People must usually travel great distances to attend teleconferences.

14 __F__ E-commerce has greatly decreased the number of goods and services available to American consumers.

15 __T__ The Speaker of the House of Representatives is always a member of the majority party.

(continued)

SKILLS

Part Two: Test Your Skills

IDENTIFY POLITICAL SYMBOLS (4 points each)

Directions Look at the image below to answer the following questions.

16 Does this image represent a small part of government or does it represent a larger government? The United States flag represents the entire United States government, not just a particular branch of the government.

17 Where have you seen this symbol? Possible responses: Flags are flown by individuals and federal buildings, such as post offices. Flags are also reproduced on coins, paper money, and official documents.

18 During what holidays would you be most likely to see this symbol displayed? Possible response: Independence Day, Veterans Day, Flag Day, and Memorial Day

19 What do the 13 stripes on the flag represent? What do the 50 stars represent? The stripes represent the 13 original colonies. The stars represent the 50 states.

20 Why do you think the flag is a good representation of the United States? Possible response: The 13 stripes represent the country's history. The pattern of stars shows that all the states come together in one national government.

(continued)

APPLICATION / WRITING

Part Three: Apply What You Have Learned

21 **PROBLEMS AND SOLUTIONS** (10 points)

Describe the cause of each problem listed below, and write a solution that has been used to help solve the problem. One cause is provided.

Problems of Growth	Cause	Solution
traffic jams	too many vehicles on highways and streets	Possible response: improved public transportation
environmental pollution	Possible response: Chemicals have gotten into the water supply.	Possible response: Harmful chemicals can be limited or banned to stop pollution.
too much trash	Possible response: Communities do not have enough space to dispose of garbage.	Possible response: recycling materials

22 **ESSAY** (10 points)

Today, the United States is part of a global economy in which countries trade goods around the world. Write a paragraph describing factors that increase trade among countries.

Possible response: Global trade is made possible by modern communication and transportation systems. Governments also must agree to allow the passage of goods between countries. Free-trade agreements that limit tariffs and taxes encourage international trade. Because resources can be unevenly divided, supply and demand can set up conditions that encourage trade between countries.

Introduce the Chapter

PAGES 490–491

OBJECTIVES

- Interpret information in visuals.
- Use critical thinking skills to organize and analyze information.

Access Prior Knowledge

Ask students if they have ever seen the residence of a famous person or national leader on television. What did these places tell them about the people who live there?

Visual Learning

Picture Have students look at the picture of the White House and describe what they see. Why has this image become a national symbol? Answers may vary, but should reflect that the White House is the center of American government.

Locate It Map Washington, D.C., is located on the eastern bank of the Potomac River and is bordered by Maryland and Virginia.

THE WHITE HOUSE

For over two hundred years, the White House has symbolized the executive branch. In 1800, President John Adams and his wife Abigail became the White House's first residents. Since then, the building has been home to 41 United States Presidents. On average, the White House receives hundreds of visitors a day.

LOCATE IT

MARYLAND

Washington, D.C.

VIRGINIA

White House

490 ▪ Unit 7

BACKGROUND

Picture In 1800, the United States government moved to Washington, D.C., from Philadelphia. President John Adams and his family moved into the unfinished mansion just a few months before leaving office. At the time the White House was a spectacular building in an isolated setting. Today the White House is surrounded by a bustling, developed area. The Adamses made the best of living in the new executive mansion, although it was difficult at first to host official social functions with only a handful of finished rooms.

BACKGROUND

Quotation After serving under George Washington as Vice President, John Adams (1735–1826) became the second President of the United States in 1797. His term ended in 1801, not long after he and his family had become the first occupants of the White House. Letters written between Adams and his wife, Abigail, have become important historical documents, revealing much about life and politics in the late 1700s.

· CHAPTER ·

13

The United States Today

66I pray Heaven to bestow the best of blessings on this house and all that shall hereafter inhabit it. 99

—John Adams, letter to Abigail Adams, November 2, 1800

⭐ Focus Skill — Fact and Opinion

A **fact** is a statement that can be proven to be true. An **opinion** is an individual's view of something that is shaped by that person's feelings.

As you read this chapter, be sure to do the following.

• Separate facts from opinions about the modern United States.

Read and Respond

Read aloud the title and the quotation. Have students discuss how the quotation from 1800 is connected to the title of this chapter.

Quotation Have a volunteer read the quotation aloud.

Q What does John Adams mean by wishing for "blessings" on the White House?

A Students might suggest that Adams wishes success for the nation and its leaders.

⭐ Focus Skill — Fact and Opinion

Have students complete a graphic organizer to show facts and opinions related to the topic of the chapter.

• A graphic organizer can be found on page 132 of the Activity Book.

• Remind students to read carefully.

• A completed graphic organizer appears on page 132 of the Activity Book, Teacher's Edition.

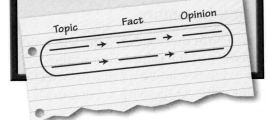

WORD WORK

Preview Vocabulary Have students use a three-column chart to list and define the lesson vocabulary terms. They can list the terms and definitions in the first two columns. Students should use the last column to make notes that will help them remember what the terms mean.

Term	Definition	Notes

MAKE IT RELEVANT

Discussion Topics You and your students might enjoy discussing these topics about the image of the United States in today's world.

■ What feature or characteristic of the United States is most impressive to you?

■ When people visit the United States for the first time, what impressions might they have of it?

OBJECTIVES

- Explain the reasons for population growth in the United States.
- Analyze cultural and ethnic diversity within the United States.
- Explain how cultural differences affect life in the United States.
- Describe the influence of technology on the way people in the United States live and work.

 Fact and Opinion
pp. 491, 492, 495, 497, 520

Vocabulary

SEE READING AND VOCABULARY TRANSPARENCY 7-2 OR THE WORD CARDS ON PP. V55–V56.

Sun Belt p. 493   **Internet** p. 496

ethnic group   **teleconference**
p. 494   p. 497

 When Minutes Count

Ask students to skim the lesson to find at least two facts about the population of the United States.

Quick Summary

This lesson discusses the growth and diversity of the population of the United States and explains how technology affects the way Americans live and work.

 Motivate

Set the Purpose

Big Idea Make sure that students understand the meaning of the word *diversity* as used in the Big Idea statement.

Access Prior Knowledge

Have students discuss what they have learned about why people came to the United States in the past.

FACT AND OPINION

As you read, look for facts and opinions about people's ways of life.

BIG IDEA
Technology and diversity have affected the way people in the United States live and work.

VOCABULARY

Sun Belt
ethnic group
Internet
teleconference

 FAST FACT Today about one of every ten people in the United States was born in another country.

The American People Today

People have been coming to the Americas since before history was recorded. Over time, the United States has become a nation of many cultures. The nation has changed in other ways, too.

A Growing Nation

More than 291 million people live in the United States today, and that number is rising fast. During the 1990s alone, the population of the United States grew by almost 33 million people—the largest ten-year increase in the country's history.

The population of the United States is growing for two reasons. More people are being born in the United States, and more people are moving to this country. People who are born in the United States or who have at least one parent who is a United States citizen are automatically citizens of our country.

Many immigrants have become naturalized citizens. To become a naturalized citizen, a person must have lived in the United States for at least five years (or three if married to a citizen). Then that person must apply for citizenship and pass a test to show that he or she understands United States history and government. Finally, the person must take part in a ceremony in which he or she promises to be loyal to the United States.

Many immigrants become citizens of the United States each year.

WORD WORK

Prefixes Instruct students to look through the lesson for vocabulary terms highlighted in yellow. After students locate the terms and read their definitions, have them identify the vocabulary terms that contain prefixes. Internet, teleconference Allow students to work in pairs to identify the meanings of the prefixes. Encourage them to predict the meanings before confirming them in a dictionary.

READING SKILL

Fact and Opinion Remind students that a fact is a statement that can be proven true. Explain that statements that include numbers or statistics are usually facts. Ask them to identify at least one fact on page 492. Possible facts: More than 281 million people live in the United States; during the 1990s, the population increased by almost 33 million people; and the 33 million increase was the largest 10-year increase in the United States ever.

The Sun Belt of the United States

Legend:
- Sunbelt region
- • Fast-growing city

0 200 400 Miles
0 200 400 Kilometers
Albers Equal-Area Projection

GEOGRAPHY THEME

Regions Many Americans are attracted to the warm and sunny weather of the Sun Belt.

What cities in Arizona are growing fast?

In the past, most immigrants came to the United States from Europe. Today, most immigrants come from countries in Asia and Latin America. Like immigrants in the past, they come seeking freedom and new opportunities for a better life. Many seek refuge from war, weak economies, and poor living conditions in their homelands.

Most new immigrants, like most other Americans, live in metropolitan areas. In fact, about four of every five people in the United States live in metropolitan areas. About one-third of all Americans live in metropolitan areas of more than 5 million people.

More than half of the American people live in the ten states with the greatest populations—California, Texas, New

York, Florida, Illinois, Pennsylvania, Ohio, Michigan, New Jersey, and Georgia. However, the population of every state is growing.

Although the population of every region of the United States is growing, different regions are growing at different rates. Much of the nation's growth has taken place in the **Sun Belt**, a wide area of the southern United States that has a mild climate all year. The Sun Belt stretches from the Atlantic coast to the Pacific coast. Places in the Sun Belt region began growing during World War II. One reason for this growth was the development of air conditioning.

Air conditioning was introduced in the early twentieth century. It was first used in movie theaters and railroad cars.

Chapter 13 ▪ 493

A Diverse Nation

Read and Respond

Culture and Society Point out that almost all people in the United States are descended from immigrants. Ask students to name ways that each ethnic group has contributed to the culture of the United States.

Culture and Society Using the information on page 494, ask students to make a bar graph that shows the breakdown of people in the United States. Ask students to rank the populations from largest to smallest based on ethnic background.

 Students might enjoy researching information about different areas of the United States. Have them visit The Learning Site at **www.harcourtschool.com.**

Culture and Society Explain to students that people who have moved to the United States from a country in Latin America are sometimes called Latinos. Then challenge them to explain the similarities and differences that may exist between Latinos from Brazil and Latinos from Costa Rica. Latinos from Brazil would speak Portuguese, and Latinos from Costa Rica would speak Spanish. Both may speak English.

Culture and Society Tell students that the cultural diversity of the United States influences all of its citizens. Peer groups in schools or communities may be made up of people from many different backgrounds with many unique perspectives.

Q How can diverse peer groups influence personal development?

A Diverse groups can teach people about different customs and new ways to see the world.

Immigrants who share a culture sometimes choose to settle in the same neighborhood. One example of this is Chinatown in San Francisco, California.

In the 1920s, the first fully air-conditioned office building, the Milam Building in San Antonio, Texas, was constructed. As air conditioning spread across the Sun Belt in the 1950s, it helped make living there more comfortable. Millions of people moved to the region, built homes and started businesses, and forever changed the environment.

The Sun Belt stretches across parts of both the South and the West. In recent years, both of these regions have grown faster than other regions of the United States. The West is the fastest-growing region of the United States, but the South has the largest population of any region. Almost 100 million people live in states in the South.

REVIEW How did the use of air-conditioning change the Sun Belt? Millions of people moved to the region and built homes and businesses.

A Diverse Nation

The population of the United States is growing quickly. At the same time, the United States is becoming a more diverse nation. In fact, the United States has one of the world's most diverse populations in terms of ancestry. Today about 210 million Americans are of European background. Almost 35 million are African Americans, and more than 10 million are of Asian background. About two and a half million people in the United States are Native Americans.

Hispanic Americans make up the fastest-growing ethnic

494 ■ Unit 7

group in the nation. An **ethnic group** is a group of people from the same country, of the same race, or with a shared culture. A little more than 1 in 10 Americans, or about 35 million people, are of Hispanic descent. More than three-fourths of them live in the South or West. California and Texas have the largest Hispanic populations, but the state with the highest percentage of Hispanic residents is New Mexico. In New Mexico more than 4 of every 10 people are of Hispanic background.

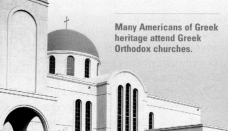

Many Americans of Greek heritage attend Greek Orthodox churches.

MAKE IT RELEVANT

In Your Community Talk with students about the ethnic diversity in their community. What ethnic groups are represented? Have a volunteer make a list of the groups mentioned in discussion. Encourage students to interview members of their families or neighbors for anecdotes that answer the questions "What ethnic groups are in our community?" and "What customs did they bring with them?"

INTEGRATE MATHEMATICS

Figuring Percentages Use the population information on page 494, and review with students how to figure percentages. Ask students to find the percentage of the United States population that is descended from European Americans, Asian Americans, Hispanic Americans, African Americans, and Native Americans. 72%, 3%, 12%, 12%, and 1%, respectively

Most people in the United States are either immigrants or descendants of immigrants. Some people's families have been living in the United States for hundreds of years. Others have come to live in this country only recently. Instead of arriving on ships, as immigrants often did in the past, most immigrants today arrive by plane at one of the nation's international airports.

Some people who have immigrated to this country still speak the language of the country in which they were born. So do some of their descendants. In fact, about one-fifth of all schoolchildren in the United States today speak a language other than English at home. Most of them speak Spanish.

Some Americans continue to dress in the styles of their homelands or take part in customs, celebrations, or traditions that are unique to their culture. Cultural differences among Americans can also be seen in the kinds of music people listen to, the foods they eat, and the religious groups they belong to.

Having so many different cultures has made the United States a more diverse place. At the same time, it has given Americans a richer life. Over the years, people from each culture have contributed to American life. Cultural differences help explain why people in the United States often seem so different from one another in so many ways.

Although Americans are different from one another, they also have much in common. Americans share a deep belief in individual rights. Most Americans support the government, which is based on representation and the consent of the people. Americans also value our economic system, which supports free enterprise and the ideas of competition, open opportunity, and private property. These common beliefs help unite Americans.

REVIEW In what ways can one see cultural differences among Americans?

🔲 FACT AND OPINION

• HERITAGE •

Epiphany

For many Hispanic families in the United States, the Christmas season does not end on December 25. It continues with Epiphany, or Three Kings Day, which is celebrated on January 6. According to tradition, 12 days after the birth of Jesus, the Three Kings, or Wise Men, arrived to present the newborn child with gifts. The night before Epiphany, many Hispanic children leave snacks out for the Kings. The children hope to find candy and presents waiting for them the next day. Other Epiphany traditions include eating special ring-shaped cakes called roscones and attending Three Kings Day parades.

Read and Respond

Culture and Society Point out to students that the United States celebrates its diversity as one of its great strengths. The tragedy of the World Trade Center attack in September 2001 reminded many Americans that we are of every race, religion, and ethnicity. In a speech Mayor Rudolph Giuliani of New York City said, "Our diversity has always been our greatest source of strength. It's the thing that renews us and revives us in every generation— our openness to new people from all over the world. . . We are defined as Americans by our beliefs—not by our ethnic origins, our race or our religion."

Q **What beliefs do most Americans share?**

A beliefs in individual rights, representative government, and economic freedom

• HERITAGE •

Epiphany

Discuss Epiphany with students. Ask students to describe special holidays or events they celebrate in the month of December. Point out that some December celebrations, such as Christmas, Hanukkah, and Kwanzaa, are celebrated primarily by people of a certain religious or ethnic background. Encourage students to describe holiday traditions that are unique to their cultural background.

INTEGRATE LANGUAGE ARTS

Descriptive Writing
Invite students to research or to take part in an event that involves people from different ethnic groups, and to write about their experience. Students might attend an event at a cultural center or attend a heritage parade. They should take notes and then use them to write descriptions of the event and their experiences.

READING SOCIAL STUDIES

Summarizing Remind students that a summary includes only the main ideas or key points of a passage. Have students work in pairs to identify the main idea of each paragraph in the section and to use the main ideas to write a summary. Challenge students to use their own words.

Changing Ways of Life

Read and Respond

Culture and Society Ask students to list the kinds of technology that are available to people every day. *cellular phones, personal computers, handheld computers, and the Internet* In discussion, ask students to explain how improvements made in the field of communication have benefited individuals and society.

• SCIENCE AND TECHNOLOGY •

The Microchip

Review the discussion of the microchip with students. Ask them to identify a machine they have recently used that includes a microchip.

Q **How do you think a technological development such as the microchip has affected the economy of the United States?**

A Possible answer: microchips allow workers to work more efficiently and encourage the development of new consumer products, helping the economy.

Read and Respond

Economics Point out that the Internet helps businesses, customers, and ordinary people communicate in new ways. Challenge students to identify other communications technologies that influenced economic activity in the United States in the past.

3 Close

Summarize Key Content

- The population of the United States has grown substantially, in part because of immigration.
- The United States population is becoming more diverse.
- Technology has changed the way Americans live, communicate, and work.

Changing Ways of Life

As the United States becomes more diverse, it is changing in other ways, too. Today many Americans use microwave ovens, play video games, and listen to music on compact discs. Other advances in technology, such as computers, cellular telephones, and facsimile, or fax, machines, also affect how people live and communicate. These machines also allow people to conduct business faster.

Computers first came into widespread use after World War II. At that time computers were so big that just one would fill an entire room. Then, in 1958, scientists working independently in Texas and California each invented the silicon chip. This tiny device can now store millions of bits of computer information. Silicon chips have allowed businesses to make smaller, faster, and cheaper computers.

Today millions of computers are used in businesses and in homes and schools throughout the world. Many people even run their own businesses from their homes with the use of the Internet. The **Internet** is a network that links computers around the world for the exchange of information.

The United States Department of Defense set up a computer network in the late 1960s for military communications. The network changed and grew over the years. In 1992, the World Wide Web came into use. It allows millions of people to send and receive electronic mail, or e-mail, as well as electronic documents, pictures, and sounds.

• SCIENCE AND TECHNOLOGY •

The Microchip

The integrated circuit, or microchip, was one of the twentieth century's greatest inventions. Introduced in 1959, the microchip helped reduce the size of all types of electronic machines. It did so by letting hundreds of electronic parts be put on a single silicon chip half the size of a paper clip. Starting in the early 1970s, microchips were used to run handheld calculators. Today microchips are used in everything from personal computers to space satellites.

Today many computers like the one above are very compact. Early computers, however, were bulky machines (below). They often filled an entire room.

STUDY/RESEARCH SKILLS

Using the Internet Encourage students to use the Internet to research space and oceanic exploration. Discuss how technology enables the exploration of these frontiers. Ask students to review earlier discussions of the western frontier in Unit 2. Then have each student write a short paragraph comparing these new frontiers to the western frontier.

EXTEND AND ENRICH

Journal Entry Direct students to write a journal entry that discusses how their own community reflects the information in the lesson. For example, has their community grown in the last decade? Is their community ethnically diverse? Has technology changed the way people live or do business? Encourage students to visit the library or the local chamber of commerce or to consult local newspapers. Lead a discussion in which students share their findings.

Using the Internet, people can shop for clothing, cars, or any other item online. They can check on bank accounts, transfer money, pay bills, make reservations, and do many other tasks. They can also reach government agencies, libraries, and other online sites to research almost any subject.

Another change in people's lives is the ability to travel much faster from one place to another. Each year more than 700 million people travel on jet airplanes. In just a few hours they can travel from city to city or halfway around the world to visit family members. People also travel to attend business meetings. However, people do not have to travel at all to communicate directly with others. They can hold a teleconference—a conference, or meeting, that uses electronic machines to connect people. Having a teleconference allows people from all over the world to

Satellites (left) can be used to take pictures of the Earth from space. Scientists study these images for many purposes, such as weather research.

communicate directly with one another by turning on a computer or dialing a telephone.

Advances in technology have changed people's lives in other ways, too. Doctors can use tiny video cameras attached to plastic tubes to see inside a person. Eye doctors now use laser beams to help correct eye problems. The way some automobile drivers find directions has changed, too. Today, automobiles can be equipped with a Global Positioning System (GPS) receiver. These receivers use satellites to help find a driver's location anywhere on Earth. Drivers can then receive directions through the GPS.

REVIEW **What is the Internet?** A network that links computers around the world for the exchange of information.

LESSON 1
REVIEW

Focus Skill **FACT AND OPINION** The United States has one of the world's most diverse populations in terms of ancestry. Is this statement a fact or an opinion? How do you know?

❶ **BIG IDEA** How have technology and diversity affected the way Americans live and work?

❷ **VOCABULARY** Write a description of the **Sun Belt.**

❸ **SCIENCE AND TECHNOLOGY** How have advances in technology helped people?

❹ **CRITICAL THINKING—Analyze** Compare and contrast today's immigrant groups and immigrant groups from 100 years ago.

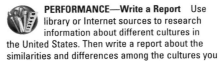
PERFORMANCE—Write a Report Use library or Internet sources to research information about different cultures in the United States. Then write a report about the similarities and differences among the cultures you researched.

Chapter 13 ▪ 497

RETEACH THE LESSON

Graphic Organizer Offer students the following chart. Have students fill in each section with one fact or idea that they learned in each subsection. Remind students that they may use the book to find or confirm information.

A Growing Nation (p. 492)	A Diverse Nation (p. 494)	Changing Ways of Life (p. 496)
Much of America's population growth is in the Sun Belt.	The United States has a diverse ethnic population.	New technology has affected the way Americans communicate and do their work.

Predictions Invite students to check their written predictions. Then ask students to make general statements about the immigrant experience.

● USE READING AND VOCABULARY TRANSPARENCY 7-2. **7-2** TRANSPARENCY

Assess
Lesson 1 Review—Answers

 FACT AND OPINION Fact; official figures about the population can confirm the statement.

❶ **BIG IDEA** Diversity has given Americans a richer life as different cultures merge with American culture. Technology has made it easier to communicate, travel, and work.

❷ **VOCABULARY** The **Sun Belt** is a wide area of the southern United States, from the Atlantic coast to the Pacific coast, which is rapidly growing in population.

❸ **SCIENCE AND TECHNOLOGY** Advances in technology have improved communication and made many kinds of work easier.

❹ **CRITICAL THINKING—Analyze** One hundred years ago most immigrants arrived by boat; today most arrive on airplanes. As in the past, many of today's immigrants come to the United States to find freedom and start a new life.

Performance Assessment Guidelines Students' reports should include specific examples of similarities and differences among the cultures they researched.

ACTIVITY BOOK

Use ACTIVITY BOOK, pp. 124–125, to reinforce and extend student learning.

Skill Lesson

PAGES 498–499

OBJECTIVES

- Use diagrams and maps to collect, analyze, and interpret data.
- Apply critical thinking skills to organize and use information from diagrams and maps.

Vocabulary

cartogram p. 498

WORD CARDS

See pp. V55–V56.

1 Motivate

Why It Matters

Explain to students that a cartogram is one of many special tools that geographers use to present information about a place. Ask students what other visual tools they could use to show population. a table, a circle graph, a bar graph

SKILLS

Use a Cartogram

VOCABULARY
cartogram

▶ WHY IT MATTERS

One way to show the population of different places is to use a cartogram. A **cartogram** is a diagram that gives information about places by the size shown for each place. Knowing how to read a cartogram can help you quickly compare information about different places.

▶ WHAT YOU NEED TO KNOW

Some maps of the United States base the size of each state on its land area. With a cartogram, a state's size is based on a geographical statistic. On the cartogram on page 499, size is based on population. A population cartogram shows the states as their sizes would be if each

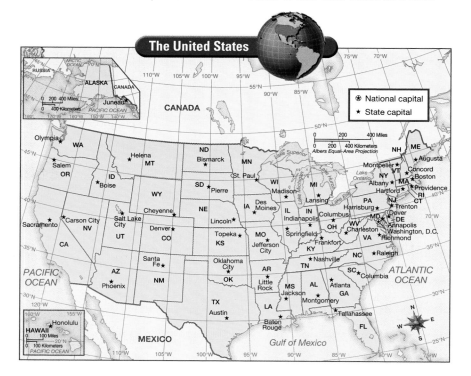

The United States

⊛ National capital
★ State capital

WORD WORK

Word Origins The term *cartotogram* is of French origin. The first part, *cart-*, comes from the French *carte,* meaning "card or map." The ending *-gram* traces its origins to the Greek *gramma,* meaning "letter or writing." It is also the root of the modern English words *grammar* and *gram.* Taken together, *cartogram* literally means "writing in map form." Ask students to think of other words that use these word parts. cartographer, diagram, telegram

MAKE IT RELEVANT

At School Lead the class in a discussion about statistical information they could gather about their class. Suggest statistics such as height, number of members in students' households, and travel time to school each day. Choose three types of statistics, and gather the data with the class using a survey or a show of hands. Record the data on the board. Have students make maps of the classroom. Then have students make cartograms based on the data recorded on the board.

Population Cartogram of the United States

One square equals 500,000 people

person had the same amount of land. A state with many people would be much bigger than a state with few people. When states are shown this way, you can quickly compare populations around the country.

➡ PRACTICE THE SKILL

The map on page 498 is a political map of the United States. The size of each state is based on its land area. Compare the size of New Jersey with the size of South Dakota. South Dakota is larger in land area. The cartogram on this page is a population cartogram. The size of each state is based on population. Compare the sizes of New Jersey and South Dakota again. Although New Jersey has a smaller land area than South Dakota, it is shown larger than South Dakota on the cartogram because it has more people.

Continue to compare land area and population to answer these questions.

1 Which state has more land area, Pennsylvania or Montana?

2 Which of those states is shown larger on the cartogram? Why is it shown larger?

3 What does the cartogram tell about Alaska when you compare its size on the political map?

➡ APPLY WHAT YOU LEARNED

With a partner, brainstorm other ideas for cartograms. What other statistics could be shown in this way to help people compare and contrast states? Make a cartogram of the United States that is based on other statistics besides population statistics. Then prepare a list of questions that could be answered by looking at your cartogram.

Chapter 13 ■ 499

CHART AND GRAPH SKILLS

2 Teach

What You Need to Know

Have students compare the sizes of states in the map and on the cartogram. Encourage students to analyze the data by combining prior knowledge with the new information presented. Use this data to make inferences and draw conclusions about the populations of states.

Practice the Skill—Answers

Briefly discuss the advantages of using a cartogram. Then have students answer the questions in this section.

1 Montana

2 Pennsylvania, because it has a larger population

3 Alaska has a large area of land and a small population.

3 Close

Apply What You Learned

Students should research statistics and create cartograms based on the data they collect. Prompt students to use several different question formats on their quizzes, such as multiple choice, fill-in-the blank, and critical thinking questions.

ACTIVITY BOOK

Use ACTIVITY BOOK, pp. 126–127, to give students additional practice using this skill.

TRANSPARENCY

Use SKILL TRANSPARENCIES 7-1A and 7-1B.

EXTEND AND ENRICH

Make Historical Cartograms
Have students use an almanac or the Internet to research the populations of their own state and the states bordering it for each decade over the last fifty years. Then have students make 5 population cartograms, one for each decade. Ask students to compare the cartograms and discuss how the population of the region has changed.

RETEACH THE SKILL

Write a Paragraph Have students write a paragraph that describes how cartograms show information and why cartograms are useful. Encourage students to share their paragraphs with a classmate.

OBJECTIVES

■ Analyze the effects of the growth of the American population.

■ Analyze environmental challenges that result from population growth in the United States.

 Fact and Opinion pp. 491, 500, 502, 503, 520

Vocabulary

SEE READING AND VOCABULARY TRANSPARENCY 7-3 OR THE WORD CARDS ON PP. V55–V56.

rapid-transit system p. 501

 When Minutes Count

Read aloud the Big Idea statement at the beginning of the lesson. Then ask students to examine the photographs and captions in the lesson and identify how each one relates to the Big Idea.

Quick Summary

This lesson examines the effects of the dramatic population growth of the United States and of efforts to conserve and repair natural resources.

 Motivate

Set the Purpose

Big Idea Help students understand that a significant event, such as population growth, presents challenges as well as benefits for the people of the United States.

Access Prior Knowledge

Have students discuss what they have learned about the growth and changes in the population of the United States. What benefits do they see as a result of the growth? What drawbacks do they see in their own lives?

· LESSON ·

FACT AND OPINION

As you read, look for facts and opinions about the growing population.

BIG IDEA
Growth has affected the United States and its natural resources.

VOCABULARY
rapid-transit system

2 The Challenges of Growth

In 1790 the first census of the United States counted 3,929,214 people living in the country. Today more than 291 million people live in the United States. By the year 2050, experts estimate the nation's population will be more than 400 million. With this growth have come challenges.

The Effects of Growth

Since that first census more than two hundred years ago, the population of the United States has continued to grow. Over time, quiet towns with small populations and a handful of buildings have grown into large cities. As those cities and the suburbs around them continue to grow, they often spread out over larger and larger areas. Land that was once used for farming is now used for houses, stores, office buildings, and highways.

Across the country many communities are choosing to manage urban growth by passing laws to control it. These laws not only limit where buildings may go, but what kinds of buildings may be built in an area. The laws set aside areas of land to be used only for homes, offices, or businesses, such as shopping centers. In some cases, the laws say the land cannot be used for buildings.

About eight out of every ten people live in or near large cities. Areas that were once undeveloped, such as this Florida neighborhood, are now home to large communities.

500

REACH ALL LEARNERS

English as a Second Language Stress to students the difference between causes and effects. Work with students to reinforce the idea that a cause is an event that makes something happen. An effect is the result of an event or a cause. Also, point out the difference between the words *effect* and *affect*. Ask students to identify causes and effects discussed in the lesson.

BACKGROUND

American Roadways Suburbs and urban growth are made possible by a complex system of roads. Up until the 1900s, most roads outside of cities were not paved; in fact, most were hardly more than trails. Once steam locomotives became a popular way to travel in the 1840s, the government invested in building railroads. It was not until the 1920s, when the automobile became popular, that roads were paved across the country.

As the population grows and the spread of urban areas continues, the need for more services, such as fire protection, also increases.

Some people disagree with placing limits on how land can be used. They believe that it is unfair to restrict use of land that has valuable resources. Some believe that private ownership of land also can help to conserve it. This is because the land's owner usually wants to protect his or her land and use its resources wisely so it will remain valuable in the future.

Rapid population growth has presented many other challenges for the American people. As the nation's population has grown, so has the number of vehicles on its highways and city streets. In many places roads are often jammed with cars, trucks, and buses. This is especially true during rush hour, the time when people are going to work or going home. To help keep traffic

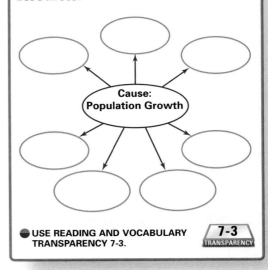

Directing traffic helps keep city streets from jamming up.

moving, some cities now use computers to control traffic lights. Others use electronic highway signs to warn drivers of problems and to suggest other routes they can take.

To help reduce the number of vehicles on their streets, many cities have worked to improve their public transportation systems. These cities have added more bus lines and built rapid-transit systems. A **rapid-transit system** is a passenger transportation system that uses elevated or underground trains or both.

A growing population means growth in the amount of services that are needed. For example, more electricity is needed for people to run their homes and businesses. More people also means that increases are needed in other services.

Graphic Organizer Provide students with the following cause-and-effect graphic organizer. Ask them to fill in the organizer as they read about the effects of population growth on cities and on natural resources.

Cause: Population Growth

● USE READING AND VOCABULARY TRANSPARENCY 7-3.

7-3 TRANSPARENCY

2 Teach

The Effects of Growth

Read and Respond

Culture and Society Have students identify some ways in which the automobile has affected daily life in the United States. Ask students to list the ways the automobile is useful in their lives. Answers will vary but should include transportation to and from school, shopping, trips, and vacations.

Economics Explain to students that urban growth brings with it challenges such as changing property values, increased crime, the need for new roads and sewers, and the need for higher taxes to pay for schools, parks, and municipal buildings.

Q How is land mostly modified in growing urban areas?

A Most of the land is used for buildings and streets.

In Your State Direct students to look at a map of their state and to identify the major highways and railroad lines. Ask students to make a generalization, based on the map, about how easy it is for people to travel from place to place within the state and out of state.

Create Mental Images Direct students to jot down mental images that come to mind as they read the subsection. Then ask volunteers to share the images with the class. Challenge students to create a complete picture by identifying sounds, smells, and other sensations that appeal to the senses.

Challenges for the Environment

Read and Respond

Culture and Society Challenge students to analyze how scientific discoveries and technological innovations have changed the environment. Students may respond that the discoveries and innovations have helped people develop new uses for resources, allowed people to use resources more efficiently, and have helped in the development of new sources of energy.

3 Close

Summarize Key Content

- Population growth has led to the growth of urban areas, causing heavy traffic, the need for more public services, and changes in government.
- Population growth has also benefited the United States through the increase in new ideas from the growing number of people and the improvement of transportation and communication systems.
- People and the government have taken steps to preserve natural resources.

502 ▪ Unit 7

Water, garbage collection, education, health care, and police and fire protection must meet the demands of a growing population.

Changes in population mean changes in government. An increase in population can affect a state's representation in Congress. When a state's population changes, the number of seats it has in the House of Representatives can change also.

Population growth also has its benefits. Having more people helps increase the number of new ideas that can lead to new inventions and new and better ways of doing things. Population growth can also help businesses grow by increasing the market for many goods and services. Having more people also encourages improvements in transportation and communication systems.

REVIEW How have many cities reduced the number of vehicles on their streets?

🌐 FACT AND OPINION

Challenges for the Environment

As the population continues to grow, so does a greater need for natural resources. As a nation it is our responsibility to use our natural resources wisely. Over the years some people have damaged the nation's natural ecosystems. Water, land, and even wildlife have been affected.

However, through conservation efforts, some of the damage has been repaired. For example, at one time the American bald eagle was on the endangered species list. There were only about 417 pairs of the eagles left in the United States.

This slide is made of recycled materials. Many everyday products can be made from recycled materials.

They have worked to improve their public transportation system by adding more bus lines and building rapid-transit systems.

To help save the endangered birds, laws were passed banning a chemical that was getting into the water supply. This chemical poisoned the fish eaten by the eagles. By 1998 there were more than 5,000 pairs of American bald eagles in the United States.

Another way to help preserve natural resources is to recycle. Countries with large populations, such as the United States, produce large amounts of trash. To solve this problem, many communities across the nation recycle.

Trash containing materials such as metal, glass, plastic, and paper is used to make new products. Many factories use recycled materials instead of new natural resources to make their products. Everyday items such as videocassettes, playground equipment, and clothing, can be made from recycled materials.

As in the past, Americans continue to rely on natural resources to meet their wants and needs. Today, however, most

National preserves, such as this one in Alabama, help to protect natural resources.

people understand the need to help protect the nation's natural resources for future Americans and to make sensible plans about how those natural resources are used.

REVIEW How do many communities try to solve their trash problems? *by recycling*

LESSON 2 REVIEW

 FACT AND OPINION In the lesson, find examples of one statement that is fact and one that is opinion.

❶ **BIG IDEA** How has the growth of the United States population affected the land and its natural resources?

❷ **VOCABULARY** What are the benefits of using a rapid-transit system?

❸ **HISTORY** What helped save the American bald eagle?

❹ **GEOGRAPHY** Why do some people disagree with placing limits on how land can be used?

❺ **CRITICAL THINKING—Hypothesize** By the year 2050 over 400 million people may be living in the United States. What new problems do you think Americans will have in that time? How might the increase in population benefit Americans?

 PERFORMANCE—Interview a Person Interview a parent, a grandparent, or someone else older than you to find out what your city or town was like when he or she was your age. Have your questions ready before the interview. Write down the answers and present them to your class.

 FACT AND OPINION Possible answer: Fact: more than 281 million people live in the United States; Opinion: it is unfair to restrict use of land that has valuable resources.

❶ **BIG IDEA** Population growth has increased the use of land and natural resources.

❷ **VOCABULARY** A **rapid-transit system** decreases pollution and traffic congestion.

❸ **HISTORY** banning a dangerous chemical

❹ **GEOGRAPHY** Some people believe that private owners will make the best decisions about how to protect land.

❺ **CRITICAL THINKING—Hypothesize** Possible answer: The limited resources of land and water may be a challenge. The population increase may result in new ideas about how to solve these problems.

Performance Assessment Guidelines Students' interviews should include their own questions as well as their subject's answers. Suggest that students work in pairs to proofread each other's interviews before submitting them.

ACTIVITY BOOK

Use ACTIVITY BOOK, p. 128, to reinforce and extend student learning.

EXTEND AND ENRICH

Roundtable Discussion Arrange students into two teams. One team should research and form ideas about the benefits of urban growth. The other should research and generate ideas about the need for protecting the environment. Then have students from each team meet with those of the opposing view to discuss how urban growth can be accomplished without harming the environment.

RETEACH THE LESSON

Oral Exercise Conduct an oral exercise in which you guide students through all the causes and effects discussed in the lesson. Start by asking, "What is one effect of urban growth?" Call on one student and repeat his or her answer. Then ask, "Did this effect cause something else?" (For example, traffic is an effect of urban growth and is the cause of improved public transportation.) If there is no answer, then continue the exercise by asking, "What is another effect of urban growth?"

Lesson 3

PAGES 504–509

 Fact and Opinion pp. 491, 504, 506, 509, 520

Vocabulary

SEE READING AND VOCABULARY TRANSPARENCY 7-4 OR THE WORD CARDS ON PP. V55–V58.

diverse economy p. 504	**interdependent** p. 507
high-tech p. 505	**international trade** p. 507
Information Age p. 505	**free-trade agreement** p. 508
e-commerce p. 506	**global economy** p. 508

 When Minutes Count

Have students scan the lesson to find the meaning of each of the lesson vocabulary terms. Then ask them to use the terms in sentences.

Quick Summary

This lesson describes the American economy and how the free enterprise system works.

 **Motivate**

Set the Purpose

Big Idea Be sure that students understand the word *economy*.

Access Prior Knowledge

Have students discuss what they have learned about the diversity of the American population.

3

 FACT AND OPINION

As you read, look for facts and opinions about our nation's diverse economy.

BIG IDEA
The economy of the United States has changed in recent years.

VOCABULARY
diverse economy
high-tech
Information Age
e-commerce
interdependent
international trade
free-trade agreement
global economy

The American Economy

Just as the people of the United States have become more and more diverse over time, so has the nation's economy. A **diverse economy** is one that is based on many kinds of industries. Our nation's diverse economy has created many new kinds of jobs for American workers. It has also changed the kinds of jobs that most of them do to earn a living.

A Changing Economy

Many American workers continue to do the traditional jobs that they have always done. Some people farm the land, fish the waters, cut down trees, and mine the earth for mineral resources. Others construct highways and buildings. Many others—more than 18 million—work in factories, where together they produce more manufactured goods than any other nation in the world.

While all of those jobs remain important parts of the American economy today, more Americans now work in

While some people continue to work in traditional jobs, advances in technology have increased the number of high-tech jobs available to Americans.

504 Unit 7

Analyze Graphs The graph shows the number of Americans who work in different kinds of industries. Today more Americans, such as this doctor (below), work in the service industry than in any other kind of industry.

◈ About how many more Americans work in the service industry than in the trade and transportation industry?

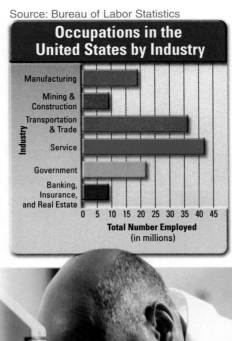

Occupations in the United States by Industry

(Bar graph showing Total Number Employed (in millions) by Industry)
- Manufacturing
- Mining & Construction
- Transportation & Trade
- Service
- Government
- Banking, Insurance, and Real Estate

Scale: 0 5 10 15 20 25 30 35 40 45

Total Number Employed (in millions)

service jobs than in any other kind of jobs. In fact, about one-third of all workers have service jobs, such as working in restaurants, repairing cars, or providing health care. If other kinds of service work are included, such as jobs in government, banks, and stores, about four out of every five workers in the United States hold service jobs.

Many changes in the kinds of jobs people do have come about because of advances in technology. In recent years, high-technology, or high-tech, industries have been of growing importance to the American economy. **High-tech** industries are those that invent, build, or use computers and other kinds of electronic equipment. For example, some high-tech industries study robotics, or the science of how to use robots. The new devices produced by these high-tech industries have made it easier to trade goods and services.

The early 1970s marked the beginning of the **Information Age**. This period in history has been defined by the growing amount of information available to people. In fact, most of what is known about the human body has been learned in the past 40 years.

Today, organizing and storing information and getting the information to people when they need it is a major industry.

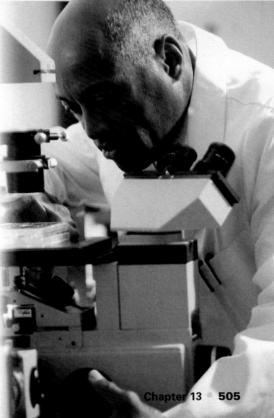

Chapter 13 ■ 505

---

2 Teach

A Changing Economy

Read and Respond

Economics Challenge students to think of what people need or want today and what kinds of products people work to make. Possible response: The need for better, faster computers and high technology cause people to design those products.

Visual Learning

Bar Graph Have students think of jobs that would be included in the service category. doctors, nurses, repairmen, restaurant workers, day-care workers, etc.
CAPTION ANSWER: about 5 million

Read and Respond

Economics Ask students to think about what they have learned and what they know about the economic development of the United States. Then challenge them to explain how Americans' ideas about equality and progress have affected the economic development of the nation. Students' responses may include that American ideas have helped the nation develop an economy that includes a diverse workforce, equal opportunities, and a variety of industries.

Read and Respond

Culture and Society Ask students to speculate on the effects of advanced medical care on the size of the population in the United States.

Q **What kind of new jobs might advances in medicine create?**

A Jobs for researchers to develop new technology and products, workers at companies to make the new products, and an increased number of health care professionals to provide more kinds of care.

Economics Ask whether any student or an adult in his or her family has researched products on the Internet or purchased anything online. Ask students how online shopping might affect business at local stores. Then discuss with them how a greater number of choices available on the Internet might affect consumers.

Economics Explain to students that companies in the United States provide technology services around the world. Point out that many United States computer and software systems are used in commerce and defense industries worldwide. Then discuss with students how technological advances in the United States affect its role in world affairs.

Visual Learning

Photograph Ask students to study the photographs and read the caption. Point out that many of the new high-tech jobs require education in very specific fields. Ask students how the availability of education might affect the development of new technologies and economic growth.

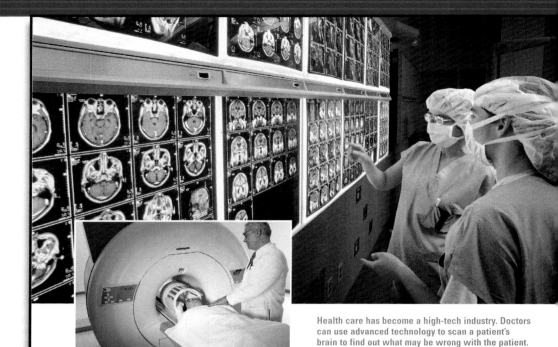

Health care has become a high-tech industry. Doctors can use advanced technology to scan a patient's brain to find out what may be wrong with the patient.

Much of this work is done electronically, through private computer networks or through public Web sites. Setting up and managing these computer systems is a growing field for workers.

New technologies are also changing the way people buy and sell goods and services. The rise of electronic commerce, or **e-commerce**, means that both large and small companies can market their products worldwide. E-commerce has greatly increased the number of goods and services available to American consumers. It has also enabled thousands of Americans to run full-time or part-time businesses from their homes. In 1999, American businesses and individual consumers spent a total of $659 billion on e-commerce purchases. More than 90 percent of this total was made up of business-to-business

sales, or businesses selling things to one another.

New technologies are also changing the part of the American economy that relates to medicine and science. High-tech advances in the field of medicine have already changed the way doctors treat disease. For example, the use of lasers in surgery has helped millions of people.

As technology and knowledge advance, the possibility of additional scientific discoveries increases. Scientific discoveries will likely change the American economy even more in time. Technology used in the area of space exploration has already given the United States many new pictures of different parts of space.

REVIEW How have new technologies changed people's lives?
FACT AND OPINION
by changing the work people do, the way doctors treat disease, and the way people buy and sell goods and services

Types of Resources As the United States economy grows, different types of resources are needed. Natural resources, such as oil and timber, come from the environment. Most major corporations also need human resources, or workers, and capital resources, or machines and other goods made by people.

Note Taking Offer students some guidance on taking notes on each section of the lesson. Remind students to include the heading of each subsection as well as boldfaced vocabulary terms and their definitions. Students may also jot down key words and phrases. Finally, they should write and answer the Review question at the end of each subsection. Students' answers should include the key words they wrote in their notes.

A Global Economy

Each day, people in different states and in different regions of the United States exchange natural resources, finished products, and services. That is because no one state or region has all the natural resources that people and businesses there may need or want. And no one state or region can produce all the goods and services that people may need or want.

North Carolina, for example, grows too little cotton to supply all of its textile mills, so mill owners there buy cotton from other states. In turn, farmers in those states may buy cotton clothing made by workers in North Carolina. In this way people in different states are interdependent—they depend on one another for natural resources, finished products, and services.

The United States and other countries are also interdependent. Modern transportation and communication systems have made it easier for people in one country to trade with people in other countries. Goods from the United States are exported to places all over the world. At the same time, the United States imports many goods from other countries. This international trade, or trade among nations, allows people in the United States and in other countries to buy goods that their own countries do not make or grow. The United States' most important international trading partners are Canada, China, Britain, Germany, Japan, and Mexico. The United States imports oil from members of the Organization of Petroleum Exporting Countries, or OPEC.

This man is working on an American brand of automobile in a factory in Beijing, China. Below, cars in Japan await shipment overseas.

A Global Economy

Read and Respond

Geography Ask students to consider the natural resources in their region of the country. What resources does their region provide? Then invite students to name products that their region does not produce. Guide students to see that without regional and global trade, people in their region would not have all the things they need.

Visual Learning

Photograph Ask students how the photographs demonstrate the importance of transportation for global trade. Point out that the cars might be shipped to a port in the United States. Have students speculate how cars made in other countries reach their town to be sold locally.

Read and Respond

History Ask a volunteer to describe the triangular trade routes which flourished when the United States was a colony of Britain. Ask students to describe similarities and differences between that trading system and today's global economy.

Economics Tell students that the interdependence of national economies through global trade increased during the second half of the twentieth century. Point out that most countries now import and export large amounts of goods.

Q How might an increase in imports affect a country's economy?

A Imports bring new goods into the country, but companies at home may sell fewer of their goods.

A Free Enterprise Economy

Read and Respond

Economics Explain to students that any market economy, including that of the United States, has some basic institutions. These include consumers, who use goods and services; businesses, which produce goods and services; and government organizations.

Close

Summarize Key Content

- In recent years, high-tech and service jobs have become more important in the American economy.
- Scientific and technological advances have made trade and communications with other countries easier.
- In a free enterprise economy, people own and run their own businesses and produce goods or services that are in demand.

To increase international trade, many countries, including the United States, have signed free-trade agreements. A **free-trade agreement** is a treaty in which countries agree not to charge tariffs, or taxes, on goods they buy from and sell to each other. Such an agreement gives industries in each of the trading nations the chance to compete better. In 1994, Mexico, Canada, and the United States put the North American Free Trade Agreement, or NAFTA, into effect. One of NAFTA's goals has been to assist the movement of goods and services across national borders. As a result, the number

a treaty in which countries agree not to charge tariffs on goods they buy from and sell to each other

508 ■ Unit 7

of goods and services available to people in all three nations has increased.

International trade adds much to the economy of the United States. The United States also interacts with other countries in other ways. Many companies in the United States have offices and factories in other countries. Many companies from other countries also have businesses in the United States. Almost 5 million people in the United States work in businesses owned by people in other countries. This means that the nations of the world are now part of a **global economy**, the world market in which companies from different countries buy and sell goods and services.

REVIEW What is a free-trade agreement?

A Free Enterprise Economy

The United States has a free enterprise economy. In this type of market economy, producers offer goods or services that consumers want to buy. Companies produce a greater supply when demand rises. Price affects demand, and demand affects price. For example, few people would buy a computer game that cost $1,000. Demand for the product would be low, and the company would produce only a few games. If the price of the game is $10, many more people will buy it. Demand for the product will be high, so the company will produce many games.

In a free enterprise economy, people own and run their own businesses. In other kinds of economies, the government owns businesses. It tells factory

Many people in the United States, such as this Virginia couple, run their businesses from their homes.

Under the free enterprise system, Americans can open a wide variety of businesses, such as this store in Waitsfield, Vermont.

managers what goods to produce, how to produce them, and how much to charge for them. In the United States, these decisions are made by business owners.

The freedom that American businesses have has led to the creation of many new products. For example, some of today's largest computer companies were started in people's homes. The people who began these businesses were free to design their products any way they wished. As a result, consumers have been able to choose from a wide variety of products.

Another benefit of a free enterprise economy is that anyone, even a young person, can start a business. Some of the many businesses young people have started include everything from dog-walking services to Web site design companies.

REVIEW In what kind of economy are people allowed to own and run their own businesses?
a free enterprise economy

LESSON 3 REVIEW

FACT AND OPINION Price affects demand, and demand affects price. Is this statement a fact or an opinion? Explain.

1 **BIG IDEA** How has the economy of the United States changed in recent years?

2 **VOCABULARY** Explain how **e-commerce** is a part of the nation's **diverse economy**.

3 **HISTORY** When did the Information Age begin?

4 **ECONOMICS** In what ways do entrepreneurs affect the American economy?

5 **CRITICAL THINKING—Analyze** How has the interdependence of different countries increased in the modern economy?

PERFORMANCE—Conduct a Survey Survey your classmates and ask them what kinds of jobs they would like to have when they are older. Find out how many of your classmates want to have traditional jobs and compare that to how many of your classmates want to have either high-tech or service jobs.

Chapter 13 ▪ 509

Assess

Lesson 3 Review—Answers

FACT AND OPINION Fact: The sentence can be proven true.

1 **BIG IDEA** The economy of the United States has become more diverse, creating new kinds of jobs for American workers.

2 **VOCABULARY** Possible answer: **E-commerce** allows many companies to compete for business in today's **diverse economy**.

3 **HISTORY** in the early 1970s

4 **ECONOMICS** Possible answer: They create a wide variety of products for consumers to choose from.

5 **CRITICAL THINKING—Analyze** Modern transportation and communication systems have made it easier for people in one country to trade with those in another. This leads to greater dependence on products from other countries.

Performance Assessment Guidelines Students' surveys should mention how many students were polled and list their answers without revealing who said what. Suggest that students make a chart of the careers mentioned by their classmates. Students may also present the information in different ways. For example, they might show what careers girls and boys preferred.

ACTIVITY BOOK

Use ACTIVITY BOOK, p. 129, to reinforce and extend student learning.

RETEACH THE LESSON

Graphic Organizer Have students complete the following graphic organizer. Allow them to read through the lesson to check or confirm information.

What is the free enterprise system?
The free enterprise system means anybody can begin a business if he or she can supply a product or a service that consumers want to buy.

The American Economy

How has it changed?
More people in America work in service jobs than any other kind of job.

Why is it global?
A global economy is helpful as it brings in natural resources from other places.

OBJECTIVES

- Identify the roles of the federal government.
- Compare and contrast the responsibilities of state and federal governments.
- Describe the duties and responsibilities of citizens.
- Explain the importance of patriotism and good citizenship.

 Fact and Opinion pp. 491, 510, 514, 515, 520

Vocabulary

SEE READING AND VOCABULARY TRANSPARENCY 7-5 OR THE WORD CARDS ON PP. V57–V58.

responsibility p. 512	**jury** p. 513
register p. 513	**volunteer** p. 514
informed citizen p. 513	**patriotism** p. 515

 When Minutes Count

Have pairs of students work together to find the answers to the subsection review questions.

Quick Summary

This lesson discusses the roles, structure, and powers of the government. It also focuses on the responsibilities and duties of American citizens.

 **Motivate**

Set the Purpose

Big Idea Make sure students understand the word *citizen* as it is used in the Big Idea statement.

Access Prior Knowledge

Have students discuss the challenges American citizens face as the population grows. What kinds of problems will government need to solve?

 FACT AND OPINION
As you read, look for facts and opinions about government and citizens.

BIG IDEA
The role of government affects the main rights and responsibilities of American citizens.

VOCABULARY
responsibility
register
informed citizen
jury
volunteer
patriotism

Government and the People

The Constitution of the United States of America, which became law in 1788, set up the government for the nation. More than 200 years later, government leaders still look to the Constitution to help guide their actions. The American people also look to the Constitution to protect their rights and freedoms.

The Federal System

The federal system created by the Constitution divides political power between the national, or federal, government and the state governments. The federal government is the country's largest government system.

From the United States capital in Washington, D.C., the federal government affects the economic and social activities of all Americans. Federal government runs programs to help people who are poor, aged, or disabled. It tests foods and drugs for safety and sets

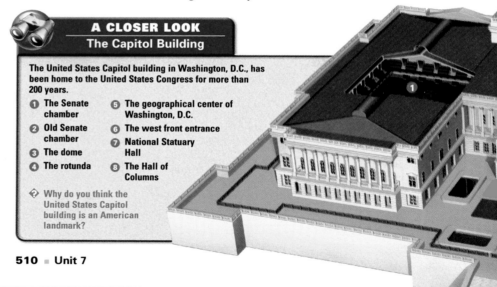

A CLOSER LOOK
The Capitol Building

The United States Capitol building in Washington, D.C., has been home to the United States Congress for more than 200 years.

1. The Senate chamber
2. Old Senate chamber
3. The dome
4. The rotunda
5. The geographical center of Washington, D.C.
6. The west front entrance
7. National Statuary Hall
8. The Hall of Columns

◈ Why do you think the United States Capitol building is an American landmark?

510 ■ Unit 7

REACH ALL LEARNERS

English as a Second Language Allow students to work in pairs and to spend extra time on the details of the federal system. Also, consider displaying photographs of the landmarks mentioned on page 511.

WORD WORK

Suffixes Point out that some of the vocabulary terms in this lesson have suffixes. Work with students to identify the suffixes and to create a list with the suffixes and their definitions. Challenge students to think of other words that have the suffixes *–ity* and *–ism*.

standards to control pollution. It deals with the governments of other nations, and it sets trade rules with them. The federal government is also in charge of space exploration, air travel safety, and national parks, forests, historic sites, and museums.

Many famous landmarks across the country are associated with the federal government. These include the Statue of Liberty in New York Bay, the White House in Washington, D.C., and Mount Rushmore in South Dakota. They are not just places to visit. They are patriotic symbols that remind Americans of the things that unite them as a people.

Americans are also united by the political parties to which they belong. The United States is a representative government, which means that its leaders are elected by citizens. These leaders represent the citizens who belong to their party. The two main political parties are the Republican and Democratic parties. In Congress, the party with the most members in each house is known as the majority party. The party with fewer members is called the minority party.

The most powerful officer of the House of Representatives is the Speaker of the House. No member of the House may speak until called upon by the Speaker. The Speaker is always a member of the majority party and has usually served in Congress for many years.

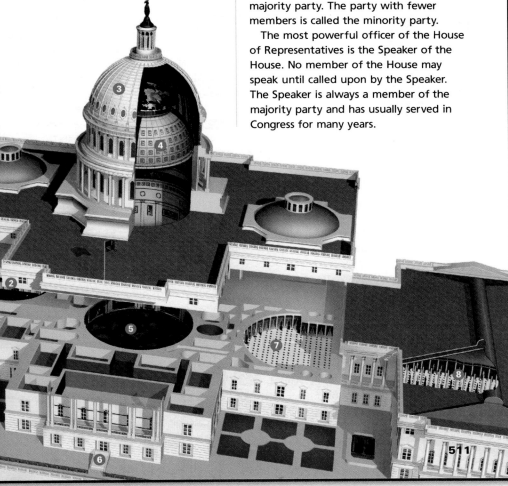

511

K-W-L Chart Have students fill out a K-W-L chart to organize their thinking about the lesson material.

K	W	L
American citizens have responsibilities.	What are the responsibilities of citizens?	

● USE READING AND VOCABULARY TRANSPARENCY 7-5.

7-5
TRANSPARENCY

2 Teach

The Federal System

A CLOSER LOOK

The Capitol Building

Ask students to read the caption and locate the places in the illustration. Explain that the Capitol building was built on the exact geographical center of the District of Columbia. Encourage students to discuss the significance of building the Capitol at this location.
CAPTION ANSWER: The Capitol houses the federal government and is a symbol of democracy.

Read and Respond

Civics and Government Remind students that each state sends two senators to the Senate and a certain number of representatives to the House of Representatives. The number of representatives per state is based on that state's population. Ask students how many representatives their state sends to Washington, D.C., and to identify the political party of each representative. Responses will vary.

Advanced Learners
Challenge advanced students to discuss the structure of the federal government. Have them work in small groups to create a poster or other presentation of the organization of the three branches of the federal government and their duties. legislative makes laws; executive carries out laws; judicial interprets laws

School Prayer Because of separation of church and state, the federal government does not get involved with religious matters. Citizens are free to decide for themselves when and how they want to worship. For example, the Supreme Court ruled that prayers should not be allowed in public schools because the schools are paid for in part by federal tax revenues.

Read and Respond

Government Inform students that there are about 3 million civilians employed by the federal government, more than 4 million by state governments, and more than 11 million by local governments. Illustrate the information by using the following circle graph.

Government Employees

58% Local
18% Federal
24% State

Civic Affairs

Read and Respond

Civics and Government Explain to students that all local and state governments form, debate, and carry out public policy. Although local governments are created by state governments, they still have their own powers. Some small-town governments work together with other local governments to provide basic services. Ask students to discuss why state and local governments are important.

History Read aloud the opening paragraph of the Constitution and have students state its purpose.

• HERITAGE •

Uncle Sam

American history is filled with heroes, but only a few of them have been preserved as cartoons. During the War of 1812, Samuel Wilson, owner of a New York meat-packing business, helped supply the United States Army with beef. Wilson's supply wagons were marked with the initials *U.S.* It was reported that *U.S.* stood for *Uncle Sam* Wilson. In fact, the letters stood for *United States.* The name caught on and in 1868 the great political cartoonist Thomas Nast created the first Uncle Sam cartoon.

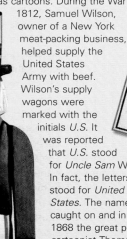

The most powerful officers of the Senate are the majority leader and the minority leader. These people help direct the actions of their party in the Senate. Since most state congresses are modeled after the federal Congress, these offices also exist at the state level.

Federal, state, and local governments have some of the same powers. They can tax citizens, and spend and borrow money. Tax money is used to provide services such as schools and roads. Each state has its own constitution and laws. However, state laws and activities must not conflict with the United States Constitution. In turn, the activities of local governments must

512 ▪ Unit 7

not conflict with state and national government laws. The mayor of a city, for example, has less authority than the governor of a state.

On every level of government federal, state, and local leaders attempt to fulfill their roles as government officials. Some of these leaders, such as state representatives to Congress, are elected by the voters. Others, such as federal judges, are appointed, or named, by a specific governing body. For example, in 2000 Hillary Rodham Clinton was elected to the United States Senate by the voters of New York. Supreme Court Justice Sandra Day O'Connor, on the other hand, was appointed to her position by the President of the United States.

REVIEW What are some powers that the federal and state governments share? the rights to tax and to spend and borrow money

Civic Affairs

The Constitution says that citizens who meet the age requirements have the right to vote and the right to hold public office. All residents in the United States—citizens and noncitizens alike—have freedom of speech, freedom of the press, freedom of religion, and freedom to gather in groups. Laws passed by the United States Congress and by state governments can give people other rights, too.

With these rights come responsibilities. A **responsibility** is a duty—something that a person is expected to do. With the right to vote, for example, comes the responsibility of voting. Most state governments say that a citizen who wants to take part in an election must **register** to vote, or show that he or she lives where the voting takes place. This is an important responsibility because every vote matters in an election. This was very clear in the 2000 presidential election when only a few hundred votes made the difference in George W. Bush's win over Al Gore.

With freedom of speech and freedom of the press comes the responsibility of being an informed and active citizen. An **informed citizen** is one who knows what is happening in the community, the state, the nation, and the world. An informed citizen is more likely to see other people's points of view.

Citizens who feel strongly about an issue can work to influence policies and decisions. They can contact their representatives by writing letters or making phone calls. Today e-mail provides another way to stay in touch with government leaders.

The responsibilities of citizens are not written in the Constitution, but they follow naturally from what is written there. For example, the Constitution says that every person charged with a crime will be judged by a jury. A **jury** is a group of citizens who decide a case in court. Citizens must be willing to be members of a jury if called upon to serve. The Constitution gives Congress the authority to raise money to run the nation. Citizens must be willing to pay taxes if the nation is to run smoothly.

Besides voting, obeying the laws, defending the nation, serving on a jury, and paying taxes, some citizens take a more active part in the government. One way citizens take action is by taking part in political campaigns.

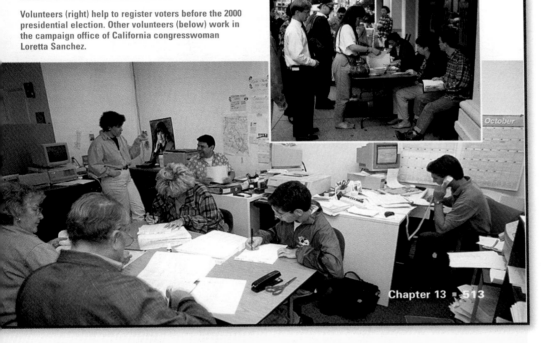

Volunteers (right) help to register voters before the 2000 presidential election. Other volunteers (below) work in the campaign office of California congresswoman Loretta Sanchez.

Chapter 13 — 513

Read and Respond

Culture and Society Remind students that basic rights are important in American society. Stress that the belief in human rights, or fundamental rights, lies at the heart of the United States citizenship and enables people to worship as they wish, speak freely, and read and write what they choose.

Civics and Government Explain to students that a constitutional democracy such as the United States succeeds because citizens take positions of leadership. Point out that most school, community, state, and national leaders are elected, or chosen by the people they will represent. Ask students to discuss appropriate criteria for leadership at all four levels.

Civics and Government Inform students that in the 2000 Presidential election between Governor George W. Bush and Vice President Al Gore there was a 327-vote difference out of 6 million votes cast in Florida. Emphasize to students that was an incredibly close margin! That would be about equivalent to a 1-vote margin in an election with 18,000 votes cast.

Q Why is it important that all citizens vote in elections?

A Every vote cast makes a difference in who is elected. And the person elected makes a difference in each citizen's life.

Visual Learning

Photograph Inform students that many people who work on campaigns and help register voters are volunteers. By performing these services, the volunteers are participating in the government.

Working Together

Read and Respond

Civics and Government Tell students that citizens can work together in large interest groups to influence government policies. Interest groups may work to protect the environment, provide for the homeless, or improve healthcare.

· HERITAGE ·

Pledge of Allegiance

Inform students that the wording of the Pledge of Allegiance has been changed twice over the years. For nearly forty years, students pledged only to "my flag." In 1923, Congress made the change to "the flag of the United States of America." Thirty years later, the words "under God" were added. Have students recite the Pledge of Allegiance and explain its meaning.
---

3 Close

Summarize Key Content

- The federal government conducts thousands of activities that affect the lives of Americans.
- State governments are similar to the federal government but they have different powers.
- Citizens have many rights but have a responsibility to vote, become informed, and serve on juries.
- By working together to support the nation and by being good citizens, Americans uphold the work of the original founders of the nation.

Some citizens go from door to door, handing out information on their candidates or on issues. Other citizens telephone voters to remind them to go to the polls on election day. Most campaign workers are **volunteers**, or people who work without pay.

The most common way citizens take part in politics is by joining a political party. Most registered voters are members of either the Republican or Democratic party. However, a growing number of voters are choosing to register as independents. These voters are not connected to any organized party.

Members of organized parties can be chosen to serve as delegates to their party's national convention. These conventions, which take place every four years, are where presidential candidates are selected. Every state sends a certain number of delegates to each convention. The greater the state's population, the more delegates it can send. These delegates then vote on who their party will nominate as its presidential candidate.

Citizens can also be candidates themselves. One person who decided to take an active part in government is Patty Murray. As a parent volunteer, she lobbied for more money for education. In 1992 she ran for office and won, becoming the first woman to represent the state of Washington in the United States Senate.

REVIEW How can people today contact government leaders?

FACT AND OPINION
by writing letters, sending e-mail, or making phone calls

Working Together

The writers of the United States Constitution were not sure their government would last. No other nation had ever had a government quite like the one described by the Constitution. No other people had ever had all of the rights that

Elected officials and local citizens hold a city council meeting in Gloucester, Massachusetts.

514 ■ Unit 7

EXTEND AND ENRICH

Prepare a Citizenship Pamphlet
Have students work in small groups to prepare a pamphlet that explains the responsibilities and duties of a good citizen. Students may use the information in this chapter as well as other sources. Encourage students to use clip art and graphics that will help make their points.

INTEGRATE LANGUAGE ARTS

Write a Letter
Encourage students to use reference sources to find the names of their local or state representatives. Lead a discussion to identify important issues in your community or state and encourage students to express their opinion about one of these issues. Then ask students to write a letter expressing their opinions to one of the local or state representatives.

American citizens enjoyed. But would the people be able to keep their government going and protect their freedoms over time? The country would need good citizens—citizens who would work for the common good.

Past republics, like that of ancient Rome, broke up partly because the people grew greedy and selfish. To keep the nation strong, Americans would have to keep the spirit that had given the nation its independence and its Constitution. They would need to show **patriotism**, or love of country. Patriotism is more than simply waving the American flag at special times. The writers of the Constitution knew that Americans would have to be good citizens all the time.

REVIEW What are good citizens?

citizens who work for the common good of the country

LESSON 4 REVIEW

 FACT AND OPINION The most powerful officer of the House of Representatives is the Speaker of the House. Is this statement a fact or an opinion? Explain.

1 BIG IDEA What are the roles of government and citizens in the United States?

2 VOCABULARY Use the word **register** in a sentence about voting.

3 CIVICS AND GOVERNMENT What are some of the responsibilities that come with the rights of United States residents?

4 CRITICAL THINKING—Analyze How does the United States government reflect the purposes and values of American citizens?

 PERFORMANCE—Write a Letter The role of government leaders is to work for the good of the people they represent. Write a letter to one of your local, state, or national leaders telling this person how he or she could improve life in your community.

Chapter 13 ■ 515

READING SOCIAL STUDIES

K-W-L Chart Pair students and have them compare their K-W-L charts.

K	W	L
American citizens have responsibilities.	What are the responsibilities of citizens?	Citizens should be informed citizens, vote, and participate in government.

● USE READING AND VOCABULARY TRANSPARENCY 7-5.

7-5 TRANSPARENCY

Assess

Lesson 4 Review—Answers

FACT AND OPINION Fact: the statement can be proven true.

1 BIG IDEA The government's role is to protect and govern citizens; citizens pay taxes and obey the laws of the land.

2 VOCABULARY Once you **register**, you may vote in elections.

3 CIVICS AND GOVERNMENT voting, being an informed and active citizen, serving on a jury, paying taxes, defending the nation

4 CRITICAL THINKING—Analyze Citizens elect government leaders who represent their beliefs and values.

 Performance Assessment Guidelines Students' letters should mention at least one specific concern that students have.

ACTIVITY BOOK

Use ACTIVITY BOOK, p. 130, to reinforce and extend student learning.

RETEACH THE LESSON

Graphic Organizer Ask students to complete the following Venn diagram to reinforce the lesson.

State
• deals with local governments
• funds state parks, forests, historic sites, and museums
• builds and maintains roads, schools, and public buildings
• maintains state military reserves

Both
• provide aid to poor, aged, disabled
• set standards for pollution control

Federal
• maintains Federal branches of military
• maintains national parks, forests, historic sites, and museums
• deals with foreign governments
• conducts research
• tests food and drugs
• space travel

Skill Lesson

PAGES 516–517

OBJECTIVES

- Identify important political symbols that represent American beliefs and principles.
- Explain how political symbols contribute to our national identity.

1 Motivate

Why It Matters

Explain to students that political symbols have been used for centuries to identify governments, armies, and rulers. Today, political symbols are often used to show allegiance or to convey information quickly.

2 Teach

What You Need to Know

Have students study the description of political symbols. Ask students to identify places where they see political symbols. If students have difficulty, ask them to visualize a dollar bill and name some of the symbols printed there.

·SKILLS· Identify Political Symbols

➡ WHY IT MATTERS

People often recognize sports teams, clubs, and other organizations by their symbols. The same is true for political parties, the President, Congress, the Supreme Court, and even voters. Being able to identify political symbols and what they stand for can help you better understand news reports, political cartoons, and other sources of information.

➡ WHAT YOU NEED TO KNOW

Two of the country's most famous political symbols are animals. The donkey represents the Democratic party. The elephant represents the Republican party. The donkey was probably first used to represent President Andrew Jackson, a Democrat, in the 1830s. Later the donkey became a symbol for the entire party. Cartoonist Thomas Nast introduced the elephant as a symbol of the Republican party in 1874. Both of these symbols are still used today.

One of the symbols for the national government is Uncle Sam. The bald eagle and the Statue of Liberty are other symbols for our government. Buildings are often used as political symbols. The White House is a symbol for the President, and the United States Capitol is a symbol for Congress.

516 ■ Unit 7

INTEGRATE ART

Make a Symbol

Organize students into small groups. Encourage students to generate ideas for symbols of their classroom or school. Have students design a school symbol, using pens and markers. Display school symbols in the classroom.

BACKGROUND

Thomas Nast Born in Germany, Nast came to the United States in 1846 when he was six years old. He studied art at the National Academy of Design and began his career at 15 as a draftsman for an illustrated newspaper. By age 18, Nast was working at *Harper's Weekly*, one of the most influential publications of the Gilded Age. Soon his pro-Union, pro-abolitionist cartoons on Civil War activities were being published regularly in *Harper's Weekly*. Nast popularized the Democratic party's donkey and created the elephant for the Republican party. His political cartoons criticizing New York City's corrupt "Boss" Tweed during the 1870s eventually led to Tweed's arrest.

➡ PRACTICE THE SKILL

When you see a political symbol, answer the following questions to help you understand its meaning.

❶ Do you recognize the symbol? Does it stand for the whole national government or only part of the national government? Does it stand for a person or group that is involved in government, such as a political party or organization?

❷ Where did you see the symbol? If it appeared in a magazine, did the writer give you any clues about its meaning?

❸ Does it include any captions or other words that help explain what the symbol means? A symbol labeled "To Protect and Serve," for example, might tell you that it stands for the police.

❹ Why do you think the symbol is a good representation of the person or group it stands for?

❺ When do you think you are most likely to see the symbol?

➡ APPLY WHAT YOU LEARNED

Look through current news magazines, in the editorial pages of newspapers, or on the Internet. Cut or print out an example of a political symbol and paste it on a sheet of paper. Below the symbol, write a brief description of what it stands for.

The elephant (left) is the symbol of the Republican party. The donkey (below) is the symbol of the Democratic party.

CITIZENSHIP SKILLS

Chapter 13 ■ 517

Practice the Skill—Answers

Have the students work through the questions listed in Practice the Skill. Choose a symbol from a current publication and use it to model the questions.

Close

Apply What You Learned

Have students search current publications for examples of political symbols. Students may also wish to search the Internet for the Web sites of political parties and action groups for more political symbols. When students have written descriptions for their examples, display their work in the classroom.

EXTEND AND ENRICH

Research State Symbols Tell students that each state has its own political symbols. Have students do research to identify the state seal, flag, bird, and tree and other symbols of their own state. Encourage students to research the symbols of a nearby state.

RETEACH THE SKILL

Evaluate Symbols Organize students into groups. Have each group choose two symbols of the United States and discuss them. Have groups consider when and where they are most likely to see the symbols. Ask them to use critical thinking skills to evaluate why their choices are fitting symbols of the United States.

Examine Primary Sources

OBJECTIVES

- Identify political buttons as an effective campaigning technique.
- Compare and contrast the effectiveness of examples of political memorabilia from our nation's past.

1 Motivate

Set the Purpose

Political buttons are one way in which candidates rally support from voters. By studying these political buttons, students will determine symbols and phrases candidates used to gain support.

Access Prior Knowledge

Ask students if they have ever owned a button on which appeared a funny or wise saying. Point out that politicians also use buttons to spread their political messages.

2 Teach

Read and Respond

Tell students that some of the earliest political buttons to appear in this country appeared with the first United States President—George Washington. These early buttons were actually brass clothing buttons that had been engraved. How do political buttons today differ from buttons used on clothing? Students may say that instead of being permanently sewn on, political buttons are temporarily pinned to clothes.

EXAMINE PRIMARY SOURCES

Political Buttons

Political candidates often think of clever ways to make themselves known to voters. They distribute buttons and other materials to rally enthusiasm and support of voters. Political buttons can list or show ideas that are important to a candidate's campaign. Many people wear political buttons to show their support for a candidate. Some people choose to wear political buttons to show they support an elected leader.

This title identifies the button's purpose.

The photographs on this button show who was elected.

The eagle is a patriotic symbol of the United States.

The elephant is a political symbol of the Republican party.

Red, white, and blue are the colors of the American Flag.

BACKGROUND

More About the Time Each President of the United States has sworn the same oath upon entering office. That oath, which is set forth in Article II, Section 1 of the Constitution of the United States, reads as follows:

"I do solemnly swear (or affirm) that I will faithfully execute the office of President of the United States, and will, to the best of my ability, preserve, protect, and defend the Constitution of the United States."

INTEGRATE LANGUAGE ARTS

Expressive Writing Ask small groups of students to use newspapers, magazines, and other reference materials to research the current President. Their assignment is to determine what kind of political button would reflect one of this President's beliefs or policies. Once the group has chosen a topic, have members work together to think of a clever way it could be phrased on a political button. Have group representatives share each group's 'button text' with the class.

This handkerchief (above) is from Grover Cleveland's presidential campaign.

OUR CHOICE

Political buttons show a variety of information. The postcard (left) is from William Taft's presidential campaign.

ACTIVITY

Write to Explain Imagine you are running for an elected office. Design a political button for your supporters to wear. Write a paragraph that explains the information on your button.

RESEARCH

Visit The Learning Site at **www.harcourtschool.com** to research other primary sources.

Analyze the Primary Source
Answers

❶ A political button worn by a supporter indicates that someone strongly favors a particular candidate; political buttons worn by supporters can make a face more familiar to other voters.

❷ In addition to the handkerchief and postcard shown here, students may list items such as calendars, business cards, and embossed pencils.

❸ Flags, ribbons, eagles, an elephant, World War II poster, and the colors red, white, and blue.

3 Close

Activity

Write to Explain Have students actually create the political button they have designed by cutting out a circle of paper on which the design is replicated. Each student should then pin the finished 'button' to his or her clothes with a safety pin.

Research

Students will find a variety of political artifacts at The Learning Site at **www.harcourtschool.com**.

Ask each student to choose one of the political artifacts at the site and then identify what the political artifact symbolizes.

INTERNET RESOURCES

THE LEARNING SITE

Go to **www.harcourtschool.com** for a DIRECTORY OF PRIMARY SOURCES.

EXTEND AND ENRICH

Write a Report Ask each student to choose one of the public figures pictured on these political buttons. Tell students to research and write reports on the persons that they have chosen. Explain that their reports should answer these questions: *When might the button have been used? Did the person win or lose the election? In what year(s) did the person run for office?* Ask volunteers to read aloud their completed reports to the class.

RETEACH

Compare and Contrast Have each student choose two of the political buttons pictured. Tell students to write paragraphs comparing and contrasting the figures, symbols, and colors used by each button. Ask them to determine which political button made a more favorable impression on them as future voters. Have volunteers read aloud their paragraphs to the class.

Chapter 13 Review

 FACT AND OPINION

Students may use the graphic organizer that appears on page 132 of the Activity Book. Answers appear in the Activity Book, Teacher's Edition.

Think & Write

Write a List of Questions Students' lists of questions will vary based on the students' interests and concerns. They may include immigration, new technologies, the environment, the economy, or the President's views on responsible citizenship.

Write a Poem Students' poems will vary, depending upon their opinions regarding the qualities of the United States that make it a great nation. Topics may range from the opportunities offered to its citizens to the assistance it provides to other nations.

ACTIVITY BOOK

A copy of the graphic organizer appears in the ACTIVITY BOOK on page 132.

TRANSPARENCY

The graphic organizer appears on READING AND VOCABULARY TRANSPARENCY 7-6.

---

13 Review and Test Preparation

 Fact and Opinion

Copy the following graphic organizer onto a separate sheet of paper. Use the information you have learned to identify facts and opinions about the United States.

Facts and Opinions About the United States
The Population of the United States

Fact	Opinion
More than 291 million people live in the United States.	_____ _____ _____

 THINK & WRITE

Write a List of Questions Imagine that the President of the United States has scheduled a trip to visit your school and to spend time with your class. Write a list of questions you would like to ask the President.

Write a Poem Many patriotic poems have been written about the United States over the course of its history. Think of the things that make the United States a great nation, and then write a poem that honors the country.

520 ■ Chapter 13

TEST PREPARATION

Review these tips with students:

- Read the directions before reading the questions.
- Read each question twice, focusing the second time on all the possible answers.
- Take the time to think about all the possible answers before deciding on an answer.
- Move past questions that give you trouble, and answer the ones you know. Then return to the difficult items.

UNIT PROJECT

Progress Check Students may wish to make a chart listing countries people have come from, reason they have come to the United States, and contributions groups have made to the United States.

520 ■ **CHAPTER 13**

USE VOCABULARY

For each pair of terms, write a sentence that explains how the terms are related.

1 **Internet** (p. 496), **teleconference** (p. 497)

2 **interdependent** (p. 507), **global economy** (p. 508)

3 **register** (p. 513), **informed citizen** (p. 513)

RECALL FACTS

Answer these questions.

4 In what ways can people contact their representatives?

5 Why was the Pledge of Allegiance written?

Write the letter of the best choice.

6 Today most new immigrants to the United States come from countries in—
A Europe and South America.
B Asia and Europe.
C Asia and Latin America.
D Africa and South America.

7 Under a free enterprise system—
F people can own and run their own businesses.
G the government owns most businesses.
H most people work in agriculture.
J the government tells businesses what to charge for goods and services.

8 The two main political parties in the United States today are the—
A Republican and Federalist parties.
B Federalist and Democratic parties.
C Republican and Democratic parties.
D Democratic and Whig parties.

9 The most common way American citizens take part in politics is by—
F running for office.
G volunteering as campaign workers.
H joining a political party.
J serving on a jury.

THINK CRITICALLY

10 How does immigration continue to shape the United States today?

11 What do you think might happen if cities did not try to manage urban growth?

12 How have American jobs changed over the last 100 years?

13 Why do you think the United States has remained a strong nation for so long?

APPLY SKILLS

Use a Cartogram
Review the map and the cartogram in the skill on pages 498–499. Then answer the following questions.

14 Why is New Jersey shown larger than Maine on the cartogram?

15 Which West Coast state has the smallest population?

Identify Political Symbols

16 Write down the names of the last five United States Presidents. Then use the Almanac in the back of your textbook to find out their political parties. Decide which party symbol would be used to represent each President.

Think Critically

10 People come from many different countries, bringing with them customs and traditions that diversify the culture of the United States.

11 They may risk becoming overcrowded.

12 More Americans work in foreign-owned companies, and many people rely upon new technologies and other innovations, such as the microchip and the Internet, to do their work.

13 The framers of the Constitution created a document that provided a strong enough balance of structure and flexibility to suit the nation's changing needs.

Apply Skills

Use a Cartogram

14 because it has more people

15 Oregon

Identify Political Symbols

16 Students should correctly identify the last five Presidents and their parties, using appropriate symbols to represent each one's party.

ACTIVITY BOOK

Use the CHAPTER 13 TEST PREPARATION on page 133 of the Activity Book.

ASSESSMENT

Use the CHAPTER 13 TEST on pages 109–112 of the Assessment Program.

Use Vocabulary

1 Innovations such as the **Internet** and **teleconferencing** allow people to communicate without having to travel.

2 **Interdependence** among nations has led to the development of a larger **global economy**.

3 An **informed citizen** who is **registered** to vote is able to take part in the political process.

Recall Facts

4 letter, phone call, and e-mail (p. 513)

5 for students to recite on Columbus Day (p. 515)

6 C (p. 493)

7 F (p. 508)

8 C (p. 514)

9 H (p. 514)

Chapter 14 Planning Guide Partners in the Hemisphere

LESSON	PACING	OBJECTIVES	VOCABULARY
Introduce the Chapter pp. 522–523	1 Day	■ Interpret information in visuals. ■ Use critical thinking skills to organize and analyze information.	**Word Work:** Preview Vocabulary, p. 523
1 Mexico pp. 524–528	1 Day	■ Describe the geography and cultural heritage of Mexico. ■ Identify changes over time in Mexico's government, from its days as a republic to its current status as a democratic nation. ■ Identify leaders in Mexico's government, such as Vicente Fox. ■ Analyze the relationship between the growth of Mexico's cities and the growth of the middle class.	**middle class** **interest rate** **Word Work:** Compound Terms, p. 524
2 Central America and the Caribbean pp. 529–533	1 Day	■ Describe the geography and people of Central America and the Caribbean. ■ Identify the challenges of living in a tropical climate. ■ Describe the governments of Central America and the Caribbean.	**commonwealth** **embargo** **free election** **Word Work:** Word Origins, p. 529
CHART AND GRAPH SKILLS **Read Population Pyramids** pp. 534–535	1 Day	■ Interpret information in a population pyramid. ■ Gather and organize information using a population pyramid.	**population pyramid** **life expectancy** **median age**

READING	INTEGRATE LEARNING	REACH ALL LEARNERS	RESOURCES
Compare and Contrast, p. 523			
Reading Social Studies: **Anticipation Guide,** p. 525 **Compare and Contrast,** p. 525 Reading Social Studies: **Graphic Organizer,** p. 526 Reading Social Studies: **Anticipation Guide Responses,** p. 528	Language Arts **Informative Writing,** p. 527	**Auditory Learners,** p. 526 **Extend and Enrich,** p. 528 **Reteach the Lesson,** p. 528	**Activity Book,** p. 134 **Reading and Vocabulary Transparency 7-7**
Reading Social Studies: **Graphic Organizer,** p. 530 Reading Social Studies: **Reread to Clarify,** p. 532 Reading Social Studies: **Graphic Organizer Responses,** p. 533	Science **Hurricanes,** p. 531	**Extend and Enrich,** p. 533 **Reteach the Lesson,** p. 533	**Activity Book,** p. 135 **Reading and Vocabulary Transparency 7-8** Internet Resources
	Language Arts **Write a Scientific Summary,** p. 534	**Extend and Enrich,** p. 535 **Reteach the Skill,** p. 535	**Activity Book,** pp. 136–137 **Skill Transparency 7-3**

LESSON	PACING	OBJECTIVES	VOCABULARY
3 South America pp. 536–540	2 Days	■ Describe the geography and people of South America. ■ Describe how South American countries gained their independence and some of the problems that came with it. ■ Identify new challenges facing South America.	**standard of living** **liberate** **deforestation**
4 Canada pp. 541–545	1 Day	■ Describe the geography of Canada. ■ Describe Canada's history, from first settlement to self-government. ■ Explain why some citizens want to secede from Canada. ■ Identify Canada's role in the world economy.	**province** **separatist** **Word Work:** Preview Vocabulary, p. 541
MAP AND GLOBE SKILLS **Use a Time Zone Map** pp. 546–547	1 Day	■ Analyze and interpret a time zone map. ■ Compare time in different parts of the Western Hemisphere.	**time zone**
Chapter Review and Test Preparation pp. 548–549	1 Day		

READING	INTEGRATE LEARNING	REACH ALL LEARNERS	RESOURCES
Reading Social Studies: **Study Questions,** p. 537 Reading Social Studies: **Study Question Responses,** p. 540	Science **Identify Unique Species,** p. 537	**Kinesthetic Learners,** p. 538 **Below Level Learners,** p. 539 **Extend and Enrich,** p. 540 **Reteach the Lesson,** p. 540	**Activity Book,** p. 138 🌐 **Reading and Vocabulary Transparency 7-9** 💻 Internet Resources
Reading Social Studies: **Summarize,** p. 542 Reading Social Studies: **Summarize Responses,** p. 545	Music **Canadian Music,** p. 544	**Below-Level Learners,** p. 541 **Auditory Learners,** p. 543 **Extend and Enrich,** p. 545 **Reteach the Lesson,** p. 545	**Activity Book,** p. 139 🌐 **Reading and Vocabulary Transparency 7-10** 💻 Internet Resources
		Extend and Enrich, p. 547 **Reteach the Skill,** p. 547	**Activity Book,** pp. 140–141 🌐 **Skill Transparency 7-4** 💿 **GeoSkills CD-ROM**
		Test Preparation, p. 548	**Activity Book,** pp. 142–143 🌐 **Reading and Vocabulary Transparency 7-11** ✅ **Assessment Program, Chapter 14 Test,** pp. 113–116

Activity Book

LESSON 1

Name _____ Date _____

Mexico

Directions Write the letter next to each event listed below in the appropriate place on the time line.

a. In the early 1900s, Mexican leaders write a new constitution that includes land for farmers and a six-year limit on presidents' terms.

b. Soon after the Mexican economy starts to recover, Mexico elects its first president from the Partido Acción Nacional (PAN), Vicente Fox.

c. United States President George W. Bush meets with Mexican President Vicente Fox to show the importance of ties between the two nations.

d. In the late 1900s Mexico, Canada, and the United States sign the North American Free Trade Agreement (NAFTA).

e. Mexico wins its independence.

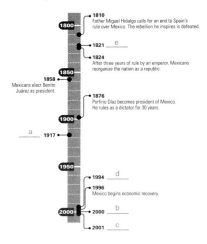

1800 — **1810** Father Miguel Hidalgo calls for an end to Spain's rule over Mexico. The rebellion he inspires is defeated.

— **1821** _e_

— **1824** After three years of rule by an emperor, Mexicans reorganize the nation as a republic.

1850 —

1858 Mexicans elect Benito Juárez as president.

— **1876** Porfirio Díaz becomes president of Mexico. He rules as a dictator for 30 years.

1900 —

_a_ — **1917**

1950 —

— **1994** _d_

— **1996** Mexico begins economic recovery.

2000 — **2000** _b_

— **2001** _c_

Use after reading Chapter 14, Lesson 1, pages 524–528.

LESSON 2

Name _____ Date _____

Central America and the Caribbean

Directions Answer the questions below.

❶ What seven countries make up Central America? Belize, Guatemala, Honduras, El Salvador, Nicaragua, Costa Rica, Panama

❷ What crops are grown in the countries of Central America? bananas, beans, coffee, corn, cotton, and sugarcane

❸ Which natural events challenge the residents of islands in the Caribbean? volcanic eruptions, earthquakes, tropical storms, hurricanes, droughts, heavy rains, mudslides, and flooding

❹ What kind of government does Cuba have? a communist dictatorship

❺ Which Caribbean islands are part of the United States? Puerto Rico, the Virgin Islands

❻ How is the government of Costa Rica similar to the government of the United States? It is a democracy with three branches of government and a president elected to a four-year term.

SKILL PRACTICE

Name _____ Date _____

CHART AND GRAPH SKILLS
Read Population Pyramids

Directions Study the population pyramid of Costa Rica below. Then write a paragraph that explains to another student what the pyramid reveals about the population of Costa Rica. As you write, try to answer these questions:

❶ What is a population pyramid?

❷ Which part of the pyramid is the largest? What does this mean?

❸ Which part of the pyramid is the smallest? What does this mean?

❹ Does the pyramid show any differences between females and males?

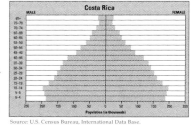

Source: U.S. Census Bureau, International Data Base.

❺ About how many Costa Ricans are in your age group?

Students' paragraphs should include the following:

1) A population pyramid shows the division of a country's population by age and sex.   2) The largest part is males and females aged 10–14. There are more people in this group than in any other group in Costa Rica.   3) The smallest part is males aged 75–79. This is the smallest population group in Costa Rica. 4) There are more young men than young women in Costa Rica, about the same number of middle-aged men and women, and slightly more older women than men.   5) For 10-year olds: more than 400,000 people in age group; for 9-year olds: about 400,000 people in age group

(continued)

Use after reading Chapter 14, Skill Lesson, pages 534–535.

SKILL PRACTICE

Name _____ Date _____

Directions The population pyramid on the left represents the population of Mexico in 1980. The population pyramid on the right illustrates what the Mexican population might look like in 2030. Use the information from the two pyramids to answer the questions below.

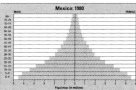 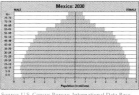

Source: U.S. Census Bureau, International Data Base.   Source: U.S. Census Bureau, International Data Base.

❻ About how many people were 20–24 years old in 1980? about 6 million in 2030? about 10 million

❼ Which age group was the smallest in 1980? 80+ years old in 2030? 80+ years old

❽ Which age group was the largest in 1980? 0–4 years old in 2030? 10–14 years old

❾ What is the predicted approximate increase in the number of people 50–54 years old between 1980 and 2030? about 6 million

❿ Do any gender/age groups show a predicted decrease between 1980 and 2030? yes

If so, which one(s)? males and females 0–4 years old

⓫ About how many people were less than 15 years old in 1980? about 30 million

---

LESSON 3

Name _____ Date _____

South America

Directions Read each statement below. If the statement is true, write *T* in the blank. If the statement is false, write *F* in the blank.

1 __F__ Most of South America is covered in tropical rain forest.

2 __T__ Scientists feel that it is important to preserve the rain forests of South America because of their potential medical benefits.

3 __F__ At one time Spain controlled all of South America.

4 __F__ All *mestizos* come from South America.

5 __T__ The American Revolution encouraged people in South American colonies to fight for their independence.

6 __T__ Simón Bolívar was one of the leaders of the efforts to free South American colonies.

7 __F__ Simón Bolívar believed that the former South American colonies had so much in common that they could join together as a single nation.

8 __T__ In the new, independent countries of South America, dictators or armies often took control of the political process.

9 __T__ Reformers in South America have worked to help small farmers own their land.

LESSON 4

Name _____ Date _____

Canada

Directions Circle the letter of the best answer.

1 Which best represents the flag of Canada?

A.   B.   (C.)   D.

2 Which is a prairie province of Canada?
(F.) Alberta   H. Ontario
G. Quebec   J. Nunavut

3 Which ocean does **not** border Canada?
A. Arctic   C. Pacific
(B.) Indian   D. Atlantic

4 Which best describes the relationship between Canada and Great Britain right after the British North America Act of 1867?
F. Independent nation   H. Commonwealth partner
G. Conquered territory   (J.) Representative government

5 Who is the official leader of the executive branch of the Canadian government?
A. The Parliament   (C.) The British monarch
B. The prime minister   D. The governor-general

6 Who runs the executive branch of the Canadian government on a day-to-day basis?
F. The Parliament   H. The British monarch
(G.) The prime minister   J. The governor-general

7 Which nation buys the majority of Canada's exports?
A. France   C. Great Britain
B. Australia   (D.) the United States

SKILL PRACTICE

Name _____ Date _____

MAP AND GLOBE SKILLS
Use a Time Zone Map

Directions Use the time zone map below to answer the questions.

United States Time Zones

Eastern time zone · Central time zone · Mountain time zone · Pacific time zone · Alaska time zone · Hawaii-Aleutian time zone

1 How many time zones cover the 50 states? __6__

2 Which of these cities are in the Central time zone: Chicago, Dallas, Denver?
Chicago, Dallas

3 When it is 8:00 A.M. in New York City, what time is it in Los Angeles?
5:00 A.M.

4 When it is 3:30 P.M. in Chicago, what time is it in Honolulu?
11:30 A.M.

(continued)

SKILL PRACTICE

Name _____ Date _____

Directions Use the time zone map to complete the chart below.

Western Hemisphere Time Zones

When the time is . . .	The time is . . .
5 2:00 A.M. in Buenos Aires	11:00 P.M. in Chicago
6 1:00 P.M. in São Paulo	12:00 P.M. in La Paz
7 6:30 A.M. in Los Angeles	9:30 A.M. in Lima
8 3:45 P.M. in Houston	4:45 P.M. in Bogotá
9 2:00 P.M. in Rio de Janeiro	10:00 A.M. in Phoenix
10 11:30 A.M. in Managua	11:30 A.M. in Mexico City
11 9:15 P.M. in Caracas	8:15 P.M. in Washington, D.C.

Name _____ Date _____

The United States, Canada, and Mexico

Directions Complete this graphic organizer by comparing and contrasting the United States, Canada, and Mexico.

THE UNITED STATES AND CANADA		THE UNITED STATES AND MEXICO	
↓	↓	↓	↓
SIMILARITIES	**DIFFERENCES**	**SIMILARITIES**	**DIFFERENCES**
Both Canada and the United States were once under British rule.	Today, Canada's executive branch is still headed by Britain's monarch while the United States government is fully independent.	Mexico and the United States both have democratic governments.	The president of Mexico can serve only one six-year term, but the President of the United States can serve two four-year terms.

Use after reading Chapter 14, pages 522–547.

© Harcourt

· CHAPTER · Name _____ Date _____

14 Test Preparation

Directions Read each question and choose the best answer. Then fill in the circle for the answer you have chosen. Be sure to fill in the circle completely.

❶ Which two civilizations have created the cultural heritage of Mexico?
Ⓐ PRI and PAN
Ⓑ *Mestizo* and French
Ⓒ Native American and Spanish
Ⓓ North American and South American

❷ Which do many of the Central American and Caribbean nations have in common?
Ⓕ Land area
Ⓖ Population size
Ⓗ Threat of hurricanes
Ⓙ Communist governments

❸ Which word best describes the political history of Haiti?
Ⓐ Isolated
Ⓑ Unstable
Ⓒ Communist
Ⓓ Democratic

❹ Which person led the efforts to free parts of South America from colonial rule?
Ⓕ Fidel Castro
Ⓖ Simón Bolívar
Ⓗ Jean-Bertrand Aristide
Ⓙ Father Miguel Hidalgo

❺ Which two nations in the Western Hemisphere share a border of almost 4,000 miles?
Ⓐ Colombia and Brazil
Ⓑ Colombia and Panama
Ⓒ United States and Mexico
Ⓓ United States and Canada

© Harcourt

Use after reading Chapter 14, pages 522–547.

COMMUNITY RESOURCES

Experts on International Relations

_____
_____
_____
_____
_____

Experts on Mexico

_____
_____
_____
_____
_____

Experts on Canada

_____
_____
_____
_____
_____

Experts on South America

_____
_____
_____
_____
_____

Chapter 14 Assessment

CONTENT / VOCABULARY

·CHAPTER·

14 Test

Name _____ Date _____

Part One: Test Your Understanding

MULTIPLE CHOICE (4 points each)

Directions Circle the letter of the best answer.

1 What two cultures does a mestizo heritage blend?
A Native American and French
B French and Austrian
C Spanish and French
D Native American and Spanish

2 Which of the following rulers governed Mexico for more than 30 years?
F an Austrian prince
G dictator Porfirio Díaz
H Father Miguel Hidalgo
J President Benito Juárez

3 Mexico's 1917 constitution ensured that—
A only PAN candidates could be elected as president.
B the PRI party would have to share power.
C presidents could serve for only six years.
D people's political choices would increase.

4 Many cities in northern Mexico grew during the twentieth century because—
F they were located in a federal district.
G they encouraged people to move from cities to farms.
H interest rates increased greatly.
J many factories were built there.

5 What is the main language of most Central American countries?
A English
B Spanish
C French
D African languages

6 Which Central American country has three branches of government like those of the United States?
F Cuba
G Haiti
H Puerto Rico
J Costa Rica

(continued)

Chapter 14 Test

CONTENT / VOCABULARY

Name _____ Date _____

7 In the late 1700s and early 1800s, people in South America wanted—
A to colonize Central America.
B independence from European countries.
C goods from North America.
D economic freedom.

8 Simón Bolívar and José de San Martín were important figures in South America because they—
F established sugarcane and coffee plantations.
G supported the French Revolution.
H worked to make South American colonies independent.
J helped settle the area for the Dutch.

9 The Quebec Act of 1774—
A included a Charter of Rights and Freedoms.
B made Canada and New Zealand partner nations in the British Commonwealth.
C created Nova Scotia, Quebec, and the Dominion of Canada.
D allowed French settlers in Canada to maintain their laws, language, and religion.

10 Canada's strongest economic partnership is with—
F Mexico.
G the United States.
H France.
J Britain.

MATCHING (4 points each)

Directions Match the descriptions on the left with the terms on the right. Then write the correct letter in the space provided.

11 __C__ when one nation refuses to trade with another

12 __A__ a type of Canadian political region

13 __E__ a percentage amount banks charge when they loan money

14 __D__ when many trees in an area are cut down

15 __B__ a kind of territory that governs itself

A province
B commonwealth
C embargo
D deforestation
E interest rate

(continued)

Chapter 14 Test

SKILLS

Name _____ Date _____

Part Two: Test Your Skills

READ A POPULATION PYRAMID (5 points each)

Directions Use the population pyramid to answer the following questions.

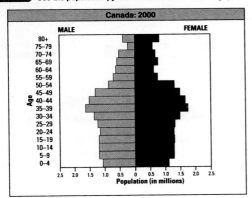

Source: U.S. Census Bureau, International Data Base.

16 In the year 2000 what age group had the largest number of people in Canada?
The largest group was people aged 35–39 years.

17 In the year 2000 what age group had the smallest number of people in Canada?
The group of people aged 75–79 was the smallest.

18 In which age groups are there more females than males? all but ages 60–64

19 What general statement can you make about Canada's population from this pyramid? Possible response: The largest group of Canadian citizens is between the ages of 30 and 49.

(continued)

Chapter 14 Test

APPLICATION / WRITING

Name _____ Date _____

Part Three: Apply What You Have Learned

20 SEQUENCING (10 points)

The list below describes some of the many governments that have ruled in Mexico. Put this list of governments in order on the time line below.

Governments in Mexico

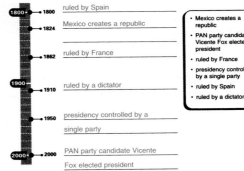

21 ESSAY (10 points)

Many people in Central America, South America, and Canada have struggled to attain self-government. Write a paragraph that describes one region discussed in the chapter and explains how people there have changed the way that their area is ruled.

Possible responses: Many countries were European colonies for a long time. Simón Bolívar and José de San Martín led many South American countries to gain independence from Spain. Canada gradually gained more independence from Great Britain. Haiti has had problems maintaining a stable democracy.

_____

_____

Chapter 14 Test

Introduce the Chapter

PAGES 522–523

OBJECTIVES

- Interpret information in visuals.
- Use critical thinking skills to organize and analyze information.

Access Prior Knowledge

Ask students to share experiences they have had with their neighbors. Why is it important to maintain good relations with neighbors?

Visual Learning

Picture Have students examine the photograph. As a class, discuss how these images suggest the content of this chapter.

Locate It Map Washington, D.C. is located on the Potomac River. The city of Washington, D.C., is on federal land, and is not part of any state.

ORGANIZATION OF AMERICAN STATES FLAG GARDEN

The Organization of American States, or OAS, was formed in 1890. It is the world's oldest regional organization. Today, the OAS is made up of 35 Western Hemisphere nations. It has four official languages—English, Spanish, French, and Portuguese.

LOCATE IT

MARYLAND
Washington, D.C.
VIRGINIA
Organization of American States Flag Garden

BACKGROUND

Picture The flags in the picture represent the countries that are part of the Organization of American States (OAS). Countries as large as Canada and as small as Trinidad are among the organization's members. With its headquarters in Washington, D.C., the OAS promotes social justice, supports international law, and believes that an attack against a member nation is an attack against all OAS members. The OAS works to settle disputes peacefully.

BACKGROUND

Quotation President George W. Bush, elected in November 2000, is the son of George Bush, who was President of the United States from 1989–1993. Not since John Adams (1796) and his son, John Quincy Adams (1824), were each elected President have both a father and son been Presidents of the United States. President George W. Bush's State Department speech was one of his first speeches as President.

14

Partners in the Hemisphere

" Our future cannot be separated from the future of our neighbors. "
—George W. Bush, State Department speech, February 15, 2001

 Compare and Contrast

To **compare** two things is to find out how they are alike. To **contrast** them is to find out how they are different.

As you read this chapter, be sure to do the following.

• Compare and contrast the issues and events involving the United States and its neighbors.

Chapter 14 ■ 523

Read and Respond

As students read the title, ask them in which hemisphere they live. The Western Hemisphere includes Greenland, Canada, the United States, Mexico, Central America, South America, and the Caribbean islands.

Quotation Have a volunteer read the quotation aloud.

Q To whom does the word "neighbors" refer?

A Answers will vary, but should reflect that President Bush is referring to neighboring countries. He considers our country to be part of a global community.

 Compare and Contrast

Have students use a graphic organizer to illustrate the similarities and differences they identify about key topics in the chapter.

• Students will find a compare-and-contrast graphic organizer on page 142 of the Activity Book.

• A completed graphic organizer can be found on page 142 of the Activity Book, Teacher's Edition.

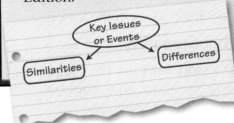

WORD WORK

Preview Vocabulary Have students list the vocabulary terms from each lesson of the chapter and write what they already know about each term in a chart like the one shown. Then have students read the chapter, and record the definitions in the third column.

Term	What I Know about the Term	Definition

MAKE IT RELEVANT

Discussion Topics As you teach the chapter, generate discussion with students using these topics. The topics encourage students to think beyond the borders of the United States.

■ What other countries have you visited in the Western Hemisphere? How were they the same as or different from the United States?

■ What makes a "good" neighbor—either in your community or in the global community?

■ Who are the United States' closest neighbors?

OBJECTIVES

- Describe the geography and cultural heritage of Mexico.
- Identify changes over time in Mexico's government, from its days as a republic to its current status as a democratic nation.
- Identify leaders in Mexico's government, such as Vicente Fox.
- Analyze the relationship between the growth of Mexico's cities and the growth of its middle class.

 Compare and Contrast
pp. 523, 524, 525, 528, 548

Vocabulary

SEE READING AND VOCABULARY TRANSPARENCY 7-7 OR THE WORD CARDS ON PP. V59–V60.

middle class	interest rate
p. 528	p. 528

 When Minutes Count

Have students examine the map on page 525. Use the map to help discuss main ideas in the lesson.

Quick Summary

This lesson describes the geography, history, economy, and people of Mexico.

 Motivate

Set the Purpose

Big Idea Explain to students that Mexico is a collection of states with diverse lands, people, and histories.

Access Prior Knowledge

Ask students to review what they know about the war between Mexico and the United States.

Mexico

| 1800 | 1900 | PRESENT |

 COMPARE AND CONTRAST
As you read, compare and contrast facts about Mexico.

BIG IDEA
Mexico's people, history, and economy have played an important role in the history of the United States.

VOCABULARY
middle class
interest rate

In 1521 the Spanish conquistador Hernando Cortés conquered the Aztec Empire and claimed Mexico for Spain. For the next 300 years, Mexico remained under Spanish rule. Then, in 1821, a revolution ended Spain's rule, and Mexico became an independent country.

Independence, however, did not immediately bring peace. For many years afterward, the people of Mexico struggled to build an orderly society. The Mexican Constitution of 1917 reorganized the country's government and led to closer ties with the United States. Today, the two countries are major trading partners.

The Land and People of Mexico

Mexico is a land with many mountains. Two mountain ranges, the Sierra Madre Occidental on the west and the Sierra Madre Oriental on the east, stretch along Mexico's coasts. Between these mountains lies the Mexican Plateau, a region of rich farmland

FAST FACT Two states in Mexico share part of their names with a state in the United States—California.

WORD WORK

Compound Terms Point out that the vocabulary terms for this lesson are compound terms and that the words *middle, class, interest,* and *rate* have several different meanings by themselves. Invite students to work in groups to prepare sentences that show the many different meanings of the individual words as well as the compound terms *middle class* and *interest rate.*

BACKGROUND

Mexico Today About 100 million people live in Mexico today, the vast majority of them in urban areas such as Mexico City. Mexico's wealth of natural resources has led to the growth of industries such as silver mining and oil production. Tourism is one of Mexico's fastest-growing industries and its most important after oil.

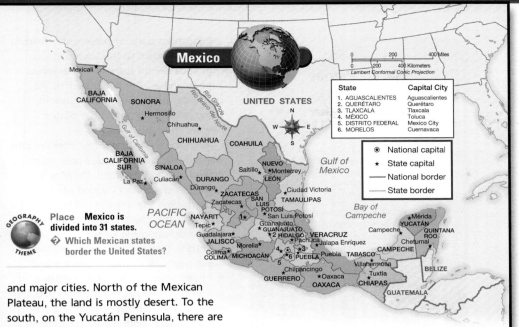

Mexico

State	Capital City
1. AGUASCALIENTES	Aguascalientes
2. QUERÉTARO	Querétaro
3. TLAXCALA	Tlaxcala
4. MÉXICO	Toluca
5. DISTRITO FEDERAL	Mexico City
6. MORELOS	Cuernavaca

⊛ National capital
★ State capital
— National border
— State border

Place Mexico is divided into 31 states.
❖ Which Mexican states border the United States?

and major cities. North of the Mexican Plateau, the land is mostly desert. To the south, on the Yucatán Peninsula, there are both rain forests and grassy plains.

Most people in Mexico today trace their cultural heritage to two main groups—Native American and Spanish. In fact, more than 60 percent of the people are mestizos, people of mixed Indian and Spanish ancestry. Mexicans continue to honor the contributions of both groups with public history displays and celebrations.

REVIEW **What two groups have mainly influenced Mexico's culture and people?**
COMPARE AND CONTRAST
Native American and Spanish

These hikers (left) are in the rugged desert of Mexico's Baja Peninsula.

Mexico, a Republic

Most of the wealth and power in colonial Mexico belonged to people of pure Spanish ancestry. Other Mexicans had few opportunities. In September 1810, Father Miguel Hidalgo (mee•GAYL ee•DAHL•goh) gave a speech in his church calling for a revolution against Spain. Hidalgo's rebel army was later defeated, but his actions were not forgotten. The revolution continued, and in 1821 Mexico gained its independence.

In time, Mexico became a republic. The Mexican people, however, had little experience with self-government. Presidents were no sooner elected than they were forced out of office by their enemies. During those same years, Mexico lost most of its northern lands to the United States. Texas, which won its independence from Mexico in 1836, became part of the United States in 1845.

Chapter 14 ▪ 525

Focus Skill

READING SKILL

Compare and Contrast Ask students to compare the struggles of the Mexican people to establish a republic to that of the British colonists in America in the 1770s. Encourage students to research both movements and to report their findings in brief summaries.

---

2 Teach

The Land and People of Mexico

Read and Respond

Geography Reinforce to students that the majority of Mexico is highlands or mountains, with very little suitable farming land.

Visual Learning

Map Help students locate the state of Mexico on the map on page 525. Explain that Mexico is both the name of the country and the name of a member state.
CAPTION ANSWER: Baja California, Sonora, Chihuahua, Coahuila, Nuevo León, and Tamaulipas

Mexico, a Republic

Read and Respond

History Explain that in the years following Mexico's independence, the country was run by a series of select groups seeking personal gains. As a result, there was inefficiency in Mexico's government.

Fiestas Patrias

Explain that *Diez y Seis de Septiembre* has the same significance to the people in Mexico as the Fourth of July does to people in the United States. Ask students to compare the celebrations of the two holidays. Both feature speeches, patriotic songs and dances, and parades.

Read and Respond

Culture and Society Explain that the Mexican Revolution began in response to dissatisfaction with Díaz's policies. Inform students that the revolution lasted for a decade and involved struggles among various factions for control of the country. Explain that many of the reforms sought during the revolution were realized in the Constitution of 1917, such as workers' rights and limits on a president's tenure.

Fiestas Patrias

Each year the Mexican people celebrate two national holidays known as the *Fiestas Patrias*, or festivals of the country. The first of these holidays, *Cinco de Mayo*, or May 5, honors Mexico's victory over the French at Puebla on May 5, 1862. The second holiday, *Diez y Seis de Septiembre*, or September 16, is Mexico's national independence day. Both celebrations often feature speeches, patriotic songs, dances, and parades.

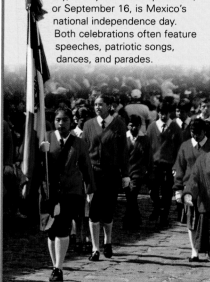

Three years later, following a war with the United States, Mexico agreed to give up most of its remaining northern lands to the United States. These lands included present-day California, Utah, and Nevada and parts of New Mexico, Arizona, Colorado, and Wyoming. In return, the United States paid Mexico $15 million. Mexico later sold

526 ▪ Unit 7

the southern parts of present-day Arizona and New Mexico to the United States.

In 1861 Benito Juárez (HWAHR•ays), a Zapotec Indian, became president. As president, Juárez helped bring about many reforms, including the private ownership of land.

From the start, Juárez had enemies who wanted him out of office. Those enemies looked to France for help. On May 5, 1862, French soldiers invaded Mexico and attacked the city of Puebla. Though greatly outnumbered, the Mexicans at Puebla defeated the French.

Despite their loss at Puebla, the French eventually took control of Mexico and removed Juárez from office. Within a few years, however, the Mexican people rebelled. Juárez became president again.

After Juárez died, the dictator Porfirio Díaz (pour•FEER•yoh DEE•ahs) ruled for more than 30 years. Díaz ordered railroads built and factories enlarged. Díaz brought economic growth to Mexico, but problems remained. Many poor farmers lost their land. When Díaz took control, 20 percent of the people owned land. Thirty years later, only 2 percent of the people owned land.

In 1910 many Mexican farmers and other groups fought against the dictatorship. Díaz resigned, but the fighting continued in Mexico. When the fighting ended, the leaders of the revolution took control of Mexico. They wrote a new constitution that limited the time a president could serve to a six-year term.

Benito Juárez

Mexican Cession Ask students to consider the lands acquired in the Mexican Cession.

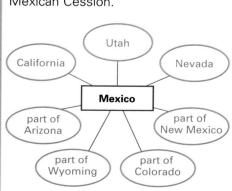

Graphic Organizer Organize students into pairs, and have them use information from this lesson to create a time line of the political history of Mexico. Remind students that the purpose of a time line is to show events over a period of time. Ask advanced learners to expand their time lines to include events before 1821.

Auditory Learners Ask students to work in pairs or small groups and take turns reading aloud the subsection Mexico, a Republic. Each student should read aloud two or three paragraphs at a time. Listening students may take notes. Then have students discuss the details they heard.

Mexico City, like all large cities, has crowded streets. Air pollution from automobile exhaust is often a problem in the city.

LOCATE IT

Mexico City

MEXICO

Many government-owned farms were divided among farm families.

While more people owned land, they still had few political choices. For more than 70 years, a single party controlled the presidency. Candidates from other political parties were elected to the Mexican Congress, but only those from the Partido Revolucionario Institucional (PRI) became president.

The election of July 2000 changed everything. Mexicans chose Vicente Fox, from the Partido Acción Nacional (PAN), as their new president. When asked how difficult his job as president would be, Fox replied, "The challenge is gigantic, but so are our resources. In Mexico we have a saying, 'Every newborn child comes with a gift.' Democracy will bring us lots of benefits and hope."

REVIEW **How does the Mexican constitution limit a president's power?** A president can serve only a six-year term.

A Growing Middle Class

Mexico is divided into 31 states and one federal district. The federal district contains Mexico City, Mexico's capital. About 9 million people live in Mexico City. About 9 million more people live in its metropolitan area, making Mexico City one of the world's most populated metropolitan areas.

Mexico City is just one of the large cities that lie on the Mexican Plateau. In fact, more than half of Mexico's population lives in this region. Other large cities on the Mexican Plateau include Monterrey, Guadalajara, and Puebla. Each of these cities has more than a million people.

Many cities in Mexico have grown as people have moved from rural areas to cities to find new jobs and better wages. In recent years, many new factories have been built in northern Mexico.

Chapter 14 527

INTEGRATE LANGUAGE ARTS

Informative Writing
Ask students to research and write short reports explaining the causes and effects of Mexican people moving to cities. Students may focus on the economic, cultural, or political impacts that such a move would bring. Encourage students to use reference sources, including encyclopedias and the Internet, in their research.

A Growing Middle Class

Read and Respond

Civics and Government Explain that the Federal District in Mexico City is equivalent to the District of Columbia in the United States. Inform students that both areas are seats of national government.

Visual Learning

Photograph Direct students' attention to the picture of Mexican president Vicente Fox and United States President George W. Bush on page 528. Explain that both leaders have worked closely with political parties other than their own to pass legislation.

Q **What leadership qualities do both President Fox and President Bush share?**

A Answers may vary, but should reflect that both leaders share the leadership quality of cooperation.

3 Close

Summarize Key Content

- Mexico is a land of mountains, plateaus, deserts, and rain forests.
- Mexico's people trace their heritage to two main groups, Native Americans and the Spanish.
- Mexico struggled for many years to become a republic and succeeded in the year 2000, when Vicente Fox was elected president.
- Mexico has become a nation of major cities in which people work largely in manufacturing and other related industries.

READING SOCIAL STUDIES

Anticipation Guide Have students check their responses to the Anticipation Guide.

1. The people of Mexico trace their heritage to ~~three~~ main groups. two

2. Mexico lost the land that is now Texas as a result of a war with the United States.

3. Mexico's trade with Canada nearly ~~tripled~~ after the signing of the North American Free Trade Agreement in 1994. doubled

● USE READING AND VOCABULARY TRANSPARENCY 7-7. **7-7 TRANSPARENCY**

Assess

Lesson 1 Review—Answers

 COMPARE AND CONTRAST The land in northern Mexico is mostly desert; the land in the Yucatán includes rain forests and grassy plains.

❶ **BIG IDEA** in the Mexican Plateau

❷ **VOCABULARY** The growth of manufacturing in Mexico has led to the growth of a **middle class**.

❸ **TIME LINE** in 1821

❹ **HISTORY** It wanted to remove Benito Juárez from office.

❺ **CRITICAL THINKING—Analyze** Challenges might include overcrowding, pollution, and poverty.

 Performance Assessment Guidelines Check students' bar graphs. Then ask students to research data for the current year and add it to their graphs.

ACTIVITY BOOK

Use ACTIVITY BOOK, p. 134, to reinforce and extend student learning.

George W. Bush's first international trip as President of the United States was to visit with Mexican president Vicente Fox. The trip emphasized the strong ties between the two nations.

As a result, Ciudad Juárez, Matamoros, Tijuana, and other cities near the United States border have all grown quickly.

The growth of manufacturing and other industries in Mexico also led to the growth of a large **middle class**, an economic level between the poor and the wealthy. Today, Mexico's middle class is one of the largest in the Americas.

In 1994, however, even middle-class families found buying most products difficult. The value of the peso, Mexico's basic unit of money, suddenly dropped. That caused prices in Mexico to rise sharply. **Interest rates**, the amounts that banks charge to loan money, rose as high as 80 percent. To help, the United States arranged $52 billion in loans to Mexico. Had the Mexican economy collapsed, it would have had a terrible effect on the world economy.

The Mexican economy also improved in 1994 when Canada, Mexico, and the United States put the North American Free Trade Agreement into effect. The year before NAFTA began, trade between the United States and Mexico totaled $80 billion a year. By 2000 that figure was $230 billion. Clothing, shoes, and other goods are made in Mexico and imported by the United States.

REVIEW Why did Mexico's middle class grow larger? because of the growth in manufacturing and other industries

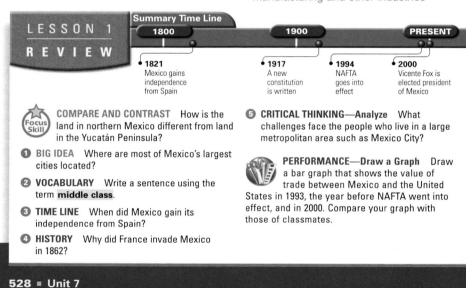

LESSON 1 REVIEW

Summary Time Line

1800 — 1900 — PRESENT

● 1821 Mexico gains independence from Spain
● 1917 A new constitution is written
● 1994 NAFTA goes into effect
● 2000 Vicente Fox is elected president of Mexico

COMPARE AND CONTRAST How is the land in northern Mexico different from land in the Yucatán Peninsula?

❶ **BIG IDEA** Where are most of Mexico's largest cities located?

❷ **VOCABULARY** Write a sentence using the term **middle class**.

❸ **TIME LINE** When did Mexico gain its independence from Spain?

❹ **HISTORY** Why did France invade Mexico in 1862?

❺ **CRITICAL THINKING—Analyze** What challenges face the people who live in a large metropolitan area such as Mexico City?

PERFORMANCE—Draw a Graph Draw a bar graph that shows the value of trade between Mexico and the United States in 1993, the year before NAFTA went into effect, and in 2000. Compare your graph with those of classmates.

528 ■ Unit 7

EXTEND AND ENRICH

Research Ask students to research the relations between Mexico and the United States before, during, and after the Mexican-American War. Students may report their findings in a round-table discussion.

RETEACH THE LESSON

Graphic Organizer Have students fill in the graphic organizer with facts from each subsection. Remind students that they may use the text to find or confirm information. Direct students to identify on their own the main topics covered in the lesson.

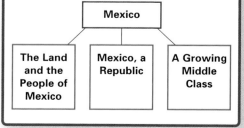

Mexico
- The Land and the People of Mexico
- Mexico, a Republic
- A Growing Middle Class

528 ■ **UNIT 7**

Central America and the Caribbean

1880   1940   PRESENT

Like the United States, many nations in Central America and the Caribbean have a history of democracy. Costa Rica has a long democratic tradition. So does Puerto Rico, with its ties to the United States. In some places in the region, however, people continue to struggle for democracy and economic security.

The Land and People

The geography of the nations of Central America and the Caribbean is as varied as the backgrounds of the people who live there. Towering mountains, sandy beaches, dense forests, and remote islands are just some of the features that mark these two regions.

COMPARE AND CONTRAST
As you read, compare and contrast events in Central American and Caribbean countries.

BIG IDEA
Central American and Caribbean countries have various regions, common heritages, and face similar challenges.

VOCABULARY
commonwealth
embargo
free election

On the outskirts of Guatemala City, a large volcano looms.

LOCATE IT

MEXICO

GUATEMALA

Guatemala City

Chapter 14 · 529

WORD WORK

Word Origins Write the word *commonwealth* on the board, and ask students to break the word into two parts, *common* and *wealth.* Explain that the word dates to the Middle Ages, when *commun welthe* referred to a community's general well-being. Explain that today the word may refer to a group of people or a state, such as the Commonwealth of Massachusetts, or to a specific political body, such as the Commonwealth of Independent States.

BACKGROUND

The United States in Central America The United States became involved in the development of Central America at the start of the 1900s, when Panama declared its independence and invited the United States to build a canal that would connect the Pacific and Atlantic oceans. The Panama Canal took ten years to complete and was considered a significant engineering achievement. The United States controlled the canal until 2000 when the rights reverted to Panama.

Lesson 2
PAGES 529–533

OBJECTIVES

- Describe the geography and people of Central America and the Caribbean.
- Identify the challenges of living in a tropical climate.
- Describe the governments of Central America and the Caribbean.

Compare and Contrast
pp. 523, 529, 531, 533, 548

Vocabulary
SEE READING AND VOCABULARY TRANSPARENCY 7-8 OR THE WORD CARDS ON PP. V59–V60.

commonwealth	free election
p. 532	p. 533
embargo p. 532	

When Minutes Count

Have students read about the Arecibo Observatory on page 532. Then invite them to tell in their own words what they just read.

Quick Summary

This lesson describes the various features and people of Central America and the Caribbean.

1 Motivate

Set the Purpose

Big Idea Explain that Central American and Caribbean countries share common heritages and face similar challenges.

Access Prior Knowledge

Have students discuss what they know about life in Central America and the Caribbean. How is life there similar to life in the United States? How is it different?

Graphic Organizer Suggest that students work in pairs to make web diagrams about Central America and the Caribbean. As students read, they should build web diagrams by writing key words, phrases, or concepts that relate to their region. After reading, students should compare their diagrams.

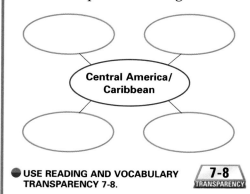

● USE READING AND VOCABULARY TRANSPARENCY 7-8.

7-8
TRANSPARENCY

2 Teach

The Land and People

Read and Respond

Geography Explain that Central America is essentially a land bridge that unites the ecosystems of North America and South America. Inform students that as a result, Central America features a mixture of plant and animal species from both continents.

Visual Learning

Map Direct students' attention to the map on page 530. Explain that the Caribbean Sea separates Central America from the Caribbean countries.

Q **Which Central American countries border both the Caribbean Sea and the Pacific Ocean?**

A Guatemala, Honduras, Nicaragua, Costa Rica, and Panama

CAPTION ANSWER: the Bahamas

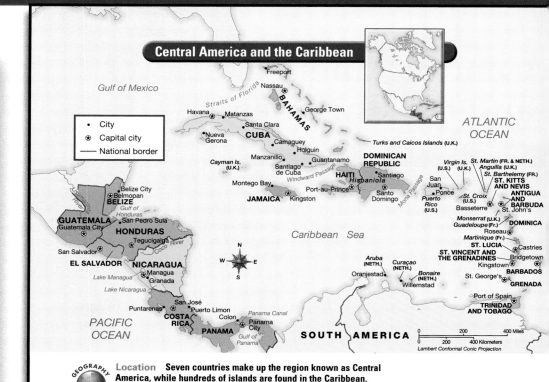

Central America and the Caribbean

- City
- ⊛ Capital city
- — National border

GEOGRAPHY THEME

Location Seven countries make up the region known as Central America, while hundreds of islands are found in the Caribbean.

◈ Which Caribbean country lies farthest north?

Traveling south from Mexico, a visitor would pass through Belize (buh·LEEZ), Guatemala (gwah·tuh·MAH·luh), Honduras, El Salvador, Nicaragua (nih·kuh·RAH·gwah), Costa Rica, and Panama. These seven countries form the 202,000 square miles (523,140 sq km) called Central America. Almost all the Central American countries have mountains. Volcanoes, some still active, formed the mountains. Ash from the volcanoes made the surrounding land fertile.

The Pacific Ocean forms the western borders of all the Central American countries except Belize. The Caribbean Sea, which is part of the Atlantic Ocean, forms the eastern borders of all the Central American countries except El Salvador.

Rain forests brighten the landscapes of Guatemala and Costa Rica. Costa Rica especially wants to preserve its rain forests' rich variety of plant and animal life. About 25 percent of Costa Rica's land has been set aside as nature preserves.

The fertile land of Central America is farmed to produce crops such as bananas, sugarcane, coffee, corn, cotton, and beans. Fishing is an important industry in Belize. Some countries, such as Guatemala and Panama, also have mineral resources.

People who live on islands in the Caribbean grow many of the same kinds

530 ▪ **Unit 7**

Mapping Central America Ask students to picture in their minds the arrangement of countries in Central America. Have students work in groups to make a map showing the order and placement of the countries.

Hispaniola The island of Hispaniola consists of mountain ranges, long valleys, and plains. It was visited in 1492 by Christopher Columbus and today is home to the nations of Haiti and the Dominican Republic. Haiti occupies the western one-third of the island and the Dominican Republic occupies the eastern two-thirds.

of crops as people in Central America, and they earn their livings in similar ways. Among the hundreds of islands in the Caribbean are Cuba, Puerto Rico, the Bahamas, Jamaica, and Hispaniola.

European explorers first visited these islands in the late 1400s and early 1500s. The beauty of the tropical islands and the rich land impressed the explorers. Today, visitors come for the islands' lovely beaches and warm climates.

Despite the beauty and the rich land, places in the Caribbean and Central America face special challenges. Earthquakes are common in Central America, and tropical storms often bring heavy rains to both regions. Hurricane Georges, for example, hit the eastern Caribbean, Haiti, and the Dominican Republic in September 1998. The storm caused more than $1.5 billion in damages.

One month later, Hurricane Mitch roared into the western Caribbean, with winds that reached 180 miles (290 km) per hour. The storm then came ashore in Honduras, where its heavy rains caused mudslides in Central America. The storm killed more than 10,000 people and injured about 13,000.

Many of the people who live in Central America and the Caribbean are of Spanish and Native American descent. Many people of African descent also live in the regions. Their ancestors were brought from Africa as slaves. The main language in most of the countries is Spanish, but in some countries most people speak either English, French, or Dutch.

REVIEW What are two major challenges shared by Central America and the Caribbean?
COMPARE AND CONTRAST earthquakes and tropical storms

In 1998 Hurricane Mitch (below) hit the Caribbean island of Guanaja (right), destroying most buildings and boat docks.

55 mph   PRESSURE: 923 MB   CUBA

(YUCATAN)

JAMAICA

Chapter 14   531

Photograph Explain that hurricane season lasts from June to November and that during that time, hurricanes are a threat to many people and places. Central America is one of the two regions in the world with the highest recorded hurricane activity each year.

Q Where is the hurricane located in the satellite photograph?

A Students should indicate that the hurricane is located in between Jamaica and Mexico.

Read and Respond

Culture and Society Many forms of popular music come from the Caribbean Islands. The merengue began in the Dominican Republic and is based on both Spanish and African musical styles. Calypso music, which is based on West African work songs, began in Trinidad during the 1800s. It is music of celebration, but it also tells of social and political problems. Another type of Latin American music called salsa began in Cuba and Puerto Rico. Salsa combines the rhythm of African drums with brass instruments.

Culture and Society Inform students that languages and cultures vary not only among islands, but sometimes within them. Explain that the island of Saint Martin is shared by two governments, the French and the Dutch. Explain that the Dutch control the southern one-third of the island, which is known for sandy beaches and thriving tourism. The French control the northern two-thirds of the island, known for its abundant fishing.

Q How is the island of Saint Martin organized?

A Saint Martin is divided into two nations—the Dutch part, known for tourism, and the French part, renowned for its fishing.

STUDY/RESEARCH SKILLS

Using the Internet Tell students that people in areas in and around the Caribbean must deal with environmental problems caused by hurricanes. Encourage students to use the Internet to research some methods of hurricane preparation. Ask students to share their solutions with the class.

INTEGRATE SCIENCE

Hurricanes Hurricanes are large, spiraling storm systems that can travel for thousands of miles and can reach wind speeds of 186 miles per hour (300 km/hr). A hurricane usually starts as a low-pressure system over an ocean. Winds blow into the low-pressure area, and Earth's rotation causes them to spiral around it. If a storm's winds reach speeds of 74 miles per hour (120 km/hr), the storm is classified as a hurricane.

Government in the Regions

Read and Respond

Civics and Government Explain to students that in a capitalist country like the United States, people own land and businesses. Inform students that in a communist country such as Cuba, the government owns the land and businesses.

Q **What are some advantages of a capitalist government?**

A People can own their own land and businesses.

· SCIENCE AND TECHNOLOGY ·

The Arecibo Observatory

Explain that until the 1940s, most of the world's observatories were in the Northern Hemisphere. Inform students that after World War II, scientists realized they lacked information about the skies over the Southern Hemisphere. Soon observatories were built in Chile and Australia as well as in Puerto Rico. Help students find star charts that show constellations from both the Northern and Southern hemispheres.

 **Close**

Summarize Key Content

- Central America and the Caribbean have features such as mountains, beaches, dense forests, and remote islands, as well as tropical climates that present many challenges.
- All nations in Central America and the Caribbean, except for Cuba, have democratic governments, but many have achieved democracy only recently.

Fidel Castro has ruled Cuba since 1959.

Government in the Regions

For the first time in recent history, almost all the nations in Central America and the Caribbean have some form of democratic government. Cuba, which is a communist dictatorship, is the exception.

Both Puerto Rico and Cuba came under United States control in 1898, after the Spanish-American War. Puerto Rico was made a United States territory, but Cuba became an independent country in 1902. In 1952 Puerto Rico became a **commonwealth**, a kind of territory that governs itself. As citizens of a territory, Puerto Ricans hold United States citizenship. The United States Virgin Islands is another United States territory in the Caribbean.

Since 1959 Fidel Castro has ruled Cuba as a communist dictator. In an effort to end communism in Cuba, the United States government set up an economic embargo against the nation in 1960. An **embargo** is one nation's refusal to trade goods with another. Cuba's economy has been weakened by the embargo, but Cuba still remains a communist nation. Meanwhile, many Cuban Americans in the United States continue to hope that Cuba will become a democracy.

At Castro's request, Pope John Paul II visited Cuba in January 1998. Although

---

· SCIENCE AND TECHNOLOGY ·

The Arecibo Observatory

In the late 1950s, American scientist William E. Gordon was searching for a site to build a space observatory. Because of what Gordon wished to study, the observatory had to be able to see a certain part of the sky, near the equator. The site finally chosen was Arecibo (ah•rah•SEE•boh) in northwest Puerto Rico. Today, the Arecibo Observatory has the world's largest single-dish radio telescope. The dish has a 1000-foot (305-m) diameter and covers 20 acres. The telescope has helped locate planets outside our solar system.

BACKGROUND

Puerto Rico In 1898, as a result of the Spanish-American War, Puerto Rico became part of the United States. In 1952 Puerto Rico drafted its own constitution and became a United States commonwealth. Today, Puerto Rico has a governor and a local government that operates in much the same way that a state's does. Over time, citizens of Puerto Rico have discussed statehood.

READING SOCIAL STUDIES

Reread to Clarify To ensure understanding of the text, ask students to write brief summaries of each subsection. Then have students reread each subsection to confirm their summaries.

the Roman Catholic Church is not outlawed, its members cannot join the Communist party, which controls housing and jobs. In honor of the Pope's visit, Castro allowed Christmas to be celebrated in public for the first time in many years.

Many democratic governments in Central America and the Caribbean have struggled to survive. Costa Rica has been the most stable democracy. Like the United States, Costa Rica has three branches of government.

Despite being the second-oldest republic in the Western Hemisphere, after the United States, Haiti has had a history of military takeovers of its government. For much of its history, Haiti was ruled by dictators.

At other times, however, the people of Haiti have freely elected their leaders. In 1990 Haiti held a **free election**—one that offers a choice of candidates, instead of a single candidate. Jean-Bertrand Aristide (air•ih•STEED) was elected, but military leaders soon took over. Aristide escaped to the United States. To help end military rule and return Aristide to office, the United States sent troops to Haiti in 1994. Soon Aristide returned to office.

Since that time, Haiti has held other free elections. Most people in Haiti are hopeful that their government will remain a democracy.

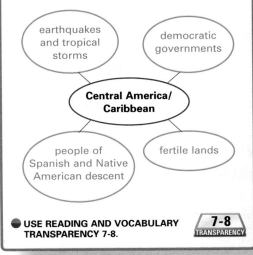
Former president of Haiti, Jean-Bertrand Aristide

REVIEW What nation in the Caribbean continues to be a communist country? Cuba

LESSON 2 REVIEW

Summary Time Line

1880 — 1940 — PRESENT

- **1898** Cuba, the Philippines, and Puerto Rico are under United States control
- **1952** Puerto Rico becomes a United States commonwealth
- **1990** Haiti holds free elections
- **1998** Pope John Paul II visits Cuba

 COMPARE AND CONTRAST How are the governments of Costa Rica and Cuba different?

1 BIG IDEA What do all the countries in Central America and the Caribbean, except Cuba, have in common?

2 VOCABULARY What is a **commonwealth**?

3 TIME LINE When did Puerto Rico become a commonwealth?

4 HISTORY Why did the United States send troops to Haiti in 1994?

5 CRITICAL THINKING—Analyze How might an embargo affect a country?

 PERFORMANCE—Make a Mobile Make a mobile about the land and the people of Central America and the Caribbean. Include pictures that represent the region's physical features and products. Use your mobile to describe the region to other students.

Chapter 14 ■ 533

EXTEND AND ENRICH

United Nations Session
Organize students into pairs, and have each pair represent a country from the lesson in a United Nations meeting. Students should discuss at least two issues affecting the country they represent. When students have completed their meeting, ask them to summarize what they have learned about the region as a whole.

RETEACH THE LESSON

Chart Ask students to complete the chart below with details from the lesson. Students may refer to the lesson for additional information.

	Features	Challenges
Central America and the Caribbean	• diverse land and people • grow a variety of crops	• hurricanes • earthquakes

READING SOCIAL STUDIES

Graphic Organizer Have students check their graphic organizers against the one below.

earthquakes and tropical storms

democratic governments

Central America/ Caribbean

people of Spanish and Native American descent

fertile lands

● USE READING AND VOCABULARY TRANSPARENCY 7-8.

7-8 TRANSPARENCY

Assess

Lesson 2 Review—Answers

 COMPARE AND CONTRAST Like the United States, Costa Rica is a democracy with three branches of government. Cuba is a communist country run by a dictator.

1 BIG IDEA They all are democracies.

2 VOCABULARY A **commonwealth** is a kind of territory that governs itself.

3 TIME LINE in 1952

4 HISTORY to help return President Jean-Bertrand Aristide to office

5 CRITICAL THINKING—Analyze It could weaken a nation's economy.

Performance Assessment Guidelines Students' mobiles should show a variety of products and physical features from the region.

ACTIVITY BOOK

Use ACTIVITY BOOK, p. 135, to reinforce and extend student learning.

Skill Lesson

PAGES 534–535

OBJECTIVES

- Interpret information in a population pyramid.
- Gather and organize information using a population pyramid.

Vocabulary

population pyramid p. 534

median age p. 534

life expectancy p. 534

WORD CARDS

See pp. V59–V60.

1 Motivate

Why It Matters

Explain that population pyramids can provide valuable information about a country or society. Inform students that scientists can use data from different countries to draw conclusions about factors such as birth rates, death rates, and the general health of the people.

INTEGRATE LANGUAGE ARTS

Write a Scientific Summary Ask students to review the population pyramid of Puerto Rico on page 535. Have students interpret the major findings of the pyramids and use them to write brief outlines. From these outlines, ask students to write short summaries about Puerto Rico's population.

· SKILLS · CHART AND GRAPH

Read Population Pyramids

VOCABULARY

population pyramid
life expectancy
median age

➡ WHY IT MATTERS

A graph that shows the division of a country's population by age is called a **population pyramid**. Each side of the graph is divided by age. One side of the graph shows the female population. The other side of the graph shows the male population.

Two factors affect the shape of the population pyramid—a country's birth rate and its death rate. The birth rate is the number of children born each year for every 1,000 people in the country. The death rate is the number of people who die each year for every 1,000 people in the country.

A population pyramid also gives a picture of a country's **life expectancy**, the number of years people can expect to live. This number varies from country to country. It tells in general how long people in a country live, but it does not say how long any one person will live.

A population pyramid also shows the country's median age. The word *median* means "middle." Half the people in the country are older than the **median age**, and half are younger.

Four generations of the same family can be seen in this photograph.

534 ■ Unit 7

BACKGROUND

Life Expectancy The life expectancy for Americans has steadily risen over the last century to its current average of 77 years. In 1900 the average was 47 years. The increase in life span has come as factors such as childhood diseases and poor sanitation have been reduced through scientific and public-health advances. Scientists cite those improvements along with a history of good health, a healthful diet, and regular exercise as keys to living long and productive lives. Many scientists believe that life expectancy may be further extended, but probably not much beyond an ultimate age of 120.

Population Pyramid: Puerto Rico

Source: U.S. Census Bureau, International Database

▶ WHAT YOU NEED TO KNOW

The population pyramid shown above gives the population of Puerto Rico. Notice how it is divided into age groups, with the youngest at the bottom and the oldest at the top. The left side of the population pyramid shows the number of males in each age group. The right side shows the number of females. If you want to know the number that a whole age group represents, add together the number of males and the number of females in that age group. For example, in the 10–14 age group, there are about 152,000 males and about 150,000 females. So there are about 302,000 persons age 10–14 in Puerto Rico.

The pyramid's shape indicates how rapidly Puerto Rico's population is growing. The very wide parts of the pyramid show that the greatest number of people are under 29 years of age. The top of the pyramid indicates that fewer people are over 70 years of age.

▶ PRACTICE THE SKILL

Use the population pyramid to answer the following questions.

1. Find your age group on the population pyramid. About how many boys in Puerto Rico are in that age group? About how many girls?

2. In which age groups are there more females than males?

3. Which age group is the largest?

4. About how many people in Puerto Rico have lived 80 years or longer?

5. What general statement can you make about Puerto Rico's population from this pyramid?

▶ APPLY WHAT YOU LEARNED

Think about the ages of people in your own family or in your class at school. Draw a population pyramid that shows the number of people of different ages in your family or class.

Chapter 14 ▪ 535

CHART AND GRAPH SKILLS

---

2 Teach

What You Need to Know

Direct students' attention to the population pyramid. Ask students why the number of people decreases in the higher age groups. As people age, many die. Have students compare the number of males in the pyramid with the number of females. There are more males at lower age levels but more females at higher age levels.

Practice the Skill—Answers

1. about 152,000 boys and about 151,000 girls
2. 30–34, 35–39, 40–44, 45–49, 50–54, 55–59, 60–64, 65–69, 70–74, 75–79, 80+
3. 20–24
4. about 100,000
5. Females in Puerto Rico tend to live longer than do males.

3 Close

Apply What You Learned

Check to ensure that students' pyramids are constructed with younger people at the bottom of the pyramid and older people at the top.

ACTIVITY BOOK

Use ACTIVITY BOOK, pp. 136–137, to give students additional practice using this skill.

TRANSPARENCY

Use SKILL TRANSPARENCY 7-3.

EXTEND AND ENRICH

Compare and Contrast Ask students to research and locate population maps of two areas, states, or countries and to draw conclusions about the information in them. Have students write brief summaries based on their conclusions. Ask volunteers to share their summaries with the class.

RETEACH THE SKILL

Make a Population Pyramid Organize students into groups and ask them to locate and use information from the 2000 census to construct a population pyramid of their state. Encourage students to use calculators to convert numbers into percentages.

Lesson 3

PAGES 536–540

OBJECTIVES

- Describe the geography and people of South America.
- Describe how South American countries gained their independence and some of the problems that came with it.
- Identify new challenges facing South America.

 Compare and Contrast
pp. 523, 536, 539, 540, 548

Vocabulary

SEE READING AND VOCABULARY TRANSPARENCY 7-9 OR THE WORD CARDS ON PP. V61–V62.

standard of living p. 536   **deforestation** p. 540

liberate p. 538

 When Minutes Count

Ask students to write down the lesson vocabulary terms and their definitions. Then ask volunteers to explain how each term relates to the Big Idea of the lesson.

Quick Summary

This lesson describes the geography, history, and development of South America.

1 Motivate

Set the Purpose

Big Idea Inform students that South America's many geographic differences led its countries to develop on their own rather than as one nation.

Access Prior Knowledge

Ask students to state what they know about the British colonies' quest for independence from Britain. How was it similar to South America's situation? How was it different?

536 ■ UNIT 7

·LESSON·

3

 COMPARE AND CONTRAST
As you read, compare and contrast countries in South America.

BIG IDEA
The land and people of South America have an important effect on the world's health and economy.

VOCABULARY
standard of living
liberate
deforestation

South America

1800   1900   PRESENT

South America's diversity can be seen in its lands, climates, and resources. Across the continent, landforms range from towering mountains to broad plateaus and plains. Climates range from tropical in the north to arid and desert in the south. The continent has abundant natural resources, but some of them have not yet been fully developed. Since the countries of South America differ in their economic development, their standards of living also vary widely. A **standard of living** is a measure of how well people in a country live.

South America and Its People

South America, the fourth largest continent, covers more than twice the area of the continental United States. Only Africa has a less indented coastline than South America. Because of this, there are few good harbors along most of South America's coasts.

The Andes Mountains extend 4,500 miles (7,250 km) along the western side of South

LOCATE IT
Caracas
VENEZUELA
Angel Falls

536 ■ Unit 7

STUDY/RESEARCH SKILLS

Using Reference Sources
Organize students in groups and assign each group a South American country to research. Have groups answer the following questions:

- How large is the country, and how many people live in it?
- What is the country's capital?
- What are the main industries in the country's economy?

Ask groups to orally present their findings to the class.

America, from the Caribbean in the north to the continent's southern tip. East of the Andes are areas of plateaus and plains, including the Guiana Highlands in the north and the Pampas and Patagonia to the south. Three major river systems—the Río de la Plata, the Orinoco (ohr•ee•NOH•koh), and the Amazon— run like veins through the continent's lowlands. Many of these lowlands lie in the tropics. Rain forests, with unique animals and plants, cover much of the land along the Amazon and along many of the other rivers in the region.

While much of South America is hot and humid, some areas are dry and cold. West of the snowcapped Andes, along the coast of northern Chile, is the Atacama Desert. It is the world's driest desert. So little rain falls there that people have found ways to capture moisture from the early morning fogs. The southern part of the continent is cold for much of the year.

Native peoples lived in South America for thousands of years. Then, in the 1500s, Spain, Portugal, and other European countries began to build colonies there.

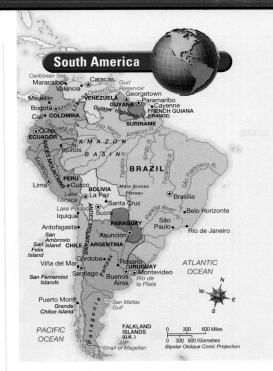

South America

Location There are 13 countries on the continent of South America. Of those 13, Brazil is the largest.

◈ How are Bolivia and Paraguay different from the other countries of South America?

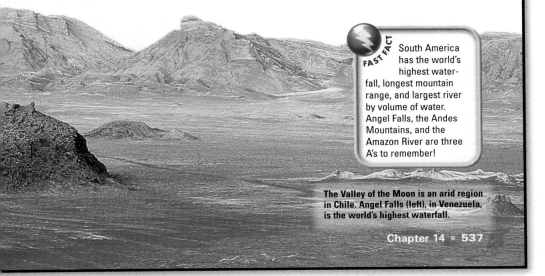

FAST FACT
South America has the world's highest waterfall, longest mountain range, and largest river by volume of water. Angel Falls, the Andes Mountains, and the Amazon River are three A's to remember!

The Valley of the Moon is an arid region in Chile. Angel Falls (left), in Venezuela, is the world's highest waterfall.

Chapter 14 ▪ 537

---

2 Teach

South America and Its People

Read and Respond

Geography Explain that although part of South America extends north of the equator, it also extends farther south than any other continent except Antarctica. Inform students that this results in vast climatic and ecological differences across the continent.

GO ONLINE Students might be interested in learning more about the countries of South America. Have them visit The Learning Site at **www.harcourtschool.com.**

Visual Learning

Map Ask students to study the map on page 537. Explain that Brazil covers an area of 3,300,171 square miles (8,546,783 sq km), or roughly half the total area of South America.

Q **Which nations border Brazil?**

A French Guiana, Suriname, Guyana, Venezuela, Colombia, Peru, Bolivia, Paraguay, Uruguay, and Argentina CAPTION ANSWER: They are landlocked.

• BIOGRAPHY •

Simón Bolívar   1783–1830

Character Trait: Leadership

Simón Bolívar fought for nine years for his homeland's independence. In 1821 he and his troops defeated the Spanish in Venezuela. Two years earlier Bolívar had helped Colombia win its freedom. He and his troops later defeated the Spanish in Bolivia and Peru. Because of his contributions to the independence of many nations, he is known as *El Libertador*, or The Liberator.

MULTIMEDIA BIOGRAPHIES **GO ONLINE**
Visit The Learning Site at
www.harcourtschool.com
to learn about other famous people.

Europeans soon ruled most of the continent.

During the late 1700s and early 1800s, political independence became a goal for many people in South America. They had observed the success of the 13 British colonies in North America in breaking free of British rule and forming the United States. In the early 1800s, colony after colony in South America declared its independence—usually through revolution.

Simón Bolívar (see•MOHN boh•LEE•var) in Venezuela and José de San Martín

538 ■ Unit 7

(sahn mar•TEEN) in Argentina were key figures in the struggle to **liberate**, or set free, these colonies. By 1828 all of Spain's and Portugal's colonies in South America had become independent. By the mid-1800s most parts of South America had been liberated.

Bolívar hoped for a single nation in South America but knew how unlikely that would be. "[South] America is separated by climatic differences, geographical diversity, conflicting interests, and dissimilar characteristics," he said. Each country developed on its own, often fighting over borders with its neighbors.

REVIEW **What was the goal of many people in South America in the early 1800s?**
political independence

Old Problems in New Countries

Even after independence, most of the people in South America had little say in government. Wealth was concentrated in the hands of a few landowners, and political matters were in the hands of dictators or armies. The people lacked the education necessary to make changes. They were also unschooled in the ways of self-government.

Various reformers throughout South America began working to solve these problems.

This statue of José de San Martín is in Cordoba, Argentina.

One solution was to redistribute the land so that individuals could own small farms. During the colonial period large haciendas, which were similar to plantations in the southern United States, were common. Since the 1960s, land reform supporters have enjoyed some victories, but many farmers still do not own the land on which they work.

REVIEW What were some problems the newly independent countries faced?

🌐 COMPARE AND CONTRAST

New Problems for All Countries

Many South American countries continue to face the problems of poverty, unemployment, and keeping their democracies. Land use has once again become a major issue. In places, Indian tribes have protested land development,

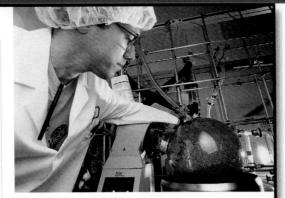

Many scientists are working to solve problems related to the destruction of the rain forests.

which they believe disturbs centuries-old patterns of life. These tribes are beginning to take legal measures to regain their ancestral lands.

In addition, many scientists are concerned over the destruction of the rain forests in some areas of South America.

little experience in democracy, little education, and wealth and land in the hands of a few people

• GEOGRAPHY •

Galápagos Islands
Understanding Places and Regions

Six hundred miles (966 km) west of Ecuador in the Pacific Ocean are the 19 islands called the Galápagos. They were once called the Enchanted Isles, and pirates were known to bury treasure there. Today, the islands are best known for the bird and animal species that are found nowhere else. Among these are 13 species of finches, large lizards, and huge land turtles. The Spanish word for these turtles, *galápagos*, gave the islands their name.

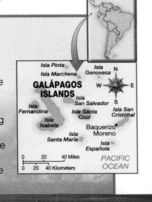

GALÁPAGOS ISLANDS

Isla Pinta
Isla Marchena
Isla Genovesa
Isla Fernandina
Isla San Salvador
Isla Santa Cruz
Isla San Cristóbal
Isla Isabela
Baquerizo Moreno
Isla Santa María
Isla Española

N W E S

0 20 40 Miles
0 20 40 Kilometers

PACIFIC OCEAN

Chapter 14 ▪ 539

• GEOGRAPHY •

Galápagos Islands
Understanding Places and Regions Explain that Charles Darwin, the nineteenth century scientist, developed some of his ideas about evolution while visiting the Galápagos Islands. He believed that species changed over time and that the changes came in response to the environment. Darwin's ideas were supported by the variations of finches he saw living on the islands. He noticed that finches on different islands had developed different physical characteristics. Inform students that Darwin believed the finches, as a species, had adapted to their environments.

New Problems for All Countries

Read and Respond

Geography Explain to students that deforestation also can lead to destruction of various habitats and the possible extinction of certain plants and animals.

3 Close

Summarize Key Content

- South America's diverse landscape includes mountains, major river systems, deserts, and rain forests.
- Most of the colonies of South America gained their independence in the early 1800s under the leadership of Simón Bolívar and José de San Martín.
- Following independence, many South American countries encountered problems of poverty, poor education, and rule by dictatorship.
- Today South American countries face many modern problems, including poverty, unemployment, and deforestation.

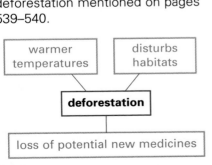

Assess

Lesson 3 Review—Answers

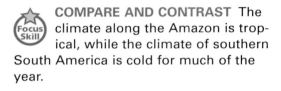

COMPARE AND CONTRAST The climate along the Amazon is tropical, while the climate of southern South America is cold for much of the year.

❶ **BIG IDEA** Simón Bolívar and José de San Martín helped most South American countries fight for independence.

❷ **VOCABULARY** Simón Bolívar helped **liberate** the people of South America from Spanish rule.

❸ **TIME LINE** by 1828

❹ **HISTORY** They were key figures in the struggle to liberate South America from Spanish rule.

❺ **CRITICAL THINKING—Analyze** If deforestation is not controlled the nation's natural resources may be lost.

Hikers journey toward the Upsala Glacier in *Los Glaciares* National Park, Argentina. The Upsala Glacier is the largest glacier in South America.

Across South America, rain forests are cleared for their valuable wood or to build new farms, towns, and roads. As the forests are cut down and burned, carbon dioxide is released into the atmosphere and there are fewer trees to absorb it. Some scientists believe that having more carbon dioxide in the atmosphere leads to warmer temperatures, which scientists term the *greenhouse effect*.

Scientists have begun to explore the use of rain forest plants for medicine. Although less than 1 percent of the plants in the rain forest have been tested for medical benefits, about 25 percent of western medicines come from rain forest plants. Destroying these plants may prevent new medicines from being discovered.

Brazil has worked to slow this **deforestation**, or the widespread cutting down of forests. Not only has the rate of cutting slowed, but lands have been set aside for protection. The Amazon region now has several plant and animal reserves, national parks, and national forests.

REVIEW What kinds of lands have been set aside for protection in the Amazon region? plant and animal reserves, national parks, and national forests

LESSON 3 REVIEW

Summary Time Line
1800 — 1900 — PRESENT

• 1828
All of Spain's and Portugal's South American colonies are independent

 COMPARE AND CONTRAST How is the climate of southern South America different from the climate along the Amazon?

❶ **BIG IDEA** How did most countries in South America gain independence?

❷ **VOCABULARY** Use the word **liberate** in a sentence that explains its meaning.

❸ **TIME LINE** When did the last of Spain's and Portugal's South American colonies gain independence?

❹ **HISTORY** Who were Simón Bolívar and José de San Martín?

❺ **CRITICAL THINKING—Analyze** Why is it important for government leaders to make informed decisions to slow deforestation?

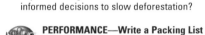 **PERFORMANCE—Write a Packing List** The climate and geography of parts of South America are very different. Imagine that you will be taking a trip across the continent. Tell where you will visit, and write a packing list of the clothes and supplies you might need there.

540 ■ Unit 7

Canada

Canada's red and white maple leaf flag is a familiar symbol to many Americans. Canada and the United States share one of the longest borders in the world, and about two-thirds of all Canadians live within 100 miles of the United States border. Geography, however, is just one reason why the two nations have such strong ties to each other.

A Varied Landscape

In land area, Canada is the second-largest country in the world. It covers more than 40 percent of North America. Canada, like the United States, stretches from the Atlantic Ocean to the Pacific Ocean, and from a 3,987-mile (6,416-km) southern border shared with the continental United States to islands in the Arctic Ocean. Canada's people may live near mountains, lakes, forests, prairies, or tundra.

A wide variety of climates and landforms can be found in Canada. Cattle graze on fertile prairie land. This glacier (inset) is in northern Alberta.

Chapter 14 ■ 541

· LESSON ·

4

COMPARE AND CONTRAST
As you read, compare and contrast Canada and the United States.

BIG IDEA
Canada is a land of great variety and has strong ties to the United States.

VOCABULARY
province
separatist

Lesson 4
PAGES 541–545

OBJECTIVES

- Describe the geography of Canada.
- Describe Canada's history, from first settlement to self-government.
- Explain why some citizens want to secede from Canada.
- Identify Canada's role in the world economy.

Compare and Contrast
pp. 523, 541, 542, 545, 548

Vocabulary

SEE READING AND VOCABULARY TRANSPARENCY 7-10 OR THE WORD CARDS ON PP. V61–V62.

province p. 542   **separatist** p. 544

When Minutes Count

Have students examine the map on page 542. Use the map as a springboard to discuss Canada's geography and history.

Quick Summary

This lesson describes Canada's geography and history and its place in today's world economy.

1 Motivate

Set the Purpose

Big Idea Discuss with students the long history that Canada shares with the United States.

Access Prior Knowledge

Have students review what they learned about European colonization of North America in the 1600s. Why did Europeans come to North America? What did they hope to gain?

REACH ALL LEARNERS

Below-Level Learners
Ask students for words or phrases that they associate with Canada. Write their responses on the board. After students have read the lesson, return to the list to correct or confirm items on it.

WORD WORK

Preview Vocabulary Ask students to preview each vocabulary word and its definition. Then have each student use both words in a sentence. Many citizens of the **province** of Quebec are **separatists** who favor seceding from Canada.

CHAPTER 14   ■   541

Summarize Ask students as they read the lesson to use the following chart to summarize characteristics of Canada.

Land	• _____
	• _____
Government	• _____
	• _____
Economy	• _____
	• _____

● USE READING AND VOCABULARY TRANSPARENCY 7-10.

7-10
TRANSPARENCY

2 Teach

A Varied Landscape

Read and Respond

Civics and Government Point out that Canada's first provinces were founded in 1867.

Students might be interested in learning more about the provinces and territories of Canada. Have them visit The Learning Site at **www.harcourtschool.com.**

Culture and Society Inform students that although Canada has the second-largest land area of any country in the world, its population is only as large as California's.

Visual Learning

Map Explain that like the United States, Canada has one national capital. It also has many provincial capitals that are like state capitals in the United States.

ℚ What is Canada's capital?

A Ottawa

CAPTION ANSWER: Quebec is the largest province and Nunavut is the largest territory.

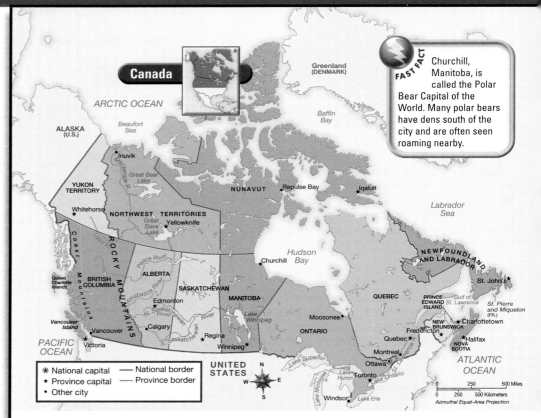

Regions This map shows the 10 provinces and 3 territories of Canada.
◈ Which Canadian province is the largest? Which territory is the largest?

Canada is a land of variety. The low Coast Mountains extend along the Pacific coast, while farther inland are the towering Rockies. The Interior Plains cover the central part of Canada. To the northeast is the Canadian Shield, a huge region of poor, rocky soil. Southeast of the Canadian Shield is the St. Lawrence Lowlands. This region has most of Canada's people and industries. The Appalachian Mountains extend into southeastern Canada.

Canada has many rivers and lakes that provide natural resources. Four of the five Great Lakes help define its southern border.

Canada has 10 provinces and 3 territories. A **province** is a political region similar to a state in the United States. Each province has its own government, and it can take many actions without the approval of the national government.

REVIEW How is western Canada different from central Canada?

⊕ **COMPARE AND CONTRAST**

Western Canada has mountains, while central Canada has plains.

542 ▪ Unit 7

Journey to Self-Government

Thousands of years ago, Canada's first settlers entered the region, probably over a land bridge from Asia. Many of the descendants of these early settlers still live in Canada today. They are known as the First Nation peoples.

Canada's flag

The Vikings first explored what is now eastern Canada around A.D. 1000, but other European explorers did not reach Canada until about 500 years later. Both Britain and France wanted to control Canada's vast lands, and each nation sent explorers to claim land. After wars in Europe and North America, France lost its Canadian holdings to Britain. In the Quebec Act of 1774, Britain agreed that French settlers in Canada could keep their own laws, language, and religion.

In 1867 the British Parliament passed the British North American Act. This act, which united all of Canada into one nation, also served as Canada's first constitution. It gave Canada a representative government, but Britain held the final word in Canadian affairs.

In 1931 the British Parliament passed the Statute of Westminister. It allowed Canada to conduct its own foreign affairs, but Canada still remained partly under British rule. Canada also became a partner in the British Commonwealth of Nations, the name given to territories that give allegiance to the British crown.

Canadians wanted more control over their own government and decisions. A new constitution in 1982 permitted constitutional amendments without approval from the British Parliament.

LOCATE IT

Ottawa
ONTARIO

Members of the Canadian Senate (inset) meet inside the Parliament Building, in Ottawa.

Journey to Self-Government

Read and Respond

Culture and Society Inform students that the first inhabitants of Canada had developed complex societies well before the first Europeans landed there. Explain that the word *canada* comes from an Iroquois word meaning "village" or "community."

Culture and Society Explain that by the mid-1700s, there were about 1.5 million British colonists living in North America. Ask students to consider ways in which the British influence continues to be felt today in Canada. Most citizens of Canada speak English, and the national government includes features modeled after the British system of government.

Visual Learning

Picture Direct students to the picture of the national flag of Canada on page 543. Point out that the flag, featuring a red maple leaf on a white background, was officially adopted in 1964. Explain that the maple leaf has historically been a Canadian symbol and that red and white have been Canada's official colors since 1921.

REACH ALL LEARNERS

Auditory Learners
Invite students to work with partners to read aloud the subsection Journey to Self-Government. While one partner reads, the other should construct a time line based on the information. Students should take turns reading and preparing the time line. Review the time lines as a class.

QUESTIONS KIDS ASK

Q How do members of Canada's Senate differ from members of its House of Commons?

A Members of the Canadian Senate are appointed and may hold their offices until the age of 75. Representatives who serve in the House of Commons are elected by Canadian voters. Elections are held at least once every five years.

New Solutions to Old Problems

Read and Respond

Civics and Government Discuss advantages and disadvantages of becoming an independent country.

POINTS OF VIEW
Should Quebec Secede?

Encourage students to analyze the two viewpoints.

Analyze the Viewpoints— Answers

❶ Marc-Andre Bedard believes that Quebec's identity deserves sovereign standing. Pierre Trudeau believes that Quebec's secession would hurt the confederation of Canada.

❷ Encourage students to ask at least five people for their views on the subject.

A World Partner

Read and Respond

Geography Point out that the St. Lawrence Seaway was the final link in a waterway that extends about 2,340 miles (3,766 km) from Duluth, Minnesota, to the Atlantic Ocean.

3 Close

Summarize Key Content

- Canada's geographical features include mountains, lakes, forests, prairies, and tundra.
- Canada was settled by Europeans hundreds of years ago.
- Some citizens of Quebec hope to preserve their culture by forming their own country.
- Canada has a history of cooperation with the United States.

POINTS OF VIEW
Should Quebec Secede?

Almost since Britain won control of New France in 1763, Quebec has struggled to hold on to its French heritage. Some French Canadians of Quebec have tried to win Quebec's independence from Canada.

MARC-ANDRE BEDARD, a leader of the separatist movement

❝ Are we a people or are we not? If we are, we should be sovereign. We should be at the table with the international community. ❞

PIERRE TRUDEAU, former Canadian prime minister

❝ It would be disastrous. . . . It would mean a major setback in the course of history. And the burden would lie with those who would like to break up one of history's greatest achievements—the Canadian federation. ❞

Analyze the Viewpoints
❶ What views does each person hold?
❷ **Make it Relevant** Choose an issue about which the people in your class or community have different views. Find out what people think about the issue.

In Montreal (below), signs such as this one are in both French and English.

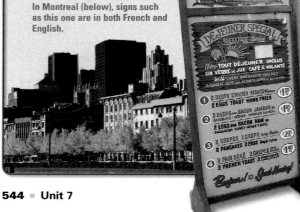

544 ■ Unit 7

The constitution also included a Charter of Rights and Freedoms, similar to the United States Bill of Rights. Canada's independence was complete.

Canada's executive branch is still headed by Britain's monarch, who appoints a representative, the governor-general. Daily governmental affairs, however, are handled by the prime minister. He or she is a member of the ruling majority party of the House of Commons. Along with the Senate, the House of Commons makes up the Canadian Parliament.

REVIEW What did the Constitution of 1982 do? It allowed constitutional amendments without approval from Britain and made Canada independent.

New Solutions to Old Problems

For a long time, many Quebec citizens, called **separatists**, have wanted to form a separate country in order to preserve their French culture. In 1998 a vote to secede from Canada failed. The Canadian Supreme Court then ruled that Quebec could not secede unless the rest of Canada agreed.

Like the people of Quebec, the native peoples of Canada want to preserve their culture. In 1999 Nunavut, part of the Northwest Territories, became Canada's third territory. Most of the people who live in Nunavut are Inuit. They plan to govern the territory of Nunavut according to the traditional means of consensus, or the agreement of the community.

REVIEW Why do separatists want to secede from Canada? They wish to preserve their French culture.

BACKGROUND

Canadian Imports and Exports Manufactured goods comprise the bulk of Canada's imports. Important Canadian exports include newsprint, lumber, wheat, machinery, natural gas, and telecommunications equipment.

INTEGRATE MUSIC

Canadian Music Explain to students that Canada has a rich tradition of music. Invite students to find examples of both traditional and modern Canadian music that reflect the country's cultural heritages. Ask students to play recordings or to perform the songs themselves before commenting on the music.

A World Partner

Canada has economic partnerships with many countries, but it has the greatest cooperation with the United States. The United States and Canada are major trading partners. In 1987 the two countries signed a free trade agreement that was a forerunner to NAFTA. Today, more than 80 percent of Canada's exports go to the United States, and Canada gets about 70 percent of its imports from the United States.

One of the greatest examples of cooperation between the two neighbors was the construction of the St. Lawrence Seaway. The St. Lawrence River flows nearly 800 miles (1,287 km) from Lake Ontario to the Atlantic Ocean, but parts of the river are not deep enough for large ships to navigate. The St. Lawrence Seaway also includes the Welland Ship Canal, built between Lake Ontario and Lake Erie to bypass Niagara Falls. Construction of the St. Lawrence Seaway

This photograph shows the first ship to enter the locks of the St. Lawrence Seaway in April of 1959.

was completed in 1959. This allowed large ships to reach the Great Lakes from the Atlantic Ocean.

REVIEW What is one example of cooperation between Canada and the United States?
trade; building the St. Lawrence Seaway

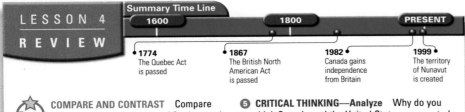

LESSON 4 REVIEW

Summary Time Line

1600	1800	PRESENT

- **1774** The Quebec Act is passed
- **1867** The British North American Act is passed
- **1982** Canada gains independence from Britain
- **1999** The territory of Nunavut is created

 COMPARE AND CONTRAST Compare and contrast the residents of Quebec and the residents of Nunavut.

① **BIG IDEA** Why does Canada have strong ties to the United States?

② **VOCABULARY** What is a **province**?

③ **TIME LINE** Which occurred first, the Quebec Act or the British North American Act?

④ **GEOGRAPHY** What are the three main mountain ranges in Canada?

⑤ **CRITICAL THINKING—Analyze** Why do you think Canada and the United States cooperated to build the St. Lawrence Seaway?

PERFORMANCE—Draw a Map Use your textbook, library books, and the Internet to draw a map of Canada. Find the location of each of Canada's major landforms, and label them on your map. Also show each of Canada's provinces and territories.

Chapter 14 ▪ 545

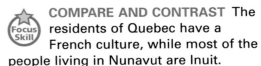

CHAPTER 14 ▪ **545**

Skill Lesson

OBJECTIVES

- Analyze and interpret a time zone map.
- Compare time in different parts of the Western Hemisphere.

Vocabulary

time zone p. 546

WORD CARDS

See pp. V61–V62.

1 Motivate

Why It Matters

Ask volunteers if they have ever made telephone calls to friends or family members who live in a different region from them. Explain that with these calls, they may have had to take into account a time difference. For example, explain that calls made late in the evening in the West could wake people living in the East where it is several hours later. Emphasize that all parts of a single time zone observe the same time.

·SKILLS·
MAP AND GLOBE

Use a Time Zone Map

VOCABULARY
time zone

➡ WHY IT MATTERS

"What time is it?" The answer depends on where you are. That is because people who live in different parts of the world set their clocks at different times.

For centuries people used the sun to determine time. When the sun was at its highest point in the sky, it was noon. However, the sun cannot be at its highest point all around the Earth at the same time. As the Earth rotates, the sun is directly overhead in different places at different times. The sun is past its highest point at places east of where you are, and it has not yet reached its highest point at places west of you.

In the 1800s Charles Dowd of the United States and Sandford Fleming of Canada developed the idea of dividing the Earth into time zones. A **time zone** is a region in which a single time is used. To figure out the time in a place, you can use a time zone map like the one on page 547.

➡ WHAT YOU NEED TO KNOW

Dowd and Fleming divided the Earth into 24 time zones. A new time zone begins every fifteenth meridian, starting at the prime meridian. In each new time zone to the west, the time is one hour earlier than in the time zone before it.

The map on page 547 shows the time zones in the Western Hemisphere. Find Dallas, in the central time zone. Now find New York City. It is in the eastern time zone, which is just east of the central time zone. The time in the central time zone is one hour earlier than the time in the eastern time zone. If it is 5:00 P.M. in the central time zone, it is 6:00 P.M. in the eastern time zone.

➡ PRACTICE THE SKILL

Use the time zone map of the Western Hemisphere to answer these questions.

❶ In which time zone is Los Angeles?

❷ If it is 10:00 A.M. in Los Angeles, what time is it in San Antonio?

❸ In which time zone is Puerto Rico?

While the sun sets in Honolua Bay, Hawaii, it is already dark in other places in the United States.

546 ▪ Unit 7

BACKGROUND

Daylight Saving Time The idea for a daylight saving time was first put forth by Benjamin Franklin, who wrote about it in a 1784 essay. Years later during World War II, several countries, including Australia, Britain, and the United States, adopted summer daylight saving time to conserve fuel for the war effort. Today, we still use this system. On the first Sunday in April, clocks are set ahead one hour so that it gets dark "later" and people can work longer without turning on lights. On the last Sunday in October, clocks are set back to standard time so that it gets light "earlier" and fewer people have to get up in the dark. The saying "Spring forward, fall back" reminds us which way to turn our clocks. Three states—Arizona, Hawaii, and Indiana—do not currently use daylight saving time.

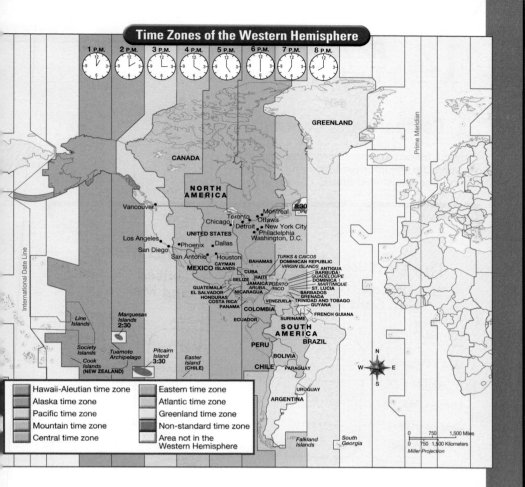

Time Zones of the Western Hemisphere

1 P.M. 2 P.M. 3 P.M. 4 P.M. 5 P.M. 6 P.M. 7 P.M. 8 P.M.

GREENLAND

CANADA

NORTH AMERICA

Vancouver

8:30

Toronto Montreal
Chicago Ottawa
Detroit New York City
Philadelphia
Washington, D.C.

Los Angeles
San Diego
Phoenix Dallas
San Antonio Houston

UNITED STATES

MEXICO
CAYMAN ISLANDS
BAHAMAS
TURKS & CAICOS
DOMINICAN REPUBLIC
VIRGIN ISLANDS ANTIGUA
BARBUDA
GUADELOUPE
DOMINICA
MARTINIQUE
ST. LUCIA
BARBADOS
GRENADA
CUBA
BELIZE
HAITI
JAMAICA PUERTO
ARUBA RICO
GUATEMALA
EL SALVADOR
HONDURAS NICARAGUA
COSTA RICA
PANAMA
VENEZUELA TRINIDAD AND TOBAGO
GUYANA
COLOMBIA
FRENCH GUIANA
ECUADOR
SURINAME
SOUTH AMERICA
PERU BRAZIL
BOLIVIA
CHILE PARAGUAY
URUGUAY
ARGENTINA

Line Islands
Marquesas Islands 2:30
Society Islands
Tuamoto Archipelago
Cook Islands (NEW ZEALAND)
Pitcairn Island 3:30
Easter Island (CHILE)

International Date Line

Prime Meridian

Falkland Islands
South Georgia

0 750 1,500 Miles
0 750 1,500 Kilometers
Miller Projection

N W E S

Hawaii-Aleutian time zone	Eastern time zone
Alaska time zone	Atlantic time zone
Pacific time zone	Greenland time zone
Mountain time zone	Non-standard time zone
Central time zone	Area not in the Western Hemisphere

④ If it is 3:00 P.M. in Puerto Rico, what time is it in Philadelphia? in Houston?

⑤ If it is 6:00 A.M. in San Diego, what time is it in Toronto?

⑥ Imagine that you are in Honduras. Is the time earlier than, later than, or the same as in Chicago?

➡ **APPLY WHAT YOU LEARNED**

Record the current time where you live. Now figure out the time in Montreal, Canada; Vancouver, Canada; Venezuela; and Argentina. Explain why it might be useful to know the time in different places.

Practice your map and globe skills with the **GeoSkills CD-ROM.**

Chapter 14 ■ 547

MAP AND GLOBE SKILLS

CHAPTER 14 ■ 547

Chapter 14 Review

 COMPARE AND CONTRAST

Students may use the graphic organizer that appears on page 142 of the Activity Book. Answers appear in the Activity Book, Teacher's Edition.

Think & Write

Write a Postcard Students' postcards should display accurate references to the diversity of South America's land, resources, climate, and people. They may wish to depict the lowlands of the tropics or the snowcapped mountains of the Andes.

Write a Wise Saying Students' sayings should display their understanding of the benefits that can be derived from maintaining peaceful and supportive relationships with our neighbors. They may wish to reference the economic benefits offered through trade relations or the mutual protection that can be derived through alliances.

ACTIVITY BOOK

A copy of the graphic organizer appears in the ACTIVITY BOOK on page 142.

TRANSPARENCY

The graphic organizer appears on READING AND VOCABULARY TRANSPARENCY 7-11.

---

14 Review and Test Preparation

 Compare and Contrast

Copy the following graphic organizer onto a separate sheet of paper. Use the information you have learned to compare and contrast the United States, Canada, and Mexico.

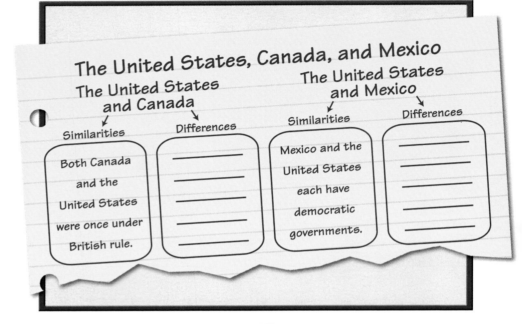

The United States, Canada, and Mexico

The United States and Canada — Similarities: Both Canada and the United States were once under British rule. — Differences:

The United States and Mexico — Similarities: Mexico and the United States each have democratic governments. — Differences:

THINK & WRITE

Write a Postcard Imagine you are traveling through South America on a family vacation. Write a postcard to a friend describing the natural wonders you have seen. Be sure to mention where these places are located.

Write a Wise Saying Having a good relationship with one's neighbors is important for both people and nations. Write a wise saying about the importance of the United States maintaining good relations with its neighbors.

548 ■ Chapter 14

TEST PREPARATION

Review these tips with students:

■ Read the directions before reading the questions.

■ Read each question twice, focusing the second time on all the possible answers.

■ Take the time to think about all the possible answers before deciding on an answer.

■ Move past questions that give you trouble, and answer the ones you know. Then return to the difficult items.

UNIT PROJECT

Progress Check Encourage students to complete their charts. Then have them select what they would like to show or make for their cultural fair.

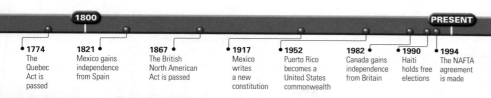

1774 The Quebec Act is passed

1821 Mexico gains independence from Spain

1867 The British North American Act is passed

1917 Mexico writes a new constitution

1952 Puerto Rico becomes a United States commonwealth

1982 Canada gains independence from Britain

1990 Haiti holds free elections

1994 The NAFTA agreement is made

USE VOCABULARY

Identify the term that correctly matches each definition.

middle class (p. 528)

interest rate (p. 528)

free election (p. 533)

province (p. 542)

1 the amount that banks charge to loan money

2 a political region

3 people who are economically between the rich and the poor

4 a political race that offers a choice of candidates

RECALL FACTS

Answer these questions.

5 Why are *Fiestas Patrias* important for many Mexican Americans?

6 How is the territory of Nunavut different from other Canadian territories?

Write the letter of the best choice.

7 The purpose of NAFTA is to—
A protect French Canadian culture.
B continue an embargo on exports from Cuba.
C increase trade among the United States, Canada, and Mexico.
D bring democracy to all the nations of Central America and the Caribbean.

8 Benito Juárez was the first Native American president of—
F Mexico.
G Bolivia.
H El Salvador.
J Costa Rica.

9 Which of the following Canadian provinces has stated a wish to secede?
A Alberta
B New Brunswick
C Quebec
D British Columbia

THINK CRITICALLY

10 Why is immigration such an important issue for the United States and Mexico?

11 Why do you think some Latin American countries have had difficulty forming stable governments?

12 What might happen if Quebec decides to secede from Canada?

APPLY SKILLS

Read Population Pyramids
Review the population pyramid on page 535. Then answer the following questions.

13 What age group makes up the smallest part of the population?

14 In which age groups are there more males than females?

Use a Time Zone Map
Find the Bahamas on the time zone map on page 547. Then answer the following questions.

15 If it is 9:00 A.M. in the Bahamas, what time is it in Dallas?

16 If it is 12:00 P.M. in the Bahamas, what time is it in Vancouver?

Chapter 14 ■ 549

Apply Skills

Read Population Pyramids

13 75–79

14 under 5, 5–9, 10–14, 15–19, 20–24, 25–29

Use a Time Zone Map

15 8:00 A.M.

16 9:00 A.M.

ACTIVITY BOOK

Use the CHAPTER 14 TEST PREPARATION on page 143 of the Activity Book.

ASSESSMENT

Use the CHAPTER 14 TEST on pages 113–116 of the Assessment Program.

Use Vocabulary

1 interest rate (p. 528)
2 province (p. 542)
3 middle class (p. 528)
4 free election (p. 533)

Recall Facts

5 It honors their victory over the French in 1862 and their national independence. (p. 526)

6 Most of the population is Inuit, and they plan to govern themselves in the traditional way. (p. 544)

7 C (p. 545)
8 F (p. 526)
9 C (p. 544)

Think Critically

10 It has a large impact on each country's economy and culture.

11 Students may observe that people continue to fight for control of some of the countries, and the people cannot elect leaders.

12 People may fight to keep Quebec a part of Canada.

Washington, D.C.

OBJECTIVES

- Locate major centers of government in the United States.
- Use visual material to learn about the history of the United States.

Summary

Washington, D.C., home of the national government, has many museums, memorials, and buildings that honor the history of the United States.

1 Motivate

Get Ready

Point out that Washington, D.C., is not part of any state. It was established to house the federal government. Many people visit Washington, D.C., every year to see its many monuments and memorials. Ask whether any students have visited Washington, D.C. Encourage them to share their experiences with the class.

2 Teach

What to See

Direct students to the photographs of sites in Washington, D.C. Ask students the following questions:

- *Which sites shown in the photographs house part of the government?*
- *Where can you learn about the history of space travel?*
- *What other kinds of items might be on display at the National Archives?*

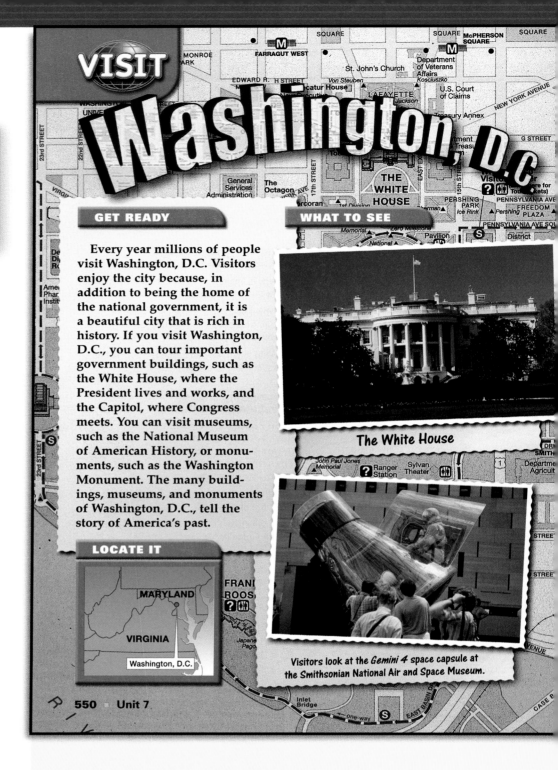

VISIT Washington, D.C.

GET READY

Every year millions of people visit Washington, D.C. Visitors enjoy the city because, in addition to being the home of the national government, it is a beautiful city that is rich in history. If you visit Washington, D.C., you can tour important government buildings, such as the White House, where the President lives and works, and the Capitol, where Congress meets. You can visit museums, such as the National Museum of American History, or monuments, such as the Washington Monument. The many buildings, museums, and monuments of Washington, D.C., tell the story of America's past.

LOCATE IT

MARYLAND

VIRGINIA

Washington, D.C.

WHAT TO SEE

The White House

Visitors look at the *Gemini 4* space capsule at the Smithsonian National Air and Space Museum.

550 ■ Unit 7

MAKE IT RELEVANT

In Your Community Ask students to identify a memorial or monument in their community. Have them write short reports on the memorial or monument, including when it was built and whom or what it honors. Invite volunteers to read their reports to the class.

REACH ALL LEARNERS

English as a Second Language Pair students who are acquiring English with English-speaking classmates. Have partners study the feature together. Tell partners to discuss the reading and summarize the information in their own words.

The Capitol

The Washington Monument

The Declaration of Independence is displayed at the National Archives.

The United States Botanic Garden has more than 10,000 varieties of plants.

TAKE A FIELD TRIP

A VIRTUAL TOUR
Visit The Learning Site at **www.harcourtschool.com** to take virtual tours of places of interest in the United States.

 **A VIDEO TOUR**
Check your media center or classroom library for a videotape tour of Washington, D.C.

Unit 7   551

Take a Field Trip

Direct students to research one memorial or museum that can be found in Washington, D.C. Students may want to learn more about the Washington Monument, the Lincoln Memorial, the Smithsonian, or the Capitol building.

A Virtual Tour Depending on the availability of computers, suggest that students work individually, in pairs, or in small groups to view the virtual tour. Encourage them to research monuments throughout the United States as they explore the Web sites. Students may use what they learn on their virtual tours as background information for the Unit Project.

GO ONLINE   **INTERNET RESOURCES**

THE LEARNING SITE Go to **www.harcourtschool.com** for a listing of Web sites focusing on places of interest in the United States.

A Video Tour Ask students to jot down three questions that can be answered by the CNN video tour of Washington, D.C., as they are watching it. Then have students exchange questions with a partner. Partners should answer each other's questions. Ask students to make sure that their partners arrived at the correct answers.

VIDEO

Use the CNN/Turner Learning TAKE A FIELD TRIP videotape of Washington, D.C.

BACKGROUND

The Washington Monument
This monument, honoring George Washington, is the tallest structure in Washington, D.C. It stands 555 feet $5\frac{1}{2}$ inches tall (about 169 m). People can travel by elevator from the lobby to the observation deck, 500 feet up (152 m). The walls in the lobby are 15 feet (5 m) thick. The thickness of the walls decreases as you go up and the walls are only 18 inches (46 cm) thick at the observation level.

EXTEND AND ENRICH

Make a Brochure Challenge students to create travel brochures for Washington, D.C. Tell them to include at least four major sites in their brochures. Encourage them to be creative and to share their brochures with their classmates.

Unit 7 Review and Test Preparation

PAGES 552–554

Visual Summary

Students' newspaper headlines should clearly describe the pictures.

- **The United States is home to people from all over the world** Because people of many different cultures have come to live in the United States, it is a diverse nation.

- **Today more Americans work in service jobs than in any other kinds of jobs** About one-third of all workers in the United States have jobs in the service industry.

- **Mexico City is one of the largest metropolitan areas in the world** More than half of Mexico's population lives in or near Mexico City.

- **Jean Bertrand-Aristide becomes Haiti's president** In 1990 Aristide was elected.

- **Simón Bolívar helps win independence for many present-day Latin American countries** Bolívar is known as *El Libertador*.

- **The St. Lawrence Seaway allows ships to travel from the Atlantic Ocean to the Great Lakes** The Seaway was built by people in the United States and Canada.

Use Vocabulary

1. rapid-transit system
2. register
3. Sun Belt
4. embargo

·UNIT·

7 Review and Test Preparation

VISUAL SUMMARY

Write a Newspaper Headline Study the pictures and captions below to help you review Unit 7. Then choose one of the pictures. Write a newspaper headline that goes along with the picture you have chosen.

USE VOCABULARY

Use a term from this list to complete each of the sentences that follow.

Sun Belt (p. 493)
rapid-transit system (p. 501)
register (p. 513)
embargo (p. 532)

1. A _____ moves passengers on an underground train.

2. Before a citizen can vote, that person must _____.

3. Much of the recent growth in the United States has taken place in the _____.

4. An _____ occurs when one nation refuses to trade goods with another.

RECALL FACTS

Answer these questions.

5. How has the Information Age affected science?

6. How has NAFTA affected trade between the United States, Canada, and Mexico?

Write the letter of the best choice.

7. The fastest-growing ethnic group in the United States today is—
   A Hispanic Americans.
   B African Americans.
   C Asian Americans.
   D Irish Americans.

8. About one-third of all American workers have jobs in the—
   F federal government.
   G banking, insurance, and real estate industry.
   H service industry.
   J medical profession.

Visual Summary

The United States is home to people from all over the world. p. 492

Today more Americans work in service jobs than in any other kinds of jobs. p. 505

Mexico City is one of the largest metropolitan areas in the world. p. 527

552

Recall Facts

5. It has greatly increased knowledge about the human body. (p. 505)

6. It has increased the number of goods and services available to people in all three nations. (p. 508)

7. A (p. 494)

8. H (p. 505)

Think Critically

9. Students may suggest that it makes their opinion heard or that it helps leaders know which party's policies are backed by the most citizens, helping them to better serve the nation's needs.

10. Students may observe that the Mexican people may have been ready for a change and they wanted to find out how another party would improve life in Mexico.

11. Students' answers will vary.

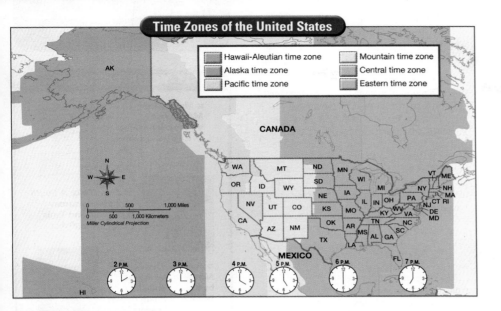

Time Zones of the United States

Hawaii-Aleutian time zone	Mountain time zone
Alaska time zone	Central time zone
Pacific time zone	Eastern time zone

AK

CANADA

N
W E
S

0   500   1,000 Miles
0   500   1,000 Kilometers
Miller Cylindrical Projection

WA MT ND MN VT ME
OR ID SD WI NH
    WY NE IA MI NY MA
NV UT CO KS IL IN OH PA CT RI
CA   MO KY WV VA NJ DE
    AZ NM OK AR TN NC MD
            TX MS AL GA SC
                LA FL

MEXICO

2 P.M. 3 P.M. 4 P.M. 5 P.M. 6 P.M. 7 P.M.

HI

THINK CRITICALLY

9 Why is voting an important part of a citizen's responsibility?

10 Why do you think the Mexican people chose to elect Vicente Fox as president in 2000?

11 What might happen if Quebec decides to secede from Canada?

APPLY SKILLS

Use a Time Zone Map
Use the map to answer the following questions.

MAP AND GLOBE SKILLS

12 What is the time difference between New Jersey and New Mexico?

13 What is the time difference between Oklahoma and Montana?

ean-Bertrand Aristide becomes Haiti's resident. p. 533

Simón Bolívar helps win independence for many present-day Latin American countries. p. 538

The St. Lawrence Seaway allows ships to travel from the Atlantic Ocean to the Great Lakes. p. 545

553

TEST PREPARATION

Review these tips with students:

■ Read the directions before reading the questions.

■ Read each question twice, focusing the second time on all the possible answers.

■ Take the time to think about all the possible answers before deciding on an answer.

■ Move past questions that give you trouble, and answer the ones you know. Then return to the difficult items.

ASSESSMENT

Use the UNIT 7 TEST on pages 117–125 of the Assessment Program.

Apply Skills

Use a Time Zone Map
12 two hours
13 one hour

Unit Activities

Make a Mural

Assign each group one of the following monuments: the Washington Monument, the Lincoln Memorial, the Statue of Liberty, or Mount Rushmore. Explain that their mural should include a label as well as a description of the features of their assigned monument.

 Performance Assessment Guidelines Look for evidence that students understand their monument's features and its historic significance and that they have clearly and creatively communicated them through their mural.

Prepare a Newscast

Suggest that students use material presented in this unit in their newscasts. They may also wish to enhance the information provided in the text by performing outside research in newspapers and other periodicals.

 Performance Assessment Guidelines Make sure that students have based their newscasts on facts they read about in this unit or in current periodicals that they have used in their research.

Complete the Unit Project

Suggest that each group make a contribution to the cultural fair. Students may wish to invite students from other classes to attend.

 Performance Assessment Guidelines Check to make sure that students have selected symbols, colors, foods, and traditions from their selected cultures.

Unit Activities

 Visit The Learning Site at www.harcourtschool.com for additional activities.

 ### Make a Mural

Work with a group of your classmates to create a mural of famous United States monuments. First, decide which monuments you want to show on your mural. Some examples include the Washington Monument, the Lincoln Memorial, the Statue of Liberty, and Mount Rushmore. After choosing the monuments you wish to show, draw or paint them on a posterboard. Remember to label each monument. Finally, display your mural with those of your classmates.

 ### Prepare a Newscast

Work in a group to prepare a newscast on a meeting between the President of the United States and a leader of a Western Hemisphere nation. Each member of your group should have a job, such as researcher, writer, reporter, or anchorperson. When planning your newscast, include information about the other nation and its relationship with the United States. When you are finished, present your newscast to your class.

554 ■ Unit 7

VISIT YOUR LIBRARY

■ *My Mexico— México mío* by Tony Johnston. G. P. Putnam's Sons.

■ *Angel Falls: A South American Journey* by Martin and Tanis Jordan. Kingfisher.

■ *Journey Through the Northern Rainforest* by Karen Pandell. Penguin Putnam Books for Young Readers.

COMPLETE THE UNIT PROJECT

A Cultural Fair Work with a group of your classmates to finish the unit project—presenting a cultural fair. Look over your notes describing the different cultures discussed in this unit. Use these notes to decide what to include in your cultural fair. Your fair may feature posters representing different art forms or styles of dress. You may also wish to feature different kinds of foods or music. Finally, hold your cultural fair.

Visit Your Library

Encourage independent reading after students' study of the issues and challenges facing the United States today with these books or books of your choice. Additional books are listed on the Multimedia Resources, on page 483D of this Teacher's Edition.

Easy *My Mexico-México mío* by Tony Johnston. G. P. Putnam's Sons, 1996. This book offers poems about Mexico in both English and Spanish.

Average *Angel Falls: A South American Journey* by Martin and Tanis Jordan. Kingfisher, 1995. This story explores the wonder of the rainforest.

Challenging *Journey Through the Northern Rainforest* by Karen Pandell. Penguin Putnam Books for Young Readers, 1999. In this book students will read about the changes taking place in the rainforest.

For Your Reference

Almanac

Facts About the States

State Flag	State	Year of Statehood	Population*	Area (sq. mi.)	Capital	Origin of State Name
	Alabama	1819	4,486,508	50,750	Montgomery	Choctaw, *alba ayamule*, "one who clears land and gathers food from it"
	Alaska	1959	643,786	570,374	Juneau	Aleut, *alayeska*, "great land"
	Arizona	1912	5,456,453	113,642	Phoenix	Papago, *arizonac*, "place of the small spring"
	Arkansas	1836	2,710,079	52,075	Little Rock	Quapaw, "the downstream people"
	California	1850	35,116,033	155,973	Sacramento	Spanish, a fictional island
	Colorado	1876	4,506,542	103,730	Denver	Spanish, "red land" or "red earth"
	Connecticut	1788	3,460,503	4,845	Hartford	Mohican, *quinnitukqut*, "at the long tidal river"
	Delaware	1787	807,385	1,955	Dover	Named for Lord de la Warr
	Florida	1845	16,713,149	54,153	Tallahassee	Spanish, "filled with flowers"
	Georgia	1788	8,560,310	57,919	Atlanta	Named for King George II of England
	Hawaii	1959	1,244,898	6,450	Honolulu	Polynesian, *hawaiki* or *owykee*, "homeland"
	Idaho	1890	1,341,131	82,751	Boise	Invented name with unknown meaning

---

State Flag	State	Year of Statehood	Population*	Area (sq. mi.)	Capital	Origin of State Name
	Illinois	1818	12,600,620	55,593	Springfield	Algonquin, *iliniwek*, "men" or "warriors"
	Indiana	1816	6,159,068	35,870	Indianapolis	*Indian + a*, "land of the Indians"
	Iowa	1846	2,936,760	55,875	Des Moines	Dakota, *ayuba*, "beautiful land"
	Kansas	1861	2,715,884	81,823	Topeka	Sioux, "land of the south wind people"
	Kentucky	1792	4,092,891	39,732	Frankfort	Iroquoian, *ken-tah-ten*, "land of tomorrow"
	Louisiana	1812	4,482,646	43,566	Baton Rouge	Named for King Louis XIV of France
	Maine	1820	1,294,464	30,865	Augusta	Named after a French province
	Maryland	1788	5,458,137	9,775	Annapolis	Named for Henrietta Maria, Queen Consort of Charles I of England
	Massachusetts	1788	6,427,801	7,838	Boston	Massachusett tribe of Native Americans, "at the big hill" or "place of the big hill"
	Michigan	1837	10,050,446	56,809	Lansing	Ojibwa, "large lake"
	Minnesota	1858	5,019,720	79,617	St. Paul	Dakota Sioux, "sky-blue water"
	Mississippi	1817	2,871,782	46,914	Jackson	Indian word meaning "great waters" or "father of waters"
	Missouri	1821	5,672,579	68,898	Jefferson City	Named after the Missouri Indian tribe. *Missouri* means "town of the large canoes."

* latest available population figures

Almanac ■ **R3**

State Flag	State	Year of Statehood	Population*	Area (sq. mi.)	Capital	Origin of State Name
	Montana	1889	909,453	145,566	Helena	Spanish, "mountainous"
	Nebraska	1867	1,729,180	76,878	Lincoln	From an Oto Indian word meaning "flat water"
	Nevada	1864	2,173,491	109,806	Carson City	Spanish, "snowy" or "snowed upon"
	New Hampshire	1788	1,275,056	8,969	Concord	Named for Hampshire County, England
	New Jersey	1787	8,590,300	7,419	Trenton	Named for the Isle of Jersey
	New Mexico	1912	1,855,059	121,365	Santa Fe	Named by Spanish explorers from Mexico
	New York	1788	19,157,532	47,224	Albany	Named after the Duke of York
	North Carolina	1789	8,320,146	48,718	Raleigh	Named after King Charles II of England
	North Dakota	1889	634,110	70,704	Bismarck	Sioux, *dakota*, "friend" or "ally"
	Ohio	1803	11,421,267	40,953	Columbus	Iroquois, *oheo*, "great water"
	Oklahoma	1907	3,493,714	68,679	Oklahoma City	Choctaw, "red people"
	Oregon	1859	3,521,515	96,003	Salem	Unknown; generally accepted that it was taken from the writings of Maj. Robert Rogers, an English army officer
	Pennsylvania	1787	12,335,091	44,820	Harrisburg	*Penn* + *sylvania*, meaning "Penn's woods"

State Flag	State	Year of Statehood	Population*	Area (sq. mi.)	Capital	Origin of State Name
	Rhode Island	1790	1,069,725	1,045	Providence	From the Greek island of Rhodes
	South Carolina	1788	4,107,183	30,111	Columbia	Named after King Charles II of England
	South Dakota	1889	761,063	75,898	Pierre	Sioux, *dakota*, "friend" or "ally"
	Tennessee	1796	5,797,289	41,220	Nashville	Name of a Cherokee village
	Texas	1845	21,779,893	261,914	Austin	Native American, *tejas*, "friend" or "ally"
	Utah	1896	2,316,256	82,168	Salt Lake City	From the Ute tribe, meaning "people of the mountains"
	Vermont	1791	616,592	9,249	Montpelier	French, *vert*, "green," and *mont*, "mountain"
	Virginia	1788	7,293,542	39,598	Richmond	Named after Queen Elizabeth I of England
	Washington	1889	6,068,996	66,582	Olympia	Named for George Washington
	West Virginia	1863	1,801,873	24,087	Charleston	From the English-named state of Virginia
	Wisconsin	1848	5,441,196	54,314	Madison	Possibly Algonquian, "the place where we live"
	Wyoming	1890	498,703	97,105	Cheyenne	From Delaware Indian word meaning "land of vast plains"
	District of Columbia		570,898	67		Named after Christopher Columbus

* latest available population figures

Almanac

Facts About the Western Hemisphere

Country	Population*	Area (sq. mi.)	Capital	Origin of Country Name
North America				
Antigua and Barbuda	67,897	171	St. Johns	Named for the Church of Santa María la Antigua in Seville, Spain
Bahamas	297,477	5,382	Nassau	Spanish, *bajamar*, "shallow water"
Barbados	277,264	166	Bridgetown	Means "bearded"—probably referring to the beard like vines early explorers found on its trees
Belize	266,440	8,867	Belmopan	Mayan, "muddy water"
Canada	32,207,113	3,851,788	Ottawa	Huron-Iroquois, *kanata*, "village" or "community"
Costa Rica	3,896,092	19,730	San José	Spanish, "rich coast"
Cuba	11,263,429	42,803	Havana	Origin unknown
Dominica	69,655	291	Roseau	Latin, *dies dominica*, "Day of the Lord"
Dominican Republic	8,715,602	18,815	Santo Domingo	Named after the capital city
El Salvador	6,470,379	8,124	San Salvador	Spanish, "the Savior"
Grenada	89,258	133	St. George's	Origin unknown
Guatemala	13,309,384	42,042	Guatemala City	Indian, "land of trees"
Haiti	7,527,817	10,714	Port-au-Prince	Indian, "land of mountains"
Honduras	6,669,789	43,278	Tegucigalpa	Spanish, "profundities" —probably referring to the depth of offshore waters
Jamaica	2,695,867	4,244	Kingston	Arawak, *xamayca*, "land of wood and water"
Mexico	104,907,991	761,602	Mexico City	Aztec, *mexliapan*, "lake of the moon"
Nicaragua	5,128,517	49,998	Managua	from *Nicarao*, the name of an Indian chief

Country	Population*	Area (sq. mi.)	Capital	Origin of Country Name
Panama	2,960,784	30,193	Panama City	From an Indian village's name
Saint Kitts and Nevis	38,763	101	Basseterre	Named by Christopher Columbus—Kitts for St. Christopher, a Catholic saint; Nevis, for a cloud-topped peak that looked like *las nieves*, "the snows"
Saint Lucia	162,157	239	Castries	Named by Christopher Columbus for a Catholic saint
Saint Vincent and the Grenadines	116,812	150	Kingstown	May have been named by Christopher Columbus for a Catholic saint
Trinidad and Tobago	1,104,209	1,980	Port-of-Spain	Trinidad, from the Spanish word for "trinity"; Tobago, named for tobacco because the island has the shape of a person smoking a pipe
United States of America	290,342,554	3,794,083	Washington, D.C.	Named after the explorer Amerigo Vespucci

South America

Country	Population*	Area (sq. mi.)	Capital	Origin of Country Name
Argentina	38,740,807	1,068,296	Buenos Aires	Latin, *argentum*, "silver"
Bolivia	8,586,443	424,162	La Paz/Sucre	Named after Simón Bolívar, the famed liberator
Brazil	182,032,604	3,286,470	Brasília	Named after a native tree that the Portuguese called "bresel wood"
Chile	15,665,216	292,258	Santiago	Indian, *chilli*, "where the land ends"
Colombia	41,662,073	439,733	Bogotá	Named after Christopher Columbus
Ecuador	13,710,234	109,483	Quito	From the Spanish word for *equator*, referring to the country's location
Guyana	702,100	83,000	Georgetown	Indian, "land of waters"
Paraguay	6,036,900	157,046	Asunción	Named after the Paraguay River, which flows through it
Peru	28,409,897	496,223	Lima	Quechua, "land of abundance"
Suriname	435,449	63,039	Paramaribo	From an Indian word, *surinen*
Uruguay	3,413,329	68,039	Montevideo	Named after the Uruguay River, which flows through it
Venezuela	24,654,694	352,143	Caracas	Spanish, "Little Venice"

* latest available population figures

Almanac ▪ **R7**

Almanac

Facts About the Presidents

1 George Washington

1732–1799
Birthplace:
Westmoreland County, VA
Home State: *VA*
Political Party: *None*
Age at Inauguration: *57*
Served: *1789–1797*
Vice President:
John Adams

2 John Adams

1735–1826
Birthplace: *Braintree, MA*
Home State: *MA*
Political Party: *Federalist*
Age at Inauguration: *61*
Served: *1797–1801*
Vice President:
Thomas Jefferson

3 Thomas Jefferson

1743–1826
Birthplace:
Albemarle County, VA
Home State: *VA*
Political Party:
Democratic-Republican
Age at Inauguration: *57*
Served: *1801–1809*
Vice Presidents:
Aaron Burr,
George Clinton

4 James Madison

1751–1836
Birthplace:
Port Conway, VA
Home State: *VA*
Political Party:
Democratic-Republican
Age at Inauguration: *57*
Served: *1809–1817*
Vice Presidents:
George Clinton,
Elbridge Gerry

5 James Monroe

1758–1831
Birthplace:
Westmoreland County, VA
Home State: *VA*
Political Party:
Democratic-Republican
Age at Inauguration: *58*
Served: *1817–1825*
Vice President:
Daniel D. Tompkins

6 John Quincy Adams

1767–1848
Birthplace: *Braintree, MA*
Home State: *MA*
Political Party:
Democratic-Republican
Age at Inauguration: *57*
Served: *1825–1829*
Vice President:
John C. Calhoun

7 Andrew Jackson

1767–1845
Birthplace:
Waxhaw settlement, SC
Home State: *TN*
Political Party:
Democratic
Age at Inauguration: *61*
Served: *1829–1837*
Vice Presidents:
John C. Calhoun,
Martin Van Buren

8 Martin Van Buren

1782–1862
Birthplace: *Kinderhook, NY*
Home State: *NY*
Political Party:
Democratic
Age at Inauguration: *54*
Served: *1837–1841*
Vice President:
Richard M. Johnson

9 William H. Harrison

1773–1841
Birthplace: *Berkeley, VA*
Home State: *OH*
Political Party: *Whig*
Age at Inauguration: *68*
Served: *1841*
Vice President:
John Tyler

10 John Tyler

1790–1862
Birthplace: *Greenway, VA*
Home State: *VA*
Political Party: *Whig*
Age at Inauguration: *51*
Served: *1841–1845*
Vice President: *none*

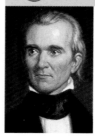

11 James K. Polk

1795–1849
Birthplace:
near Pineville, NC
Home State: *TN*
Political Party:
Democratic
Age at Inauguration: *49*
Served: *1845–1849*
Vice President:
George M. Dallas

12 Zachary Taylor

1784–1850
Birthplace:
Orange County, VA
Home State: *LA*
Political Party: *Whig*
Age at Inauguration: *64*
Served: *1849–1850*
Vice President:
Millard Fillmore

13 Millard Fillmore

1800–1874
Birthplace: *Locke, NY*
Home State: *NY*
Political Party: *Whig*
Age at Inauguration: *50*
Served: *1850–1853*
Vice President: *none*

Home State refers to the state of residence when elected.

14 Franklin Pierce

1804–1869
Birthplace: *Hillsboro, NH*
Home State: *NH*
Political Party:
Democratic
Age at Inauguration: *48*
Served: *1853–1857*
Vice President:
William R. King

15 James Buchanan

1791–1868
Birthplace:
near Mercersburg, PA
Home State: *PA*
Political Party:
Democratic
Age at Inauguration: *65*
Served: *1857–1861*
Vice President:
John C. Breckinridge

16 Abraham Lincoln

1809–1865
Birthplace:
near Hodgenville, KY
Home State: *IL*
Political Party:
Republican
Age at Inauguration: *52*
Served: *1861–1865*
Vice Presidents:
Hannibal Hamlin,
Andrew Johnson

17 Andrew Johnson

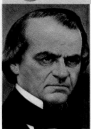

1808–1875
Birthplace: *Raleigh, NC*
Home State: *TN*
Political Party:
National Union
Age at Inauguration: *56*
Served: *1865–1869*
Vice President: *none*

18 Ulysses S. Grant

1822–1885
Birthplace:
Point Pleasant, OH
Home State: *IL*
Political Party:
Republican
Age at Inauguration: *46*
Served: *1869–1877*
Vice Presidents:
Schuyler Colfax,
Henry Wilson

19 Rutherford B. Hayes

1822–1893
Birthplace:
near Delaware, OH
Home State: *OH*
Political Party:
Republican
Age at Inauguration: *54*
Served: *1877–1881*
Vice President:
William A. Wheeler

20 James A. Garfield

1831–1881
Birthplace: *Orange, OH*
Home State: *OH*
Political Party:
Republican
Age at Inauguration: *49*
Served: *1881*
Vice President:
Chester A. Arthur

21 Chester A. Arthur

1829–1886
Birthplace: *Fairfield, VT*
Home State: *NY*
Political Party:
Republican
Age at Inauguration: *51*
Served: *1881–1885*
Vice President: *none*

22 Grover Cleveland

1837–1908
Birthplace: *Caldwell, NJ*
Home State: *NY*
Political Party:
Democratic
Age at Inauguration: *47*
Served: *1885–1889*
Vice President:
Thomas A. Hendricks

23 Benjamin Harrison

1833–1901
Birthplace: *North Bend,*
OH
Home State: *IN*
Political Party:
Republican
Age at Inauguration: *55*
Served: *1889–1893*
Vice President:
Levi P. Morton

24 Grover Cleveland

1837–1908
Birthplace: *Caldwell, NJ*
Home State: *NY*
Political Party:
Democratic
Age at Inauguration: *55*
Served: *1893–1897*
Vice President:
Adlai E. Stevenson

25 William McKinley

1843–1901
Birthplace: *Niles, OH*
Home State: *OH*
Political Party:
Republican
Age at Inauguration: *54*
Served: *1897–1901*
Vice Presidents:
Garret A. Hobart,
Theodore Roosevelt

26 Theodore Roosevelt

1858–1919
Birthplace: *New York, NY*
Home State: *NY*
Political Party:
Republican
Age at Inauguration: *42*
Served: *1901–1909*
Vice President:
Charles W. Fairbanks

27 William H. Taft

1857–1930
Birthplace: *Cincinnati, OH*
Home State: *OH*
Political Party:
Republican
Age at Inauguration: *51*
Served: *1909–1913*
Vice President:
James S. Sherman

28 Woodrow Wilson

1856–1924
Birthplace: *Staunton, VA*
Home State: *NJ*
Political Party:
Democratic
Age at Inauguration: *56*
Served: *1913–1921*
Vice President:
Thomas R. Marshall

29 Warren G. Harding

1865–1923
Birthplace:
Blooming Grove, OH
Home State: *OH*
Political Party:
Republican
Age at Inauguration: *55*
Served: *1921–1923*
Vice President:
Calvin Coolidge

30 Calvin Coolidge

1872–1933
Birthplace:
Plymouth Notch, VT
Home State: *MA*
Political Party:
Republican
Age at Inauguration: *51*
Served: *1923–1929*
Vice President:
Charles G. Dawes

31 Herbert Hoover

1874–1964
Birthplace: *West Branch, IA*
Home State: *CA*
Political Party:
Republican
Age at Inauguration: *54*
Served: *1929–1933*
Vice President:
Charles Curtis

32 Franklin D. Roosevelt

1882–1945
Birthplace: *Hyde Park, NY*
Home State: *NY*
Political Party:
Democratic
Age at Inauguration: *51*
Served: *1933–1945*
Vice Presidents:
John N. Garner, Henry A. Wallace, Harry S. Truman

33 Harry S. Truman

1884–1972
Birthplace: *Lamar, MO*
Home State: *MO*
Political Party:
Democratic
Age at Inauguration: *60*
Served: *1945–1953*
Vice President:
Alben W. Barkley

34 Dwight D. Eisenhower

1890–1969
Birthplace: *Denison, TX*
Home State: *NY*
Political Party:
Republican
Age at Inauguration: *62*
Served: *1953–1961*
Vice President:
Richard M. Nixon

35 John F. Kennedy

1917–1963
Birthplace: *Brookline, MA*
Home State: *MA*
Political Party:
Democratic
Age at Inauguration: *43*
Served: *1961–1963*
Vice President:
Lyndon B. Johnson

36 Lyndon B. Johnson

1908–1973
Birthplace:
near Stonewall, TX
Home State: *TX*
Political Party:
Democratic
Age at Inauguration: *55*
Served: *1963–1969*
Vice President:
Hubert H. Humphrey

37 Richard M. Nixon

1913–1994
Birthplace: *Yorba Linda, CA*
Home State: *NY*
Political Party:
Republican
Age at Inauguration: *56*
Served: *1969–1974*
Vice Presidents:
Spiro T. Agnew, Gerald R. Ford

38 Gerald R. Ford

1913–
Birthplace: *Omaha, NE*
Home State: *MI*
Political Party:
Republican
Age at Inauguration: *61*
Served: *1974–1977*
Vice President:
Nelson A. Rockefeller

39 Jimmy Carter

1924–
Birthplace: *Plains, GA*
Home State: *GA*
Political Party:
Democratic
Age at Inauguration: *52*
Served: *1977–1981*
Vice President:
Walter F. Mondale

40 Ronald W. Reagan

1911–2004
Birthplace: *Tampico, IL*
Home State: *CA*
Political Party:
Republican
Age at Inauguration: *69*
Served: *1981–1989*
Vice President:
George Bush

41 George Bush

1924–
Birthplace: *Milton, MA*
Home State: *TX*
Political Party:
Republican
Age at Inauguration: *64*
Served: *1989–1993*
Vice President:
Dan Quayle

42 William Clinton

1946–
Birthplace: *Hope, AR*
Home State: *AR*
Political Party:
Democratic
Age at Inauguration: *46*
Served: *1993–2001*
Vice President:
Albert Gore

43 George W. Bush

1946–
Birthplace: *New Haven, CT*
Home State: *TX*
Political Party:
Republican
Age at Inauguration: *54*
Served: *2001–*
Vice President:
Richard Cheney

R10 ■ Reference

American Documents

THE DECLARATION OF INDEPENDENCE

In Congress, July 4, 1776.
The unanimous Declaration of the
thirteen United States of America,

When in the Course of human events it becomes necessary for one people to dissolve the political bands which have connected them with another, and to assume among the powers of the earth, the separate and equal station to which the Laws of Nature and of Nature's God entitle them, a decent respect to the opinions of mankind requires that they should declare the causes which impel them to the separation.

We hold these truths to be self-evident, that all men are created equal, that they are endowed by their Creator with certain unalienable Rights, that among these are Life, Liberty and the pursuit of Happiness.
That to secure these rights, Governments are instituted among Men, deriving their just powers from the consent of the governed,
That whenever any Form of Government becomes destructive of these ends, it is the Right of the People to alter or to abolish it, and to institute new Government, laying its foundation on such principles and organizing its powers in such form, as to them shall seem most likely to effect their Safety and Happiness. Prudence, indeed, will dictate that Governments long established should not be changed for light and transient causes; and accordingly all experience hath shown, that mankind are more disposed to suffer, while evils are sufferable, than to right themselves by abolishing the forms to which they are accustomed. But when a long train of abuses and usurpations, pursuing invariably the same Object evinces a design to reduce them under absolute Despotism, it is their right, it is their duty, to throw off such Government, and to provide new Guards for their future security.

Such has been the patient sufferance of these Colonies; and such is now the necessity which constrains them to alter their former Systems of Government. The history of the present King of Great Britain is a history of repeated injuries and usurpations, all having in direct object the establishment of an absolute Tyranny over these States. To prove this, let Facts be submitted to a candid world.

He has refused his Assent to Laws, the most wholesome and necessary for the public good.
He has forbidden his Governors to pass Laws of immediate and pressing importance, unless suspended in their operation till his Assent should be obtained; and when so suspended, he has utterly neglected to attend to them.

Preamble
The Preamble tells why the Declaration was written. It states that the members of the Continental Congress believed the colonies had the right to break away from Britain and become a free nation.

A Statement of Rights
The opening part of the Declaration tells what rights the members of the Continental Congress believed that all people have. All people are equal in having the rights to life, liberty, and the pursuit of happiness. The main purpose of a government is to protect the rights of the people who consent to be governed by it. These rights cannot be taken away. When a government tries to take these rights away from the people, the people have the right to change the government or do away with it. The people can then form a new government that respects these rights.

Charges Against the King
The Declaration lists more than 25 charges against the king. He was mistreating the colonists, the Declaration says, in order to gain total control over the colonies.

The king rejected many laws passed by colonial legislatures.

The king made the colonial legislatures meet at unusual times and places.

The king and the king's governors often dissolved colonial legislatures for disobeying their orders.

The king stopped people from moving to the colonies and into the western lands.

The king prevented the colonists from choosing their own judges. The king chose the judges, and they served only as long as the king was satisfied with them.

The king hired people to help collect taxes in the colonies.

The king appointed General Thomas Gage, commander of Britain's military forces in the Americas, as governor of Massachusetts.

The king expected the colonists to provide housing and supplies for the British soldiers in the colonies.

The king and Parliament demanded that colonists pay many taxes, even though the colonists did not agree to pay them.

Colonists were tried by British naval courts, which had no juries.

Colonists accused of treason were sent to Britain to be tried.

He has refused to pass other Laws for the accommodation of large districts of people, unless those people would relinquish the right of Representation in the Legislature, a right inestimable to them and formidable to tyrants only.

He has called together legislative bodies at places unusual, uncomfortable, and distant from the depository of their public Records, for the sole purpose of fatiguing them into compliance with his measures.

He has dissolved Representative Houses repeatedly, for opposing with manly firmness his invasions on the rights of the people.

He has refused for a long time, after such dissolutions, to cause others to be elected; whereby the Legislative powers, incapable of Annihilation, have returned to the People at large for their exercise; the State remaining in the mean time exposed to all the dangers of invasion from without, and convulsions within.

He has endeavored to prevent the population of these States; for that purpose obstructing the Laws for Naturalization of Foreigners; refusing to pass others to encourage their migrations hither, and raising the conditions of new Appropriations of Lands.

He has obstructed the Administration of Justice, by refusing his Assent to Laws for establishing Judiciary powers.

He has made Judges dependent on his Will alone, for the tenure of their offices, and the amount and payment of their salaries.

He has erected a multitude of New Offices, and sent hither swarms of Officers to harass our people, and eat out their substance.

He has kept among us, in times of peace, Standing Armies without the Consent of our legislatures.

He has affected to render the Military independent of and superior to the Civil power.

He has combined with others to subject us to a jurisdiction foreign to our constitution, and unacknowledged by our laws; giving his Assent to their Acts of pretended Legislation:

For quartering large bodies of armed troops among us:

For protecting them, by a mock Trial, from punishment for any Murders which they should commit on the Inhabitants of these States:

For cutting off our Trade with all parts of the world:

For imposing Taxes on us without our Consent:

For depriving us in many cases, of the benefits of Trial by Jury:

For transporting us beyond Seas to be tried for pretended offenses:

For abolishing the free System of English Laws in a neighboring Province, establishing therein an Arbitrary government, and enlarging its Boundaries so as to render it at once an example and fit instrument for introducing the same absolute rule into these Colonies:

For taking away our Charters, abolishing our most valuable Laws, and altering fundamentally the Forms of our Governments:

For suspending our own Legislatures, and declaring themselves invested with power to legislate for us in all cases whatsoever.

He has abdicated Government here, by declaring us out of his Protection and waging War against us.

He has plundered our seas, ravaged our Coasts, burnt our towns, and destroyed the lives of our people.

He is at this time transporting large Armies of foreign Mercenaries to complete the works of death, desolation and tyranny, already begun with circumstances of Cruelty & perfidy scarcely paralleled in the most barbarous ages, and totally unworthy the Head of a civilized nation.

He has constrained our fellow Citizens taken Captive on the high Seas to bear Arms against their Country, to become the executioners of their friends and Brethren, or to fall themselves by their Hands.

He has excited domestic insurrections amongst us, and has endeavored to bring on the inhabitants of our frontiers, the merciless Indian Savages, whose known rule of warfare, is an undistinguished destruction of all ages, sexes and conditions.

In every stage of these Oppressions We have Petitioned for Redress in the most humble terms: Our repeated Petitions have been answered only by repeated injury. A Prince, whose character is thus marked by every act which may define a Tyrant, is unfit to be the ruler of a free people.

Nor have We been wanting in attentions to our British brethren. We have warned them from time to time of attempts by their legislature to extend an unwarrantable jurisdiction over us. We have reminded them of the circumstances of our emigration and settlement here. We have appealed to their native justice and magnanimity, and we have conjured them by the ties of our common kindred to disavow these usurpations, which, would inevitably interrupt our connections and correspondence. They too have been deaf to the voice of justice and of consanguinity. We must, therefore, acquiesce in the necessity, which denounces our Separation, and hold them, as we hold the rest of mankind, Enemies in War, in Peace Friends.

We, therefore, the Representatives of the united States of America, in General Congress, Assembled, appealing to the Supreme Judge of the world for the rectitude of our intentions, do, in the Name, and by Authority of the good People of these Colonies, solemnly publish and declare, That these United Colonies are, and of Right ought to be Free and Independent States; that they are Absolved from all Allegiance to the British Crown, and that all political connection between them and the State of Great Britain, is and ought to be totally dissolved; and that as Free and Independent States, they have full Power to levy War, conclude Peace, contract Alliances, establish Commerce, and to do all other Acts and Things which Independent States may of right do.

The king allowed General Gage to take military action to enforce British laws in the colonies.

The king hired Hessian mercenaries and sent them to fight the colonists.

The king's governor in Virginia promised freedom to all enslaved people who joined the British forces. The British also planned to use Indians to fight the colonists.

The Declaration explained the efforts of the colonists to avoid separation from Britain. But the colonists said that the king had ignored their protests. Because of the many charges against the king, the writers of the Declaration concluded that he was not fit to rule free people.

A Statement of Independence The writers declared that the colonies were now free and independent states. All ties with Britain were broken. As free and independent states, they had the right to make war and peace, to trade, and to do all the things free countries could do.

To support the Declaration, the signers promised one another their lives, their fortunes, and their honor.

And for the support of this Declaration, with a firm reliance on the protection of divine Providence, we mutually pledge to each other our Lives, our Fortunes and our sacred Honor.

John Hancock

NEW HAMPSHIRE
Josiah Bartlett
William Whipple
Matthew Thornton

MASSACHUSETTS
John Adams
Samuel Adams
Robert Treat Paine
Elbridge Gerry

NEW YORK
William Floyd
Philip Livingston
Francis Lewis
Lewis Morris

RHODE ISLAND
Stephen Hopkins
William Ellery

NEW JERSEY
Richard Stockton
John Witherspoon
Francis Hopkinson
John Hart
Abraham Clark

PENNSYLVANIA
Robert Morris
Benjamin Rush
Benjamin Franklin
John Morton
George Clymer
James Smith
George Taylor
James Wilson
George Ross

DELAWARE
Caesar Rodney
George Read
Thomas McKean

MARYLAND
Samuel Chase
William Paca
Thomas Stone
Charles Carroll of Carrollton

NORTH CAROLINA
William Hopper
Joseph Hewes
John Penn

VIRGINIA
George Wythe
Richard Henry Lee
Thomas Jefferson
Benjamin Harrison
Thomas Nelson, Jr.
Francis Lightfoot Lee
Carter Braxton

SOUTH CAROLINA
Edward Rutledge
Thomas Heyward, Jr.
Thomas Lynch, Jr.
Arthur Middleton

CONNECTICUT
Roger Sherman
Samuel Huntington
William Williams
Oliver Wolcott

GEORGIA
Button Gwinnett
Lyman Hall
George Walton

Members of the Continental Congress stated that copies of the Declaration should be sent to all Committees of Correspondence and to commanders of the troops and that it should be read in every state.

Resolved, That copies of the Declaration be sent to the several assemblies, conventions, and committees, or councils of safety, and to the several commanding officers of the continental troops; that it be proclaimed in each of the United States, at the head of the army.

R14 ■ Reference

THE CONSTITUTION OF THE UNITED STATES OF AMERICA

Preamble*

We the people of the United States, in order to form a more perfect Union, establish justice, insure domestic tranquillity, provide for the common defense, promote the general welfare, and secure the blessings of liberty to ourselves and our posterity, do ordain and establish this Constitution for the United States of America.

ARTICLE I
THE LEGISLATIVE BRANCH
SECTION 1. CONGRESS

All legislative powers herein granted shall be vested in a Congress of the United States, which shall consist of a Senate and House of Representatives.

SECTION 2. THE HOUSE OF REPRESENTATIVES

(1) The House of Representatives shall be composed of members chosen every second year by the people of the several states, and the electors in each state shall have the qualifications requisite for electors of the most numerous branch of the state legislature.

(2) No person shall be a Representative who shall not have attained to the age of twenty-five years, and been seven years a citizen of the United States, and who shall not, when elected, be an inhabitant of that state in which he shall be chosen.

(3) Representatives [*and direct taxes*]** shall be apportioned among the several states which may be included within this Union, according to their respective numbers [*which shall be determined by adding to the whole number of free persons, including those bound to service for a term of years, and excluding Indians not taxed, three-fifths of all other persons*]. The actual enumeration shall be made within three years after the first meeting of the Congress of the United States, and within every subsequent term of ten years, in such manner as they shall by law direct. The number of Representatives shall not exceed one for every 30,000, but each state shall have at least one Representative [; *and until such enumeration shall be made, the State of New Hampshire shall be entitled to choose three; Massachusetts eight; Rhode Island and Providence Plantations one; Connecticut five; New York six; New Jersey four; Pennsylvania eight; Delaware one; Maryland six; Virginia ten; North Carolina five; South Carolina five; and Georgia three*].

*Titles have been added to make the Constitution easier to read. They did not appear in the original document.

**The parts of the Constitution that no longer apply are printed in italics within brackets [ ]. These portions have been changed or set aside by later amendments.

Preamble
The introduction to the Constitution states the purposes and principles for writing it. The writers wanted to set up a fairer form of government and to secure peace and freedom for themselves and for future generations.

Congress
Congress has the authority to make laws. Congress is made up of two groups of lawmakers: the Senate and the House of Representatives.

(1) Election and Term of Members
Qualified voters are to elect members of the House of Representatives every two years. Each member of the House of Representatives must meet certain requirements.

(2) Qualifications
Members of the House of Representatives must be at least 25 years old. They must have been citizens of the United States for at least seven years. They must live in the state that they will represent.

(3) Determining Apportionment
The number of representatives a state may have depends on the number of people living in each state. Every ten years the federal government must take a census, or count, of the population in every state. Every state will have at least one representative.

(4) Filling Vacancies
If there is a vacancy in representation in Congress, the governor of the state involved must call a special election to fill it.

(5) Special Authority
The House of Representatives chooses a Speaker as its presiding officer. It also chooses other officers as appropriate. The House is the only government branch that may impeach, or charge, an official in the executive branch or a judge of the federal courts for failing to carry out his or her duties. These cases are tried in the Senate.

(1) Number, Term, and Selection of Members
Each state is represented by two senators. Until Amendment 17 was passed, state legislatures chose the senators for their states. Each senator serves a six-year term and has one vote in Congress.

(2) Overlapping Terms and Filling Vacancies
One-third of the senators are elected every two years for a six-year term. This grouping allows at least two-thirds of the experienced senators to remain in the Senate after each election. Amendment 17 permits state governors to appoint a replacement to fill a vacancy until the next election is held.

(3) Qualifications
Senators must be at least 30 years old. They must have been citizens of the United States for at least nine years. They must live in the state that they will represent.

(4) President of the Senate
The Vice President acts as chief officer of the Senate but does not vote unless there is a tie.

(5) Other Officers
The Senate chooses its other officers and a president pro tempore, who serves if the Vice President is not present or if the Vice President becomes President. *Pro tempore* is a Latin term meaning "for the time being."

---

(4) When vacancies happen in the representation from any state, the executive authority thereof shall issue writs of election to fill such vacancies.

(5) The House of Representatives shall choose their Speaker and other officers; and shall have the sole power of impeachment.

SECTION 3. THE SENATE

(1) The Senate of the United States shall be composed of two Senators from each state [*chosen by the legislature thereof*], for six years, and each Senator shall have one vote.

(2) [*Immediately after they shall be assembled in consequence of the first election, they shall be divided as equally as may be into three classes. The seats of the Senators of the first class shall be vacated at the expiration of the second year, of the second class at the expiration of the fourth year, and of the third class at the expiration of the sixth year, so that one-third may be chosen every second year; and if vacancies happen by resignation, or otherwise, during the recess of the legislature of any state, the executive thereof may make temporary appointments until the next meeting of the legislature, which shall then fill such vacancies.*]

(3) No person shall be a Senator who shall not have attained to the age of thirty years, and been nine years a citizen of the United States, and who shall not, when elected, be an inhabitant of that state for which he shall be chosen.

(4) The Vice President of the United States shall be President of the Senate, but shall have no vote, unless they be equally divided.

(5) The Senate shall choose their other officers, and also a President *pro tempore*, in the absence of the Vice President, or when he shall exercise the office of the President of the United States.

(6) The Senate shall have the sole power to try all impeachments. When sitting for that purpose, they shall be on oath or affirmation. When the President of the United States is tried, the Chief Justice shall preside; and no person shall be convicted without the concurrence of two-thirds of the members present.

(7) Judgment in cases of impeachment shall not extend further than to removal from office, and disqualification to hold and enjoy any office of honor, trust, or profit under the United States; but the party convicted shall nevertheless be liable and subject to indictment, trial, judgment and punishment, according to law.

SECTION 4. ELECTIONS AND MEETINGS
(1) The times, places, and manner of holding elections for Senators and Representatives shall be prescribed in each state by the legislature thereof; but the Congress may at any time by law make or alter such regulations, [*except as to the places of choosing Senators*].

(2) The Congress shall assemble at least once in every year, [*and such meeting shall be on the first Monday in December, unless they shall by law appoint a different day*].

SECTION 5. RULES OF PROCEDURE
(1) Each house shall be the judge of the elections, returns and qualifications of its own members, and a majority of each shall constitute a quorum to do business; but a smaller number may adjourn from day to day, and may be authorized to compel the attendance of absent members, in such manner and under such penalties as each house may provide.

(2) Each house may determine the rules of its proceedings, punish its members for disorderly behavior, and, with the concurrence of two-thirds, expel a member.

(3) Each house shall keep a journal of its proceedings, and from time to time publish the same, excepting such parts as may in their judgment require secrecy; and the yeas and nays of the members of either house on any question shall, at the desire of one-fifth of those present, be entered on the journal.

(6) Impeachment Trials
If the House of Representatives votes articles of impeachment, the Senate holds a trial. A two-thirds vote is required to convict a person who has been impeached.

(7) Penalty for Conviction
If convicted in an impeachment case, an official is removed from office and may never hold office in the United States government again. The convicted person may also be tried in a regular court of law for any crimes.

(1) Holding Elections
Each state makes its own rules about electing senators and representatives. However, Congress may change these rules at any time. Today congressional elections are held on the Tuesday after the first Monday in November, in even-numbered years.

(2) Meetings
The Constitution requires Congress to meet at least once a year. That day is the first Monday in December, unless Congress sets a different day. Amendment 20 changed this date to January 3.

(1) Organization
Each house of Congress may decide if its members have been elected fairly and are able to hold office. Each house may do business only when a quorum—a majority of its members—is present. By less than a majority vote, each house may compel absent members to attend.

(2) Rules
Each house may decide its own rules for doing business, punish its members, and expel a member from office if two-thirds of the members agree.

(3) Journal
The Constitution requires each house to keep records of its activities and to publish these records from time to time. The House Journal and the Senate Journal are published at the end of each session. How each member voted must be recorded if one-fifth of the members ask for this to be done.

(4) Adjournment
When Congress is in session, neither house may take a recess for more than three days without the consent of the other.

(1) Pay and Privileges
Members of Congress set their own salaries, which are to be paid by the federal government. Members cannot be arrested or sued for anything they say while Congress is in session. This privilege is called congressional immunity. Members of Congress may be arrested while Congress is in session only if they commit a crime.

(2) Restrictions
Members of Congress may not hold any other federal office while serving in Congress. A member may not resign from office and then take a government position created during that member's term of office or for which the pay has been increased during that member's term of office.

(1) Money-Raising Bills
All money-raising bills must be introduced first in the House of Representatives, but the Senate may suggest changes.

(2) How a Bill Becomes a Law
After a bill has been passed by both the House of Representatives and the Senate, it must be sent to the President. If the President approves and signs the bill, it becomes law. The President can also veto, or refuse to sign, the bill. Congress can override a veto by passing the bill again by a two-thirds majority. If the President does not act within ten days, two things may happen. If Congress is still in session, the bill becomes a law. If Congress ends its session within that same ten-day period, the bill does not become a law.

(3) Orders and Resolutions
Congress can pass orders and resolutions, some of which have the same effect as a law. Congress may decide on its own when to end the session. Other such acts must be signed or vetoed by the President.

(4) Neither house, during the session of Congress, shall, without the consent of the other, adjourn for more than three days, nor to any other place than that in which the two houses shall be sitting.

SECTION 6. PRIVILEGES AND RESTRICTIONS

(1) The Senators and Representatives shall receive a compensation for their services, to be ascertained by law and paid out of the Treasury of the United States. They shall in all cases, except treason, felony, and breach of the peace, be privileged from arrest during their attendance at the session of their respective houses, and in going to and returning from the same; and for any speech or debate in either house, they shall not be questioned in any other place.

(2) No Senator or Representative shall, during the time for which he was elected, be appointed to any civil office under the authority of the United States, which shall have been created, or the emoluments whereof shall have been increased, during such time; and no person holding any office under the United States shall be a member of either house during his continuance in office.

SECTION 7. MAKING LAWS

(1) All bills for raising revenue shall originate in the House of Representatives; but the Senate may propose or concur with amendments as on other bills.

(2) Every bill which shall have passed the House of Representatives and the Senate shall, before it become a law, be presented to the President of the United States; if he approve, he shall sign it, but if not, he shall return it, with his objections, to that house in which it shall have originated, who shall enter the objections at large on their journal, and proceed to reconsider it. If after such reconsideration two-thirds of that house shall agree to pass the bill, it shall be sent, together with the objections, to the other house, by which it shall likewise be reconsidered, and, if approved by two-thirds of that house, it shall become a law. But in all such cases the votes of both houses shall be determined by yeas and nays, and the names of the persons voting for and against the bill shall be entered on the journal of each house respectively. If any bill shall not be returned by the President within ten days (Sundays excepted) after it shall have been presented to him, the same bill shall be a law, in like manner as if he had signed it, unless the Congress by their adjournment prevent its return, in which case it shall not be a law.

(3) Every order, resolution, or vote to which the concurrence of the Senate and House of Representatives may be necessary (except on a question of adjournment) shall be presented to the President of the United States; and before the same shall take effect, shall be approved by him, or being disapproved by him, shall be repassed by two-thirds of the Senate and House of Representatives, according to the rules and limitations prescribed in the case of a bill.

SECTION 8. POWERS DELEGATED TO CONGRESS
The Congress shall have power
(1) To lay and collect taxes, duties, imposts and excises, to pay the debts and provide for the common defense and general welfare of the United States; but all duties, imposts and excises shall be uniform throughout the United States;

(2) To borrow money on the credit of the United States;

(3) To regulate commerce with foreign nations, and among the several states and with the Indian tribes;

(4) To establish an uniform rule of naturalization, and uniform laws on the subject of bankruptcies throughout the United States;

(5) To coin money, regulate the value thereof, and of foreign coin, and fix the standard of weights and measures;

(6) To provide for the punishment of counterfeiting the securities and current coin of the United States;

(7) To establish post offices and post roads;

(8) To promote the progress of science and useful arts by securing for limited times to authors and inventors the exclusive right to their respective writings and discoveries;

(9) To constitute tribunals inferior to the Supreme Court;

(10) To define and punish piracies and felonies committed on the high seas and offenses against the law of nations;

(1) Taxation
Only Congress has the authority to raise money to pay debts, defend the United States, and provide services for its people by collecting taxes or tariffs on foreign goods. All taxes must be applied equally in all states.

(2) Borrowing Money
Congress may borrow money for national use. This is usually done by selling government bonds.

(3) Commerce
Congress can control trade with other countries and between states.

(4) Naturalization and Bankruptcy
Congress decides what requirements people from other countries must meet to become United States citizens. Congress can also pass laws to protect people who are bankrupt, or cannot pay their debts.

(5) Coins, Weights, and Measures
Congress can coin money and decide its value. Congress also decides on the system of weights and measures to be used throughout the nation.

(6) Counterfeiting
Congress may pass laws to punish people who make fake money, bonds, or stamps.

(7) Postal Service
Congress can build post offices and make rules about the postal system and the roads used for mail delivery.

(8) Copyrights and Patents
Congress can issue patents and copyrights to inventors and authors to protect the ownership of their works.

(9) Federal Courts
Congress can establish a system of federal courts under the Supreme Court.

(10) Crimes at Sea
Congress can pass laws to punish people for crimes committed at sea. Congress may also punish United States citizens for breaking international law.

(11) Declaring War
Only Congress can declare war.

(12) The Army
Congress can establish an army, but it cannot vote enough money to support it for more than two years. This part of the Constitution was written to keep the army under civilian control.

(13) The Navy
Congress can establish a navy and vote enough money to support it for as long as necessary. No time limit was set because people thought the navy was less of a threat to people's liberty than the army was.

(14) Military Regulations
Congress makes the rules that guide and govern all the armed forces.

(15) The Militia
Each state has its own militia, now known as the National Guard. The National Guard can be called into federal service by the President, as authorized by Congress, to enforce laws, to stop uprisings against the government, or to protect the people in case of floods, earthquakes, and other disasters.

(16) Control of the Militia
Congress helps each state support the National Guard. Each state may appoint its own officers and train its own guard according to rules set by Congress.

(17) National Capital and Other Property
Congress may pass laws to govern the nation's capital (Washington, D.C.) and any land owned by the government.

(18) Other Necessary Laws
The Constitution allows Congress to make laws that are necessary to enforce the powers listed in Article I. This clause has two conflicting interpretations. One is that Congress can only do what is absolutely necessary to carry out the powers listed in Article I. The other is that Congress may stretch its authority in order to carry out these powers, but not beyond limits established by the Constitution.

---

(11) To declare war, grant letters of marque and reprisal, and make rules concerning captures on land and water;

(12) To raise and support armies, but no appropriation of money to that use shall be for a longer term than two years;

(13) To provide and maintain a navy;

(14) To make rules for the government and regulation of the land and naval forces;

(15) To provide for calling forth the militia to execute the laws of the Union, suppress insurrections and repel invasions;

(16) To provide for organizing, arming, and disciplining the militia, and for governing such part of them as may be employed in the service of the United States, reserving to the states, respectively, the appointment of the officers, and the authority of training the militia according to the discipline prescribed by Congress;

(17) To exercise exclusive legislation in all cases whatsoever, over such district (not exceeding ten miles square) as may, by cession of particular states, and the acceptance of Congress, become the seat of government of the United States, and to exercise like authority over all places purchased by the consent of the legislature of the state in which the same shall be, for the erection of forts, magazines, arsenals, dock-yards, and other needful buildings; —and

(18) To make all laws which shall be necessary and proper for carrying into execution the foregoing powers, and all other powers vested by this Constitution in the government of the United States, or in any department or officer thereof.

SECTION 9. POWERS DENIED TO CONGRESS

(1) [*The migration or importation of such persons as any of the states now existing shall think proper to admit shall not be prohibited by the Congress prior to the year 1808; but a tax or duty may be imposed on such importation, not exceeding 10 dollars for each person.*]

(2) The privilege of the writ of habeas corpus shall not be suspended, unless when in cases of rebellion or invasion the public safety may require it.

(3) No bill of attainder or ex post facto law shall be passed.

(4) [*No capitation or other direct tax shall be laid, unless in proportion to the census or enumeration herein before directed to be taken.*]

(5) No tax or duty shall be laid on articles exported from any state.

(6) No preference shall be given by any regulation of commerce or revenue to the ports of one state over those of another; nor shall vessels bound to, or from, one state, be obliged to enter, clear, or pay duties in another.

(7) No money shall be drawn from the Treasury, but in consequence of appropriations made by law; and a regular statement and account of the receipts and expenditures of all public money shall be published from time to time.

(1) Slave Trade
Some authority is not given to Congress. Congress could not prevent the slave trade until 1808, but it could put a tax of ten dollars on each slave brought into the United States. After 1808, when a law was passed to stop slaves from being brought into the United States, this section no longer applied.

(2) Habeas Corpus
A writ of habeas corpus is a privilege that entitles a person to a hearing before a judge. The judge must then decide if there is good reason for that person to have been arrested. If not, that person must be released. The government is not allowed to take this privilege away except during a national emergency, such as an invasion or a rebellion.

(3) Special Laws
Congress cannot pass laws that impose punishment on a named individual or group, except in cases of treason. Article III sets limits to punishments for treason. Congress also cannot pass laws that punish a person for an action that was legal when it was done.

(4) Direct Taxes
Congress cannot set a direct tax on people, unless it is in proportion to the total population. Amendment 16, which provides for the income tax, is an exception.

(5) Export Taxes
Congress cannot tax goods sent from one state to another or from a state to another country.

(6) Ports
When making trade laws, Congress cannot favor one state over another. Congress cannot require ships from one state to pay a duty to enter another state.

(7) Public Money
The government cannot spend money from the treasury unless Congress passes a law allowing it to do so. A written record must be kept of all money spent by the government.

(8) Titles of Nobility and Gifts
The United States government cannot grant titles of nobility. Government officials cannot accept gifts from other countries without the permission of Congress. This clause was intended to prevent government officials from being bribed by other nations.

(1) Complete Restrictions
The Constitution does not allow states to act as if they were individual countries. No state government may make a treaty with other countries. No state can print its own money.

(2) Partial Restrictions
No state government can tax imported goods or exported goods without the consent of Congress. States may charge a fee to inspect these goods, but profits must be given to the United States Treasury.

(3) Other Restrictions
No state government may tax ships entering its ports unless Congress approves. No state may keep an army or navy during times of peace other than the National Guard. No state can enter into agreements called compacts with other states without the consent of Congress.

(1) Term of Office
The President has the authority to carry out our nation's laws. The term of office for both the President and the Vice President is four years.

(2) The Electoral College
This group of people is to be chosen by the voters of each state to elect the President and Vice President. The number of electors in each state is equal to the number of senators and representatives that state has in Congress.

(3) Election Process
This clause describes in detail how the electors were to choose the President and Vice President. In 1804 Amendment 12 changed the process for electing the President and the Vice President.

---

(8) No title of nobility shall be granted by the United States; and no person holding any office of profit or trust under them, shall, without the consent of the Congress, accept of any present, emolument, office, or title, of any kind whatever, from any king, prince, or foreign state.

SECTION 10. POWERS DENIED TO THE STATES
(1) No state shall enter into any treaty, alliance, or confederation; grant letters of marque and reprisal; coin money; emit bills of credit; make anything but gold and silver coin a tender in payment of debts; pass any bill of attainder, ex post facto law, or law impairing the obligation of contracts, or grant any title of nobility.

(2) No state shall, without the consent of the Congress, lay any imposts or duties on imports or exports, except what may be absolutely necessary for executing its inspection laws; and the net produce of all duties and imposts, laid by any state on imports or exports, shall be for the use of the Treasury of the United States; and all such laws shall be subject to the revision and control of the Congress.

(3) No state shall, without the consent of Congress, lay any duty of tonnage, keep troops, or ships of war in time of peace, enter into any agreement or compact with another state, or with a foreign power, or engage in war, unless actually invaded, or in such imminent danger as will not admit of delay.

ARTICLE II
THE EXECUTIVE BRANCH
SECTION 1. PRESIDENT AND VICE PRESIDENT
(1) The executive power shall be vested in a President of the United States of America. He shall hold his office during the term of four years, and together with the Vice President, chosen for the same term, be elected as follows:

(2) Each state shall appoint, in such manner as the legislature thereof may direct, a number of electors, equal to the whole number of Senators and Representatives to which the state may be entitled in the Congress; but no Senator or Representative, or person holding an office of trust or profit under the United States, shall be appointed an elector.

(3) [*The electors shall meet in their respective states, and vote by ballot for two persons, of whom one at least shall not be an inhabitant of the same state with themselves. And they shall make a list of all the persons voted for, and of the number of votes for each; which list they shall sign and certify, and transmit sealed to the seat of the government of the United States, directed to the president of the Senate. The president of the Senate shall, in the presence of the Senate and House of Representatives, open all the certificates, and the votes shall then be counted. The person having the greatest number of votes shall be the President, if such number be a majority of the whole number of electors appointed; and if there be more than one who have such majority, and have an equal number of votes, then the House of Representatives shall immediately choose by ballot one of them for President; and if no person have*

a majority, then from the five highest on the list the said House shall in like manner choose the President. But in choosing the President the votes shall be taken by states, the representation from each state having one vote: A quorum for this purpose shall consist of a member or members from two-thirds of the states, and a majority of all the states shall be necessary to a choice. In every case, after the choice of the President, the person having the greatest number of votes of the electors shall be the Vice President. But if there should remain two or more who have equal votes, the Senate shall choose from them by ballot the Vice President.]

(4) The Congress may determine the time of choosing the electors, and the day on which they shall give their votes; which day shall be the same throughout the United States.

(5) No person except a natural-born citizen [*or a citizen of the United States, at the time of the adoption of this Constitution,*] shall be eligible to the office of the President; neither shall any person be eligible to that office who shall not have attained to the age of thirty-five years, and been fourteen years a resident within the United States.

(6) [*In case of the removal of the President from office, or of his death, resignation, or inability to discharge the powers and duties of the said office, the same shall devolve on the Vice President, and the Congress may by law provide for the case of removal, death, resignation or inability, both of the President and Vice President, declaring what officer shall then act as President, and such officer shall act accordingly, until the disability be removed, or a President shall be elected.*]

(7) The President shall, at stated times, receive for his services, a compensation, which shall neither be increased nor diminished during the period for which he shall have been elected, and he shall not receive within that period any other emolument from the United States, or any of them.

(8) Before he enter on the execution of his office, he shall take the following oath or affirmation:—"I do solemnly swear (or affirm) that I will faithfully execute the office of President of the United States, and will to the best of my ability, preserve, protect, and defend the Constitution of the United States."

SECTION 2. POWERS OF THE PRESIDENT
(1) The President shall be Commander in Chief of the Army and Navy of the United States, and of the militia of the several states, when called into the actual service of the United States; he may require the opinion, in writing, of the principal officer in each of the executive departments, upon any subject relating to the duties of their respective offices, and he shall have power to grant reprieves and pardons for offenses against the United States, except in cases of impeachment.

(4) Time of Elections
Congress decides the day the electors are to be elected and the day they are to vote.

(5) Qualifications
The President must be at least 35 years old, be a citizen of the United States by birth, and have been living in the United States for 14 years or more.

(6) Vacancies
If the President dies, resigns, or is removed from office, the Vice President becomes President.

(7) Salary
The President receives a salary that cannot be raised or lowered during a term of office. The President may not be paid any additional salary by the federal government or any state or local government. Today the President's salary is $400,000 a year, plus expenses for things such as housing, travel, and entertainment.

(8) Oath of Office
Before taking office, the President must promise to perform the duties faithfully and to protect the country's form of government. Usually the Chief Justice of the Supreme Court administers the oath of office.

(1) The President's Leadership
The President is the commander of the nation's armed forces and of the National Guard when it is in service of the nation. All government officials of the executive branch must report their actions to the President when asked. The President can excuse people from punishment for crimes committed.

(2) Treaties and Appointments
The President has the authority to make treaties, but they must be approved by a two-thirds vote of the Senate. The President nominates justices to the Supreme Court, ambassadors to other countries, and other federal officials with the Senate's approval.

(3) Filling Vacancies
If a government official's position becomes vacant when Congress is not in session, the President can make a temporary appointment.

Duties
The President must report to Congress on the condition of the country. This report is now presented in the annual State of the Union message.

Impeachment
The President, the Vice President, or any government official will be removed from office if impeached, or accused, and then found guilty of treason, bribery, or other serious crimes. The Constitution protects government officials from being impeached for unimportant reasons.

Federal Courts
The authority to decide legal cases is granted to a Supreme Court and to a system of lower courts established by Congress. The Supreme Court is the highest court in the land. Justices and judges are in their offices for life, subject to good behavior.

(1) General Authority
Federal courts have the authority to decide cases that arise under the Constitution, laws, and treaties of the United States. They also have the authority to settle disagreements among states and among citizens of different states.

---

(2) He shall have power, by and with the advice and consent of the Senate, to make treaties, provided two-thirds of the senators present concur; and he shall nominate, and by and with the advice and consent of the Senate, shall appoint ambassadors, other public ministers and consuls, judges of the Supreme Court, and all other officers of the United States, whose appointments are not herein otherwise provided for, and which shall be established by law; but the Congress may by law vest the appointment of such inferior officers, as they think proper, in the President alone, in the courts of law, or in the heads of departments.

(3) The President shall have power to fill up all vacancies that may happen during the recess of the Senate, by granting commissions which shall expire at the end of their next session.

SECTION 3. DUTIES OF THE PRESIDENT

He shall from time to time give to the Congress information of the state of the Union, and recommend to their consideration such measures as he shall judge necessary and expedient; he may, on extraordinary occasions, convene both houses, or either of them, and in case of disagreement between them, with respect to the time of adjournment, he may adjourn them to such time as he shall think proper; he shall receive ambassadors and other public ministers; he shall take care that the laws be faithfully executed, and shall commission all the officers of the United States.

SECTION 4. IMPEACHMENT

The President, Vice President and all civil officers of the United States, shall be removed from office on impeachment for, and conviction of, treason, bribery, or other high crimes and misdemeanors.

ARTICLE III
THE JUDICIAL BRANCH
SECTION 1. FEDERAL COURTS

The judicial power of the United States shall be vested in one Supreme Court, and in such inferior courts as the Congress may from time to time ordain and establish. The judges, both of the supreme and inferior courts, shall hold their offices during good behavior, and shall, at stated times, receive for their services a compensation, which shall not be diminished during their continuance in office.

SECTION 2. AUTHORITY OF THE FEDERAL COURTS

(1) The judicial power shall extend to all cases, in law and equity, arising under this Constitution, the laws of the United States, and treaties made or which shall be made, under their authority; to all cases affecting ambassadors, other public ministers and consuls; to all cases of admiralty and maritime jurisdiction; to controversies to which the United States shall be a party; to controversies between two or more states; [*between a state and citizens of another state;*] between citizens of different states; —between citizens of the same state claiming lands under grants of different states, [*and between a state or the citizens thereof, and foreign states, citizens, or subjects.*]

(2) In all cases affecting ambassadors, other public ministers and consuls, and those in which a state shall be party, the Supreme Court shall have original jurisdiction. In all the other cases before mentioned, the Supreme Court shall have appellate jurisdiction, both as to law and fact, with such exceptions, and under such regulations as the Congress shall make.

(3) The trial of all crimes, except in cases of impeachment, shall be by jury; and such trial shall be held in the state where the said crimes shall have been committed; but when not committed within any state, the trial shall be at such place or places as the Congress may by law have directed.

SECTION 3. TREASON
(1) Treason against the United States shall consist only in levying war against them, or in adhering to their enemies, giving them aid and comfort. No person shall be convicted of treason unless on the testimony of two witnesses to the same overt act, or on confession in open court.

(2) The Congress shall have power to declare the punishment of treason, but no attainder of treason shall work corruption of blood, or forfeiture except during the life of the person attainted.

ARTICLE IV
RELATIONS AMONG STATES
SECTION 1. OFFICIAL RECORDS
Full faith and credit shall be given in each state to the public acts, records, and judicial proceedings of every other state. And the Congress may by general laws prescribe the manner in which such acts, records, and proceedings shall be proved, and the effect thereof.

SECTION 2. PRIVILEGES OF THE CITIZENS
(1) The citizens of each state shall be entitled to all privileges and immunities of citizens in the several states.

(2) A person charged in any state with treason, felony, or other crime, who shall flee from justice, and be found in another state, shall on demand of the executive authority of the state from which he fled, be delivered up, to be removed to the state having jurisdiction of the crime.

(3) [*No person held to service or labor in one state, under the laws thereof, escaping into another, shall in consequence of any law or regulation therein, be discharged from such service or labor, but shall be delivered up on claim of the party to whom such service or labor may be due.*]

---

(2) Supreme Court
The Supreme Court can decide certain cases being tried for the first time. It can review cases that have already been tried in a lower court if the decision has been appealed, or questioned, by one side.

(3) Trial by Jury
The Constitution guarantees a trial by jury for every person charged with a federal crime. Amendments 5, 6, and 7 extend and clarify a person's right to a trial by jury.

(1) Definition of Treason
Acts that may be considered treason are making war against the United States or helping its enemies. A person cannot be convicted of attempting to overthrow the government unless there are two witnesses to the act or the person confesses in court to treason.

(2) Punishment for Treason
Congress can decide the punishment for treason, within certain limits.

Official Records
Each state must honor the official records and judicial decisions of other states.

(1) Privileges
A citizen moving from one state to another has the same rights as other citizens living in that person's new state of residence. In some cases, such as voting, people may be required to live in their new state for a certain length of time before obtaining the same privileges as citizens there.

(2) Extradition
At the governor's request, a person who is charged with a crime and who tries to escape justice by crossing into another state may be returned to the state in which the crime was committed.

(3) Fugitive Slaves
The original Constitution required that runaway slaves be returned to their owners. Amendment 13 abolished slavery, eliminating the need for this clause.

(1) Admission of New States
Congress has the authority to admit new states to the Union. All new states have the same rights as existing states.

(2) Federal Property
The Constitution allows Congress to make or change laws governing federal property. This applies to territories and federally owned land within states, such as national parks.

Guarantees to the States
The federal government guarantees that every state have a republican form of government. The United States must also protect the states against invasion and help the states deal with rebellion or local violence.

Amending the Constitution
Changes to the Constitution may be proposed by a two-thirds vote of both the House of Representatives and the Senate or by a national convention called by Congress when asked by two-thirds of the states. For an amendment to become law, the legislatures or conventions in three-fourths of the states must approve it.

(1) Public Debt
Any debt owed by the United States before the Constitution went into effect was to be honored.

(2) Federal Supremacy
This clause declares that the Constitution and federal laws are the highest in the nation. Whenever a state law and a federal law are found to disagree, the federal law must be obeyed so long as it is constitutional.

(3) Oaths of Office
All federal and state officials must promise to follow and enforce the Constitution. These officials, however, cannot be required to follow a particular religion or satisfy any religious test.

SECTION 3. NEW STATES AND TERRITORIES
(1) New states may be admitted by the Congress into this Union; but no new state shall be formed or erected within the jurisdiction of any other state; nor any state be formed by the junction of two or more states, or parts of states, without the consent of the legislatures of the states concerned as well as of the Congress.

(2) The Congress shall have power to dispose of and make all needful rules and regulations respecting the territory or other property belonging to the United States; and nothing in this Constitution shall be so construed as to prejudice any claims of the United States, or of any particular state.

SECTION 4. GUARANTEES TO THE STATES
The United States shall guarantee to every state in this Union a republican form of government, and shall protect each of them against invasion; and on application of the legislature, or of the executive (when the legislature cannot be convened) against domestic violence.

ARTICLE V
AMENDING THE CONSTITUTION
The Congress, whenever two-thirds of both houses shall deem it necessary, shall propose amendments to this Constitution, or, on the application of the legislatures of two-thirds of the several states, shall call a convention for proposing amendments, which, in either case, shall be valid to all intents and purposes, as part of this Constitution, when ratified by the legislatures of three-fourths of the several states, or by conventions in three-fourths thereof, as the one or the other mode of ratification may be proposed by the Congress; provided that [*no amendment which may be made prior to the year 1808 shall in any manner affect the first and fourth clauses in the Ninth Section of the First Article; and that*] no state, without its consent, shall be deprived of its equal suffrage in the Senate.

ARTICLE VI
GENERAL PROVISIONS
(1) All debts contracted and engagements entered into, before the adoption of this Constitution, shall be as valid against the United States under this Constitution, as under the Confederation.

(2) This Constitution, and the laws of the United States which shall be made in pursuance thereof, and all treaties made, or which shall be made, under the authority of the United States, shall be the supreme law of the land; and the judges in every state shall be bound thereby, anything in the Constitution or laws of any state to the contrary notwithstanding.

(3) The Senators and Representatives before mentioned, and the members of the several state legislatures, and all executive and judicial officers, both of the United States and of the several states, shall be bound by oath or affirmation, to support this Constitution; but no religious test shall ever be required as a qualification to any office or public trust under the United States.

ARTICLE VII
RATIFICATION

The ratification of the conventions of nine states, shall be sufficient for the establishment of this Constitution between the states so ratifying the same.

Done in convention by the unanimous consent of the states present the seventeenth day of September in the year of our Lord one thousand seven hundred and eighty seven and of the independence of the United States of America the Twelfth. In witness whereof we have hereunto subscribed our names.

George Washington—President and deputy from Virginia

Ratification
In order for the Constitution to become law, 9 of the 13 states had to approve it. Special conventions were held for this purpose. The process took 9 months to complete.

DELAWARE
George Read
Gunning Bedford, Jr.
John Dickinson
Richard Bassett
Jacob Broom

MARYLAND
James McHenry
Daniel of St. Thomas Jenifer
Daniel Carroll

VIRGINIA
John Blair
James Madison, Jr.

NORTH CAROLINA
William Blount
Richard Dobbs Spaight
Hugh Williamson

SOUTH CAROLINA
John Rutledge
Charles Cotesworth Pinckney
Charles Pinckney
Pierce Butler

GEORGIA
William Few
Abraham Baldwin

NEW HAMPSHIRE
John Langdon
Nicholas Gilman

MASSACHUSETTS
Nathaniel Gorham
Rufus King

CONNECTICUT
William Samuel Johnson
Roger Sherman

NEW YORK
Alexander Hamilton

NEW JERSEY
William Livingston
David Brearley
William Paterson
Jonathan Dayton

PENNSYLVANIA
Benjamin Franklin
Thomas Mifflin
Robert Morris
George Clymer
Thomas FitzSimons
Jared Ingersoll
James Wilson
Gouverneur Morris

ATTEST: William Jackson, secretary

Basic Freedoms
The Constitution guarantees our five basic freedoms of expression. It provides for the freedoms of religion, speech, the press, peaceable assembly, and petition for redress of grievances.

Weapons and the Militia
This amendment protects the right of the state governments and the people to maintain militias to guard against threats to their public order, safety, and liberty. In connection with that state right, the federal government may not take away the right of the people to have and use weapons.

Housing Soldiers
The federal government cannot force people to house soldiers in their homes during peacetime. However, Congress may pass laws allowing this during wartime.

Searches and Seizures
This amendment protects people's privacy and safety. Subject to certain exceptions, a law officer cannot search a person or a person's home and belongings unless a judge has issued a valid search warrant. There must be good reason for the search. The warrant must describe the place to be searched and the people or things to be seized, or taken.

Rights of Accused Persons
If a person is accused of a crime that is punishable by death or of any other crime that is very serious, a grand jury must decide if there is enough evidence to hold a trial. People cannot be tried twice for the same crime, nor can they be forced to testify against themselves. No person shall be fined, jailed, or executed by the government unless the person has been given a fair trial. The government cannot take a person's property for public use unless fair payment is made.

AMENDMENT 1 (1791)***
BASIC FREEDOMS

Congress shall make no law respecting an establishment of religion, or prohibiting the free exercise thereof; or abridging the freedom of speech, or of the press; or the right of the people peaceably to assemble, and to petition the government for a redress of grievances.

AMENDMENT 2 (1791)
WEAPONS AND THE MILITIA

A well-regulated militia, being necessary to the security of a free state, the right of the people to keep and bear arms shall not be infringed.

AMENDMENT 3 (1791)
HOUSING SOLDIERS

No soldier shall, in time of peace, be quartered in any house, without the consent of the owner; nor in time of war, but in a manner to be prescribed by law.

AMENDMENT 4 (1791)
SEARCHES AND SEIZURES

The right of the people to be secure in their persons, houses, papers, and effects, against unreasonable searches and seizures, shall not be violated; and no warrants shall issue but upon probable cause, supported by oath or affirmation, and particularly describing the place to be searched, and the persons or things to be seized.

AMENDMENT 5 (1791)
RIGHTS OF ACCUSED PERSONS

No person shall be held to answer for a capital, or otherwise infamous crime, unless on a presentment or indictment of a grand jury, except in cases arising in the land or naval forces, or in the militia, when in actual service in time of war or public danger; nor shall any person be subject for the same offense to be twice put in jeopardy of life or limb; nor shall be compelled in any criminal case to be a witness against himself; nor be deprived of life, liberty, or property, without due process of law; nor shall private property be taken for public use without just compensation.

*** The date beside each amendment is the year that the amendment was ratified and became part of the Constitution.

AMENDMENT 6 (1791)
RIGHT TO A FAIR TRIAL

In all criminal prosecutions, the accused shall enjoy the right to a speedy and public trial, by an impartial jury of the state and district wherein the crime shall have been committed, which district shall have been previously ascertained by law, and to be informed of the nature and cause of the accusation; to be confronted with the witnesses against him; to have compulsory process for obtaining witnesses in his favor, and to have the assistance of counsel for his defense.

AMENDMENT 7 (1791)
JURY TRIAL IN CIVIL CASES

In suits at common law, where the value in controversy shall exceed 20 dollars, the right of trial by jury shall be preserved, and no fact tried by a jury shall be otherwise re-examined in any court of the United States, than according to the rules of the common law.

AMENDMENT 8 (1791)
BAIL AND PUNISHMENT

Excessive bail shall not be required, nor excessive fines imposed, nor cruel and unusual punishments inflicted.

AMENDMENT 9 (1791)
RIGHTS OF THE PEOPLE

The enumeration in the Constitution, of certain rights, shall not be construed to deny or disparage others retained by the people.

AMENDMENT 10 (1791)
POWERS OF THE STATES AND THE PEOPLE

The powers not delegated to the United States by the Constitution, nor prohibited by it to the states, are reserved to the states respectively, or to the people.

AMENDMENT 11 (1798)
SUITS AGAINST STATES

The judicial power of the United States shall not be construed to extend to any suit in law or equity, commenced or prosecuted against one of the United States or citizens of another state, or by citizens or subjects of any foreign state.

Right to a Fair Trial
A person accused of a crime has the right to a public trial by an impartial jury, locally chosen. The trial must be held within a reasonable amount of time. The accused person must be told of all charges and has the right to see, hear, and question any witnesses. The federal government must provide a lawyer free of charge to a person who is accused of a serious crime and who is unable to pay for legal services.

Jury Trial in Civil Cases
In most federal civil cases involving more than 20 dollars, a jury trial is guaranteed. Civil cases are those disputes between two or more people over money, property, personal injury, or legal rights. Usually civil cases are not tried in federal courts unless much larger sums of money are involved or unless federal courts are given the authority to decide a certain type of case.

Bail and Punishment
Courts cannot treat harshly people accused of crimes or punish them in unusual or cruel ways. Bail is money put up as a guarantee that an accused person will appear for trial. In certain cases bail can be denied altogether.

Rights of the People
The federal government must respect all natural rights, whether or not they are listed in the Constitution.

Powers of the States and the People
Any powers not clearly given to the federal government or denied to the states belong to the states or to the people.

Suits Against States
A citizen of one state cannot sue another state in federal court.

Election of President and Vice President
This amendment replaces the part of Article II, Section 1, that originally explained the process of electing the President and Vice President. Amendment 12 was an important step in the development of the two-party system. It allows a party to nominate its own candidates for both President and Vice President.

AMENDMENT 12 (1804)
ELECTION OF PRESIDENT AND VICE PRESIDENT

The electors shall meet in their respective states, and vote by ballot for President and Vice President, one of whom, at least, shall not be an inhabitant of the same state with themselves; they shall name in their ballots the person voted for as President, and in distinct ballots the person voted for as Vice President, and they shall make distinct lists of all persons voted for as President, and of all persons voted for as Vice President, and of the number of votes for each, which lists they shall sign and certify, and transmit, sealed, to the seat of government of the United States, directed to the President of the Senate; the President of the Senate shall, in the presence of the Senate and House of Representatives, open all the certificates, and the votes shall then be counted; the person having the greatest number of votes for President shall be the President, if such a number be a majority of the whole number of electors appointed; and if no person have such majority; then from the persons having the highest numbers not exceeding three on the list of those voted for as President, the House of Representatives shall choose immediately, by ballot, the President. But in choosing the President, the votes shall be taken by states, the representation from each state having one vote; a quorum for this purpose shall consist of a member or members from two thirds of the states, and a majority of all the states shall be necessary to a choice. [And *if the House of Representatives shall not choose a President whenever the right of choice shall devolve upon them, before the fourth day of March next following, then the Vice President shall act as President, as in the case of the death or other constitutional disability of the President.*] The person having the greatest number of votes as Vice President, shall be the Vice President, if such number be a majority of the whole number of electors appointed, and if no person have a majority, then, from the two highest numbers on the list the Senate shall choose the Vice President; a quorum for the purpose shall consist of two thirds of the whole number of Senators, and a majority of the whole number shall be necessary to a choice. But no person constitutionally ineligible to the office of President shall be eligible to that of Vice President of the United States.

End of Slavery
People cannot be forced to work against their will unless they have been tried for and convicted of a crime for which this means of punishment is ordered. Congress may enforce this by law.

AMENDMENT 13 (1865)
END OF SLAVERY

SECTION 1. ABOLITION

Neither slavery nor involuntary servitude, except as a punishment for crime whereof the party shall have been duly convicted, shall exist within the United States, or any place subject to their jurisdiction.

SECTION 2. ENFORCEMENT

Congress shall have power to enforce this article by appropriate legislation.

Citizenship
All persons born or naturalized in the United States are citizens of the United States and of the state in which they live. State governments may not deny any citizen the full rights of citizenship. This amendment also guarantees due process of law. According to due process of law, no state may take away the rights of a citizen. All citizens must be protected equally under law.

AMENDMENT 14 (1868)
RIGHTS OF CITIZENS

SECTION 1. CITIZENSHIP

All persons born or naturalized in the United States and subject to the jurisdiction thereof, are citizens of the United States and of the state wherein they reside. No state shall make or enforce any law which shall abridge the privileges or immunities of citizens of the United States, nor shall any state deprive any person of life, liberty, or property, without due process of law; nor deny to any person within its jurisdiction the equal protection of the laws.

SECTION 2. NUMBER OF REPRESENTATIVES

Representatives shall be apportioned among the several states according to their respective numbers, counting the whole number of persons in each state, [*excluding Indians not taxed*]. But when the right to vote at any election for the choice of electors for President and Vice President of the United States, representatives in Congress, the executive and judicial officers of a state, or the members of the legislature thereof, is denied to any of the [*male*] inhabitants of such state, being [*twenty-one years of age and*] citizens of the United States, or in any way abridged, except for participation in rebellion or other crime, the basis of representation therein shall be reduced in the proportion which the number of such [*male*] citizens shall bear to the whole number of [*male*] citizens [*twenty-one years of age*] in such state.

SECTION 3. PENALTY FOR REBELLION

No person shall be a Senator or Representative in Congress, or elector of President and Vice President, or hold any office, civil or military, under the United States, or under any state, who, having previously taken an oath, as a member of Congress, or as an officer of the United States, or as a member of any state legislature, or as an executive or judicial officer of any state, to support the Constitution of the United States, shall have engaged in insurrection or rebellion against the same, or given aid or comfort to the enemies thereof. But Congress may, by a vote of two thirds of each house, remove such disability.

SECTION 4. GOVERNMENT DEBT

The validity of the public debt of the United States, authorized by law, including debts incurred for payment of pensions and bounties for services in suppressing insurrection or rebellion, shall not be questioned. But neither the United States nor any state shall assume or pay any debt or obligation incurred in aid of insurrection or rebellion against the United States, [*or any claim for the loss or emancipation of any slave;*] but all such debts, obligations, and claims shall be held illegal and void.

SECTION 5. ENFORCEMENT

The Congress shall have power to enforce, by appropriate legislation, the provisions of this article.

AMENDMENT 15 (1870)
VOTING RIGHTS
SECTION 1. RIGHT TO VOTE

The right of citizens of the United States to vote shall not be denied or abridged by the United States or by any state on account of race, color, or previous condition of servitude.

SECTION 2. ENFORCEMENT

The Congress shall have power to enforce this article by appropriate legislation.

AMENDMENT 16 (1913)
INCOME TAX

The Congress shall have power to lay and collect taxes on incomes, from whatever source derived, without apportionment among the several states, and without regard to any census or enumeration.

Number of Representatives
Each state's representation in Congress is based on its total population. Any state denying eligible citizens the right to vote will have its representation in Congress decreased. This clause abolished the Three-fifths Compromise in Article I, Section 2. Later amendments granted women the right to vote and lowered the voting age to 18.

Penalty for Rebellion
No person who has rebelled against the United States may hold federal office. This clause was originally added to punish the leaders of the Confederacy for failing to support the Constitution of the United States.

Government Debt
The federal government is responsible for all public debts. It is not responsible, however, for Confederate debts or for debts that result from any rebellion against the United States.

Enforcement
Congress may enforce these provisions by law.

Right to Vote
No state may prevent a citizen from voting simply because of race or color or condition of previous servitude. This amendment was designed to extend voting rights to enforce this by law.

Income Tax
Congress has the power to collect taxes on its citizens, based on their personal incomes rather than on the number of people living in a state.

Direct Election of Senators
Originally, state legislatures elected senators. This amendment allows the people of each state to elect their own senators directly. The idea is to make senators more responsible to the people they represent.

AMENDMENT 17 (1913)
DIRECT ELECTION OF SENATORS

SECTION 1. METHOD OF ELECTION

The Senate of the United States shall be composed of two Senators from each state, elected by the people thereof, for six years; and each Senator shall have one vote. The electors in each state shall have the qualifications requisite for electors of the most numerous branch of the state legislatures.

SECTION 2. VACANCIES

When vacancies happen in the representation of any state in the Senate, the executive authority of such state shall issue writs of election to fill such vacancies: *Provided*, that the legislature of any state may empower the executive thereof to make temporary appointments until the people fill the vacancies by election as the legislature may direct.

SECTION 3. EXCEPTION

[*This amendment shall not be so construed as to affect the election or term of any Senator chosen before it becomes valid as part of the Constitution.*]

Prohibition
This amendment made it illegal to make, sell, or transport liquor within the United States or to transport it out of the United States or its territories. Amendment 18 was the first to include a time limit for approval. If not ratified within seven years, it would be repealed, or canceled. Many later amendments have included similar time limits.

AMENDMENT 18 (1919)
BAN ON ALCOHOLIC DRINKS

SECTION 1. PROHIBITION

[*After one year from the ratification of this article the manufacture, sale, or transportation of intoxicating liquors within, the importation thereof into, or the exportation thereof from the United States and all territory subject to the jurisdiction thereof for beverage purposes is hereby prohibited.*]

SECTION 2. ENFORCEMENT

[*The Congress and the several states shall have concurrent power to enforce this article by appropriate legislation.*]

SECTION 3. RATIFICATION

[*This article shall be inoperative unless it shall have been ratified as an amendment to the Constitution by the legislatures of the several states as provided in the Constitution, within seven years from the date of the submission hereof to the states by the Congress.*]

Women's Voting Rights
This amendment protected the right of women throughout the United States to vote.

AMENDMENT 19 (1920)
WOMEN'S VOTING RIGHTS

SECTION 1. RIGHT TO VOTE

The right of citizens of the United States to vote shall not be denied or abridged by the United States or by any state on account of sex.

SECTION 2. ENFORCEMENT

Congress shall have power to enforce this article by appropriate legislation.

Terms of Office
The terms of the President and the Vice President begin on January 20, in the year following their election. Members of Congress take office on January 3. Before this amendment newly elected members of Congress did not begin their terms until March 4. This meant that those who had run for reelection and been defeated remained in office for four months.

AMENDMENT 20 (1933)
TERMS OF OFFICE

SECTION 1. BEGINNING OF TERMS

The terms of the President and Vice President shall end at noon on the 20th day of January, and the terms of Senators and Representatives at noon on the 3rd day of January, of the years in which such terms would have ended if this article had not been ratified; and the terms of their successors shall then begin.

SECTION 2. SESSIONS OF CONGRESS

The Congress shall assemble at least once in every year, and such meeting shall begin at noon on the 3rd day of January, unless they shall by law appoint a different day.

SECTION 3. PRESIDENTIAL SUCCESSION

If, at the time fixed for the beginning of the term of the President, the President-elect shall have died, the Vice President-elect shall become President. If a President shall not have been chosen before the time fixed for the beginning of his term, or if the President-elect shall have failed to qualify, then the Vice President-elect shall act as President until a President shall have qualified; and the Congress may by law provide for the case wherein neither a President-elect nor a Vice President-elect shall have qualified, declaring who shall then act as President, or the manner in which one who is to act shall be selected and such person shall act accordingly until a President or Vice President shall be qualified.

SECTION 4. ELECTIONS DECIDED BY CONGRESS

The Congress may by law provide for the case of the death of any of the persons from whom the House of Representatives may choose a President whenever the right of choice shall have devolved upon them, and for the case of the death of any of the persons from whom the Senate may choose a Vice President whenever the right of choice shall have devolved upon them.

SECTION 5. EFFECTIVE DATE

[*Sections 1 and 2 shall take effect on the 15th day of October following the ratification of this article.*]

SECTION 6. RATIFICATION

[*This article shall be inoperative unless it shall have been ratified as an amendment to the Constitution by the legislatures of three fourths of the several states within seven years from the date of its submission.*]

AMENDMENT 21 (1933)
END OF PROHIBITION

SECTION 1. REPEAL OF AMENDMENT 18

The eighteenth article of amendment to the Constitution of the United States is hereby repealed.

SECTION 2. STATE LAWS

The transportation or importation into any state, territory, or possession of the United States for delivery or use therein of intoxicating liquors, in violation of the laws thereof, is hereby prohibited.

SECTION 3. RATIFICATION

[*This article shall be inoperative unless it shall have been ratified as an amendment to the Constitution by conventions in the several states, as provided in the Constitution within seven years from the date of the submission hereof to the states by Congress.*]

Sessions of Congress
Congress meets at least once a year, beginning at noon on January 3. Congress had previously met at least once a year beginning on the first Monday of December.

Presidential Succession
If the newly elected President dies before January 20, the newly elected Vice President becomes President on that date. If a President has not been chosen by January 20 or does not meet the requirements for being President, the newly elected Vice President becomes President. If neither the newly elected President nor the newly elected Vice President meets the requirements for office, Congress decides who will serve as President until a qualified President or Vice President is chosen.

End of Prohibition
This amendment repealed Amendment 18. This is the only amendment to be ratified by state conventions instead of by state legislatures. Congress felt that this would give people's opinions about prohibition a better chance to be heard.

AMERICAN DOCUMENTS

Two-Term limit for Presidents
A President may not serve more than two full terms in office. Any President who serves less than two years of a previous President's term may be elected for two more terms.

Presidential Electors for District of Columbia
This amendment grants three electoral votes to the national capital.

Ban on Poll Taxes
No United States citizen may be prevented from voting in a federal election because of failing to pay a tax to vote. Poll taxes had been used in some states to prevent African Americans from voting.

Presidential Vacancy
If the President is removed from office or resigns from or dies while in office, the Vice President becomes President.

AMENDMENT 22 (1951)
TWO-TERM LIMIT FOR PRESIDENTS
SECTION 1. TWO-TERM LIMIT

No person shall be elected to the office of the President more than twice, and no person who has held the office of President, or acted as President, for more than two years of a term to which some other person was elected President shall be elected to the office of the President more than once. [*But this article shall not apply to any person holding the office of President when this article was proposed by the Congress, and shall not prevent any person who may be holding the office of President, or acting as President, during the term within which this article becomes operative from holding the office of President, or acting as President, during the remainder of such term.*]

SECTION 2. RATIFICATION

[*This article shall be inoperative unless it shall have been ratified as an amendment to the Constitution by the legislatures of three-fourths of the several states within seven years from the date of its submission to the states by the Congress.*]

AMENDMENT 23 (1961)
PRESIDENTIAL ELECTORS FOR DISTRICT OF COLUMBIA
SECTION 1. NUMBER OF ELECTORS

The District constituting the seat of Government of the United States shall appoint in such manner as Congress may direct:

A number of electors of President and Vice President equal to the whole number of Senators and Representatives in Congress to which the District would be entitled if it were a state, but in no event more than the least populous state; they shall be in addition to those appointed by the states, but they shall be considered, for the purposes of the election of President and Vice President, to be electors appointed by a state, and they shall meet in the District and perform such duties as provided by the twelfth article of amendment.

SECTION 2. ENFORCEMENT

The Congress shall have power to enforce this article by appropriate legislation.

AMENDMENT 24 (1964)
BAN ON POLL TAXES
SECTION 1. POLL TAX ILLEGAL

The right of citizens of the United States to vote in any primary or other election for President or Vice President, for electors for President or Vice President, or for Senator or Representative in Congress, shall not be denied or abridged by the United States or any state by reason of failure to pay any poll tax or other tax.

SECTION 2. ENFORCEMENT

The Congress shall have power to enforce this article by appropriate legislation.

AMENDMENT 25 (1967)
PRESIDENTIAL SUCCESSION
SECTION 1. PRESIDENTIAL VACANCY

In case of the removal of the President from office or of his death or resignation, the Vice President shall become President.

SECTION 2. VICE PRESIDENTIAL VACANCY

Whenever there is a vacancy in the office of the Vice President, the President shall nominate a Vice President who shall take the office upon confirmation by a majority vote of both houses of Congress.

SECTION 3. PRESIDENTIAL DISABILITY

Whenever the President transmits to the President pro tempore of the Senate and the Speaker of the House of Representatives his written declaration that he is unable to discharge the powers and duties of his office, and until he transmits to them a written declaration to the contrary, such powers and duties shall be discharged by the Vice President as Acting President.

SECTION 4. DETERMINING PRESIDENTIAL DISABILITY

Whenever the Vice President and a majority of either the principal officers of the executive departments or of such other body as Congress may by law provide, transmit to the President pro tempore of the Senate and the Speaker of the House of Representatives their written declaration that the President is unable to discharge the powers and duties of his office, the Vice President shall immediately assume the powers and duties of the office as Acting President.

Thereafter, when the President transmits to the President pro tempore of the Senate and the Speaker of the House of Representatives his written declaration that no inability exists, he shall resume the powers and duties of his office unless the Vice President and a majority of either the principal officers of the executive department or of such other body as Congress may by law provide, transmit within four days to the President pro tempore of the Senate and the Speaker of the House of Representatives their written declaration that the President is unable to discharge the powers and duties of his office. Thereupon Congress shall decide the issue, assembling within 48 hours for that purpose if not in session. If the Congress, within 21 days after receipt of the latter written declaration, or, if Congress is not in session, within 21 days after Congress is required to assemble, determines by two-thirds vote of both houses that the President is unable to discharge the powers and duties of his office, the Vice President shall continue to discharge the same as Acting President; otherwise the President shall resume the powers and duties of his office.

AMENDMENT 26 (1971)
VOTING AGE

SECTION 1. RIGHT TO VOTE

The right of citizens of the United States, who are 18 years of age or older, to vote shall not be denied or abridged by the United States or any state on account of age.

SECTION 2. ENFORCEMENT

The Congress shall have the power to enforce this article by appropriate legislation.

AMENDMENT 27 (1992)
CONGRESSIONAL PAY

No law, varying the compensation for the services of the Senators and Representatives, shall take effect, until an election of Representatives shall have intervened.

Vice Presidential Vacancy
If the office of the Vice President becomes open, the President names someone to assume that office and that person becomes Vice President if both houses of Congress approve by a majority vote.

Presidential Disability
This section explains in detail what happens if the President cannot continue in office because of sickness or any other reason. The Vice President takes over as acting President until the President is able to resume office.

Determining Presidential Disability
If the Vice President and a majority of the Cabinet inform the Speaker of the House and the president pro tempore of the Senate that the President cannot carry out his or her duties, the Vice President then serves as acting President. To regain the office, the President has to inform the Speaker and the president pro tempore in writing that he or she is again able to serve. But, if the Vice President and a majority of the Cabinet disagree with the President and inform the Speaker and the president pro tempore that the President is still unable to serve, then Congress decides who will hold the office of President.

Voting Age
All citizens 18 years or older have the right to vote. Formerly, the voting age was 21 in most states.

Congressional Pay
A law raising or lowering the salaries for members of Congress cannot be passed for that session of Congress.

THE NATIONAL ANTHEM

The Star-Spangled Banner

"The Star-Spangled Banner" was written by Francis Scott Key in September 1814 and adopted as the national anthem in March 1931. The army and navy had recognized it as such long before Congress approved it.

During the War of 1812, Francis Scott Key spent a night aboard a British warship in the Chesapeake Bay while trying to arrange for the release of an American prisoner. The battle raged throughout the night, while the Americans were held on the ship. The next morning, when the smoke from the cannons finally cleared, Francis Scott Key was thrilled to see the American flag still waving proudly above Fort McHenry. It symbolized the victory of the Americans.

There are four verses to the national anthem. In these four verses, Key wrote about how he felt when he saw the flag still waving over Fort McHenry. He wrote that the flag was a symbol of the freedom for which the people had fought so hard. Key also told about the pride he had in his country and the great hopes he had for the future of the United States.

(1)
Oh, say can you see by the dawn's early light
What so proudly we hail'd at the twilight's last gleaming,
Whose broad stripes and bright stars through the perilous fight
O'er the ramparts we watch'd were so gallantly streaming?
And the rockets' red glare, the bombs bursting in air,
Gave proof through the night that our flag was still there.
Oh, say does that star-spangled banner yet wave
O'er the land of the free and the home of the brave?

(2)
On the shore dimly seen through the mists of the deep,
Where the foe's haughty host in dread silence reposes,
What is that which the breeze, o'er the towering steep,
As it fitfully blows, half conceals, half discloses?
Now it catches the gleam of the morning's first beam,
In full glory reflected now shines in the stream.
'Tis the star-spangled banner, oh, long may it wave
O'er the land of the free and the home of the brave!

(3)
And where is that band who so vauntingly swore
That the havoc of war and the battle's confusion
A home and a country should leave us no more?
Their blood has wash'd out their foul footstep's pollution.
No refuge could save the hireling and slave
From the terror of flight or the gloom of the grave,
And the star-spangled banner in triumph doth wave
O'er the land of the free and the home of the brave.

(4)
Oh, thus be it ever when freemen shall stand
Between their lov'd home and the war's desolation!
Blest with vict'ry and peace may the heav'n-rescued land
Praise the power that hath made and preserv'd us a nation!
Then conquer we must, when our cause it is just,
And this be our motto, "In God is our Trust,"
And the star-spangled banner in triumph shall wave
O'er the land of the free and the home of the brave.

THE PLEDGE OF ALLEGIANCE

I pledge allegiance to the Flag
of the United States of America,
and to the Republic
for which it stands,
one Nation under God, indivisible,
with liberty and justice for all.

The flag is a symbol of the United States of America. The Pledge of Allegiance says that the people of the United States promise to stand up for the flag, their country, and the basic beliefs of freedom and fairness upon which the country was established.

American Documents ■ R37

Biographical Dictionary

The Biographical Dictionary lists many of the important people introduced in this book. The page number tells where the main discussion of each person starts. See the Index for other page references.

A

Adams, John *1735–1826* Second U.S. President and one of the writers of the Declaration of Independence. p. 62

Adams, Samuel *1722–1803* American Revolutionary leader who set up a Committee of Correspondence in Boston and helped form the Sons of Liberty. p. 50

Addams, Jane *1860–1935* American reformer who brought the idea of settlement houses from Britain to the United States. With Ellen Gates Starr, she founded Hull House in Chicago. pp. 207–208

Albright, Madeleine *1937–* First woman to be appointed U.S. secretary of state. p. 441

Aldrin, Edwin, Jr. *1930–* American astronaut who was one of the first people to set foot on the moon. p. 432

Anderson, Robert *1805–1871* Union commander of Fort Sumter; he was forced to surrender to the Confederacy. p. 118

Anthony, Susan B. *1820–1906* Women's suffrage leader who worked to enable women to have the same rights as men. p. 247

Aristide, Jean-Bertrand (air•ih•STEED, ZHAHN bair•TRAHN) *1953–* Freely elected president of Haiti; he was overthrown in 1991 but was returned to office in 1994. p. 533

Armstrong, Louis *1901–1971* Noted jazz trumpeter who helped make jazz popular in the 1920s. pp. 288–289

Armstrong, Neil *1930–* American astronaut who was the first person to set foot on the moon. p. 432

Austin, Stephen F. *1793–1836* Moses Austin's son. He carried out his father's dream of starting a United States colony in Texas. p. 71

B

Balboa, Vasco Núñez de (bahl•BOH•uh, NOON•yays day) *1475–1519* Spanish explorer who, in 1513, became the first European to reach the western coast of the Americas—proving to Europeans that the Americas were separate from Asia. p. 31

Banneker, Benjamin *1731–1806* African American mathematician and astronomer who helped survey the land for the new capital of the United States. p. 64

Barrett, Janie Porter *1865–1948* African American teacher who founded a settlement house in Hampton, Virginia. p. 208

Barton, Clara *1821–1912* Civil War nurse and founder of the American Red Cross. p. 127

Begin, Menachem (BAY•guhn) *1913–1992* Israeli prime minister; signed peace treaty with President Anwar Sadat of Egypt. p. 456

Bell, Alexander Graham *1847–1922* American inventor and educator; he invented the telephone in 1876. p. 201

Bellamy, Francis *1800s* Writer of patriotic oath that came to be called the Pledge of Allegiance. p. 515

Berlin, Irving *1888–1989* American songwriter who moved to New York City from Russia in 1893. p. 167

Berry, Chuck *1926–* American rock and roll performer. p. 419

Bessemer, Henry *1813–1898* British inventor of a way to produce steel more easily and cheaply than before. p. 159

Bolívar, Simón (boh•LEE•var, see•MOHN) *1783–1830* Leader of independence movements in Bolivia, Colombia, Ecuador, Peru, and Venezuela. p. 538

Bonaparte, Napoleon (BOH•nuh•part, nuh•POH•lee•uhn) *1769–1821* French leader who sold all of the Louisiana region to the United States. pp. 66–67

Bonavita, Rosina *1900s* American factory worker during World War II who became the model for "Rosie the Riveter," representing women working to produce goods needed for the war. pp. 349–350

Boone, Daniel *1734–1820* American who was one of the first pioneers to cross the Appalachians. p. 65

Booth, John Wilkes *1838–1865* Actor who assassinated President Abraham Lincoln. p. 141

Breckinridge, John *1821–1875* Democrat from Kentucky who ran against Abraham Lincoln in the 1860 presidential election. p. 117

Brezhnev, Leonid (BREZH•nef) *1906–1982* Leader of the Communist party of the Soviet Union from 1964 until his death in 1982. President Nixon's 1972 visit with him in the Soviet Union led to arms control and began a period of détente. pp. 452–453

Brown, John *1800–1859* American abolitionist who seized a weapons storehouse to help slaves rebel. He was caught and hanged. p. 113

Brown, Linda *1943–* African American student whose family was among a group that challenged public-school segregation. pp. 420–421

Bruce, Blanche K. *1841–1898* Former slave who became U.S. senator from Mississippi. p. 143

Burchfield, Charles *1893–1967* American painter. p. 288

Bush, George *1924–* Forty-first U.S. President. He was President at the end of the Cold War and during Operation Desert Storm. pp. 461, 462–464, 465–466, 523

Bush, George W. *1946–* Forty-third U.S. President; son of George Bush, he won the closest presidential election in history. pp. 470–471, 473, 513

C

Caboto, Giovanni (kah•BOH•toh, joh•VAH•nee) *1450?–1499?* Italian explorer who, in 1497, sailed from England and landed in what is now Newfoundland, though he thought he had landed in Asia. The English gave him the name John Cabot. p. 30

Calhoun, John C. *1782–1850* Vice President under John Quincy Adams and Andrew Jackson. He was a strong believer in states' rights. pp. 100–101, 117

Calvert, Cecilius *1605–1675* First proprietor of the Maryland Colony. p. 43

Capone, Alphonse *1899–1947* American gangster during Prohibition Era. pp. 282–283

Cardozo, Francis L. *1837–1903* African American who became secretary of state and state treasurer in South Carolina. p. 143

Carnegie, Andrew *1835–1919* Entrepreneur who helped the steel industry grow in the United States. pp. 159, 160

Carter, Jimmy *1924–* Thirty-ninth U.S. President. He brought about a peace agreement between Israel and Egypt. pp. 456–457, 458

Cartier, Jacques (kar•TYAY, ZHAHK) *1491–1557* French explorer who sailed up the St. Lawrence River and began a fur-trading business with the Hurons. p. 33

Castro, Fidel *1926–* Leader who took over Cuba in 1959 and made it a communist nation. pp. 429, 532

Catt, Carrie Chapman *1859–1947* President of the International Woman Suffrage Alliance. pp. 247–248

Cavelier, René-Robert (ka•vuhl•YAY) *See* La Salle.

Chamberlain, Neville *1869–1940* British prime minister; met with Hitler and Mussolini in hopes of preventing invasions and war. p. 335

Champlain, Samuel de (sham•PLAYN) *1567?–1635* French explorer who founded the first settlement at Quebec. p. 33

Charles I *1600–1649* English king who chartered the colonies of Massachusetts and Maryland. pp. 39, 40, 43

Charles II *1630–1685* English king who granted charters for the New Hampshire Colony and the Carolina Colony. Son of Charles I and Henrietta Maria. pp. 41, 44

Chavez, Cesar *1927–1993* Labor leader and organizer of the United Farm Workers. p. 439

Chisholm, Shirley *1924–* First African American woman elected to Congress. p. 438

Churchill, Sir Winston Leonard Spencer *1874–1965* British prime minister during World War II. pp. 337, 390

Clark, William *1770–1838* American explorer who aided Meriwether Lewis in an expedition through the Louisiana Purchase. p. 67

Clay, Henry *1777–1852* Representative from Kentucky who worked for compromises on the slavery issue. pp. 102–103

Clay, Lucius *1897–1978* U.S. Army officer; he oversaw Berlin Airlift. pp. 392–393

Clinton, Hillary Rodham *1947–* Wife of William Clinton; senator of New York. p. 512

Clinton, William *1946–* Forty-second U.S. President. Economic recovery occurred during his presidency; second President to be impeached. pp. 465–467, 468–470

Cochran, Jacqueline *1910?–1980* American aviator; director of Women's Air Force Service Pilots, or WASPs. p. 350

Collins, Michael *1930–* American astronaut who remained in the lunar orbiter during the *Apollo 11* moon landing. p. 432

Columbus, Christopher *1451–1506* Italian-born Spanish explorer who, in 1492, sailed west from Spain and thought he had reached Asia but had actually reached islands near the Americas, lands that were unknown to Europeans. pp. 29–30

Coolidge, Calvin *1872–1933* Thirtieth U.S. President; as governor of Massachusetts, he restored order during a police strike. p. 246

Cooper, Peter *1791–1883* American manufacturer who built *Tom Thumb*, one of the first locomotives made in the United States. p. 80

Copland, Aaron *1900–1990* American composer. p. 289

Cornish, Samuel *1795–1858* African American who, in 1827, helped John Russwurm found an abolitionist newspaper called *Freedom's Journal*. p. 112

Coronado, Francisco Vásquez de (kawr•oh•NAH•doh) *1510?–1554* Spanish explorer who led an expedition from Mexico City into what is now the southwestern United States in search of the Seven Cities of Gold. p. 32

Cortés, Hernando (kawr•TEZ) *1485–1547* Spanish conquistador who conquered the Aztec Empire. pp. 32, 524

Crazy Horse *1842?–1877* Sioux leader who fought against General George Custer. p. 155

Cullen, Countee *1903–1946* African American writer and poet during the Harlem Renaissance. p. 290

D

da Gama, Vasco (dah GA•muh) *1460?–1524* Portuguese navigator who sailed from Europe, around the southern tip of Africa, and on to Asia between 1497 and 1499. p. 29

Davis, Jefferson *1808–1889* United States senator from Mississippi who became president of the Confederacy. p. 117

Dawes, William *1745–1799* American who, along with Paul Revere, warned the Patriots that the British were marching toward Concord. p. 50

de Soto, Hernando (day SOH•toh) *1496?–1542* Spanish explorer who led an expedition into what is today the southeastern United States. p. 31

Dempsey, William (Jack) *1895–1983* American boxer. p. 287

Dewey, George *1837–1917* American naval commander who destroyed the Spanish fleet and captured Manila Bay in the Spanish-American War. p. 194

Dewey, Thomas Edmund *1902–1971* Republican candidate who challenged Harry S. Truman for the presidency in 1948 election. p. 411

Dias, Bartolomeu (DEE•ahsh) *1450?–1500* Portuguese navigator who, in 1488, became the first European to sail around the southern tip of Africa. p. 29

Díaz, Porfirio *1830–1915* Mexican dictator. p. 526

Disney, Walter Elias *1901–1966* American film producer, cartoon creator, and builder of theme parks. p. 307

Douglas, Stephen A. *1813–1861* American legislator who wrote the Kansas-Nebraska Act and debated Abraham Lincoln in a race for a senate seat from Illinois. pp. 115–116

Douglass, Frederick *1817–1895* Abolitionist speaker and writer who had escaped from slavery. p. 113

Drake, Edwin *1819–1880* American pioneer in oil industry; became first to drill for petroleum. p. 161

Drew, Charles *1904–1950* American physician who developed an efficient way to store blood plasma in blood banks. p. 348

Du Bois, W. E. B. (doo•BOYS) *1868–1963* African American teacher, writer, and leader who helped form the National Association for the Advancement of Colored People (NAACP). p. 218

E

Earhart, Amelia *1897–1937* American aviator; first woman to cross the Atlantic in an airplane. pp. 279–280

Edison, Thomas *1847–1931* American who invented the phonograph and the electric lightbulb; he also built the first power station to supply electricity to New York City. pp. 162–163, 164–165, 201

Eisenhower, Dwight D. *1890–1969* Thirty-fourth U.S. President and, earlier, American general who led the D day invasion. pp. 362, 364, 384, 415, 419, 454

Ellicott, Andrew *1754–1820* American clockmaker who helped survey the land for the new capital of the United States. p. 64

Ellington, Edward Kennedy (Duke) *1899–1974* Band leader who became well-known playing jazz during the 1920s. pp. 289, 290

F

Ferdinand, Francis *1863–1914* Archduke of Austria-Hungary; his assassination sparked the outbreak of World War I. pp. 227–228

Ferdinand II *1452–1516* King of Spain who—with Queen Isabella, his wife—sent Christopher Columbus on his voyage to find a western route to Asia. p. 30

Fitzgerald, F. Scott *1896–1940* American writer. p. 288

Fong, Hiram L. *1906–* Chinese immigrant who settled in Hawaii; became first Chinese American senator. p. 169

Ford, Gerald *1913–* Thirty-eighth U.S. President. He became President when Richard Nixon resigned. The Vietnam War ended during his term. pp. 453, 455-456

Ford, Henry *1863–1947* American automobile manufacturer who mass-produced cars at low cost by using assembly lines. pp. 202–204, 277

Fox, Vicente *1942–* Elected president of Mexico in 2000. p. 527

Franco, Francisco *1892–1975* Spanish dictator. p. 334

Frank, Anne *1929–1945* Jewish girl who kept a diary describing her family's hiding during Nazi occupation of the Netherlands; they were later found and sent to concentration camps. pp. 367–368

Franklin, Benjamin *1706–1790* American leader who was sent to Britain to ask Parliament for representation. He was a writer of the Declaration of Independence, a delegate to the Constitutional Convention, and a respected scientist and business leader. p. 59

Friedan, Betty *1921–* Writer who helped set up the National Organization for Women to work for women's rights. p. 439

Fulton, Robert *1765–1815* American engineer and inventor who created the first commercial steamboat. p. 79

G

Gagarin, Yury Alekseyevich *1934–1968* Soviet cosmonaut; first human to orbit Earth. p. 431

Gage, Thomas *1721–1787* Head of the British army in North America and colonial governor. p. 50

Garrison, William Lloyd *1805–1879* American abolitionist who started a newspaper called *The Liberator*. p. 112

George III *1738–1820* King of Britain during the Revolutionary War. p. 47

Gershwin, George *1898–1937* American composer. p. 289

Gibbs, Jonathan C. *1800s* African American who became secretary of state in Florida; helped set up public school system. p. 143

Glenn, John H., Jr. *1921–* American astronaut who was the first person from the United States to orbit Earth. Former U.S. senator. p. 432

Gorbachev, Mikhail (gawr•buh•CHAWF, mee•KAH•eel) *1931–* Leader of the Soviet Union from 1985 to 1991. He improved relations with the United States and expanded freedom in the Soviet Union. pp. 459–460, 461, 464

Gordon, William E. *1918–* American scientist who established the Arecibo Observatory in Puerto Rico. p. 532

Gore, Albert *1948–* Vice President under President William Clinton. Defeated by George W. Bush in the 2000 election—the closest presidential election in history. pp. 470, 513

Granger, Gordon *1822–1876* Union general who read the order declaring all slaves in Texas to be free. p. 146

Grant, Ulysses S. *1822–1885* Eighteenth U.S. President and, earlier, commander of the Union army in the Civil War. pp. 129, 132, 133, 135, 139

Greeley, Horace *1811–1872* American journalist and political leader; publisher of a newspaper called the *New York Tribune*. p. 125

Groves, Leslie *1896–1970* American general and head of the project to develop the atomic bomb. p. 378

H

Hallidie, Andrew S. *1836–1900* American inventor of the cable car. p. 209

Hamilton, Alexander *1755–1804* American leader in calling for the Constitutional Convention and winning support for it. He favored a strong national government. pp. 62, 63

Hammond, James Henry *1807–1864* Senator from South Carolina. p. 106

Hancock, John *1737–1793* Leader of the Sons of Liberty in the Massachusetts Colony. p. 50

Harding, Warren G. *1865–1923* Twenty-ninth U.S. President. p. 246

Haynes, Elwood *1857–1925* Indiana inventor who developed the first gasoline-powered automobile, in 1894. p. 202

Hearst, William Randolph *1863–1951* American newspaper publisher; owner of *New York Journal*; known for yellow journalism. p. 193

Hemingway, Ernest *1899–1961* American writer. p. 288

Henry *1394–1460* Henry the Navigator, prince of Portugal, who set up the first European school for training sailors in navigation. p. 29

Hidalgo, Miguel *1753–1811* Mexican priest who called for a revolution against Spain in 1810. p. 525

Hirohito *1901–1989* Emperor of Japan from 1926 until his death. p. 334

Hitler, Adolf *1889–1945* Nazi dictator of Germany. His actions led to World War II and the killing of millions of people. pp. 333, 335, 336, 363, 366, 368

Holiday, Eleanora (Billie) *1915–1959* American jazz singer. p. 290

Holly, Charles Hardin (Buddy) *1936–1959* American rock and roll performer. p. 419

Hooker, Thomas *1586?–1647* Minister who helped form the Connecticut Colony. His democratic ideas were adopted in the Fundamental Orders. pp. 40–41

Hoover, Herbert *1874–1964* Thirty-first U.S. President. When the Great Depression began, he thought that the economy was healthy and conditions would improve. pp. 296, 302–304

Hopper, Edward *1882–1967* American painter. p. 288

Houston, Sam *1793–1863* President of the Republic of Texas and, later, governor of the state of Texas. p. 117

Hudson, Henry *?–1611* Explorer who sailed up the Hudson River, giving the Dutch a claim to the area. p. 34

Huerta, Dolores *1930–* Labor leader and organizer, along with Cesar Chavez, of the United Farm Workers. p. 439

Hurston, Zora Neale *1903–1960* African American novelist and one of the best-known Harlem writers. p. 290

Hussein, Saddam *1937–* Leader of Iraq. pp. 463, 464

Hutchinson, Anne Marbury *1591–1643* English-born woman who left Massachusetts because of her religious beliefs. She settled near Providence, which joined with other settlements to form the Rhode Island Colony. p. 40

Isabella I *1451–1504* Queen of Spain who—with King Ferdinand, her husband—sent Columbus on his voyage to find a western route to Asia. p. 30

Jackson, Andrew *1767–1845* Seventh U.S. President and, earlier, commander who won the final battle in the War of 1812. As President he favored a strong Union and ordered the removal of Native Americans from their lands. pp. 69–70, 100, 101

Jackson, Thomas (Stonewall) *1824–1863* Confederate general. pp. 122, 130

Jay, John *1745–1829* American leader who wrote letters to newspapers, defending the Constitution. He became the first chief justice of the Supreme Court. p. 62

Jefferson, Thomas *1743–1826* Third U.S. President and the main writer of the Declaration of Independence. pp. 51, 62, 63, 66, 67

Jenney, William *1832–1907* American engineer who developed the use of steel frames to build tall buildings. pp. 160, 208–209

John I *1357–1433* King of Portugal during a time of great exploration. Father of Prince Henry, who set up a school of navigation. p. 29

Johnson, Andrew *1808–1875* Seventeenth U.S. President. Differences with Congress about Reconstruction led to his being impeached, though he was found not guilty. pp. 141, 143

Johnson, Lyndon B. *1908–1973* Thirty-sixth U.S. President. He started Great Society programs and expanded U.S. involvement in the Vietnam War. pp. 431, 436, 437, 448, 449, 451

Joliet, Louis (zhohl•YAY, loo•EE) *1645–1700* French fur trader who with Jacques Marquette and five others explored North American lakes and rivers for France. p. 33

Joplin, Scott *1868–1917* American composer; known as the King of Ragtime. p. 209

Joseph *1840?–1904* Nez Perce chief who tried to lead his people to Canada after they were told to move onto a reservation. p. 155

Juárez, Benito *1806–1872* Served twice as president of Mexico; made many reforms. p. 526

Kalakaua (kah•lah•KAH•ooh•ah) *1836–1891* Hawaiian king who tried but failed to keep Americans from taking over the Hawaiian Islands. p. 191

Kennedy, John F. *1917–1963* Thirty-fifth U.S. President. He made the Soviet Union remove its missiles from Cuba; later introduced the bill that became known as the Civil Rights Act of 1964. pp. 428–431, 432

Kennedy, Robert *1925–1968* American politician and attorney general. p. 429

King, Dr. Martin Luther, Jr. *1929–1968* African American civil rights leader who worked for integration in nonviolent ways. King won the Nobel Peace Prize in 1964. pp. 421, 422, 435–438

La Follette, Robert *1855–1925* Wisconsin governor who began many reforms in his state, including a merit system for government jobs. pp. 214–215

La Salle, René-Robert Cavelier, Sieur de (luh•SAL) *1643–1687* French explorer who found the mouth of the Mississippi River and claimed the whole Mississippi Valley for France. p. 34

Lawrence, Jacob *1917–2000* African American artist; his parents took part in the Great Migration. pp. 170, 171, 238

Leahy, William *1875–1959* American navy admiral; opposed the use of the atom bomb. p. 378

Lee, Robert E. *1807–1870* United States army colonel who gave up his post to become commander of the Confederate army in the Civil War. pp. 125, 129, 130, 131, 133, 135

LeMay, Curtis *1906–1990* American air force officer; directed Berlin Airlift. p. 393

L'Enfant, Pierre Charles *1754–1825* French-born American engineer who planned the buildings and streets of the new capital of the United States. p. 64

Lewis, Meriwether *1774–1809* American explorer chosen by Thomas Jefferson to be a pathfinder in the territory of the Louisiana Purchase. p. 67

Lewis, Sinclair *1885–1951* American novelist. p. 288

Liliuokalani, Lydia (lih•lee•uh•woh•kuh•LAH•nee) *1838–1917* Hawaiian queen who tried but failed to bring back the Hawaiian monarchy's authority. p. 191

Lincoln, Abraham *1809–1865* Sixteenth U.S. President, leader of the Union in the Civil War, and signer of the Emancipation Proclamation. pp. 114–119, 125, 126, 131, 132, 140–141

Lincoln, Mary Todd *1818–1882* Wife of Abraham Lincoln. p. 141

Lindbergh, Charles *1902–1974* Airplane pilot who was the first to fly solo between the United States and Europe. pp. 278–279

Longstreet, James *1821–1904* Former Confederate general who wanted the South to build more factories; considered a scalawag. p. 148

MacArthur, Douglas *1880–1964* Commander of Allied forces in the Pacific during World War II. pp. 304, 388, 394, 413

Madison, James *1751–1836* Fourth U.S. President. He was a leader in calling for the Constitutional Convention, writing the Constitution, and winning support for it. p. 62

Magellan, Ferdinand (muh•JEH•luhn) *1480?–1521* Portuguese explorer who, in 1519, led a fleet of ships from Spain westward to Asia. He died on the voyage, but one of the ships made it back to Spain, completing the first trip around the world. p. 31

Malcolm X *1925–1965* African American leader who disagreed with the views of Dr. Martin Luther King, Jr., on nonviolence and integration. p. 438

Marconi, Guglielmo (mahr•KOH•nee, gool•YEL•moh) *1874–1937* Italian who invented the radio. p. 201

Marquette, Jacques (mar•KET, ZHAHK) *1637–1675* Catholic missionary who knew several American Indian languages. With Louis Joliet, he explored lakes and rivers for France. p. 33

Marshall, George C. *1880–1959* U.S. secretary of state who developed the European Recovery Program, also known as the Marshall Plan, after World War II. p. 391

Marshall, Thurgood *1908–1993* NAACP lawyer who argued the school segregation case that the Supreme Court ruled on in 1954 and, later, was the first African American to serve on the Supreme Court. pp. 421, 438

Martí, José (mar•TEE) *1853–1895* Cuban writer and patriot who worked for Cuban independence from Spain. p. 192

McCarthy, Joseph Raymond *1908–1957* American politician; accused many individuals of being communists. p. 420

McKay, Claude *1890–1948* African American writer during the Harlem Renaissance. p. 290

McKinley, William *1843–1901* Twenty-fifth U.S. President. The Spanish-American War was fought during his term. p. 195

Miller, Doris (Dorie) *1919–1944* African American seaman who was awarded the Navy Cross for his bravery during the Japanese attack on Pearl Harbor, December 7, 1941. p. 344

Monroe, James *1758–1831* Fifth U.S. President. He established the Monroe Doctrine, which said that the United States would stop any European nation from expanding its American empire. p. 69

Morton, Ferdinand Joseph La Menthe (Jelly Roll) *1885–1941* American jazz musician. p. 288

Motecuhzoma (maw•tay•kwah•SOH•mah) *1466–1520* Emperor of the Aztecs when they were conquered by the Spanish. He is also known as Montezuma. p. 32

Murrow, Edward Roscoe *1908–1965* American journalist who reported from London during Battle of Britain. pp. 337–338

Mussolini, Benito (moo•suh•LEE•nee, buh•NEE•toh) *1883–1945* Ruler of Italy from 1922 until 1943, most of that time as dictator. pp. 333, 335, 363, 366

Nast, Thomas *1840–1902* American cartoonist who created the "Uncle Sam" character. p. 512

Nimitz, Chester W. *1885–1966* Commander of U.S. Pacific fleet during World War II. p. 373

Nixon, Richard M. *1913–1994* Thirty-seventh U.S. President. He tried to end the Vietnam War, he reduced tensions with communist nations, and he resigned the presidency because of the Watergate scandal. pp. 451–453, 455

O

O'Connor, Sandra Day *1930–* First woman to be appointed to the United States Supreme Court. pp. 441, 512

Oglethorpe, James *1696–1785* English settler who was given a charter to settle Georgia. He wanted to use debtors from England to help settle it. p. 44

O'Keeffe, Georgia *1887–1986* American painter who developed her own style of showing abstract studies of color and light. p. 288

Oppenheimer, Julius Robert *1904–1967* Director of the Manhattan Project, which developed the atom bomb. p. 376

Otis, James *1725–1783* Massachusetts colonist who spoke out against British taxes and called for "no taxation without representation." p. 48

P

Paine, Thomas *1737–1809* Author of a widely read pamphlet called *Common Sense,* in which he attacked King George III and called for a revolution to make the colonies independent. p. 50

Parks, Rosa *1913–* African American woman whose refusal to give up her seat on a Montgomery, Alabama, bus started a year-long bus boycott. p. 421

Paterson, William *1745–1806* Constitutional delegate from New Jersey who submitted the New Jersey Plan, under which each state would have one vote, regardless of population. p. 61

Penn, William *1644–1718* Proprietor of Pennsylvania under a charter from King Charles II of Britain. Penn was a Quaker who made Pennsylvania a refuge for settlers who wanted religious freedom. p. 42

Perot, H. Ross *1930–* Texas business person who ran for President in the 1992 election against George Bush and William Clinton. pp. 465–466

Pickett, George *1825–1875* Confederate general who led the charge at Gettysburg; he was forced to retreat. p. 130

Polo, Marco *1254–1324* Explorer from Venice who spent many years in Asia in the late 1200s. He wrote a book about his travels that gave Europeans information about Asia. p. 28

Ponce de León, Juan (POHN•say day lay•OHN) *1460–1521* Spanish explorer who landed on the North American mainland in 1513, near what is now St. Augustine, Florida. p. 31

Powell, Colin L. *1937–* Chairman of the Joint Chiefs of Staff during the Gulf War; became U.S. secretary of state in 2001. p. 464

Presley, Elvis *1935–1977* American rock and roll performer. p. 419

Pulitzer, Joseph *1847–1911* American journalist and newspaper publisher; owner of *New York World.* p. 193

R

Randolph, Edmund *1753–1813* Virginia delegate to the Constitutional Convention who wrote the Virginia Plan, which stated that the number of representatives a state would have in Congress should be based on the free population of the state. p. 61

Reagan, Ronald *1911– 2004* Fortieth U.S. President. His meetings with Soviet leader Mikhail Gorbachev led to a thaw in the Cold War, including advances in arms control. pp. 458–460

Revels, Hiram R. *1822–1901* First African American elected to the U.S. Senate. p. 143

Revere, Paul *1735–1818* American who warned the Patriots that the British were marching toward Concord, where Patriot weapons were stored. p. 50

Riis, Jacob (REES) *1849–1914* Reformer and writer who described the living conditions of the poor in New York City. pp. 206–207

Robinson, Bill (Bojangles) *1878–1949* African American tap dancer. p. 290

Rockefeller, John D. *1839–1937* American oil entrepreneur who joined many refineries into one business, called the Standard Oil Company. pp. 161–162

Roebling, John *1806–1869* Engineer and industrialist who designed suspension bridges. p. 160

Rogers, Will *1879–1935* American comedian during the Great Depression. p. 306

Roosevelt, Eleanor *1884–1962* Wife of Franklin Delano Roosevelt; one of the most active First Ladies. p. 312

Roosevelt, Franklin Delano *1882–1945* Thirty-second U.S. President. He began New Deal programs to help the nation out of the Great Depression, and he was the nation's leader during most of World War II. pp. 308–310, 313, 332, 340–341, 344–345, 348, 353, 362, 367, 375

Roosevelt, Theodore *1858–1919* Twenty-sixth U.S. President. Hero of the Spanish-American War. He showed the world America's strength, made it possible to build the Panama Canal, and worked for progressive reforms and conservation. pp. 194–195, 196, 215–217

Root, George Frederick *1820–1895* American composer and teacher. p. 99

Ross, Edmund G. *1826–1907* Senator from Kansas who voted to acquit President Andrew Johnson. p. 143

Ross, John *1790–1866* Chief of the Cherokee nation. He fought in U.S. courts to prevent the loss of the Cherokees' lands in Georgia. Though he won the legal battle, he still had to lead his people along the Trail of Tears to what is now Oklahoma. p. 70

Russwurm, John *1799–1851* Helped Samuel Cornish found an abolitionist newspaper called *Freedom's Journal* in 1827. p. 112

Ruth, George (Babe) *1895–1948* American baseball player. p. 287

BIOGRAPHICAL DICTIONARY

Biographical Dictionary ■ **R43**

S

Sacagawea (sa•kuh•juh•WEE•uh) *1786?–1812?* Shoshone woman who acted as an interpreter for the Lewis and Clark expedition. p. 68

Sadat, Anwar (suh•DAT) *1918–1981* Egyptian president; signed peace treaty with Prime Minister Menachem Begin of Israel. p. 456

San Martín, José de (sahn mar•TEEN) *1778–1850* Leader of an independence movement in Argentina. p. 538

Santa Anna, Antonio López de *1794–1876* Dictator of Mexico; defeated Texans at the Alamo. p. 71

Sarnoff, David *1891–1971* American communications executive; he planned to broadcast music to radios in people's homes. p. 286

Scott, Dred *1795?–1858* Enslaved African who took his case for freedom to the Supreme Court and lost. p. 104

Seward, William H. *1801–1872* Secretary of state in the cabinet of Abraham Lincoln. pp. 107, 189

Shays, Daniel *1747?–1825* Leader of Shays's Rebellion, which showed the weakness of the government under the Articles of Confederation. p. 59

Shepard, Alan, Jr. *1923–1998* American astronaut; first American to fly in space. p. 432

Sherman, William Tecumseh *1820–1891* Union general who, after defeating Confederate forces in Atlanta, led the March to the Sea, on which his troops caused great destruction. pp. 132, 133

Sitting Bull *1831–1890* Sioux leader who fought against General George Custer. p. 155

Slater, Samuel *1768–1835* Textile pioneer who helped bring the Industrial Revolution to the United States by providing plans for a new spinning machine. p. 77

Smalls, Robert *1839–1915* African American who delivered a Confederate steamer to the Union forces. p. 127

Smith, Bessie *1894 or 1898–1937* African American blues singer. p. 288

Smith, John *1580–1631* English explorer who, as leader of the Jamestown settlement, saved its people from starvation. p. 34

Sprague, Frank *1857–1934* American inventor who built the trolley car, an electric streetcar. p. 211

Squanto *See* Tisquantum.

Stalin, Joseph *1879–1953* Dictator of the Soviet Union from 1924 until his death. pp. 334, 336, 390

Stanton, Elizabeth Cady *1815–1902* American reformer who organized the first convention for women's rights. pp. 111, 247

Starr, Ellen Gates *1860–1940* Reformer who, with Jane Addams, founded Hull House in Chicago. p. 208

Stowe, Harriet Beecher *1811–1896* American abolitionist who, in 1852, wrote the book *Uncle Tom's Cabin.* p. 112

T

Taft, William Howard *1857–1930* Twenty-seventh U.S. President; initiated dollar diplomacy with other nations. p. 228

Taney, Roger B. (TAW•nee) *1777–1864* Supreme Court chief justice who wrote the ruling against Dred Scott. p. 105

Tarbell, Ida *1857–1944* Reporter during the Progressive Era; investigated John D. Rockefeller's Standard Oil Company. p. 214

Tisquantum *1585?–1622* Native American who spoke English and who helped the Plymouth Colony. p. 35

Tojo, Hideki *1884–1948* Japanese general who was named prime minister when military seized Japan's government. p. 334

Tompkins, Sally *1833–1916* Civil War nurse who eventually ran her own private hospital in Richmond, Virginia. She was a captain in the Confederate army, the only woman to achieve such an honor. p. 127

Trudeau, Pierre *1919–2000* Twice-elected prime minister of Canada who helped defeat the separatist movement of Quebec. p. 544

Truman, Harry S. *1884–1972* Thirty-third U.S. President. He ordered the atom bomb to be dropped on Japan to end World War II; he later sent American soldiers to support South Korea in 1950. pp. 367, 375, 377, 391, 410–411, 412

Truth, Sojourner *1797?–1883* Abolitionist and former slave who became a leading preacher against slavery. p. 113

Tubman, Harriet *1820–1913* Abolitionist and former slave who became a conductor on the Underground Railroad. She led about 300 slaves to freedom. p. 111

Tunney, Gene *1898–1978* American boxer. p. 287

Turner, Nat *1800–1831* Enslaved African who led a rebellion against slavery. p. 109

Tweed, William (Boss) *1823–1878* New York City political boss who robbed the city of millions of dollars. pp. 213–214

V

Vespucci, Amerigo (veh•SPOO•chee, uh•MAIR•ih•goh) *1454–1512* Italian explorer who made several voyages from Europe to what many people thought was Asia. He determined that he had landed on another continent, which was later called America in his honor. pp. 30–31

W

Wald, Lillian *1867–1940* Reformer who started the Henry Street Settlement in New York City. p. 208

Warren, Earl *1891–1974* Chief justice of the Supreme Court; he wrote the 1954 decision against school segregation. p. 421

Washington, George *1732–1799* First U.S. President, leader of the Continental Army during the Revolutionary War, and president of the Constitutional Convention. pp. 50, 52, 53, 58, 62–64

Waters, Ethel *1896–1977* African American singer and actress. p. 290

BIOGRAPHICAL DICTIONARY

Weaver, Robert *1907–1997* Secretary of Housing and Urban Development; first African American to serve in a President's Cabinet. p. 438

Welch, Joseph *1890–1960* American lawyer; represented the U.S. Army in a televised hearing before Joseph McCarthy. p. 420

Westinghouse, George *1846–1914* American inventor who designed an air brake for stopping trains. p. 159

White, Edward Higgins, II *1930–1967* American astronaut; first U.S. astronaut to walk in space. p. 432

Whitney, Eli *1765–1825* American inventor who was most famous for his invention of the cotton gin and his idea of interchangeable parts, which made mass production possible. p. 77

Williams, Roger *1603?–1683* Founder of Providence, in what is now Rhode Island. He had been forced to leave Massachusetts because of his views. pp. 39–40

Wilson, Samuel *1766–1854* American meat packer who inspired the "Uncle Sam" national symbol. p. 512

Wilson, Woodrow *1856–1924* Twenty-eighth U.S. President. He brought the country into World War I after trying to stay neutral. He favored the League of Nations, but the Senate rejected U.S. membership in the league. pp. 228, 229, 230, 237, 241, 242–243, 244, 248

Winthrop, John *1588–1649* Puritan leader who served several times as governor of the Massachusetts Bay Colony. He helped form confederation among people of New England and served as its first president. p. 39

Woods, Granville T. *1856–1910* African American who improved the air brake and developed a telegraph system for trains. p. 159

Wright, Frank Lloyd *1867–1959* American architect known for producing unusual buildings. pp. 281, 282

Wright, Orville *1871–1948* Pioneer in American aviation who—with his brother, Wilbur—made and flew the first successful airplane, at Kitty Hawk, North Carolina. pp. 204–205

Wright, Wilbur *1867–1912* Pioneer in American aviation who—with his brother, Orville—made and flew the first successful airplane, at Kitty Hawk, North Carolina. pp. 204–205

Y

Yeltsin, Boris *1931–* President of Russia who worked with President Clinton to reduce the number of nuclear weapons. p. 469

Z

Zedong, Mao (MOW zeh•DUNG) *1893–1976* Communist leader of China who invited President Richard Nixon to visit his country in 1972. p. 452

Zimmermann, Arthur *1864–1940* Germany's foreign secretary; he sent a telegram during World War I to a German ambassador to Mexico offering Mexico an alliance with Germany and support in reconquering lost territory. p. 229

Gazetteer

The Gazetteer is a geographical dictionary that will help you locate places discussed in this book. The page number tells where each place appears on a map.

A

Abilene A city in central Kansas on the Smoky Hill River; a major railroad town. (39°N, 97°W) p. 152

Alberta One of Canada's ten provinces; located in western Canada. p. 542

Amazon River The longest river in South America, flowing from the Andes Mountains across Brazil and into the Atlantic Ocean. p. 537

Andes Mountains (AN•deez) The longest chain of mountains in the world; located along the entire western coast of South America. p. 537

Antietam (an•TEE•tuhm) A creek near Sharpsburg in north central Maryland; site of a Civil War battle in 1862. (39°N, 78°W) p. 134

Antigua An island in the eastern part of the Leeward Islands, in the eastern West Indies. p. 530

Appomattox (a•puh•MA•tuhks) A village in central Virginia; site of the battle that ended the Civil War in 1865; once known as Appomattox Court House. (37°N, 79°W) p. 134

Atlanta Georgia's capital and largest city; located in the northwest central part of the state; site of a Civil War battle in 1864. (33°N, 84°W) pp. 134, 493

Austin The capital of Texas; located in south central Texas. (30°N, 97°W) p. 493

B

Bahamas An island group in the North Atlantic Ocean; located southeast of Florida and north of Cuba. p. 530

Baja California A peninsula in northwestern Mexico extending south-southeast between the Pacific Ocean and the Gulf of California. p. 525

Barbados An island in the Lesser Antilles, West Indies; located east of the central Windward Islands. p. 530

Barbuda A flat coral island in the eastern West Indies. p. 530

Baxter Springs A city in the southeastern corner of Kansas. (37°N, 94°W) p. 152

Belgrade The capital of Serbia. (44°N, 20°E) p. 227

Belmopan (bel•moh•PAN) A town in Central America; capital of Belize. (17°N, 88°W) p. 530

Bennington A town in the southwestern corner of Vermont; site of a major Revolutionary War battle in 1777. (43°N, 73°W) p. 52

Bogotá A city in South America, located on the plateau of the Andes; capital of Colombia. (4°N, 74°W) p. 537

Boise (BOY•zee) Idaho's capital and largest city; located in the southwestern part of the state. (44°N, 116°W) p. 493

Brandywine A battlefield on Brandywine Creek in southeastern Pennsylvania; site of a major Revolutionary War battle in 1777. (40°N, 76°W) p. 52

Brasília A city in South America on the Tocantins River; capital of Brazil. (15°S, 48°W) p. 537

British Columbia One of Canada's ten provinces; located on the west coast of Canada and bordered by the Yukon Territory, the Northwest Territories, Alberta, the United States, and the Pacific Ocean. p. 542

Buenos Aires A city in South America; the capital of Argentina. (34°S, 58°W) p. 537

Bull Run A stream in northeastern Virginia; flows toward the Potomac River; site of Civil War battles in 1861 and in 1862. p. 134

C

Calgary A city in southern Alberta, Canada; located on the Bow River. (51°N, 114°W) p. 542

Camden A city in north central South Carolina, near the Wateree River; site of a major Revolutionary War battle in 1780. (34°N, 81°W) p. 52

Canal Zone A strip of territory in Panama, through which the Panama Canal runs. p. 196

Canary Islands An island group in the Atlantic Ocean off the northwest coast of Africa. (28°N, 16°W) p. 37

Caracas (kuh•RAH•kuhs) A city in northern Venezuela; capital of Venezuela. (10°N, 67°W) p. 537

Caribbean Sea A part of the Atlantic Ocean between the West Indies and Central and South America. p. 530

Cayenne A city on the northwestern coast of Cayenne Island, in northern South America; capital of French Guiana. (5°N, 52°W) p. 537

Chancellorsville (CHAN•suh•lerz•vil) A location in northeastern Virginia, just west of Fredericksburg; site of a Civil War battle in 1863. (38°N, 78°W) p. 134

Charleston A city in southeastern South Carolina; a major port on the Atlantic Ocean; once known as Charles Town. (33°N, 80°W) pp. 52, 134

Charlotte The largest city in North Carolina; located in the south central part of the state. (35°N, 81°W) p. 493

Charlottetown The capital of Prince Edward Island, Canada; located in the central part of the island. (46°N, 63°W) p. 542

Chattanooga (cha•tuh•NOO•guh) A city in southeastern Tennessee; located on the Tennessee River; site of a Civil War battle in 1863. (35°N, 85°W) p. 134

Cheyenne (shy•AN) The capital of Wyoming; located in the southeastern part of the state. (41°N, 105°W) p. 152

Chicago A city in Illinois; located on Lake Michigan; the third-largest city in the United States. (42°N, 88°W) p. 152

Chickamauga (chik•uh•MAW•guh) A city in northwestern Georgia; site of a Civil War battle in 1863. (35°N, 85°W) p. 134

Chihuahua A city and state in northern Mexico. (28°N, 85°W) p. 525

Cold Harbor A location in east central Virginia, north of the Chickahominy River; site of Civil War battles in 1862 and in 1864. (38°N, 77°W) p. 134

Concord A town in northeastern Massachusetts, near Boston; site of a major Revolutionary War battle in 1775. (42°N, 71°W) p. 52

Cowpens A town in northwestern South Carolina; located near the site of a major Revolutionary War battle in 1781. (35°N, 82°W) p. 52

Cuba An island country in the Caribbean; the largest island of the West Indies. (22°N, 79°W) pp. 430, 530

D

Dallas A city in northeastern Texas; located on the Trinity River. (33°N, 97°W) p. 493

Denver Colorado's capital and largest city. (40°N, 105°W) pp. 152, 493

Dodge City A city in southern Kansas; located on the Arkansas River; once a major railroad center on the Santa Fe Trail. (38°N, 100°W) p. 152

Dominica (dah•muh•NEE•kuh) An island and a republic in the West Indies; located in the center of the Lesser Antilles between Guadeloupe and Martinique. p. 530

Dominican Republic A country in the West Indies, occupying the eastern part of Hispaniola. p. 530

Durango A city and state in northwestern central Mexico. (24°N, 104°W) p. 525

E

Edmonton The capital of Alberta, Canada; located in the south central part of the province on both banks of the North Saskatchewan River. (53°N, 113°W) p. 542

El Paso A city at the western tip of Texas; located on the Rio Grande. (32°N, 106°W) p. 493

Ellsworth A city in central Kansas. p. 152

F

Falkland Islands A British colony in the Atlantic Ocean; located east of the Strait of Magellan. p. 537

Fort Donelson A fort located in northwestern Tennessee; site of a major Civil War battle in 1862. p. 134

Fort Lauderdale A city in southeastern Florida along the Atlantic coast. p. 493

Fort Sumter A fort on a human-made island, off the coast of South Carolina, in Charleston Harbor; site of the first Civil War battle, in 1861. (33°N, 80°W) p. 134

Fort Wagner A fort near Charleston, South Carolina; site of a Civil War battle in 1863. p. 134

Fort Worth A city in northern Texas; located on the Trinity River. (33°N, 97°W) p. 493

Franklin A city in central Tennessee; site of a major Civil War battle in 1864. (36°N, 87°W) p. 134

Fredericksburg A city in northeastern Virginia; located on the Rappahannock River; site of a Civil War battle in 1862. (38°N, 77°W) p. 134

Fredericton The capital of New Brunswick, Canada; located in the southwestern part of the province. (46°N, 66°W) p. 542

G

Galápagos Islands Nineteen islands off the coast of Ecuador; home to many unique animal species. p. 539

Gatun Lake (gah•TOON) A lake in Panama; part of the Panama Canal system. p. 196

Georgetown A city in South America; located at the mouth of the Demerara River; capital of Guyana. (6°N, 58°W) p. 537

Germantown A residential section of present-day Philadelphia, on Wissahickon Creek, in southeastern Pennsylvania; site of a major Revolutionary War battle in 1777. (40°N, 75°W) p. 52

Gettysburg A town in southern Pennsylvania; site of a Civil War battle in 1863. (40°N, 77°W) p. 134

Grenada (grah•NAY•duh) An island in the West Indies; the southernmost of the Windward Islands. p. 530

Guadalajara A city in western central Mexico; capital of Jalisco state. (20°N, 103°W) p. 525

Guánica (GWAHN•ih•kah) A town in southwestern Puerto Rico; located on Guánica Harbor. (18°N, 67°W) p. 194

Guantánamo Bay (gwahn•TAH•nah•moh) A bay on the southeastern coast of Cuba. p. 430

Guatemala City Capital of Guatemala; largest city in Central America. (14°N, 90°W) p. 530

Guiana Highlands (gee•AH•nuh) Highland area in northern South America. p. 537

Guilford Courthouse (GIL•ferd) A location in north central North Carolina, near Greensboro; site of a major Revolutionary War battle in 1781. (36°N, 80°W) p. 52

Gulf of Panama A large inlet of the Pacific Ocean; located on the southern coast of Panama. p. 196

H

Haiti A country in the West Indies; occupies the western part of the island of Hispaniola. p. 530

Halifax The capital of the province of Nova Scotia, Canada; a major port on the Atlantic Ocean; remains free of ice all year. (44°N, 63°W) p. 542

Hampton Roads A channel in southeastern Virginia that flows into Chesapeake Bay; site of a Civil War naval battle in 1862 between two ironclad ships, the *Monitor* and the *Merrimack*. p. 134

Havana The capital of Cuba; located on the northwestern coast of the country. (23°N, 82°W) pp. 194, 430

Hiroshima The Japanese city upon which the first atom bomb was dropped in World War II. p. 377

Hispaniola (ees•pah•NYOH•lah) An island in the West Indies made up of Haiti and the Dominican Republic; located in the Caribbean Sea between Cuba and Puerto Rico. pp. 30, 530

Honolulu (hah•nuhl•OO•loo) Hawaii's capital and largest city; located on Oahu. (21°N, 158°W) pp. 190, 342

Houston A city in southeastern Texas; third-largest port in the United States; leading industrial center in Texas. (30°N, 95°W) p. 493

Iceland An island country in the North Atlantic Ocean; between Greenland and Norway. p. 366

Inchon (ihn•CHON) A city in northwestern South Korea. (36°N, 127°E) p. 412

Iqaluit (ee•KAH•loo•iht) The capital of Nunavut, Canada; located on the eastern coast. p. 542

Iron Curtain An imaginary barrier separating communist Eastern European countries from the West during the Cold War years. p. 393

Isthmus of Panama (IS•muhs) A narrow strip of land that connects North America and South America. p. 30

Iwo Jima A Japanese island; the site of major battles during World War II. p. 377

Jacksonville A city in northeastern Florida; located near the mouth of the St. Johns River. (30°N, 82°W) p. 493

Jamaica (juh•MAY•kuh) An island country in the West Indies; south of Cuba. p. 530

Kahoolawe (kah•hoh•uh•LAY•vay) One of the eight main islands of Hawaii; located west of Maui. pp. 190, 342

Kaskaskia (ka•SKAS•kee•uh) A village in southwestern Illinois; site of a major Revolutionary War battle in 1778. (38°N, 90°W) p. 52

Kauai (kah•WAH•ee) The fourth-largest of the eight main islands of Hawaii. pp. 190, 342

Kennesaw Mountain (KEN•uh•saw) An isolated peak in northwestern Georgia, near Atlanta; site of a Civil War battle in 1864. p. 134

Kings Mountain A ridge in northern South Carolina and southern North Carolina; site of a Revolutionary War battle in 1780. p. 52

Kingston A commercial seaport in the West Indies; capital of Jamaica. (18°N, 76°W) p. 530

La Paz A city in South America; capital of Bolivia. (16°S, 68°W) p. 537

Lanai (luh•NY) One of the eight main islands of Hawaii. pp. 190, 342

Las Vegas (lahs VAY•guhs) A city in southeastern Nevada. (36°N, 115°W) p. 493

Lexington A town in northeastern Massachusetts; site of the first battle of the Revolutionary War, in 1775. (42°N, 71°W) p. 52

Lima (LEE•mah) The capital of Peru; located on the Rímac River. (12°S, 77°W) p. 537

Little Bighorn A location near the Little Bighorn River in southern Montana; site of a fierce battle in 1876 between Sioux and Cheyenne Indians and United States Army soldiers led by General George Armstrong Custer. p. 154

Long Island An island located east of New York City and south of Connecticut; lies between Long Island Sound and the Atlantic Ocean. p. 52

Los Angeles The largest city in California; second-largest city in the United States; located in the southern part of the state. (34°N, 118°W) p. 493

M

Madeira (mah•DAIR•uh) An island group in the eastern Atlantic Ocean, off the coast of Morocco. p. 37

Managua A city in Central America; capital of Nicaragua; located on the south shore of Lake Managua. (12°N, 86°W) p. 530

Manitoba (ma•nuh•TOH•buh) A province in central Canada; bordered by Nunavut, Hudson Bay, Ontario, the United States, and Saskatchewan; located on the Interior Plains of Canada. p. 542

Maui (MOW•ee) The second-largest island in Hawaii. pp. 190, 342

Mérida A city in southeastern Mexico; capital of Yucatán state. (21°N, 89°W) p. 525

Mexico City A city on the southern edge of the Central Plateau of Mexico; the present-day capital of Mexico. (19°N, 99°W) p. 525

Minneapolis The largest city in Minnesota; located in the southeast central part of the state, on the Mississippi River; twin city with St. Paul. (45°N, 93°W) p. 162

Mobile Bay An inlet of the Gulf of Mexico; located off the coast of southern Alabama; the site of a Civil War naval battle in 1864. p. 134

Molokai (mah•luh•KY) One of the eight main islands of Hawaii. pp. 190, 342

Montenegro An independent state in southeastern Europe on the Balkan Peninsula. p. 227

Monterrey A city in northeastern Mexico; capital of Nuevo León state. (25°N, 100°W) p. 525

Montevideo (mon•tuh•vih•DAY•oh) A seaport city located in the southern part of the north shore of La Plata estuary; capital of Uruguay. (35°S, 56°W) p. 537

N

Nagasaki Japanese city upon which the second atom bomb was dropped, resulting in the end of World War II. p. 377

Nashville The capital of Tennessee; site of a Civil War battle in 1864. (36°N, 87°W) pp. 134, 493

Nassau A city on the northeastern coast of New Providence Island; capital of the Bahamas. (25°N, 77°W) p. 530

New Brunswick One of Canada's ten provinces; bordered by Quebec, the Gulf of St. Lawrence, Northumberland Strait, the Bay of Fundy, the United States, and Nova Scotia. p. 542

New Guinea (GIH•nee) An island of the eastern Malay Archipelago; located in the western Pacific Ocean, north of Australia. p. 377

New Orleans The largest city in Louisiana; a major port located between the Mississippi River and Lake Pontchartrain. (30°N, 90°W) p. 134

Newfoundland and Labrador (NOO•fuhn•luhnd) One of Canada's ten provinces; bordered by Quebec and the Atlantic Ocean. p. 542

Newton A city in south central Kansas. (38°N, 97°W) p. 152

Niihau (NEE•how) One of the eight main islands of Hawaii. pp. 190, 342

Normandy A region of northwest France; site of the Allied D day invasion on June 6, 1944. p. 366

Northwest Territories One of Canada's three territories; located in northern Canada. p. 542

Nova Scotia (NOH•vuh SKOH•shuh) A province of Canada; located in eastern Canada on a peninsula. p. 542

Nunavut (NOO•nuh•voot) One of Canada's three territories; formed in 1999 and inhabited mostly by Inuit peoples. p. 542

O

Oahu (oh•AH•hoo) The third-largest of the eight main islands of Hawaii; Honolulu is located there. pp. 190, 342

Oaxaca (wuh•HAH•kuh) A city and state in southern Mexico. (17°N, 96°W) p. 525

Ogallala (oh•guh•LAHL•uh) A city in western Nebraska on the South Platte River. (41°N, 102°W) p. 152

Ontario (ahn•TAIR•ee•oh) One of Canada's ten provinces; located between Quebec and Manitoba. p. 542

Orinoco River A river in Venezuela in northern South America. p. 537

Orlando A city in central Florida. (28°N, 81°W) p. 493

Ottawa (AH•tuh•wuh) The capital of Canada; located in Ontario on the St. Lawrence Lowlands. (45°N, 75°W) p. 542

P

Pampas (PAHM•puhs) The plains of South America; located in the southern part of the continent, extending for nearly 1,000 miles. p. 537

Panama Canal A canal across the Isthmus of Panama; extends from the Caribbean Sea to the Gulf of Panama. p. 196

Panama City The capital of Panama; located in Central America. (9°N, 80°W) p. 530

Paramaribo (par•ah•MAR•uh•boh) A seaport city located on the Suriname River; capital of Suriname. (5°N, 55°W) p. 537

Paraná River (par•uh•NAH) A river in southeast central South America; formed by the joining of the Rio Grande and the Paranaíba River in south central Brazil. p. 537

Patagonia A barren tableland in South America between the Andes and the Atlantic Ocean. p. 537

Pearl Harbor An inlet on the southern coast of Oahu, Hawaii; the Japanese attacked an American naval base there on December 7, 1941. p. 342

Pecos River (PAY•kohs) A river in eastern New Mexico and western Texas; empties into the Rio Grande. p. 152

Perryville A city in east central Kentucky; site of a major Civil War battle in 1862. (38°N, 90°W) p. 134

Petersburg A port city in southeastern Virginia; located on the Appomattox River; site of a series of Civil War battles from 1864 to 1865. (37°N, 77°W) p. 134

Philippine Islands A group of more than 7,000 islands off the coast of southeastern Asia, making up the country of the Philippines. p. 30

Phoenix Capital and largest city of Arizona; located in south central Arizona. (34°N, 112°W) p. 493

Port of Spain A seaport in the northwestern part of the island of Trinidad; capital of Trinidad and Tobago. (10°N, 61°W) p. 530

Port-au-Prince A seaport located on Hispaniola Island, in the West Indies, on the southeastern shore of the Gulf of Gonâve; capital of Haiti. (18°N, 72°W) p. 530

Portland (OR) Oregon's largest city and principal port; located in the northwestern part of the state on the Willamette River. (46°N, 123°W) p. 493

Prince Edward Island One of Canada's ten provinces; located in the Gulf of St. Lawrence. p. 542

Princeton A borough in west central New Jersey; site of a major Revolutionary War battle. (40°N, 75°W) p. 52

Puebla A city and state in southeastern central Mexico. (19°N, 98°W) p. 525

Pueblo (PWEH•bloh) A city in Colorado. p. 152

Pueblo Bonito (PWEH•bloh boh•NEE•toh) Largest of the prehistoric pueblo ruins; located in Chaco Culture National Historical Park, New Mexico. p. 23

Pusan (poo•SAHN) A city in the southeast corner of South Korea. (35°N, 129°E) p. 412

Q

Quebec (kwih•BEK) The capital of the province of Quebec, Canada; located on the northern side of the St. Lawrence River; the first successful French settlement in the Americas; established in 1608. (47°N, 71°W) p. 542

R

Raleigh (RAW•lee) The capital of North Carolina; located in the east central part of the state. (36°N, 79°W) p. 493

Regina (rih•JY•nuh) The capital of Saskatchewan, Canada; located in the southern part of the province. (50°N, 104°W) p. 542

Richmond The capital of Virginia; a port city located in the east central part of the state, on the James River; capital of the Confederacy. (38°N, 77°W) p. 134

Rio de Janeiro A city and commercial seaport in southeastern Brazil, on the southwestern shore of Guanabara Bay. (23°S, 43°W) p. 537

Río de la Plata A river on the southeastern coast of South America. p. 537

S

Sacramento The capital of California; located in the north central part of the state, on the Sacramento River. (39°N, 121°W) p. 493

Salt Lake City Utah's capital and largest city; located in the northern part of the state, on the Jordan River. (41°N, 112°W) p. 493

San Antonio A city in south central Texas; located on the San Antonio River; site of the Alamo. (29°N, 98°W) p. 493

San Diego A large port city in southern California; located on San Diego Bay. (33°N, 117°W) p. 493

San Francisco The second-largest city in California; located in the northern part of the state, on San Francisco Bay. (38°N, 123°W) pp. 196, 493

San José A city in Central America; capital of Costa Rica. (10°N, 84°W) p. 530

San Juan (SAN WAHN) Puerto Rico's capital and largest city. (18°N, 66°W) pp. 194, 530

San Juan Hill A hill in eastern Cuba; captured by Cuban and American troops during the Spanish-American War in 1898. p. 194

San Salvador One of the islands in the southern Bahamas; Christopher Columbus landed there in 1492. p. 37

Santa Fe (SAN•tah FAY) The capital of New Mexico; located in the north central part of the state. (36°N, 106°W) p. 493

Santiago (san•tee•AH•goh) A seaport on the southern coast of Cuba; second-largest city in Cuba. (20°N, 75°W) p. 194

Santo Domingo The capital of the Dominican Republic. (18°N, 70°W) p. 530

São Francisco River A river in eastern Brazil; flows north, northeast, and east into the Atlantic Ocean. p. 537

São Paulo (SOW POW•loh) A city in southeastern Brazil; capital of São Paulo state. p. 537

Saratoga A village on the western bank of the Hudson River in eastern New York; site of a major Revolutionary War battle in 1777; present-day Schuylerville. (43°N, 74°W) p. 52

Saskatchewan (suh•SKA•chuh•wahn) One of Canada's ten provinces; located between Alberta and Manitoba. p. 542

Savannah The oldest city and a principal seaport in southeastern Georgia; located in the southeastern part of the state, at the mouth of the Savannah River. (32°N, 81°W) pp. 52, 134

Seattle The largest city in Washington; a port city located in the west central part of the state, on Puget Sound. (48°N, 122°W) p. 493

Sedalia (suh•DAYL•yuh) A city in west central Missouri. (39°N, 93°W) p. 152

Seoul The capital of South Korea; located in the northwestern portion of nation. (37°N, 127°E) p. 412

Serbia An independent state in southeastern Europe on the Balkan Peninsula. p. 227

Shiloh (SHY•loh) A location in southwestern Tennessee; site of a major Civil War battle in 1862; also known as Pittsburg Landing. (35°N, 88°W) p. 134

Sierra Madre Occidental (see•AIR•ah MAH•dray ahk•sih•den•TAHL) A mountain range in western Mexico, running parallel to the Pacific coast. p. 525

St. John's A city on the southeastern coast of Canada, on the Atlantic Ocean; the capital of Newfoundland and Labrador. (47°N, 52°W) p. 542

St. Joseph A city in northwestern Missouri on the Missouri River. (40°N, 95°W) p. 152

St. Lucia An island and an independent state of the Windward Islands; located in the eastern West Indies, south of Martinique and north of St. Vincent. p. 530

St. Paul The capital of Minnesota; located in the eastern part of the state, on the Mississippi River. (45°N, 93°W) p. 162

Strait of Magellan (muh•JEH•luhn) The narrow waterway between the southern tip of South America and Tierra del Fuego; links the Atlantic Ocean with the Pacific Ocean. p. 30

Sucre (SOO•kray) A city in Bolivia, South America. (19°S, 65°W) p. 537

Suriname A country in north central South America. p. 537

T

Tallahassee The capital of Florida; located in the state's panhandle. (34°N, 84°W) p. 493

Tegucigalpa (teh•goo•see•GAHL•puh) A city in Central America; capital of Honduras. (14°N, 87°W) p. 530

Toledo (tuh•LEE•doh) A port city in northwestern Ohio located at the southwestern corner of Lake Erie. (42°N, 84°W) p. 162

Toronto The capital of the province of Ontario, Canada; located near the northwestern end of Lake Ontario; largest city in Canada. (43°N, 79°W) p. 542

Trenton The capital of New Jersey; located in the west central part of the state; site of a major Revolutionary War battle in 1776. (40°N, 75°W) p. 52

Trinidad and Tobago An independent republic made up of the islands of Trinidad and Tobago; located in the Atlantic Ocean off the northeastern coast of Venezuela. p. 530

Tucson (TOO•sahn) A city in southern Arizona; located on the Santa Cruz River. (32°N, 111°W) p. 493

V

Valley Forge A location in southeastern Pennsylvania, on the Schuylkill River; site of General George Washington's winter headquarters during the Revolutionary War. (40°N, 75°W) p. 52

Vancouver Canada's eighth-largest city; located where the northern arm of the Fraser River empties into the Pacific Ocean. (49°N, 123°W) p. 542

Veracruz (veh•rah•KROOZ) A state in Mexico; located in the eastern part of the country, on the Gulf of Mexico. (19°N, 96°W) p. 525

Vicksburg A city in western Mississippi; located on the Mississippi River; site of a major Civil War battle in 1863. (32°N, 91°W) p. 134

Victoria The capital of British Columbia, Canada; located on Vancouver Island. (48°N, 123°W) p. 542

Vincennes (vihn•SENZ) A town in southwestern Indiana; site of a Revolutionary War battle in 1779. (39°N, 88°W) p. 52

Wabash River (WAW•bash) A river in western Ohio and Indiana; flows west and south to the Ohio River, to form part of the Indiana-Illinois border. p. 52

West Indies The islands enclosing the Caribbean Sea, stretching from Florida, in North America, to Venezuela, in South America. p. 37

West Point A United States military post since the Revolutionary War; located in southeastern New York on the western bank of the Hudson River. p. 52

Whitehorse The capital of the Yukon Territory, Canada; located on the southern bank of the Yukon River. (60°N, 135°W) p. 542

Winnipeg The capital of the province of Manitoba, Canada; located on the Red River. (50°N, 97°W) p. 542

Yellowknife The capital of the Northwest Territories in Canada; located on the northwestern shore of Great Slave Lake at the mouth of the Yellowknife River. (62°N, 114°W) p. 542

Yorktown A small town in southeastern Virginia; located on Chesapeake Bay; site of the last major Revolutionary War battle, in 1781. (37°N, 76°W) p. 52

Yucatán Peninsula (yoo•kah•TAN) A peninsula in southeastern Mexico and northeastern Central America. p. 525

Yukon Territory One of Canada's three territories; bordered by the Arctic Ocean, the Northwest Territories, British Columbia, and Alaska. p. 542

Glossary

The Glossary contains important social studies words and their definitions. Each word is respelled as it would be in a dictionary. When you see this mark ´ after a syllable, pronounce that syllable with more force than the other syllables. The page number at the end of the definition tells where to find the word in your book.

add, āce, câre, pälm; end, ēqual; it, īce; odd, ōpen, ôrder; tŏŏk, pōōl; up, bûrn; yōō as *u* in *fuse*; oil; pout; ə as *a* in *above*, e in *sicken*, i in *possible*, o in *melon*, u in *circus*; check; ring; thin; this; zh as in *vision*

A

abolitionist (a•bə•li´shən•ist) A person who wanted to end slavery. p. 112

absolute location (ab´sə•lōōt lō•kā´shən) The exact location of any place on Earth. p. 36

acquittal (ə•kwi´təl) A verdict of not guilty. p. 143

adapt (ə•dapt´) To adjust ways of living to land and resources. p. 6

address (ə•dres´) A formal speech. p. 131

advertisement (ad•vər•tīz´mənt) A public announcement that tells people about a product or an opportunity. p. 167

advertising (ad´vər•tīz•ing) Information that a business provides about a product or service to make people want to buy it. p. 276

agriculture (a´grə•kul•chər) Farming. p. 22

alliance (ə•lī´əns) A formal agreement. p. 227

ally (a´lī) A partner in an alliance. p. 227

amendment (ə•mend´mənt) A change. p. 62

analyze (a´nəl•īz) To look closely at how parts of an event connect with one another and how the event is connected to other events. p. 3

anarchist (a´nər•kist) A person who is against any kind of government. p. 195

architect (är´kə•tekt) A person who designs buildings. p. 282

armistice (är´mə•stəs) An agreement to stop fighting a war. p. 194

arms control (ärmz kən•trōl´) Limiting the number of weapons that each nation may have. p. 453

arms race (ärmz rās) A time during which one country builds up weapons to protect itself against another country. p. 390

assassinate (ə•sa´sən•āt) To murder a leader by sudden or secret attack. p. 141

assembly line (ə•sem´blē līn) System of building things in which a moving belt carries parts from worker to worker. p. 202

aviation (ā•vē•ā´shən) Air travel. p. 204

B

baby boom (bā´bē bōōm) The 15 years following World War II during which 50 million babies were born in the United States. p. 386

balanced budget (ba´lənst bu´jət) A government plan for spending in which it does not spend more money than it makes. p. 302

bias (bī´əs) A personal feeling for or against someone or something. p. 73

black codes (blak kōdz) Laws limiting the rights of former slaves in the South. p. 142

blockade (blä•kād´) To use ships to isolate a port or island. p. 429

boom (bōōm) A time of fast economic growth. p. 150

border state (bôr´dər stāt) During the Civil War, a state—Delaware, Kentucky, Maryland, or Missouri—between the North and the South that was unsure which side to support. p. 123

boycott (boi´kät) The refusal to buy certain goods. p. 48

bureaucracy (byōō•rä´krə•sē) The many workers and groups that are needed to run government programs. p. 309

bust (bust) A time of quick economic decline. p. 151

C

candidate (kan´də•dāt) A person chosen by a political party to run for office. p. 465

capital (ka´pə•təl) The money needed to set up or improve a business. p. 161

cardinal direction (kärd´nal də•rek´shən) One of the main directions: north, south, east, or west. p. A3

carpetbagger (kär´pət•ba•gər) A Northerner who moved to the South to take part in Reconstruction governments. p. 147

cartogram (kär´tə•gram) A diagram that gives information about places by the size shown for each place. p. 498

cash crop (kash krop) A crop that is grown to be sold. p. 43

casualty (ka´zhəl•tē) A person who has been wounded or killed in a war. p. 125

cause (kôz) An event or an action that makes something else happen. p. 27

cease-fire (sēs•fīr´) A temporary end to a conflict. p. 453

charter (chär´tər) An official paper in which certain rights are given by a government to a person or business. p. 39

chronology (krə•nä´lə•jē) Time order. p. 2

civic participation (si´vik pär•ti´sə•pā´•shən) Being concerned with and involved in issues related to the community, state, country, or world. p. 9

civics (si´viks) The study of citizenship. p. 9

civil rights (si´vəl rīts) The rights guaranteed to all citizens by the Constitution. p. 218

civilian (sə•vil´yən) A person who is not in the military. p. 344

civilization (si•və•lə•zā´shən) A culture that usually has cities and well-developed forms of government, religion, and learning. p. 23

classify (kla´sə•fī) To group. p. 315

climograph (klī´mə•graf) A chart that shows the average monthly temperature and the average monthly precipitation for a place. p. 156

code (kōd) A set of laws. p. 109

cold war (kōld wôr) A war fought mostly with propaganda and money rather than with soldiers and weapons. p. 393

colony (kä´lə•nē) A settlement ruled by another country. p. 32

commercial industry (kə•mûr´shəl in´dəs•trē) An industry that is run to make a profit. p. 279

commission (kə•mi´shən) A special committee. p. 214

commonwealth (kä´mən•welth) A kind of territory that governs itself. p. 532

communism (kä´myə•ni•zəm) A political and economic system in which all industries, land, and businesses are owned by the government. p. 239

commute (kə•myōōt´) To travel back and forth to work. p. 281

compass rose (kum´pəs rōz) A circular direction marker on a map. p. A3

competition (käm•pə•ti´shən) The contest among companies to get the most customers or sell the most goods. p. 49

compromise (käm´prə•mīz) To reach an agreement by having each party give up some of what it wants. p. 60

concentration camp (kon•sən•trā´shən kamp) A prison camp. p. 333

Confederacy (kən•fe´də•rə•sē) The group of eleven states that left the Union, also called the Confederate States of America. p. 117

confederation (kən•fə•də•rā´shən) A loose group of governments working together. p. 26

conquistador (kän•kēs´tə•dôr) An explorer or soldier sent by Spain to conquer and claim large areas of North and South America. p. 31

conservation (kän•sər•vā´shən) The protection of the environment by keeping natural resources from being wasted or destroyed. p. 216

constitution (kän•stə•tōō´shən) A plan of government. p. 41

consumer good (kən•sōō´mər gŏŏd) A product made for personal use. p. 269

culture (kul´chər) A way of life. p. 10

D

D day (dē dā) June 6, 1944, the day the Allies worked together in Europe in the largest water-to-land invasion in history. p. 364

declaration (de•klə•rā´shən) An official statement. p. 48

deficit (de´fə•sət) A shortage. p. 459

deforestation (dē•fôr•ə•stā´shən) The widespread cutting down of forests. p. 540

democracy (di•mä´krə•sē) A government in which the people rule. p. 69

demonstration (de•mən•strā´shən) A public show of a group's feelings about a cause. p. 435

depression (di•pre´shən) A time when industries do not grow and many people are out of work. p. 300

desegregate (dē•se´gri•gāt) To remove racial barriers. p. 411

détente (dā•tänt´) An easing of tensions, especially between the United States and the Soviet Union. p. 453

developing country (di•ve´lə•ping kun´trē) A country that does not have modern conveniences such as good housing, roads, schools, and hospitals. p. 429

dictator (dik´tā•tər) A leader who has total authority to rule. p. 71

dictatorship (dik´tā•tər•ship) A government in which the dictator, or head of the government, has total authority. p. 333

distortions (di•stôr´shənz) The purposeful errors that enable cartographers to make flat maps. p. 198

diverse economy (də•vûrs´ i•kä´nə•mē) An economy based on many kinds of industries. p. 504

diversity (də•vûr´sə•tē) Great differences among the people. p. 24

doctrine (däk´trən) A government plan of action. p. 69

dollar diplomacy (dä´lər di•plō´mə•sē) A policy in which the United States government gave money to other nations in return for some U.S. control over the actions of those nations. p. 228

dove (duv) A person who was against the Vietnam War. p. 450

E

e-commerce (ē•kä´mərs) The buying and selling of goods and services through computers. p. 506

economics (e•kə•nä´miks) The study of how people use resources to meet their needs. p. 8

economist (i•kä´nə•məst) A person who studies the economy. p. 300

economy (i•kä´nə•mē) The way people of a state, region or country use resources to meet their needs. p. 8

effect (i•fekt´) Something that happens as a result of an event or action. p. 27

electoral college (i•lek´tə•rəl kä´lij) A group of electors who vote for the President and Vice President. p. 62

emancipation (i•man•sə•pā´shən) The freeing of enslaved peoples. p. 109

embargo (im•bär´gō) One nation's refusal to trade goods with another. p. 532

empire (em´pīr) A conquered land of many people and places governed by one ruler. p. 32

entrepreneur (än•trə•prə•nûr´) A person who sets up and runs a business. p. 159

equality (i•kwä´lə•tē) Equal rights. p. 112

ethnic group (eth´nik grŏŏp) A group of people from the same country, of the same race, or with a shared culture. p. 494

GLOSSARY

executive branch (ig•ze´kyə•tiv branch) The part of government that carries out the laws. p. 60

expedition (ek•spə•di´shən) A journey. p. 30

F

fact (fakt) A statement that can be checked and proved true. p. 291

fascism (fa´shi•zem) A political idea in which power is given to a dictator and the freedoms of individuals are taken away. p. 333

federal system (fe´də•rəl sis´təm) A system of government in which national and state authorities share the responsibility of governing. p. 60

flow chart (flō chärt) A diagram that uses arrows to show the order in which events happen. p. 250

frame of reference (frām uv ref´•rəns) A set of ideas that determine how a person understands something. pp. 3, 106

free election (frē i•lek´shən) Election that offers a choice of candidates instead of a single candidate. p. 533

free enterprise (frē en´tər•prīz) An economic system in which people are able to start and run their own businesses with little control by the government. p. 158

free state (frē stāt) A state that did not allow slavery before the Civil War. p. 101

free world (frē wûrld) The United States and its allies. p. 391

freedmen (frēd´mən) The men, women, and children who had once been slaves. p. 145

free-trade agreement (frē•trād´ ə•grē´mənt) A treaty in which countries agree not to charge tariffs, or taxes, on goods they buy from and sell to each other. p. 508

front (frənt) A battle line. p. 362

fugitive (fyōō´jə•tiv) A person who is running away from something. p. 109

G

generalization (jen•ə•rə•lə•za´shən) A statement that summarizes the facts. p. 274

geography (jē•ä´grə•fē) The study of Earth's surface and the way people use it. p. 6

global economy (glō´bəl i•kä´nə•mē) The world market in which companies from different countries buy and sell goods and services. p. 508

government (gu´vərn•mənt) A system by which people of a community, state, or nation use leaders and laws to help people live together. p. 9

grid system (grid sis´təm) An arrangement of lines that divide something, such as a map, into squares. p. A3

H

hawk (hôk) Person who supported the Vietnam War. p. 450

heritage (her´ə•tij) Culture that has come from the past and continues today. p. 10

high-tech (hī•tek´) Based on computers and other kinds of electronic equipment. p. 505

hijack (hī´jak) To illegally take control of an aircraft or other vehicle. p. 472

historical empathy (hi•stôr´i•kəl em´pə•thē) An understanding of the thoughts and feelings people of the past had about events in their time. p. 3

historical map (hi•stôr´i•kəl map) A map that provides information about a place at a certain time in history. p. 370

history (hi•stə•rē) Events of the past. p. 2

Holocaust (hō´lə•kôst) The mass murder during World War II of European Jews and other people whom Adolf Hitler called "undesirable." p. 368

homesteader (hōm´sted•ər) Person living on land granted by the government. p. 152

hostage (hos´tij) A prisoner held until the captors' demands are met. p. 457

human feature (hyōō´mən fē´chər) Something created by humans, such as a building or road, that alters the land. p. 6

human resource (hyōō´mən rē´sôrs) A worker who brings his or her own ideas and skills to a job. p. 163

hydroelectric dam (hī•drō•i•lek´trik dam) Dam that uses the water it stores to produce electricity. p. 314

I

immigrant (i´mi•grənt) A person from one country who comes to live in another country. p. 42

impeach (im•pēch´) To accuse a government official, especially the President, of a crime. p. 470

imperialism (im•pir´ē•ə•liz•əm) The building of an empire. p. 192

import (im´pôrt) A product brought in from another country. p. 42

indentured servant (in•den´chərd sûr´vənt) A person who agreed to work for another person for a certain length of time in exchange for passage to North America. p. 43

independence (in•də•pen´dəns) The freedom to govern on one's own. p. 51

Industrial Revolution (in•dus´trē•əl re•və•lōō´shən) A time of complete change in how things were made, in which people began using machines instead of hand tools. p. 76

inflation (in•flā´shən) An economic condition in which more money is needed to buy goods and services than was needed earlier. p. 450

Information Age (in•fər•mā´shən āj) A period of history defined by the growing amount of information available to people. p. 505

informed citizen (in•fôrmd´si´tə•zən) Someone who knows what is happening in the community. p. 513

inset map (in´set map) A smaller map within a larger one. p. A3

installment buying (in•stâl´mənt bī´ing) Taking home a product after paying only part of a price and then making monthly payments until the product is paid for. p. 269

GLOSSARY

integration (in•tə•grā´shən) The bringing together of people of all races. p. 421

interchangeable parts (in•tər•chān´jə•bəl pärts) Identical machine-made parts, any of which may be used to make or repair an item. p. 77

interdependent (in•tər•di•pen´dənt) Depending on other states and regions for natural resources, finished products, and services. p. 507

interest (in´trəst) The fee a borrower pays to a lender for the use of money. p. 270

interest rate (in´trəst rāt) An amount that a bank charges to lend money. p. 528

intermediate direction (in•tər•mē´dē•it də•rek´shən) One of the in-between directions: northeast, northwest, southeast, southwest. p. A3

international trade (in•tər•na´shə•nəl trād) Trade among nations. p. 507

Internet (in´tər•net) A network that links computers around the world for the exchange of information. p. 496

investor (in•ves´tər) Someone who uses money to buy or make something that will yield a profit. p. 297

island hopping (ī´lənd hä´ping) The fighting by the Allied forces to win only certain key islands as they worked their way toward an invasion of Japan. p. 373

isolation (ī•sə•lā´shən) The policy of remaining separate from other countries. p. 244

isthmus (is´məs) A narrow strip of land that connects two larger landmasses. p. 196

J

jazz (jaz) A music style influenced by the music of West Africa as well as by spirituals and blues. p. 288

judicial branch (jŏŏ•di´shəl branch) The part of government that settles differences about the meaning of laws. p. 60

jury (jûr´ē) A group of citizens who decide a case in court. p. 513

L

labor union (lā´bər yŏŏn´yən) A group of workers who join together to improve their working conditions. p. 245

land use (land yŏŏs) The way in which most of the land in a place is used. p. 274

legislative branch (le´jəs•lā•tiv branch) The part of government that makes the laws. p. 60

legislature (le´jəs•lā•chər) The lawmaking branch of a government. p. 34

liberate (li´bə•rāt) To set free. p. 538

life expectancy (līf ik•spek´tən•sē) The number of years a person can expect to live. p. 534

lines of latitude (līnz uv la´tə•tŏŏd) Lines that run east and west on a map or globe. p. 36

lines of longitude (līnz uv lon´jə•tŏŏd) Lines that run north and south on a map or globe. p. 36

location (lō•kā´shən) The place where something can be found. p. 6

locator (lō´kā•tər) A small map or picture of a globe that shows where an area on the main map is found in a state, on a continent, or in the world. p. A3

long drive (lông drīv) A trip made by ranchers to lead cattle to market or to the railroads. p. 151

M

manifest destiny (ma´nə•fest des´tə•nē) The belief that the United States should someday stretch from the Atlantic Ocean to the Pacific Ocean. p. 71

map key (map kē) A part of a map that explains what the symbols on a map stand for. p. A2

map scale (map skā l) A part of a map that compares a distance on the map to a distance in the real world. p. A3

map title (map tī´təl) Words on a map that tell the subject of the map. p. A2

mass production (mas prə•duk´shən) The system of producing large amounts of goods at one time. p. 78

median age (mē´dē•ən āj) An age in years that half of the people in a country are older than and half are younger than. p. 534

meridians (mə•ri´dē•ənz) Lines of longitude. p. 36

merit system (mer´ət sis´təm) A system through which a person is tested to make sure he or she can do the job before the job is offered. p. 215

middle class (mi´dəl klas) An economic level between the poor and the wealthy. p. 528

migrant worker (mī´grənt wûr´kər) Someone who moves from place to place with the seasons, harvesting crops. p. 439

migration (mī•grā´shən) The movement of people. p. 21

militarism (mil´ə•tə•ri•zem) The idea that using military force is a good way to solve problems. p. 226

military draft (mil´ə•ter•ē draft) A way of making the people of a nation join the armed forces. p. 230

minimum wage (mi´nə•məm wāj) The lowest amount of money by law that a person can be paid per hour. p. 313

mission (mi´shən) A small religious settlement. p. 33

missionary (mi´shə•ner•ē) A person sent out by a church to spread its religion. p. 32

modify (mä´də•fī) To change. p. 6

monopoly (mə•no´pə•lē) A company that has little or no competition. p. 215

N

nationalism (na´shə•nel•i•zem) Pride in one's country. p. 69

navigation (na•və•gā´shən) The study or act of planning and controlling the course of a ship. p. 29

neutral (nŏŏ´trəl) Not taking a side in a conflict. p. 229

GLOSSARY

new immigration (nōō i•mə•grā´shən) People who came from southern and central Europe and other parts of the world after 1890 to settle in North America. p. 167

no-man's-land (nō´manz•land) In a war, land not controlled by either side and filled with barbed wire, land mines, or bombs buried in the ground. p. 235

nonviolence (nän•vī´ə•ləns) The use of peaceful ways to bring about change. p. 421

old immigration (ōld i•mə•grā´shən) People who came from northern and western Europe before 1890 to settle in North America. p. 166

open range (ō´pən rānj) Land on which animals can graze freely. p. 153

opinion (ə•pin´yən) A statement that tells what a person thinks or believes. p. 291

opportunity cost (ä•pər•tōō´nə•tē kôst) The value of what a person gives up in order to get something else. p. 355

oral history (ôr´əl his´tə•rē) Stories, events, or experiences told aloud by a person who did not have a written language or who did not write down what happened. p. 2

panhandle (pan´han•dəl) A portion of land that sticks out like the handle of a pan. p. 189

parallel time lines (par´ə•lel tīm līnz) Two or more time lines that show the same period of time. p. 380

parallels (par´ə•lelz) Lines of latitude. p. 36

patriotism (pā´trē•ə•ti•zəm) Love of one's country. p. 515

pension (pen´shən) Retirement income paid to people who stop working at a certain age. p. 312

petroleum (pə•trō´lē•əm) Oil. p. 161

physical feature (fi´zi•kəl fē´chər) A land feature that has been made by nature. p. 6

pioneer (pī•ə•nir´) A person who first settles a place. p. 65

point of view (point uv vyōō) How a person sees things. p. 3

political boss (pə•li´ti•kəl bôs) An elected official—often a mayor—who has many dishonest employees and who is able to control the government with the help of those employees. p. 213

population density (po•pyə•lā´shən den´sə•tē) The number of people living in 1 square mile or 1 square kilometer of land. p. 474

population pyramid (po•pyə•lā´shən pir´ə•mid) A graph that shows the division of a country's population by age. p. 534

prediction (pri•dik´shən) A decision about what might happen next, based on the way things are. p. 232

prejudice (pre´jə•dəs) An unfair feeling of hate or dislike for members of a certain group because of their background, race, or religion. p. 168

primary source (prī´mer•ē sôrs) A record of an event made by a person who saw or took part in it. p. 4

prime meridian (prīm mə•ri´dē•ən) The meridian marked 0 degrees and that runs north and south through Greenwich, England. p. 37

progressive (prə•gre´siv) A person who worked to improve life for those who were not wealthy. p. 213

prohibition (prō•hə•bi´shən) The plan to stop people in the United States from drinking alcoholic beverages. p. 219

projections (prə•jek´shənz) The different kinds of maps cartographers use to show the Earth. p. 198

propaganda (prä•pə•gan´də) Information designed to help or hurt a cause. p. 232

proprietary colony (prə•prī´ə•tər•e kä´lə•nē) A colony owned and ruled by one person. p. 42

prospector (präs´pek•tər) A person who searches for gold, silver, or other mineral resources. p. 151

province (prä´vəns) A political region similar to a state in the United States. p. 542

rapid-transit system (ra´pəd tran´sət sis´təm) A passenger transportation system that uses elevated or underground trains or both. p. 501

ratify (ra´tə•fī) To approve. p. 61

rationing (rash´ən•ing) The limiting of the supply of what people can buy. p. 351

recession (ri•se´shən) A period of slow economic activity. p. 463

Reconstruction (rē•kən•struk´shən) The time during which the South was rebuilt after the Civil War. p. 140

recycling (rē•sī´kəl•ing) Using items again. p. 351

refinery (ri•fī´nə•rē) A factory in which materials, especially fuels, are cleaned and made into usable products. p. 151

refugee (ref´yōō•jē) A person who seeks shelter and safety in a country other than his or her own. p. 383

region (rē´jən) An area of Earth in which many features are similar. p. 6

register (re´jə•stər) To sign up to vote by showing proof that the voter lives where the voting takes place. p. 513

regulation (re•gyə•lā´shən) A rule or an order. p. 169

relocation camp (rē•lō•kā´shən kamp) During World War II, an army-style settlement in which Japanese Americans were forced to live. p. 353

renaissance (re´nə•säns) A time of great interest and activity in the arts. p. 290

representation (re•pri•zen•tā´shən) The action of having someone speaking for another. p. 48

republic (ri•pub´lik) A form of government in which people elect representatives to govern the country. p. 60

reservation (re•zər•va´shən) An area of land set aside by the government for use only by Native Americans. p. 154

resist (ri•zist´) To act against. p. 109

responsibility (ri•spän•sə•bi´lə•tē) A duty; something a person is expected to do. p. 512

retreat (ri•trēt´) To fall back. p. 122

revolution (re•və•lōō´shən) A sudden, complete change, such as the overthrow of a government. p. 47

royal colony (roi´əl kä´lə•nē) A colony ruled directly by a monarch. p. 43

rural (rûr´əl) Of or like the country; away from the city. p. 280

S

satellite (sa´tə•līt) An object that orbits a planet. p. 423

scalawag (ska´li•wag) A rascal; someone who supports something for his or her own gain. p. 148

scandal (skan´dəl) An action that brings disgrace. p. 453

secede (si•sēd´) To leave. p. 117

secondary source (se´kən•der•ē sôrs) A record of an event written by someone who was not there at the time. p. 5

secret ballot (sē´kret ba´lət) A voting method in which no one knows how anyone else voted. p. 148

sectionalism (sek´shən•ə•li•zəm) Regional loyalty. p. 100

segregated (se´gri•gā•təd) Set apart or separated because of race or culture. p. 363

segregation (se•gri•gā´shən) The practice of keeping people in separate groups based on race or culture. p. 148

separatist (se´pə•rə•tist) A person in a province who wants his or her country to become a separate nation to preserve a culture. p. 544

settlement house (se´təl•mənt hous) A community center where people can learn new skills. p. 208

sharecropping (sher´kräp•ing) A system of working the land in which the worker was paid with a "share" of the crop. p. 147

siege (sēj) A long-lasting attack. p. 194

skyscraper (skī´skrā•pər) A tall steel-frame building. p. 209

slave state (slāv stāt) A state that allowed slavery before the Civil War. p. 101

slavery (slā´və•rē) The practice of holding people against their will and making them carry out orders. p. 33

society (sə•sī´ə•tē) A human group. p. 10

standard of living (stan´dərd uv li´ving) A measure of how well people in a country live. p. 536

states' rights (stāts rīts) The idea that the states, rather than the federal government, should have final authority over their own affairs. p. 100

stock (stäk) A share of a business or company. p. 271

stock market (stäk mär´kət) A place where people buy and sell shares of a company or business. p. 271

strategy (stra´tə•jē) A long-range plan. p. 123

strike (strīk) The stopping of work in protest of poor working conditions. p. 245

suburb (su´•bərb) A community or neighborhood that lies outside a city. p. 281

Sun Belt (sun belt) A wide area of the southern United States that has a mild climate all year. p. 493

superpower (sōō´pər•pou•ər) A nation that is one of the most powerful in the world. p. 388

T

tariff (tar´əf) A tax on goods brought into a country. p. 100

technology (tek•nä´lə•jē) The use of scientific knowledge or tools to make or do something. p. 22

teleconference (te´li•kän•frəns) A conference, or meeting, that uses electronic machines to connect people. p. 497

tenement (te´nə•mənt) A poorly built apartment building. p. 167

territory (ter´ə•tôr•ē) Land that belongs to a national government but is not a state and is not represented in Congress. p. 66

terrorism (ter´ər•i•zəm) The use of violence to promote a cause. p. 472

textile (tek´stīl) Cloth. p. 76

theory (thē´ə•rē) A possible explanation. p. 20

time zone (tīm zōn) A region in which a single clock time is used. p. 546

trade-off (trād´ôf) A giving up of one thing in return for another. p. 355

transcontinental railroad (trans•kän•tə•nen´təl rāl´rōd) The railway line that crossed North America. p. 158

treaty (trē´tē) An agreement between countries. p. 53

trial by jury (trī´əl bī jûr´ē) The judging of a person accused of a crime by a jury of fellow citizens. p. 42

U

underground (un´dər•ground) Done in secret. p. 110

unemployment (un•im•ploi´mənt) The number of workers without jobs. p. 301

urban (ûr´bən) Of or like a city. p. 280

V

veteran (ve´tə•rən) A person who has served in the armed forces. p. 383

veto (vē´tō) To reject. p. 468

V-J Day (vē•jā´ dā) Victory over Japan Day; August 15, 1945, the day in World War II on which Japan agreed to surrender and fighting stopped. p. 378

volunteer (vä•lən•tir´) A person who works without pay. p. 514

Y

yellow journalism (ye´lō jər´nəl•i•zəm) Style of newspaper writing in which reporters exaggerate the facts of a story in order to sell newspapers. p. 193

GLOSSARY

Index

Page references for illustrations are set in italic type. An italic *m* indicates a map. Page references set in boldface type indicate the pages on which vocabulary terms are defined.

INDEX